NORTHERN WEI (386–534)

OXFORD STUDIES IN EARLY EMPIRES

Series Editors
Nicola Di Cosmo, Mark Edward Lewis, and Walter Scheidel

State Power in Ancient China and Rome
Edited by Walter Scheidel

The Confucian-Legalist State
A New Theory of Chinese History
Dingxin Zhao

Cosmopolitanism and Empire
Universal Rulers, Local Elites, and Cultural Integration in the Ancient Near East
and Mediterranean
Edited by Myles Lavan, Richard E. Payne, and John Weisweiler

Power and Public Finance at Rome, 264–49 BCE
James Tan

The Jiankang Empire in Chinese and World History
Andrew Chittick

Reign of Arrows
The Rise of the Parthian Empire in the Hellenistic Middle East
Nikolaus Leo Overtoom

Empires and Communities in the Post-Roman and Islamic World, c. 400–1000 CE
Edited by Walter Pohl

Roman and Local Citizenship in the Long Second Century CE
Edited by Myles Lavan and Clifford Ando

Northern Wei (386–534)
A New Form of Empire in East Asia
Scott Pearce

Northern Wei (386–534)

A New Form of Empire in East Asia

Scott Pearce

OXFORD
UNIVERSITY PRESS

Oxford University Press is a department of the University of Oxford. It furthers the University's objective of excellence in research, scholarship, and education by publishing worldwide. Oxford is a registered trade mark of Oxford University Press in the UK and certain other countries.

Published in the United States of America by Oxford University Press
198 Madison Avenue, New York, NY 10016, United States of America.

© Oxford University Press 2023

All rights reserved. No part of this publication may be reproduced, stored in a retrieval system, or transmitted, in any form or by any means, without the prior permission in writing of Oxford University Press, or as expressly permitted by law, by license, or under terms agreed with the appropriate reproduction rights organization. Inquiries concerning reproduction outside the scope of the above should be sent to the Rights Department, Oxford University Press, at the address above.

You must not circulate this work in any other form and you must impose this same condition on any acquirer.

Library of Congress Control Number: 2022059419

ISBN 978-0-19-760039-9

DOI: 10.1093/oso/9780197600399.001.0001

Printed by Integrated Books International, United States of America

Contents

Maps   vii
Acknowledgments   ix
Abbreviations   xi
Genealogies   xiii
Prologue: Defining Our Arenas   xvii

SECTION I. On Sources

1. The Emperor Taiwu and the Creation of History   3
2. History Writing and Its Discontents   12

SECTION II. Origins

3. Growth from Out Decay   23
4. Myths of Origin   47

SECTION III. A Dynasty Takes Shape

5. The Interloper   59
6. Establishing a State   82

SECTION IV. Creating an Empire

7. The Way of War   93
8. The World Shegui Entered   114
9. The World Shegui Created   133
10. Troubling Innovation   157

SECTION V. Pingcheng as Center of a World

11. The Wei Army 169
12. The Wolf Lord 187
13. Hunting and Gathering in the Land of Dai 202

SECTION VI. End Games

14. A Transitional Age 235
15. The Two Buddhas 255
16. To Luoyang 263
17. Downfall of a Theatre State 283

Summing Up; Looking Ahead 298

Bibliography 305
Index 341

Maps

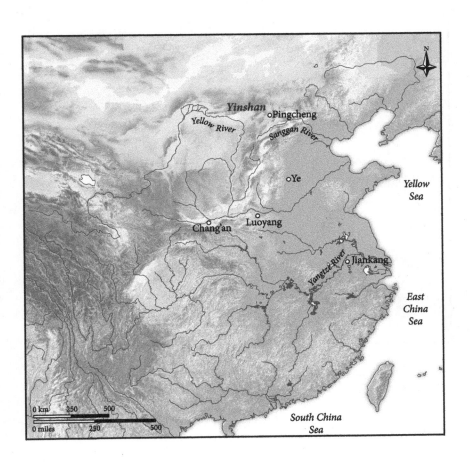

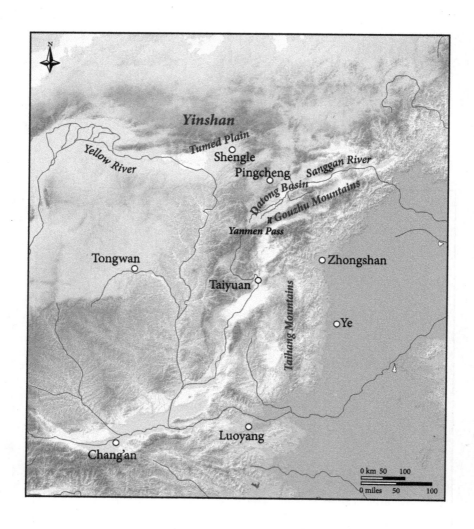

Acknowledgments

Thanks go first and foremost to my father, John Pearce, a biologist who taught me that I needed to look at the world; and then to Denis Twitchett, a historian who began the process of teaching me how to look at a particular part of the world in a particular way.

A long time coming, this book commenced with Denis. Completion was facilitated by a sabbatical afforded me in 2015–2016 by my home institution, Western Washington University, in Bellingham, Washington.

Looking back, I would like to express my appreciation to James Geiss, too quickly gone, who kindly served as a guide for me in graduate school at Princeton.

More recently, thanks are due to Nicola Di Cosmo of the Institute for Advanced Study, who helped me correct a couple of key terms; and to Fan Zhang of Tulane for reviewing my attempt to incorporate archaeological findings into my own efforts at social and political history.

All remaining errors are, of course, my own.

Abbreviations

JOURNALS

BMFEA	Bulletin of the Museum of Far Eastern Antiquities
BSOAS	Bulletin of the School of Oriental and African Studies
EMC	Early Medieval China
HJAS	Harvard Journal of Asiatic Studies
JAH	Journal of Asian History
JAOS	Journal of the American Oriental Society
JAS	Journal of Asian Studies
JESHO	Journal of the Economic and Social History of the Orient
LSYJ	Li shi yan jiu
PFEH	Papers on Far Eastern History
TP	T'oung Pao
WW	Wen wu

REFERENCE WORK

HYDCD	Han yu da ci dian

PRIMARY TEXTS

All are standard Zhonghua shu ju editions

BQS	Bei Qi shu
BS	Bei shi
HHS	Hou Han shu
HS	Han shu
JS	Jin shu
NQS	Nan Qi shu

SGZ	San guo zhi
SJ	Shi ji
SoS	Song shu
WS	Wei shu
ZZTJ	Zi zhi tong jian

Genealogies

SUCCESSION OF TAGHBACH KHAGHNATE, TO SHEGUI, ACCORDING TO *WEI SHU*

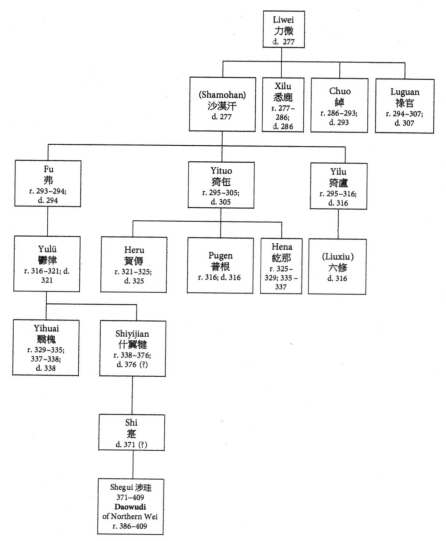

Genealogies xv

Monarchs of Northern Wei

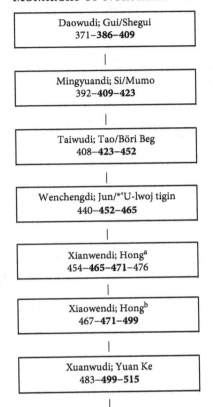

Daowudi; Gui/Shegui
371-**386-409**

Mingyuandi; Si/Mumo
392-**409-423**

Taiwudi; Tao/Böri Beg
408-**423-452**

Wenchengdi; Jun/*'U-lwoj tigin
440-**452-465**

Xianwendi; Hong[a]
454-**465-471**-476

Xiaowendi; Hong[b]
467-**471-499**

Xuanwudi; Yuan Ke
483-**499-515**

Xiaomingdi; Yuan Xu
510-**515-528**

Minor successors
528-535

Prologue: Defining Our Arenas

As the thinker Zhuang Zhou (fl. fourth century BCE) observed long ago, the world is a vast ocean of great currents and little eddies, all part of the larger world, but each with a meaning in and of itself. But because of our need to impose order, of a sort, upon chaos, we humans regularly attempt to limit the limitless, and stretch our manufactured labels across the world. And then, of course, we confuse our labels with the world itself.

In this volume we will examine a mid-size eddy that took shape in the early centuries of the Common Era among the disparate peoples and uneven terrains of East Asia. This was a new people—the *Taghbach (Ch. Tuoba)—who emerged in the highlands south of the Yinshan Mountains in modern Inner Mongolia to create a new sort of empire in continental East Asia, the Northern Wei (386–534).[1] The underlying aim of this study will be to make an effort at least to see this regime in and of itself, attempting to look past the various sets of labels that have from the beginning been imposed upon it; the cages in which history constructors have attempted to place it.

History, of course, is always incomplete, consisting largely of what the people who write history have chosen—consciously or unconsciously—to write about, usefully supplemented by material remains, to the degree that coffins and drinking cups can describe a world. Since the people who created Northern Wei were an oral culture of Inner Asian derivation, the main textual account of their history composed by writers recruited from among their subjects in the literate Chinese world, we really have only glimpses of the women and men who brought that state into being. The incomplete nature of our knowledge of these people is portrayed—both physically and metaphorically—in this book's cover photo, a glimpse of such an individual from the damaged wall of a mid-sixth-century tomb.[2] Unfortunately, all we get of such people are glimpses. For the most part,

---

1. Here, and elsewhere, the asterisk indicates a reconstructed term, not taken from actual text.
2. The tomb, located at Xinzhou, just south of the Datong Basin, the fifth-century seat of Northern Wei power, seems to date from the sixth-century successor regimes, Eastern Wei or Northern Qi: see Shanxisheng kao gu yan

at least, their own words are not heard; there is no *Secret History of the Mongols* we can read alongside the histories that emerged from within Chinese tradition. An effort needs to be made to see something of the complexity of such figures in the particular age under consideration here. And that, to make clear, is the point of this book.

Each form that emerges from the stuff of the world has, of course, its own importance. But Northern Wei is also important in the broader currents of time in that it is the earliest major example of the new sort of East Asian empire that began to emerge in the early centuries CE, in the aftermath of collapse of the Han and Xiongnu empires.[3] Formed by armies organized from out of Inner Asian populations, states of this sort would go on over the next 1,000 years or more repeatedly to extend rule over Chinese populations in the highly productive lowlands to the south.[4] These were regimes such as those of the Khitans (10th–12th centuries) and the Jurchen (12th–13th centuries), the Mongols (13th–14th centuries) and the Manchus (17th–20th centuries), which though showing evolution and significant difference from one to the next, would as a category dominate much of East Asian history.

* * *

Our discussion needs to begin with straightforward (if tentative) definitions of the main geographical labels that will be applied in this study: Inner Asia, Central Asia, and the Chinese world. Various scholars use these in various ways, at times without sufficient explanation. The set of definitions put forth here is created for a particular purpose—the history of Northern Wei. They took shape on the basis of specifics of geography, historical role, and contiguity of cultures and languages

---

jiu suo 山西省考古研究所 et al., "Shanxi Xinzhoushi Jiuyuangang Bei chao bi hua mu" 山西忻州市九原岗北朝壁画墓, *Kao gu* 2015.7: 51–74. This particular photo from the tomb is taken from: http://www.gov.cn/jrzg/2013-12/25/content_2554334.htm; 4 October 2022.

3. The distinctive nature of Northern Wei in the history of East Asia, and of the Chinese world, is observed by, among others, Charles Holcombe in his *The Genesis of East Asia: 221 B.C.–A.D. 907* (Honolulu: University of Hawai'i Press, 2001), 131–44. In his important recently published book, *The Jiankang Empire in Chinese and World History* (Oxford: Oxford University Press, 2020), 7, Andrew Chittick refers to this sort of state as "Sino-steppe empires."

4. An early but still useful discussion of relationships between Chinese worlds and those of Inner Asia is given in Owen Lattimore, *The Inner Asian Frontier of China* (Boston: Beacon Press, 1951). More problematic but still frequently cited is Thomas Barfield, *The Perilous Frontier: Nomadic Empires and China* (Cambridge, MA: Blackwell, 1989); see the review by Ruth Dunnell in *JAS* 50.1 (1991): 126–27. A more recent summation and debate with Barfield is given in Nicola Di Cosmo, "China-Steppe Relations in Historical Perspective," in *Complexity of Interaction along the Eurasian Steppe Zone in the First Millennium CE*, ed. Jan Bemmann and Michael Schmauder (Bonn: Vor- und Frühgeschichtliche Archäologie, Rheinische Friedrich-Wilhelms-Universität, 2015), 49–72. Di Cosmo's main point here is to reject Barfield's notion that Inner Asian states emerged in reaction to developments in the Chinese world; instead, he insists that they emerged of themselves, far from the frontier, through internal Inner Asian struggles, and only then turned toward the rich products of the Chinese world. This idea will be interesting to follow through our discussion of Northern Wei in the following chapters; it is also interesting to compare it, *mutatis mutandis*, with the appearance in the 16th and 17th centuries of European states on the world stage, which in the midst of centuries of ongoing internal struggle turned outward to harvest the wealth of more developed parts of the world.

seen through study of that regime. Others, concentrating on different periods, may well define them differently.

Thus, "Inner Asia" refers here to the high, relatively dry grasslands that extend for more than 500 miles north of the Tianshan and Yinshan mountain chains, and stretch from Ukraine, through Kazakhstan into the territories of Mongolia and the Inner Mongolia province of the modern Zhonghua Renmin Gongheguo (the "People's Republic of China," hereafter PRC). Since the collapse of the Xiongnu empire in the first century CE, these lands of desert and grass have historically been dominated by groups speaking Mongolic and Turkic languages. Though geographically and ecologically quite distinct, the great northeastern river valley of Manchuria might for this period at least be included on an honorary basis, still playing a relatively minor part in the larger East Asian world.

Our "Central Asia" consists of the world of mountains and deserts that lies west of the Gansu Corridor and its northwestern terminus, the modern PRC city of Jiuquan, and includes the Tarim Basin and the Pamirs to the edges of the Persian and South Asian worlds. The populations of these regions have been more diverse than those of Inner Asia, including Turkic groups (parts of this region have come to be called "Turkestan"), but also Iranians and other Indo-European groups. Though nomads frequently controlled these regions, and at times physically relocated to inhabit them, they are in nature quite different from the Inner Asian territories to the north, defined by oasis states that were key points on the ancient international trade routes that have come to be called the "Silk Roads."

The Chinese world emerged more than 3,000 years ago as the "heartland" or "hub" of East Asia. Centered on the densely populated lowlands of East Asia's two great rivers, the Yellow River and the Yangtze (though certainly extending beyond), these lands formed a productive agricultural economy that became the base of rich forms of material production and cultural influence. Given a unity of a sort by a set of closely related languages, Chinese peoples have also been united by a shared, "literary" Chinese, related to but distinct from the spoken tongues.[5] Central to the body of texts enshrined in Literary Chinese was the original Chinese canon, a set of authoritative "classics" believed for the most part to date back to the ancient Zhou dynasty (1045/1040–256 BCE), and passed on from generation to generation by the Ru, the "men of the book," or "text masters," who in English are often referred to as "Confucians." Drawing on their canon, the Ru portrayed a vision of the proper order of state and society, along with a distinct set of ethics, centered on the duty of child to parent (see more discussion of this in Chapter 3).

---

5. See Jerry Norman, *Chinese* (Cambridge and New York: Cambridge University Press, 1988), Chapter 4.

In using the term "Chinese world," it must, of course, be acknowledged that one could also refer to an "Inner Asian world," or "the world of Central Asia." There is not, however, the same need, since for neither Inner Asia nor Central Asia is there the assumption embedded in the term "China" that there is somehow a rough contiguity of political and cultural boundaries. In his recent study of *The Jiankang Empire*, Andrew Chittick has properly reminded us of the problematic nature of the terms "China" and "Chinese," which are "convenient shorthand, a sweeping generalization for many different things."[6] Most pointedly, until perhaps the early modern period, there was not a unified, self-conscious "Chinese" ethnicity. In his study of the formation and nature of the Jiankang empire, Chittick prefers to look at particular groups along the Yangtze, which had their own vernacular languages (in some cases perhaps not even of the Sinitic language family), and their own local interests and loyalties. "China" is thus divided by Chittick into a "Sino-steppe Zone" centered on the Yellow River plains and a "Sino-Southeast Asian Zone" along the Yangtze.

These are good points, and rethinking is needed on these matters. It will be noted, however, that there is a "Sino-" in each of those zones. If a shared "Chinese" ethnicity did not emerge from the Han empire, with common action and a clear sense of the Other, this author does see an evolving "Chinese" cultural field, the "seamless web" described long ago in lecture heard from the author's teacher, Frederick Mote. Whether or not the rough-and-ready generals who held the throne at Jiankang always listened to them, there were in that city learned gentlemen—Ru—who exercised some level of authority by controlling and reciting texts in a written language that, though different from their own spoken, was clearly related to it. Competitions and debates can be seen with their cousins in the Yellow River region ("cousins" here used both metaphorically and literally). Their situation was simply not the same as that of the broader "Sinosphere," the world where the Chinese classics had taken root within elites but the native language was not Chinese.

Thus, this author will continue to use the "convenient shorthand" of "Chinese" in this book, perhaps particularly because, as will be seen in discussion below, there was in the Yellow River region at least a clear distinction between those, on the one hand, who spoke a Chinese language, and claimed descent from the vanished Han empire; and, on the other hand, the Northern Wei overlords, whose mother tongue continued for many generations to be Inner Asian.[7]

6. Chittick, *The Jiankang Empire*, 10–11; and this author's review of the book in *EMC* 26 (2020): 114–19. Chittick is building on concerns raised by others in the last few years, including Hugh Clark, "What's the Matter with China? A Critique of Teleological History," *JAS* 77.2 (2018): 295–314; and Victor Mair, "The North(west)ern Peoples and the Recurrent Origins of the 'Chinese' State," in *Teleology of the Modern Nation-State: Japan and China*, ed. Joshua Fogel (Philadelphia: University of Pennsylvania Press, 2005), 46–84.
7. Though these groups grew together over the centuries, clear distinction can still be seen in the sixth century in a famous comment of the military man Gao Huan (496–547), contrasting Xianbei and "people of Han": *Zi zhi tong jian* [hereafter ZZTJ] 157.4882. Yang Shaoyun, in his "Becoming Zhongguo, Becoming Han: Tracing and

The term "China," however, will be put aside. Though it can be argued that seamless cultural webs do exist, those webs never fit precisely into the political limits of states; sometimes not really at all. A "Chinese world" perhaps corresponded most closely with state lines during the empire of Qin and Han, from which in many ways it was birthed (including new forms of administrative and social organization, which through a network of walled government centers allowed for efficient counting and taxation of the *Han ren*, "people of Han"). Good argument can be made that "China," the label used in various forms among the Germanic and Romance languages, derives from the great unifying power, "Qin."[8] The real complexity of the situation, however, immediately becomes apparent in the term used by Russians and others to refer to at least part of these same territories: "Kitai"—"Cathay"—which was taken from an empire centered in Inner Asia that controlled and extracted wealth from a part of the Chinese world, but actually quite a small part.

With the Khitan we see the dominant model of the East Asian state that first took shape under Northern Wei. Over many centuries, such empires controlled parts at least of both Inner Asia and the Chinese territories, with different forms of administration used in different parts of the realm, and complex cultural struggles, interactions, and entanglements among the originally distinct populations.

The term "China" (perhaps as opposed to "Chinese") is thus of abstract and elusive meaning. If used, it needs to be used with care, with clear explanation of its meaning in any particular application. For this author, "Chinese world" is preferable, referring to a field of cultural sway and economic activity, not to any particular political entity. This field would, of course, exert enormous influence over Northern Wei, as did the Inner Asian world from which its founders originally emerged. The modern scholar Luo Xin has summed this up by saying that states such as Northern Wei "are a part of ancient Chinese history," but at the same time "an integral part" of Inner Asia.[9] But in this study our main aim will be to look on Northern Wei in and of itself, to locate its people in the particular

---

Reconceptualizing Ethnicity in Ancient North China, 770 B.C.–A.D. 581" (MA thesis, National University of Singapore, 2007), 79–83, discusses development in the Yellow River region in the period under discussion of the term "Han ren" as an identity label, even if that term did not yet refer to a fully shaped ethnicity. Chittick (*The Jiankang Empire*, 35), for his part, constructed a term of his own for people from the Yellow River who fled south with the empire's collapse: *zhong ren* 中人, drawing on the concept of the Yellow River plains as containing the "central states" 中國.

8. Derk Bodde, "The State and Empire of Ch'in," in *Cambridge History of China*, Vol. 1, *The Ch'in and Han Empires, 221 B.C.–A.D. 220*, ed. Denis Twitchett and Michael Loewe (New York: Cambridge University Press, 1986), 20.

9. Luo Xin, "Chinese and Inner Asian Perspectives on the History of the Northern Dynasties (386–589) in Chinese Historiography," in *Empires and Exchanges in Eurasian Late Antiquity: Rome, China, Iran, and the Steppe, ca. 250–750*, ed. Nicola Di Cosmo and Michael Maas (Cambridge: Cambridge University Press, 2018), 168.

places—on the hills, along the slopes—they themselves knew and loved, and to try at least to refer to its people by names they themselves might recognize.

Those names have not survived in their original forms. From a language related to Mongolic, they come down to us only in transcriptions in Chinese characters, scattered through Chinese histories.[10] At this early point in the study we will touch on only one: the original name of Northern Wei's ruling clan. This has come down to us as 拓跋, pronounced in modern Mandarin as "Tuoba" (reconstructed in Middle Chinese as *Thaek-beat),[11] but also appears on an eighth-century Orkhon stele in the Turkic version of "Tabgatch." It has, however, been plausibly suggested on the basis of broader linguistic studies that in Turkic the inner consonants were reversed (a metathesis) and that the original name—as rendered most recently by Andrew Shimunek—was "*Taghbach."[12] This is, of course, hypothetical reconstruction. But for this author, at least, that is preferable to use of the transcription "Tuoba," the modern Mandarin pronunciation of the Chinese characters that 1,500 years ago were used to transcribe the actual name, and so if anything even further from the original than *Taghbach.[13] From this point on, we will use "Taghbach" to refer to our subjects' name, and having made clear that this is a reconstruction, the asterisk will be put aside (as will also be the case with other frequently seen reconstructions).

There are several interpretations of the meaning of the name Taghbach. The canonical Chinese history of Northern Wei, *Wei shu*, says it is "ruler of the earth," or more literally "earth ruler," *tagh* (Middle Chinese *thaek*) meaning "earth," and *bach* (MC *beat*) meaning "ruler." This theory is supported by among others the modern scholar Christopher Beckwith.[14] Making a number of suggestions, Peter Boodberg has said his favorite is "mountain-crossers," which conforms

---

10. The Northern Wei "national language," *guo yu*, has been characterized by Andrew Shimunek, *Languages of Ancient Southern Mongolia and North China: A Historical-Comparative Study of the Serbi or Xianbei Branch of the Serbi-Mongolic Language Family* (Wiesbaden: Harrassowitz Verlag, 2017), 13, as of the *Serbi (Xianbei) language family, a sister of the Mongolic languages, both descending from "proto-Serbi-Mongolic."

11. Reconstruction of the Middle Chinese is taken from Paul Kroll, *A Student's Dictionary of Classical and Medieval Chinese* (Leiden and Boston: Brill, 2015), 605, 6 (and by Kroll from William H. Baxter and Laurent Sagart, *Old Chinese: A New Reconstruction* [Oxford: Oxford University Press, 2014]).

12. Shimunek, *Languages of Ancient Southern Mongolia and North China*, xxvi, 52; borrowing from Christopher Beckwith, *Empires of the Silk Road: A History of Central Asia from the Bronze Age to the Present* (Princeton, NJ: Princeton University Press, 2009), 103 note 29, where he renders the name *Taghbač. For more discussion, see also Peter Golden, *An Introduction to the History of the Turkic Peoples: Ethnogenesis and State-formation in Medieval and Early Modern Eurasia and the Middle East* (Wiesbaden: Harrassowitz, 1992), 73–74.

13. Tim Robinson put it so well, for a different part of the world, in his *Connemara: Listening to the Wind* (Dublin and New York: Penguin Ireland, 2006), 81: "Irish placenames dry out when anglicized, like twigs snapped off from a tree. And frequently the places too are degraded, left open to exploitation for lack of a comprehensible name to point out their natures or recall their histories."

14. *Wei shu* [hereafter WS] 1.1. Christopher Beckwith, "On the Chinese Names for Tibet, Tabghatch and the Turks," *Archivum Eurasiae Medii Aevi* 14 (2005): 10–12, suggests this is a borrowing from Chinese. Discussion of these issues goes back to Uchida Ginpū 内田吟風, *Kita Ajia shi kenkyū* 北アジア史研究, Vol. 2, *Senpi Jūzen Tokketsu hen* 鮮卑柔然突厥篇 (Kyōto: Dōhōsha, 1975), 96. While Beckwith in the article cited above suggests *bach* derives from the Indic word *pati*, "ruler," An-king Lim, "On the Etymology of T'o-pa," *Central Asiatic Journal* 44.1 (2000): 40, suggests it is transcription of the Turkic term "beg," "lord," which we'll see in Chapter 1.

to Taghbach mythology given in *Wei shu*'s "Prefatory Annals" (though that is mythology).[15] Others have proposed that the name derives from intermarriage of *Serbi (Chinese Xianbei, the language group of which the Taghbach originally formed a part) with Xiongnu, meaning "*Serbi father, Xiongnu mother."[16] Whether or not this is the actual origin of the name, we do know that the Taghbach developed from mixed populations, and for generations had intermarried with groups affiliated with the Xiongnu. Other suggestions are found as well.[17] When mulling these over, it is useful to keep in mind Boodberg's wisdom in saying that "a primary ethnic name has no etymology";[18] and to wonder whether the Northern Wei emperors—who as we shall see below did not quite know where their forebears had lived—actually knew the meaning of the name their ancestors had at some point taken up. How often does an American named "Smith" think of the metal-work of far-off ancestors?

Going beyond this, however, it needs to be acknowledged that the Wei lords were not even simply the "Taghbach." As is the case with human beings in general, at least some elements of this group were in a never-ending process of transformation, along multiple lines. At a certain point, as we shall see below, a Taghbach monarch abandoned that name and came to style his line with the Chinese name "Yuan." The dynastic name "Wei" itself was a relatively late addition. We'll try to keep up with these people in the course of their changes.

But a core did persist through these changes. Across the centuries, our evolving royal line built and led cavalry armies, organized in various ways, to exert control over other peoples and new territories—to build an empire. When they abandoned such activities, the dynasty quickly fell. Power came from the point of an arrow; abandonment of the mounted archer led to its disappearance.[19]

* * *

15. Peter Boodberg, "The Language of the T'o-Pa Wei," rpt. in *Selected Works of Peter A. Boodberg*, ed. Alvin P. Cohen (Berkeley: University of California Press, 1979), 238–39.

16. Ma Changshou, 馬長壽, *Wuhuan yu Xianbei* 烏桓與鮮卑 (Shanghai: Shanghai ren min chu ban she, 1962), 30–33. "*Serbi" is, of course, also a reconstruction (see Shimunek, *Languages of Ancient Southern Mongolia and North China*, 39) from the Chinese transcription鮮卑, pronounced in modern Mandarin as "Xianbei," in the Middle Chinese reconstruction *Sjen pjie (Kroll, *Student's Dictionary*, 493, 11). Hereafter, the asterisk on the name will be dropped. An even more frequently used reconstruction is *Särbi, put forth by E. G. Pulleyblank, "The Chinese and Their Neighbors in Prehistoric and Early Historic Times," in *The Origins of Chinese Civilization*, ed. David N. Keightley (Berkeley: University of California Press, 1983), 453. The author must make clear that he has adopted the Shimunek version out of a desire for consistency; no claim is made as to which of these is the more reliable.

17. See Boodberg, "Marginalia to the Histories of the Northern Dynasties," rpt. in *Selected Works of Peter A. Boodberg*, 280–83; and ZZTJ 77:2459.

18. Boodberg, "Marginalia to the Histories of the Northern Dynasties," 280.

19. For an example of persistence over time, see the study by Bao Yuzhu 宝玉柱 of a Northern Wei guard unit, the Karqin, that in later centuries evolved into a distinct Inner Asian polity that played a role in the Mongols' empire: "Kalaqin yuan liu: Bei Wei shi qi de Helazhen 喀喇沁源流：北魏时期的曷剌真," *Man yu yan jiu* (2013.1): 96–104. Descendants of the Taghbach royal house also appear to have been the organizers of the later Tangut regime: see the discussion of Ruth Dunnell in her *The Great State of High and White: Buddhism and State Formation in Eleventh-Century Xia* (Honolulu: University of Hawai'i Press, 1996), 40–45.

On to some practical matters.

In terms of primary (Chinese) textual sources, for the "standard"—in some sense the canonical—dynastic histories and for the great early modern Chinese history, *Zi zhi tong jian*, I use the Zhonghua shu ju editions, as noted in the list of abbreviations.

Parts of *Wei shu*—the dynasty's "standard" history within the Chinese historiographical tradition—have been lost, interestingly, often key chapters on princes and empresses (see discussion in Chapter 2).[20] These were reconstructed during the early modern Song dynasty largely on the basis of *Bei shi*, a seventh-century overview of the states—including Northern Wei—that ruled the Yellow River region in the fifth and sixth centuries. For passages from *Wei shu* chapters reconstructed using *Bei shi*, I will first cite *Bei shi*, then *Wei shu* in parentheses. When a *Wei shu* chapter is older than its equivalent in *Bei shi*, unless there is a significant discrepancy I will cite only *Wei shu*, and not include the derivative passage from *Bei shi*.

Over the last several decades there has emerged a huge and rapidly growing body of secondary study, interpreting and reinterpreting the slender body of primary sources that has come down to us. Some is very good; much is entangled in modern efforts to assert correspondence of early medieval peoples and regimes with the accident of contemporary state lines. For this author, among the best in Chinese has been the work of earlier scholars such as Lü Simian and Tang Zhangru; and more recently, Yan Yaozhong and Luo Xin. In Japanese, perhaps the most important works are those of Maeda Masana, Tamura Jitsuzō, Kawamoto Yoshiaki, and Matsushita Ken'ichi. The textual sources have, of course, also been greatly enriched by increasingly sophisticated interpretation of material remains: among the most important recent such works are those of Albert Dien, Bonnie Cheng and Chin-yin Tseng, and the PhD thesis of Zhang Fan that will no doubt soon become a monograph. This book will not, however, attempt to be a restatement of the contemporary field of study of "early medieval China"; in interest of space, citation of secondary sources has been selective.

The organization of time is a key way in which societies create a distinct identity. In the traditional Chinese world from which the histories we use derive, years were measured by monarchs' reign periods, and the year itself on the basis of a lunar calendar; this system was then adopted by the Taghbach lords. But compromising with the demands of modernity, this work places events in the "Common Era" calendar. Years of the Common Era—the Gregorian calendar—do not, of course, precisely match those of traditional Chinese calendar that is

---

20. See discussion of these chapters in two articles by Jennifer Holmgren in *Monumenta Serica*, Vol. 35 (1981–1983): "Social Mobility in the Northern Dynasties: A Case Study of the Feng of Northern Yen" (19–32) and "Women and Political Power in the Traditional T'o-Pa Elite: A Preliminary Study of the Biographies of Empresses in the *Wei-Shu*" (33–74).

the basis for our histories; I will use the ordinal assignment given in the modern Zhonghua shu ju edition of *Zi zhi tong jian*, while making sure to describe the season in which events took place, and for a few key events, place them in the Common Era calendar.

At certain places in the narrative I supply reconstructions of Middle Chinese. This is not so much an attempt to reconstruct the Taghbach *guo yu*, but to remind the reader that we are using a modern, Mandarin pronunciation of the characters being used for transcription of another people's language.

For reconstruction of Middle Chinese, I have used Paul Kroll's *Student's Dictionary of Classical and Medieval Chinese*, which draws on Baxter and Sagart's *Old Chinese* (as noted in note 10). In these reconstructions of Middle Chinese, I have for the sake of convenience dropped the "-X" for rising and "-H" for departing tones as in the very limited uses being made here of this system, they confuse more than inform: as Baxter and Sagart themselves say, these are not necessarily accurate descriptions of sound, but only an attempt to place the character's pronunciation on contemporary rhyme tables.[21]

---

21. Baxter and Sagart, *Old Chinese*, 14, 11.

SECTION I.

On Sources

Although the historian draws on multiple sources of information, generally at least a central role is played by the primary source, by the stories contemporaries or near-contemporaries have written down and presented as meaningful description of significant events. But since stories of this sort tend to be "an agreed-upon fable" (*une fable convenue*), as the exiled Napoleon is quoted saying, we must confront our texts with a skeptical attitude. In the two chapters in Section I we pursue this issue within the particular circumstances of the Taghbach empire.

Chapter 1 looks at the creation—or fabrication—of history, a common practice in ancient times, and in modern. Although sometimes made out of whole cloth, generally at least this involves rearrangement, innuendo, or, as in the case of the Gaxian Cave, proclamation of a powerful truth on the basis of questionable claims, in order to seek a quite practical end.

In Chapter 2 we turn to the often distinctive role of those who write history within the larger world in which they live. When the historian is a participant in an established tradition, the account will be not just accurate record keeping, but organized on the basis of shared assumptions and preoccupations; will be shaped by ideas of what the world should be rather than what it actually is. One who plays such a role can be a victim of it, perhaps at times because the historian speaks truth to power, but of equal or even greater frequency, because the historian replaces the interests of the patron with his own, as we clearly see in the case of Cui Hao.

The Emperor Taiwu and the Creation of History

In the year 443, the Taghbach emperor of the Northern Wei received a delegation from a people who lived far to the north, along the Nenjiang River in Manchuria. Riding more than a thousand miles south, they had brought gifts for the emperor, and also a declaration that still further to the northwest, in the dense forests of the eastern foothills of the Khingan Mountains, was a stone shrine used centuries before by the emperor's ancestors.

As is often the case in this period, we do not directly know the name used by the people from whom these agents came. We do have a phonetic transcription in Literary Chinese, the language of administration used by many in medieval East Asia, including the scribes of the Wei emperors: "Wuluohou" 烏洛侯, which one modern scholar has reconstructed as "*Olakkô."[1] The region in which these people lived—far from the Chinese world of the time, though today a part of Heilongjiang province in the People's Republic of China (PRC), around the town of Qiqihar—was (and is) bitterly cold in the winter, regularly dropping down to −10 degrees Fahrenheit and below. To survive those months, the Olakkô lived in pit dwellings. Apparently ancestors of the Mongols, in the warm months they grew millet to supplement the meat and dairy products they took from hunting and livestock.[2] Though the different settlement groups each had their own hereditary chieftains, there was no overall lord; it is not clear who exactly sent the "envoys," or whom exactly they represented.

The court they entered was at the emperor's capital of Pingcheng, the modern city of Datong in the far north of the PRC's province of Shanxi. Pingcheng, originally a Chinese name, meant "the walled [city] of pacification." First used under the Han (206 BCE–220 CE), the name had originally proclaimed that Chinese

---

1. On the reconstruction as *Olakkô, see Christopher Atwood, "Some Early Inner Asian Terms Related to the Imperial Family and the Comitatus," *Central Asiatic Journal* 56 (2012–2013): 62. A brief account of this people is given in WS 100.224. Later mentions are made in several texts from the Tang, where variant transcriptions are given. For broader treatment of the issue of Chinese as East Asian court language, see Peter Kornicki, *Languages, Scripts and Chinese Texts in East Asia* (Oxford: Oxford University Press, 2018).

2. See Mi Wenping 米文平, "Wuluohou yan jiu 烏洛侯研究," in his *Xianbei shi yan jiu* 鮮卑史研究 (Zhengzhou: Zhongzhou gu ji chu ban she, 1994), 188–209; and Jan Janhunen, *Manchuria: An Ethnic History* (Helsinki: Finno-Ugrian Society, 1996), 184, 193.

empire's conquest and pacification of this central section of its northern frontier. The meaning had now been reversed. A huge military base in the highlands, this was the site from which the Wei emperor and his immediate ancestors, men of Inner Asian derivation, had over the previous fifty years pacified—conquered—the Yellow River territories of what had been the Han. The name would appear again in East Asian history.[3] One of the names taken by the regime—Wei—was also a borrowing from the Chinese language. It had been used repeatedly by previous regimes in the Chinese world, and to distinguish it the Taghbach Wei came to be referred within the Chinese historiographical tradition as "Northern Wei." Borrowings of this sort—adoption of Chinese titles by frontier regimes—would be seen repeatedly in later East Asian history, including use by the proto-Mongol Khitans—relatives of the Taghbach—of the Chinese name for the Liao River as one title for their northeast Asian regime. As seen above, it also went the other way, as with Western peoples' use of "Kitai" ("Cathay") to designate what they knew of the Chinese world.

Reflecting this ethnic and linguistic complexity, the man who sat on the Northern Wei throne in 443 presented himself under various guises, with names drawn from various tongues. In Inner Asian language, it seems, he was known as Böri Beg, "the Wolf Lord": *böri* being a Turkic term for that key Inner Asian cultural icon, the wolf; and *beg*, a widely used Inner and Central Asian term meaning "chief" or "lord."[4] It needs noted that this appellation appears only in the

---

3. Some 300 years later, Heijōkyō (Ch. Pingcheng-jing) 平城京 was an alternative name given to the Nara capital of the Yamato state (710–784). It is, of course, difficult to assess the connection with Northern Wei. Even more difficult to assess is the use of the name Pyongsong 平城 by the North Korean regime for a city established in 1969, about 10 miles north of Pyongyang 平壤.

4. For appearance of this name in southern histories, see *Song shu* (hereafter SoS) 95.2330; *Nan Qi shu* (hereafter NQS) 57.983. The fullest transcription is given in SoS 95.2352: 佛狸伐 *fo li fa*, in Middle Chinese (hereafter MC) Bjut-li Bjot. See also Luo Xin 罗新, "Bei Wei Taiwudi de Xianbei ben ming 北魏太武帝的鲜卑本名," rpt. in his *Zhong gu bei zu ming hao yan jiu* 中古北族名号研究 (Beijing: Beijing da xue chu ban she, 2009), 166–74; Peter A. Boodberg, "Selections from *Hu T'ien Han Yüeh Fang Chu*," rpt. in *Selected Works of Peter A. Boodberg*, 74–78, 99–102. Peter Golden reads *böri* as a Turkic borrowing from Iranian ("Wolves, Dogs and Qïpchaq religion," *Acta Orientalia Hungarica* 50.1–3 [1997]: 87–97, here 92), and quotes (p. 91 note 27) J. P. Mallory (*In Search of the Indo-Europeans* [London: Thames and Hudson, 1989]), 110, as describing the wolf as a symbol of warrior groups that "operate outside the normal jurisdiction of society." Golden goes on with a quote from an Orkhon inscription telling that "the army of my father, the Qaghan, was like a wolf, his enemy were like sheep." The personal guard of the Türk Khaghans was termed "Böri." As for the term *beg*: this is Luo Xin's reading of SoS 95.2352's 伐 *fa*, which he suggests is a term that probably originated from Sogdiana, with multiple Inner Asian variants, including the Ottoman *bey*. See use in E. Denison Ross and Vilhelm Thomsen, "The Orkhon Inscriptions: Being a Translation of Professor Vilhelm Thomsen's Final Danish Rendering," *Bulletin of the School of Oriental Studies, University of London* 5.4 (1930): 865; Carter Findley, *The Turks in World History* (Oxford: Oxford University Press, 2005), 45; and an article on "beg" in *Encyclopedia Iranica* (http://www.iranicaonline.org/articles/beg-pers, accessed December 17, 2018), where the author Peter Jackson tells us that "*Beg* is a Turkish title meaning 'lord' or 'chief,' later 'prince,' equivalent to the Arabic-Persian *amīr*." In personal correspondence, Christopher Atwood has suggested an alternative reading of *fa*, suggesting instead that it stands for the suffix "-bar," an "otherwise non-extant title with the pronunciation 'bar' and of uncertain meaning," though it clearly means something on the order of "lord," as seen in the later Turkic term "elteber." If that theory is correct, this may have been a unique term in the Taghbach language; in Atwood's interpretation, the Turkic "böri" was the borrowing. For a proposal of what was the actual Taghbach word for "wolf," see Shimunek, *Languages of Ancient Southern Mongolia and North China*, 128–29.

histories of Wei's Yangtze rivals, and not in the dynasty's own Chinese-language history, *Wei shu*, written after the regime's fall by the Chinese historian Wei Shou, who for reasons to be discussed below generally swept Inner Asian origins under the rug. Still, this ruler had made an impression in the Chinese world: the name continued to be used, as a title of honor, for a "Böri Shrine" dedicated to the Wei emperor that survived into the 1200s.[5]

In general, however, we shall simply refer to this man by the Chinese title bestowed after his death: Taiwudi, the "great martial emperor" (r. 426–451), Taiwu for short. Taiwu was indeed an imposing military figure, who over the course of his career completed his dynasty's main work and brought to an end the fighting that had for generations been waged over the rich farmlands of the Yellow River plains. A key tax base of the Han empire, this region would play a breadbasket role in East Asian history something like that of Egypt in the classical Mediterranean, though on a much larger scale. Many powerful men had competed for control after the Han collapse, most recently Taiwu's grandfather, who in the year 396 had marched an army down from the Pingcheng highlands to seize the plains from another regime, also of Inner Asian origin. Taiwu finished the conquests by destroying other rivals still active in the surrounding belt of peripheral highlands; the last of these was Northern Liang (397–439) in the Gansu Corridor to the west, which was taken in 439, just four years before the coming of the Olakkô ambassadors.

Change was now in the air. The first major phase of Wei history, with its focus more or less exclusively on organizing and using armies, had come to an end. Later stages would see more attention to efforts to explain and justify the regime and its activities, while more efficiently extracting from its subjects the fruits of their labors. For the latter, experiment over decades would eventually lead in the late fifth century to the Equal Fields system, a new system to control and tax land and harvest, which would for centuries provide a sound fiscal base for succeeding empires and armies (see Chapter 15). This would, however, be for the future; in 443, progress on this front had not gone far. More important during the latter part of Taiwu's reign were the beginnings of efforts to legitimize the Wei state. The stone shrine was one of these.

A key theme in this book will be the complex attempts by conquerors of Inner Asian origin to define and redefine themselves and their world—the Land of Dai, in which lay the city of Pingcheng—as they grew increasingly involved with rich lands densely populated by ethnic Chinese; or, looking at the issue from the other side, efforts by Chinese to lead the conqueror in directions they found more palatable.[6] Over the generations, different approaches were taken by different

---

5. See Cai Zongxian 蔡宗憲, "Bei Wei Taiwudi de ji si ji qi yi xiang de zhuan bian 北魏太武帝的祭祀及其意象的轉變," *Zao qi Zhongguo shi yan jiu* 6.1 (2014): 1–28.

6. Struggles seen in many societies, of course. Scholars of New Qing History have made important contributions in their study of the Manchu empire of the 17th through the 20th centuries. See, for example, Mark

figures. The later Wei emperor Xiaowen (r. 471–499), in the face of strong opposition, decisively rejected the ways of his ancestors to adopt what was at least his own vision of a Chinese order based on Chinese canon. Fifty years before, his great-great-grandfather, the military man Taiwu, took a more ad hoc approach. Under the guidance of a key figure of his administration, the Chinese minister Cui Hao, the emperor gave state support to a Daoist sect and to an imperial Confucian academy. But alongside this, in an effort to maintain the solidarity of the Inner Asian men who made up his army, were affirmations of deep ties to the northlands. It was from such lands that the Olakkô party came in 443, speaking to the emperor of a "stone shrine" they claimed had been used by his ancestors.

The so-called shrine was in fact a naturally formed cave, rediscovered more than 1,500 years later, in 1980, some three miles northwest of the capital of the Oroqen Autonomous Banner (Ch. 鄂伦春自治旗), in the far northeastern corner of the PRC's province of Inner Mongolia (50°38′ latitude and 123°38′ longitude). This has come to be called the Gaxian Cave.[7] In the eastern foothills of the northern extension of the Khingan Mountains, the cave is located in a region of wooded hills through which runs the Gan River, a branch of the Nenjiang. Facing south-southwest, the mouth is an opening in a low granite cliff, from which the cavity extends roughly northward for about 300 feet, with a ceiling that is at its highest point more than 60 feet tall. Though Taiwu enjoyed calling this the "shrine of the ancestors," archaeological findings show the most important use of this natural enclosure was as a place of habitation for Neolithic bands. Apart from a few shards of pottery, all the implements dug up there by modern archaeologists are stone or bone, including arrowheads used to hunt dogs and deer. Those who dwelt in the Gaxian Cave were hunter-gatherers. The cave's most basic function seems to have been to protect its inhabitants from the snows of a harsh natural environment. In modern times, at least, there is heavy precipitation (up to 20 inches a year) and temperatures that in winter are even colder than those of the Nenjiang River area, going down to as low as −40° F. This extreme was somewhat tempered inside the cave, with low temperatures of less than −5.[8]

Though they may have come from this general region, there is no real proof that it was Taiwu's distant forebears who had dwelt—or worshipped—in this Stone Age habitation.[9] There were hundreds of bands scattered throughout this

---

Elliott, "Whose Empire Shall It Be? Manchu Figuration of Historical Process in the Early Seventeenth Century," in *Time, Temporality and Imperial Transition*, ed. Lynn A. Struve (Honolulu: Association for Asian Studies and University of Hawai'i Press, 2005), 31–72.

7. Mi Wenping, "Xianbei shi shi de fa xian yu chu bu yan jiu 鲜卑石室的发现与初步研究," *WW* (1981.2): 1–7. Charles Holcombe, "The Xianbei in Chinese History," *EMC* 19 (2013): 15 note 67, suggests the name "Gaxian" 嘎仙 may be Chinese transcription of an Oroqen (Elunchun) term for "old home."

8. Chen Cheng-siang (Chen Zhengxiang) 陳正祥, *Cao yuan di guo: Tuoba Wei wang chao zhi xiang shuai* 草原帝國: 拓跋魏王朝之興衰 (Hong Kong: Zhonghua shu ju [Xianggang] you xian gong si, 1991), 4.

9. Ma Changshou, *Wuhuan yu Xianbei*, 239, drawing on Taiwu's use of the Gaxian Cave to invent tradition, put forth the still generally accepted suggestion that Taiwu's ancestors came from this region. Many accept this claim, but for a well-argued rejection of the necessity of a particular link between these people and the Gaxian Cave, see

region, and no clear linkage of any group in particular with the Gaxian Cave. Be that as it may, the emperor accepted the claim, and put a very public face upon it.[10] An imperial secretary was now sent north to the cave, where for the emperor he delivered an announcement to Heaven, and made sacrifices of a horse and an oxen, designated for Heaven and Earth and secondarily for the imperial ancestors.[11] We don't know what language the announcement was mouthed in, but a Chinese version was transcribed on the cave wall, where in 1980 it was rediscovered and copied down by modern archaeologists. Long before that, a variant form had been incorporated into the mid-sixth-century *Wei shu*.[12]

There are a few interesting differences between what is present in *Wei shu* and what was actually carved into the cave wall. In the latter, the inscription closes with announcement that the sacrifices were given to Heaven and Earth, and that sharing in this were the dynasty's male and female ancestors, referred to respectively as "khaghan" (*kehan* 可寒) and "khaghtun" (*kedun* 可敦), recently emergent Inner Asian terms for royalty, male and female respectively.[13] Unsurprisingly, these terms do not appear in the *Wei shu* variant. Both versions, however, share identical passages putting forth the announcement's main theme: although Taiwu's forefathers had come south to become lords of the Yellow River plain, the "rise of the royal enterprise began with the august ancestors" 王業之興, 起自皇祖 of the far north. "How could [this cave] be called a remote region, where, my head bowed, I come before the Prince [of Heaven]? All know the old temple is not ruined, is not gone" 豈謂幽遐, 稽首來王. 具知舊廟, 弗毀弗亡.[14] The Wei empire consisted of many peoples, and many languages; it seems quite likely that this propaganda was put forth orally in other versions, in other tongues, as we see a thousand years later in more concrete written form on the multilingual stelae of the Manchus.

Yang Jun 样军, "Tuoba Xianbei zao qi li shi bian wu 拓拔鲜卑早期历史辩误," *Shi xue ji kan* (2006.4): 127–29; and also Holcombe, "Xianbei," 16.

10. Though not the origin of the ideas put forth in this chapter—having been read by this author after the chapter was written—similar ideas are put forth in interesting ways by (Randolph) R. A. Ford, "The Gaxian Cave 嘎仙洞 Inscription: the Perpetuation of Steppe Tradition under the Northern Wei Dynasty," *Archivum Eurasiae Medii Aevi* 20 (2013): 23–66; and Luo Xin 罗新, "Min zu qi yuan de xiang xiang yu zai xiang xiang—yi Gaxian dong de liang ci fa xian wei zhong xin 民族起源的想像与再想像—以嘎仙洞的两次发现为中心," *Wei shi* (2013.2): 5–25.

11. WS 4A.95, 108.2738–39, 100.2224; *Bei shi* (hereafter BS) 94.3132.

12. WS 108A.2738. Though generally accepted, one must, of course, keep in mind the possibility that the inscription in the cave is a forgery.

13. Mi Wenping, "Xianbei shi shi de fa xian yu chu bu yan jiu," 2–3. Cf. Mi Wenping, "Gaxian dong Bei Wei shi ke zhu wen kao shi 嘎仙洞北魏石刻祝文考释," in *Wei Jin Nan bei chao shi yan jiu* 魏晋南北朝史研究 (Chengdu: Sichuan sheng she hui ke xue yuan chu ban she, 1986), 353; and *Xianbei shi shi xun fang ji* 鲜卑石室寻访记 (Jinan: Shandong hua bao chu ban she, 1997), 55. See Shimunek, *Languages of Ancient Southern Mongolia and North China*, 162, for mention of this term at the cave, and its connection with the Qifu 乞伏 people (we here use Shimunek's transcription style for the term); Boodberg, "Language of the T'o-pa Wei," 225–26, who in an early but perceptive set of comments discusses why the title was certainly in use by the Taghbach; and also Holcombe, "Xianbei," 15–16. And see Chapter 5 note 53.

14. The characters 來王 are drawn from *Shijing*, "Yinwu" ("The warriors of Yin"), in the "Shangsong" chapter.

In reality, however, as the account of this given in the dynasty's history itself says, the cave was a long way away from the rich, powerful state created by the Wei emperors on the edge of the Chinese world. The number given—"more than 4,000 *li*"—is in fact both a goodly distance and startlingly accurate: a *li* being about a third of a mile, this comes to some 1,300 miles, the distance given by Google Maps for a drive (on modern highways) from Oroqen down to Datong. In the *Wei shu* introduction to the announcement set up in the cave, we are told that the Wei ancestors had "come south, and this land became distant and removed."[15] Distant and removed, Taiwu had no clear knowledge of where his people had come from, despite his excitement at the news brought by the Olakkô. Nor did the Olakkô necessarily know much about either cave or Taghbach, themselves being relatively recent migrants to the area.[16]

The emperor's eager acceptance of this as his ancestors' home, despite any real knowledge to that effect, tells us more about the circumstances of Taiwu's own time than it does about dynastic origin. Borrowing a key insight of the thinker Xunzi (fl. third century BCE) for application to this particular incident, it might be said that the rituals enacted at the cave were in truth more for Taiwu and his contemporaries than for gods and ancestors. In them, we see the unfolding nature of the emperor's relationships with the men of his armies, and with the peoples of the forests and grasslands that lay to the north. By Taiwu's time, the Wei hold on the rich agricultural lands south of Pingcheng had become relatively secure. Control of the steppe was less so.

Though holding the highlands north of the Yellow River plain, the Wei did not directly rule most of the lands past these, certainly not the rich grasslands north of the Gobi Desert. The early Wei emperors instead intimidated and despoiled these regions with armies periodically led forth from the "city of pacification," and thus curbed raiding, attempted to stunt the growth of independent new powers on the steppe, and seized the regions' resources: its herds of sheep and goats, horses and humans. The wealth thus obtained was a major basis of the power they enjoyed vis-à-vis their rivals in and around the Chinese territories.[17] As recently as fourteen years before, in 429, Taiwu had launched a great campaign against what amounted to the new steppe empire, the Rouran 柔然, in which he seized a million head of livestock and a comparable number of nomads for forced resettlement in the belt of grasslands just north of Pingcheng, which lay between the Yinshan Mountains and the Gobi Desert.[18]

---

15. WS 108A.2738–39.
16. Yang Jun, "Tuoba Xianbei zao qi li shi bian wu," 127–28.
17. See discussion in an important early contribution to the field, Kenneth Klein's "The Contributions of the Fourth Century Xianbei States to the Reunification of the Chinese Empire" (Ph.D. diss., UCLA, 1980), 114–17; and in Wang Wanying 王万盈's very useful *Zhuang xing qi de Bei Wei cai zheng yan jiu* 转型期的北魏财政研究 (Beijing: Guang ming ri bao chu ban she, 2006), 5–6.
18. The Rouran (Jou-jan) seem to be linked in some way with the Pannonian Avars: see summation of the argument in Beckwith, *Empires of the Silk Road*, 390–91, endnote 18. For more general studies of the Rouran, see Zhou

Less successful, however, was Taiwu's steppe campaign of 443. It was in the third month of that year that the Olakkô mission—interestingly, the only one ever recorded in the *Wei shu* annals—came to Pingcheng. In the next month, the emperor went north to visit the great assembly point he had set up the previous year northwest of the capital, on the north face of the Yinshan Mountains, as a base for another invasion of the steppe. In the sixth month, back in the capital, Taiwu held a great review of the troops in the western suburbs, close by the dynasty's main shrine to its high god, Heaven. The campaign began three months later, at the beginning of autumn.[19] Abandoning his baggage train for a quick march, and dividing his forces to proceed along different routes, Taiwu reassembled the army up in the valley of the Orkhon River (a base, of course, of several later steppe empires). The *Wei shu* annals seem to avoid discussion of the campaign, simply referring the reader to *Wei shu*'s "Account of the Rouran," which itself says little more than that the Rouran khaghan fled, so the emperor returned south.[20] The situation was, however, far more complex.

Even before the campaign, argument raged at court about the wisdom of launching another huge raiding party against the steppe peoples. The main figure opposing, whose name is given in *Wei shu* as Liu Jie, was a military man serving as director of the secretariat (*shangshu ling*), who (quite duplicitously, in view of the 429 campaign) argued that there was no booty to be had for the troops up north, and that "it's not like the broad farmlands, with their stores of grain waiting for us to come."[21] All the ministers, we are told, supported Liu's view with the exception of the Chinese advisor, Cui Hao, who persuaded the emperor that the northern campaign could and should be done.

Probably because of this lack of support from key leaders of the military, the campaign did not go well. One example would be the overall commander of the operation, whose name is also given in Sinicized form as "Feng Ta," who is described not only as jumping sides to the Rouran, but also helping them develop an ultimately unsuccessful plan to cut the Wei army's supply train.[22] Furthermore, the armies did not meet the emperor in the Orkhon Valley at the appointed time.

Weizhou 周伟洲, *Chile yu Rouran* 敕勒与柔然 (Shanghai: Shanghai ren min chu ban she, 1983); and a new study by Rong Xinjiang, "The Rouran Qaghanate and the Western Regions during the Second Half of the Fifth Century Based on a Chinese Document Newly Found in Turfan," in *Great Journeys across the Pamir Mountains*, ed. Huaiyu Chen and Xinjiang Rong (Leiden and Boston: Brill, 2018), 59–82.

19. WS 4B.95–96; ZZTJ 124.3899–901.

20. WS 4B.96, 103.2294. The *Song shu* (95.2338) "Account of the Braidhead Caitiffs," aka the Taghbach, a useful but not necessarily reliable supplement, states that Taiwu "suffered a great defeat and retreated."

21. WS 28.688–89. See a general overview of these events in the useful, multivolume work of Zhang Jinlong 张金龙, *Bei Wei zheng zhi shi* 北魏政治史, 9 vols. (Lanzhou: Gansu jiao yu chu ban she, 2008), 3:31–34. Though Liu Jie's family came from among the Murong in southern Manchuria, he was likely of Xiongnu origin: see Yao Weiyuan 姚薇元, *Bei chao Hu xing kao* 北朝胡姓考 (Beijing: Zhonghua shu ju, 1962), 38–52.

22. Mention of the defection is made in the annals, with a fuller account in the biography of the Wei general in charge of transportation: WS 4B.96, 37.856. Another defector was an uncle of the future empress dowager Wenming, who would come to dominate the court in the 470s and 480s: WS 83A.1818.

The fault for this was laid on Liu Jie, who is said to have doctored the orders; he and his family were all put to death. To this were added charges that a brother of Taiwu had conspired with Liu to seize the throne if the emperor was killed by the Rouran after arriving at the Orkhon, leading to the deaths of three princes of the house and several other generals.[23]

With this as context, the announcement to Heaven at the ancient, distant cave perhaps takes on a new significance. Though there is no clear evidence to link them, there is an interesting juxtaposition to these events. The Olakkô mission would have arrived in the midst of the fierce court debates about the northern campaigns, giving perhaps a new meaning to the question in the *Wei shu* announcement, "How could this [cave] be called a remote region . . .? All know the old temple is not ruined, is not gone." Statements that have come down to us as dry passages in books are, of course, the distillation of words spoken (or shouted) by real actors in the court, and beyond. Here, perhaps, the emperor was attempting to call forth symbols to reinforce loyalties in the "nation" his ancestors had built around Pingcheng, on a more specific level implicitly adding, "Go north, young men." Unfortunately for Taiwu, and Cui Hao, much of the soldiery seem not to have wanted to go north to fight their cousins on the steppe, but wished instead to expand their conquests and appropriate wealth from the rich Chinese territories to the south.

Nonetheless, the mission to the cave would have been an opportunity to attempt to spread Wei propaganda through the northern lands themselves. The party sent by Taiwu in response to arrival of the Olakkô was traveling a different path from the armies, which would have gone northwest across the Gobi, at least supposedly to meet at the Orkhon. Riding instead to the northeast, the embassy would have taken a route that led from Pingcheng (Datong), over the Yinshan (mod. Daqing) Mountains to the edge of the Mongolian plateau, which they would then have skirted, probably going past modern Zhangjiakou, then up the west side of the Khingans to the great defile just southeast of Xilin Gol (the route of the modern highway G303), and then up the range's east side to the cave, again, about 1,300 miles.[24] Assuming the party could push their horses to go thirty miles a day—much of the route is rolling grassland—that would be about a month and a half, in which this ancient Lewis and Clark expedition would presumably stop from time to time to communicate with the locals through interpreters, if necessary, and advertise the power and glory of the Wei empire, and then repeat this on the way home.

Perhaps this, and other forms of propaganda, in addition to their very real power, contributed to equation by steppe peoples of the Wei monarchy with the rich Chinese territories they ruled. Some three centuries after Taiwu, Türk lords

---

23. WS 4B.97, 28.689; BS 16.602–3 (WS 17.414–15).
24. For confirmation that these men were riding, see such comment in the inscription given in WS 104A.2738.

were placing inscribed tablets in the Orkhon Valley, on which, as mentioned in the Prologue, they referred to the Tang empire as the Tabgatch, which it has been persuasively suggested is the Turkic, metathesized version of Taghbach, the clan name of the long-defunct Wei dynasty, from whose military establishment Tang had sprung.

2

History Writing and Its Discontents

In 450, seven years after the stone cave mission, came another incident illustrating the complexities of Taiwu's world: the execution of the Chinese official Cui Hao, who had over previous decades emerged as a major figure in the Wei court. As we shall see below, Cui Hao pursued many endeavors there. One was that of chronicler, continuing an historiographical tradition that, having achieved maturity within the Han empire, was now using Chinese words and worldviews to attempt to describe, really repackage, a very different people, who had created a very different state.

Taiwu and his predecessors had actively recruited into their regime leaders from the conquered territories, one important such group being Chinese men of the "gentle" arts, classicists who maintained a canon that held its own promise of order in the world. Those who preserved and transmitted the Chinese classics—the Ru—drew authority from authoritative texts and so possessed a power of suasion, for those interested in being persuaded.[1] Though rough comparison can be made to similar figures in other systems of complex thought and belief, with other canons, the position of the Ru was never as clearly institutionalized as were counterparts in some other societies. Despite such difference, all complex societies have had individuals who use canon to uphold their understanding of social order, while at times using the authority so obtained to seek their own ends.[2]

Cui Hao was a key such figure in early Wei, revered by later generations of Ru. His lineage traced itself back to the town of Qinghe, a district on the Yellow River flatlands near the modern town of the same name in PRC's Hebei province. The line had first emerged some two centuries before, in the late stages of collapse of

---

1. For an overview, see Michael Nylan, *The Five "Confucian" Classics* (New Haven, CT: Yale University Press, 2001).
2. One approach is seen in the notion of "communitarianism" put forth by Tanigawa Michio 谷川道雄, *Chūgoku chūsei shakai to kyōdōtai* 中国中世社会と共同体 (Tokyo: Kokusho Kankōkai, 1976); partially translated by Joshua Fogel, *Medieval Chinese Society and the Local "Community"* (Berkeley: University of California Press, 1985). Such ideas can, of course, be taken too far and veer into a utopian romanticism; there has always been abuse of authority. But in a balanced analysis of Tanigawa's ideas, Charles Holcombe (*In the Shadow of the Han* [Honolulu: University of Hawai'i Press, 1994], 46) speaks of the power in this society (and no doubt many others) of the patron-client relationship, and that "the most significant fracture lines separating competing from cooperating groups fall vertically along hierarchical networks of patron-client relationships rather than horizontally between socioeconomic classes." Part of what imparted authority to the patron in the "shadow of the Han" was direct or indirect position as a guardian of the texts. See more discussion of this in Chapter 8.

the old Chinese empire, when an ancestor had served high office under an earlier dynasty also named Wei, that of the Chinese Cao family of the Three Kingdoms (220–265).³ With the final collapse of Han's successors in the early fourth century, later members of the line served several of the non-Chinese "Sixteen Kingdoms" that for generations contested control of the Yellow River region. We will discuss this group in more detail below, here simply noting that one member of the line was Cui Hao's father, Cui Hong, who was serving the Later Yan (384–407) regime of the northeastern Murong people—another branch of the Serbi—when in 396 Taghbach armies came south to seize the plains.⁴ At this point, Cui the Father fled, but he was soon apprehended and brought back on horseback to the military encampment of the founder of Northern Wei, the emperor Daowu (r. 386–409), who wished to use him, both to buttress his legitimacy among his newly acquired Chinese subjects, and more practically as a scribe for the newly created empire; as mentioned above, Literary Chinese at this time was still the only effective written language available in East Asia. Building on the accomplishments of his father, Cui Hao became an important figure in the emerging regime, playing a variety of roles in Taiwu's court. Here, however, we focus on the one that proved fatal: history writing.

By the fourth century BCE, during the age of incessant warfare that preceded Han, the writing of history in the Chinese tradition had become the province of gentlemen from within the Ru tradition, who by judging what had been done in a disordered world were able to present and maintain a vision of order, a "patterned past," and on this basis attempt to maintain—or create—an orderly present; in ancient times and modern, history is often written to make a set of claims as to what the world *should* be. In this model of history as moral teaching, the history writer does not merely narrate events, but "inscribes their interpretation on the reader's mind."⁵

Whether or not Daowu quite wanted this tradition "inscribed on his mind," he did in the midst of his state-building projects order a colleague of Cui Hong, Deng Yuan, to produce a Chinese history of his dynasty as it then stood.⁶ Though the craft of history writing had developed before the Han as ideally at least an occupation of the independent and righteous scholar, placing judgment upon

---

3. For an overall study of the Qinghe Cui, see Xia Yan 夏炎, *Zhong gu shi jia da zu Qinghe Cui shi yan jiu* 中古世家大族清河崔氏研究 (Tianjin: Tianjin gu ji chu ban she, 2004); and Jennifer Holmgren, "The Making of an Élite: Local Politics and Social Relations in Northeastern China during the Fifth Century A.D.," *PFEH* 30 (1984): 1–79.

4. WS 24.620–23. In this account, Cui Hong 宏 is listed by his cognomen Xuanbo, since his given name offended the taboo against the later Wei emperor Xiaowen's Chinese name, which was also Hong.

5. David Schaberg, *A Patterned Past: Form and Thought in Early Chinese Historiography* (Cambridge, MA: Harvard University Press, 2001); the quote taken from a review and discussion of Schaberg's book by Martin Kern, *HJAS* 63.1 (2003): 277.

6. For an overview of Northern Wei history officials, see Niu Runzhen 牛润珍, "Bei Wei shi guan zhi du yu guo shi zuan xiu" 北魏史官制度与国史纂修, *Shi xue shi yan jiu* (2009.2): 16–29.

the acts of power-holders, this activity had a way of becoming intertwined with power and those who held it. If not directly for his written work, the famous early Han historian Sima Qian, for instance, suffered an ignominious and well-known fate at the hands of the emperor Wudi (r. 141–87 BCE).[7] Speaking of later periods, the modern scholar Étienne Balazs complains that "*history was written by officials for officials*" (his italics), which despite appreciable overlap is not quite the same as the gentleman.[8] For his part, at the beginning of the Northern Wei state, Deng Yuan is an interesting and quite typical representative of the "Chinese world" at this time. His family originated from among the Qiang, a Tibetan people who in the early centuries CE had percolated into western Han territories and greatly vexed the empire. Deng's grandfather—whose personal name is given as "Qiang" (as in "Mr. Deng, the Qiang")—served as a general under the Former Qin (351–394), a powerful but short-lived regime that emerged from the northwestern lands where the Qiang lived. Though grandfather was a military man, the grandson Deng Yuan was "widely read in the [Chinese] classics" and through that tradition "knew much of ancient matters."[9] In the ongoing debate as to whether the "Chinese world" is defined by culture or descent, Deng is evidence for the former.[10]

Having followed his father when he took up a posting with Later Yan (384–409), Deng Yuan—like Cui Hong—found himself on the Yellow River plains when Daowu invaded in 396. Recruited by the invader as a secretary, Deng now teamed up with Cui Hao's father on a variety of projects including court ceremony, law, and music. He was also charged by the Wei monarch with compiling a history of the dynasty. Though in his biography this is described as nothing very grand—"ten or so chapters of nothing more than a sequence, by year and month, of the daily events [of the emperor]"—it has been speculated that Deng in his work on music also tapped into the "songs of Dai," the dynasts' songs of their own deeds and those of their ancestors, which were regularly sung at feasts and sacrifices, and in the back quarters of the Pingcheng palace. According to this theory, having been involved in translating these from Daowu's native language into written Chinese—perhaps thus participating to some extent in their

---

7. To wit, castration. See Stephen Durrant et al., *The Letter to Ren An & Sima Qian's Legacy* (Seattle: University of Washington Press, 2016).
8. Étienne Balazs, "A Guide to History as Bureaucratic Practice," in his *Chinese Civilization and Bureaucracy*, tr. H. M. Wright (New Haven, CT: Yale University Press, 1964), 135.
9. WS 24.634–35.
10. Yuri Pines discusses "inclusive" as opposed to "exclusive" perceptions of Chinese identity in his "Beasts or Humans: Pre-imperial Origins of the 'Sino-Barbarian' Dichotomy," in *Mongols, Turks and Others: Eurasian Nomads and the Sedentary World*, ed. Reuven Amitai and Michal Biran (Leiden and Boston: Brill, 2005), 60–62; and similar discussion is given by Michael Brose, *Subjects and Masters: Uyghurs in the Mongol Empire* (Bellingham: Center for East Asian Studies, Western Washington University, 2007), 259–60, where he looks at the choices held by Uyghurs who served the Mongol empire within Chinese territories from a "*repertoire* of options depending on the situation." Aspects of an "exclusive" nature of Chinese identity under the Tang are, on the other hand, seen in Marc Abramson, *Ethnic Identity in Tang China* (Philadelphia: University of Pennsylvania Press, 2008).

construction as well—Deng then drew upon them in his history project to compile at least a preliminary draft of the "prefatory annals," the record of Daowu's ancestors, which 150 years or so later were drawn upon to form the first chapter of the dynasty's history, the *Wei shu* compiled in the 550s by Wei Shou (506–572), after the dynasty's collapse.[11]

Deng was later put to death by Daowu—according to our sources, for unrelated issues—and historical compilation was shelved for several decades.[12] It was resumed in earnest under Daowu's grandson, Taiwu, who in 439 ordered Cui Hao to serve as director of a team of compilers, charging him with the somewhat contradictory goals of producing a truthful record of the past (*shi lu* 實錄) while also praising "those who still raise up war banners" to march off on the dynasty's campaigns.[13] After completion, Cui's "National Records" (*Guo ji*) were carved onto tablets and put out for a grand display to the west of the outer walls of Pingcheng, on the avenue that led to the dynasty's Altar of Heaven. This was a mistake. Complaints soon surfaced among "northern men"—that is military men of Inner Asian origin, the core of the regime—that in the work there were "inappropriate" (given in Chinese translation of their words as *bu dian* 不典) passages that revealed "unseemly affairs of the [Taghbach] nation" (*guo e*). Cui Hao's chronicle has not survived as a volume on its own, and we do not know what exactly the complaints were about. Nevertheless, they soon became formal charges and Cui was executed in 450, along with dozens of kith and kin.[14]

The reasons for this event are murky and it is unbelievable that demands for Cui's death were not silently propelled by such unmentioned issues as court politics and tensions between different groups within the regime.[15] We'll discuss

---

11. WS 24.635, 109.2828. The modern scholar who put this theory forth was Tian Yuqing 田余庆, "'Dai ge,' 'Dai ji,'" he Bei Wei guo shi" 《代歌》、《代记》和北魏国史, in his *Tuoba shi tan* (Beijing: Sheng huo du shu xin zhi san lian shu dian, 2003), 217–243. If Tian is correct, or even if he is not, it is interesting to wonder when the *Dai ge* were composed; it seems likely that even if older elements were incorporated, the "songs" took full shape from the time of occupation of the "old lands of the Xiongnu," the Tumed Plain, as we shall discuss in Chapter 5.

12. Pushing his speculations even further, Tian ("'Dai ge,'" 231ff.) goes on to suggest that Deng's execution—ascribed in *Wei shu* to involvement through a kinsman in a treason case—was directly linked to his history writing. It must be noted that in the text there is not even a hint of this connection, and Tian may be extrapolating back from later events, which we shall get to shortly; this author is not convinced by this particular argument.

13. WS 35.823–24.

14. WS 35.826; BS 21.789; ZZTJ 125.3941–44. Not used in *Wei shu*, perhaps because of continuing ethnic tensions, it is the early Tang *Bei shi* that explicitly states that it was "northerners" 北人 who voiced complaint to Taiwu; this word usage is then picked up by the Song-dynasty *Zi zhi tong jian*. In the *Wei shu* version it is simply "those who passed back and forth" 往來行者 who complained.

15. There is a tendency by some modern scholars to deny the existence of ethnic tensions within the Wei realm, and the Wei government, and instead focus on the "merging together" 融合 of different groups. There certainly was ongoing cooperation of men of diverse background within the state apparatus. This does not, of course, tell us what they said about each other after going home. Ethnic tension existed there, of course, as it unfortunately has existed everywhere. It certainly existed in the Han, as we see in description of circus-like performances put on for the emperor, which in the midst of gymnastics and magic put figures of Serbi and Qiang up on a pole on a wagon to be shot at with arrows: David R. Knechtges, tr., *Wen xuan: or, Selections of Refined Literature*, 3 vols. (Princeton, NJ: Princeton University Press, 1982), 1: 234–35. It took on even more ferocious form with decay of Han and its third-century successors, and a new emergence of competition and struggle between disparate groups. Thus we see the complaints of the late Western Jin official Jiang Tong (d. 310) regarding a barbarian infestation of the Wei

these possibilities in more detail in Chapter 12. But certainly the proximate cause was history, and its publication, and perhaps more to the point, the complexities of bringing the oral history of one people into the written language of another, and into the web of assumption and bias those written forms entailed.

Cui Hao's death was a shocking event for the Chinese gentlemen who had been brought to Pingcheng to serve the dynasty. It was, however, the last death caused by history writing. After another break, these projects were resumed at the court, though it is interesting to note that in the tumult of the dynasty's collapse they were briefly taken over by men of the military establishment.[16]

Despite these favorable changes, the compiler of the ultimate product, Wei Shou, must still have been a bit nonplussed when he was "assured" by his patron Gao Huan, the general behind the throne of one of Northern Wei's two successors, Eastern Wei (534–550), that "my reputation in later ages is in your hands—don't say I don't know that" 我後世身名在卿手，勿謂我不知.[17] With power comes danger. But things had changed in the century since Cui Hao's killing, and Wei Shou emerged from the adventure physically unscathed. Perhaps not emotionally, however. When in 554 he presented to the throne[18] his final product, *Wei shu*, the "Documents of Wei," he was set upon by a barrage of vociferous criticisms, coming from powerful contemporaries who said that "the history stank" (*hui shi* 穢史), because too little had been said in it about their ancestors under Northern Wei, or too much of the wrong sort of thing. Protected by the ruler, Wei Shou simply made a few minor changes.[19]

Complaint continued, however, this being an age when genealogy—along with its pretensions and falsifications—was of great importance.[20] Over time, the complaints changed. Under the Sui dynasty (581–618), the emperor asked for a rewrite, dissatisfied with *Wei shu*'s assumption that legitimacy had lain with the eastern line of Northern Wei's successor regimes, rather than those of the west from which his regime had sprung.[21] The alternate version, however, did not catch on, and among the "Standard Histories" of the Chinese historiographical

---

Valley (*Jin shu* [hereafter JS] 56.1531–32); and the 349 pogrom incited by the Chinese Ran Min against non-Chinese groups, which resulted in more than 200,000 deaths (ZZTJ 98.3099–100). And tensions continued to exist after Northern Wei, as seen in the Eastern Wei army: see *Bei Qi shu* (hereafter BQS) 21.295. Massacres, of course, took place on many sides, and Chinese were not necessarily involved, as we see in a story of the Wei founder, Daowu, who became enraged at a man who had gone down to Chang'an and become "too much of a Qiang," leading to the fellow's execution: WS 28.686.

16. WS 81.1794. The results of the work of "men of Dai" were, however, pitifully small.
17. BQS 37.486; BS 56.2029; WS 104.2325.
18. By this time, the throne had been taken from Eastern Wei by the general's son, a man of the Gao family, who had established a Northern Qi dynasty (550–577).
19. BQS 37.488, 491.
20. It is particularly interesting, then, that Jennifer Holmgren's article on this subject uses Wei Shou as an example: "Lineage Falsification in the Northern Dynasties: Wei Shou's Ancestry," *PFEH* 21 (1980): 1–16.
21. For detailed discussion of this attempt at a rewrite, see Albert Dien, "Wei Tan and the Historiography of the *Wei-shu*," in *Studies in Early Medieval Chinese Literature and Cultural History*, ed. Paul W. Kroll and David R. Knechtges (Provo, UT: T'ang Studies Society, 2003): 399–466.

tradition it is Wei Shou's work that has come down to us.[22] To this must be added "more or less," since over time in the archives of Tang and its successors parts of the book were lost. Out of the original 114 chapters (*juan*), 29 were missing or incomplete when in the eleventh century, under the Song dynasty, efforts were made to restore this (and many other) books, as part of an (early) modern process of rediscovering the past.[23] The Song scholars made up the loss by drawing on various works of the Tang period, most important being the seventh-century *Bei shi*, a general history of Northern Wei and its sixth-century successors, which had borrowed heavily from *Wei shu*, among other sources. How the original chapters were lost is not clear: perhaps physical decay of a book that people had lost interest in; perhaps—for some of the chapters—furtive destruction by men too interested in it, still unhappy about treatment of forebears.

Overall, *Wei shu* is certainly a version of the dynasty's history constructed from within the context of the dramatic and imposed Sinicizing reforms of its last decades. As already noted above, one prominent feature of these processes was the rewrite in Chinese of the names of all the actors of earlier times. Still, the general attitude of modern scholars is that, though having major gaps, the book we assign to Wei Shou really does not stink but is overall a fairly good effort by a series of Chinese historians in the fifth and sixth centuries, using their own writing system, to report on an alien regime that had seized control of their homelands. Blessedly, for the modern historian at least, little energy seems to have been given by these men to produce history as moral judgment. Though far from perfect, *Wei shu* was a serious effort in an ongoing process to gather what they could of documents and reported conversations into an emerging whole.

Translation was, of course, crucial to this process, though it is barely mentioned in *Wei shu* and a quick skim might leave the reader thinking the speeches and debates given in the book were actually in Chinese. Especially in the dynasty's early generations, this was not the case at all: the speeches and debates, the folk tales and popular jingles that inhabit *Wei shu* and at least occasionally seem to bring real insight of the age and its inmates, were all originally in other tongues, only later translated into Chinese by Cui Hao and others. Important Chinese servitors of the Wei throne such as Cui or Deng Yuan were certainly multilingual, but "interpreter-clerks" (*yi ling shi* 譯令史) also played essential roles in the early Wei, in history writing and many other government activities.[24] These pieces have

---

22. For more detail on the book and its history, see Zhang Li 张莉, *Wei shu yan jiu* 魏书研究 (Beijing: Hua wen chu ban she, 2009), which has drawn on many works, but perhaps most importantly Zhou Yiliang 周一良, "Wei Shou zhi shi xue" 魏收之史学, in his *Wei Jin Nan bei chao shi lun ji* (Beijing: Zhonghua shu ju, 1963), 236–72. In English, see Holmgren, "The Northern Wei as a Conquest Dynasty," *PFEH* 40 (1989): 1–8.

23. Zhang, *Wei shu yan jiu*, 11.

24. Regarding the role of interpreters in history writing, see comments in the eighth-century *Shitong* 史通 of Liu Zhiji 劉知幾 (661–721) (*Shi tong tong shi* 史通通釋, with comm. by Pu Qilong [Taipei: Jiusi chu ban you xian gong si, 1978], 11.315). More generally, *Wei shu*'s "Monograph on Offices and Clans" (113.2973) mentions establishment of interpreters in the early Wei bureaucracy in general. And see also Zheng Qinren 鄭欽仁, *Bei Wei guan liao ji gou yan jiu xu pian* 北魏官僚機構研究續篇 (Taibei: Dao he chu ban she, 1995), 215–44; Charles O. Hucker,

thus been translated twice: for this book from Chinese into English, but originally from an Inner Asian language (or languages) into Chinese. No doubt much has been lost, in both stages of this process. More study is needed of the evolution of transcription and translation within the Chinese historiographical tradition, both to bring deeper understanding of that tradition, and to remind us more clearly that the authors of *Wei shu* are chronicling an "other."[25]

The need for translation was of course more pressing for speech than for documents, since in this period virtually all documents were written in Chinese; again, this is the reason Wei lords eagerly sought scribes among the conquered population. The earliest preserved evidence we have for Inner Asian writing dates only to the late sixth century.[26] Sporadic efforts were made under Wei to compile books in the "national tongue" (*guo yu*), but none survives and we have little more than titles—in Chinese, of course—in *Sui shu*'s "Monograph on Bibliography," compiled in the early Tang (618–907). These were presumably efforts to use (or adapt) Chinese characters to give phonetic transcription of the *guo yu*, seen in *Wei shu* with a few dozen names and terms, and with fuller development in several interesting later forms among the Japanese, the Khitans, and others.[27] As for the language family to which the Wei *guo yu* belonged, we have only a few dozen words and names transcribed into Chinese, and disagreement persists as to whether it was Turkic or an early form of Mongolian, though most recent work leans toward the latter. It was, at any rate, an Inner Asian language.[28] Whatever its roots, it is, in fact, quite likely that it was a distinct creole developed from sustained mingling in the Wei army, over centuries, of Inner Asians from different language groups.[29]

A Dictionary of Official Titles in Imperial China (Stanford, CA: Stanford University Press, 1985), 268 no. 2981; and Shimunek, *Languages of Ancient Southern Mongolia and North China*, 150, 350–51.

25. Good work has already begun in Rachel Lung's *Interpreters in Early Imperial China* (Amsterdam and Philadelphia: John Benjamins Publishing Company, 2011).

26. See Alexander Vovin, "A Sketch of the Earliest Mongolic Language: the Brāhmī Bugut and Khüis Tolgoi Inscriptions," *International Journal of Eurasian Linguistics* 1 (2019): 162–97. More famous, of course, are the Orkhon inscriptions, a century or so later.

27. For more discussion on this topic, see Chapter 9.

28. The debate began with Paul Pelliot ("Les mots à *h*- initial," *Journal Asiatique* 206 [1925]: 255) and Peter Boodberg ("Language of the T'o-pa Wei"), arguing for Turkic on the one hand; and on the other, Lajos (Louis) Ligeti ("Le Tabghatch, un dialecte de la langue Sien-pi," in *Mongolian Studies*, ed. Louis Ligeti [Budapest: Akadémiai Kiadó, 1970], 265–308), arguing for ties to Mongolic languages. In recent decades, consensus has emerged that the Taghbach *guo yu* is not Turkic. Some say it is Mongolic: Alexander Vovin, "Once Again on the Tabgač Language," *Mongolian Studies* 29 (2007): 199; while as seen above (Prologue, note 9), Shimunek, *Languages of Ancient Southern Mongolia and North China*, 13, says it is a sister language: "the Mongolic branch (including the modern Mongolian languages, Middle Mongol, and its immediate ancestors) and the Serbi branch (including Khitan, Taghbach, T'u-yü-hun, and others) are sister branches of a common proto-language, i.e., Proto-Serbi-Mongolic." This author uses "Inner Asian language" in preference to "Altaic," in recognition of most linguists' rejection of the latter as an actual language family.

29. It seems quite likely, in fact, that Chinese vocabulary came to be incorporated as well: see Zhu Dawei 朱大渭 et al., *Wei Jin Nan bei chao she hui sheng huo shi* 魏晋南北朝社会生活史 (Beijing: Zhongguo she hui ke xue chu ban she, 1998), Kindle ed., Chapter 12, Section 3. For more on this, see Chapter 9.

Because of this distance in language—and beyond that worldview—the compilers of the materials that ended up as *Wei shu* deserve praise, if historians have a need for praise. But it must be remembered that there was much about which these men—strangers in the strange land of the Taghbach court at Pingcheng—were not even aware, or if aware did not fully understand. As seen in the photo on the cover of this book, much of that world was half seen by the outsider, if seen at all. This was particularly true in the regime's early years, with the existence of such things as the shadowy "inner court" of the emperor and his generals, barely described in *Wei shu* though it actually ran the state, as opposed to the "outer court" cobbled together by men such as Deng Yuan and Cui Hong in an attempt to mime the rituals and administrative structures of a vanished empire. For reasons quite understandable, Deng and Cui and their immediate successors (and some modern historians, as well) were much more concerned with the latter, despite the fact that originally at least it exercised much less real power within the regime.[30] Despite this "tyranny of inscription,"[31] we will in this book carry on the efforts of these early historians to catch a few more glimpses of these men, and women, and their movement through the world.

---

30. A key theme of the important study by Yan Yaozhong 严耀中, *Bei Wei qian qi zheng zhi zhi du* 北魏前期政治制度 (Changchun: Jilin jiao yu chu ban she, 1990), the insights of which we will repeatedly come across in this study.

31. A comment applied by Peter Perdue to discussion of the Manchu regime, more than a thousand years later in his "Military Mobilization in Seventeenth and Eighteenth Century China, Russia, and Mongolia," *Modern Asian Studies* 30.4 (1996): 784.

SECTION II.

Origins

In order to understand a world that is forever changing, we are told by an author of a section of the commentary of the famous *Book of Changes*, one must "look up to contemplate the patterns of the skies, and look down to examine the lines of the earth," and then go on to "trace the beginnings [of things] back to their origins, then turn to pursue them to their end." 原始反終 ("Xici" 1.4).

We will attempt to borrow that ancient wisdom for this book. Though giving less attention to the patterns of the skies, in Chapter 3 we examine in detail the lines of those parts of the earth across which the Taghbach moved in their early endeavors. And in terms of time, in that same chapter we will trace that people back to their origins, origins that came long before they took the name "Northern Wei." They first appeared in the early centuries of the Common Era, as part of the re-emergence of populations—members of the Serbi language family—who had earlier been pushed to the edges by the wars of East Asia's first two empires: that of Han and that of the Xiongnu. With decay of those two empires, hundreds of small Serbi bands gradually moved into the Yinshan region—the frontier between Han and the Xiongnu. They were drawn there by offers—from both sides—of reward for mercenary service. With collapse of first the Xiongnu, and then of Han, they would come to act not as servants but as lords.

In Chapter 4 we turn to an origin myth ascribed to the Taghbach, contained in writings that came forth over generations from the brushes of the Taghbach lords' Chinese scribes, eventually to be incorporated into the sixth-century "Documents of Wei," *Wei shu*. In it is described a frequently seen theme of human mythology: a great journey of people, who in the course of the journey become *a* people. Myths, of course, must always be used with care.

Growth from Out Decay

Interesting in and of themselves, the Taghbach have a broader historical importance, having established a new, complex model of empire within the East Asian world. The road traveled to reach that point was long. It began, as all roads do, at a particular intersection of time and space.

The space was the band of frontier highlands that stretched from the upper bend of the Yellow River into the Datong Basin and then east to the Chengde region.

The time was an age of collapse of older empire—two of them, in fact.

One of the two empires was that created in 221 BCE through the kingdom of Qin's forcible unification of the "warring states" that had for centuries contested control of—while in some sense creating—the Chinese world.[1] Though Qin quickly fell, its empire was taken over in modified form by the new dynasty of Han (206 BCE–220 CE), which would rule for some four centuries and then yield to several generations of successors before the empire's final collapse in the early fourth century CE.

In the deserts and grasslands to the north was the other empire, that of the Xiongnu, which had also emerged in the late third century BCE and whose rule at its height extended from the Tarim Basin in the west to the Khingan mountains in the east, from the forests of Siberia in the north to the frontier highlands that uneasily separated the two empires.[2]

The Han and Xiongnu empires were very differently organized polities, and these two realms—separated and distinguished by the line of the "Great Wall"—have at times been described in terms of stark difference: the "sown" of the Chinese world, as opposed to the "steppe" of the Xiongnu; or at a cruder level, "civilization" vs. "barbarism." As many have discussed over the last several decades, however, this is a caricature, the reality being far more complex.[3] The

---

1. See Yuri Pines et al., *Birth of an Empire: The State of Qin Revisited* (Berkeley: University of California Press, 2014).

2. See Nicola Di Cosmo, *Ancient China and Its Enemies* (Cambridge and New York: Cambridge University Press, 2002).

3. See various reconsiderations of the nature of the Xiongnu empire, including Nicola Di Cosmo, "Ethnogenesis, Co-evolution and Political Morphology of the Earliest Steppe Empire: The Xiongnu Question Revisited," in *Xiongnu Archaeology: Multidisciplinary Perspectives of the First Steppe Empire in Inner Asia*, ed. Ursula Brosseder and Bryan K. Miller (Bonn: Vor- und Frühgeschichtliche Archäologie, Rheinische Friedrich-Wilhelms-Universität Bonn, 2011), 35–48; William Honeychurch, *Inner Asia and the Spatial Politics of Empire: Archaeology, Mobility, and*

lines drawn by humans on maps, even those imposed upon the land, often represent wish more than reality. At times more solid are the lines and borders that come forth from the earth itself, whether set in rock or marked by water, so we'll begin by turning to a real and important line that runs throughout this study, the Yinshan Mountains, the spine of an important length of the highlands contested by the Han and Xiongnu empires.[4]

The Yinshan begin at the northwest corner of the Ordos loop, the great northern loop of the Yellow River (in Literary Chinese, showing its importance, it is just "the River," He 河), where they rise to their highest heights, almost a mile and half above sea level. The range then runs east for some 600 miles, turning into a broad belt of highlands running north of the modern cities of Hohhot, Datong, and Beijing to end in the Chengde region. These mountains took shape in a complex and extended process of folding and thrusting of the earth's crust that occurred more than 100 million years ago, long before any of the human events recounted in this book, though recent in terms of the history of the planet itself.[5]

Despite the power of water, it has not yet succeeded in wearing these mountains down. It is in fact the Yinshan range that creates the River's loop, blocking its northward flow toward the Gobi Desert and forcing it east, in which direction it proceeds for several hundred miles before it encounters the roughly north-south ranges of Shanxi province, at which point it turns again for a long leg to the south, before making a last sharp turn east to enter the vast Yellow River Plain and eventually the sea (in this period, flowing north of the Shandong Peninsula). In multiple ways, the Yinshan create real environmental disjunction. South of them, rivers' waters run east and south into the sea. Included among these are, of course, the River itself, as well as the Sanggan, which originates in the highlands just east of the great loop. On the *yin*, the north side of the Yinshan, rivers run north into grasslands and desert, often simply going dry in the process.[6]

At various times humans have tried to reinforce these natural walls, and exclude others from this region, by erecting "long walls" (*chang cheng*, aka, the "Great Wall")—extended ramparts—that have run both north and south of the

---

Culture Contact (New York: Springer, 2015); and Bryan Kristopher Miller, "The Southern Xiongnu in Northern China: Navigating and Negotiating the Middle Ground," in *Complexity of Interaction along the Eurasian Steppe Zone in the First Millennium CE*, ed. Jan Bemmann and Michael Schmauder (Bonn: Vor- und Frühgeschichtliche Archäologie, Rheinische Friedrich-Wilhelms-Universität, 2015), 127–98. For the historiography involved, see Nicola Di Cosmo, "Ethnography of the Nomads and 'Barbarian' History in Han China," in *Intentional History: Spinning Time in Ancient Greece*, ed. Lin Foxhall et al. (Stuttgart: Franz Steiner Verlag, 2010), 306.

4. For an overview of the Yinshan, and the Khangai Mountains to the northwest, see Yoshida Jun'ichi 吉田順一, "Hangai to Kageyama" ハンガイと陰山, *Shikan* 102 (1980): 48–61.

5. Brian J. Darby et al., "Structural Evolution of the Southwestern Daqing Shan, Yinshan Belt, Inner Mongolia, China," in *Paleozoic and Mesozoic Tectonic Evolution of Central and Western Asia* (Boulder, CO: Geological Society of America, 2001): 199–214.

6. Lattimore, *Inner Asian Frontiers of China*, 21–23. For an overview of the geography, see Zhao Songqiao, *Physical Geography of China* (Beijing: Science Press; New York: John Wiley and Sons, 1986): 164–66.

Yinshan.[7] But neither the Yinshan themselves, nor these human-made barriers, have ever created an absolute line of demarcation for different kinds of humans and different kinds of human activity. Or for that of nature: during the last period of glaciation, fierce winds blowing south from the Gobi went over the Yinshan to drop on the regions south of the mountains the fine and fertile dust called loess.[8]

One of the areas covered by loess blowing south from the Mongolian Plateau is the plateau of the Ordos, within the River's great loop, a combination of grassland and, the further west one goes, desert. This is bounded on the east by the River, and then moving further east by two parallel sets of northeast-tending mountain chains, the Lüliang and then the Taihangs, formed by the same processes of fold and thrust that created the Yinshan. These ranges were also covered with loess, especially in the north, though to a lesser degree than the Ordos. As rain has run off from the loess-covered hills, it has carved out the spiderweb-like networks of ravines and gullies that are a regular feature of this area. In the east, the region is contained by the Taihang Mountains, which at some points rise to almost two miles high. Then, on the eastern side of the Taihang, one suddenly plunges down to the flatlands through which the River flows after its last turn to the east at the southern end of the mountain chain. To the character "He," "River," the Chinese have added the descriptor "Yellow," because the great waterway picks up the yellowish loess as it rushes through the highlands. Upon entering the flatlands, the waters spread and slow, and the loess drops out of the water to gradually raise the riverbed. Across millennia, this has led to floods every few centuries—most recently in the 1930s—that have been a bane upon the humans who lived there. Still, particularly in early times, the periodic spread of fertile loess soil across the plains made them a rich base for agricultural production, and for the granaries and treasuries of regimes that learned to exploit it.

Both the Yellow River Plain and the Ordos Plateau are of importance in the history of the Taghbach. The center of their drama, however, was played out on two distinct but neighboring regions tucked between. The first was the Tumed Plain, a northeastern spur of the Ordos Plateau, divided from the main part by the curve of the River as it turns to the south. East and slightly south of this, separated by a chain of high hills, is the basin of the upper Sanggan River—the Datong Basin—which under the Taghbach became the core of their "land of Dai."

With average height of something more than 3,000 feet above sea level, the Tumed Plain was called by the Chinese the "land within the clouds," Yunzhong 雲中. An inverted triangle of about 6,000 square miles, its northern border was defined by the Daqing (Mongol: Dalanhar) mountains, a section of the Yinshan

---

7. Often misleadingly translated as "Great Wall," as this author did just above. On the myth and meaning of the ramparts erected on the frontiers, see Arthur Waldron, *The Great Wall of China: From History to Myth* (Cambridge and New York: Cambridge University Press, 1990).

8. T. R. Treager, *A Geography of China* (London: University of London Press, 1965): 211–15; Yi-fu Tuan, *A Historical Geography of China* (Piscataway, NJ: AldineTransaction, 2008), 15–17.

that separated the Tumed Plain from the open steppe, and on its southwestern side by the Yellow River. The southeast line is marked by the hills that are also the northwestern edge of the Datong Basin. Shielded by the Yinshan from the open steppelands to the north, the Tumed Plain is a transitional zone between northern grasslands and the lands of the sedentary farmer. Situated in the lee of the mountains, which wring out much of what is left in the clouds as they move north, it is better watered than the open steppe, receiving in modern times 15 inches (some 400 mm) a year, while the territories north of the mountains, on the other side of the 400 mm line, get a foot or less.[9] The rainfall on the Tumed Plain is supplemented by southward runoff from the mountains, most significantly the "Great Black" River (Da Hei He), which flows southwest to join the Yellow River.

The mountains also block the freezing winds that come south from Mongolia's continental climate, making the plain milder than it would otherwise be, though not as mild as some might like. Winters are long—lasting about five months. In modern times the average temperature of the coldest month, January, is about 10° F, and can plunge far below that, to −20° F or lower. And during the period under consideration, temperatures in this region were a bit cooler than in either the Han or the Tang.[10] Spring also comes late here; it is not until April that ice finally begins to break up on the rivers. During its short growing season, however, temperatures rise into the 70s or 80s, and during this time, grain—wheat, millet, and kaoliang—can be grown. And it can grow quickly, this being "[t]he most fertile land outside the Great Wall."[11] Sustained agriculture has always been possible there, and in the age of trains and tractors it has become a predominantly Chinese, agrarian region.[12] Through much of its history, however, the Tumed Plain was a land if not exclusively of shepherds, at least ruled by those who came from that stock. In the sixteenth century the Tumed Mongol leader Altan Khan

---

9. Xiao Ke 晓克 et al., *Tumote shi* 土默特史 (Hohhot: Nei Menggu jiao yu chu ban she, 2008), 2. For further discussion of the crucial "400 mm line" of annual rainfall, see Anke Hein, ed., *The "Crescent-shaped Cultural-communication Belt": Tong Enzheng's Model in Retrospect* (Oxford: Archaeopress, 2014); and Han Maoli 韩茂莉, "Li shi shi qi Zhongguo jiang yu shen suo de di li ji chu" 历史时期中国疆域伸缩的地理基础, *Zhongguo wen hua yan jiu* (2016.2): 71–79.

10. Mandred Domrös and Peng Gongbin, *The Climate of China* (Berlin: Springer-Verlag, 1988), 132. Zheng Jingyun 鄭景雲 et al., "Wei Jin Nan bei chao shi qi de Zhongguo dong bu wen du bian hua" 魏晉南北朝時期的中國東部溫度變化, *Di si ji yan jiu* (2005.2): 129–40, suggest two particular cold troughs, one from the 270s into the 350s going 0.5° C (about 1° F) below the norm in our times, another from the 450s to the 530s, about 0.9° C lower; while Wang Lihua 王利華, *Zhongguo nong ye tong shi: Wei Jin Nan bei chao juan* 中國農業通史：魏晉南北朝卷 (Beijing: Zhongguo nongye chubanshe, 2009), 2–3, suggests a several Celsius degree lower temperature in this period than in the 20th century. Zou Yi et al., "The Decline of Pingcheng: Climate Change Impact, Vulnerability and Adaptation in the Northern Wei Dynasty, China," *Journal of Historical Geography* 58 (2017): 12–22, suggest that situations of cooling and drought worsened in the late 470s. See also the broad study of the effect of climate and war and politics in this age by Zhang Min 張敏, *Sheng tai shi xue shi ye xia de Shi Liu Guo Bei Wei xing shuai* 生态史学视野下的十六国北魏兴衰 (Wuhan: Hubei ren min chu ban she, 2004).

11. Treager, *Geography of China*, 209. Again, caution is needed in use of the term "Great Wall"; see note 7.

12. *Nei Menggu zi zhi qu jing ji di li* 内蒙古自治区经济地理, comp. Gang Ge'er 钢格尔 et al. (Beijing: Xin hua chu ban she, 1992), map facing p. 18.

established in this place his "Blue City," Köke qota, or Hohhot (in Chinese transcription, Huhehaote), which now has a population of almost 3 million.

Across the hills on the southeast, and from center to center only about 150 miles away, lies the Datong Basin. This is the northernmost and largest of the loess-covered valleys and basins in the modern PRC province of Shanxi.[13] Watered by the Sanggan, which beginning in hills in the southwest then runs east-northeast through the basin's lower register, the district has historically been more tightly integrated into the Chinese world of farmers than the Tumed Plain. In the Ming period, the line of hills that separated the Datong Basin from the Tumed Plain was reinforced by construction of a particularly great set of ramparts.

But the connection of the Datong basin with the Chinese world may have been largely a matter of propinquity. It is a region very much to itself. While the Tumed Plain's Great Black River flows southwest into the River, and the rivers of central and southern Shanxi flow to the Fen and then to the Yellow River at a much lower point, the Sanggan flows east through the Yinshan highlands, then into other rivers northwest of Beijing and ultimately out into the Bohai Bay. The climate of the Datong Basin is not very different from that of the Tumed Plain. In modern times, Hohhot, on the Tumed Plain, and Datong, in the basin of the upper Sanggan, both reach into the mid-80s F in July, going down to about −10° F in January. At least in the 21st century, Hohhot receives more rain than Datong, getting about five inches in June, its rainiest month, and more than four in July, while Datong receives about 4.25 inches in its month with the most precipitation, July.[14]

For century after century, as the modern scholar Owen Lattimore tells us, these "uplands were fought for by herdsmen from Inner Asia and cultivators from China, though it was not the optimum environment for either way of life."[15] This is perhaps more true for the farmer, for whom the land was "a little too high and a little too poor." Though not full open steppe, these regions could be a rich base for the pastoralist. During the Han period, before the cooling that began in the third century, we are told that in the Yinshan region in general "the grasses

---

13. Treager, *Geography of China*, 211–15.
14. These figures based on results from 2000 to 2012, on www.worldweatheronline.com (last accessed 6 August 2019). See also Domrös and Peng, *Climate of China*, 95, 144–45, whose figures from Hohhot (#58 in the tables)—on the Tumed Plain—and Datong (#59)—in the Sanggan Basin—show that during the period 1951–1980, the latter is slightly less cold in winter, while the two are about the same in spring and summer. Their crops are the same. (Once again, it must be pointed out that in the Period of Division, weather was somewhat colder; see note 10.) Figures on precipitation are even more interesting, showing that in our time, at least, Datong receives about 12 percent less of rain a year than Hohhot (384 mm a year as opposed to 436, and so below the 400 mm line), which receives almost as much at the central Shanxi city of Taiyuan, 150 miles south of Datong (459 mm). Horinger, the site of the early Taghbach capital of Shengle, on the south side of the Tumed Plain, does worse than either, going down to −5° F in January, and not over 80° in July—no doubt because it is on the *yin* side of the mountains dividing the Tumed Plain from the Sanggan basin, while Hohhot is on the *yang* side of the Yinshan.
15. Lattimore, *Inner Asian Frontiers of China*, 413, 414. See also Anatoly Khazanov's discussion of their ambiguous nature in his *Nomads and the Outside World* (Cambridge and New York: Cambridge University Press, 1984), 46.

and forests were lush, the birds and beasts were plenty" 草木茂盛，多禽獸.[16] Showing the changeable nature of the region—the fact that it could be inhabited by different sorts of people, and incorporated into different sorts of states—one line of the Ming ramparts was constructed on the north side of the Datong Basin, while a second was put on the basin's southern edge, in the region of the important Yanmen Pass, which through the Gouzhu Mountains 句注山 could connect the basin with the more secure holdings of central Shanxi. Over the centuries, several famous battles were fought between Inner Asians and Chinese in and around this region. In Western academia, at least, discussion of this "belt of marginal lands" began some 75 years ago, with Lattimore's seminal work *Inner Asian Frontiers of China*. Some misapprehensions have been corrected, and new insights added, of particular importance being Tong Enzheng's development of the idea of a "crescent" zone, part of which was the Yinshan frontier zone.[17] Still, Lattimore contributed a great deal by pointing out that these territories had a "political importance of their own," and as we shall see, an identity as well.[18]

Inhabited from the fourth millennium BCE by scattered communities of Neolithic foragers, who supplemented their diets with horticulture, the second millennium saw transition in these territories—from a Chinese point of view the "Northern Zone" (*bei fang*)—to the use of bronze and a mixed economy of farming and animal rearing, not terribly different from peoples to the south.[19]

By the middle of the first millennium BCE, however, apparently influenced by broader developments on the steppelands to the west, some of these groups had abandoned sedentary life to become fully nomadic pastoralists. But only some: the map that archaeology gives of this period shows complexity, with different groups living in this region, with different forms of economy and

---

16. *Han shu* (hereafter HS) 94B.3803. See also Rafe De Crespigny, *Northern Frontier: The Policies and Strategy of the Later Han Empire* (Canberra: Faculty of Asian Studies, Australian National University, 1984), 34–35; and Emma Bunker, *Ancient Bronzes of the Eastern Eurasian Steppes from the Arthur M. Sackler Collections* (New York: Arthur M. Sackler Foundation, 1997), 55. On the richness of the Yinshan region for herding during Northern Wei, see Sagawa Eiji 佐川 英治, "You mu yu nong geng zhi jian—Bei Wei Pingcheng lu yuan de ji neng ji qi bian qian" 游牧与农耕之间—北魏平城鹿苑的机能及其变迁, in *Zhongguo zhong gu shi yan jiu: Zhongguo zhong gu shi qing nian xue zhe lian yi hui hui kan* 中國中古史研究: 中国中古史青年学者联谊会会刊 (Beijing: Zhonghua shu ju, 2011), 116 (this is a translation of Sagawa's original "Yūboku to nōkō no aida—Hokugi Heijō no Rakuen no kinō to sono hensen" 遊牧と農耕の間—北魏平城の鹿苑の機能とその変遷, *Okayama Daigaku bungaku bu kiyo* 47 [2007]).

17. For an overview of Tong's work, see Hein, ed., *The "Crescent-shaped Cultural-communication Belt"*; and discussion of the crescent in the unfolding of East Asian history in Jessica Rawson, "China and the Steppe: Reception and Resistance," *Antiquity* 91 (2017): 375–88.

18. Lattimore, *Inner Asian Frontiers of China*, 423, 422. See also the positive comments on Lattimore made in recent work by Gideon Shelach, *Prehistoric Societies on the Northern Frontiers of China* (London and Oakville, CT: Equinox, 2009), 3; William Honeychurch, "Alternative Complexities: The Archaeology of Pastoral Nomadic States," *Journal of Archaeological Research* 22.4 (2014): 307; and Honeychurch, *Inner Asia and the Spatial Politics of Empire*, 7.

19. Shelach, *Prehistoric Societies*, 47; Nicola Di Cosmo, "The Northern Frontier in Pre-imperial China," in *Cambridge History of Ancient China*, ed. Michael Loewe and Edward L. Shaughnessy (Cambridge and New York: Cambridge University Press, 1999), 889–90.

production.[20] The modern scholar Gideon Shelach has, however, shown that these diverse frontier groups had already begun to develop a shared regional identity of their own, becoming increasingly conscious of their distinction from their neighbors to the north and to the south, at the same time that they were becoming increasingly involved with those neighbors.[21] This identity took on physical form in horse sacrifices in graves, along with decorated knives and daggers, and most famously, bronze plaques, often sewn onto clothing, which commonly represented animals, in local variation of a pattern of motifs seen across the Eurasian steppelands. These images were often quite ferocious, frequent themes being the tiger, or the wolf, killing prey.[22] Symbols of fierce domination worn on the body accompanied the creation among the frontier populations of a new sort of militaristic elite.[23] Part at least of that militaristic elite eventually developed into nomadic aristocracies, which seem to have begun to dominate groups more firmly fixed to the land.[24] As Lattimore suggested long ago, this distinctive identity would continue to evolve for millennia. A middle point in its development is Northern Wei.[25]

Besides being from another's viewpoint, the Chinese records for events in this region in the second and early first millennia BCE—the only records—are also very sparse. We get more at least of these outsiders' view in the early centuries BCE, with increasing numbers of received texts, culminating in the first century BCE compilation of the *Shi ji* (*Records of the Grand Historian*) of Sima Qian, at least one of the templates that Cui Hao later drew on for his Wei history.[26] Though more attention was now given to nearby societies, the frontier was still not, of course, the center of these chroniclers' attention.

During the period of warring Chinese states, from the fifth through third centuries BCE, the regimes that had grown out of the body of the old Zhou monarchy contended ever more fiercely, while groups in the frontier zone were becoming increasingly involved in the wars to the south, at times allying with one of the warring parties against another.[27] Regimes of the Chinese world now began

---

20. Shelach, *Prehistoric Societies*, 13; and Di Cosmo, *Ancient China and Its Enemies*, 45–46, 171, citing Yao Congwu, *Liao Jin Yuan shi lun wen (shang)*, in Vol. 5 of *Yao Congwu xian sheng quan ji* (Taibei: Zheng zhong shu ju, 1981).

21. Shelach, *Prehistoric Societies*, 109–11, 144; Honeychurch, *Inner Asia and the Spatial Politics of Empire*, 8; and also Bunker, *Ancient Bronzes*, 40ff.

22. Bunker, *Ancient Bronzes*, 57.

23. Di Cosmo, *Ancient China*, 65–68; Shelach, *Prehistoric Societies*, 90.

24. Di Cosmo, *Ancient China*, 87–89.

25. Shelach, *Prehistoric Societies*, 152; and also Di Cosmo, *Ancient China*, 45–46. Lattimore should have looked more at Northern Wei; and more generally, in terms of the name of his book, it could of course have also been called the "Chinese frontier of Inner Asia." Jonathan Skaff, in his *Sui-Tang China and Its Turko-Mongol Neighbors* (Oxford: Oxford University Press, 2012), Chapter 2, looks at the "China-Inner Asian Borderlands" in a later period. Frontier societies have, of course, played important roles in many parts of the world. One example would be the empire of the Avars, in the Carpathian Basin, at the eastern edge of Europe: see Walter Pohl, *The Avars: A Steppe Empire in Central Europe, 567–822* (Ithaca, NY, and London: Cornell University Press, 2018).

26. This is one of the main themes of Di Cosmo's *Ancient China*.

27. See Di Cosmo, *Ancient China*, 116–24, in which section he discusses "non-Chou [i.e., Zhou] as allies," and "non-Chou as resources."

to seize territories in the frontier region, to expand bases for tax and conscription, turn the flank on rivals in the interior, and, no doubt, also to attempt to thwart the growth there of new varieties of warring states. They would succeed, for a time.

Though relationships along the borders were certainly multifaceted, Chinese accounts from the early Zhou on make it clear that raiding parties were coming south to seize grain and goods.[28] Other East Asian power centers would eventually emerge, but in early times in particular the Chinese warring states were "central states," in a variety of ways. One of these was as a center for the accumulation and redistribution of wealth, drawing upon a rich and growing agricultural base, which supported what early became one of the world's most highly developed centers of commerce and manufacture, including early versions of industrial mass production.[29]

There can be no doubt that mobile groups from the north raided south to tap these treasuries, storehouses, and granaries, as is seen in many parts of the world.[30] On the other side, however, Chinese lords were, of course, doing something similar, seizing from rivals lands and populations, who were then subjected to increasingly efficient and systematic forms of extraction of labor and product. Efforts were made to do this in adjacent non-Chinese territories as well. Polities to the north and west had posed threats to Chinese states during the eighth and seventh centuries. In the early centuries BCE, however, the aggressors in the borderlands were the heirs of Zhou.[31] In fact, it may have been incursions from Zhou states that stimulated the rise of full nomadic pastoralism.[32]

The first such effort made in the Tumed-upper Sanggan region came in the early fifth century BCE, with a viscount of the principality of Zhao, who bore the sobriquet Wuxu 毋恤, "The Merciless." The Zhao lords occupied central Shanxi, with frequent contacts with the peoples who lived just to the north. The mother of Wuxu himself was, in fact, of non-Chinese extraction, and for this reason his

---

28. In his *By Steppe, Desert, and Ocean* (Oxford: Oxford University Press, 2015), Barry Cunliffe notes that a key feature of our species is our "intense acquisitiveness . . . [our] passion to take ownership of commodities" (1); and see also the work of the anthropologist Mary Helms, especially *Craft and the Kingly Ideal: Art, Trade and Power* (Austin, TX: University of Texas Press, 1993). Nicola Di Cosmo, "China-Steppe Relations," 51, 58, is one of many recent scholars to point out that agriculture in various forms is found on the steppe, and insist that nomads did not need to raid for grains. It must, however, be pointed out that, since we need to look at the diversity and complexity of the steppe, the evidence of some agriculture in and around the steppe, at some times, does not mean that all herding populations, at all times, had access to such produce; this was a delicate set of relationships, which could very well collapse, or have existed for some and not others. We will discuss more on the "hungry empire" of Northern Wei below.

29. See Lothar Ledderose, *Ten Thousand Things: Module and Mass Production in Chinese Art* (Princeton, NJ: Princeton University Press, 2000).

30. See the incessant and ongoing raiding that occurred across the Scots-English borders in the late Middle Ages, where both sides learned "a system of armed plunder, from neighbours as well as from subjects of the opposite realm": George Fraser MacDonald, *The Steel Bonnets* (New York: Knopf, 1972), 29–30.

31. Di Cosmo, "China-Steppe Relations," 60.

32. Shelach, *Prehistoric Societies*, 71.

father looked down upon him when he was young.[33] According to a tale told in *Shi ji*, however, one day the father sent Wuxu and his brothers to seek a "precious token" on Mount Chang, on the northern edge of Zhao (mod. Hengshan, in the same range as the Yanmen Pass to the southwest).[34] While the others fruitlessly pursued material treasures, Wuxu came back to report that "I've already found the token." When asked what this was, the son proceeded to say that "From the peak of Mount Chang, one can look down upon Dai. Dai—it can be taken" 從常山上臨代，代可取也, Dai—the Datong Basin—being a non-Chinese principality to the north, famous for its horses.[35] For this, the father made Wuxu heir.

The lord of Dai, though according to Shelach much aware of the distinctive nature of his land and his people, had taken to wife a Zhao woman, Wuxu's sister. In 457 BCE the Merciless One invited his brother-in-law to join him for a feast by the Yanmen pass, where he showed the import of his name by having his men beat the barbarian lord to death with wine ladles. He then continued across the Gouzhu Mountains into the Datong Basin to take Dai.[36] From this point on, the *Shi ji* passage on this topic tells us, Zhao was in direct contact with the Hu, in this period at least a generic term for "mounted nomad,"[37] though this is apparently a reference to Dai's neighbors to the north, and not to those people themselves, who would have been that part of the frontier population who lived relatively settled lives, with a mix of farming and ranching.[38]

There followed 150 years or so of general peace, and growing trade, with horses and furs going south, silks and ornaments coming north.[39] At the end of the fourth century, however, these patterns changed significantly, under the first

---

33. There are several mentions of members of the Zhao royal house marrying non-Chinese. See Shen Changyun 沈长云, *Zhao guo shi gao* 赵国史稿 (Beijing: Zhonghua shu ju, 2000), 107.

34. *Shi ji* (hereafter SJ) 43.1789.

35. See discussion of the nature and location of Dai in Jaroslav Průšek, *Chinese Statelets and the Northern Barbarians in the Period 1400–300 B.C.* (New York: Humanities Press, 1971), 189–92; and of the origin of this polity in the sixth century BCE, when the Jin regime from which Zhao later emerged drove non-Chinese north of the Gouzhu Mountains: Shen, *Zhao guo shi gao*, 113. We know of this polity only through Chinese text, and so don't know the linguistic origin of the word "Dai." What we do know is that Inner Asian rulers of parts of the Chinese world often played with names: Mark Elliott, "Manchu (Re)Definitions of the Nation in the Early Qing," *Indiana East Asian Working Papers on Language and Politics in Modern China* 7 (1996): 61, points out that the Chinese name for the Manchu dynasty, "Da (or Dai) Qing" 大清, was pronounced in Manchu as "Daicing" (the "c" pronounced like English "ch"), which in Manchu meant "warrior," and so "the warrior dynasty."

36. Di Cosmo, *Ancient China*, 128–29. The Zhao clan had up to this point been part of the larger state of Jin. These seizures of territory led to establishment of Zhao as an independent state: Lattimore, *Inner Asian Frontiers of China*, says "[t]he newly invaded territory north of the headwaters of the Fen was not drawn inward to the state of Chin [Jin] but broke away from it, forming the new state of Chao [Zhao]" (416). Despite her brother's treacherous nature, the sister is said to have grieved her husband's death to the point of committing suicide: Shen, *Zhao guo shi gao*, 114.

37. Di Cosmo, *Ancient China*, 127, 129, defines Hu as a blanket term meaning "mounted bowmen who practiced pastoral nomadism as their main economic activity." See also Shimunek, *Languages of Ancient Southern Mongolia and North China*, 37 note 1.

38. SJ 43.1793, 110.2885; and Průšek, *Chinese Statelets*, 223–24. This is part of what Di Cosmo, in his "Northern Frontier in Pre-imperial China," 951, describes as "the shrinkage of the intermediate area inhabited by semipastoral people."

39. Di Cosmo, *Ancient China*, 131–33.

Zhao lord to arrogate the title "king" (*wang*), Wuling 武靈 ("Martial Spirit"). Pressed by rivals to the east and west, and perhaps reacting to the emergence of fully developed cavalry among the northern pastoralists,[40] Wuling now sought to extend and solidify his control over the frontier region. He began in 307 BCE by taking a tour of the perimeters of his realm, going north to the Datong Basin then west to the banks of the River, after which he instituted the much-mentioned plan "to take nomad garb and mounted archery in order to teach (them to) the hundred names" 將胡服騎射以教百姓, his subjects, that is to say, those whose family names were on census registers for purposes of taxation and conscription.[41] The "hundred names" who were to be taught certainly included the frontier folk of Dai, who if not nomads were well accustomed to the horse, and were now being incorporated into the king's army.[42] This is confirmed by the rapidity with which an effective cavalry force was raised: it was just one year later that Wuling began a series of campaigns that swept from Dai west to defeat the frontier peoples known in Chinese as the Loufan and "Forest Barbarians" (Lin Hu) and seize the "[lands] below the Yinshan Mountains" all the way to the western corner of the River's loop.[43]

Along with this came a proposal that the court and the army wear the dress of the "barbarian." "I doubt not at all the efficacy of the Hu costume," said Wuling, "my only qualm is to hear the laughter of the empire" 寡人非疑胡服也，吾恐天下笑之.[44] Here we see presented, in the not entirely reliable text *Zhan guo ce*, a fascinating inverse to a Sinicizing policy of the Northern Wei emperor Xiaowen, 800 years later, which we shall discuss in detail in Chapter 16. And as occurred under Xiaowen, some bitterly resisted. In the *Zhan guo ce* anecdote, a royal kinsman says, "[T]oday, Your Majesty, you want a new beginning and a departure from custom. Barbarian clothing is not thought well of in the world, and wearing it would not be something which would instruct people and make the proprieties

---

40. Shelach, *Prehistoric Societies*, 71; with reference to Di Cosmo, *Ancient China*, 134–38.
41. SJ 43.1806; ZZTJ 3.104.
42. Shen, *Zhao guo shi gao*, 115; on p. 163, we are told of establishment southeast of Hohhot of a cavalry base 騎邑. Emma Bunker (*Ancient Bronzes*, 24) has suggested that cast-silver bridle ornaments were given by Zhao to frontier horse herders; and Robin D. S. Yates, "The Horse in Early Chinese Military History," in *Jun shi zu zhi yu zhan zheng* 軍事組織與戰爭, ed. Huang Kewu (Taibei: Zhong yang yan jiu yuan li shi yu yan yan jiu suo, 2002), 49, suggests that cavalry had probably begun to appear in Warring States armies decades before. See also the general comments on such use in Di Cosmo, *Ancient China*, 125. Nicola Di Cosmo, "The Origins of the Great Wall," *The Silk Road* 4.1 (2006): 19, suggests that the northern ramparts were built as "part of a system designed to enclose and establish exclusive access to a precious reservoir of human and material resources," to wit, cavalry recruited from the frontier populations.
43. SJ 43.1811, 110.2885; ZZTJ 3.106. The suggestion of the source of the cavalry is confirmed by the statement in the SJ 43 passage that "the Minister of Dai, Zhao Gu, ruled the Hu, and summoned their soldiers" 代相趙固主胡, 致其兵.
44. *Zhan guo ce* 戰國策 (Shanghai: Shanghai gu ji chu ban she, 1978), 2: 19.654–55; tr. J. I. Crump, *Chan-kuo tsʾe* (Oxford: Clarendon, 1970), 297. The book, it must be noted, is fundamentally a collection of anecdotes, collected when and where it is not entirely clear. As Crump, the translator, bluntly tells us, it "is not a history" (*Chan-kuo tsʾe*, 11). Care needs taken in its use, but here at least it is elaborating events described in (somewhat) more reliable historical texts.

禮 complete. If the garment be outlandish, intentions become disordered; when custom is flouted, the people become rebellious. So it is that one who rules a country does not clothe himself in strange garments. The Middle Kingdoms have no affinity for barbarian activities, so this action of yours is not something which teaches the people and makes the proprieties complete." To which the king replied, "[T]he niceties of deportment and the standardizing of clothing are for the regulation of common men and have no place in the discussions of superior men."[45] And so, according to *Zhan guo ce*, the matter was decided.

Among the territories being brought under Wuling's control was the region around the modern town Liangcheng, by Lake Daihai, in the hills separating the Tumed Plain and the Datong Basin. On the basis of excavated burials, some have suggested that it is the "cradle of the Xiongnu," the first great steppe empire.[46] If the forefathers of the Xiongnu had been there when Wuling arrived—and the name Xiongnu does not appear in the *Shi ji* account of these events—they would presumably have been driven out of the new regions of Zhao control, perhaps south across the River into the Ordos, or north beyond the ramparts (*chang cheng* 長城) that Zhao constructed to separate the zone of their supposed control from the steppes to the north. One line of these ran through the southern foothills of the Yinshan, while another line ran north of the mountains. Remnants still survive.

The walls would have served multiple purposes. One was undoubtedly to prevent raiding into the newly claimed Zhao territories. Being for the most part rammed earth constructions that were originally 11 to 12 feet high, these were not at all the imposing structures built 2,000 years later by Ming.[47] Interlopers could certainly have found a way to get over them. Nevertheless, it would have been much harder to bring their mounts over, and since raiding parties seem to have frequently been small, ad hoc adventures,[48] they wouldn't have had the time or manpower to breach the wall.[49] But the walls served other purposes as well. One of these might have been an effort to cut off yearly cycles of nomadic movement, with summers spent on the open grasslands north of the Yinshan and then

45. *Zhan guo ce* 2: 19.663; tr. Crump, *Chao kuo ts'e*, 302–3.
46. Di Cosmo, *Ancient China*, 77.
47. Arthur Waldron, *The Great Wall of China*; Di Cosmo, *Ancient China*, 147, and on p. 144 mentioning their use of natural barriers to keep building to a minimum; Gai Shanlin 盖山林 and Lu Sixian 陆思贤, "Yinshan nan lu de Zhao chang cheng" 阴山南麓的赵长城, in *Zhongguo chang cheng yi ji diao cha bao gao ji* 中国长城遗迹调查报告集, ed. Wen wu bian ji wei yuan hui (Beijing: Wen wu chu ban she, 1981), 21–24. See also the fascinating article by Jessica Wapner, "Do Walls Change How We Think?," *New Yorker*, 28 March 2019.
48. See the numbers given for Xiongnu raiding parties (some at least having but 90, or even 40) by Enno Giele, "Evidence for the Xiongnu in Chinese Wooden Documents from the Han Period," in *Xiongnu Archaeology: Multidisciplinary Perspectives of the First Steppe Empire in Inner Asia*, ed. Ursula Brosseder and Bryan K. Miller (Bonn: Vor- und Frühgeschichtliche Archäologie, Rheinische Friedrich-Wilhelms-Universität Bonn, 2011), 72–73.
49. Mark Edward Lewis, *The Early Chinese Empires: Qin and Han* (Cambridge, MA: The Belknap Press of Harvard University Press, 2007), 130, more specifically suggests that the walls served to keep northern raiding parties from absconding with the herds of Han subjects who lived within the walls.

retreat south of the mountains in an effort to protect their herds and flocks from the worst of winter's cold.[50] Once again, while individual humans would almost certainly have been able to scramble over the ramparts, they wouldn't be able to bring with them their sheep and goats to graze on the "lush grasslands" Zhao now claimed as its own. The walls also cut off trade and contact of newly created Zhao subjects with the nomads who may heretofore have been their kinsmen, or masters; that is to say, they attempted to prevent the creation of complex polities out of the diverse populations of the larger region.[51] And perhaps most fundamentally, the walls kept the "hundred names" from escaping onto the steppe and so escaping the control exerted over them by the Zhao lord through the systems that had evolved in the Chinese interior.[52]

These efforts were not entirely effective.[53] Archaeological surveys of the region around Liangcheng at this time show that while administratively controlled population centers were established on the farmlands around Lake Daihai, homesteads depending on a more mixed economy were also scattered across outlying regions, perhaps in an effort to evade Zhao control.[54] But some success must have been gotten from the wall building, since Zhao was not alone in such efforts.[55] To the west, Qin was also imposing physical limits on movement and mingling in what had been a porous frontier region, building their own set of ramparts that led from Ningxia to the northeastern bend of the River, where they seem to have laid down a challenge to Zhao by crossing that great waterway to establish an outpost on the east side, at the mouth of the Tumed Plain's Great Black River.[56] Similar construction was conducted by Zhao's eastern Chinese neighbor, Yan, which is said to have pushed the "Hu of the east" (Dong Hu 東胡) back hundreds of miles beyond their newly created barriers. Again, however, archaeological reports tell us that some indigenous groups remained among those on the south side of the walls. Though it is not clear if these populations had previously been autonomous, or subjects of a confederation of "Eastern Hu," we do know

---

50. De Crespigny, *Northern Frontier*, 31; Di Cosmo, "Origins of the Great Wall."

51. For comments on the power gained by nomads through control of farmland and peasants, see Abbas Alizadeh, "Archaeology and the Question of Mobile Pastoralism in Late Prehistory," in *The Archaeology of Mobility: Old World and New World*, ed. Hans Barnard and Willeke Wendrich (Los Angeles: Cotsen Institute of Archaeology, University of California, 2008), 80.

52. See Lattimore, *Inner Asian Frontiers of China*, 484. For the use of walls to prevent escape of Han subjects to the Xiongnu, see the quotation in Giele, "Xiongnu in Chinese Wooden Documents," 62: "As to those who abscond and make over to the Xiongnu or the other barbarians ... all these are to be cut in half at the waist." Sebastian Junger, in his *Tribe: On Homecoming and Belonging* (New York and London: Twelve, 2016), 9–10, points out that in early stages of European colonization of North America, of those immigrants who went over to the natives none returned to their original community.

53. Shelach, *Prehistoric Societies*, 2–3, quoting Lattimore, *Inner Asian Frontiers of China*, 25; they did not create a rigid distinction between "steppe and sown."

54. See Gregory G. Indrisano, "Subsistence, Environment Fluctuation and Social Change: A Case Study in South Central Inner Mongolia" (Ph.D. diss., University of Pittsburgh, 2006).

55. Miller, "The Southern Xiongnu," 140.

56. SJ 110.2885–86; Di Cosmo, *Ancient China*, 138–58, esp. 147, 149.

that they now became a source of cavalry for the Yan army, as had happened with Zhao.[57] As for those who built these walls, we can assume they were men already bound into the system of census, taxation and corvée, called up to enclose others within that system. In an important recent study, *Against the Grain*, James Scott has on a worldwide basis discussed the bound nature of the settled farmer and systematic extraction of part of such an individual's produce.[58]

This system of census, taxation, and corvée was at the heart of the state system emerging in the Chinese world in the fourth and third centuries BCE, best known in Qin of course, but appearing among its rivals as well. In fact, with addition of the canon of authoritative texts that reached full development during the Han period—the "Chinese classics"—this is one way to define the Chinese world, at least in its early stages.[59] The system of control and extraction was implemented by Zhao and its rival expansionists not only with walls, but with placement of new administrative centers in the occupied frontier territories; power often lies in imposition of names. For Zhao, in the east was established a new unit of local administration, a commandery (*jun* 郡), bearing an old name, Dai. This version was located in the vicinity of the modern town of Yuxian 蔚縣, along the middle Sanggan, in the mountains north of modern Beijing (about 100 miles east of the Northern Wei Dai, which would be centered on the upper Sanggan). The Datong Basin itself was placed under a commandery re-entitled Yanmen, after the pass through which the Merciless One had led his army to take these territories, after murdering their lord. The western of the three imposed Zhao commanderies was Yunzhong, on the Tumed Plain.

These attempts to impose order did not bring peace. Conflict grew between Zhao and increasingly militarized frontier populations.[60] But it grew far more dramatically among the Chinese states themselves. In 228 BCE, Qin conquered Zhao, a surviving member of the royal house fleeing north to try to hold out as King of Dai.[61] Six years later, that fell as well, along with Yan.

---

57. Di Cosmo, *Ancient China*, 155; and restated more succinctly in his "Origins of the Great Wall."
58. James Scott, *Against the Grain: A Deep History of the Earliest States* (New Haven, CT: Yale University Press, 2017).
59. There are, of course, many ways to define the Chinese world. For a good summation, see Robin Yates, "Introduction: Empire of the Scribes," in *Birth of an Empire: The State of Qin Revisited*, ed. Yuri Pines et al. (Berkeley: University of California Press, 2014), 141, who describes the emergence of "an unprecedentedly powerful, centralized, and hierarchically organized bureaucratic state," which "attempted to subject, control, and exploit the physical and material resources of all individuals and groups living within its boundaries." See also efforts to define an "East Asian Heartland," which though diverse collectively became the "roots of Chinese civilization," by John S. Major and Constance A. Cook, in their *Ancient China* (Abingdon and New York: Routledge, 2017), 10–15; and Shelach, *Prehistoric Societies*, 5, where he admits that though anachronistic for the very early period under discussion, the term is "both convenient and purposeful," since "[m]uch of what we can call the Chinese culture of the early Imperial period—such as the written Chinese language, important texts, social and political norms, religious beliefs and artistic expressions—were already present and significant during the first half of the first millennium BCE." Of more general interest are the chapters in Thomas S. Mullaney, ed., *Critical Han Studies: The History, Representation and Identity of China's Majority* (Berkeley: University of California Press, 2012).
60. Di Cosmo, *Ancient China*, 152.
61. SJ 6.233, 235.

The Qin First Emperor's work was completed in the next year. Wishing to maintain the power of his dynasty for "ten thousand generations," the founder now implemented a wide-ranging set of programs to solidify central control over the conquered territories. The dynasty itself was short-lived, but these actions would profoundly change the nature of East Asia, for centuries, perhaps millennia. Though most were imposed upon the Chinese world, the newly created empire's interior, one at least was on the northern frontier: in 215 the Qin general, Meng Tian, was sent north with an army of 300,000 to take control of the Ordos and adjacent regions, including the Tumed Plain and the Datong Basin.[62] The walls built by Zhao and Yan were now linked together in a combined set of ramparts spanning Qin's entire northern border. With unification of the Chinese territories, control of the frontier territories had been raised to a new order.

The Xiongnu had been present as a power in the frontier region for at least several decades before the Meng Tian campaign of occupation, having already engaged in military struggle with Zhao, Qin, and Yan.[63] But as the modern scholar Nicola Di Cosmo has well described, the crisis of expulsion from their apparent homeland in the Ordos region now precipitated both transformation and growth into a major imperial power in East Asia, no doubt based on broad preexisting ties that stretched throughout the northern lands.[64] With collapse of Qin after the First Emperor's death came collapse of Qin's artificially constructed frontier districts, and the southward flight of those who had been compelled to settle and defend them. Unmanned, the ramparts no longer impeded, and the Xiongnu leader Touman led his followers across the walls to retake at least some of the contested lands of the Ordos.[65]

---

62. SJ 6.252, 88.2565–66, 110.2886; the latter gives the lesser number of 100,000. See also Di Cosmo, *Ancient China*, 174–75.

63. A Zhao general, "Li the Shepherd" 李牧, is said to have had particular success fighting back the Xiongnu; see SJ 81.2449; Di Cosmo, *Ancient China*, 154.

64. Di Cosmo, *Ancient China*, 89. William Honeychurch, in his recent *Inner Asia and the Spatial Politics of Empire*, has done a good job pulling together great amounts of archaeological study in Mongolian and Russian to demonstrate growth during the first millennium BCE of linkages between communities in central and northern Mongolia, which existed within a north-south network of relationships that led from those regions, down into the Ordos and then into the Chinese world. He agrees with Di Cosmo in insisting (vs. Thomas Barfield and others) that the Xiongnu state did not emerge in response to the Chinese empire. In the opinion of this author, however, he pushes this matter too far, going on to argue that the origins of the Xiongnu empire came from the regions in Mongolia in which, coincidentally, he has concentrated his research. In the midst of this, arguing for a completely autochthonous origin to the Xiongnu regime, he simply rejects the abundant mentions in Chinese history showing Xiongnu origins and early activities in the frontier region. These sources are, of course, both biased and incomplete; but it is not appropriate to dismiss them out of hand on the basis of sheer conjecture emerging from the existence of cultural and material interaction in regions to the north. In fact, Honeychurch does so only selectively, since he opens the book with an account of the confrontation of Liu Bang and Modun at Pingcheng. The only real proof he raises to make his point is: (1), the growth of regional ties mentioned above, and (2), that burials at his sites don't demonstrate violent death around the time of formation of the Xiongnu empire. It should not be necessary to say that this empire, like any empire, did not emerge only on the basis of military action. There is no reason why, taking shape in the frontier region in the midst of crisis, the Xiongnu did not take military action against rivals to the east and west, while diplomatically riding north to build new kinds of alliance with those with whom they had long-standing relations.

65. SJ 110.2887–88.

A struggle between father and son now led to the former's murder followed by the explosive rise of the parricide, Modun, as the first great Xiongnu lord.⁶⁶ Apparently building alliances in the lands to the north, Modun then turned west to attack a group called the Yuezhi, forcing at least their leadership out of the East Asian theater and asserting control over trade moving through the Tarim Basin. To the east, in the tales put forth by Han historians, Modun repeatedly accommodated demands of the lord of the Eastern Hu, until the latter finally demanded territorial concessions, whereupon the outraged Modun led a campaign to rout his eastern rival.⁶⁷ Those of the defeated who could are said to have fled to the north or east, beyond the Xiongnu empire; those who could not came under Xiongnu control. Among the former are people called—in the modern Mandarin pronunciation of the name's Chinese transcription—the Xianbei 鮮卑, or in the reconstruction used in this book, the Serbi. Among those who became subjects of the Xiongnu were the Wuhuan (also transcribed into Chinese as Wuwan), who now paid a heavy regular tribute of livestock and pelts to the Xiongnu lord, the *chanyu*.⁶⁸ According to Chinese sources, the bound Wuhuan and the free Serbi were culturally and linguistically closely related.⁶⁹ A shared language—or related set of languages—was probably the main thing binding these peoples together.

While civil war raged within the Chinese interior, Modun retook all the Xiongnu lands in the Ordos, gaining a closeness to the emerging Han capital of Chang'an (mod. Xi'an) that must have made its lords uncomfortable. "War," as a Chinese observer noted, "is their business."⁷⁰ The center of the *chanyu*'s activity—the portable tent palace from which he ruled—was, however, further

---

66. SJ 110.2888. Nicola Di Cosmo, "Ethnography of the Nomads and 'Barbarian' History in Han China," 307–8, suggests this story may originally be from Xiongnu oral sources. Honeychurch (*Inner Asia and the Spatial Politics of Empire*, 224) has expressed doubt about this story specifically, not entirely accurately stating that Beckwith and Di Cosmo support his view. It must be pointed out that under the Taghbach there are several, reasonably verifiable father-killings. Regarding the origins of the name "Xiongnu," which is a Chinese transcription, there are various theories: see an overview in Peter Golden, *An Introduction to the History of the Turkic Peoples: Ethnogenesis and State-formation in Medieval and Early Modern Eurasia and the Middle East* (Wiesbaden: O. Harrassowitz, 1992), 58. Similar issues are found with this people's monarchical title, *chanyu* or *shanyu* 單于, which is again Chinese transcription of a not-clearly-known original; Beckwith, *Empires of the Silk Road*, 387 note 7, proposes the reconstruction *Darya. As for the name of the first major *chanyu*, the Chinese characters on which it is based are read in several different ways: Modun, Modu, Maodun; Beckwith, *Empires of the Silk Road*, 387 note 8, has suggested it may come from "Hero," Bayatur, a widely used name in Inner Asia, containing the Iranian "bay" or "beg," meaning "lord." As seen above, a case has been made that the Wolf Lord's name also contained this term.
67. SJ 110.2889.
68. De Crespigny, *Northern Frontier*, 367. Failure by the Wuhuan to pay one's duty is said to have resulted in seizure of family as hostages.
69. *San guo zhi* (hereafter SGZ) 30.835. For general discussion of the Wuhuan (also transcribed as Wuwan), see Ma Changshou, *Wuhuan yu Xianbei*; and Nina Duthie, "The Nature of the *Hu*: Wuhuan and Xianbei Ethnography in the *San guo zhi* and *Hou Han shu*," EMC 25 (2019): 23–41. Some scholars link the Wuhuan to the later Avar (or Awar): Pulleyblank, "Chinese and Their Neighbors," 453; Shimunek, *Languages of Ancient Southern Mongolia and North China*, 55–57. Christopher Atwood has suggested the Chinese transcription "Wuhuan" came from a word originally meaning "war," a vanguard suicide unit to which Inner Asian nobles were assigned as punishment: "Some Early Inner Asian Terms Related to the Imperial Family and the Comitatus," 56.
70. SJ 110.2899 (tr. Burton Watson, *Records of the Grand Historian of China* [New York: Columbia University Press, 1961]: 2: 171), a comment attributed to the Chinese defector Zhonghang Yue (SJ 110.2899–901). In recent decades, some scholars have correctly felt a need to refute a caricature of Inner Asian populations as simply warlike creatures

north, apparently ranging across the frontier districts from Yunzhong to Dai; what Modun called these regions is unknown to us, though the toponym Dai—whatever its original source—could like much in East Asia have been shared by many peoples, belonging to none.[71] Modun's institutions, it must be noted, were quite distinct from those of the Chinese world. Central to them was the *chanyu*'s army, organized on a decimal basis, a practice that may have come indirectly from the Achaemenid empire of Iran. This would later reappear among the Taghbach and many other Inner Asian polities.[72] It is important to remember that although the Xiongnu state was quite different from the Han in terms of organizational form and symbol set, and with much less in terms of material output, it was still a political and military power of the East Asian world, an empire in its own right.[73]

Emerging victorious from the Chinese civil war, the first emperor of the Han dynasty, Liu Bang (d. 195 BCE), attempted to re-establish control of the frontier region, sending an agent to take control of Mayi, "Horse Town" (mod. Shuozhou)—obviously a mart for horse trading—which lay at the bottom of the Datong Basin, on the north side of the Yanmen Pass. There the Han representative was immediately seized by the Xiongnu, defected—as did many in this period—and in the year 200 BCE led the *chanyu*'s forces south to the strategic town of Taiyuan, on the Fen River in the center of what is now the province of Shanxi.[74] Challenged, Liu Bang then himself led an army against the invaders. Using a classic steppe tactic, the Xiongnu immediately withdrew, luring the Han army through the passes and up into the Datong Basin. Riding ahead of the main force, the Han emperor and his following arrived at the Qin outpost of Pingcheng, the "city of pacification," where they camped on the flat peak of White Top (Baideng) Hill, just northeast of modern Datong. There, according to the story, he was immediately encircled by 400,000 picked Xiongnu cavalry and for seven days cut off from his larger army in a tense standoff. In the end, however, he was released and withdrew to the south. Modun then withdrew as well.

---

seen among historians of both the ancient Chinese world and the modern West. Thus, see Di Cosmo's criticism of the Zhonghang Yue comment, in "Origins of the Great Wall," 15. It is certainly the case that not all of the many groups inhabiting Inner Asia over the millennia have been militarized populations, but some societies—or groups within societies—certainly were; see the assertion by Denis Sinor that in the Turkic and Mongolic languages there was no native word for "soldier," since "military service was a natural occupation": "The Inner Asian Warriors," *JAOS* 101.2 (1981): 135.

71. SJ 110.2891–92. And see Waldron, *The Great Wall of China*, 106; and Di Cosmo, *Ancient China*, 189, who suggests that the Tumed Plain and Datong Basin were perhaps the Xiongnu monarch's personal domain.

72. Di Cosmo, "China-Steppe Relations," 59–60, and "Ethnogenesis," 47. It was, of course, most famous with the Mongols, for whom Temujin borrowed this system from a neighbor on the steppe: see Igor de Rachewiltz, *The Secret History of the Mongols: A Mongolian Epic Chronicle of the Thirteenth Century*, 2 vols. (Leiden and Boston: Brill, 2004), 1: 35, 410.

73. Here interest can be had from the work of Pekka Hämäläinen, who moving away from a single, dominant model of state and civilization in his *Comanche Empire* (New Haven, CT: Yale University Press, 2008) describes a loosely organized empire that can be compared to that of the Xiongnu; this work was brought to my attention by mention in Bryan Miller's "The Southern Xiongnu." See also discussion of "state" or "polity" in Honeychurch, *Inner Asia and the Spatial Politics of Empire*, 58–59.

74. SJ 110.2894, 93.2634; ZZTJ 11.377–78. And see discussion of these events in Di Cosmo, *Ancient China*, 190–92; Honeychurch, *Inner Asia and the Spatial Politics of Empire*, 1–2.

The negotiations that followed would lead to "brotherly" relations between the two dynasties. Han was able to resume control over at least certain outposts in the region, including Dai, Yanmen and Yunzhong, perhaps among other things as entrepôts for trade in horses, livestock, and furs.[75] For what it is worth, in the Chinese description of the arrangement the Xiongnu lord ruled all north of the Qin ramparts, the Han lord all to the south.[76] In Chinese, the relationship thus established was called *heqin*, or "amicable kinship." Under its provisions, marriage ties were established between the two dynasties, and regular tribute payments sent to the *chanyu*.[77] Its underlying logic rested on two key features: the ability of the Xiongnu, though much fewer in number, to marshal potent and mobile cavalry forces; and the enormous wealth of the Han empire, based on the much larger number of its productive and taxable subjects.

Though important, this was just one source from which the Xiongnu court drew revenue to maintain its power by maintaining its armies. Others included tribute from Inner Asian vassals, and control of trade routes, both familiar east-west ones, and others that moved goods along the north-south axis.[78] The Xiongnu empire was not entirely dependent on interaction with the Chinese world.[79] Neither, however, did it wish to neglect that major funding source. The regular extraction of wealth from the Chinese world was undoubtedly an important aspect of the Xiongnu empire, as it would be for that of the Taghbach.

On the Han side, several generations of "august god-kings," *huang di*, were undoubtedly told that it was both less expensive and more effective to give "gifts" to the Xiongnu than go to war with them. Some at least at the Chang'an court, however, came increasingly to resent the situation, taking up the idea of Chang'an as center of the world, with the corollary that those at the edges should accept the role of vassal.[80] This would have been exacerbated by the loose control that the *chanyu*, willingly or not, exercised over his subjects along the frontier. Small-scale raiding into Chinese settlements there, as a kind of pick-up game for those in the mood for the "callous fun of reiving," was an ongoing issue.[81]

---

75. SJ 110.2895. On the isolated nature of these administrative centers in the frontier regions—as "islands" of imperial control—see Miller, "Southern Xiongnu," 151
76. SJ 110.2902.
77. SJ 110.2894; Di Cosmo, *Ancient China*, 193–96.
78. Di Cosmo, *Ancient China*, 188.
79. Di Cosmo, *Ancient China*, 169–70.
80. It must also be noted that not all in Chang'an or the larger Chinese world—or among the Xiongnu—thought this way: see discussion in Michael Nylan, "Review: Talk about 'Barbarians' in Antiquity," *Philosophy East and West* 62.4 (2012): 580–601, including the very insightful comment (590) that the identities of the ancients "were far more complexly constructed than our own impoverished identities today, which are apt to boil down to gender and/or sexual preference, national identity, and consumer preferences." For discussion of the "tributary system," see Tansen Sen and Victor Mair, *Traditional China in Asian and World History* (Ann Arbor, MI: Association for Asian Studies, 2012), 33.
81. Di Cosmo, *Ancient China*, 217, 221; Giele, "Xiongnu in Chinese Wooden Documents," 70–75. Such raiding was, no doubt, also greatly enjoyed by the raiders. Graham Robb describes memories "of the sheer callous fun of

Chang'an's desire to exert more secure control over the claimed frontier territories took concrete shape in the reign of that dynasty's "martial emperor," Wudi (r. 141–87 BCE). Wudi's father and grandfather—the two preceding Han emperors—had begun to build up cavalry forces to defend the capital region. Wudi completed the process, often using captives or mercenary units taken from the Xiongnu or other groups, borrowing from Zhao a practice that would persist for centuries within Chinese regimes.[82] Having thus remade the Han military, the emperor turned aggressively on the *chanyu*; by 119 BCE he had been forced out of the Ordos and adjoining frontier regions and so compelled to move the center of his activities to the lands north of the Gobi.[83] The Xiongnu leaders seem to have greatly regretted this loss of territory. In a memorial submitted almost 200 years later, a Han official reported that "the elders of the frontier say that 'Since the Xiongnu lost the Yinshan, when passing that [place] there's never a time that they don't weep'" 邊長老言匈奴失陰山之後，過之未嘗不哭也.[84]

To fill the space on the newly taken frontier—and interestingly prefiguring Taghbach policy 500 years later—Wudi had hundreds of thousands of Chinese farmers transported north.[85] Yunzhong—the Tumed Plain—now came to 173,270 head of tax-paying subjects on its census registers.[86] A modern archaeological survey of the area around the Daihai Lake—in a small valley in the mountains between the Tumed Plain and the Datong Basin—shows a much greater concentration of population—presumably the transportees—around administrative centers.[87] But these were outposts in a region imperfectly held. Blanket control was never established in these highlands, as evidenced by the many small forts that were scattered through the region, much more numerous than those in the interior.[88] These stood not just against invasion, but against the indigenous

---

reiving (i.e., raiding) in its glory days"—in what had been the borderlands between England and Scotland, before union in the early 17th century led to efforts to suppress these activities—"when humble farmers played practical jokes on the high and mighty, burned down their houses and mills, galloped over the mosses under a harvest moon and stole anything that moved": *The Debatable Land: The Lost World between Scotland and England* (New York and London: W. W. Norton, 2018), 178.

82. SJ 110.2909, 111.2939, the latter mentioning how, grieving for the death of his general Huo Qubing, the emperor Wudi had armored troops from "dependent states" line the road from Chang'an to his tomb at Maoling. The commanders of Wudi's troops were at times Xiongnu themselves: see SJ 111.2941. For development of the Han cavalry, see Di Cosmo, *Ancient China*, 199–200, 204, 232–34. Interesting discussion is given by Catrin Kost, "Heightened Receptivity: Steppe Objects and Steppe Influences in Royal Tombs of the Western Han Dynasty," *JAOS* 137.2 (2017): 373, on "evidence for the appropriation of the north and its artifacts" by the lords of Former Han, whose tombs contained classic Inner Asian belt plaques, and models of archers with Phrygian caps, using the way of the *chanyu* to redefine and enhance their own status within the Chinese world.

83. SJ 110.2910–11; HS 94A.3770.

84. HS 94B.3803; and see translation of this document in Garett P. S. Olberding, *Dubious Facts: The Evidence of Early Chinese Historiography* (Albany: State University of New York Press, 2012), 210.

85. SJ 110.2911; Di Cosmo, *Ancient China*, 240–41.

86. HS 28B.1620.

87. This is the focus of the dissertation of Indrisano, "Subsistence, Environment Fluctuation and Social Change."

88. Chen Bo and Gideon Shelach, "Fortified Settlements and the Settlement System in the Northern Zone of the Han Empire," *Antiquity* 88 (2014): 237; HS 49.2286.

frontier populations that had remained, and resented occupation by Chang'an. It was the Xiongnu head that had been displaced, not necessarily the body.

Han was changing, too, slowly, then very suddenly with the usurpation of Wang Mang (r. 9–23). The man who resumed Han rule in 25 CE was a distant descendant of the Liu imperial line, his polity quite distinct from Former Han. With its capital now moved east to the western edge of the Yellow River Plain, to the ancient city of Luoyang, Later Han was dependent on private armies and their leaders, the universal military draft of the original Han long since abandoned.[89] More particularly, the frontier was changing as well. For half a century, Xiongnu—not content simply to weep as they passed by—had been percolating back into the frontier region, or reasserting a presence that had never been entirely lost. In the midst of the wars that ousted Wang Mang, a Xiongnu took up the Chinese name Liu Wenbo—the "earl of culture," with the surname of the Han royal house—and occupied the Ordos and all the districts south of the Yinshan.[90] Though the Earl of Culture was eventually dislodged by the Later Han founder, the frontier had now clearly resumed its ethnic complexity, with Chinese farmers in the valleys surrounded by groups allied to the *chanyu*, and others as well, such as the Wuhuan, the former Xiongnu subjects, who beginning in Wudi's reign had been settled by Han in the frontier districts to serve as scouts and auxiliary units against their former masters.[91] In a memorial to the throne toward the end of Former Han, by an official arguing against accepting a beleaguered *chanyu*'s request to lead his party south into the frontier districts, one of the arguments made was that the border was already porous, with too much movement back and forth, as slaves, bandits, the poor, and former Xiongnu subjects fled across the ramparts to join the Xiongnu.[92]

Luoyang did still exercise a measure of power in the region, and settlements and outposts it re-established would survive into the early third century.[93] At least part of the reason for persistence of Han power there would have been Han generosity, its regular distribution of its manufactures to Inner Asian polities.[94]

---

89. Mark Edward Lewis, "Han Abolition of Universal Military Service," in *Warfare in Chinese History*, ed. Hans J. van de Ven (Leiden and Boston: Brill, 2000), 33–74.

90. *Hou Han shu* (hereafter HHS) 12.505–8; Miller, "Southern Xiongnu," 150–51.

91. Lin Gan 林幹, *Xiongnu tong shi* 匈奴通史 (Beijing: Ren min chu ban she, 1986), 6–7, citing HS 94B.3822. It also seems that they later were taxed by the Wei of the Cao: see SGZ 26.731, where remission of taxation is asked for Wuhuan families giving military service, the implication being that others were registered households that did pay taxes. By the Northern Wei period, the alternative term "Wuwan" simply meant "mestizo": WS 113.2971.

92. HS 94B.3804; and again see translation in Olberding, *Dubious Facts*, 210–11. C. M. Wilbur, *Slavery in China during the Former Han Period, 206 B.C.–A.D. 25* (Chicago: Field Museum, 1943), 95, 103–114, 409–10, suggests that slaves (such as those mentioned in the just-cited document) were frequently enslaved Xiongnu; the Chinese name for this people is, of course, a pun, meaning "fierce slave." Needless to say, seizure of slaves went the other way as well, Wilbur, 91.

93. Miller, "Southern Xiongnu," 166–68.

94. For one example of these processes, see Yan Liu's discussion of Han lacquerware in Manchuria in "Emblems of Power and Glory: The Han Period Chinese Lacquer Wares Discovered in the Borderlands," in *Production, Distribution and Appreciation: New Aspects of East Asian Lacquer Ware*, ed. Patricia Frick and Annette Kieser (Boston: Brill, 2018), 30–63. At an earlier phase of these relations, Zhonghang Yue had warned the *chanyu* of the allure of Han

Xiongnu lords were themselves certainly wealthy: tombs ascribed to them north of the Gobi show the enormous wealth of its elites.[95] But as a whole the Xiongnu fiscal base was, as noted above, fundamentally on a much smaller scale than that of Han.[96] Loss of both Han "gifts" and control over the east-west trade routes came at the same time as a series of succession struggles broke out within the Xiongnu regime.[97] Former subjects, such as the Wuhuan with their heavy tribute burdens, now began to turn against the *chanyu*. In 46 CE, when "the Xiongnu dynasty was in a state of chaos" with yet another internal power struggle, a party of Wuhuan attacked and routed them. Some Xiongnu now established a "northern *chanyu*" in Mongolia, while in the year 48 other groups—many no doubt already south of the Gobi—rallied around a new "southern *chanyu*."[98]

The Wuhuan were not at all politically united; for centuries dozens or hundreds of their bands had been settling in the frontier zone, and assembling on an ad hoc basis, for various ends and to ally with various parties. Their loyalties were local, not to dynasties but to effective military leaders. At times they would raid the holdings of the Han outposts in the region.[99] When they served Han, as some did some of the time, it was on a contract basis, in which they were paid, unreliable employees of the Chinese empire. After their defeat of the Xiongnu in 46 CE, 922 of their chieftains came south to Luoyang, supposedly to pledge fealty and certainly to receive gifts. Despite decline in the effectiveness of the Han tax system, Luoyang would undoubtedly have matched and exceeded what the Wuhuan gave the Chinese emperor in "tribute" of slaves, livestock and the skins

---

goods: "[W]hen you get any of the Han silks, put them on and try riding around on your horses through the brush and brambles!" See SJ 110.2899; HS 94A.3759; tr. Burton Watson, *Records of the Grand Historian, Han Dynasty II*, rev. ed. (Hong Kong and New York: Columbia University Press, 1993), 143. In later times, similar comments are made on the Turks' Orkhon Inscription: "The Chinese people, who give in abundance gold, silver, millet (?), and silk (?), have always used ingratiating words and have at their disposal enervating riches. While ensnaring them with their ingratiating talk and enervating riches, they have drawn the far dwelling peoples nearer to themselves": Ross, "The Orkhon Inscriptions," 862. Modern scholars such as Nicola Di Cosmo and William Honeychurch have in their work developed the good point that steppe peoples did not *need* Chinese goods, and that, moreover, the comments attributed to Zhonghang Yue at least are reported in Chinese texts, and show Chinese bias. Not needing, of course, is not the same as not wanting; Europeans in the 1400s and 1500s did not, of course, need pepper or porcelain, but they still spent a great deal of energy to get those things (and then to control the routes along which they were shipped). For an excellent examination of the general human desire for exotic goods, again see Mary Helms, *Craft and the Kingly Ideal*.

95. Nicola Di Cosmo, "Aristocratic Elites in the Xiongnu Empire as Seen from Historical and Archaeological Evidence," in *Nomad Aristocrats in a World of Empires*, ed. Jürgen Paul (Wiesbaden: Ludwig Reichert Verlag, 2013), 45; and Joshua Wright, William Honeychurch, and Chunag Amartuvshin, "The Xiongnu Settlements of Egiin Gol, Mongolia," *Antiquity* 89 (2009): 372–87.

96. Di Cosmo, "Ethnogenesis," 39, suggests the appearance of these tombs represents the appearance of strong local centers of power in the north, in the wake of loss of territories south of the Gobi.

97. Di Cosmo, "Ethnogenesis," 38–39, and, *Ancient China*, 247–49.

98. HHS 1B.75, 76; 89.2942–43, 90.2982; Lin Gan 林幹, ed., *Xiongnu shi liao hui bian* 匈奴史料彙編, 2 vols. (Beijing: Zhonghua shu ju, 1988), 1: 441–43.

99. Such as in 135–136, when a party seized carts, goods and cattle of tradesmen on the road across the Tumed Plain: HHS 90.2983.

of tigers and leopards.[100] The new southern *chanyu* now also swore fealty to Han, and was settled as a Han client state in the northeastern corner of the Ordos, reoccupying the region from which the dynasty had emerged some 250 years before. He too would receive pay, annually in fact.[101]

In the view of Luoyang, in return for these gifts the southern *chanyu* had a duty to "guard against the Serbi in the east; repel the Xiongnu in the north; rigorously to lead and discipline the barbarians of the four quarters and completely restore the commanderies of the (northern) frontier."[102] The southern *chanyu* may well have had different ideas. Though Han officials were posted to monitor events at his court, the southern *chanyu* was effectively lord of his own satrapy, largely carrying on the institutions and traditions of his forefathers on the northern grasslands.[103] Subjects and officials of the southern *chanyu* were now interspersed throughout the entire belt of frontier districts from Beijing to Baotou, including Yanmen and Yunzhong. Many of the Chinese of these regions at this time fled south: "the walled towns," we are told, "were deserted and empty" 城郭丘墟.[104] Between the censuses of 2 CE and 140 CE the registered population of these districts shrank dramatically, particularly in the Ordos, presumably as Chinese settlers died without replacement, returned to the interior, or fled to join camps among the nomads.[105]

100. HHS 90.2982. Barfield, *The Perilous Frontier*, 78, suggests that under Later Han, expenditures to groups on the northern and western frontiers (not just the Wuhuan) were huge, at times reaching one-third of the empire's entire payroll. In terms of slavery, Wilbur, *Slavery*, 95–96, points out that among other things, this was a form of trade. There were also Han ordinances for "rewarding Xiongnu who surrender": "those who . . . (surrender with?) . . . a horde of eight thousand persons or more will be enfeoffed as nobles with (a domain of) two thousand households and will be given five-hundred (catties of) gold (i.e., five million cash). Take the old leaders and make them (again) leaders, letting them all lead their men . . . report those who attained to military merit, and grant them peerages": Giele, "Xiongnu in Chinese Wooden Documents," 61–62 (with slight modification).

101. Miller, "Southern Xiongnu," 153.

102. HHS 1.76, 19.716.

103. In the Hohhot Museum are Later Han end eave tiles from the Zhaowan 召湾 tomb group south of Baotou, on which are written: "*Chanyu*, descended from Heaven" 單于天降 and "Barbarians of the four (directions), all submitted" 四夷盡服. Bryan Miller, "Southern Xiongnu," 147–48, quite correctly refers to these as a "façade." Still, such pieces would certainly have been made for the southern Xiongnu lord by workmen directly or indirectly in employ of Chang'an.

Miller, "The Southern Xiongnu," 148, also observes that among other things we see tombs of the Southern Xiongnu leadership that resemble not surrounding Chinese graves, but tombs from the steppe. Here he makes good arguments leading us past the more traditional view of the Southern Xiongnu voiced by Yü Ying-shih, in his "Han Foreign Relations," in *Cambridge History of China*, Vol. 1, *The Ch'in and Han Empire 221 B.C.-A.D. 220*, ed. Denis Twitchett and Michael Loewe (Cambridge: Cambridge University Press, 1986), 400–3.

104. *Dongguan Han ji jiao zhu* 東觀漢記校注 ([Zhengzhou:] Zhongzhou gu ji chu ban she, 1987) 1.12 and pp. 47–48 note 223, where it is made clear this passage relates to removal of populations from the frontier highlands. And see also HHS 1B.78, 89.2942–43, 2945. More simply, a quick comparison of the maps of *Zhongguo li shi di tu ji* 中国历史地图集, ed. Tan Qixiang 谭其骧 (Shanghai: Di tu chu ban she, 1982) for the series' Vol. II, *Qin, Xi Han, Dong Han*, and its Vol. IV, *Dong Jin Shi liu guo, Nan bei chao*, will show the enormous change in use and control of these territories.

105. Yunzhong—the Tumed Plain—which in Former Han had had a population of 173,270 (HS 28B.1620) is in the Later Han report on this district reduced to 26,430 (HHS 113[Zhi 23].3525). And see Figure 14 in Miller, "Southern Xiongnu," 150.

It is also at this time, more precisely in the year 45 CE, that the Serbi first appear in Chinese text.[106] As is frequently seen when empires' men of letters look outward—or downward—upon "the other," organized in a different and half-understood manner, the names they use have generally had a loose and evolving meaning, as is seen in the efforts of Europeans to name native peoples of the American continents.[107] This is certainly the case with the Serbi—in fact, at times at least the Chinese "Xianbei" may actually be more appropriate, revealing more about the namer than the named. As mentioned above, after Modun had routed the Eastern Hu in the late third century BCE, the Serbi are said to have remained independent by fleeing further north or further east. It is claimed that they took the name from a "great Mount Serbi," which among other things has been identified as the Khingans.[108] The name, however, is really only a loose ethnic and linguistic designator, by which Chinese referred to those of this sort who had remained free of Xiongnu control. Within these populations, we can be sure the situation was more complex.

In the texts, we are told, with the decay of Xiongnu power on the steppe in the first century CE, Serbi groups began to move down from the Khingans into those territories, some eventually joining their Wuhuan cousins in the frontier territories.[109] They too were organized in many smaller groups: in the early second century, for example, Han gave gifts and titles to 120 Serbi chieftains, who in return gave sons as hostages.[110] The proliferation of bands would have been part of Han policy; by spreading pay widely, Luoyang prevented the unruly many from becoming a united, and much more dangerous one. But this may have been the preference of the Serbi anyway. Presumably originating as small bands dwelling in the forests in and around the Khingans, they would in addition have felt resentment at the Xiongnu rout of the Eastern Hu, and the centuries of dominance that had followed. Frequently seen as a sign of primitiveness, their organization

---

106. HHS 1B.73. This was a recorded "Xianbei raid on Liaodong" commandery, in Manchuria. Holcombe, "The Xianbei," 3, mentions an embassy four years later by a party of Xianbei (HHS 90.2985).

107. For another part of Eurasia, see Peter Wells, *Beyond Celts, Germans and Scythians: Archaeology and Identity in Iron Age Europe* (London: Duckworth, 2001). The skewed nature of the "ethnography" of the "civilized" was brilliantly mocked in John Beazley's *Herodotus at the Zoo* (Oxford: Gaisford Prize, 1907), in which, in a supposedly long-lost fragment of Herodotus' history, the Greek historian is presented as describing a remote island that contained a wonderful zoo, the London Zoo: see discussion by Peter Thonemann, in a review, "Sex and Elephants," in the 31 May 2019, edition of the *Times Literary Supplement*.

108. This linkage with one or more mountains appears already in SGZ 30.835; HHS 90.2985. See also Jennifer Holmgren, *Annals of Tai: Early T'o-pa History According to the First Chapter of the "Wei shu"* (Canberra: Australian National University Press, 1982), 80 note 8; and Miao Linlin 苗霖霖, "Xianbei shan di li wei zhi kao lue" 鲜卑山地理位置考略, *Bei Hua da xue xue bao (She hui ke xue ban)* (2015.2): 60–63. For archaeological studies linking the Serbi to the Dong Hu, see Adam Theodore Kessler, *Empires beyond the Great Wall: The Heritage of Genghis Khan* (Los Angeles: Natural History Museum of Los Angeles County, 1994), 76–79; and Holcombe, "The Xianbei," 3–4.

109. See SGZ 30 and HHS 90 for the accounts of these groups, as well as Duthie, "The Nature of the *Hu*."

110. HHS 90.2986. Barfield, *Perilous Frontier*, 85, points out that for the Serbi in their early stages "authority was vested in petty chieftains."

in smaller groups may have come from a desire for a liberty of a sort. Perhaps it was also the basis for ultimately quite successful political and military experimentation in the coming century or two, and then, centuries after that, resistance in turn of some at least to the growing centralization imposed by the lords of late Northern Wei.[111]

For forty years after the first recorded Serbi appearance, the northern and southern *chanyu* waged war against each other, with regularly shifting constellations of alliances. Finally in 87 CE, between several Han campaigns against the northern *chanyu*, a great Serbi war party came from the east to defeat him, and then skin him, showing among other things their deep hostility to the Xiongnu overlords.[112] What remained of his core following soon fled far to the west.[113] It is interesting to note that though Serbi groups had over the decades repeatedly served as mercenaries for Han, in 87 CE they acted on their own. Though it was suggested within the Luoyang court that the southern *chanyu* be sent north to oversee the victors, the Han ministers didn't know who their leaders were.[114] With the flight of the northern *chanyu* to lands west, dozens of the Xiongnu's subject groupings (*bu*, often translated "tribe"[115])—comprising hundreds of thousands of people—now moved south from the grasslands to further swell the Inner Asian populations of Han's frontier provinces, including Yunzhong.[116] Of those who remained in the northlands, "more than 100,000 *luo* (encampment, or settlement group) of the leftover [subject] peoples (*zhong* 種) went to the lands east of the Liao River, where they lived interspersed [among other groups]." Showing the malleable nature of the name "Serbi," "they all now called themselves Serbi soldiers," presumably taking up Serbi language, at least in the war camps. From this time, according to the Chinese author of this passage, the Serbi

---

111. A loose analogy can be made to development of the western end of Eurasia in Walter Scheidel's *Escape from Rome: The Failure of Empire and the Road to Prosperity* (Princeton, NJ, and Oxford: Princeton University Press, 2019), where it is argued that the fall of empire—Rome—led to various sorts of innovation in the European world.

112. HHS 3.157, 89.2951; ZZTJ 47.1509. This was the culmination of "ruthless wars of revenge by formerly subject groups" against the Xiongnu lords, "which included the defilement of Xiongnu aristocratic tombs": Di Cosmo, "Aristocratic Elites," 30.

113. The party was driven west in 89 CE by a combined force of Han troops and those of the southern *chanyu*: HHS 89.2953. Alongside the regular cavalry units, we are told in the HHS 23.814 biography of the campaign's commander, "Qiang and Hu troops went forth from the (northern) passes" 羌胡兵出塞, including, no doubt, those of the Southern Chanyu.

114. HHS 41.1415–16.

115. This author resists use of the word "tribe." Though it seems to be a meaningful term for description of a kind of human organization—as seen in the work of Morton Fried, *The Notion of Tribe* (Menlo Park, CA: Cummings, 1975)—both "tribe" and its Chinese counterpart "*bu luo* 部落" have strong pejorative undertones, and also fail to convey the political complexity of Inner Asian regimes. See in this chapter, note 73; and David Sneath, *The Headless State: Aristocratic Orders, Kinship Society, and Misrepresentations of Nomadic Inner Asia* (New York: Columbia University Press, 2007).

116. The records here are somewhat confusing: HHS 89.2951 says 58 *bu* and 200,000 people; ZZTJ 47.1510 says 280,000; HHS 23.814 says 81 *bu*.

"gradually grew strong."[117] It might be more accurate to say they had already done so.[118]

This merger of populations did not just go one way. Intermarriage between Xiongnu and Serbi is frequently seen. And in the frontier region, some Serbi were still subordinate to Xiongnu, as seen in the case of the first major Serbi leader known in the Chinese sources, whose name is preserved in Chinese transcription as Tanshihuai (ca. 137–ca. 181). In a variant of the worldwide Birth of Hero story, the husband of Tanshihuai's mother was a mercenary serving in the army of the southern *chanyu*, who returned after three years to discover his wife had borne a son.[119] Spared death by the mother's claim of divine impregnation, the boy was raised by the family steward. Later, through military skills, he began to rise.

At first just one of many Serbi "big men" (*da ren*), Tanshihuai went on to build a confederation of Serbi chieftains and establish a capital just north of the Yinshan, on Danhan Mountain (in the vicinity of the modern town of Shangyi, in the PRC's Hebei province), which lay at the center of a vast if rickety new steppe empire.[120] Raiding began in 156 with an attack on Han settlements on the Tumed Plain, about 150 miles to the west, then spread across the whole frontier. A decade later, in 166, unable to check the attacks, Luoyang sought to placate Tanshihuai by granting him a princely title. Refusing the offer of delegated status with benefits, he continued to pound the Han frontier outposts.[121] In 177 a new generalship was created by the Han court—the "Smash the Serbi Commandant" 破鮮卑中郎將—whose unlucky incumbent took command of an army including the southern *chanyu*, who brought auxiliary cavalry units made up of Xiongnu and Wuhuan. Dividing into several columns, the Han force marched forth from Yunzhong and the Yanmen Pass.[122] They were routed. No doubt with hyperbole it was said that 70 or 80 percent never returned; but perhaps some of these too "now called themselves Serbi soldiers."[123] Tanshihuai—and the peoples of his confederation—had become masters of the steppe.

---

117. The first quote from SGZ 30.837 (from a fragment of a largely lost mid-third-century *Wei shu* of Wang Shen 王沈 dedicated to history of the third-century Wei dynasty of the Cao family); the second from a variant passage in HHS 90.2986. It is estimated that the *luo* settlement group generally contained two or three yurts and 20 to 30 individuals: see Uchida, *Kita Ajia shi kenkyū* 2: 34. Chen Linguo 陈琳国 points out that incorporation of the former Xiongnu subjects into emerging Serbi polities would have been a gradual process that would have taken decades: see his *Zhong gu bei fang min zu shi tan* 中古北方民族史探 (Beijing: Shang wu yin shu guan, 2010), 195.

118. K. H. J. Gardiner and R. R. C. (Rafe) de Crespigny, "T'an-shih-huai and the Hsien-pei Tribes of the Second Century A.D.," *PFEH* 15 (1977): 4–5; de Crespigny, *Northern Frontiers*, 296. And see the comments in HHS 90.2991 regarding the technological superiority of the Serbi as well, who were better able to get iron for their weaponry across the increasingly porous border: "their weapons were sharper and their horses faster than those of the Xiongnu."

119. HHS 90.2989. See discussion of this story in Gardiner and de Crespigny, "T'an-shih-huai," 16–20.

120. ZZTJ 53.1733–34. For the nature of the regime, see Yü, "Han Foreign Relations," in *Cambridge History of China*, 1: 444–45; Barfield, *Perilous Frontier*, 89–90.

121. ZZTJ 55.1796.

122. HHS 90.2993–94; SGZ 30.838; ZZTJ 57.1842–43.

123. An interesting suggestion by Gardiner and de Crespigny, "T'an-shih-huai," 36.

4

Myths of Origin

Tanshihuai's confederation was an intermediate step in the development of the increasingly active and increasingly heterogeneous populations we loosely refer to as "Serbi." With the effective end of Xiongnu rule in the lands north of the Yinshan, the frontier region took on a new importance of its own. A distinctive local identity began to reappear, accompanying the growth of local ties that took shape among the many groups, both old and new, that inhabited the region. As the Han court had dreaded, the small and numerous bands that had destroyed the Xiongnu now began to experiment with ways to coalesce into larger polities and larger armies. While Han settlements were still maintained in the frontier zone—often with significant power and prestige—these were isolated outposts in a land increasingly of its own.[1] It was into this world of uncertainty and opportunity that the Taghbach would soon appear.

As seen above, before Tanshihuai the Wuhuan and Serbi bands had been many and autonomous, choosing their leaders through election or acclamation.[2] And the power of these men had been limited to leadership in war; within the settlement groups, within the household, one "followed the plans of the women" 從婦人計, a practice that may have echoes in later ages.[3] Enormous change, however, seems to have taken place during the decades of the great confederation: in contrast to the hundreds of chieftains mentioned a century or two before, we are told in the Chinese history *San guo zhi* that Tanshihuai had under him just a few dozen magnates, each leading his own following, and apparently giving shape to new polities, some of which would prove to be enduring.[4]

A title used in the Chinese text to refer to these subordinate leaders—"great commander" (*da shuai* 大帥)—seems like the Arabic term *emir*, or the Latin *dux*, to have contained the twin meanings of "commander" and "ruler."[5] From this time the leadership positions of Tanshihuai's "big men were passed down, from

---

1. See discussion of "dis-embedded centers" by Miller, "Southern Xiongnu," 167–68.
2. HHS 90.2979; SGZ 30.832.
3. SGZ 30.832; HHS 90.2979. Duthie, "Nature of the *Hu*," 31.
4. SGZ 30.837–38.
5. Remembering here Peter Jackson's suggestion that *beg* was an equivalent of the Arabic-Persian title *emir* (*amīr*); see Chapter 1, note 4. For *dux*/duke, OED's first definition is: "A leader; a leader of an army, a captain or general; a chief, ruler."

generation to generation" 諸大人遂世相傳襲.[6] Here we see at least the beginning among the Serbi of the principle of dynasty, with enduring authority and hereditary lines of leadership to whom the leaderless of various origins—including Xiongnu—might turn to form new sorts of polities, less clearly fixed than the territorial state but real nonetheless. It seems quite likely that it was at some point in the midst of this process—precisely when we do not know—that the title "khaghan" came to be used among the Serbi *da shuai*, supplanting *chanyu*, the imperial title of the Xiongnu.

Though a principle of dynasty began taking shape among the Serbi during the time of Tanshihuai, in the end it was not successfully applied to his own clan. The great Serbi lord died relatively young, in or around the year 181.[7] His heir, described in the Chinese sources as incompetent and greedy, was soon killed in battle and the confederation disintegrated.[8] But if anyone in the Han empire breathed a sigh of relief at this point, it would have been sucked back in panic with the rebellion of the millenarian Yellow Turbans, which broke out within the Han territories just a few years later, in 184. As an opponent of the 177 campaign of the "Smash the Serbi Commandant" had said: "Misfortunes on the frontier are no more than an irritating rash on the hands or the feet; but troubles within the central states, those are like a cancer on the breast."[9] The cancer on the breast quickly metastasized. Though the religionists were swiftly suppressed, the men within the empire who had raised armies to do so now turned on each other in a civil war that spread throughout the realm. Most at least of the fighting was in the Han interior, and when in 207 a key contestant in these wars, Cao Cao (ca. 155–220), did go north to rout a powerful Wuhuan leader in southern Manchuria who had been harboring Cao's rivals, he did not attempt to secure those territories but instead brought Wuhuan horsemen back south, to be used as crack cavalry units in his army down on the plains.[10] Key frontier administrative districts—including Yunzhong and Yanmen—were formally abolished in 215.[11]

Controlling the Yellow River plains, Cao Cao had presented himself as regent of the Han. But with his death in 220 came the end of Han as well. Cao's son now

---

6. HHS 90.2994.

7. ZZTJ 58.1860 places this event in the year corresponding to 181; HHS 90.2994 simply places the event in Han's Guanghe reign period (178–183). Gardiner and de Crespigny, "T'an-shih-huai," 24, 38–39, explore possibilities, including the suggestion he died in 180. Tanshihuai's birth year is given as ca. 137 on the basis of extrapolating 45 years in which he lived back from 181.

8. HHS 90.2994.

9. A comment by the well-known late Han scholar Cai Yong (132–192): HHS 90.2992.

10. SGZ 30.835; Rafe de Crespigny, *Imperial Warlord: A Biography of Cao Cao, 155–220* (Leiden: Brill, 2010), 230–39. Cao Cao's victory was also celebrated in a poem telling of how the Wuhuan lord had "yielded his head," and informing the reader that "the divine martial prowess," of Cao, "inspired awe beyond the seas, There shall be no worry about looking back at the north": Xiaofei Tian, "Remaking History: The Shu and Wu Perspectives in the Three Kingdoms Period," *JAOS* 136.4 (2016): 730. For a broader discussion of the use of nomad auxiliaries in armies of the Chinese interior, see Giele, "Xiongnu in Chinese Wooden Documents," 69; and Lewis, "Han Abolition of Universal Military Service," 47–48.

11. SGZ 1.45; JS 14.428; Chen, *Bei fang min zu*, 188.

took the throne and established a new dynasty, the Wei 魏 (220–266)—the "Cao Wei" of the Chinese historiographical tradition—which stood in opposition to two rivals in the south. After a few decades, this period of Three Kingdoms came to an end, and most at least of the old Han territories were briefly reunified, under the Western Jin regime (266–316), which having taken power from within the Wei court at Luoyang went on to conquer the southern regimes. With the fall of Western Jin in the early fourth century, the empire created by Qin 500 years before finally came to an end.

In the north, a second, lesser Serbi confederation took shape in the 220s and early 230s. But when its leader Kebineng was killed in 235 by a Wei assassin, that crumbled as well.[12] From this point, very different sorts of polities began to emerge among the Serbi, more compact but more stable, now tied to specific territories containing both steppe and farmland and so using an innovative new form of statecraft, a system of dual administration, that is, separate governance for pastoralists, on the one hand, and farmers, on the other.[13] The emirs of Tanshihuai's confederation had been held together by the leader's personal charisma. With his death they began to go their own ways; two generations later, much the same occurred with the assassination of Kebineng. The only name on the list given in *San guo zhi* of Tanshihuai's great commanders with clear links to a later regime is that of the Murong 慕容.[14] They may have been part of the Kebineng confederation as well. At any rate, the first date given in the Chinese source *Jin shu* for the Murong was 237—two years after Kebineng's death—when having moved his following to southern Manchuria and established a polity there, the first Murong leader mentioned is said to have participated in a northeastern campaign of the Cao Wei army.[15]

The Taghbach do not explicitly appear on the list of Tanshihuai's emirs, though as we shall see below there are hints that this group may have participated in some form or another. Nevertheless, in 248, just a decade after the Murong had established their regime in southern Manchuria, there is reference in Chinese sources of the appearance in the "old lands of the Xiongnu" of the Taghbach founder Liwei.[16]

* * *

12. SGZ 30.839–40.
13. Barfield, *Perilous Frontier*, 104. This carried on into the Taghbach state, as discussed by Klein, "Contributions of the Fourth Century Xianbei States," 113–14.
14. SGZ 30.838 (citing the mid-third-century *Wei shu*); Holmgren, *Annals of Tai*, 9. Shimunek, *Languages of Ancient Southern Mongolia and North China*, 51, suggests a reconstruction of "Murong" as *BaglU; Nie Hongyin 聂 鸿 音, "Xianbei yu yan jie du shu lun" 鲜卑语言解读述论, *Min zu yan jiu* (2001.1): 65–66, suggests "Moyo." Various theories of the name origin are discussed in Gerhard Schreiber, "The History of the Former Yen Dynasty," *Monumenta Serica* 14 & 15 (1949–1956): 392–93.
15. JS 108.2803; WS 95.2060; ZZTJ 73.2319.
16. For discussion of the "old lands of the Xiongnu," see Wu Youjiang 毋有江, *Bei Wei zheng zhi di li yan jiu* 北魏政治地理研究 (Beijing: Ke xue chu ban she, 2018), 2–6.

Prior to their appearance in the "old lands," we really know the Taghbach only through the origin myth presented in the first chapter of *Wei shu*, its "Prefatory Annals" (*xu ji* 序紀). Myths can be delightful. But since they exist fundamentally not to describe but to define and justify, they always conceal as much as they reveal, just as do we humans who invent them. Whether in ancient times or in modern, even if they contain elements of truth they are fundamentally fabrication. Special care must be given to genealogical myth that has been orally transmitted, as by the early, pre-literate Taghbach. People can in part at least imagine their own line of ancestors, or invent it; sometimes they take it from others; sometimes others invent it for us.[17]

It is not quite clear who invented the origin myths that eventually took shape as the *Wei shu* "Prefatory Annals." As mentioned in Chapter 1, the Wei lords do seem to have carried with them memories—tales, myths—that had for generations been passed down orally, in songs of their own language.[18] Eventually written down by Chinese scribes, and relocated into those men's mental universe, these were ultimately incorporated into Wei Shou's sixth-century history. Some modern scholars accept these, in whole or in part. Others do not.[19] This author tends to agree with Jennifer Holmgren, who has suggested that for the period up to Liwei, "Wei Shou had little more than distorted oral tradition," then perceptively adds, "and his own Chinese literary heritage." Turning to the issue of how the *Wei shu* origin myth was constructed, she goes on to say that "fictitious genealogical links such as these were naturally built up backwards, over a period of time."[20] Holmgren is certainly correct in this. Parts of the *Wei shu* story are clearly late additions, such as the opening section, where it is stated that the Taghbach were descendants of a son of the mythological Chinese Yellow Emperor who had been sent to the far north.[21] The most interesting question here is, perhaps,

---

17. James Fentress and Chris Wickham, *Social Memory* (Cambridge, MA: Blackwell, 1992), 77–81; Jack Goody, *The Power of the Written Tradition* (Washington, DC: Smithsonian Institution Press, 2000), 31–32.

18. Tian Yuqing discusses these "Songs of Dai" in his *Tuoba shi tan*, 217–43.

19. A good overview of the many positions taken on this by East Asian scholars—primarily divided between those leaning toward doubt about the use of myth to trace history, and those leaning toward acceptance—is given in Zhang, *Bei Wei zheng zhi shi*, 1: 55–61.

20. Holmgren, *Annals of Tai*, 18, 21. In this regard, see also Yao Dali 姚大力, "Lun Tuoba Xianbei bu de zao qi li shi: Du '*Wei shu* Xuji'" 论拓跋鲜卑部的早期历史—读《魏书序纪》, *Fudan xue bao (She hui ke xue ban)* (2005.2): 19–27.

21. WS 1.1. It is said, however, that such mention had been made almost a century before, in 306, on a stele that we will touch on in Chapter 5; it must be noted, however, that the stele itself has not been recovered, and we have only a copy of its text in Wei Shou's *Wei shu*. The process of installing the Yellow Emperor as ultimate ancestor is explicitly described in *Wei shu*'s "Ritual Monograph" (108A.2734) as being the result of a 398 petition to the throne, in the midst of adopting other symbols from the Chinese empire such as the dynasty's element, number, and color. See Sonoda Shunsuke 園田 俊介, "Hokugi Tō Seigi jidai ni okeru Senpi Takubatsushi (Gen-shi) no sosen densetsu to sono keisei" 北魏・東西魏時代における鮮卑拓跋氏(元氏)の祖先伝説とその形成, *Shiteki* 27 (2005): 63–80; and Yang, "Tuoba Xianbei zao qi li shi bian wu," 126–27. As Yang points out, the process of disentangling this myth began with several of the fine early modern historians of the Song. And as has been pointed out by Michael Nylan in her *Philosophy East and West* 2012 review of Erich Gruen's *Rethinking the Other in Antiquity* (Princeton, NJ: Princeton University Press, 2011), emergent groups have often in human history appropriated the ancestors of "the other." For the Yellow Emperor in early Chinese religion, see Mark Edward Lewis, "The Mythology

when Taghbach themselves began to believe these things, and which ones did the believing.

The first descendant of the Yellow Emperor's northern son mentioned in the "Prefatory Annals" was given the name "Original Equality" (Shijun 始均); it is hard to tell whether this comes from the primal memories of the Taghbach, or from Zhuangzi, or from an ancient Chinese sociologist.[22] While Shijun for some reason reappeared in the Chinese world (to serve the mythical emperor Shun), his descendants were far to the north again, removed from the Xiongnu and other barbarians who in age after age "did harm to the central provinces (*zhong zhou*)," that is, the Chinese territories. In contrast to the baleful Xiongnu, the Wei ancestors "had no contact with southern Xia"—again, the lands of the Chinese—"and thus, we do not hear of them in the records." In this deft construction, the Taghbach are relieved of guilt for other nomads' sins, while explanation is given for their absence from early Chinese historical writings.[23] It is not entirely clear for what audience this was composed.

From this, the "Prefatory Annals" proceed to a long king list consisting of suspiciously monosyllabic names—not at all like the multisyllabic transcriptions of real Taghbach names received in the texts—suggesting that even if the list in some sense came from Taghbach memory, it had been significantly revised and incorporated into ritual text developed by Chinese officials.[24] Problems leap out almost immediately with the first figure on the list, "Mao" 毛, the "completing emperor" 成皇帝, of whom it is said that his "awesome [power] shook the northlands," so that he came to be lord of 36 "nations" (*guo* 國) and 99 "clans" (*da xing* 大姓). As the modern scholar and refreshing skeptic Lü Simian (1884–1957) made clear, these are evocative symbols: 99 plus 1 (Mao's own clan) equals 100; and 36 is a term that—beginning with the establishment in 221 BCE of the 36 commanderies of the Qin empire—was another way in the Chinese tradition to refer to "totality."[25] They are not to be taken seriously as a description of the following of "Mao" up in the dense forests of the Khingans. Furthermore, on the king list

---

of Early China," in *Early Chinese Religion*, Part 1, *Shang through Han* (Leiden and Boston: Brill, 2008), 1: 564–69; and also Robert Ford Campany, *Making Transcendents: Ascetics and Social Memory in Early Medieval China* (Honolulu: University of Hawai'i Press, 2009), 201–7.

22. WS 1.1; and Holmgren's discussion in *Annals of Tai*, 79 note 5.
23. Holmgren, *Annals of Tai*, 80 note 6.
24. Tamura Jitsuzō 田村實造, *Chūgoku shijō no minzoku idōki: Goko, Hokugi jidai no seiji to shakai* 中国史上の民族移動期: 五胡・北魏時代の政治と社會 (Tokyo: Sōbunsha, 1985), 185, citing Shiratori Kurakichi 白鳥庫吉, *Dong Hu min zu kao* 東胡民族考 (Shanghai: Shang wu yin shu guan, 1934), 122. Many others have discussed these matters.
25. See Lü Simian 呂思勉, *Du shi zha ji* 讀史札記 (Taibei: Muduo chu ban she, 1983), 809; Tang Zhangru 唐长孺, "Tuoba guo jia de jian li ji qi feng jian hua" 拓跋國家的建立及其封建化, in his *Wei Jin Nan bei chao shi lun cong* (Beijing: Sheng huo, du shu, xin zhi san lian shu dian, 1955), 193–94; and Huang Lie 黄烈, "Tuoba Xianbei zao qi guo jia de xing cheng" 拓拔鲜卑早期国家的形成, in *Wei Jin Sui Tang shi lun ji*, ed. Zhongguo she hui ke xue yuan li shi yan jiu suo, Wei Jin Nan Bei chao Sui Tang shi yan jiu shi (Beijing: Zhongguo she hui ke xue chu ban she, 1983), 67. "36 *guo*" was also used in Later Han with reference to the "western regions" of eastern Turkestan, with an equal likelihood that it did not reflect reality: see ZZTJ 45.1448.

leading to the first historical Taghbach ruler—the mid-third century Liwei—are 81 names, this apparently being another numerological construct deriving from Chinese tradition, since 81 equals 9^2 and 9 in the *Book of Changes* is the number designating the active male principle.[26] Some modern scholars suggest that the entire king's list of the "Prefatory Annals" needs to be viewed with skepticism; that we do not see a real hereditary line until the late third-century figure Liwei (see just below).[27] Though hard to prove, this is quite possible: even if the idea of dynasty had begun to take shape among the Serbi in general several generations before, that does not mean a Taghbach dynasty had yet taken shape.

But before turning to the more reliably historical, we will look a bit more at this list in terms of the relationship between history and mythology, with particular reference here to migration, an important aspect of the origin myth of the Taghbach, and many other groups. Such stories do need to be examined with skepticism. Because of their use and misuse by European nationalists, after World War II historians and archaeologists broadly rejected stories of mass movement of "peoples." And it is indeed true that some modern scholars have been much too credulous in accepting the tales of Taghbach migration given in the "Prefatory Annals," occasionally descending into efforts at detailed itinerary across time and space.[28] But though understandable, the reaction to myths of *Völkerwanderung* seems to have gone too far. Counterargument could begin simply by pointing out the obvious, massive movements of populations in the first decades of the 21st century.[29] Giving more nuance to the issue, scholars of late antiquity in Europe have in the last several decades demonstrated the reality of movement of small, transformative groups, often warriors.[30] Thus, it is possible that the Taghbach were indeed newcomers, from lands far to the northeast, as they are often described in Chinese sources. It is, however, also possible that the third-century Liwei—an interloper—appropriated the myths of others. With the sources we have, it is really impossible to say which is true.

With these matters in mind, we turn back to examination of the Taghbach origin myth as myth. On the list of "emperors" that follow Mao, most provide

---

26. Lü, *Du shi zha ji*, 809.
27. Tamura, *Chūgoku shijō no minzoku idōki*, 184; Holmgren, *Annals of Tai*, 20–22.
28. Anthony Snodgrass, a specialist on Mediterranean archaeology, in his "Archaeology in China: a View from the Outside," in *China's Early Empires: A Re-appraisal*, ed. Michael Nylan and Michael Loewe (Cambridge: Cambridge University Press, 2010), 233, suggests that although "[t]he documentary record available from Qin and Han times seems to me superior, in almost all respects, to that of any of the contemporary or somewhat earlier western Iron Age cultures," "[i]s there any risk that archaeologists, encouraged by the wealth of this documentary record, might become too deferential to it, too reluctant to depart from the framework it imposes?"
29. Questioning of this new orthodoxy began even before the 21st century, with David Anthony, in the aptly named article "Migration in Archaeology: The Baby and the Bathwater," *American Anthropologist*, n.s., 92 (1990): 895–914.
30. P. J. Heather, *Empires and Barbarians* (London: Macmillan, 2009), 33–35; and Guy Halsall, *Barbarian Migration and the Roman West, 376–568* (Cambridge: Cambridge University Press, 2007), Chapters 13 and 14. For the Eurasian steppe, see Shelach, *Prehistoric Societies*, 134–37.

nothing but Chinese-style imperial title,[31] monosyllabic name (or "taboo name," *hui* 諱), and then "died" 崩. This is interrupted twice by longer entries, both of which assign to the individual the name (or title) Tuiyin 推寅 (MC *Thwoj yij), which is at one point described as a transcribed foreign term, glossed in proper Chinese as *zuan yan* 鑽研, "boring through," meaning one who leads the people in migration through difficult obstacles such as mountains.[32]

In the title's first appearance in the genealogy, this Tuiyin is said to have "moved south to a great swamp, whose circumference was more than a thousand *li*, its soil dark and sodden."[33] If the Taghbach ancestors did come from the far northeastern slopes of the Khingans—the general region of the Gaxian Cave—many modern scholars have assumed this to mean that Tuiyin "bored through" that mountain chain, leading his people west to live along Hulun Nur, a huge lake on the steppelands west of the Khingans, in what is now the far northeastern corner of the PRC's Inner Mongolia. It is possible that we do see here real ancestral memories. The lake's modern circumference of 277 miles comes close to meeting the description in this of the "swamp's" circumference as being "more than a thousand *li*" (a *li* being about a third of a mile). Grave sites have also been found near the lake, with the animal sacrifices of pastoralists.[34] Although those buried in these graves were non-literate, and so left no written statement of identity, discovery among the human remains of braids does suggest that they may have been of the Manchurian or Northern Serbi, for whom the braid is described as a distinctive characteristic, at least in early times.[35] But we cannot on this basis possibly assume that those found in these graves were the particular ancestors of Taiwu, as some modern scholars

---

31. It will be noted that—a thousand years later, it is true—the early modern historian Sima Guang replaced the Chinese *huang di* in his version of this list with "khaghan" (*ke han*): ZZTJ 77.2459. In ZZTJ 80.2548 Sima also calls Liwei a "khaghan."
32. WS 1.2. This is the literal meaning of a term generally used to denote the more abstract concept of "deep study": *Han yu da ci dian* 汉语大词典 (hereafter *HYDCD*), 12 vols. (Shanghai: Han yu da ci dian chu ban she, 1993), 11B: 1436. See Boodberg, "Language of the T'o-Pa Wei," 234, who linked this to what he called the "Gog and Magog Complex" of Inner Asian myth.
33. See the slightly different translation in Holmgren, *Annals of Tai*, 52.
34. Two grave sites were found in this area in the 1960s, one east of the lake at Wangong, the other at Jalainur (Ch. Zhalainuoer), 25 miles north of the lake, almost on the border with Mongolia. For a summary, see Su Bai 宿白, "Dong bei, Nei Menggu di qu de Xianbei yi ji—Xianbei yi ji ji lu zhi yi" 东北、内蒙古地区的鲜卑遗迹—鲜卑遗迹辑录之一, *WW* (1977.5), rpt. in *Zou chu shi ku Bei Wei wang chao*, ed. Jin Zhao and Alede'ertu (Beijing: Wen hua yi shu chu ban she, 2010), 396–98; and tr. by David Fridley, "Xianbei Remains in Manchuria and Inner Mongolia: Record of Xianbei Remains, Part One," *Chinese Studies in Archaeology* 1.2 (1980): 18–27. See also Albert Dien, "A New Look at the Xianbei and Their Impact on Chinese Culture," in *Ancient Mortuary Traditions of China: Papers on Chinese Ceramic Funerary Sculptures*, ed. George Kuwayama (Los Angeles: Los Angeles County Museum of Art, 1991), 41–43; and Wei Jian 魏坚, ed., *Nei Menggu di qu Xianbei mu zang de fa xian yu yan jiu* 内蒙古地区鲜卑墓葬的发现与研究 (Beijing: Ke xue chu ban she, 2004), Chapter 10.
35. Huang, "Tuoba zao qi guo jia," 64–65. In accounts of the Northern Wei rulers in standard histories of contemporary Jiankang regimes, the Taghbach are referred to as "braid-heads": this is mentioned in NQS 57.983, and embedded in the very title of *Song shu* 95, "The Braid-head Caitiffs" 索虜. Shimunek, *Languages of Ancient Southern Mongolia and North China*, 52 note 75, suggests this was a "folk etymology" of the term *suo*, which referred to the Scythians. This could, of course, be a conflation of their real hairstyle with association with Scythians.

have done.³⁶ As is the case with Gaxian, these could be the leavings of any one of the hundreds of bands active in these regions in the early centuries CE.

Nevertheless, it is useful to see what we can of those buried near Hulun Nur, whoever they may have been. On the basis of Chinese manufactures found within, the graves are tentatively dated from the early centuries CE, by which time the Xiongnu empire was in decline, though elements of its culture can still be seen in the presence of decorative bronze ornaments with distinctive Xiongnu animal designs.³⁷ There was increased mingling and merger of disparate groups in these regions, with encounters between established populations and those that had fled Xiongnu control to the north and east but now began moving south and west. It will be remembered that a passage in the Chinese sources states that with the Xiongnu collapse in the late first century, Xiongnu—or better, groups that had been under Xiongnu overlordship—now "called themselves Serbi" 自號鮮卑.³⁸ Under such circumstances, intermarriage seems quite likely to follow, and both ancient text and modern DNA studies suggest mingling of bloodlines.³⁹ If "pure blood" has ever existed for any group, it did not exist for the Serbi.

Scattered traces of Chinese influence are also seen in the Hulun Nur graves. It is on the basis of dated, Chinese-made items found at Hulun Nur that these graves are dated to the Eastern Han (25–220 CE). These pieces included such fine manufactures as lacquer ware, a TLV mirror, and embroidery bearing the widely used Chinese phrase "as one wishes" (*ruyi*).⁴⁰ Objects of great value, difficult to obtain in the steppelands, these would have been status markers, playing a part similar to Ming porcelain in Europe a thousand or so years later. It would be a fascinating project to reconstruct the movement of these goods into the

---

36. Many scholars have linked these sites with the migrating Taghbach of *Wei shu*. An important early argument made for this is in the paper written by Su Bai in the piece cited in note 34, or the map provided by Wei, *Nei Menggu di qu Xianbei mu zang*, Map #30, facing p. 234. See the introduction of doubt on this matter by Dien, "New Look at the Xianbei," 42–43; and Lin Sheng-Chih 林聖智, "Bei Wei Shaling bi hua mu yan jiu" 北魏沙嶺壁畫墓研究, *Zhong yang yan jiu yuan li shi yu yan yan jiu suo ji kan* 83.1 (2012): 7.

37. Su, "Dong bei, Nei Menggu di qu de Xianbei yi ji—Xianbei yi ji ji lu zhi yi," 398. A good depiction of some of the pieces with animal design is given in Wei, *Nei Menggu di qu Xianbei mu zang*, 221.

38. HHS 90.2986; SGZ 30.837 gives an interesting variant of this by saying they began "to call themselves Serbi troops" 自號鮮卑兵. See also Chen, *Bei fang min zu*, 194.

39. A recent study suggests DNA linkages between Xiongnu and Taghbach (or Serbi): Yu Changchun 于长春 et al., "Tuoba Xianbei he Xiongnu zhi jian qin yuan guan xi de yi chuan xue fen xi" 拓拔鮮卑和匈奴之間親緣关系的遗传学分析, *Yi chuan/Hereditas* (2007.10): 1223–29. This issue is, of course, made complex by the fact that each of these groups is ill-defined and apparently itself heterogeneous; see the comments of Di Cosmo, "Aristocratic Elites," 48–49. For the diversity of constituent elements through text, see Ma, *Wuhuan yu Xianbei*, 248–54; and a key contribution to this field, Yao, *Bei chao Hu xing kao*, 25–266. For an example of the heterogeneity of another such group, see Scott Pearce, Audrey Spiro, and Patricia Ebrey, "Introduction," in *Culture and Power in the Reconstitution of the Chinese Realm, 200–600*, ed. Scott Pearce, Audrey Spiro, and Patricia Ebrey (Cambridge, MA: Harvard University Press, 2001), 6–7. As noted above, one modern scholar (Ma, *Wuhuan yu Xianbei*, 30–33) suggests the meaning of "Tuoba" was "Serbi father, Xiongnu mother," which even if not the real etymology reflects the reality of a joining of disparate groups.

40. Su, "Dong bei, Nei Menggu di qu de Xianbei yi ji—Xianbei yi ji ji lu zhi yi," 398; Dien, "New Look at Xianbei," 42.

northlands, if that were possible. Presumably, however, the traces of grain also found in the graves were of local cultivation.[41]

Whether or not the Hulun Nur was actually the "great swamp" alongside which the origin myth says the Taghbach dwelt for a time, it goes on to say that after six "reigns" had transpired there a "spirit man" (*shen ren*) addressed the nation (*guo*), saying, "This land is wild and remote. It will not allow us to build a capital. We should move again."[42] The chieftain being old, he passed his authority on to his son, who is only the second figure on this long list who seems to have held a name of actual Inner Asian origin, in the transcription Jiefen 詰汾 (MC *Khjit bjun). We are not told if the aged father arrived in the promised land (nothing more is said of him), but since it was he who at least began the process of leading them forth from the swampland, he too was given the epithet *tuiyin*, the "one who bores through."[43] As we shall see below, it seems to have been the son, Jiefen, who finally arrived.

Pointing out the similarity in sound with the name Tuiyan 推演 seen in the *San Guo zhi* list of Tanshihuai's emirs from the third quarter of the second century, some scholars have suggested identity with one or another of the two Tuiyins in the *Wei shu* "Prefatory Annals." Others reject this. Once again, certainty is not to be had. The "Prefatory Annals" make no claim to membership in Tanshihuai's confederation, nor even mention of its existence. Furthermore, there were many big men active at this time, and our scanty sources show many shared common Inner Asian names.[44]

Despite these uncertainties, Jiefen does lead us to firmer historical ground. As seems often to happen in exoduses, at one point the people wished to stop. But their resistance ended when a divine beast appeared, with a body like a horse and a call like an ox (some suggest this was a deer or reindeer[45]), which now led them on for several more years till in the end—in the mid-third century—they "first came to live in the old lands of the Xiongnu," the Tumed Plain. And here, despite the imperfections of text, we pass on to something beginning to resemble actual, verifiable history.

---

41. Cheng, *Cao yuan di guo*, 16–17. See also Nicola Di Cosmo, "Ancient Inner Asian Nomads: Their Economic Basis and Its Significance in Chinese History," *JAS* 53.4 (1994): 1092–126. In the *San guo zhi* account on the Wuhuan and Serbi (30.832), however, it is noted that "for rice, they depend on the central states" (Duthie, "Nature of the Hu," 32).

42. WS 1.2. This is, of course, a preposterous statement, clearly inserted into the record at a time when the Taghbach *did* have a capital city.

43. WS 1.2, 112B.2927.

44. Gardiner and de Crespigny, "T'an-shih-huai," 42. For skeptical views of this claim, see also Huang, "Tuoba Xianbei zao qi guo jia," 73–74, who suggests the correspondence is hard to accept and that Tanshihuai's confederation instead had an indirect effect; support for this argument is given by Yang, "Tuoba Xianbei zao qi li shi bian wu," 129–30.

45. Du Shiduo 杜士铎, ed., *Bei Wei shi* 北魏史 (Taiyuan: Shanxi gao xiao lian he chu ban she, 1992), 50–51; Sun Wei 孙危, *Xianbei kao gu xue wen hua yan jiu* 鲜卑考古学文化研究 (Beijing: Kexue chubanshe, 2007), 73; Chen Sanping, *Multicultural China in the Early Middle Ages* (Philadelphia: University of Pennsylvania Press, 2012), 53. Bunker, *Ancient Bronzes*, 91–92, mentions appearance of the image of a mythical winged quadruped on bronze belt plaques found in early Xianbei tombs.

SECTION III.

A Dynasty Takes Shape

A fascinating and quite distinctive feature of the human species is the dynasty: not only did we at a certain point begin to vest in some individuals the right to rule—to command labor from others, and impose punishment up to and including death—but this right became the possession of a family, a "dynasty," transferrable in various ways from one family member to another. This phenomenon is also quite new. It was just five millennia ago—a blink of the eye in the course of our species' history—that dynasties began to take shape in the Mediterranean world and Mesopotamia. A bit later it appeared in the Chinese world, and much later among the Xiongnu in Inner Asia. And as seen above, in the second century CE it took shape among the Serbi, as part of a larger development among various northeast Asian groups.

There were many different Serbi polities and so many different Serbi dynasties. Chapter 5, "The Interloper," describes the establishment of one of them, that of the Taghbach, in the third century. Despite claims of dynastic myth, the rule of the Taghbach line can only reliably be dated to the time of Liwei, an upstart and intruder who appeared in the frontier highlands in a vacuum left by the disappearance of Xiongnu power, and on the eve of collapse of Han's last heir, the Western Jin. Becoming a khaghan in the Yinshan region, he used the two key technologies of any state: coercive force and manipulative symbol.

Liwei's death in 277 led to sudden collapse. It is characteristic, however, in the development of early polities to see peaks and valleys, times of aggregation and then times of dispersal. In the end, the dynasty maintained itself as a symbol of authority in the world it inhabited and so survived. Sixty years later another Taghbach dynast, a great-great-grandson of Liwei named Shiyijian (r. 338–376), came to rule a solidly established state, with the power to draft, the power to tax, and the power to enforce law. This is the theme of Chapter 6.

These events, it must be noted, are not mere prologue to Northern Wei. Taken together, they form the opening acts of a longer play, in which names would change, but much at least of the substance would carry on.

5

The Interloper

For the Taghbach, the reliable intersection of myth and history comes in the mid-third century, on the Tumed Plain, in a person clearly referred to both in the "Prefatory Annals" of the dynasty's own *Wei shu*, and also in an entirely separate source, the *Jin shu* ("Documents of Jin"), which though not formally completed until the early Tang, drew on archives of the Jin dynasty (266–420) that would have been kept down at Jiankang (mod. Nanjing).[1] The name given for the Taghbach leader is, of course, a Chinese transcription, pronounced in modern Mandarin as Liwei 力微 (MC *Lik mjɨj). It may be that while incorporating this Inner Asian name into the Chinese writing system the transcriber also made a pun, as is seen with some frequency: the literal Chinese meaning of the two chosen characters is "strength faded," a reference perhaps to the inglorious end of his career that we will see below. In the *Wei shu* "Prefatory Annals," he is said to be the son of Jiefen and grandson of the one who had at least begun the process of "boring through."[2]

Parts of the *Wei shu* account of Liwei's career are quite implausible. It states, for instance, that the first year of his "reign" (*yuan nian*) was a *gengzi* year in the Chinese cycle of 60, which in context of the more solid dates *Jin shu* gives for his life could only have been the year 220. No further date or event is provided until the year 248. In terms of death date, *Wei shu* more believably states Liwei died in 277, adding the perhaps more improbable suggestion that he had ruled his nation for 58 years, and lived through 104. If this were true, it would mean that he was born in 174, while Tanshihuai was still alive at the helm of his powerful confederation.[3] Though it is not impossible that an individual could live to such a ripe old age, it seems much more likely that at some later time a clever historian or ritual master placed his "enthronement" in the last year of Han, displacing the Wei (220–265) of the Chinese Cao clan with the ancestor of the Taghbach Wei. This is given indirect support by the lack of any mention of this man in the *San guo zhi*, which covers the Cao Wei years; it is only in the 270s that his name appears in *Jin shu* as a threat

---

1. See *Jin shu*, Introduction, 1.
2. WS 1.2.
3. WS 1.5. Sima Guang, in ZZTJ 80.2548 (supported by JS 36.1057, though without a clear date), accepts the year of death, without repeating the suggested age.

on the northern frontier, after the Sima clan had seized the Cao throne in 266 to establish their own (Western) Jin dynasty (266–316). If we push the initial stages of Liwei's career up a few decades, to perhaps around 240, it would contain all believably dated events in Liwei's career, while also placing his time of significant activity after the death of Kebineng in 235, in the midst of the remaking of the frontier region with the emergence of nascent dynasties that followed the collapse of the last significant attempt to create a Serbi steppe empire on the Xiongnu model.[4]

If the year of his "accession" is open to doubt, more so is the means of his birth. We are told that early on, while hunting up in the hills, the father Jiefen suddenly saw a screened carriage descending from the heavens, from which stepped a beautiful maiden, surrounded by doughty guardsmen.[5] Taken aback, Jiefen asked who she was, to which she replied, "I am a daughter of Heaven. I have been charged to mate with you 相偶." That night they lay together, and the next morning she said, "Next year, on this same day, we will meet again at this place." Her words spoken, she was gone, "departing like wind or rain." And sure enough, when Jiefen returned the next year she was there to hand him a baby, saying, "This is my lord's son. Watch over him well, for your progeny shall follow [one after another], and in their time be monarchs." And then she was gone for good.

Some reality may be teased out of this variant of the worldwide myth of divine birth. First of all, in this story a claim of irregular succession is attached to Liwei, a generation or two after the notion of dynasty is said during the time of Tanshihuai to have taken firm shape among the Serbi. Some have quite plausibly suggested this interjection of the divine indicates instead a break in the kinship of the leaders, and self-insertion of an avid warrior of low status—from who knows what kind of group?—who rose in the midst of crisis and opportunity.[6] Studies of other peoples sometimes show an interloper maintaining the origin myth of those from whom he has taken power.[7] This possibility might be confirmed by an apparent early split in the Taghbach, which led to another group with apparently the same underlying Inner Asian name, differently transcribed into Chinese as "Tufa" 禿髮.[8] This line is said to have sprung from a "brother" of Liwei, the "eldest son" of Jiefen, who had left the "old lands of the Xiongnu" and led his own following west to the Gansu Corridor where, generations later, descendants ruled the minor Southern Liang regime, from 397 to 414.[9] One possibility is that this

---

4. Doubts for the 220 date are expressed by, among others: Lü, *Du shi zha ji*, 813; Tamura, *Chūgoku shijō no minzoku idōki*, 182, 195; Yao, "Lun Tuoba Xianbei bu de zao qi li shi," 23.

5. WS 1.2–3.

6. Tamura, *Chūgoku shijō no minzoku idōki*, 184, suggests that establishment of hereditary leadership appears only with Liwei, and that there was probably not a "line" before him—at least of *this* kind of ruler; and see Nicola Di Cosmo's theory of crystallization of rule in the midst of crisis: "State Formation and Periodization in Inner Asian History," *Journal of World History* 10.1 (1999): 15–16.

7. Herwig Wolfram, *History of the Goths* (Berkeley: University of California Press, 1988), 36–40.

8. See Shimunek, *Languages of Ancient Southern Mongolia and North China*, 52–53.

9. Boodberg, "Language of the T'o-Pa Wei," 222–23, 229; WS 41.919, 99.2200; JS 126.3141; WS 99.2200; *Xin Tang shu* 75A.3361. The "appended record" of the Tufa clan and their Southern Liang regime is *juan* 126 of *Jin shu*.

was not just a branch of the original Taghbach clan, but the core of the original clan itself, forced out by Liwei; as we shall see below, he was a usurper. It is interesting to note that neither of these two groups is mentioned in Chinese texts until quite late; in the mentions of frontier threats given in *Jin shu* in the 270s there is no mention at all of "Tuoba" (or "Tufa") as group or dynasty, but only reference to "Liwei" as an individual.[10] It is, of course, only when "barbarians" reach a certain level of potency that "the civilized" care much about them, or the way they refer to themselves.

In the birthing of Liwei by a mysterious female appears another interesting feature of this myth, the apparent mingling and bonding of different groups, an ongoing process in Taghbach history. To the examples seen above of modern DNA studies suggesting intermarriage between Xiongnu and Serbi can be added the writings of fifth- and sixth-century histories of Jiankang regimes, who state that "the braid-headed caitiffs," the Taghbach, were of Xiongnu descent.[11] Though at times descending into gossip, slander, and simple misunderstanding, in these quite separate lines of historical compilation can be found interesting tidbits (to be used, of course, with caution). Linked to the possibility of intermarriage in the *Wei shu* story is the hint of an early effort to separate an emerging aristocratic patriline from relatives through marriage, an important basis for alliance in early Taghbach history. The passage on Liwei's birth ends by stating that people of that age said, "The emperor Jiefen had no wife's family; the emperor Liwei no uncle's family."[12] Whatever the reality in the mid-third century, this would as we shall see be actively implemented under Northern Wei.

Much of the above is conjecture. But one thing we do know for sure: it is for some reason the nature of our species to grant authority to those claiming such mythical descent, if of course they can get others to believe (or at least accept) the story. And despite significant overlay of myth and legend, Liwei is the first fully historical character on the *Wei shu* king list, not only on the basis of confirmation by *Jin shu*, but also by reason of a *Wei shu* account of his career that, though slim, gives much more detail than any earlier figure.[13] Furthermore,

---

10. JS 36.1057; a reference in the annals to the same set of events (dated 277) refers to "the Serbi Liwei": JS 3.67. "Tuoba" appears in *Jin shu* only with reference to Northern Wei monarchs. It is interesting to compare this to treatment in Chinese text of Tanshihuai a century before. There is also no mention of "Tufa" in the Jin annals until 397: JS 10.249.

11. NQS 57.983 states this directly. SoS 95.2321 weaves a more complex story, telling how a Han official, Li Ling, surrendered to the Xiongnu (under whom "there were hundreds or thousands of groups, each with their own name" 有數百千種, 各立名號), and that the "braidhead line," coming from a union of Chinese father and Xiongnu mother, was one of these. For an overview of this theme, see Wen Haiqing 溫海清, "Bei Wei, Bei Zhou, Tang shi qi zhui zu Li Ling xian xiang shu lun" 北魏, 北周, 唐时期追祖李陵现象述论, *Min zu yan jiu* (2007.3): 73–80. While, as mentioned above, it has been speculated that "Tuoba" means "Serbi father, Xiongnu mother" (Ma, *Wuhuan yu Xianbei*, 30–33), a similar assertion is made about a branch of the Xiongnu, the Tiefu, who in their *Wei shu* account (95.2054) are said to have been "Xiongnu [Hu] father, Serbi mother."

12. WS 1.3. And see Tian, *Tuoba shi tan*, 16.

13. JS 3.65, 67. In the annals of *Jin shu*, in the year corresponding to 275 (Xianning 1), it is briefly mentioned that "the Serbi Liwei sent his son to present tribute." This doesn't seem to have done the job, and two years later we

62   *A Dynasty Takes Shape*

150 years later the founder of Northern Wei took Liwei as his apical ancestor; in the "Prefatory Annals" king list, he is entitled "inaugural ancestor" (*shi zu* 始祖) and "spirit origin emperor" (*shen yuan di* 神元帝). The book's "Monograph on Ritual" describes him as "beginning of the imperial enterprise" 帝業, 神元為首.¹⁴ One might interpret this as meaning that the Taghbach dynasty began with this man in the third century, despite the "Prefatory Annals" claim of a line stretching back to the Yellow Emperor.

The world in which Liwei began his imperial enterprise, the "old lands of the Xiongnu," had long consisted of an expanding collection of different peoples pursuing different ways: Xiongnu and Chinese, Wuhuan and Serbi, and no doubt others as well.¹⁵ In the time of Liwei's emergence, however, two things had changed. One was the disappearance of powerful neighbors: the impending collapse of the Chinese empire to the south, with its efficient extraction of tax from a huge peasant base, on the basis of which the frontier populations had been subsidized; and the already arrived-at demise of empire in the steppelands to the north, where efforts to recreate on the steppe a great confederation of the Serbi—those of Tanshihuai and Kebineng—had for a time at least come to an end. The other was the beginning in the frontier zone of efforts to bind together populations into territorially fixed states, part of a much broader tendency seen throughout northeastern Asia at this time, extending all the way to the archipelago that would in time evolve into "Nihon."¹⁶ In the frontier highlands region, the most successful of these emergent regimes would in the end be that of the Taghbach, who by hammering together an effective nation over the first century of their history laid the foundation for eventual construction of a new sort of empire in East Asia.

In the beginning, however, the dynasty's founder began his career as a minor interloper. Though the "Prefatory Annals" put forth the claim that he and his forebears had led a group newly arrived on the frontier, the first substantive record of Liwei's career given in *Wei shu* states that, attacked by rivals, he had

---

are told that a Jin general was sent against him. In the biography of the Jin general, Wei Guan (JS 36.1057), a bit more detail is given of him as a recalcitrant power in the frontier region west of present-day Beijing during the Taishi reign (266–274). Another support for the historicity of this figure is description of later members of the imperial family as being his descendants, in one case explicitly as his great-grandson: WS 14.345.

14. WS 1.3, 108A.2746. He is in the Monograph also described as the central and earliest figure sacrificed to by the Northern Wei founder, Daowu (WS 108A.2734–35). As we shall see below, he was until the time of the emperor Xiaowen (r. 471–499) conceived as the royal line's apical and defining ancestor.

15. According to JS 97.2548, at the time of the collapse of Han, Xiongnu had settled in the frontier region where "they lived interspersed with Han people" 與漢人雜處, in a situation "much the same as the registered households" 與編戶大同. Over time, the text goes on to say, their numbers "gradually increased" 漸滋.

16. This involved, among other things, spread of some cultural forms from the Chinese world and their incorporation in neighboring emergent states, particularly to the northeast; see Gina Lee Barnes, *Archaeology of East Asia: The Rise of Civilization in China, Korea and Japan* (Oxford and Philadelphia: Oxbow Books, 2015), esp. Chapters 13–15. The growth of new centers in East Asia is explored with particular reference to the Japanese archipelago by Jóhann Páll Árnason, *The Peripheral Centre: Essays on Japanese History and Civilization* (Melbourne: Trans Pacific Press, 2002).

lost whatever following—"nation"—he had had as "the people of the *guo* had scattered" 國民離散.¹⁷ Rather than being an independent leader, Liwei was attached to 依於 one of the real powers of the Yinshan region, the leader of a group called in *Wei shu* Moluhui.¹⁸ It was the Moluhui headman, not Liwei, who led a subsequent attack on "the rivals," and then, defeated and unhorsed, fled on foot. He did get a horse, but in the end his line lost the kingdom to the one who supplied the mount: Liwei.

At first not even knowing the name of the underling who had saved him, upon learning his identity the Moluhui leader, or so *Wei shu* tells us, offered to give half his nation to Liwei. When the offer was declined, he instead gave Liwei "his beloved daughter," and allowed him to lead his own following—whatever that was—to the northeast, away from the tempestuous frontier region and back north across the Yinshan to the region around "Long Creek" (Chang chuan), in the open steppelands east of modern Ulanqab, Inner Mongolia, now unimpeded by what was left of the long ramparts of the Han empire, which had come to an end about twenty years before.¹⁹

Over the years, we are told, word of Liwei's charisma spread through the northern lands and his company grew, his scattered former following regathering around him 諸舊部民,咸來歸附. In interesting new studies of ethnogenesis in Europe's early medieval period, it is made clear that the creation of new polities generally took shape in the "coalescence of diverse groups of people around a small aristocratic core, as a result of the political and military success of the latter."²⁰ Apparently a broad pattern of human behavior, this is a good description of what Liwei was doing as he began the process of creating a new nation, the binding together of disparate groups on the basis of shared challenges and triumphs, while forging common ideas of history and destiny. This was not

---

17. WS 1.3. The rivals were peoples of the "western district," who seem to have been "Serbi" (here apparently referring to slaves who had fled Xiongnu control and renamed themselves; see Yao, *Bei chao Hu xing kao*, 5–6, where Yao suggests the Taghbach themselves may originally have been such a group, as were their "Tufa" cousins: JS 126.3141) under loose Chinese control in the Cao Wei period, located to the west in the Baotou area on the north side of the Yellow River's northern loop: see mention of a group by this name in SGZ 30.839. Huang Lie, in his "Tuoba Xianbei zao qi guo jia de xing cheng," 71, points out that the "western district" people were diverse as all the others in this region, made up not just of Serbi groups, but also Xiongnu, Gaoche, and even Qiang. For location see WS 95.2054; Li Daoyuan 酈道元 (d. 527), *Shui jing zhu shu* 水經注疏, comm. by Yang Shoujing 楊守敬 (1839–1915) et al., 3 vols. (Nanjing: Jiangsu gu ji chu ban she, 1989), 1: 212, 222. A century later, Taghbach lords were still fighting "refractory bandits of the western district" 西部叛賊: WS 1.16.

18. For background on this group, see Yao, *Bei chao Hu xing kao*, 175–80. An alternative form of Moluhui, Hedouling, is included in the Gaoche account in *Wei shu*: WS 103.2312; Yao, *Bei chao Hu xing kao*, 175. In late Wei, the name was converted to the single-syllable form Dou, the form it generally takes in *Wei shu*. Yao, *Bei chao Hu xing kao*, 178—perhaps stretching the evidence—suggests that because in the sixth-century Northern Zhou period a fellow with the name Dou, a Sinicized form of the clan title, spoke the Serbi tongue, he at least must have been a Serbi. See also Shimunek, *Languages of Ancient Southern Mongolia and North China*, 131–32.

19. WS 1.3. In the *Zhongguo li shi di tu ji*, 4: No. 53, a "Chang chuan cheng" 长川城 is placed west of the modern town of Shangyi; see also Holmgren, *Annals of Tai*, 81 note 12, 131 map 5.

20. Halsall, *Romans and Barbarians*, 457; and see also Eberhard, *History of the Goths*, 39, who speaks of "small successful clans, the bearers of prestigious traditions, [which] emigrated and became founders of new *gentes*."

simply a modern phenomenon.[21] Nor was it new in East Asia—it has been persuasively argued that this had been done earlier among the Zhou states, Qin being the most successful.[22]

The emerging Taghbach polity had the complexity those who look will see in any "nation," an "ill-born" mob of the sort so well described in Daniel Defoe's "True-born Englishman," in which "With Hengist, Saxons; Danes with Sueno came, / In search of plunder, not in search of fame. / Scots, Picts, and Irish from th' Hibernian shore, / And conqu'ring William brought the Normans o're. / All these their barb'rous offspring left behind, / The dregs of armies, they of all mankind."[23] The complexity of the Taghbach nation is described in more direct form in *Wei shu*'s "Monograph of Offices and Clans." This is a very idiosyncratic chapter of the book, without counterpart in any other of the "standard dynastic histories" of the Chinese historiographical tradition. While the first section of this chapter is conventional, providing rosters of ranked government posts created in the late Wei, it is the second section that is unique, being a list of the polities or tribes—the "clans" (*shi* 氏)—that came together to create the larger whole. Sans the explicitly religious aspects, it reminds one of Japan's *Kojiki*, which with its long lists of tutelary deities in the first section was actually describing the real groups that also in the early centuries CE participated in the emergence of the Yamato monarchy.[24] Some of the "clans" listed in *Wei shu* might have been of long standing; others were themselves "ill-born mobs"—in Chinese, "sundry households," *za hu* 雜戶—such as those seen in many regimes of this period, including that of the fourth-century power Fu Jian, whose army contained "7,000 sundry households, [from] 12 sorts of barbarians" 雜戶七千, 夷類十二.[25]

The "Monograph of Offices and Clans" tells of emergence of the innermost layers of the Taghbach onion under Tuiyin II, by the "great swamp," with division of the subjects among the clan's brothers to create eight distinct but related lines: the royal line itself as well as seven cadet branches.[26] These were aristocratic

---

21. For discussion of the linkage of nation and ethnicity, the capacity for its "invention," and the origins of these processes, see Azar Gat, *Nations: The Long History and Deep Roots of Political Ethnicity and Nationalism* (Cambridge: Cambridge University Press, 2013), 3, 24, *et passim*; and the debate on these topics including Gat, Chris Wickham et al., in *Nations and Nationalism* 21.3 (2015): 383–402.

22. Gideon Shelach and Yuri Pines, "Secondary State Formation and the Development of Local Identity: Change and Continuity in the State of Qin (770–221 B.C.)," in *Archaeology of Asia*, ed. Miriam T. Stark (Malden, MA: Blackwell, 2006), 219–22, mentioning, among other things, the importance within such phenomena of new possibilities for "upward mobility routes for commoners" (220), which is certainly seen within Northern Wei and many other militarized regimes.

23. This complexity of the Taghbach nation is confirmed by Huang Lie, "Tuoba Xianbei zao qi guo jia de xing cheng," 71–72. It seems to contrast with Azar Gat's presentation of early Rome, in which different language groups "fused almost without a trace" (*Nations*, 19).

24. Roy Starrs, "The *Kojiki* as Japan's National Narrative," in *Asian Futures, Asian Traditions*, ed. Edwina Palmer (Folkestone, Kent: Global Oriental, 2005), 28.

25. From a stele inscription cited by Chen Yuping 陈玉屏, *Wei Jin Nan bei chao bing hu zhi du yan jiu* 魏晋南北朝兵户制度研究 (Chengdu: Ba Shu shu she, 1988), 180. For his part, the warlord Shi Le established a "commander of the refugees" 流人都督 (JS 112.2867).

26. WS 113.3005–6. Two were later added to make ten in all.

lines, quite distinct from the subject populations, who now "took control" (*she ling*) of the share of the subject populations—the *guo ren*—allotted to them. The subject populations would have included Serbi, groups speaking Turkic languages, and others as well.[27] The description given in the Monograph was, however, at best a simplification; written down centuries later, by Chinese authors, it is unclear how well it portrays the reality of the Taghbach in the third century as opposed to later construction and systematization.[28] The cadet branches seem to have been created over a long period—not as a single event—and even if that was not the case, members of the royal line continued to be transferred into them, in a way somewhat resembling use of Genji and Heike by the Japanese imperial house.[29] Furthermore, they were names of complex polities—"tribes," if one prefers to use the term—and not names of patrilineal descent groups, as was the dominant form of social organization in the Chinese world.[30] However they took shape, these groups had importance in the early Wei: they were not to intermarry and until the reforms of the emperor Xiaowen, in the late fifth century, they alone were allowed to participate in the imperial house's funerals and ancestral rituals.

The second stratum of the emerging Taghbach polity, the peoples said to have been gathered together by Liwei, are called in the Monograph "incorporated clans" (*nei ru xing*), that is to say, groups that, theoretically at least, became a permanent part of the emerging Taghbach body politic.[31] Beyond this were the "clans of the four quarters" (*si fang xing*), describing loose and volatile relationships with neighboring

---

27. For the ethnic backgrounds of some of these groups, see discussion of a cadet branch of the royal clan, the Hegu 紇骨 (renamed under Xiaowen as Hu 胡), discussed in Yao, *Bei chao Hu xing kao*, 9, which was originally the name of a Turkic-speaking group brought under control of the Taghbach royal house. See a general discussion of the composite nature of Inner Asian regimes, which were generally "a collection of different peoples, lands and languages," in Di Cosmo, "China-Steppe Relations," 65; and Fried, *Notion of Tribe*, 27–28.

28. Holmgren, *Annals of Tai*, 20–22, 112–15, theorizes that the story of formation of eight (or ten) clans were both invention (made in the late fourth or early fifth centuries), and also the basis for constructing the generations between the two Tuiyins. On p. 21, however, she does suggest it does a better job than the annals.

29. E.g., the dynast who renamed the Taghbach regime Northern Wei in the late fourth century giving a first cousin, once removed, one of these names, "Zhangsun" 長孫, "elder grandson": *Xin Tang shu* 72A.2409; in the commentary in ZZTJ 104.3279–3280, Hu Sanxing points out the discrepancy with the Monograph's claim for the name's origin. Furthermore, Zhangsun is itself a late Wei reassignment—the line's original name was transcribed into Chinese as Baba 拔拔: WS 113.3005, and note 23 on p. 3019; and for another example, see ZZTJ 115.3624. Luo, "Bei Wei Taiwudi de Xianbei ben ming," 128, suggests that this name means something like "beg-beg," "lord-lord."

30. We will see in Chapter 16, the efforts of the later emperor Xiaowen to reorganize Taghbach society along the lines of the Chinese patrilineal family, that had been the main unit of production, control, and extraction of goods and labor for the state.

31. WS 113.3006–11. While there may be some truth in the WS 1.3 statement that "all the old subject groups came to resubmit" to Liwei, it is clear from the "Monograph on Offices and Clans" that many other groups came as well. Here and just below, the term "clan" is a translation not of *shi* but of *xing*. As Albert Dien pointed out long ago, in discussion of the Edict of 495 in his article "Elite Lineages and the T'o-pa Accommodation: A Study of the Edict of 495," *JESHO* 19.1 (1976): 74 note 39, the term *xing* "seems to refer to a number of things, and its precise meaning in any instance must be inferred from the context." It is here a borrowed term referring to Inner Asian groups constructed no doubt in various ways that were being incorporated into the Taghbach polity. I use here the English translation "clan" to give a sense of the term's ambiguity as applied to Inner Asian populations, whatever the term precisely meant in the Chinese world.

peoples, whose "chieftains ruled their own people," allying with the Taghbach when the Taghbach were strong, and not when they were not.[32] These listings need to be used with caution, and there were doubtlessly retroactive revisions and adjustments, but this does seem to describe at least a process that began with Liwei of drawing peoples into a new confederation. Some of these had long inhabited the old lands of the Xiongnu. Others, like the Taghbach themselves, were apparently recent migrants.

In 248 the Moluhui headman died. Fearing—for good reason—that his brothers-in-law would not accept his claim to be rightful heir, Liwei now had "brave troopers" kill his wife, his rivals' sister. Rushing to the scene of her murder, they too were killed. Having despatched his in-laws—and apparently overthrown an at least incipient dynasty—he is said to have gone to "completely absorb their people" 盡并其眾.[33] Undoubtedly with exaggeration, we are told he could now assemble a force of 200,000 light cavalry, able to shoot the bow on horseback (though apparently still without the advantage of the stirrup, as we shall discuss below).[34] A decade later, in 258, having built his power on the open steppe, Liwei moved back to the rich grasslands of the Tumed Plain and the old town of Shengle 盛樂, which lay against the hills that defined the plain's southeast border, near modern Horinger.[35] For more than a century, Shengle would serve as the main defined base of Taghbach power. The importance of buildings for these people should not, however, be overstated, and it is not clear how much time the Taghbach elite actually spent in fixed structures constructed on what remained of Han rammed-earth foundations. Other cities built for nomads have been identified by modern scholars as serving mainly as storage sites for grain and valuables.[36] Power was at this time on horseback, not at writing desks, and we frequently see shifts to other centers. It would be generations before the Taghbach fully sedentarized; most of their lives were still spent in felt tents.[37]

---

32. Some of these were eventually conquered; others, such as the Murong (WS 113.3012), at times dominated the Taghbach.

33. WS 1.3, 13.322. The claim of "complete absorption" seems not to have been true. The Moluhui/Hedouling are not listed among the incorporated clans in the "Monograph on Offices and Clans" but among the "clans of the four quarters" (WS 113.3012). Citing Yao Weiyuan, Jennifer Holmgren, "Women and Political Power in the Traditional T'o-pa Elite," 37, points out that the Moluhui were not in fact fully incorporated into the Taghbach regime until the time of the Northern Wei founder, a century or so later.

34. WS 1.3. Even if this number had some basis in fact, it needs remembered that at this time of Taghbach history, such a number represents every mature male of the ruler's people. For the stirrup, see Albert Dien, "The Stirrup and Its Effect on Chinese Military History," Ars Orientalia 16 (1986): 33–56; and discussion of the stirrup in Chapter 11.

35. During the Han, this was called Chengle 成樂: HHS, Monographs 23.3525.

36. See Nancy Steinhardt, *Chinese Architecture in an Age of Turmoil, 200–600* (Honolulu: University of Hawai'i Press, 2014), 27, citing comments by Fu Xinian on use of the Xiongnu town of Tongwan primarily as a storage depot. Huang, "Tuoba Xianbei zao qi guo jia de xing cheng," 81–82, suggests, however, that beginning with Liwei the Taghbach did use towns and fixed structures as places of at least occasional habitation. For an overall history of the century when the Taghbach regime based itself (primarily at least) in and around Shengle, see Wang Kai 王凱, *Bei Wei Shengle shi dai* 北魏盛乐时代 (Hohhot: Nei Menggu ren min chu ban she, 2003).

37. For an overview of such dwelling places, see Peter A. Andrews, *Felt Tents and Pavilions: The Nomadic Tradition and Its Interaction with Princely Tentage*, 2 vols. (London: Melisende, 1999).

In spring of this same year, 258, Liwei summoned the headmen of his confederation for a great sacrifice to Heaven (Tengri, in the Turkic version of the name), an assertion of overlordship that in Inner Asia went back to the Xiongnu and would continue with the rise of the Türks.[38] Refusing, the leader of one group, the Bai, was put to death.[39] As a consequence, "no one" among the onlookers "did not tremble in fear."[40] Standing on the two legs of lordship—religion and violence—the charismatic newcomer had established his own complex polity.[41] One may surmise that it was at this time that Liwei took the title "khaghan."

While some groups submitted to Liwei's imposed confederation, and some at least acknowledged his overlordship, others voted with their feet by fleeing the region. One such group, previously mentioned, was the Tufa, the group said to have been led by Liwei's "brother." Another would be the Qifu, a classic example of the complexity of these emerging polities. The Qifu consisted of several separate groups that had come down from the north into the Yinshan region.[42] Only one—the core Qifu clan—was clearly Serbi; at least some of the others spoke Turkic languages. As they entered the Yinshan region, we are told in the version of origin myth given in *Jin shu*, the Qifu encountered a "huge reptile" (*ju hui*), with the shape of a dragon. To this, they sacrificed a horse, praying, "If you are a good spirit, then open the gate; if an evil spirit, then through the stopper we will not pass." Suddenly the dragon was gone, and in its place appeared a boy—an interloper—who in a manner something like Liwei grew up to be "Khaghan of the Qifu, the Demi-god," gathering diverse peoples to create the emerging Qifu nation.[43] Here again, as with the Taghbach on a much larger scale, we see Serbi interloper as crystallizing agent, along with appearance of the new monarchical title "khaghan."

---

38. For the Xiongnu, see Huang, "Tuoba Xianbei zao qi guo jia de xing cheng," 75; SJ 110.2892. For the Türks, see Denis Sinor, "The Making of a Great Khan," in *Altaica Berolinensia: The Concept of Sovereignty in the Altaic World*, ed. Barbara Kellner-Heinkele (Wiesbaden: Harrassowitz, 1993), 249. As Sinor says, beginning with the Xiongnu, this was an important source of authority, "charisma" (*qut*), for Inner Asian lords. Among the Xiongnu, it is said to have taken place in the fifth month, at a site called Dragon Castle, west of Ulan Bator; see Di Cosmo, *Ancient China*, 172. Heaven was also, of course, important as a source of authority in the Chinese world. But Di Cosmo ("Ethnogenesis," 46) rejects that the Xiongnu borrowed this concept from lands south. In fact, the borrowing could possibly have gone the opposite way; it has been suggested that although many borrowings in the frontier regions came from the Chinese world, the use of oracle bones originated in the north: Shelach, *Prehistoric Societies*, 121.

39. For discussion of the Bai 白, "White," people, see Zhang Jihao 張繼昊, *Cong Tuoba dao Bei Wei—Bei Wei wang chao chuang jian li shi de kao cha* 從拓跋到北魏 — 北魏王朝創建歷史的考察 (Taibei: Dao xiang chu ban she, 2003), Chapter 2; Yao, *Bei chao Hu xing kao*, 294–96; and Edwin G. Pulleyblank, "Ji Hu: Indigenous Inhabitants of Shaanbei and Western Shanxi," in *Opuscula Altaica: Essays Presented in Honor of Henry Schwarz*, ed. Edward H. Kaplan and Donald W. Whisenhunt (Bellingham: Center for East Asian Studies, Western Washington University, 1994), 524–25.

40. WS 1.3.

41. For discussion of the rise of the charismatic leader more generally in Inner Asian history, with authority gained from the divine, suppression of aristocracy through construction of a strong central army, and establishment of family succession, see Di Cosmo, "State Formation and Periodization in Inner Asian History," 19–22.

42. JS 125.3113; WS 99.2198; Hong Tao 洪濤, *San Qin shi* 三秦史 (Shanghai: Fudan da xue chu ban she, 1992), 129–32.

43. See Peter Boodberg, "Selections from *Hu T'ien Han Yüeh Fang Chu*," 103; and Hong Tao, *San Qin shi*, 130.

While it remained in the Yinshan region, this group would have been one of the many rivals of Liwei, and the Moluhui: a successor to the holy boy "brought together many tribes; the tribal army gradually grew stronger." But in or around 266—eight years after Liwei had established his polity as the dominant group in the Yinshan region—the Qifu leader led a migration of 5,000 households to the southwest, passing, in stages, through the Ordos, into Ningxia and thence into Gansu, where more than a century later they founded perhaps the most minor of all the minor Sixteen Kingdoms, the "Western Qin" (385–431).[44]

Remaining in the Yinshan region was Liwei, who in 261, five years before the Qifu flight, sent his son and assumed heir Shamo Han 沙漠汗 (or "the Shamo Khaghan," "han" apparently an abbreviation of the new Serbi title) down to Luoyang, where he remained as a hostage for six years during the transition from Cao rule to that of the Sima.[45] In 275 he made a briefer trip, apparently a trade mission to purchase silks. Returning the same year, he en route encountered Jin's General-in-chief for Northern Campaign, Wei Guan, who viewed the Shamo Khaghan as dangerous and detained him at his base at Taiyuan in central Shanxi.[46] Two years later, having received a charge from Luoyang to "chastise the Serbi Liwei"[47]—presumably because of conflict with Jin subjects in the frontier region[48]—the general released the son, with the aim of using his return to provoke internal power struggles and so undercut the father's position; to make Liwei's "strength fade." Unaware of the plot, the Shamo Khaghan now continued leading the 100 wagons full of textiles he had acquired at Luoyang up the valley of the Fen River. Most people delight in pretty goods from far-off places, and the frontier elites prized such difficult-to-obtain goods as status markers.[49] It was certainly intended that these would be distributed to the lords by Liwei (or perhaps Shamo Khaghan), as one way of building prestige and influence.

---

44. See discussion in Hong, *San Qin shi*; the "appended record" of Western Qin is in *juan* 125 of *Jin shu*.
45. WS 1.4–5, JS 3.65. The idea of the nature of Shamo Han's name comes from the suggestion of Sima Guang in ZZTJ 80.2548. "Shamo" in Chinese means "sandy desert." If not a translation from Taghbach into Chinese (or perhaps even if), then the transcription contains a pun, meaning "Lord of the Sandy Desert." See a tentative suggestion regarding the meaning of "Shamo" by Boodberg, "Selections from *Hu T'ien Han Yüeh Fang Chu*," 104, and an alternative for "shamohan" on p. 125. Also, there are questions about the dating of this event: WS (1.4) says Shamo Khaghan originally went in 261, then again in 267, and last in 275; whereas the first mention of such an event in *Jin shu* (3.65) is in 275 (Sima Guang simply incorporates both: ZZTJ 77.2459, 80.2541). See Tamura, *Chūgoku shijō no minzoku idōki*, 194.
46. WS 1.4–5; JS 36.1057; ZZTJ 80.2548–49. On the 275 trip as a trade mission, see Holmgren, *Annals of Tai*, 24.
47. JS 3.67.
48. JS 36.1057 states that Liwei and the Wuhuan to the east were both "causing trouble on the frontier" 邊害.
49. See note 94 in Chapter 3, for the warnings given by Zhonghang Yue to the Xiongnu lord regarding desire for exotica from the Han empire, and similar comments on the eighth-century Orkhon inscriptions. The power on the steppe that came from redistribution of prestige goods is described in William Honeychurch, "From Steppe Roads to Silk Roads: Inner Asian Nomads and Early Interregional Exchange," in *Nomads as Agents of Social Change: The Mongols and Their Eurasian predecessors*, ed. Reuven Amitai and Michal Biran (Honolulu: University of Hawai'i Press, 2015), 50–87.

It did not, however, work out that way. Just past the Yanmen Pass, at the town of Yinguan, a last outpost of the Chinese empire, Shamo Khaghan encountered a delegation of lords sent south by Liwei. From the start, these men were suspicious of the interloper's son. Their suspicion deepened as they saw how he had changed down in the Chinese metropolis: tipsy, we are told, Liwei's son took up a pellet-bow—a technology not yet known to the Taghbach—to bring a bird down for them. It seems that among these men there was also resistance to another innovation: the organizational technology of dynasty that had begun to emerge among the Serbi a few generations before. This, no doubt, was the fear underlying their (as always in these early times, translated and paraphrased) statement that "if he takes over leadership of the nation, he'll change the old ways" 若繼國統，變易舊俗.[50] Perhaps these men—many whose families had long dwelt in this region—particularly resented that this would be a dynasty of interlopers and usurpers.[51] So the lords now fled north to hector Liwei with complaints that Shamo Khaghan was a threat to the regime. By this time a confused old man—if not actually in his 100s, certainly in his 80s—Liwei had himself grown distant from his son during his years in Luoyang, and according to our account in the end broke down Lear-like to say, "what we can't bear, we should be rid of."[52] Returning south to intercept Shamo Khaghan's caravan, the lords killed the young upstart. Of mixed mind on this matter, and distressed by his son's fate, Liwei now fell ill.

It was Wei Guan who brought the first act of the Taghbach drama to an end. Carrying on the time-honored strategy of *divide et impera*, the Jin general had bought off a key figure in the confederation, a "Wuhuan prince," who now came to Shengle to announce to the lords there that "the Khaghan (Liwei) resents that you defamed and then killed the heir. Now he wishes to gather all the chieftains' eldest sons and kill them."[53] Abandoning Liwei, the lords scattered. Shortly thereafter, the old man died, perhaps of grief.

This was a pattern that would be repeated several times over the next century. As seen in many early polities, for its first century the Taghbach regime was

---

50. WS 1.4. It seems clear to this author that Liwei was attempting at least to establish dynastic succession, continuing the trends that had begun a century before under Tanshihuai. A different view is given by Cheng Fangyi in "Remaking Chineseness: The Transition of Inner Asian Groups in the Central Plain during the Sixteen Kingdoms Period and Northern Dynasties" (PhD diss., University of Pennsylvania, 2018), 102.

51. Tamura, *Chūgoku shijō no minzoku idōki*, 196.

52. WS 1.5. It should be noted that while Shamo Han had been in the south, the father had come to prefer another son: ZZTJ 80.2548.

53. See ZZTJ 80.2548; WS 1.5. Though these two passages are roughly parallel, it should be noted that WS uses "His Highness" 上, while the early modern *Zi zhi tong jian* (which I have used for the translation above) refers to Liwei as "khaghan" 可汗, with an insertion by the 13th-century commentator Hu Sanxing that "Xianbei lords were already at this time referred to as khaghans." This is indirectly confirmed by other sources: the chapter on the Ruanruan (Rouran) in *Wei shu* (103.2291) makes the fascinating statement that the title "khaghan" 可汗 taken up by the Rouran lords "was like [when] the Wei say *huang di*." *Ke han* 可汗 is also used for the Qifu, as seen above, and the Tuyuhun, a branch of the Murong (descended from a Murong [Tuhe] lord also named Shegui 涉歸, though transcribed differently from the Taghbach lord of the same name) who had built their own domain down in the region of modern Qinghai province: WS 101.2233. And for description in the early Tang *Bei shi* of the Türk

highly dependent on leaders' skill and personality and so would have peaks and valleys.⁵⁴ Still, despite initial rejection of dynastic succession—as had occurred with Tanshihuai himself, a century before—the record conveyed in the "Prefatory Annals" portrays the usurper Liwei as having established a transmissible authority that subsequently led at least some of the peoples of the Yinshan region repeatedly to raise his heirs up as leaders. Caution is of course needed here. The genealogy given in *Wei shu* for the century after Liwei is complex and at times confusing. There is a real possibility that control of the region was contested, and that rival lines have been conflated into one. That said, a century or so after his passing Liwei *was* designated as "inaugural ancestor" of a newly created (Northern) Wei dynasty.⁵⁵

In immediate terms, however, as Wei Guan and Luoyang had wished, the death of the "inaugural ancestor" in 277 led to the confederation's fragmentation: "all the groups defected, and the realm was in chaos." The "Prefatory Annals" tell us that what remained of the polity was ruled for almost two decades by sons of Liwei, and then by a son of Shamo Khaghan, the last again with a suspiciously monosyllabic name, Fu 弗.⁵⁶ Little is said of these men, but incorporation of groups seems to have gradually begun to expand again, since when another individual said to be a son of Liwei, Luguan 禄官, took up overlordship in 294 he divided the realm into three parts, perhaps inheriting the idea from Tanshihuai, and before him the Xiongnu.⁵⁷ The politics underlying this is not described—it quite likely represents different power blocs within the regime and

confederation that took shape under the later Northern Dynasties and Sui, the name is used very frequently. For more on "khaghan," see Chapter 1 note 13; Luo Xin 罗新, "Kehan hao zhi xing zhi" 可汗号之性质, in his *Zhong gu bei zu ming hao yan jiu*, 1–26; and Zhang, *Bei Wei zheng zhi shi*, 1: 112–27. As for Wuhuan turning against Liwei, Wei Guan's biography in *Jin shu* says "in the east were the Wuhuan, the west had Liwei. Both caused trouble on the frontier. Guan divided the two caitiffs, which then caused a rift based on [mutual] mistrust. Thereupon, the Wuhuan submitted and Liwei died of grief" (JS 38.1057). The Wuhuan played a powerful role in the emerging Taghbach state; for an overview, see Tian Yuqing, *Tuoba shi tan*, 108–203; Misaki Yoshiaki 三崎良章, "Bei Wei zheng quan xia de Wuhuan" 北魏政权下的乌桓, in *Wei Jin Nan bei chao shi de xin tan suo*, ed. Lou Jing 楼劲 (Beijing: Zhongguo she hui ke xue chu ban she, 2015), 173–84.

54. See discussion of this in Joyce Marcus, "The Peaks and Valleys of Archaic States: An Extension of the Dynamic Model," in *Archaic States*, ed. Gary M. Feinman and Joyce Marcus (Santa Fe, NM: School of American Research Press, 1998), 59–94; and also in Francis Allard, "Introduction: Power, Monumentality, and Mobility," in *Social Complexity in Prehistoric Eurasia*, ed. Bryan K. Hanks and Katheryn M. Linduff (Cambridge and New York: Cambridge University Press, 2009), 328, where Allard points out that "periods characterized by demographic aggregation—as evidenced, for example by public works or military campaigns—are invariably followed by periods that appear to be more decentralized." Below we will give more attention to definitions of "state."

55. WS 2.34, 108A.2734. The fabrication of monarchical lineage took place in many states in northeast Asia around this time. See Edward J. Kidder's discussion of questionable genealogy in the rulers of the archipelago's emerging state in his *Himiko and Japan's Elusive Chiefdom of Yamatai: Archaeology, History, and Mythology* (Honolulu: University of Hawai'i Press, 2007); and on the other end of Eurasia, similar issues for the Goths discussed by Peter Heather, *Goths and Romans, 332–489* (Oxford: Clarendon Press, 1991), 19.

56. WS 1.5. The name "Fu" might have been assigned because the fellow's original, Altaic name was forgotten, but Tamura, *Chūgoku shijō no minzoku idōki*, 197, expresses skepticism regarding the supposed "successors" of Liwei. It is possible that these have been inserted to construct a link between Liwei and the Yulü line, which we will discuss below.

57. WS 1.5–6; ZZTJ 82.2614. For the idea regarding borrowing of the practice, see Du, *Bei Wei shi*, 60.

struggles for leadership within the multiple branches of the family (or possibly, between different families)—but in practical terms Luguan held the eastern division, the grasslands east and northeast of Hebei's Zhangjiakou, bordering on the territories of another powerful northern people, the Yuwen, with whom the Taghbach had marriage ties. To his nephew, Shamo Khaghan's eldest son, Yituo 猗㐌,[58] was assigned the central zone, the steppe north of Shenhe Slope 參合陂 (located northeast of Datong, near modern Yanggao[59]), the region of Tanshihuai's headquarters. Yituo's younger brother, Yilu 猗盧, was based at "the old city of Shengle," on the Tumed Plain.

Among the triumvirs, the two sons of Shamo Khaghan are represented in *Wei shu* as the more significant; Luguan is given little if any place in the recorded events. For his part, the elder brother, Yituo, established a Taghbach practice that would be seen for centuries, leading a five-year campaign that pushed far to the north and west on the steppe, and forced many steppe peoples into at least temporary submission. Located more firmly in the liminal zone, the younger son of Shamo Khaghan, Yilu, was for his part transporting various unattached people of nomadic descent 雜胡 from the Taiyuan region up to the north loop of the Yellow River, presumably to produce grain there. A bit later a Chinese native of the frontier region, Wei Cao 衛操, originally an unrelated subordinate of Wei Guan, attached himself to the Taghbach, bringing with him a group of refugees—Chinese and Wuhuan alike—fleeing the civil war that had broken out in the Jin interior. This group—of several tens of thousands—must have supported themselves with farming while also serving as a militia of the sort that at this time littered the landscape of the Yellow River plains.[60]

The triumvirate as a whole is said to have been able to field an army of more than 400,000 mounted archers. Once again, this is likely an exaggeration—meaning something like "twice as big as Liwei's big army"—but if not would amount to all adult men of a population of over a million.[61] Whatever the actual size, many at least of these cavalrymen were attached to their own lord, only indirectly obligated to the Taghbach overlord. Use of the directly attached Chinese militia (or other resettled groups), and employment of their leaders as personal advisors, would certainly have strengthened the Taghbach leader's position,

---

58. *HYDCD* 1: 646 gives the pronunciation of this character as "yi," a position supported by Victor Xiong (in his review of "Dawn of a Golden Age," *American Journal of Archaeology Online Publications*, January 2005, accessed 13 August 2019). The *ZZTJ* commentary (85.2701), however, gives "tuo," which we shall use here.
59. For more on location of this site, see note 67.
60. WS 1.6–7, 23.599. For the guess at a number, see how many together fled back south twenty years later: WS 1.9. For the development of such groups in the midst of the empire's collapse, see Jin Fagen 金發根, *Yongjia luan hou bei fang de hao zu* 永嘉亂後北方的豪族 (Taibei: Zhongguo xue shu zhu zuo jiang zhu wei yuan hui, 1964). For several generations, refugees had been fleeing the empire's slow collapse, some seeking protection among various groups on the northern frontier: SGZ 26.731.
61. WS 1.6.

giving him counterweight to local aristocrats, who were at one and the same time allies and rivals.

At any rate, this would have been a good time to have a big army. The one remaining empire they bordered, the last echo of the Han, was in the process of disappearing. In 291, members of the Jin royal house, the Sima, began fighting each other in the Disorders of the Eight Princes, a suicidal conflict that would persist until the Luoyang regime had destroyed itself. While a member of the ruling house would eventually be installed at the city of Jiankang (mod. Nanjing) down on the Yangtze, to reign over a quite different "Eastern Jin" (317–420) regime, in the vacuum in the northern territories came a new flowering of states established by peripheral (or peripheralized) populations that had for centuries served the empire while seeking indirectly to draw on its wealth. To do so directly would now be the effort of these peoples' "sixteen kingdoms," as they are pigeonholed in Chinese historical accounts.

The first of the Sixteen Kingdoms, which for a time at least called itself Han, was established in southern Shanxi by the Xiongnu Liu Yuan, an heir to Modun and more recently to a Southern *Chanyu*, who also, however, claimed the surname of the Han imperial family through a marriage between the two imperial houses that had taken place long before. Originally serving as commander in a Sima prince's army, disgust with the princes' war eventually caused Liu Yuan to strike out on his own and claiming the Han mandate attempt to restore the empire. The effort was not successful, and in fact, after Liu Yuan's death in 310 a successor changed the name, a bit ironically, to Zhao.

Whatever claim to legitimacy Liu Yuan had had (we shall discuss him in more detail in Chapter 8), for the Taghbach he was a Xiongnu rival, so they chose to side with the Sima against him as they assumed a minor role in fighting in what had been the Jin interior. This began in 304, when Yituo—responding to a request from the embattled governor of Bingzhou (seat at Taiyuan), the Jin duke Sima Teng—together with his brother Yilu led a force down south of Taiyuan. Winning a skirmish with Liu Yuan's forces they then returned north, having had little impact on the larger picture.[62] In the next year, at the urging we are told of Wei Cao, Yituo sent another force south to rescue Sima Teng. "On behalf of the Jin," we are told, Sima Teng gave Wei Cao a general's title while awarding Yituo the title "Great Chanyu," certainly an archaizing written affirmation of the title of Khaghan he already held from his own people.[63]

It is said in the same *Wei shu* passage that Yituo was also given a "gold seal with vermillion cord." Almost fifty years ago, in the hills separating Shengle from the Datong Basin, a cache was found including a golden plaque inscribed with the Chinese characters "Yituo's Gold" 猗㐌金, portraying four supernatural

---

62. WS 1.6; ZZTJ 85.2701.
63. WS 1.6–7.

beasts, perhaps horses, portrayed as about to leap off the plaque.[64] Along with the plaque were recovered three seals, all topped with crouching camels. One, made of gold, was inscribed "Jin's Marquis Returning Xianbei to Righteousness" 晉鮮卑歸義侯; the second, also of gold, was inscribed "Jin's Marquis Returning Wuwan to Righteousness" 晉烏丸歸義侯; and the last, of silver, read "Jin's Commandant Leading Xianbei to Goodness" 晉鮮卑率善中郎將.[65] Han and its successors had for centuries been producing such seals to attempt to inveigle local frontier leaders to join into the empire's systems of rank and imperial bestowal. Recipients, for their part, certainly used such objects—as well as the exotic manufactures that came with them—to build authority within their own communities; that is what had made Tanshihuai's rejection of such bestowals especially significant. In this case we see that in the Jin view at least, Yituo's followers were Serbi (Xianbei), not Taghbach, and furthermore, that despite the actions of a Wuhuan faction in Liwei's confederation thirty years before, there were still Wuhuan in Yituo's following. But it must not be assumed that receipt of such objects implied submission to Jin. At this point, there wasn't much left of the empire's systems to be inveigled into; the immediate source of these objects—Sima Teng—was a man struggling to survive, on behalf of a regime in a state of collapse.[66]

Yituo died in this same year, 305; perhaps the cache was left as he traveled through the sacred woodlands of this area as he returned north of the Yinshan.[67] His death was marked by an early evidence of use among the Taghbach of Chinese as the language of formal written announcement, as seen in a stele

---

64. Zhang Jingming 张景明, "Nei Menggu Liangchengxian Xiaobazitan jin yin qi jiao cang" 内蒙古凉城县小坝子滩金银器窖藏, *WW* (2002.8): 50–52, 69; Su Bai 宿白, "Shengle, Pingcheng yi dai de Tuoba Xianbei—Bei Wei yi ji—Xianbei yi ji ji lu zhi er" 盛乐、平城一带的拓跋鲜卑——北魏遗迹——鲜卑遗迹辑录之二 *WW* (1977.11): 39–40; Adam Kessler, *Empires beyond the Great Wall*, 79–81. James Watt et al., eds., *China: Dawn of a Golden Age, 200–750 AD* (New Haven, CT: Yale University Press, 2004), 8–9, 127–28 no. 32, point out this plaque shows Xiongnu influence in depiction of the animals (9). Of course, there is always a possibility that this is a more recent forgery.

65. See the works cited in note 64; and mentions of such seals and their functions among the Southern Xiongnu in Miller, "Southern Xiongnu," 160–62. For a general overview, see Zhang Jingming 张景明, *Zhongguo bei fang cao yuan gu dai jin yin qi* 中国北方草原古代金银器 (Beijing: Wen wu chu ban she, 2005), 78–96.

66. Miller, "Southern Xiongnu," 162, calls the seal "a tool for structured mediation."

67. Some have suggested that the location of the cache was Yituo's home base, which we are told was the Shenhe Slope 参合陂; this is a controversy that will be discussed in greater detail in Chapter 7 note 73. Here this author will simply state preference for locating the Shenhe Slope northeast of Datong, on the edge of the open steppe. Confirming this in this particular case is the WS (1.5) statement that Yituo "dwelt north of Dai commandery's Shenhe slope" 居代郡之参合陂北. The original Dai commandery of the Chinese empire was located to the east of the upper Sanggan valley, in the area of mod. Yuxian, Hebei (and see also ZZTJ 82.2614). An interesting legend tells of how on the Shenhe Slope Yituo had spat out a bug, and in that place grew elms where none had been before: WS 1.7. Such woodlands had long been seen as sacred by frontier populations: near the town of Mayi ("Horse Town") at the bottom of the Datong Basin had been a grove sacred to the Xiongnu: SJ 110.2892. Similar practices can be seen among the Taghbach: Han Xiang 韩香, "Shi lun zao qi Xianbei zu de yuan shi sa man chong bai" 试论早期鲜卑族的原始萨满崇拜, *Heilongjiang min zu cong kan* (1995.1): 602; and Holmgren, *Annals of Tai*, 80 note 8 and 84 note 38. They also had a practical purpose: Shao Zhengkun 邵正坤, "Shi lun Xianbei zao qi de zong jiao xin yang ji qi zhuan bian" 试论鲜卑早期的宗教信仰及其转变, in *Zou chu shi ku de Bei Wei wang chao*, ed. Jin Zhao and

erected by Wei Cao with a Chinese inscription memorializing the deceased Taghbach lord.[68]

Two years later, Luguan died as well, whereupon Yilu took all three divisions under his own control. He went on to build ties in various directions, including with Liu Kun 劉琨, the last Jin governor at Taiyuan. Cut off and desperate in central Shanxi, Liu repeatedly begged Yilu to send relief forces to support his fighting with the Xiongnu and their affiliates.[69] Some of the time, Yilu granted Liu's requests. In 310 he sent his nephew Yulü 鬱律—a son of Yilu's putative brother, Fu—down to drive away the still-recalcitrant Bai people, who with Xiongnu allies were attempting to seize the valley of the Hutuo River, just south of the Yanmen Pass. Having given that favor to the Jin governor, Yilu now received the titles of Great Chanyu, and Duke of Dai. But he wanted more. Originally at least, the ducal title was an empty one, since Jin's Dai district lay to the east (in the valley of the Huliu River, near mod. Yuxian), in lands beyond Yilu's control. To give substance to the abstract, Yilu now requested formal recognition of his control of a belt of districts, including Loufan, which lay north of the Yanmen Pass in the Datong Basin. Liu had little choice in the matter, and while Yilu moved tens of thousands of families from the Tumed Plain down into the Sanggan region, Liu did what he could to move what remained there of Jin subjects south of the Gouzhu Mountains.[70] Having obtained the readily arable lands along the Sanggan, we are told that Yilu "thus flourished all the more."

Dai was, of course, very old—having begun as an independent frontier statelet, before becoming an appropriated district of the Zhao kingdom and then the Chinese empire. Now, however, the "Land of Dai" had emerged as something quite new: an eagle's nest from which a very particular people—the Taghbach—would for centuries involve themselves in the power struggles of the core regions of continental East Asia. In 315, Yilu received from Jin the title "King of Dai," in the midst of a series of unsuccessful efforts by a court without a reliable army to induce the Taghbach ruler to come to their rescue.[71] With this royal title, Jin granted Yilu the privilege of establishing the complement of secretaries and clerks prescribed within

---

Alede'ertu (Beijing: Wen hua yi shu chu ban shu, 2010), 635, points out that in addition to being sacred, the elm was important to Inner Asians, used to make such things as saddles and arrows.

68. WS 23.599–602. It needs to be noted that the stele itself has not been recovered, though a transcription of this 306 stele is given in the sixth-century *Wei shu*. If an accurate description of what was on the stele, this contains the first claim that the Taghbach had descended from the Yellow Emperor (599).

69. On Liu Kun, see Fan Zhaofei 范兆飞, "Yongjia luan hou de Bingzhou ju shi—yi Liu Kun ci Bing wei zhong xin" 永嘉乱后的并州局势——以刘琨刺并为中心, *Xue shu yue kan* (2008.3): 122–30. The reader should note that the term "Xiongnu" is used loosely here, to refer to a variety of groups of disparate ethnicity connected politically with the Southern Xiongnu in regions within the modern Shanxi and Shaanxi provinces.

70. WS 1.7; ZZTJ 87.2752–53. It seems, in fact, that this was a fait accompli, since the history of the Jiankang-based Song regime states that Yilu had begun moving his people into these districts the year before. Liu Kun's relocation was sped up in 311 by an attack by Yilu on the Bingzhou seat, Taiyuan: SoS 95.1321; JS 5.123; Uchida, *Kita Ajia shi kenkyū*, 2: 102–3.

71. WS 1.9.

the Chinese imperial structure for a *wang* ("king," or "prince"). It is not clear quite what this meant—he would die the next year—but in contrast to Tanshihuai, five or six generations before, Yituo, Yilu, and their successors seem to have enjoyed receiving titles and seals from what remained of the Jin empire. These symbols of power certainly would have made former Jin subjects more willing to serve them.[72] And they may have played a role with Inner Asian populations as well. Though the regional confederation Liwei created by force had fragmented, much at least of the inner core of dependents and followers—the *nei ru*—presumably remained, who maintained a shared belief in the mandate bestowed by Tengri upon the Taghbach khaghans. Into this mix had now been added another strand of authority, a parallel series of impressive titles and, perhaps even more important, exotic-looking gold and silver seals coming from the potentates of the fabulously wealthy empire to the south.[73] This complexity would be a centerpiece in the development of the Taghbach polity, which though apparently lacking something blue, certainly had the old, borrowed, and new.[74] The thrill of status markers—expressed in material form as a seal, or a robe, or a tweed jacket—is hardly confined to the barbarian.

A question frequently raised during this early period of Taghbach history is when it passes the line to become a state. Turning to this issue, we first need to think a little about how important that question actually is. The modern scholar William Honeychurch and others have suggested the preferability of giving attention to the complexities of the political processes of any large-scale society, without focusing on whether or not it passes someone's test to be a "state."[75] Honeychurch's point is about the Xiongnu, but this also applies to Yilu's realm: whether or not these were "states" according to one or another definition, they were complex polities with enormous importance for the larger world in which they were located. The term "tribe," though perhaps with technical significance on the chart of development of human forms of organization, fails to convey the reality of such regimes, while all too often descending into caricature. For its part, "state" can become lost in a wilderness of theory and jargon, and—like "civilization"—fraught with imposed and highly subjective judgement. Or as Richard Tapper has so succinctly put it, "there is 'state' within every tribe, and 'tribe' within every state."[76] Still, "state" does have meaning of a sort, as a reference to enduring institutional control by elites over subject populations. Attempting

---

72. For one example of Yilu's recruitment, see the account of Mo Han in WS 23.603.
73. For general discussion of such issues, see Anthony P. Cohen, *Symbolic Construction of Community* (London and New York: Tavistock Publications, 1985); and Helms, *Craft and the Kingly Ideal*.
74. For the nature of a later East Asian hybrid state, with which interesting comparison can be made, see the articles in James Millward et al., eds., *New Qing Imperial History: The Making of Inner Asian Empire at Qing Chengde* (London and New York: Routledge, 2004).
75. Honeychurch, *Inner Asia and the Spatial Politics of Empire*, 58–59; and more generally, Hämäläinen's *Comanche Empire*.
76. Richard Tapper, *The Conflict of Tribe and State in Iran and Afghanistan* (London: Croom Helm; New York: St. Martin's Press, 1983), 67. At the time the author writes this, Americans are, of course, confronting this reality head on.

compromise, this author prefers the straightforward definition of "state" put forth by the anthropologist Robert Carneiro: power to draft, power to tax, power to enforce law.[77]

Drawing on the authority of Tengri, the Khaghan Liwei had created an unstable confederation of local lords not terribly unlike those of Tanshihuai and Kebineng (though more modest in scale). The confederation broke apart when the semi-independent lords beneath him resisted the institutionalization of hereditary succession (and on top of this, killed the designated heir). Yilu, however, carried on his grandfather's project. In terms of taxation, he resettled populations on the farmable lands of the Sanggan valley and the Yellow River loop, and from them extracted grain to supplement the diets of his horse-riding followers. As for draft and law: the *Wei shu* "Monograph on Punishments" states that "to bring peace to the chaos [of the age, Yilu] then made punishment and law harsh, for every [matter] proceeding according to military regulation."[78] The only substantive example given in the description in the "Prefatory Annals" of Yilu's effort to enforce law was, however, strict deadlines for military call-up, that is to say, to fulfill one's draft obligations: "With no exceptions, all those who [came] after the scheduled time [had] their whole unit 舉部 executed. Sometimes there was an entire family holding hands and going to the execution ground. People asked, 'Where are you going?,' and they would reply, 'We must go be put to death.'" It is said that tens of thousands died this way.

These stories must be viewed with care, since they really do resemble tales told about Qin and the reasons for its fall. Still, the emerging Taghbach state was in its own way built around army, so these records—though formulaic—cannot be dismissed out of hand. If accurate, they probably describe military draft imposed on resettled groups under direct control of the Taghbach lord, rather than affiliated groups with their own lords. "The ways of the nation" had, however, heretofore been "simple and relaxed." Still not too far from the *liberté* of Original Equality, "people had not previously known prohibitions" and began to flee.

Yilu's aim of building an effective and disciplined army would remain central to Taghbach policy for centuries, even if more carrots were later added to the stick, and the program became more effective.[79] But under Yilu the powers to tax, draft, and enforce the law were not firmly in place; the man's experiments soon came

---

77. Robert L. Carneiro, "The Chiefdom: Precursor to the State," in *The Transition to Statehood in the New World*, ed. Grant D. Jones and Robert R. Kautz (Cambridge and New York: Cambridge University Press, 1981), 69. And see Di Cosmo, "China-Steppe Relations," 66, who to the right to tax, draft, and issue laws adds "the authority to represent the whole political community in diplomatic and international relations."

78. WS 111.2873, 1.9.

79. Di Cosmo, "China-Steppe Relations," 65, points out centrality of army in the formation of Inner Asian (perhaps all?) states: "There is general agreement on the fact that steppe imperial institutions were, at least initially, all military in nature, since the steppe empire can only be formed by military means. The new armies, which are no longer bands of tribesmen but complex military machines of tens of thousands of people, became the laboratory in which new institutions were born." See more in Chapter 11, "The Wei Army."

to an end, as did the man himself. It was not, however, taxes that brought Yilu down, or harsh law. What ended his life was an act seen repeatedly in Taghbach history—parricide. Having taken the basin of the upper Sanggan, Yilu had divided his realm in a new way—not horizontally but vertically, with a northern capital at Shengle, and Pingcheng as a southern capital. Remaining in the north, Yilu installed his eldest son, Liuxiu, in the Sanggan valley—the farmlands that had made the regime "flourish all the more"—in charge of a "Southern Division" 南部 of directly controlled populations, his base at a "New Pingcheng" south of the Sanggan. This arrangement, however, soon collapsed. Preferring his youngest son, and wishing to make him heir instead of Liuxiu, Yilu set out to humiliate the first-born, taking Liuxiu's prize steed to give to the youngest, and insisting that Liuxiu bow down to his brother.[80] Finally, in 316, when Yilu summoned Liuxiu and the son did not respond, the enraged father attacked. Losing the battle, he lost his life, and the life of his beloved youngest as well.[81] Liuxiu was then killed by a son of Yituo, Pugen.

This appearance of a Southern Division—implying juxtaposition against a Northern Division as well—was apparently an early form of "dual," or "complex," administration that, as mentioned in Chapter 4, had also begun to appear among the Taghbach's Murong cousins, in Manchuria, about which we have more information.[82] It would play an important role in Northern Wei, and then carry on in East Asia for centuries, among the Khitan, Manchus, and others. In this system of governance, a northern administration managed the pastoral populations directly under the court's control, while a southern administration handled the farming populations of conquered Chinese territories. Embedded in such a system was the constant possibility of struggle between north and south, Inner Asian tradition and Sinicizing reorganization. Underlying these tensions is the fundamental question of what the polity should be: a confederation with significant sharing of authority to local groups and their leaders, or a centralized regime basing its power on close control of populations, and mechanisms whereby tax and labor service can systematically be extracted from those populations. Such

---

80. This *Wei shu* story of struggle between father and son does remind one of how the Xiongnu ruler Modun was treated by his father, and many other such tales; see Di Cosmo, *Ancient China*, 175–76. Of course, one could similarly try to deny extramarital affairs as mythical construction precisely because of how frequently they appear.

81. WS 1.9; BS 15.545 (WS 14.384); ZZTJ 89.2830.

82. See Chapter 4 note 13; and Huang Lie, "Tuoba Xianbei zao qi guo jia," 79. Yan, *Bei Wei qian qi zheng zhi zhi du*, 19, points out that this was a borrowing from the early Sixteen Kingdoms of the fourth century, and perhaps long before that. According to Michael Frachetti, "Differentiated Landscape and Non-uniform Complexity among Bronze Age Societies of the Eurasian Steppe," in *Social Complexity in Prehistoric Eurasia*, ed. Bryan K. Hanks and Katheryn M. Linduff (Cambridge and New York: Cambridge University Press, 2009), 19: "Even in local settings, evidence suggests that Bronze Age steppe communities were organizationally heterogeneous—meaning they were not politically or economically centralized under a shared corpus of functional institutions." For the officers of Northern Wei's Northern and Southern Units 南北部, see Yan Gengwang 嚴耕望, "Bei Wei shang shu zhi du" 北魏尚書制度, *Li shi yu yan yan jiu suo ji kan* 18 (1948), rpt. in *Yan Gengwang shi xue lun wen xuan ji* (Taibei: Lian jing chu ban shi ye gong si, 1991), 116–22.

struggles, of course, have not existed only in East Asia, but can be seen worldwide, in ancient times and modern.

Sometimes it has been the monarchy's younger generation that leans toward greater centralization, though in this case it seems to have been the opposite, the son resenting having been sent down to the Southern Division, while the power of the father vis-à-vis the tribal aristocracy rested on an imported militia drawn from the several tens of thousands of families of Chinese and Wuhuan extraction that Wei Cao had brought north twenty years before.[83] After Yilu's death, they decided to flee, fearing that the "indigenous populations 舊人 hate [us] new folk for our bravery in battle, and wish to kill us all."[84] At the end, as *Jin shu* tells us, "this force returned to Liu Kun." They did not, however, find peace there either. Always seeking an army, Liu Kun now sought to force this group into battle against Shi Le (r. 319–333), a military man of Central Asian ancestry who was in the process of establishing the Later Zhao regime, which would come to occupy most of what had been the northern territories of the Jin empire. Arguing against Liu's demand, a leader of the group now said that, "although these are people of Jin, they have long been in the barren frontier lands, without practicing mercy or faith; it is difficult to bind them to the law. Now, within [the Taghbach state] we have gathered up the Serbi stalks of grain; and outside it we have seized the sheep and cattle of the savage Xiongnu. Furthermore, we have closed the passes and defended the defiles. Get the peasants working, let the soldiers rest . . . then we can do good deeds."[85] Refusing to listen, however, Liu Kun sent them against Shi Le, where they were defeated. In the aftermath, one unit that attempted to flee back to the Taghbach was tracked down by Shi Le's agents and wiped out. With this debacle, efforts to hold a northern outpost for Jin ended: Taiyuan fell to Shi Le that same year, and Liu Kun met his end soon after.

Though this might have presented the Taghbach with opportunity, they were not able to exploit it, as decades-long conflicts over succession now emerged between Yituo's offspring, and those descended from Yituo's brother, Fu. Pugen, the son of Yituo who had killed the parricide Liuxiu (at which point, the historical significance of Yilu's line ended), was raised up upon a felt blanket as the new khaghan, but within a month or so himself died. *Wei shu* gives no explanation for this, but goes on to describe how Yituo's wife, Madam Wei, had her dead son's newborn boy raised up as khaghan. The baby also, however, soon died (again,

---

83. WS 1.9, 23.603; JS 5.130, 62.1684; ZZTJ 89.2830. See also Tang, "Tuoba guo jia de jian li ji qi feng jian hua," 199; Zhang, *Bei Wei zheng zhi shi*, 1: 131–34 (and on p. 135 examining a different figure—300—given in the "Prefatory Annals," WS 1.9). "Wuhuan" here has lost any particular ethnic meaning, and refers to "various peoples from all over who have come to submit" 諸方雜人來附者 (WS 113.2971).

84. WS 23.603. Holmgren, *Annals of Tai*, 38, suggests that what this group feared was Pugen and the Yituo line, which wished to keep the polity's base on the grasslands.

85. JS 62.1685, 1687; WS 23.603; ZZTJ 89.2837–38, 90.2858–59.

with no explanation).⁸⁶ Power thus fell in 317 to Yulü (r. 316–321), the son of Shamo Khaghan's son Fu, who is said briefly to have reigned twenty years before.⁸⁷ It was from this line that the Northern Wei imperial house came, and in early Northern Wei Yulü was honored as the dynasty's "great ancestor" (Ch. *tai zu* 太祖, though that title was subsequently placed instead on the Northern Wei founder).⁸⁸ In addition to expanding the confederation to the east and west—a claim was later inserted that the dynasty's "great ancestor" had had a cavalry force of a million men—interest was also shown in the rich lands to the south. Hearing of the killing in 318 of the last Western Jin emperor, Yulü is purported to have said, "Now the Central Plain has no lord. Has Tengri given [this opportunity] to me?"⁸⁹ At the same time, he refused to establish ties with the Jin monarch's killer—the Xiongnu Former Zhao regime—and in the next year, when the Later Zhao ruler Shi Le sent ambassadors to Yulü, seeking to establish a relationship like that between "elder and younger brother," this request was refused as well, and Shi Le's agents put to death.

With the fall of Western Jin, East Asia changed profoundly. Frontier states could no longer obtain grain and goods from an empire that despite decline had still on a massive scale been able directly to extract such resources from its huge peasant base. Following earlier examples among the Sixteen Kingdoms, Yilu had already initiated the process of instead taking land and displaced populations. If *Wei shu* accurately describes Yulü's thinking, the Taghbach had now begun to think of taking direct and large-scale control of more such territories, deeper in the interior of what had been the Jin empire. But he and his descendants would have to wait some eighty years. Others would do this first.

Yulü's unfulfilled ambitions ended soon after, when in 321 Madam Wei, the wife of the late Yituo, staged a coup in which Yulü and dozens of lords (*da ren*) were killed (perhaps as revenge for the earlier killing of her son Pugen). Replacing the Fu line was now another son of Madam Wei and Yituo, Heru (r. 321–325). In the beginning, Madam Wei was the power behind the throne 太后臨朝, and some sneeringly called the Taghbach realm a "woman's country."⁹⁰ Perhaps we

---

86. WS 1.9. For the brief account of Yituo's wife: BS 13.491 (WS 13.322–23). Her name (as transcribed into Chinese) is given as Wei 惟 in *Bei shi*; as Qi 祁 in *Wei shu*. Since this chapter in *Wei shu* was lost and restored from *Bei shi*, which had previously been based largely on the original *Wei shu* chapter, I take the latter's version of the name—"Wei"—as more reliable. For discussion of variants in her name, see Zhang, *Bei Wei zheng zhi shi*, 1: 148ff. For discussion of her origins, see Tian, *Tuoba shi tan*, 27.

87. It is here in the Taghbach lineage that we see particular possibility of manipulation, and the insertion of other interlopers into the interloper's line. Even if this were true, however, it indicates that Liwei's clan had become worth claiming membership in. Perhaps with the Serbi principle of noble dynasty as a general model, false claims of genealogy were pervasive during this period. For a later example, see Holmgren, "Lineage Falsification in the Northern Dynasties."

88. This was done in the time of Xiaowen, when the title Taizu was assigned to Daowu. See discussion in WS 84.1852–53, 108A.2745–46, 2.47 note 14.

89. WS 1.9.

90. WS 1.10; ZZTJ 91.2891; BS 13.491 (WS 13.323). It will be noted that those calling the Taghbach a "woman's country" would have been members of Shi Le's court, sneering at the emissaries sent them to establish peace. Here

see here perpetuation of elements of the early culture of the Serbi, among whom, it will be remembered, women are said to have played a role in discussion of all matters save war.[91] Counterparts to Madam Wei's rise to power can be found in the histories of many societies; looking for Inner Asian examples, it is hard not immediately to turn to Töregene, wife of Chinggis's son and heir Ögedei; or Sorqoqtani, wife of Ögedei's brother, Tolui.[92]

A powerful individual, the Taghbach leader Madam Wei was supported by an important faction. From what little we know of the period of her rule, she attempted to stabilize the regime and its ties with neighbors, in particular the Later Zhao regime of Shi Le down on the Yellow River plains. It is not clear when Madam Wei died, but Heru is said to have assumed real leadership in 324. Perhaps deprived of his mother's effective politicking, we are now told that many in the coalition were unwilling to obey him, and so, no doubt with a reduced confederation, Heru and his court left Shengle to move to the northeast, bringing their herds and followers north of the Yinshan to establish a new headquarters on East Tree-root Mountain (Dong Mu gen shan 東木根山, about 20 miles east of mod. Ulanqab).[93] In 325 he reversed his mother's alliance with Zhao by coming to the aid of the Murong against a Yuwen army sent by Shi Le against them. The Yuwen were routed, Shi Le frustrated.[94]

Heru died later in the same year, 325, and was replaced by a younger brother, Hena (r. 325–329, 335–337). Though not directly stated in the texts, it seems that for a time at least he moved his herds and his court back south onto the Tumed Plain, since the text does tell us that he too fled north when in 327 Shi Le punished Taghbach participation in the Yuwen rout by sending the general (and future ruler) Shi Hu north to seize the Datong Basin. Hena now established his headquarters in the valley of the Yang He ("Sheep River," located near mod. Zhangjiakou), and from this base resumed alliance with the Yuwen, inducing these neighbors to attack his own confederation's powerful Helan people, close marriage allies of the Yulü line who lived not far to the west and were harboring Yihuai, a son of Yulü and a Helan woman.[95] If they were an army for hire, the

---

also is a good example of the care we need using description of the doings of one people in the language of another: for though a classical Chinese term is used to describe Madam Wei's participation in the regime's decision-making, there certainly was no Chinese-style "court" (chao 朝) that she oversaw (lin 臨). And of course, neither was there a "throne," in the European style at least.

91. HHS 90.2979.
92. See Anne F. Broadbridge, *Women and the Making of the Mongol Empire* (Cambridge: Cambridge University Press, 2018): Chapters 6 and 7.
93. WS 1.10. In light of this removal of the center of power to the north, Zhang, *Bei Wei zheng zhi shi*, 1: 142, suggests that the main base of Madam Wei's power lay with those who had resisted Yulü's ambition to seize Chinese territory. Holmgren, *Annals of Tai*, 39; Holmgren, "Women and Political Power," concurs, saying that opposition to Yulü—including his hostility to Later Zhao—led to support for her leadership. Her son, however, reversed this policy, as we see just below.
94. JS 108.2808; ZZTJ 93.2933; Holmgren, *Annals of Tai*, 39.
95. For discussion of the Helan, see Zhang, *Cong Tuoba dao Bei Wei*, Chapter 1; and Tian, *Tuoba shi tan*, 63–65.

Yuwen were not particularly good at this occupation, since their attack again failed and Yihuai remained uncaptured. Two years later, apparently under pressure from the Helan, Hena fled still further east—to live among the Yuwen—whereupon "the Helan and the lords of all the tribes" raised up their scion of the Taghbach line, Yihuai (r. 329–335, 337–338), as lord of the confederation.⁹⁶

The first thing Yihuai did was resume the policy of the now deceased matriarch of the competing faction—Madam Wei—by making peace with Later Zhao and sending them a hostage in the person of his younger half-brother, Shiyijian. In a foreshadowing of things to come, however, peace unraveled within the confederation in 335, when Yihuai, having tired of his mother's overweening brother—the Helan leader—executed the man.⁹⁷ Rejecting Yihuai, but still apparently wanting a Taghbach, the lords now brought Hena back from the Yuwen. Yihuai, for his part, fled down to the plains to join his half-brother in the Later Zhao capital, the great city of Ye (near mod. Anyang, Hebei), where he was feted by the new Zhao lord, Shi Hu (r. 334–349). The last gasp of the line of Yituo and Madam Wei came two years later, when Shi Hu sent an army north with Yihuai, his own Taghbach claimant. As support for him crumbled, Hena fled east again, this time going past the Yuwen to seek protection among the Murong of the Liao River region. Yihuai was restored.

His second reign, however, was brief; within a year or two he had died. But the volatility of the last several decades now came to an end, as the half-brother Shiyijian took power. Holding the throne for 38 years, he would be an effective ruler, who paved the way for the conquests of early Northern Wei. The first to appropriate for his regime the Chinese style of reign name, in 338 he declared the beginning of the era of "establishing the state" (*jian guo* 建國).⁹⁸

---

96. WS 1.11.
97. WS 1.11.
98. In classical Chinese in general, and in Chinese accounts of non-Chinese peoples, *guo* has multiple meanings: "dynasty," "nation," "state." In this book, as will be discussed in Chapter 9, it really refers to all three: the administrative apparatus and pre-modern "nation" that took shape around the Taghbach dynasty.

Establishing a State

Shiyijian 什翼犍 (r. 338–376) was an imposing man, said to have been more than 6½ feet tall. The modern scholar Peter Boodberg has suggested his name—in Middle Chinese the transcription was pronounced something like *Dzyip-yik-ken—may in his own language have meant "Crimson."[1] Living in a different world from his ancestors, he put forth a different image. While Taghbach were in their early period called "braid-heads," a reference to their traditional hair style, Shiyijian's hair "swept down to the ground," suggesting it was long and perhaps unbound.[2] The Taghbach lords had already begun to change in dramatic ways. They would continue to do so over the next century or two.

Ending the turbulence of the preceding decades, Shiyijian would reign over the Taghbach for 38 years, and bring to it a new stability, paving the way for Northern Wei. But his entry into that role—at the age of 19 *sui*—seems to have been difficult. This is one of several episodes in early Taghbach history where "unseemly affairs" seem to be concealed in what we have received of the "Wei documents."

Shiyijian and Yihuai were both sons of Yulü, and said to be descended from Shamo Khaghan through the man called Fu in the Chinese sources (see the chart of the dynasty's claimed family tree in front matter). But they were half-brothers: Yihuai was born of the sister of the Helan lord, while Shiyijian was born of a different woman, who came from a Wuhuan family that had taken the Chinese name Wang.[3] The *Wei shu* annals give an account of the succession that both simplifies and distorts. First stating only that in his second reign Yihuai served "one year and died" 年而崩—with no explanation at all—it then proceeds with a bit of pabulum about how on his deathbed Yihuai asked that he be succeeded by his half-brother. Another brother, Gu 孤, is then said to have gone down to the city of Ye, on the plains, to bring Shiyijian back to his homeland.[4]

---

1. Boodberg, "Selections from *Hu T'ien Han Yüeh Fang Chu*," 125.
2. WS 1.11. The figure for his height given in the text is 8 *chi* 尺. A *chi* under the Northern Wei being about 10 English inches (Duan Zhijun 段智钧 and Zhao Nuodong 赵娜冬, *Tian xia da tong: Bei Wei Pingcheng Liao Jin Xijing cheng shi jian zhu shi gang* 天下大同: 北魏平城辽金西京城市建筑史纲 [Beijing: Zhongguo jian zhu gong ye chu ban she, 2011], 19); this would have made him about 6'8". It must be noted that the same term, "swept to the ground" 委地, is also used to describe the Jin founder, Sima Yan (JS 3.49).
3. Zhang, *Bei Wei zheng zhi shi*, 1: 157 note 3.
4. WS 1.11–12.

Interestingly, the annals continue by saying that Shiyijian assumed power not at Shengle, nor up on the open steppe, but at Fanzhi 繁時, a district south of the Sanggan River recently seized by Later Zhao.

In Chinese dynastic histories, the annals are often dedicated to the lies demanded by the powers that be, while hints of something closer to truth appear—at least some of the time—in the separate biography section.[5] The account of Shiyijian's mother, Madam Wang, makes clear something was going on: when Yihuai died, we are told, "the throne was imperiled; it was the empress's strength that revived the great enterprise."[6] In what is left of Gu's biography—perhaps intentionally discarded, it was one of those reconstructed in the 1100s—we are told that objecting to Shiyijian, the lords killed yet another son of Yulü, and then insisted that Gu take the throne. The biography of this figure, again with a suspiciously monosyllabic name, then presents him as righteously insisting that he must go down to Ye to retrieve Shiyijian, who when he returned to the north "divided the realm to give half to" Gu. This is followed by a one-word sentence: "[Gu] died" 薨.[7] It is not made clear how quickly this occurred; in the "Monograph on Offices and Clans," we are told that Gu controlled the Northern Division.[8] The modern scholar Jennifer Holmgren makes the sensible suggestion that Shiyijian was backed in a succession struggle by Later Zhao—perhaps even by an army that brought him up and enthroned him at Fanzhi—but that "to depict the grandfather of the founder of Northern Wei as a usurper and pawn of the [Xiongnu] would certainly have been unacceptable."[9] He is instead depicted as "a lenient and magnanimous man, who"—as is the case with many successful politickers—"showed on his face neither anger nor joy."[10] As for the nature of the strength by which Madam Wang saved the realm, perhaps it was she who was able to work out an agreement with Later Zhao for a power-sharing arrangement between Shiyijian and Gu, which ended when Shiyijian killed his "righteous" brother. The strangeness of the situation increases when we look at the biography of Gu's son, who we are told "lost his office"—presumably his right to succession—and is said some forty years later to have incited a son of Shiyijian to kill his father.[11] These were treacherous waters for a Chinese chronicler to be out upon; it seems possible that inclusion of a more

---

5. This is the process of "concealing yet revealing" forced on historians Chinese (and otherwise) who have wished to describe what they see as truth, while moving under the thumb of men (or women) of power.
6. This is stated in the Tang-period textual reconstruction of *Bei shi*: BS 13.491 (WS 13.323).
7. BS 15.546 (WS 14.349).
8. WS 113.2972.
9. Holmgren, *Annals of Tai*, 43. Zhang, *Bei Wei zheng zhi shi*, 1: 158, makes the same suggestion. Regarding Shiyijian's relationship to Zhao, ZZTJ 96.3043 tells of a Yan envoy to Eastern Jin who says: "Shi Hu has wrapped up the territory of eight provinces; he has a million men in armor; he wishes to swallow up the Yangtze and Han rivers. From the 'Braid-heads' and the Yuwen, and all the lesser nations, there are none that do not submit."
10. WS 1.11.
11. BS 15.546 (WS 14.349); Holmgren, *Annals of Tai*, 44.

straightforward account in the *Guo ji* is what caused Cui Hao's death (though there are, of course, other possibilities).

During his 38 years on the throne, Shiyijian would combine the projects of his two great-uncles (if that was in truth the relationship): Yituo, the great campaigner, and Yilu, the institution-builder. Taking the latter issue first, having in 338 taken up the Chinese reign-title "Establishing the State," he proceeded to do so, building at least a rough version of what "state," *guo*, meant to Chinese scribes. His bureaucracy, however, was certainly not on the scale of the Chinese empires, and even when borrowing official titles from Jin, they were quite differently organized.[12] One key aspect of this was designation in 339 of attendant aides (referred to in Chinese as *jin shi* 近侍) who waited on and guarded the ruler and announced his decrees. This was the beginning of the creation of an "inner court" that we shall discuss in more detail below, a key aspect in the growth of Taghbach royal power. Another important feature of Shiyijian's state-building was re-establishment of Yilu's Northern and Southern Divisions. Their bosses, called in the Chinese text *da ren* 大人, or "magnates," were administrators—directors—not of all the populations within the state but of unattached ("miscellaneous" 雜) groups within the royal domain.[13] They continued to be distinguished from the politically distinct vassal groups, such as the Helan. In charge of the Northern Division, Gu would have been in charge of pastoralists (the director of the Southern Division would be in charge of farmers).

Shiyijian also resumed Yilu's effort to establish a law code, though without the extreme harshness of the first version. We are not told whether the laws were committed to writing (in Chinese) and, if so, how they were disseminated to the non-Chinese-speaking population; it may originally have been simply a set of oral pronouncements, similar to the Mongol *yasagh*. In terms of the code's content, as later recounted in *Wei shu*, as the state and its ruling dynasty had become more clearly defined, so the first focus of Shiyijian's law code was to protect it: the punishment for rebellion (Ch.: *da ni* 大逆) was death for the perpetrator and all his kinsfolk, regardless of gender or age.[14] Sexual morality also made an appearance, with death sentences for men and women who "did not consort in a moral manner." Besides that, the code was quite gentle, at least to the rich (as is true in many societies). It was also for a society in which the main wealth was still figured in terms of livestock. This would be the case for the royal family under

---

12. See Huang, "Tuoba Xianbei zao qi guo jia de xing cheng," 81.
13. WS 113.2971–72; Huang, "Tuoba Xianbei zao qi guo jia de xing cheng," 81. These posts were key aspects of the development of dual administration in the Taghbach regime. See Yan, *Bei Wei qian qi zheng zhi zhi du*, 47. It needs noted that their import has been misunderstood by Hucker, *Official Titles*, 340 no. 414 and 372 no. 4535. As mentioned in Chapter 5 note 83, groups and individuals of Inner Asian origin not incorporated into a vassal polity had come to be referred to by the appropriated, and now meaningless, term "Wuwan" 烏丸, that is, Wuhuan.
14. WS 111.2873; Huang, "Tuoba Xianbei zao qi guo jia de xing cheng," 83–84.

Shiyijian, and for some time thereafter.[15] On the basis of these laws, those of the elite sentenced to death (apart from rebellion, of course) would be pardoned, if their family turned over a "golden horse." For a killing among the commoners, the wrongdoing could be settled by turning over to the wounded family a coffin and 49 head of horses. For the crime of thievery, the private household in fact took precedence over the dynasty: while theft of "public belongings" (referring mostly to livestock taken from the monarch's herds) needed to be repaid at a 5-to-1 rate, a 10-to-1 rate of reimbursement was required for privately owned livestock. While crude in comparison to the voluminous Han code, clearly we see here a more solid development of the legal facet of Carneiro's definition of "state."

In addition to developments in the royal administration, Shiyijian also made efforts to build an army and expand his territories. Early in Shiyijian's section of the "Prefatory Annals" we are told that "none were not submissive" and that Shiyijian controlled the world from Ferghana to Korea.[16] This ridiculous hyperbole can be readily dismissed, if for no other reason than because the powerful Murong state lay between Korea and the land of the Taghbach. But immediately after this quote we are told that Shiyijian gathered his lords together on the Shenhe Slope, at the northeastern edge of the Datong Basin. We are not told whether they came together in a tent, or outside, on the grass—though this being June it would have been quite warm—but what they discussed was whether or not Shiyijian should have his way about establishing a standing capital city at the basin's southwestern corner, near the place where Yilu's son, Liuxiu, had had his base. Shiyijian clearly had ambitions of conquest of the southlands.

According to *Wei shu*, it was his mother, the Wuhuan woman Madam Wang, who intervened here, playing a role similar to that of Madam Wei a decade or so before, and to later figures under Northern Wei. From what little we know of her, Madam Wang played an extraordinary role in Shiyijian's life. At the time of Madam Wei's killing of Shiyijian's father, Yulü, in the massacre of 321, Madam Wang is said to have put Shiyijian—just a baby at the time—down her trousers and told him that if he wanted to survive he needed to make no noise. Following mother's command, the toddler lived to fight another day.[17] Now,

---

15. As we see in WS 28.684 and 29.697, supervision of the royal herds was a hereditary function. Those herds were also mixed with those of others, and Tuoba monarchs (for WS 28.684 this was Shiyijian's grandson and founder of Northern Wei) could become quite unhappy when mixings were not resolved to their liking.

16. WS 1.12. See Holmgren, *Annals of Tai*, 89 note 87. It is, of course, quite possible that this was a later insertion, either in the oral account, or later still by historians. SoS 95.2321 is more realistic, stating that "in the north he held the desert; in the south he occupied the Yinshan Mountains."

17. Holmgren, "Women and Power," 49, suggests that this is a false claim, showing a parallel passage from the much earlier *Shi ji*. It is, however, this author's opinion that such appropriation from an earlier history does not necessarily mean that Madam Wang did not save her son, but only that the story was framed around a borrowed set of details.

eighteen years later, on Shenhe Slope, she enjoined her son not to establish his capital south of the Sanggan: "since previous times," she says in the Chinese translation of her statement, "our dynasty has made an enterprise of mobility. And now, following troublesome events, that enterprise is not secure. If [we] dwell within walls, and one morning invaders come, it will be hard abruptly to relocate."[18] So, instead, new palaces were built up at Shengle, though it is again open to question how much even those were actually used by this *al fresco* society.

Three years later, however, in the year 342, Shiyijian returned to the Shenhe Slope, this time to build his army, and to affirm its presence to the larger world. "All the units 諸部 gathered together," we are told, "setting up altars and tournament enclosures, studying warfare and shooting arrows off the backs of their horses. This now became a regular [event]."[19] Systematized training of the khaghan's army had begun. We see a clue to centralized military development in the numbers ascribed in *Wei shu* to the armies of the Taghbach khaghans: from 200,000 in the time of Liwei, to 400,000 in the time of Yilu, to 1,000,000 in the time of Yulü. Whether accurate or not, these figures represent all the fighting-age men within the realm who would be subject to a great call-up of troops, if that could actually be done. In the time of Shiyijian, however, the Jiankang history *Song shu* gives the figure "several tens of thousands,"[20] apparently referring to the establishment of a tight-knit, central army. It probably represents as well at least the beginning of processes of bringing local lords under control, and remaking some at least as military officers in the khaghan's central army.[21]

But for a time at least, these cavalry forces would not become embroiled in the fierce conflicts unfolding across the Yellow River plains. When Shi Hu's Later Zhao regime descended into civil war after his death in 349, Shiyijian attempted a call-up of all the components of his regime to take advantage of the situation to invade the Chinese territories. This time his will was stayed not by mother but by his lords. Hearing Shiyijian's proposal that "I myself [should] lead the royal army to bring peace to all within the four seas," the lords responded that: "[We] fear this would bring no lasting gain, but instead

---

18. BS 13.491 (WS 13.323).
19. WS 1.12. The *bu* in this passage might also be translated as "tribe," though in the view of this author, "unit," as in "military unit," seems the better translation, whatever the origin and organization of those units. Regarding military assemblies, see analysis of similar events under the Manchus, some 1,500 years later, where it is said they were "a hugely authoritative affirmation of Qing imperial power," which "hammer[ed] home the notion of the state as repository of massive military strength": Joanna Waley-Cohen, *The Culture of War in China: Empire and the Military under the Qing Dynasty* (London and New York: I. B. Tauris, 2006), 72. Even if differently organized, these occasions seemingly share a similar import in the life of the regime.
20. SoS 95.2321; a much higher estimate—perhaps for total possible turnout—is given in WS 24.609.
21. See Huang, "Tuoba Xianbei zao qi guo jia de xing cheng," 76. Huang goes on in this same passage to suggest that Taghbach lords also held kinsmen of the local lords as hostages.

the grief of loss."²² Shiyijian deferred to the objections of the big men, who were also of course his generals. The place of Later Zhao in the Chinese interior was in fact taken up by another Serbi group, the Taghbach's eastern neighbor, the Murong. Emerging from southern Manchuria in the 350s their Yan regime (again, a name taken from the Chinese Warring States) emerged as a new power in the East Asian world.

The two Serbi states had early on built strong marriage ties, in the midst of intermittent hostility. In 339, a year after Shiyijian's accession, the Yan monarch Murong Huang gave a sister to the new Taghbach leader. She died, however, two years later, and in 343, when Shiyijian asked for another bride, Huang replied with a request for 1,000 head of horses, a major export item from the Land of Dai. On this occasion Shiyijian refused, to which the Murong responded with a foray into Taghbach territory. But having taken his mother's advice, Shiyijian's court had remained mobile, and so was now able simply to melt away from the incursion: "the Yan men could see nothing and so went back."²³ In the next year, 344, Murong Huang put the disagreement aside and sent a daughter to become Taghbach khaghtun. Described as an influential member of the Taghbach royal household, the second Murong wife lived until the year 360.²⁴ Two more exchanges would be made over the next couple of decades.²⁵ Tensions continued, however, as we see in 367 when Murong troops, marching through the Tumed Plain to attack nomadic groups to the north, trampled millet fields (interesting evidence for the mixed economy that already existed there). Though incensed, Shiyijian stayed his hand.²⁶

Shiyijian did, however, use his growing royal guard in a number of campaigns against other peoples. One set of these offensives, which had begun with Yituo half a century before, consisted of his own massive raids against groups whose name was transcribed into Chinese as the "Tiele," and translated as "High Carts," Gaoche.²⁷ Apparently speakers of Turkic languages, these had become the dominant people in the grasslands north of the Gobi, if as little organized as the Serbi had been several centuries before. For Shiyijian, this brutal method of augmenting the dynasty's wealth began late in his reign, in the winter of 363 (virtually all of these campaigns were mounted in the winter), when 10,000 captives were taken, and a million head of horses, oxen, and sheep. A similar amount of livestock was taken in another campaign in

22. WS 1.13.
23. ZZTJ 97.3056.
24. ZZTJ 97.3059; BS 13.491 (WS 13.323–24).
25. WS 1.14; ZZTJ 101.3191.
26. ZZTJ 101.3207.
27. WS 91.2307. See Golden, *An Introduction to the History of the Turkic Peoples*, 93–95, who suggests Tiele 鐵勒 (also transcribed as Chile 敕勒 and Dingling 丁零) may represent the Turkic name Tegrek, which may in turn have signified "cart," and so been represented in Chinese as Gaoche 高車, "high cart."

the next year, and the High Carts were attacked again in 370.[28] As seen just above, the Murong also participated in these ventures to loot steppe peoples— to take from them involuntary tribute. Under Northern Wei, these campaigns continued for decades, as a key way in which the Taghbach war-leaders, cum monarchs, stocked the royal pastures, and at the same time, distributed reward to loyal soldiery with substantial achievements on the field of battle, so as to reinforce that loyalty and motivate the men to more such achievements.[29] For the victims, these predations were, of course, one of the motivations for efforts to build a new steppe confederation under the Rouran, which first began to take shape on the steppe in the early fourth century with a man named "Baldy," who had been captured and enslaved in the time of Liwei.[30] A hirsute fellow— he received his name from his master as a joke—he later rose from servitude to become a cavalry soldier for the Taghbach khaghan, but then fled north of the Gobi to avoid punishment for breaking Yilu's martial code by not arriving on time for a call-up. There he and his descendants built up a following of fugitives. Living on the grasslands north of the Gobi, the Rouran for several decades reattached to the Taghbach khaghans as tribute-giving vassals. After the death of Shiyijian in 376, however, they would emerge as an independent steppe power.

Beginning earlier than this was a much more life-and-death struggle with the Xiongnu of the Ordos region, rooted in centuries-old struggle between Serbi and Xiongnu (though also, at times, cooperation and alliance). In the fourth year of Shiyijian's reign, 341, a descendant of the Southern Chanyu, Liu Hu (combining the appropriated surname of the Han imperial house with the personal name "Tiger"), led a party from the Ordos across the Yellow River to attack. They were, however, soundly defeated, and when Liu Hu died soon after, Shiyijian attempted to establish peace by giving his successor—Liu Wuhuan (apparently meaning something like "Liu the Mestizo")—one of his daughters.[31] It will be noted that it was in the next year that Shiyijian began yearly training assemblies for his soldiery; and from this point every six or seven years (349, 356, 362) he would lead the army to the east bank of the river to show the flag and attempt to

---

28. WS 1.14–15. The *Wei shu* account of the High Carts (103.2307–14) does not mention Shiyijian's campaigns, beginning only with the Northern Wei founder. Kenneth Klein, "Contributions of the Fourth Century Xianbei States," 78, points out that the success of the Taghbach lay in their ability first to dominate (if not directly rule) the steppelands to the north.

29. On booty, see note 17 in Chapter 1.

30. WS 103.2289. For the name, see Shimunek, *Languages of Ancient Southern Mongolia and North China*, 147–48.

31. WS 1.12, 95.2054; JS 130.3201 (here Hu 虎 is called 武, to avoid a Tang imperial taboo name; the *Jin shu* account is also somewhat inaccurate, stating that it was "the King of Dai, Yilu, who defeated Liu Hu"). Boodberg ("Selections from *Hu T'ien Han Yüeh Fang Chu*," 47–51) translates and gives commentary on the *Wei shu* 95 account. Note that this round at least of conflict between the two groups had begun in the time of Yulü.

intimidate the Xiongnu.³² His efforts were not completely successful, since in 365 Liu Wuhuan's son, Liu Weichen—who had in previous years given gifts to and sought marriage with the Taghbach—crossed the Yellow River to attack.³³ He was defeated and driven back across, and two years later, in winter, Shiyijian struck back, making the only partially frozen river passable by putting reed mats down on it. Taken by surprise, Weichen and his clan fled west. The Taghbach returned across the river with hundreds of thousands of human captives, oxen, horses, and sheep.

By 376, however, the situation had changed, as Liu Weichen had allied himself to the new power of the Yellow River Plain. This was Fu Jian—of a dynasty of Tibetan extraction based in the Wei River Valley—who had in 370 destroyed the Yan (conventionally, "Former Yan") and then gone on to reunify under his Qin regime what had been the northern territories of Western Jin. Having persuaded Fu Jian to finish the conquests by sending an army against the Taghbach as well, Liu Weichen now guided north a Qin force of 200,000.³⁴ Shiyijian could not withstand the attack and sought to escape by fleeing north of the Yinshan Mountains. Beset there by the High Carts he had been despoiling with some regularity, the Taghbach lord returned to Shengle.

In a sketchy history with many gaps, what followed thereafter is again one of those unclear passages of early Taghbach history. The histories of the southern rivals provide an almost laughable tale of how Shiyijian was not killed, but instead taken by his captors down to the Qin capital of Chang'an to learn proper manners. *Wei shu*, on the other hand—quite probably the more accurate, though masking deeper issues and possibly troubling events—states that in this emergency situation, the Taghbach lord and most of his sons were massacred by Shijun 寔君, a son of Shiyijian by a consort, who had been egged on by the son of the long-before overturned co-ruler, Gu.³⁵ At this point, the Taghbach court surrendered to Fu Jian's army, encamped some 40 miles southwest of Shengle, and "the units scattered."³⁶ It would be a decade before Shiyijian was formally

---

32. WS 1.13–14.
33. WS 1.15, 95.2055; the latter tr. by Boodberg, "Selections from *Hu T'ien Han Yüeh Fang Chu*," 52–58.
34. ZZTJ 26.3277–78.
35. For the second version, see WS 1.16; BS 15.560–1 (WS 15.369), the latter, an account of the son, being somewhat more detailed, to the extent the details are accurate. Among the issues is the suspicious resemblance of the killer's name—Shijun 寔君—to the name of the father of the eventual successor, Shi 寔. (Since most died in this incident, brief [or no] accounts are given of Shiyijian's sons in *Bei shi*.) The first version of Shiyijian's fate is supplied by SoS 95.2321 and NQS 57.983; and the Tang-period compilation *Jin shu* 113.2898–99. These are apparently based on stories and rumors circulating in the south. Overviews of the issues are given in Holmgren, *Annals of Tai*, 43ff.; Zhang, *Bei Wei zheng zhi shi*, 1: 170–74. Though eminent scholars come down on both sides in debate of which—if either—is reliable, I am inclined to agree with Zhang Jinlong that the *Wei shu* account—though almost certainly giving an incomplete account—is the more accurate. Though rumors are sometimes true, both *Song shu* and *Nan Qi shu* accounts contain fundamental mistakes, such as the claim that Shiyijian was a grandson of Yilu. The great Song historian Sima Guang follows the *Wei shu* record: ZZTJ 104.3278–81.
36. BS 15.561 (WS 15.369). In this passage, according to HYDCD 10: 653, the term *bu zhong* can mean either the units of an army, or social units. On the basis of clear development under Shiyijian of an imperial central army,

buried by his grandson and heir, among the "golden mounds" (*jinling* 金陵) located in the hills south of Shengle.³⁷

The regime established by Liwei a century before had seemingly come to an end.

I choose the former. For an attempt to reconstruct these events, see Sun Xianfeng 孙险峰, "Yinshan shan mai yu 'Qian Qin fa Dai'" 阴山山脉与"前秦伐代", *Shi xue yue kan* (2014.12): 127–29.

37. Wang, *Bei Wei Shengle shi dai*, 222, suggests this is the first recorded burial of Taghbach monarchy in a "golden tumulus," *jin ling* 金陵. The account of the reconstructed *Wei shu* chapter on empresses (15.323) does, however, make a similar statement regarding Shiyijian's mother, Madam Wang (BS 13.491; WS 13.323; according to the reconstructed *Wei shu* account, in 355). Albert E. Dien, *Six Dynasties Civilization* (New Haven, CT, and London: Yale University Press, 2007), 182 (citing an article by Li Junqing 李俊清, "Bei Wei Jinling di li wei zhi de chu bu kao cha 北魏金陵地理位置的初步考察, *Wen wu ji kan* [1990.1]: 67–74, 38), suggests the *jin ling* burials may be identified with a group of 21 tombs discovered in the vicinity of the modern town of Youyu, Shanxi, on the peaks of the hills that separate the Datong Basin from the Tumed Plain. And they do seem to have been in this area: WS 7B.181 tells us that in 497 the emperor Xiaowen arrived in Yunzhong (the Tumed Plain) and then in the course of his departure visited the Jinling tombs. But Zhao Xiaolong 赵晓龙, "Bei Wei Jinling xin tan" 北魏金陵新探, *Xue shu wen ti yan jiu* (2015.2): 13–17, holds that the "golden tumuli" were not concentrated in one location but more scattered, and that the term is simply a reference to burials of Taghbach khaghans, applying to these peoples a term borrowed from Chinese. (In Chinese, "Jinling" referred among other things to Jiankang, or Nanjing.)

SECTION IV.

Creating an Empire

The four chapters of Section IV portray the life and circumstances of a pivotal figure in Taghbach history, the Taghbach lord Shegui (r. 386–409), who expanded the family enterprise with conquest of a large part of the Yellow River plains, and gave the enterprise a new name—"Wei," or as it is filed in the Chinese historiographical tradition, "Northern Wei," to distinguish it from earlier, quite different regimes named Wei. In the process of creating an empire, he took for himself the Chinese title *huang di*, "emperor." He did not, however, abandon his dynasty's original title, the Inner Asian "khaghan."

In Chapter 7, we look at major events in Shegui's early career: how beginning in 386—barely past boyhood—he reconstructed and transformed the dynasty, which had in the previous decade collapsed under the force of invasion and the death of his grandfather, Shiyijian; how with development of his cavalry army and the ability to feed it, Shegui became a threat to a Taghbach rival, the Murong, another Serbi dynasty that had taken the Yellow River plains; and how the Khaghan led a dramatic defense against concerted Murong attacks on the Taghbach heartland. At the chapter's end, we will turn to how in 396 Shegui turned the tables, leading his army of horsemen down onto the Yellow River plains to oust the Murong from the territories they had won not long before.

The circumstances underlying Shegui's regime building are discussed in the next two chapters. Chapter 8 gives background on the situation of the Yellow River plains prior to Shegui's 396 invasion. Particular attention is paid to the tragedies that had accompanied collapse of Western Jin some eighty years before, culminating in the fall of Jin's capital of Luoyang in 311. In Chapter 9 we examine how Shegui and his heirs went on to build a new conquest polity—a nation—in the highlands to the north.

Chapter 10 gives an overview of the last years of Shegui: of the gradual unraveling of the man's mind, and his death at the age of just 39 at the hand of a son. In the process will be seen perhaps the most unsettling of many unsettling things done by Taghbach monarchs: establishment in Shegui's court of a policy that after designation of an heir apparent, the heir's mother must die.

7

The Way of War

However it had happened, Shiyijian was gone. But his dynasty was not. Since the narrow meaning at least of "Taghbach" had by this time become a royal family in search of a state, and since the royal family (if not the reigning monarch) survived, the search survived as well. Its goal was achieved a decade later, with a state transformed and made stronger by the ill winds that had blown up from the south.

During the period of interregnum, Former Qin had formally placed Dai's subject populations under the control of two Xiongnu lords: the designer of the invasion, Liu Weichen, controlling Taghbach subjects active west of the River; while the core Dai lands and at least most of its peoples were administered by Liu Kuren, a member of the Dugu (*Dʊkkʊ), the "Battle-axe Clan." Though also tracing descent from the Southern Xiongnu, the Dugu were in-laws of the Taghbach. Liu Kuren himself had served as director of Shiyijian's Southern District.[1] As for members of the royal family, those not killed in 376 had scattered. One of these was Gui, or as an apparently more accurate transcription of the original Inner Asian name, Shegui 涉珪 (MC *Dzyep-kwej).[2] According to *Wei shu*, Shegui was born in 371, up on the much frequented Shenhe Slope, and so was but five years of age (six *sui*) at the time of the Former Qin conquest. At the age of 15, in 386, he emerged as lord of a revived Taghbach regime.

As with the death of Shiyijian, the details of Shegui's early career are murky, with again a stark division between *Wei shu* and histories of the Jiankang regimes. While *Wei shu* tells us that Shegui was a grandson of Shiyijian, whose father had died when he was an infant, the southern histories suggest, among other things, that Shegui was actually a son of Shiyijian. Most scholars lean toward the former position.[3]

1. WS 23.605. Shimunek, *Languages of Ancient Southern Mongolia and North China*, 138, reconstructs Dugu as *Dʊkkʊ, "Battle-axe Clan."
2. Whereas WS uses only Gui 珪, we see Shegui in variant transcriptions in southern histories: 涉珪 in SoS 95.2322, 涉圭 in NQS 57.983 (in MC, both *Dzyep-kwej). This seems to have been a fairly common Serbi name, an instance of which appears among the Murong transcribed as 涉歸, MC *Dzyep-kwɨj (JS 108.2803); and the name of an ancestor of the Yuwen people is not written down in *Bei shi* (98.3267) since it was "Daowu's taboo name." Holmgren, *Annals of Tai*, 13, suggests this may have been not a name but an honorary title.
3. For Jiankang version: SoS 95.2321–22; NQS 57.983. The *Jin shu* account (113.2898–99) adds another wrinkle, with the claim that someone named "Yigui" 翼圭—apparently an allusion to Shegui—captured his father, Shiyijian, to hand over to the Qin army, then was taken off to Sichuan. This is a view fostered by such major

Leaving this issue aside, we turn to an interesting account in *Wei shu* (from a lost chapter, and so reconstructed using *Bei shi*) that describes how the young Shegui, somewhat like Shiyijian, had survived and then thrived under the protection and guidance of his mother. She was a daughter of the lord of the Helan, allies of the Taghbach whom we have seen before. This was a Caucasoid group famous for their dappled ponies.[4] Living in the grasslands northeast across the Yinshan from the Tumed Plain they were a powerful element in the Taghbach state, and had repeatedly intermarried with the Yulü wing of the dynasty.[5] According to the *Bei shi/Wei shu* account, the Helan woman had married Shiyijian's crown prince, who died in the year of Shegui's birth. Sadly, but typically, the history does not give her personal name.[6]

We first come upon the mother and son in their journeyings in 376, when with the arrival of the Former Qin army Shiyijian and his retinue had fled north of the Yinshan Mountains. There the royal family was harried and attacked by the High Carts, and so unable to graze their herds they now turned around to go back to the Tumed Plain. In the midst of this retreat, the five-year-old and his mother were fleeing an enemy raiding party when the linchpin came out of their wagon wheel. Here we verge into myth, as Madam Helan looked up toward her people's sky god—some version of Tengri—and said, "How can it be that the dynasty's progeny should in this way be extinguished! Truly, the gods [will] help [us]."[7] And for those who accept such linkages, it was Tengri who saved them, as they were able to ride on for another 30 miles to safety, the wheel staying put and not falling off the axle.

---

scholars as Li Ping 李凭, *Bei Wei Pingcheng shi dai* 北魏平城时代 (Beijing: She hui ke xue wen xian chu ban she, 2000), 94. Along another line, Song Qirui 宋其蕤 suggests that Shegui's mother had been married to his father, and after the latter's death, on the basis of levirate, married the grandfather, Shiyijian: *Bei Wei nü zhu lun* 北魏女主论 (Beijing: Zhongguo she hui ke xue chu ban she, 2006), 57. See summation of these points in Zhang, *Cong Tuoba dao Bei Wei*, 18–19; Tamura, *Chūgoku shijō no minzoku idōki*, 59, 83–84 note 16. But content to be mostly certain, I will again side with Zhang Jinlong, who among other things points out that it would be hard for a child of 5 (6 *sui*) to tie up his father (*Bei Wei zheng zhi shi*, 1: 171–72). His birthdate in *Wei shu* could, of course, have been changed, but in that case one wonders why a young man would have been so dependent on his mother, as he is in a detailed way shown to be in *Wei shu* in the years between 376 and 386.

4. Shing Müller, "Horses of the Xianbei, 300–600 AD: A Brief Survey," in *Pferde in Asien: Geschichte, Handel und Kultur = Horses in Asia: History, Trade and Culture*, ed. Bert G. Fragner et al. (Vienna: Verlag der Österreichischen Akademie der Wissenschaften, 2009), 189–90.

5. BS 80.2671 (WS 83A.1812). The Helan were an important polity, on which much has been written: Yao, *Bei chao Hu xing kao*, 32–38; Holmgren, *Annals of Tai*, 110–12; Zhang, *Bei Wei zheng zhi shi*, 2: 25–31; Tian, *Tuoba shi tan*, 62–76; Peter Boodberg, "Two Notes on the History of the Chinese Frontier," in *Selected Works of Peter A. Boodberg*, 261–63.

6. The original *Wei shu* chapter on the wives of the Taghbach monarchs was lost, and reconstructed in the early modern Song on the basis of *Bei shi* (Chapter 13) and other texts (WS 13.341–42 note 1). Her biography is in BS 13.492 (WS 13.324–25).

7. WS 1.16; BS 13.492 (WS 13.324). Holmgren, "Women and Political Power," 53, expresses skepticism for this tale, among other things understandably expressing doubt that the little boy had been accepted by the Taghbach as heir (a point discussed below). As for the yarn itself, however, the question is not whether it is veracious, but whether it was a Taghbach tale.

More prosaic forms of protection continued to offer themselves during the interregnum. Among the members of the coterie that took shape around Shegui, consisting of kinsmen and members of the royal guard, was a strong loyalty for one they wished to support as heir. Among these was a fellow anachronistically called in *Wei shu* Zhangsun Fei 長孫肥—more properly something like "*Bjɨj-x-x of the Baba 拔拔 clan"—a member of one of the cadet branches of the royal family, who having served in Shiyijian's guard followed Shegui into exile.[8] Constantly in the boy's company, he intimidated all around. The future monarch "deeply trusted and relied on" the man.

In terms of earthly protection, however, most important was the Dugu lord Liu Kuren, who acting out of lingering loyalty to the Taghbach monarchy protected mother and son through most of the interregnum's decade.[9] Admittedly, there was a complexity to these relationships. Before the Former Qin invasion, while Shiyijian still reigned, a favorite of the Taghbach lord had been a member of another of the cadet branches of the ruling house, the Daxi, who held the hereditary family post of manager of the royal horse herds.[10] When one of the lord's finest steeds was stolen, and it was discovered that Liu Kuren—at that time director of Dai's Southern District—had done the deed, the Daxi foreman went to get the animal back. In the process he grabbed Liu by his cascading hair and slashed one of his breasts, though from what little we know of the event this appears to have been the sum of his punishment for the crime. Years later, older and apparently wiser, Liu Kuren gave more reliable service to the ruling house.

The father's loyalty did not, however, continue under his son, Liu Xian 劉顯, who took up the role of Former Qin agent in Dai after Liu Kuren's death in 385.[11] It is claimed in *Wei shu* that Fu Jian had planned to re-establish Shegui as a vassal lord when he reached the appropriate age.[12] At the age of 14 in 385, Shegui was apparently nearing that time, and Liu Xian, wishing to retain control of the

---

8. WS 26.651. *Bjɨj is, of course, MC reconstruction of "Fei," and we can assume the full transcription (three or sometimes two Chinese characters) has been abbreviated by the *Wei shu* authors to incorporate it more comfortably into Chinese text. As mentioned above, the clan's original name "Baba" was in the late fifth century replaced with the Chinese "Zhangsun." These later forms are in *Wei shu* regularly pushed back into earlier periods; see WS 113.3006 (and correction of an error in the text on p. 3019 note 23). Holmgren, *Annals of Tai*, 112–15, suggests the cadet branches such as Baba/Zhangsun had not separated up at the "great swamp" (Hulun Nur) but were descendants of Shiyijian.

9. BS 13.492 (WS 13.324); WS 23.605–6, 2.19. See translation of WS 23 biography in Boodberg, "Selections from *Hu T'ien Han Yüeh Fang Chu*," 58–61. The biography of He Na, the Helan chieftain, tells us that mother and son briefly lived among her people before placing themselves under Liu Kuren; and also claims that he was as powerful in these territories as the Xiongnu: BS 80.2671 (WS 83A.1812).

10. WS 29.697. The name of the Daxi 達奚 clansman is given in *Wei shu* in the abbreviated form of "Xi Dan" 奚單.

11. WS 23.606; see translation in Boodberg, "Selections from *Hu T'ien Han Yüeh Fang Chu*," 61–65.

12. WS 24.610. According to *Wei shu*, this was a suggestion made to Fu Jian by a Chinese of the Dai region named Yan Feng, who had served Shiyijian and was his ambassador to the Former Qin court at the time of Dai's collapse. Yan continued to serve the Taghbach under Shegui and his successors. If this is true, it would support the idea that at least some among the Taghbach were already attempting to develop regularized succession.

Taghbach subjects, began plotting to do away with the possible heir. This being a world with many overlaying networks of information (and gossip), Madam Helan now heard of Liu Xian's scheme from the wife of the Xiongnu lord's younger brother, a Taghbach woman and sister of Shegui's father. Apparently at this time living in his compound, and well acquainted with Liu Xian (we don't know quite how well), Madam Helan now commanded Shegui and his party to escape on horseback, then incapacitated Liu Xian by getting the fellow drunk.[13] Remaining behind, the mother at the crack of dawn went to the holding pen to set the horses into a panic, which caused Liu Xian to stagger out to see what was happening. At this point, in tears, Madam Helan shouted to the Xiongnu that "just now my sons were all here. Now they're all gone! Which one of you killed them?" In this way, Madam Helan kept the (no doubt hungover) Liu from sending out a posse in pursuit, and so Shegui and his comrades were able to escape onto the steppe, to the Helan territories north of the Yinshan.

To this point at least, these adventures were just a small part of a much larger picture of turmoil and collapse that had (again) overtaken the Yellow River territories in the 380s. Former Qin had reached the peak of its power in the late 370s, controlling the Yellow River plains and adjoining regions. Fu Jian's enterprise, however, soon began to fail. In 380, Fu Luo, commander of the Qin northern armies, rebelled against his kinsman and lord.[14] He was defeated by Fu Jian (and curiously pardoned), but worse things came in 383, with failure of the Qin monarch's effort to conquer the Jiankang regime, which culminated in loss at the Battle of the Fei River (a tributary of the Huai, in mod. Anhui).[15] Former Qin now began to fall apart, with re-emergence from the wreckage of forcibly incorporated peoples and polities. In the west a new Qin ruled by a Qiang dynasty (subsequently called "Later" by historians, in contrast to the "Former" Qin of Fu Jian) emerged in the Wei River valley, while in the east a Yan regime reappeared, built by a Murong, Chui, who had previously served Former Yan and then Fu Jian (Chui's regime is also conventionally called "Later" Yan).

In winter of 384, Murong Chui invested the city of Ye, now held determinedly by a son of Fu Jian. The siege would drag on for a year and a half, in the course of which the region descended into starvation, and reports of cannibalism, among civilians and soldiers alike. Though the city finally fell in late summer of 385, Murong Chui in the end decided to place his Yan's capital at Zhongshan (mod. Dingzhou, Hebei), further north on the same distinct line where the plains meet the Taihang Mountains.[16] It is in the midst of such tumult that Shegui began his

---

13. BS 13.492 (WS 13.324); WS 2.20; ZZTJ 106.3350.
14. JS 122.3054; ZZTJ 104.3292–95.
15. ZZTJ 105.3311–13. Michael Rogers, in his *Chronicle of Fu Chien: A Case of Exemplar History* (Berkeley: University of California Press, 1968), makes the case that the scale of the battle—and Qin defeat—has been greatly exaggerated, and that the very real collapse of Fu Jian's state resulted from a more complex set of causes.
16. ZZTJ 105.3323–25, 3344, 3349, 3357.

career, fleeing the household of Liu Xian to go on to build a rival military machine in the land of Dai, in the highlands that stood directly above the new capital of Murong Chui's restored, "Later," Yan.

On the day of Shegui's escape, the Dugu lord Liu Xian eventually sobered up sufficiently to realize what Madam Helan had done. To protect her own life, that night she too fled, seeking refuge with the Taghbach wife of Liu Xian's younger brother. There she was hidden for three days in a "spirit cart"—a portable shrine which these mobile, tent-dwelling people used to bring their equally mobile gods with them.[17]

For his part, Shegui had fled directly to the Helan on the open steppe, accompanied we are told by just 21 men, and eventually by his mother.[18] On arrival, Shegui was greeted by his mother's brother He Na, the Helan leader, who is reported to have said, "[When] his majesty restores the state, [you] should remember your old servant."[19] This claimed quote does need to be taken with care; the original version of the chapter in which this is found—like many regarding royal kinfolk—is a later reconstruction. Still, the passage does go on to make a statement confirmed by various texts, that in the next year "the lords of all the units (*zhu bu da ren*) made entreaties to Na and his brothers, requesting that they raise Daowu (i.e., Shegui) up to be ruler."[20] This request was also voiced by a member of the Taghbach royal family, a great-grandson of Liwei and distant cousin of Shegui, whose name comes down to us as Heluo.[21] In the group accompanying Shegui in his flight from the Dugu to the Helan, Heluo increased its numbers by "gathering together households of old [followers], getting 300 families." Arriving among the Helan, he pressed He[lan] Na to put the 15-year-old boy up as monarch.[22]

Here again we see early confirmation of the dynasty's durable popularity. The feeling, however, was not unanimous. The apparent mediator in the process of selecting a new lord, He Na, was unwilling or unable to try for the post himself, and so accepted the demands of "all the lords" to set up his sister's son. Though described as having doubts on the matter, the Helan leader would for a time accept the situation. But his younger brother, Ran'gan, could not and laid plans for

---

17. BS 13.492 (WS 13.324).
18. WS 28.686, which calls these 21 men his "original following" 元從.
19. BS 80.2671 (WS 83A.1812). Shegui responded by saying "it shall be as uncle says." Having received a general's title from Former Qin, and supposedly the equal of Liu Kuren, He Na was based at Daning 大甯(寧), in the region of modern Zhangjiakou. The name "He Na" in *Wei shu* is, again, taken from Sinicization of names in the late Wei; the name would more properly be something like "'Na-x-x' of the Helan clan."
20. BS 80.2671 (WS 83A.1812). This is also confirmation that the notion of primogeniture had already appeared among the Taghbach, even if not held by all. For a contrary position, see Holmgren, "Women and Political Power," 53.
21. BS 15.543 (WS 14.345).
22. The oldest version of this passage, from the mid-Tang *Bei shi*, uses the non-specific term *zhu* 主, "ruler," which could be a reference to "khaghan." *Wei shu*, which for this chapter was subsequently reconstructed on the basis of *Bei shi*, uses the Chinese term we translate as "king," *wang* 王.

an assassination of the irksome Taghbach nephew. After this was thwarted by an informer, Ran'gan's feelings were for a time at least suppressed by his mother, who in this dense web of relationships happened to be a sister of Shiyijian married off to the father of Ran'gan and Na.[23]

The demands of the lords—and perhaps Ran'gan's mother as well—were fulfilled in early spring of 386, the first month of the New Year, when He Na convened a great gathering of the clans up at Ox Creek (Niuchuan), in Helan country.[24] Here the young man was raised up as King of Dai, and presumably Khaghan as well, though the latter title has been submerged in the Chinese text.[25] Like Liwei more than a century before, Shegui also made sacrifices to Heaven—Tengri—and established a Chinese reign title, Dengguo 登國, which in Chinese means "Ascending to the State," but might possibly be a mixed transcription-translation of "Tengri's State" 登[利] 國.[26] For the Taghbach lords, of course, the key was always that it was neither one nor the other—they were in a continual state of eclectically mixing and matching. No detail is given on the nature of the rituals involved; perhaps they resembled the ceremony seen 150 years later, in a very different time, when in an intentionally archaizing enthronement the last lord of the Northern Wei was placed on a black felt rug held up by seven men to present him to Heaven.[27] Accompanying Shegui's accession was re-establishment of various offices, including the directors of the Northern and Southern Divisions, in charge of the dual administration of pastoralists and farmers within the royal domain. Filling the latter was a man whose name is given in *Wei shu* as Zhangsun Song 長孫嵩, yet another member of the Baba (Zhangsun) cadet branch of the ruling family, his personal name again reduced by later historians to a one-syllable transcription.

---

23. WS 26.655; BS 80.2671 (WS 83A.1812).

24. The location of Niuchuan 牛川 is uncertain and various theories have been advanced. See Zhang, *Bei Wei zheng zhi shi*, 2: 21–24. This is unfortunate, since it is an important site in early Wei history, frequently visited by Shegui. This author is most persuaded by suggestions that it was located to the northeast, in the region of the Helan center, near mod. Zhangjiakou. See *Zhongguo li shi di tu ji*, 4: No. 52, where it is depicted to the west of Zhangjiakou; and Hu Sanxing's comment in ZZTJ 106.3357, where the Song historian states that "north of Ox Creek there is nothing but desert." For another view, that the stream was located in the Horinger region, a view difficult to ignore because of the prestige of its author, see Maeda Masana 前田正名, *Heijō no rekishi-chirigakuteki kenkyū* 平城の歴史地理学的研究 (Tokyo: Kazama Shobō, 1979), 140–45, and the map on p. 138.

25. WS 2.20; ZZTJ 106.3357–58.

26. *Dengli* 登利 being a Chinese transcription of Tengri (Tängri), an epithet regularly attached to Khaghans: Kroll, *A Student's Dictionary of Classical and Medieval Chinese*, 81. See an example of this use in reference to a Türk "Khaghan of Heaven," "Tengri Khaghan" 登利可汗: *Jiu Tang shu* 144A.5177. In SoS 95.2322 we are told of the Wei monarchs that "it was their custom to sacrifice to Heaven in the fourth month," that is, in the spring. See also Kawamoto Yoshiaki 川本芳昭, *Gi Shin Nanbokuchō jidai no minzoku mondai* 魏晋南北朝時代の民族問題 (Tōkyō: Kyūko Shoin, 1998), 276ff.

27. Boodberg, "Marginalia to the Histories of the Northern Dynasties," 308–12; and Luo Xin 罗欣, *Hei zhan shang de Bei Wei huang di* 黑毡上的北魏皇帝 (Beijing: Hai tun chu ban she, 2014), 17–18, who argues that this was the perpetuation of an Inner Asian ritual. Boodberg points out that this ritual was performed later in Inner Asian history; and it is seen among the Mongols, who are said to have been following a custom used by the Taghbach and the Türks: Rachewiltz, *The Secret History of the Mongols*, 1: 316–17.

Interestingly, this investment of Shegui on the steppe occurred just three weeks before Murong Chui declared himself emperor down on the plains at Zhongshan city.[28] Coincidental or not, Shegui, the new 15-year-old King of Dai, now quickly moved himself closer to the lowlands, within a month moving from the open steppe to the town of Shengle. Having established himself in his grandfather's stronghold, Shegui went on to rename the dynasty, calling himself the King of Wei 魏, and so borrowing from the Chinese tradition to restyle his regime after a major power of the Chinese Warring States, which had long before seized the town of Zhongshan.[29] But not all within the regime agreed with the change. As we shall see in Chapter 9, among followers of the dynasty, "Dai" had for many already taken on deep meaning. Debate about the change would continue for years.

More practically, Shegui seems also to have been distancing himself from his mother's people. In doing this he walked a tightrope, because a contest for power had broken out with his own kinsmen. Though some viewed Shegui as the proper heir, others within the family did not; there were still competing notions of which dynast should be raised up on the black felt rug.[30]

Zhangsun Song's appointment as director of the Southern Division in 386 had actually been a reappointment, since he had held the same post under Shiyijian, and with the grandfather's death in 376, Zhangsun had led his own following 部眾 of more than 700 families of "long-standing [vassals] and villagers" 舊人及鄉邑 to submit to the newly appointed overseer, Liu Kuren.[31] This possession of a heritable following—that was at one and the same time a social unit, a militia, and a unit of production—was a key aspect of this age. Like all these groups, Zhangsun's was both portable, and seeking a secure hook to attach itself to. Unhappy with Liu Kuren's son, Liu Xian, toward the end of the interregnum Zhangsun fled with his people to Wuyuan on the River's northern loop. At this time, a son of Shijun—Shijun being the one who according to *Wei shu* killed his father, Shiyijian—was himself raising an army with the aim of taking the throne. Zhangsun was considering making this fellow his lord, when he is said to have encountered a mysterious stranger—perhaps a shaman—who declared that this was "the son of a rebellious father," then "turned his ox's head" to lead Zhangsun and his people to meet with Shegui, into whose service he entered instead, with reappointment at the time of Shegui's accession as director of the Southern Division.

---

28. JS 9.235, 123.3086–87; ZZTJ 106.3358.
29. WS 2.20; ZZTJ 106.3364.
30. Jennifer Holmgren, "The Harem in Northern Wei Politics," *JESHO* 26.1 (1983): 76; Andrew Eisenberg, *Kingship in Early Medieval China* (Leiden and Boston: Brill, 2008), 32ff.; Luo Xin 罗新, "Bei Wei zhi qin kao" 北魏直勤考, in his *Zhong gu bei zu ming hao yan jiu*, 80–107.
31. BS 22.805 (WS 25.643); ZZTJ 106.3351. Following the note in *Bei shi*, 831–32 note 1, here I use the wording in WS 25.643 rather than BS 22.805. Li, *Bei Wei Pingcheng shi dai*, 42, reads *xiang yi* as "farmers" accompanying Zhangsun's people.

Shijun's son is not heard of again, but there were other claimants within the dynasty. Facing pressure from Shegui on the Tumed Plain, Liu Xian had relocated his own following to Horse Town (Mayi), just northwest of the Yanmen Pass. There he established contact with the only son of Shiyijian to have survived the massacre, Kuduo, an uncle of Shegui. Whether or not his father had been taken down to Fu Jian's Chang'an, it seems that Kuduo had, and there he was taught to read Chinese texts.[32] In 386, however, Liu Xian brought him back north as a rival to Shegui, whom Liu held to be a Helan-backed pretender. Others seem to have agreed: "the groups now became restless," we are told, and even some of Shegui's own guardsmen began to plot against him, so that once again he fled north over the Yinshan to lodge among his mother's people.[33]

Support from the Helan for Shegui was grudging, but that of others was more certain. In addition to Zhangsun Song there was a "Chong" of the Qiumuling clan, a member of a descent group allied to the Taghbach since the time of Liwei. Though a border raider as a youth, Mu Chong had also been a loyal follower of Shegui during the interregnum, apparently with no contradiction.[34] During the struggle with the uncle Kuduo, while Shegui was ensconced among the Helan up on the steppe, Chong was sent back south to spy out "the people's" feelings. Leaving behind horse and attendants, and in disguise, Mu Chong entered the camp of the Kuduo party at night. In a flash of firelight, however, he was recognized by a servant woman grinding grain, who shouted out his presence. Unable to locate his horse, Mu now stole one of the enemy's and fled into a swamp, where, in the dead of night, a white wolf approached him and let out a howl. Realizing the animal's supernatural nature, Mu leapt on the stolen horse and galloped away, just before his pursuers arrived. After returning north, Mu Chong told the tale to Shegui, who finding it extraordinary ordered Mu to make sacrifice to the wolf, a ritual that would be carried on by his heirs.

The wolf plays an interesting role in the history of the Taghbach, and of other peoples as well.[35] But though of aid here to Shegui, an army would help him more,

---

32. It has been suggested that this was part of the basis for the claim in the southern histories that Shiyijian was taken to Chang'an: Zhang, *Bei Wei zheng zhi shi*, 1: 172–73.

33. WS 2.21; BS 15.579 (WS 15.385); ZZTJ 106.3368.

34. WS 27.661–62. This clan, important in the early Wei, is the first of the *nei ru* groups in *Wei shu*'s "Monograph on Offices and Clans" (113.3006). Their original name was Qiumuling 丘穆陵, shortened to Mu under Xiaowen; his name in the *Wei shu* text is thus "Mu Chong." See Yao, *Bei chao Hu xing kao*, 25–28.

35. The wolf is of course a symbol in the mythologies of many societies, often playing a more important role than it did among the Taghbach in the making of peoples. The origins of the Mongols, for instance, was attributed to the mating of a Blue Wolf with a doe: Rachewiltz, *Secret History of the Mongols*, 1: 1, 224. Much earlier, the wolf was a prominent theme in Chinese animal art of the Bronze Age, and also among the Xiongnu: see Bunker, *Ancient Bronzes*, 49–51, and figure 194 on p. 238; and a piece ascribed to the Xiongnu, figure 241 on p. 273. It was also a prominent theme among the Türks, in the centuries after the Taghbach: see Findley, *The Turks in World History*, 38; Michael R. Drompp, "The Lone Wolf in Inner Asia," *JAOS* 131.4 (2011): 515–26; and Peter Golden, "Imperial Ideology and the Sources of Unity among the Pre-Činggisid Nomads of Western Eurasia," *Archivum Eurasiae Medii Aevi* 2 (1982): 37–76. Esther Jacobson-Tepfer, *The Hunter, the Stag, and the Mother of Animals: Image, Monument, and Landscape in Ancient North Asia* (Oxford and New York: Oxford University Press, 2015), 221, in discussing the wolf describes the "delight with the world of wild animals" taken by peoples of Inner Asia. As mentioned above,

and so he now sought support from the just-established Yan regime down on the plains. The Murong lord, Chui, agreed and sent an army up from Zhongshan against Liu Xian. Liu's candidate, Kuduo, now fled to the Ordos to seek protection from that other Xiongnu lord, Liu Weichen, who instead killed him.[36] Shegui had survived the struggle for succession.

Murong Chui's support had come from his interest in building a supportive client regime in the central highlands. In an effort to cement that relationship, he now offered Shegui gifts and titles (*wang* and *chanyu*, which was probably an archaized version of "khaghan"). But the young prince's "ambition"—we are told here by Hu Sanxing, the discerning early modern commentator to Sima Guang's *Comprehensive Mirror*—"did not lie with petty things" 其志不在小,[37] and he would not accept vassalage. He was, however, willing for a time to make do with the alliance of convenience he had with an old man—Murong Chui was at this time in his sixties—who had also just climbed the ladder of power, going in fact a bit higher than Shegui to appropriate from Han the title *huang di*, "emperor." Thus, in 387, after Liu Xian—who had holed up in central Shanxi—enraged the Yan monarch by seizing a herd of horses sent him as tribute from Liu Weichen in the Ordos, Shegui joined an army sent from Zhongshan to rout Liu. The Dugu headman then fled to a short-lived rival Murong regime also in Shanxi—known subsequently as Western Yan (384–394)—to disappear from the course of history.[38] In the *Zi zhi tong jian* passage on these events, Hu Sanxing adds another insight, saying that the best plan for the Murong would have been to "serve the interests of [each of the] two [sides, Xiongnu and Taghbach], and keep both intact, so it could be that [the Murong] would not on a later day have the catastrophe of the destruction of their state."

The "later day" would come, though quite a bit later. Freed for a time at least from Xiongnu pressure, Shegui perhaps wisely chose to bide his time against the Murong, and instead resumed his grandfather's policy of aggressive attention to the steppe, beginning a series of campaigns that would stretch over more than a decade. As with Shiyijian, the purpose of these missions was twofold: first, to attempt to weaken emerging steppe powers; while also seizing their wealth, in order to sustain and build the Taghbach army. A raid in 390, for instance, went hundreds of miles up to the Böön Tsagaan Nur lake in the southwest of modern Mongolia, to bring back 200,000—a number here applied inclusively to "horses,

---

one of the titles of the Northern Wei emperor Taiwu was "Wolf Lord"; see Chapter 1 and its note 4. For more on the theme among the Taghbach, see Yang Yongjun 杨永俊, "Lun Tuoba Xianbei de dong wu chong bai yi cun" 论拓跋鲜卑的动物崇拜遗存, rpt. in *Zou chu shi ku de Bei Wei wang chao*, ed. Jin Zhao and Alede'ertu (Beijing: Wen hua yi shu chu ban she, 2010), 2: 623–24.

36. BS 15.580 (WS 15.385–86).
37. ZZTJ 106.3372. See also the passage under the eighth month of 388 in ZZTJ 107.3385, taken from BS 15.561–62 (WS 15.370).
38. WS 23.606, 24.613; ZZTJ 107.3378–79.

cattle, sheep and goats" and "live human captives."[39] Attacks were also specifically conducted against the emerging steppe confederation of the Rouran, who would become an increasingly important element in Taghbach history. But the most dramatic of the raiding missions during Shegui's reign came in 399 against the High Carts, when the Wei army brought back almost 100,000 captives, and some 350,000 head of horses, along with much other livestock.[40] After being brought south in a huge cattle drive, these groups were forcibly settled in the strip of grasslands that lies between the Gobi and the Yinshan, some eventually placed on a kind of reservation known as the Deer Park, just north of the city of Pingcheng.[41] Having begun to convert much of his own following at least into a professional soldiery (see further discussion below), Shegui was among other things forcibly drafting new herdsmen for his flocks. These resettled nomads would for generations be a source of horses, and cavalry, and rebellion.

These campaigns would also involve another—much closer—steppe power, the Helan, who having attempted to protect their own affiliates during Wei's 390 campaign were themselves defeated in a joint Taghbach-Murong offensive. After lingering on the steppe for a month or so, Shegui returned south, on the way stopping at Ox Creek where just a few years before he had taken the throne under Helan auspice. There he received a desperate plea from his mother's brother, He Na, who in defeat had fled west, only to be attacked again, this time by an army sent from the Ordos by Liu Weichen. The nephew now played protector for his straitened uncle and drove the Xiongnu off. In the next year, 391, the eruption of struggle between He Na and his brother Ran'gan led Shegui to encourage a Yan offensive, which ended in an attack on both the Helan. Once again, Shegui stepped in to pick up the pieces. While Ran'gan was taken down to Zhongshan in captivity, the Taghbach leader was able to induce the Murong to release He Na and his following to him.[42]

Relations between the Helan and the Taghbach had now changed, the Helan having become Taghbach dependents. Here we see the beginnings of an important practice established by Shegui, his forced resettlement and sedentarization of mobile pastoralists in and around the Datong Basin.[43] This was a gradual

39. WS 2.23.
40. WS 2.34; ZZTJ 111.3486–88. On the importance of these raids onto the steppe in building Wei power, see Klein, "Contributions of the Fourth Century Xianbei States," 77–80; on seizure of goods and people as a critical contribution to the early Wei treasury, see Wang, *Zhuan xing qi de Bei Wei cai zheng yan jiu*, Chapter 1.
41. Sagawa, "You mu yu nong geng zhi jian," suggests that among its other purposes, the Deer Park served as the imperial house's ranch.
42. WS 2.23, 24; BS 80.2671 (WS 83A.1812); ZZTJ 107.3396–99.
43. Such practices are not seen only in East Asia. Bradley Parker in his chapter "What's the Big Picture? Comparative Perspectives on the Archaeology of Empire," in *The Archaeology of Imperial Landscapes: A Comparative Study of Empires in the Ancient Near East and Mediterranean World*, ed. Bleda S. Düring and Tesse Dieder Stek (New York and Cambridge: Cambridge University Press, 2018), 342, describes forcible resettlement in the Incan empire of highland herdsmen to function as more easily controlled farmers in the lowlands, suggesting similar practices may have taken place in the ancient Near East. Though it would be an exaggeration for the situation in Dai to say as Parker suggests for the Incan and neo-Assyrian empires that "[I]n an effort to limit the mobility of some

and ad hoc process, never applied systematically.⁴⁴ Some groups, including the High Carts, were allowed to retain a relative autonomy, and seem to have had prosperous leaders of their own.⁴⁵ And, as we've seen in earlier ages, not all of those in the region were mobile pastoralists. But in a clear effort to build central power, and borrowing policies earlier enacted by Fu Jian, Shegui now imposed upon the Helan, and others as well, a fundamental change, attempting to break up the polity to make its constituents direct subjects of the Taghbach monarch, no longer allowed freely to move 不聽遷徙.⁴⁶ After stating that this imposed reorganization reduced the aristocrat to the same status as all the other "registered households" (*bian hu* 編戶), He Na's biography goes on to say that though esteemed as an elder maternal uncle, He Na now "had no [men] to command," at least on the basis of personal, heritable control of specific groups.⁴⁷ It would seem that this discussion of "registered households" refers not only to He Na, but to a more general process of newly creating registered populations with a special military duty to the Taghbach khaghan that will be discussed in more detail in Chapter 11. The modern scholar Li Yanong has, however, suggested that Shegui's

indigenous populations and perhaps because grain surpluses might be more easily controlled and diverted than animal resources, imperial authorities monopolized herding thus removing it from the local economy," still we can see in and around the Datong Basin a counterpart to this: "By forcing local or resettled populations to rely on plant-based agriculture, imperial authorities effectively tied local inhabitants to particular plots of cultivatable land where they could, of course, be more easily controlled and exploited," as described above in James Scott's *Against the Grain*.

44. This key issue of early Wei history is a good example of the uneven nature of the regime's recorded history, being known only through a handful of offhand remarks. The details of the policy are not clear and there has been much discussion of the matter by modern scholars. An early and good introduction to this is to be found in Tang, "Tuoba guo jia," 204–5. See also a broad overview of various ways historians have treated this set of issues—particularly the issue of centralization vs. persistence of the power of local lords—in Matsushita Ken'ichi 松下憲一, *Hokugi Kozoku taiseiron* 北魏胡族体制論 (Sapporo: Hokkaidō Daigaku Daigakuin Bungaku Kenkyūka, 2007), Chapter 1.

45. One example may be the set of graves found on the edge of the desert, 150 miles north of Zhangjiakou, in the report by Chen Yongzhi et al., "The Results of the Excavations of the Yihe-Nur Cemetery in Zhengxiangbai Banner (2012–2014)," *The Silk Road* 14 (2016): 42–57, esp. 56.

46. For other examples by which entire groups were incorporated into Shegui's own following, see WS 2.21, 22; and Zou Da 鄒達, "Bei Wei de bing zhi" 北魏的兵制, *Da lu za zhi shi xue cong shu di yi ji* 4 (1970): 163 (in the same passage, however, Zou points out that it was because of the relative weakness of Shegui's position that this could only be on an ad hoc basis). Han Guopan 韓國磐, *Bei chao jing ji shi tan* 北朝經济試探 (Shanghai: Shanghai ren min chu ban she, 1958), 23, points out that Shegui's policies were to a significant extent continuations of Fu Jian's previous impositions; for a specific example of this, see JS 113.2899. There has been debate on the nature of the restrictions placed by Shegui on settled populations: whether they were fixed to a particular plot of farmland, or to particular yearly routes as pastoralists; see Matsushita, *Hokugi Kozoku taiseiron*, 17. It seems probable that different groups received different kinds of assignments in a complex pattern for which little evidence has been preserved. The "movement" forbidden in the Wei case may also have been both physical movement, and transfer of loyalty from one leader to another. See Peter B. Golden, *Central Asia in World History* (New York: Oxford University Press, 2011), 81, for discussion of a similar process by which Chinggis Khan splintered and reorganized previously independent polities into military/social units based on 10s; and Christopher Atwood, "Historiography and Transformation of Ethnic Identity in the Mongol Empire: the Öng'üt Case," *Asian Ethnicity* 15.4 (2014): 514–34. For general discussion of such processes among Inner Asian peoples, see also Di Cosmo, "Aristocratic Elites," 28.

47. BS 80.2672 (WS 83A.1812). The registers would necessarily have been in Chinese, with a great deal of transcription of Inner Asian names into Chinese characters. Note also that loyalties to the Helan lord did not die easily: various commanders of what had been his army raised people of Helan origin in rebellion to these measures, though the rebellion was squashed: WS 28.684.

close kinship ties with the Helan may have made their case exceptional: many previously autonomous polities seem to have been incorporated intact into the growing Taghbach military system, their rulers joining the Wei officer corps, under the khaghan's command, but hereditarily serving as officers of their own unit (in Chinese, this institution being called *shi ling bu luo* 世領部落).[48]

Having cowed or conquered the peoples in the steppes to the north, and turned powerful affines into subjects, Shegui now took direct action against that longtime Taghbach enemy, Liu Weichen. Capping a series of back-and-forth attacks, in the winter of 391 Liu Weichen's son led an army of tens of thousands from the Ordos across the River against Wei. With a force supposedly of just five or six thousand, Shegui routed the attackers, seizing their baggage train and a huge herd of more than 200,000 sheep and oxen they had brought with them, perhaps anticipating grazing rights in the Land of Dai.[49] Shegui now took the battle to the Ordos. Crossing the River at the Golden Ford, just south of the town of Wuyuan (west of modern Baotou), the Wei army from there rode 60 or 70 miles across the desert straight south to Weichen's capital. The local populations scattered as they advanced. This was the prudent thing to do. Liu Weichen and his son fled but were soon tracked down. Killed by his own men, Weichen's head was sent back to be shown to Shegui in his tent. The son, however, who had fled north across the River—seeking to escape onto the open steppe—was captured alive, along with more than 5,000 kinsmen and followers. Marched back to the River, these people were butchered there and thrown into the waters, which, we are told, ran red that day with blood. One of the few to escape was another son of Weichen who would subsequently shed the Chinese name of the Han imperial family, and instead call himself by a name in his own language, which we receive in Chinese transcription as "Helian Bobo" (MC *Xae-ljen Bwo-bwo).[50] Sixteen

---

48. *Wei shu* has three examples of *shi ling bu luo*: 28.681, 40.901, 44.987. And WS 3.62 describes a 422 southern tour of Shegui's successor, Mingyuan, who was accompanied by "vassal magnates from the four quarters, each leading their own units." See Yu Lunian 俞鹿年, *Bei Wei zhi guan zhi du kao* 北魏職官制度考 (Beijing: She hui ke xue wen xian chu ban she, 2008), 19–20. For an interesting comparison to Mongol reorganization, almost 1,000 years later, see Broadbridge, *Mongol Women*, Chapter 4, on "atomized" as opposed to confederated polities. Li Yanong 李亞農, *Zhou zu de shi zu zhi yu Tuoba zu de qian feng jian zhi* 周族的氏族制與拓跋族的前封建制 (Shanghai: Hua dong ren min chu ban she, 1954), Chapter 13, discusses the limits of this policy, to which Zhang, *Bei Wei zheng zhi shi*, 2: 44–48, signals agreement. See also discussion of the ideas of Li and others in Matsushita, *Hokugi Kozoku taiseiron*, Chapter 1; and Mou Fasong 牟发松, "Bei Wei jie san bu luo zheng ce yu ling min qiu zhang zhi zhi yuan yuan xin tan" 北魏解散部落政策与领民酋长制之渊源新探, *Huadong shi fan da xue xue bao: zhe xue she hui ke xue ban* 49.5 (2017): 1–12, who among other things draws on earlier scholars to make clear that the attempt to disorganize the Helan (and other polities) was not completed immediately, but was attempted repeatedly over time (9); and see also treatment of this by Mou and his fellow editors in *Zhongguo xing zheng qu hua tong shi, Shi liu guo Bei chao juan* 中國行政區劃通史, 十六国北朝卷, 2 vols. (vols. 6 and 7 of the set) (Shanghai: Fudan da xue chu ban she, 2017), 2: Appendix 1, 1038–84.

49. WS 2.24, 95.2055–56; ZZTJ 107.3402.

50. See his account among the appended chronicles of *Jin shu*, 130.3201–16; and a partial translation by Boodberg, "Selections from the *Hu T'ien Han Yüeh Fang Chu*," 66–73 (and on 101 he speculates that this name perhaps means *bör-bör, "Wolf-wolf").

years later, with his Xia regime (407–431), Bwobwo would for a time at least reestablish Xiongnu power in the Ordos.

A key to any state and any army is of course feeding the men, and rewarding them for their service to the lord. This would be a major issue throughout the history of the Taghbach state, for which the military was a huge part of the state's budget.[51] In the early decades of Wei, the main sources of that income were livestock and booty taken in war, supplemented by the regular great hunts that were led by the Taghbach lord.[52] This has already been seen with the raids on the steppe and seizure of the victims' livestock. The victory over Liu Weichen allowed the Taghbach to seize as much or more: gold and jewels, as well as 4 million head of livestock, were taken. The Ordos was in this period, and later in East Asian history, a key region for rearing horses. On this occasion the Taghbach took 300,000 head of the animal so vital to mounted conquerors. "The state's expenditures," we are told, "were from this much enriched."[53]

These seizures would have been used to fill the khaghan's coffers, and his huge ranches, but were also a key basis for reinforcing his ties with his nobles and generals, through bestowal on the basis of rank 班賜大臣各有差, a regular feature of early Wei campaigning.[54] We can presume that the officers who received these bestowals themselves then made further redistributions among their own followers. This top-down control of distribution of goods was vital to the development of central power; as will be seen below, later Wei khaghans struggled to maintain this control, among other things attempting to prevent aristocrats from maintaining their own craft workshops. Humans were also part of the bestowals, as we see in comments of the Chinese minister Cui Hao to Emperor Taiwu, regarding "great seizures of beautiful women, precious gems, horses and livestock making up herds." (Another important part of these bestowals would, of course, be silk garments.) Taiwu in particular was praised for his complete unselfishness in redistributing the booty taken in war. Toward the end of the fifth century these became more routinized, and the content changed from livestock and slaves to goods used as the realm's currency, grain and silk, and after the beginning of minting at Luoyang, even coin.[55]

---

51. Making an effort to calculate income and expenditure, Wang, *Zhuan xing qi de Bei Wei cai zheng yan jiu*, 67, estimates that, at times, the cost of the army reached 75 percent of the state budget. By contrast, in the United States in 2015 the military received 16 percent of total federal spending: https://en.wikipedia.org/wiki/File:U.S._Federal_Spending.png, accessed 21 December 2018.

52. See WS 110.2851; Wang, *Zhuan xing qi de Bei Wei cai zheng yan jiu*, 35ff.

53. ZZTJ 107.3402.

54. As described by Marcel Mauss in the classic *The Gift: The Form and Reason for Exchange in Archaic Societies* (New York and London: W. W. Norton, 1990), such practices are of course a worldwide phenomenon. For similar practices in Jiankang regimes, see Andrew Chittick, *Patronage and Community in Medieval China: The Xiangyang Garrison, 400–600 CE* (Albany: State University of New York Press, 2009); and for these among the Mongols, Rachewiltz, *Secret History of the Mongols*, 1: 76.

55. WS 35.819, 4B.107; and regarding routinization of the process, see Wang, *Zhuang xing qi de Bei Wei cai zheng yan jiu*, 164.

Hunting and pastoralism—the predominant way of life of most Inner Asian peoples—would for generations remain central to the dynasty and the core following from which it built its army. We have already seen hints of agriculture, however—Shiyijian's trampled millet fields—and under Shegui there were more royal efforts to build grain production in the Yinshan region. When moving south to Shengle in 386, we are informed in a very brief statement that Shegui "rested his host and charged [the men] to farm" 息眾課農.[56] It is not clear if this was permanent resettlement, or simply an ad hoc measure to feed the troops. If the former, it was part of a larger process, though one that would take generations to complete. Nomadic pastoralists are, of course, not at all unable to make such shifts of economy; nor were all the groups controlled by Shegui nomads.[57] Five years later, we see two other early efforts to get grain for populations now engaged in war rather than food production. The first came in 391, before the Ordos expedition. In the seventh month of that year, military exercises were conducted along Ox Creek, followed two months later by a surprise attack on Liu Weichen's agricultural colonies at Wuyuan, in which the grain stores were seized and the inhabitants slaughtered.[58] This may have been used among other things to support the troops in preparation for the Ordos invasion, and a campaign against the Rouran conducted just before that. Apparently still not heavily armored, as cavalry of the Chinese interior had become, these men were able to travel light.[59] There doesn't seem to have been much of a supply train in the course of the northern campaign, when Shegui asked each cavalryman to feed himself off of one of the beasts in his own string of horses, so that rapid pursuit could be maintained. In the end, the Taghbach army caught up with the Rouran and defeated them, with bestowals for all concerned.[60]

A more sustainable agriculture policy came after completion of the Ordos campaign. Having seized Wuyuan and killed Liu Weichen's kith and kin, Shegui then charged his close kinsman Yi, the Prince of Wey 衛王,[61] to re-establish

---

56. WS 2.20. And see discussion in Zhu, *Wei Jin Nan bei chao she hui sheng huo shi*, Kindle ed., Chapter 12 少數民族, Section 2 饮食.

57. See Philip Carl Salzman, *When Nomads Settle: Processes of Sedentarization as Adaptation and Response* (New York: Praeger, 1980); and Khazanov, *Nomads and the Outside World*, 46–48. As has been made clear in studies of recent decades, there has always been some agriculture on the steppe: Di Cosmo, *Ancient China*, 169–70.

58. WS 2.24.

59. For a good description of the way early Wei cavalry traveled, see JS 124.3094; in WS 24.609, we see a comment by Fu Jian to an aide sent him by Shiyijian on the eve of Fu's invasion that you "northerners are without steel armor or sharp weapons," perhaps also suggesting that they were still without stirrups (for this, see more in Chapter 11). To this, the aide replied, "the northerners are strong and brave. Up on a horse they carry three weapons, and gallop along like the wind."

60. WS 2.24, 103.2290, 24.612; ZZTJ 107.3401.

61. Note that "Wey" 衛 is properly written in Pinyin as "Wei." But though a homophone, this is a completely different word from the "Wei" 魏 in Northern Wei. I use Gwoyeu Romanization to write the former as Wey to avoid confusion, though confusion exists in this biography as well, where he is called a cousin of Shegui but may have actually been a half-brother, Shegui's mother on the basis of levirate having remarried an uncle of Shegui after the death of his father: see Holmgren, "Women and Political Power," 52; Eisenberg, *Kingship in Early Medieval China*, 39–40.

agricultural colonies on the River's northern loop, which though running through desert had since the Warring States period been a productive, though remote agricultural outpost of Chinese states and empires.[62] It is not clear what labor force was used to cultivate these fields—perhaps war captives, perhaps survivors of the 391 massacre—but being isolated, it was easy to extract grain from these peasants to support an army, as it had been over the centuries for various regimes of various origins. There were no doubt overseers to control the populations and "encourage production."[63]

The results of these innovations were mixed: *Wei shu*'s "Monograph on Food and Money" states that as of 398, since "this was an age of unceasing warfare, despite successive harvests it still was not enough for long-term sufficiency."[64] But for the leadership of Later Yan, this new source of grain production for the army to the north was a threat, which they would soon attempt to eliminate. In this same year, 391, however, a more immediate cause for conflict emerged. Down in Zhongshan, on the Yellow River Plain, Murong Chui was in need of mounts for his cavalry; he had perhaps been expecting a herd to be sent from the Ordos Xiongnu. Therefore, when a Taghbach royal kinsman came down to the Yan capital on a diplomatic mission he was detained there, in an effort to force Shegui to send "fine horses" to the Murong.[65] Civil relations between Taghbach and Murong had come to an end.[66]

Heretofore a status quo had existed: though Shegui was unwilling formally to accept junior status, he had been laboring to build and maintain his position after the interregnum and struggle for succession that followed, while Murong Chui had been preoccupied with securing the recently retaken Yellow River plains and by struggles in southern Shanxi with the "Western" Yan of a recalcitrant member of the Murong clan. Western Yan would, in fact, be the proximate cause for end of the uneasy truce and outbreak of active hostilities. When in 394 Murong Chui's Later Yan took final steps against its little Murong rival, Western Yan sought survival by repeating the actions of Jin's Bingzhou governors a century before and reaching north to plead for help from the growing power on the Tumed Plain. And that power did respond, though its army, perhaps intentionally, arrived late and had no effect on fighting among the Murong cousins. Western Yan

---

62. BS 15.562 (WS 15.371).
63. Li, *Bei Wei Pingcheng shi dai*, 48; on pp. 44–46 in the same volume, Li suggests that those settled on the Prince of Wey's agricultural colonies were herdsmen from defeated groups.
64. WS 110.2850.
65. WS 2.24. The account of the kinsman-envoy is BS 15.525 (WS 15.374). This again is a figure, given in our texts as Gu 觚, who casts confusion on the relationships within this family, since he is said to be both a son of an uncle of Shegui, and also the youngest son of Shegui's mother, Madam Helan: for a beginning of the discussion, see *Bei shi* 15.584 note 28, where it is pointed out that though he was said to have been a son of Han (a son of Shiyijian), that depending on the different dates given Han had died at the age of either three or eight. Be that as it may, the detention of Gu in Zhongshan is said to have caused Madam Helan to die of grief: BS 13.492 (WS 13.324–25); she too was buried among the Jinling imperial tombs.
66. ZZTJ 107.3400; Ma, *Wuhuan yu Xianbei*, 264.

was destroyed. Nevertheless, the die was cast. Later Yan armies now seized the key city of Taiyuan in central Shanxi, establishing their presence just across the Gouzhu Mountains from Taghbach territory in the Datong Basin. In the summer of 395, Murong Chui launched a punitive offensive against Wei, sending his son and heir Murong Bao north from Zhongshan with a force of almost 100,000 men, accompanied by several kinsmen, including Bao's brother Murong Lin.

A key strategy of Later Yan was to wrest the Wuyuan plantations away from Shegui, and so deprive him of the ability to maintain a standing army and make him again dependent on Yan. The Taghbach lord responded by moving his still highly mobile subjects—his soldiers, their families, and their herds—south across the river into the Ordos. Thus, although Murong Bao was able to take the area north of the river, seize its grain stocks, and build a fort there, what now followed was a months-long standoff across the great moat of the Yellow River, almost a quarter-mile wide, whose waters had just four years before been colored with Xiongnu blood.

This would be a life-and-death campaign for Shegui. He was, however, a master of strategy and his army a strong one. Perhaps with the benefit of hindsight, and following a regularly seen device of the Chinese historical tradition, *Wei shu* inserts into the story a Laocoön-ish warning made down in Zhongshan to the Later Yan monarch, Murong Chui, that although the young and cocky Murong heir looked down upon the northerners, Taghbach "weapons are fine, their horses strong."[67] The warning, it must be noted, was inaccurate: Murong Bao did not actually show much verve, building boats but procrastinating in their use, perhaps waiting for hunger to overtake the Taghbach. This did not happen, and during the great stalemate on the River, it was in fact the 24-year-old Shegui who showed confidence, training his troops on the bleak Ordos landscape, and sending forces out to hold the flanks; these were led by commanders who were also kinsmen, including that omnipresent figure in the wars of the Wei founding, the Prince of Wey. In mid-fall, Shegui moved his troops to face the enemy across the River. According to the more independent account given in *Jin shu*, Murong Bao was "timid and did not dare cross,"[68] but then, provoked, sent troops in vessels across the river. A wind, however, now came up that wrecked several dozen boats on the southern bank, where their men were seized by Wei troops.

Choosing on this occasion to employ psychological warfare, Shegui made a display of beneficence by allowing these men to return across the river to their army.[69] More cunning still was the Taghbach lord's manipulation of tensions and

---

67. WS 32.751. The main sources for this account are ZZTJ 108.3421–25; WS 2.26–27, 95.2067–68; JS 123.3089. See also Zhang, *Bei Wei zheng zhi shi*, 2: 73–84.

68. JS 123.3089.

69. See further discussion in Zhang, *Bei Wei zheng zhi shi*, 2: 76–77.

anxieties within the Murong leadership. A man of many years, Murong Chui had been growing increasingly infirm. Sending special forces east across the River into the Shanxi highlands, the Taghbach now began to intercept all message-bearers going back and forth from Zhongshan to the Murong army, breaking the tie between the Yan emperor and his sons on the north bank of the River. Presumably under threat of death, the captive couriers were then brought up to the south bank to shout across that "Your father is already dead! Why not hurry back?"[70] With this lie, seeds of doubt were planted in the invading army; thinking of succession, Murong Bao and his brother Murong Lin began to look upon each other with suspicion.

From this point the story as given in *Wei shu* slips in and out of the fabric of myth, woven when and where it is difficult to know. But it is still a good story.[71]

Originally, while on the road to Wuyuan, the axle of Murong Bao's carriage had broken, supposedly "for no reason." According to the prince's attendant prognosticator, this was a baleful omen and they should turn back, a suggestion his angry employer rejected. Later, after the Murong had heard the claim of the father's death, the seer still more forcefully stated that "Punishment [for your wrongdoing] has already taken shape, but if you go quickly you can escape." He then went on to announce to the larger body that "Now all of you will die in this foreign land, your bodies and bones piled up upon the heath. Crows will eat you, and insects. You will not again see your families."[72]

With growing suspicion between the two Murong princes, and mutiny breaking out in the ranks, Murong Bao now made the choice to burn his barely used boats and withdraw. This was November 23 on the Gregorian calendar, a time when though the temperatures regularly drop down into the 20s, the River is not expected to freeze. The Murong heir was apparently sure he could squabble in peace with his brother on the road home, the Taghbach army having no effective way to do a rapid, large-scale crossing of the River to pursue. A week and a day later, however, on December 1, a fierce wind came up and suddenly the river did freeze solid. Shegui and his army now set off after the invaders with a picked force of some 20,000 cavalry, roughing it with no baggage train and traveling both night and day. They caught up with the Murong army six days later, at Shenhe Slope.

As noted above, we don't clearly know the location of this place, with arguments having been made for location in the Daihai Sea region, in a sequence of valleys just across the mountains from Shengle; or for a site on the edges of the open steppe, on the northern side of the Yinshan across the mountains from

---

70. WS 95.2067.
71. Most recently, in fact, retold by the poet and historian Boyang 柏杨 (Guo Dingsheng 郭定生) in a *bai hua* translation of Chapter 27 of the *Zi zhi tong jian*: *Shenhe sha fu* 资治通鉴：参合杀俘 (Killed and Captured at Shenhe) (Shenyang: Wan juan chu ban gong si, 2015).
72. WS 95.2067.

the modern town of Yanggao.[73] Relying on the work of the modern scholar Yan Gengwang, this author leans toward the latter: measuring distance with Google Maps, the former would be just about 200 miles, so the six days of pursuit would mean a bit more than 30 miles a day. This is too easy. A horse riding briskly can go 50 or 60 miles a day, which putting the Shenhe Slope northeast of Datong—some 300 miles from Wuyuan—accords better with the rapid march described for the Wei army in its pursuit of Murong Bao. But wherever the slope was, on December 7 the Murong were encamped just east of it, on a river flowing down from a mountain above.[74] Close behind was an unseen army.

At this point, there emerges in the Yan camp another voice of baleful prophecy, the monk Tanmeng. While the Murong were by the Shenhe Slope, there appeared behind them a great wind pushing forward a bank of dark fog, like a great wall that suddenly rose above them. "This fiercely rushing wind and fog," the monk now told Murong Bao, "is an omen that the Wei army is about to arrive. You ought to send troops to stop them."[75] Not giving much credence to the words of the distraught holy man, Bao made only perfunctory efforts to respond to his entreaties. Though Bao's brother Lin was sent back with a contingent, instead of remaining vigilant against the enemy they were released for an open field hunt.

With no scouts scouting, the Wei army did arrive, and stealthily climbed up the back side of the mountain. At dawn, they emerged on the slope up above the unprepared camp. Thrown into panic, the Murong army was quickly routed.[76] Tens of thousands, we are told, fled to the river, where slipping on the ice they were trampled or drowned. Though a few thousand, including the two princes, managed to escape and return to Zhonghsan—where they discovered that their father still lived—the rest of the army now threw down their arms and held up their hands to surrender.

73. For a summation of the first view, held by Maeda Masana among others, see Wang Kai, *Bei Wei Shengle shi dai*, 246–52; this is also the location given Shenhe Slope in *Zhongguo li shi di tu ji*, Vol. 4, Map 52. For the latter view, Zhang, *Bei Wei zheng zhi shi*, 2: 79, cites the persuasive argument of Yan Gengwang 嚴耕望, *Tang dai jiao tong tu kao* 唐代交通圖考, 7 vols. (Taibei: Zhongyang yan jiu yuan li shi yu yan yan jiu suo, 1985–), 5: Appendix 8, 1397–1402, who decisively demonstrates that the Shenhe Slope—a key topographical feature seen repeatedly in Taghbach history, lay northeast of Datong. This view is supported by Yin Xian 殷宪, "Bei Wei Pingcheng shi lue" 北魏平城事略, in *Pingcheng shi gao* 平城史稿 (Beijing: Ke xue chu ban she, 2012), 187; and is buttressed by several mentions in primary text, including *Shui jing zhu shu* 2: 13.1137–38; and WS 2.41, where it is stated that in the year 403 Shegui left the capital going northeast and passed Shenhe. And see Chapter 5 note 67.

74. WS 95.2067. The Chinese version of the mountain name given here, Panyang Mountain 蟠羊山, "coiled [horn] sheep mountain," apparently contains an alternate form of *pan yang* 盤羊, the "bighorn sheep," or more particularly the Argali, which are known to live in mountainous areas in Shanxi. See Alexander K. Fedosenko and David A. Blank, "Ovis ammon," *Mammalian Species* 773 (15 July 2005): 1–15.

75. JS 123.3089. It will be noted that the parallel WS account (95.2067–68) puts the warning in the mouth of the earlier seer. This is apparently a poor cut-and-paste. ZZTJ (108.3423) follows *Jin shu* here. Supporting the idea of the Chinese text as a vessel for importation of genuinely Inner Asian elements, the idea of weather magic is a long-shared element of Inner Asian mythology—see John Andrew Boyle, "Turkish and Mongol Shamanism in the Middle Ages," *Folklore* 83.3 (1972): 190–91; Agnew Birtalan, "The Tibetan Weather-magic Ritual of a Mongolian Shaman," *Shaman* 9.2 (2001): 119; and an account in *Secret History* (Rachewiltz, *Secret History of the Mongols*, 1: 64).

76. ZZTJ 108.3424; *Shui jing zhu shu* 2: 13.1137–38.

While the Taghbach had traveled light in their pursuit, the Murong had been traveling slow, since they were carting along with them heavy baggage, no doubt including riches seized from the Shengle vaults, and grains taken from the Wuyuan granaries. These would have been recovered, along with huge amounts of Murong arms and armor, rations and sundry goods (which seem to have included Murong Bao's consorts). As was the norm, the Wei lord now distributed much of these goods "as rewards to high officials and officers, each according to rank."[77] In the same passage in the *Wei shu* annals, we are told of removal from among the prisoners of several "men of talent and learning." Neither the annals nor the *Wei shu* account of Murong Chui go on to state what happened to the thousands of those that remained. This is brought forth in other sections of the book, where we are told that although Shegui originally wished to release them as proof of Taghbach benignity, his generals did not agree. One of the commanders—a man of Wuhuan descent with marriage ties to the imperial family—stated this quite bluntly: "it's best to kill them."[78] As the seer is said to have predicted, their bodies and bones were now piled up on the heath.

The tragedy was compounded in the next year. The Murong lord Chui was by this time an old man, who had been through a great deal in his life. The last act would be the hardest of all. Having escaped the fate of the men under his command at Shenhe Slope, the 30-year-old Bao badgered his father back at Zhongshan, telling him that now was the time to deal with the Wei. And so just four months later, in the spring of 396, the enraged 70-year-old personally led a punitive expedition up to the Sanggan valley.[79] At first all went well. Defeat of the Taghbach forces garrisoning a fort on the location where Pingcheng would soon be rebuilt caused an apparent fall in Taghbach morale.[80] But proceeding north, Murong Chui led his army past Shenhe Slope where "the piles of bones stood like mountains."[81] While Chui tried to hold a sacrifice for the dead Murong soldiers, he was surrounded by men howling with grief for sons and brothers whose uncovered remains they now stood before. Mortified, spitting blood, Chui turned back. He died at Shanggu (the "upper valley," mod. Yanqing, Hebei, in the highlands north of Beijing), ironically the site attached to the princely title he had wanted to bestow on the Taghbach upstart ten years before.

Over the centuries, many Taghbach armies won many victories, but this was certainly the most important, and most remembered.[82] The sudden reversal of

---

77. WS 2.27.
78. WS 30.710. This Wuhuan was from a clan that had taken up the Chinese family name "Wang" 王; see Yao, *Bei chao hu xing kao*, 256.
79. WS 15.381.
80. ZZTJ 108.3426.
81. JS 123.3090.
82. Anthony Cohen, in his book *Belonging: Identity and Social Organisation in British Rural Cultures* (St. John's: Institute of Social and Economic Research, Memorial University of Newfoundland, 1982), discusses how the

fortunes was extraordinary. Before it had been Murong armies ascending the mountains to attack the Taghbach. Soon after victory in the north, Shegui would lead the army of the Murong's enemy down from the mountains onto the plains. The route they took threaded south through the valleys and passes of Shanxi. The banners and baggage train of the army—which supposedly numbered more than 400,000—stretched for hundreds of miles; as they passed by, we are told, "the peasants in their huts all trembled with fear."[83] Still up in the highlands, in early November 396 they took the strategic city of Taiyuan. Many, of course, won titles and riches on this campaign. Here we will just mention one—the leader of the Iranian Erzhu clan, hereditary lords of their own people who had long served the Taghbach. Having effectively led 1,700 men as auxiliaries in the southern invasion, the Erzhu headman (*ling min qiu zhang* 領民酋長) was granted hereditary control of the Xiurong Valley, just south of Yanmen Pass.[84] There he and his heirs would raise horses, and as direct vassals of the monarch give logistic support, providing horses and provisions to imperial armies on campaign. Generations later, at the end of Wei, they emerged in a very different role, as we shall see below.

In December 396, having taken Taiyuan, Shegui led his army east. Going over the Taihangs, they then descended onto the Central Plain, thousands of feet below their homeland. Though most of the walled cities on the plain quickly surrendered, the process was prolonged for almost a year by several holdouts, including the Yan capital of Zhongshan, where Murong Bao, having succeeded to his father's throne, sealed himself up, defying the invaders. Fine cavalry on an open field, the Taghbach had little experience with siege and could not breach Zhongshan's walls. During this prolonged standoff, both sides grew short of food, while sickness came to afflict the Taghbach force, killing both man and horse. At one point, hearing of a Helan rebellion in the lands up north, Shegui almost withdrew his army, though in the end a botched offensive by Murong Bao rallied the Taghbach to fight on. In April 397, the Later Yan emperor abandoned the capital to flee back to his people's homeland in southern Manchuria, brought down by an ongoing power struggle within the Murong family itself, the same reason he had abandoned the Yellow River loop a year and a half before.[85] But perhaps terrified by what they had heard of the treatment of captives up at Shenhe Slope, the inhabitants of the city themselves now refused to surrender, holding out for another half year. Under increasingly dire circumstances, they finally surrendered to the Taghbach in November 397.[86] On this occasion,

---

sense of belonging takes shape among "individual and distinct groups," describing the myths that emerge as being like "empty receptacles which are filled with local and particular experience" (13).
    83. WS 2.27; ZZTJ 108.3430.
    84. WS 74.1643–44.
    85. ZZTJ 109.3446.
    86. ZZTJ 109.3459.

Shegui's instinct for beneficence was accepted by the generals, and the people of Zhongshan were treated with relative leniency.

In this way, the Taghbach became lords of a whole new world, quite coincidentally in the same year that, at the other end of the old world, Augustine gave shape to a very different universe with his *Confessions*.[87]

---

87. According to Robin Lane Fox, *Augustine: Conversion to Confessions* (New York: Basic Books, 2015), 537, the work is "a unity, composed, in my view, between the start of Lent and Easter, 397."

The World Shegui Entered

What then was the world that Shegui had led his armies down into?
If there actually was a "dark age" in northern Europe after Rome's fall, we do not see that in the world of those who defined themselves on the basis of Han, after that empire's collapse.[1] Though deeply disrupted by the wars of the previous century, with a drop in population, those lands remained a vast network of villages and cities.[2] With its dense and potentially highly organized and productive populations, the Yellow River Plain was a prize sought eagerly by the new states that had grown up along its edges in the third and fourth centuries. The groups who created those states were, however, not so much fighting locals to conquer their lands as struggling among themselves to be the one to grab the ring. The situation was very different from that of 900 years later, with stiff and prolonged Song resistance to Mongol invasion.[3] In the fourth century, with collapse of Jin, the interior of the old empire had, for a time at least, simply been politically hollowed out. There were certainly still able warriors and skilled commanders within the Chinese world.[4] But though stored in books and remembered nostalgically by such as Cui Hao, the principles of order—most practically, the methods by which one could actually organize and maintain a large army—had temporarily vanished.[5]

Prominent among the "locals" were the Chinese "great clans" that emerged out of the empire's collapse. Until recently, at least, this has been the most studied single aspect of the medieval Chinese world.[6] A central focus for contemporary

---

1. See the comment of Dien, *Six Dynasties Civilization*, 1.
2. Chittick, *The Jiankang Empire*, Appendix B, in fact casts doubt on how large the southward migrations were.
3. Mark Strange examines the later view of the fourth-century collapse from within a threatened Song in his "An Eleventh-Century View of Chinese Ethnic Policy: Sima Guang on the Fall of Western Jin," *Journal of Historical Sociology* 20.3 (2007): 235–58.
4. See Chittick, *Patronage and Community in Medieval China*.
5. This topic is discussed at length in Charles Holcombe, *In the Shadow of the Han*.
6. In English, the most prominent works on this topic are Patricia Ebrey's *The Aristocratic Families of Early Imperial China: A Case Study of the Po-ling Ts'ui Family* (Cambridge and New York: Cambridge University Press, 1978); and the seriously flawed *The Medieval Chinese Oligarchy* (Boulder, CO: Westview Press, 1977) of David Johnson. Nuance has been added with Dennis Grafflin's "Great Family in Medieval South China," *HJAS* 41 (1981): 65–74; and Jennifer Holmgren's "Lineage Falsification in the Northern Dynasties." In Chinese, the interested reader could start with Mao Hanguang's 毛漢光 *Liang Jin Nan bei chao shi zu zheng zhi zhi yan jiu* 兩晉南北朝士族政治之研究 (Taibei: Taiwan shang wu yin shu guan, 1966), a part of which is summarized in English in his "The Evolution in the Nature of the Medieval Genteel Families," in Albert Dien's edited volume *State and Society in Early Medieval China* (Stanford, CA: Stanford University Press, 1990), 73–109. See other useful summations in Holcombe,

chroniclers—who understandably wished to write about their own kith and kin—it has also been of great interest for modern ones with interest in this particular facet of medieval East Asia. In our narrative, one such eminent descent group stands out in particular: the Cui who came originally from Qinghe commandery (the seat of which was near the modern town of the same name in Hebei province). From this line came Cui Hao, and many others from many different branches.

The surname Cui is first seen in the record in the Qinghe area during the first years of Han, at a place called Dong Wucheng ("Eastern War-town"). The record then goes blank, however, and the Cui of Qinghe 清河崔 do not emerge as significant actors until the third century CE. Like most of the Chinese medieval great clans, the Qinghe Cui took shape in the midst of imperial collapse.[7]

The rise of the Qinghe Cui began with two cousins, Cui Yan and Cui Lin, in the last decades of Han, in the midst of a growing alienation of provincial elites from the Han capital, Luoyang. This culminated with the Great Proscription of 169, in the course of which such gentlemen were expelled from the court, and in the process detached the classics—and the classics' authority—from the court as well.[8]

The older of the two Cui cousins, Yan, studied under a key figure in these developments, the scholar Zheng Xuan (127–200). Though Zheng was himself an eminent master of the texts—known among other things for work on the *Rituals of Zhou*, which we will see more of below—we cannot assume the thousands of students he drew to himself were all gentle, bookish Ru; the emerging private academies of this age were, among other things, centers of social and political dissent. Cui Yan himself is said to have "enjoyed fencing, and esteemed military matters."[9] As it transpired, he would need these skills, since in the course of his studies under Zheng Xuan another expression of dissent and separatism suddenly appeared within the empire: the rebellion of the Yellow Turbans, which

---

In the Shadow of the Han; Helwig Schmidt-Glintzer, "The Scholar-Official and His Community: The Character of the Aristocracy in Medieval China," *EMC* 1 (1994): 60–83; and Dušanka Dušana Miščevič's "Oligarchy or Social Mobility. A Study of the Great Clans of Early Medieval China," *BMFEA* 65 (1993): 5–256. Perhaps the leading figures on whom they draw are Mao Hanguang; Kawakatsu Yoshio 川勝義雄, *Chūgoku kizokusei shakai no kenkyū* 中國貴族制社會の研究 (Kyoto: Kyōto Daigaku Jinbun Kagaku Kenkyūjo, 1987); and Chen Shuang 陈爽, *Shi jia da zu yu Bei chao zheng zhi* 世家大族与北朝政治 (Beijing: Zhongguo she hui ke xue chu ban she, 1998). Interesting work in more recent times has appeared from Fan Zhaofei 范兆飞, with detailed study of clans and groups of clans; and Watanabe Yoshihiro 渡邉義浩, with study of the textual and cultural bases of these groups' authority.

7. Much of the following is drawn from Xia, *Zhong gu shi jia da zu Qinghe Cui shi yan jiu*.

8. See Rafe de Crespigny, tr., *Emperor Huan and Emperor Ling: Being the Chronicle of Later Han for the Years 157 to 189 AD as Recorded in Chapters 54 to 59 of the "Zizhi tongjian" of Sima Guang* (Canberra: Faculty of Asian Studies, Australia National University, 1989), Revised Internet Edition 2018, 223–37; and Holcombe, *Shadow of the Han*, 78, where he comments that educated gentlemen, often referred to as the "literati" (*wen ren* 文人), grew to be "legitimate repositories of public authority"—thereby replacing the court—with a "corporate sense of identity."

9. SGZ 12.367. On the growth of private academies, see Robert P. Kramers, "The Development of the Confucian Schools," in *Cambridge History of China*, Vol. 1, *The Ch'in and Han Empires, 221 B.C.–A.D. 220*, ed. Denis Twitchett and Michael Loewe (Cambridge: Cambridge University Press, 1986), 764–65.

erupted in the year 184. As the rebels drew closer to Zheng Xuan's academy in northern Shandong, the master led his students in a retreat into the hills north of modern Qingdao. In the end, running out of food, he was forced to send them on their ways. Cui Yan's way, west toward his home district, was unfortunately cut off by bandits who we are told "were everywhere." And so he wandered through the territories south of the Yellow River, the Yangtze and the Lake District. Years passed, the immediate threat receded, and he returned home. There, for a time he holed up, "amusing himself with just his zither and some books" 以琴書自娛[10]— as we are told in a familiar caricature of upper-class life at this time—before entering the service of Yuan Shao, one of the powerful generals who emerged with the Han collapse. After Yuan's death in 202, Cui Yan moved on to serve in the administration of the emerging victor of the northern wars, Cao Cao.

Cui Yan was an imposing figure, looked up to (zhan wang 瞻望) by the court officials. Drawing on the wisdom of the ancients, he was also persistently preachy, in 216 finally offending Cao Cao to the point where he was ordered to commit suicide.[11] The "eminence," wang 望, established by Cui Yan survived, however, with many descendants using the line's reputation to take a place on the stage of history after the Jin collapse, most in the north but some also in the regions controlled (if loosely) by Jiankang; perhaps what we see here is one version of Weber's "routinization of charisma."[12] Of Cui Yan's descendants, most prominent was Cui Liang (460–521), whose immediate ancestors served in the south, but who himself, three centuries after Cui Yan, would hold high office at Northern Wei's Luoyang.

Back in the third century, however, Cui Yan was actually overshadowed by his cousin, Cui Lin (d. 244). Their careers are quite distinct. Independently entering service to the Cao regime, Lin was also originally of more modest means than his kinsman. When appointed magistrate of Wu district (southwest of mod. Taiyuan, Shanxi) he "had neither horse nor carriage, and walked to office on his own."[13] Later, however, when Cao Cao put out a call for "the most virtuous administrators," Cui Lin was recommended, perhaps by reason of virtue shown through penury. After establishment of the Caos' Wei dynasty in 220, Cui Lin rose to be Inspector of Youzhou, the key northeast frontier province in the area of modern Beijing, and later held the high honorary position of Minister of Works (Sikong).[14] His progeny did well too. These included granddaughters of Cui Lin who were married into a network of powerful Chinese families, including one who became the wife of Liu Kun, the man seen above who held the

---

10. SGZ 12.367.
11. SGZ 12.369.
12. See discussion of the term wang 望, "repute" or "prestige," by Yano Chikara 矢野主税, "Mochi no igi ni tsuite" 望の意義について, Nagasaki daigaku kyōiku gakubu shakai kagaku ronsō 21 (1972): 1–16.
13. SGZ 24.679.
14. SGZ 24.681.

post of Inspector of Bingzhou in the midst of the Jin collapse. In the paternal line, five generations down, was "the divine boy of Jizhou (mod. Jizhou, Hebei)," Cui Hong, who would serve first Fu Jian and then Murong Chui before forcible incorporation into Shegui's new government. His son, Cui Hao, reached greater heights, and lower depths.[15]

These descent groups are important. But excessive focus on them obscures rather than clarifies the complex nature of states such as Northern Wei, or even the Tang empire.[16] In part conceptualized ex post facto in the Tang, in neither the Tang nor in earlier periods were these groups as enduring or as powerful as often presented. It is difficult to really call them an "aristocracy," if by that is meant the OED definition of "A ruling body of the best citizens," since though they may well have thought of themselves as the best, they really did not rule the realm, directly in their own right. Their fundamental role was that of administrative agent for others.[17]

Furthermore, though sharing the social capital of an "eminent" lineage, they typically at least didn't function with other members of the line as any kind of corporate entity; or to put it in a more concrete way, the Qinghe Cui weren't Capulets, ganging together at least to fight offense by a Montague. As hinted at above, in the story of Cui Hao, marriage networks established with other powerful families by particular branches of these lineages were in reality more important—more a source of real power—than ties of kinship on the father's side. The cousins Cui Yan and Cui Lin each followed their own trajectories, with little if any significant interaction. Even on the local level, which by the fifth century prominent men of such lineages had often left behind, we regularly see several powerful families in the same administrative district, or commandery (*jun*), and though such families had an extensive patchwork of landholdings and their own private militias, they did not regulate the lives of all of those who lived in the district. The term "eminent lineage" is a better fit here, referring to the "prestige" or "eminence" (*wang*) in which they were regarded by their neighbors, an "eminence" based on local power, augmented by broad networks of marriage connection throughout the Chinese world, and combined with the authority that some at least derived through assertion of control of text and ritual taken from the Ru tradition.[18]

---

15. For the wife, see JS 44.1259, 67.1785. For Cui Hao's descent, see Xia, *Zhong gu shi jia da zu Qinghe Cui shi yan jiu*, 69–70.
16. See Jonathan Skaff's comments in his review (*Journal of Chinese Studies* 61 [2015]: 365–69) on Nicolas Tackett's *Destruction of the Medieval Chinese Aristocracy* (Cambridge, MA: Harvard University Asia Center, 2014).
17. Commented on by many, including some in note 6, this is best summed up by Dien in his *Six Dynasties Civilization*, 14, saying, "the groups so labelled were neither powerful nor aristocratic nor clans." For discussion of how the Mongols took a very different path, employing outsiders as their ruling agents in the Chinese world, see Brose, *Subjects and Masters*.
18. Holcombe, *Shadow of the Han*, 82, discusses the "fetish with these rites" that contributed to these men's special status.

Thus, the local power wielded by such descent groups was real, but limited. Though they might under different circumstances have grown into true local aristocracies, these possibilities were truncated by the rise around them of regimes that (even in the Yangtze region) had been brought into being by monarchs and generals of very different origin and attitude (however much the latter were obscured and repackaged by the histories written by the former). Members of these Chinese great families went to serve other men's states. In the process, different members of the same line became widely scattered, with increasingly little contact, much less cooperation.

* * *

As their roles took shape within a crumbling empire, men of the eminent lineages could raise for defense militias of a few dozen, at times perhaps a few hundred. The large armies that could serve as basis for a state came from elsewhere. It may be fair to say that large armies are raised and maintained in two main ways: on the basis of loyalties of various sorts, or on the basis of material reimbursement for services rendered, or as is generally the case, some combination of the two. It seems, however, that the large armies of late Western Jin leaned strongly toward the second.

The Sima had come to power from within the court of the Wei dynasty of the Cao family. Their rise was completed in 266 when their leader ceased being power behind the throne and sat the throne himself, taking as his own the Cao capital at Luoyang. Though the city had been destroyed and its inhabitants massacred 75 years before—by the Han chancellor, Dong Zhuo, in the civil wars that would eventually end that dynasty—it had been rebuilt and repopulated to become a marvelous and thriving metropolis.[19] Among those impressed by it was, it will be remembered, Liwei's son, the Shamo Khaghan. These glories would not last.

A key theme of the last centuries of Han had been growth of localism and local power within the empire.[20] Seeking to assert control over these centrifugal forces, the Sima dynasty made princes of the blood local lords in their own right, conferring upon them real power over their fiefs and the right to maintain their own armies. This would prove disastrous for the dynasty, and end the last significant effort to maintain the old empire. Jin remained united during the 25-year-long reign of its charismatic founder Wudi (r. 266–290). With his death, however, local power immediately reasserted itself, now under the leadership of rival Sima princes. In an inter-familial power struggle known by the conventional term "disorders of the Eight Princes," the imperial kinsmen were, as one contemporary observer

---

19. For Dong Zhuo's destruction of the city, see Rafe de Crespigny, *Fire over Luoyang: A History of the Later Han Dynasty, 23–220 AD* (Leiden and Boston: Brill, 2017), 456–65.
20. Lewis, *The Early Chinese Empires*, 115–27.

noted, "loyal today, treacherous tomorrow."²¹ While the dynastic house would survive as "Eastern" Jin (317–420), it did so in much attenuated form, having lost the northlands and retreated to what they at least considered the Yangtze backwaters. New actors would now step forward to dominate the East Asian world.

The ongoing backdrop for the ugly series of tableaux through which the yearslong disorders of the eight princes have been conveyed was a sad and sympathetic figure, Wudi's heir, the "gentle emperor" Huidi 惠帝. Apparently developmentally disabled, Huidi would reign for some 17 years but rule in none, being used by first one and then another of his relatives who wished to control the realm as his regent. There are many actors within these complicated tales, and many subplots, and we will look only at a small subset, beginning with one of the eight, Sima Ying, the Prince of Chengdu, who in 304 from his stronghold at the city of Ye (just south of mod. Cixian, Hebei) had from a distance taken control of Luoyang and the emperor who resided there, while giving himself the title of "great younger brother," a most irregular form of heir apparency.²² In the summer of this year a former ally, the Prince of Donghai, Sima Yue, seized Luoyang and with the emperor in tow marched north to attack the Prince of Chengdu at Ye. His army is said to have numbered 100,000; Chengdu being much disliked, militias and private armies flocked to Donghai's "call to arms to the four quarters," "gathering like clouds" 雲集.²³ When Donghai was defeated at Ye, however, the clouds that had gathered around him quickly dissipated; these militias were private holdings in service of private interests.²⁴ The Prince of Donghai fled back to his fief (in what is now Shandong province), while Chengdu took custody and control of the emperor at Ye. To the south, an erstwhile ally of Donghai—Shangguan Si—took over the now emperor-less imperial capital, which he gave his men free rein brutally to despoil. Perhaps this was revenge for what had not long before been done in Luoyang to Shangguan's former lord, the Prince of Changsha—one of the better ones, said to have actually treated his kinsman and emperor with some respect—who while serving at the capital as regent had been seized and burnt alive.²⁵ Soon after, however, Shangguan was driven out by the man who had done the burning, Zhang Fang, a general in service of the Prince of Hejian, who held the "land within the passes," Guanzhong, the valley of the Wei River where the original Han capital, Chang'an, had been located. It was on his first visit to Luoyang half a year before that Zhang Fang had immolated the Prince of Changsha, after which he took captive some 10,000 of the city's inhabitants,

---

21. ZZTJ 86.2711. For a full study of the disorders, see Miyakawa Hisayuki 宮川尚志, *Rikuchō shi kenkyū: seiji, shakai hen* 六朝史研究: 政治・社会篇 (Tokyo: Nihon Gakujutsu Shinkōkai, 1956), Chapter 1, Sections 2 and 3.

22. JS 4.102.

23. JS 59.1618; ZZTJ 85.2696.

24. Mark Edward Lewis, *China between Empires: The Northern and Southern Dynasties* (Cambridge, MA: Belknap Press of Harvard University Press, 2009), 58–59.

25. ZZTJ 85.2693, 2698.

whom he had marched back to the Wei Valley. The brutality—the barbarism—of this age is almost unspeakable.

Up at Ye, the Prince of Chengdu had been trying to bring some proper barbarians into the mix, reaching out to the Southern Xiongnu's "worthy prince of the left" 左賢王, Liu Yuan 劉淵, for support in fighting auxiliary Serbi and Wuhuan units raised in the highlands north of Beijing by Chengdu's rival, Wang Jun, a man of the Wangs of Taiyuan, another of the eminent Chinese clans taking shape during this period.[26] Though Chengdu certainly did not realize this, with the appearance of Liu Yuan we hear the first sounds of a great turning of the gears of the politics of East Asia. Border groups had for centuries served as mercenary units in the armies of the Chinese empire. They now began the process of ceasing to be pawns on other men's chessboards, and instead to make themselves kings, at times queens. "The men of the Sima clan tear at each other," said a kinsman of Liu Yuan, "[all between] the four seas is in turmoil—now is the time to resume the enterprise of Huhanye!," the Xiongnu monarch who in the middle of the first century BCE had restored his empire's unity.[27] Persuaded, Liu Yuan now allowed himself to be raised up as Chanyu of the Xiongnu. He was, however, a cosmopolite, well acquainted with the Chinese world; his son, Liu Cong, is said to have lived in Luoyang as a boy, and was as adept at composing in written Chinese as he was at pulling a bow. As noted above, the family name Liu had, in fact, been taken on the basis of claimed kinship with the Han imperial house. At a later point in ongoing discussion of what his state might be, the Xiongnu Chanyu asked, "how does it suffice to take Huhanye as my model?" Instead, "a real man would be as [emperor] Gao[zu] of the Han, or [emperor] Wu of the Wei," the founders respectively of Han and the Wei regime of the Cao family.[28] The regime Liu Yuan went on to found—the first of the so-called Sixteen Kingdoms—would be called "Han"; he claimed not conquest but restoration. Still, he did have an army, composed of men called up from the Five Divisions of Southern Xiongnu that had been settled in Shanxi, and of "unclassified Hu," various groups of Central or Inner Asian ancestry scattered through Shanxi and Shaanxi.[29] This was a complex lot, drawn to service no doubt by a mix of monies and loyalties. Though Liu Yuan maintained some sort of discipline until his natural death, not long thereafter, control quickly slipped from his heirs into hands much more rough and ready.

Though Liu Yuan's ambitions are said to have taken shape in response to Chengdu's request, the prince seems to have remained unaware of them, and unaware that no support would be forthcoming from the Xiongnu leader. The matter became moot when advance units of Wang Jun's cavalry suddenly

26. On the Taiyuan Wangs, see Fan Zhaofei 范兆飞, *Zhong gu Taiyuan shi zu qun ti yan jiu* 中古太原士族群体研究 (Beijing: Zhonghua shu ju, 2014).
27. ZZTJ 85.2699; JS 101.2647. The first clause is literally 今司馬氏骨肉相殘.
28. ZZTJ 85.2701; JS 101.2649.
29. ZZTJ 85.2699; JS 101.2647.

appeared outside the Ye walls. The Prince of Chengdu's army now collapsed, and with a guard of just a few dozen men, and the unfortunate Huidi once again in tow, he fled south to Luoyang, some 200 miles away. Ye was taken by Wang Jun's Wuhuan and Serbi auxiliaries, and brutally plundered. Outraged when he discovered some had kidnapped Ye women and were transporting them back to the frontier, Wang executed thousands of the frontiersmen by having them thrown into the Yi River (north of mod. Baoding, Hebei).[30] This sort of soldier would not be serving Jin lords much longer. But he was becoming all the more needed by the contestants of the Jin power struggle. Though not connected to Wang Jun, it was at this time that the Taghbach began to play a minor role in the wars of the Chinese territories, as yet another scion of the Sima line, the Duke of Dongying, serving at Taiyuan as Inspector of Bingzhou, turned to the brothers Yituo and Yilu for military aid. After defeating forces of the Xiongnu ruler Liu Yuan in a minor skirmish in southwestern Shanxi, the two Taghbach lords formed a pact with the Sima duke, as independent equals.[31]

This was an age in which, through military action, "those below overcame those above" 下克上. As we see at great length in this book, this was certainly true of groups long peripheralized and dominated by the power and wealth of the Chinese empire; though a man of pedigree within the Xiongnu world, Liu Yuan was certainly looked down upon by many at least of the men of Jin. At any rate, *gekokujō* also applied to the Chinese everyman. Though he left no great progeny, and may not have been viewed as particularly eminent, Zhang Fang was a poor boy who had risen to power in the employ of the Prince of Hejian, the Sima who had gone west to take control of Guanzhong.[32] It will be remembered that in his previous residence in the grand and ancient city of Luoyang, Zhang had burnt alive the Prince of Changsha. He had since returned to that metropolis to hold it for his lord.

Having crossed the River, the emperor and the Prince of Chengdu were met by Zhang Fang and a force of 10,000 horsemen in the Mangshan hills north of Luoyang. Zhang now installed the emperor once again in the palace, and "those who had fled gradually returned; in rough form at least the imperial officialdom was complete."[33] Whatever that officialdom may have still been conducting, however, the Prince of Chengdu no longer had Huidi under his control, and was no longer a part of the decision-making process.

With the emperor as cultural capital, Zhang had taken possession of something more precious than the ancient, battered imperial capital; some sort of

30. ZZTJ 85.2701; JS 39.1147.
31. ZZTJ 85.2701. For Yilu's later alliance with Liu Kun, discussed in Chapter 5, see ZZTJ 87.2752–53.
32. For Zhang Fang's biography, see JS 60.1644–46. Zhang was originally himself from Hejian (seat near mod. Xianxian, northern Shandong), and had traveled west to Guanzhong with his prince. Of the two terms in the title of Miščević's "Oligarchy or Social Mobility," it is the latter that has the greater import in this example at least.
33. ZZTJ 85.2701; JS 44.1258.

power lay, it seems, in control of the individual to whom had been affixed the 500-year-old title "august god-king," *huang di*. Fortunately, it was a mobile treasure, since his men—a motley assortment, no doubt, of westerners—were tiring of Luoyang. All that could be looted, we are told, had more or less been looted. As clamor and complaint rose within the ranks, Zhang ordered that the imperial carriage be prepared. Tracked down to his hiding place in a bamboo grove in the back garden, the weeping emperor was forced to climb up into it.[34] Zhang's troops now carried out a final round of spoliation, seizing the women of the rear apartments while they fought over what was left in the treasury. The palace's silk hangings were cut up to use as saddle blankets. Intending to go on to burn the palaces and the imperial family's ancestral shrine—so that none might think of return—Zhang was dissuaded by the only official who had remained with the emperor, the rest having once again scattered. "Bitter talk still remains a hundred years later" of the burning of Luoyang by Dong Zhuo at the end of Han, the fellow cautioned. "For what reason would you want to inherit [that mantle]?"[35]

"Bandits are everywhere," Zhang Fang now said to the emperor, when explaining why he was being moved out of the city to the fortified encampment (*lei* 壘) Zhang had built nearby.[36] The "bandits" were, of course, Zhang's own men, against whom Luoyang's huge walls—which measured about 2.5 miles north-south, 2 miles east-west[37]—could no longer protect. After three days of rape and looting, the emperor, as well as the Prince of Chengdu, took their places in a great wagon train that Zhang Fang now led to Chang'an. There the Prince of Hejian received Huidi, and set him up in a "palace" that was in fact the prince's military headquarters.[38] And here we shall for a time detach ourselves from this ongoing parade of sorrows; with the exception of the Prince of Donghai—the leader of the failed attack on Ye, whom we shall briefly see again below—all the actors seen so far would soon be killed.

* * *

Fleeing human tragedy, we will for a time at least turn to architecture. In this century, the most significant examples of the art of building were not temples nor palaces, but fortresses, both symbol and substance of atomization of the societies that had for centuries been bound together within the empire.

---

34. ZZTJ 85.2704; JS 60.1645.
35. ZZTJ 85.2704; JS 44.1258.
36. ZZTJ 85.2704 (for location of the fort, about two miles west of the city, see Hu Sanxing's note at ZZTJ 87.2763); JS 60.1645.
37. The figures are very rough: for more precise figures of the Cao Wei walls on which the walls of the Jin city were based, see the estimates given by Dien, *Six Dynasties Civilization*, 25; and Victor Xiong, *Capital Cities and Urban Form in Pre-modern China: Luoyang, 1038 BCE to 938 CE* (London and New York: Routledge, 2017), Chapter 3.
38. ZZTJ 85.2705; JS 4.104.

Zhang Fang's fort outside of Luoyang was far from unique; hundreds of strongholds big and small had been built within the territories of the crumbling empire. Little ceramic models are frequently found in tombs of this age. Just one random sample set would be the string of them found along the Luo River, which emerging from the eastern end of the Qinling Mountains, just some fifty miles across the peaks from Chang'an, led northeast past Luoyang (the city on the "north bank of the Luo"), then up to the Yellow River. The valley of the Luo River was one path of march for invaders—or refugees—going back and forth between the Yellow River Plain and the valley of the Wei River. During the period under discussion it was littered with fortifications. Some lay east of Luoyang,[39] but proceeding west from the city, going upriver through steep mountains—as did the army of the Jiankang general, Liu Yu, in the early fifth century[40]—one would first pass by the Yunzhongwu 雲中塢, the "fortress in the clouds," where mists swirled around the high peaks (west of mod. Yiyang, Henan), then soon come upon the "one [makes it] complete" fortress (*yi quan wu* 一全塢), which though on tableland was surrounded by peaks so steep that one wall on the western side was all that was needed to keep the site secure.[41] Another ten or twenty miles west (near mod. Luoning), and about a mile and a half south of the river, was "the fortress of Golden Gate [Mountain]" (*Jinmen wu* 金門塢), with another further west on Tan Mountain (檀山), on whose lofty peak was "a fortified assembly place" 有塢聚.[42]

The fortresses had begun to take shape centuries before. In terms of both symbol and substance, they were a countercurrent to the model used by early Chinese empire-builders, who beginning in the Warring States period had made effective efforts to eliminate all middlemen in the establishment of a direct relationship between the monarch and his subjects, the solid base of the lord's power, providing him with tax and labor service, including military duty.[43] In this model, fortified structures were built by the monarch, as both local seat of his control and expression of his power. These imposed structures would continue for a century or so under Han, before local interest and local power began seriously to reassert itself within the Chinese world.

As seen in Chapter 3, during the Warring States period and into the early Han, in addition to the walled cities that were the administrative centers of commandery (*jun*) and district (*xian*), there were also fortified outposts on the frontiers. These went by various names, but perhaps the most common was *wu*

---

39. *Shui jing zhu shu* 15.1321, 1317–18.
40. From records of this Jiankang campaign came much of the information given in *Shui jing zhu shu* 15, the source of this section.
41. *Shui jing zhu shu* 15.1302, 1301.
42. *Shui jing zhu shu* 15.1298, 1296.
43. Mark Edward Lewis, *The Construction of Space in Early China* (Albany: State University of New York Press, 2006), 213.

坞 (or *wu bi* 坞壁), which meant "small fortification" (*xiao zhang* 小障) or "small enceinte" (*xiao cheng* 小城).[44]

Following the reign of the Han emperor Wudi, as over the centuries central power slowly declined, such *wu bi* began to appear in the interior, built not by the state, as outposts of state power, but as private constructions, for private interests. In many instances at least, it would be fair to call the *wu bi* "castles," in the sense of inhabited strongholds of independent local leaders struggling on their own to survive in the midst of war and disorder.[45] Some saw the fortified outposts as a form of liberation from state control: it was noted long ago that the real forts were inspiration for the "Peach Blossom Spring" fable of the poet Tao Yuanming (365–427).[46]

The first major building of such independent fortifications in the empire's interior came in the midst of the civil war provoked by the usurpation of Wang Mang (r. 9–23, as lord of the "New" dynasty), and more particularly by his efforts to use policies cloaked in the language of the ancients to reassert central control over growing local power. Han was restored by the emperor Guangwu (r. 25–57), who having emerged from among the power networks of the Henan region moved his capital from the Wei valley to Luoyang, on the western edge of the Yellow River plains. The restorer also ordered the abandonment and destruction of the castles.[47] His regime, however, was markedly different from the Former Han, being a coalition of local powers, though an enduring one. The armies were different too. Though in fact long disused, universal conscription was under Guangwu formally brought to an end.[48] Imperial troops were now made up of recruits, or local militias and private armies—or, more and more, non-Chinese mercenaries from the frontier regions.

In spite of—or perhaps because of—the lessening of central control, the Later Han saw significant economic growth, though as often happens with Gross Imperial Product, distribution of wealth was very uneven. Bankruptcy abounded and more and more land fell into fewer and fewer hands. These estates were in general at least not continuous, but wide-reaching patchworks of land, worked by sharecroppers for the sake of greatholders, in whose households were increasing numbers of slaves, servants, and private soldiers (*bu qu* 部曲).[49] Accompanying this were significant drops in taxable populations on the tax rolls: in the commandery of Yingchuan (southeast of Luoyang) for instance, one

---

44. See fuller discussion of the terms' meaning in Ku Saek-hŭi 具聖姬, *Liang Han Wei Jin Nan Bei chao de wu bi* 兩汉魏晋南北朝的坞壁 (Beijing: Min zu chu ban she, 2004), 9.

45. Ku, *Wu bi*, 37. For R. Allen Brown, *English Castles* (London: B. T. Batsford, 1962), 17, the definition of a "castle," in England at least, was that it was "the private fortress and residence of a lord."

46. See Chen Yinke 陳寅恪, "Tao hua yuan ji pang zheng" 桃花源記旁證, in his *Chen Yinke xian sheng quan ji*, 2 vols. (Taibei: Jiu si chu ban you xian gong si, 1977), 2: 1169–78.

47. Ku, *Wu bi*, 11, citing Yuan Hong 袁宏 (d. ca. 376), *Hou Han ji* 後漢記 juan 4: 壞其營壘，無使復聚.

48. Lewis, "Han Abolition of Universal Military Service," 33–36.

49. These were heritable: see examples given in JS 57.1563, 1552.

of the richest in the empire, the number of mouths on the tax rolls went from more than 2.2 million in Former Han down to fewer than 1.5 in the dynasty's second act.⁵⁰ Nevertheless, for a century or so a balance of power was maintained, the imperial center still possessing enormous resources of which the emerging local powers wished to avail themselves.

The situation began to change in the 160s, with growing tension between office-holding members of the local elites—with their expanding regional networks—and the inner Han court, increasingly manned by the ultimate outsider, the eunuch.⁵¹ In 169, in the famous purge mentioned above, the Great Proscription, large numbers of the former were barred from holding bureaucratic office at the capital, Luoyang. Returning to their towns and villages, such men now began to play two sorts of roles. In coming decades they would serve as leaders of communities struggling for physical survival in the midst of increasing chaos, using the small forts under discussion to repulse bandits, refugees, and perhaps the armies that marched back and forth across the lowlands, if those armies were in a hurry.⁵²

Some, at least, took local leadership a step further. The Han state had been instrumental in establishing as canon the Chinese classics, which at least purported to be description of perfect social and political order created by wise men of the past. With a growing vacuum of the center, educated gentlemen now took for themselves the authority of the canon and its texts, and on this basis in their own local communities (*xiao tong*) solidified for their troubled age a Ru morality, centered on duty to family and parents, "filial piety" (*xiao*).⁵³ Men such as Cui Hong thus played roles loosely comparable to text and ritual masters in other societies, even without the explicitly religious character of Abrahamic scripture or the clearly defined function of a Brahmin.⁵⁴ And having on this basis established

---

50. See Appendix 2 in Luo Tonghua 羅彤華, *Han dai de liu min wen ti* 漢代的流民問題 (Taibei: Taiwan xue sheng shu ju, 1989), 296, 303; and the description of Yingchuan in Howard L. Goodman, "Sites of Recognition: Burial, Mourning, and Commemoration in the Xun Family of Yingchuan, AD 140–305," *EMC* 15 (2009): 55–60. Overall, the empire's taxable population fell by more than 10 million, from almost 60,000,000 to just a little more than 47 (Luo, *Han dai de liu min*, 302, 309). The drop was even more dramatic in frontier commanderies like Yunzhong, which went from more than 173,000 in Former Han down to fewer than 27,000 (299, 306). In the latter case, at least, it certainly was southward flight, though part at least of the population of Han subjects was replaced by groups unwilling to register for Han's levies.

51. Lewis, *The Early Chinese Empires*, 27.

52. See a mid-sixth-century anecdote of an army passing by such a little fort, in Scott Pearce, "Who and What Was Hou Jing?," *EMC* 6 (2000): 69. Chen Shuang 陈爽 discusses what did remain of local military power in the Yellow River area in his "Lue lun Bei chao de xiang cun wu zhuang" 略论北朝的乡村武装, in *1–6 shi ji Zhongguo bei fang bian jiang, min zu, she hui guo ji xue shu yan tao hui lun wen ji*, ed. Jilin daxue gu ji yan jiu suo (Beijing: Ke xue chu ban she, 2008), 299–311.

53. See description of these processes, beginning in the Han and extending into the early medieval, in Keith Knapp, *Selfless Offspring: Filial Children and Social Order in Early Medieval China* (Honolulu: University of Hawai'i Press, 2005). If not the same, a similar line of thought was pursued by Tanigawa Michio in his studies of medieval Chinese community (*kyōdōtai*) and its leaders; see comments in Chapter 2 note 2.

54. For discussion of the power of text in the Chinese world, see Mark Edward Lewis, *Writing and Authority in Early China* (Albany: State University of New York Press, 1999), who says among other things that "the final triumph of the textual realm over the administrative reality did not take place until the fall of the Han. . . . Opposition

authority in their own village, they went beyond to serve a greater community (*da tong*).⁵⁵ To pick up on issues raised in the Introduction, it is the larger, Chinese-speaking community these men built around this canon and the ethical systems that evolved out of it, alongside and at least roughly coterminous with particular forms of social organization and administrative control formed under the empire and surviving beyond, that for this volume defines the boundaries of "Chinese" vis-à-vis other peoples in the East Asian world in this age.⁵⁶

Another, quite different alternative to the growing central vacuum appeared fifteen years later. This was the rebellion of the Yellow Turbans, an early form of Daoist religion, which Cui Yan experienced firsthand. Though eventually suppressed, the uprising led, of course, to decades of civil war among emergent military leaders, from which emerged new regional powers: in Sichuan the Shu regime (221–263), on the middle and lower Yangtze, the Wu (222–280), while the northern territories of Han—which would for a while longer still be the core regions of the Chinese world—were ruled by the "regent," Cao Cao, who until his death in 220 allowed a Han scion to sit on the throne. In 220, Cao Cao's heir ended the compromise, establishing a new Wei dynasty (220–265). In the course of these decades of civil war within a failing empire, the landscape came once again to be dotted with castles. And though the major contestants were still Chinese, the armies were increasingly made up of horsemen of Inner Asian derivation.⁵⁷ In the case of the Han Chancellor Dong Zhuo, who is remembered mostly for massacring the residents of Luoyang in 190 CE and then carrying the

---

[to the court] took the form of networks of local families bound together through ties of teacher and disciple. They were committed, with more or less sincerity, to textual studies that defined them and constituted their claim to authority. Thus when the reality of imperial power collapsed, it survived as a dream, or rather as a mass of signs, in the parallel realm formed by the canon and its associated texts. Only by recreating the order articulated in these literary works could the great families secure the honored states and the income from office that were essential to their continuity. Having been disseminated from the old philosophical traditions to the new elite through the agency of the state, the textual dream at last swallowed up the political reality" (10–11). More generally, Goody, *The Power of the Written Tradition*, 56, points out that "[w]riting helps to change not only orthodoxy but the notion of orthodoxy and, I believe, of truth and identity." Some sense of the authority held by text masters is seen in Herbert Fingarette's *Confucius: The Secular as Sacred* (New York: Harper & Row, 1972); and on the Ru canon, see Nylan, *The Five "Confucian" Classics*.

55. Note that "great community," *da tong*, using variant characters 大同, 大統, etc., appears repeatedly in era names of sixth-century regimes, of both the south and the north.

56. Li Jizhong 李继忠 and Niu Jin 牛劲 do quite a good job describing the main shape of the Chinese tradition, in this period at least, in their *Bei Wei she hui sheng huo zhi liu bian* 北魏社会生活之流变 (Changchun: Jilin da xue chu ban she, 2009), 3–4. As seen in the Introduction, in discussion of Chittick's *The Jiankang Empire*, there are many possibilities for definition of such terms as "Chinese," or "China." One useful set of approaches to this complex issue is to be had in Mullaney et al., eds., *Critical Han Studies: The History, Representation, and Identity of China's Majority*. In one chapter in that book, "*Hushuo*: The Northern Other and the Naming of the Han Chinese," Mark Elliott puts forth the interesting idea that while "Hu" was a Chinese invention, placed upon peoples to the north, "so the name 'Han'—that is, a label for people who, by descent, language and cultural practice, were recognized as Central Plains dwellers (or their descendants)—was largely the invention of the people of the steppe" (174). Elliott is in part building on the work of Yang, "Becoming Zhongguo, Becoming Han," who suggests this took full shape during the Northern Dynasties.

57. Jin, *Yongjia luan hou*, 48.

Han emperor off to the old capital of Chang'an, mercenaries were also drawn from among the Qiang, a group related to Tibetans who had for centuries been entering Han's northwestern territories. To secure his power at Chang'an, Dong also constructed at the western end of the Wei River valley a huge redoubt, with ramparts supposedly "as high as the walls of Chang'an," with storage for grain that would last 30 years.[58] He did not live long enough to enjoy the stores, being killed in 192, just two years after his arrival in Guanzhong.

But the most numerous constructions came in the midst of the final collapse of the empire, in the quarter century or so of fratricidal power struggles that followed the death of the Jin emperor Wudi in 290. Above we've given a glimpse of this; below we jump ahead five or six years to turn our eyes to the fall of Luoyang, which if not the cause of the empire's collapse was certainly a prominent symptom.

* * *

The year 310 that we borrow here from the Christian calendar was in the Chinese world the roughly overlapping fourth year of "eternal excellence," Yongjia 永嘉, the reign title of the new Jin emperor, Huaidi (r. 307–311). Things, however, were not excellent in Luoyang in this year. Huaidi and the Prince of Donghai coexisted there uneasily, amid rumors that Huaidi's predecessor, the "gentle emperor," had been poisoned by the prince. Since the previous year, armies led by the new ruler of the Xiongnu Han, Liu Cong (r. 310–318)—the one as able to read a Chinese book as pull a bow—had made forays against Luoyang from his base in the Shanxi highlands, though each was halted by unexpected reverses. Worsening the situation was a widespread infestation of locusts that in the summer of 310 had descended upon Luoyang and adjacent regions, "eating the plants, [so that the] cattle, horses and all the furry [beasts] died."[59] By early winter of that year "starvation in the capital grew daily worse. The Grand Mentor, [the Prince of Donghai, Sima] Yue, sent out messengers with emergency imperial summons[60] to call up troops from throughout the empire. The emperor addressed the messengers, saying, 'Tell all the campaign [generals], and those of the garrisons: today they can still save [us]; if later, then [they] won't make it.'"[61] Perhaps not surprisingly in this age of private militias, used for private interests, no armies arrived. One who still did see himself as a servant of the crown was the General of Southern Campaign, who from his base at Xiangyang (on the location of the modern city of the same name in Hubei) tried to send an army up to Luoyang. It was, however, cut off and defeated by a local rival, and the loyalist soon after driven from

---

58. SGZ 6.176.
59. ZZTJ 87.2749; JS 5.120.
60. More literally the "feathered, or winged, summons" (*yuxi* 羽檄), a call-to-arms with a feather attached to indicate need for immediate response: *HYDCD* 9: 641.
61. ZZTJ 87.2754; JS 5.121.

the city. Upon hearing of this, another army marching up from Jiangling (mod. Jiangling, Hubei) crumbled and then retreated.[62]

Rampaging through this turmoil, repeatedly leading his troops back and forth across the River, was an independent general who had come to be called Shi Le. Offspring of minor chieftains of Central Asian origin, long settled in the Shanxi highlands, Shi, along with many others, had been captured and sold into slavery by a Sima—the Duke of Dongying at Taiyuan, whom we've seen before negotiating with Yituo and Yilu—who thus raised monies to buy an army.[63] Though not central to the economy, enslavement was widespread in the empire in this time, and regularly drew on non-Chinese peoples; it was not for nothing that in Chinese the name "Xiongnu" means "fierce slave," or that in the Jiankang history *Song shu*, the chapter dedicated to the Taghbach was called "Braid-headed Caitiffs."[64] Shi Le, however, escaped, and went on to join a group of bandits—whose leader gave him the Chinese-style name Shi Le[65]—before submitting himself to the Xiongnu lord Liu Yuan. Shi began building his own army in 307. Liu Yuan had repeatedly tried to win over a Wuhuan leader holed up with an army of 2,000 in a fortress in the mountains east of Taiyuan, one of the many fortifications that dotted these highlands, built by Chinese and non-Chinese leaders alike.[66] Failing to coax the Wuhuan from their perch, the Xiongnu lord now sent Shi Le, under the pretense he was fleeing a crime. Accepted by the Wuhuan leader, he soon became commander of the fellow's troops, won their loyalty, and in the end—knowing the answer already—asked them whom they would prefer as their lord.[67] Liu Yuan then "bestowed" the army upon Shi. It was undoubtedly his anyway. His connection to the Xiongnu state was always contingent on his own willingness. In the end, of course, the willingness ended. In the meantime, in the name of the Liu regime, he defeated a series of local lords in their enceintes, absorbing their armies into his own.

In 310, with the city of Luoyang starving, the leaders of Donghai's forces came to talk with their prince; interestingly, though not clearly identified they are described as "[those in] military garb," *rong fu* 戎服, a term that could

---

62. ZZTJ 87.2754.
63. JS 104.2707–8. Note Shi Le's use as an unfree farmer.
64. As an example, we see the *pipa*-playing Ruan Xian's infatuation with a "Serbi slave girl" 鮮卑婢: *Shi shuo xin yu jiao jian* 世說新語校箋, comp. Xu Zhen'e 徐震堮 (Taibei: Wen shi zhe chu ban she, 1985), 23.395; tr. by Richard Mather, *A New Account of Tales of the World* (Minneapolis: University of Minnesota Press, 1976), 376–77 (with reference to JS 49.1362–64). The girl belonged to his aunt, and after fulfilling his infatuation he is said to have written the aunt, telling her that "The Hu barbarian slave girl has now given birth to a Hu barbarian son." For another example of reference to Serbi as slave, see *Shi shuo xin yu jiao jian* 27.456 (Mather, tr. *New Account*, 443). And see also Huang, "Tuoba Xianbei zao qi guo jia," 84–90.
65. ZZTJ 86.2710; JS 104.2709.
66. For discussion of *wu bi* controlled by non-Chinese, see Zhang Mingming 张明明 and Fan Zhaofei 范兆飞, "Shi liu guo Bei Wei shi qi de wu bi jing ji" 十六国北魏时期的坞壁经济, *Zhongguo she hui jing ji shi yan jiu* (2011.2): 14–21.
67. ZZTJ 86.2732; JS 104.2710.

also mean "barbarian garb." The wish of these men was to take the army from Luoyang—nestled in the far southwestern corner of the Yellow River plains—down to Xuchang, about 100 miles to the southeast, where they could block Shi Le's roamings. No doubt they also wished to go to a place that could better supply them food. Though Donghai was convinced, the emperor was not, saying, "the altars of the dynasty rest on Your Lordship—how can you go far off, and so abandon the [imperial] seat?"[68] Replying that it was for the best, Donghai marched east with 40,000 men, and most of what was left of the government. Left in a city increasingly gripped by hunger was the emperor, as well as Donghai's wife and son. Bodies, we are told, began to pile up in the throne halls. Bandits openly prowled the streets.

Bypassing Xuchang, Donghai now based his army and tent government in a fortified district seat another 100 miles southeast. There, four months later, he died. The reason given is grief for two comrades, killed by a Jin rival acting on the command of the very angry emperor. If it was actually sorrow that killed the man, the roots may have gone much deeper. Tribulations, goes a Chinese proverb, don't come singly. For Donghai, they followed into death. His army now became a huge funerary procession, conveying the prince back to his fief in Shandong. In a tableau that seems scripted for a B movie, the procession was intercepted by Shi Le at "Peaceful Town" (Ningping cheng 寧平城, the mod. Ningpingzhen, Henan) in "Bitter District" (Kuxian 苦縣).[69] Encircled by Shi's cavalry, in the face of a withering rain of arrows, Jin troops trampled and climbed up on each other. In the end, we are told, all that was left was a hill of corpses. A string of princes and lords were now brought forward to be interrogated by Shi Le as to what had befallen Jin. Answering with whining pleas, each was rewarded with a blade's edge. One, however, stood apart, replying with the brief and solemn comment that "what more babbling is needed about today's events?" At first wishing to spare this fellow, Shi Le was in the end dissuaded by a lieutenant who pointed out that "in the end we will have no use for the Jin princes." He was, however, spared the dishonor of decapitation, instead being put to death by having a wall pushed over upon him. Now turning to the dead, Shi Le burnt Donghai's coffin, proclaiming that "this man"—and all his kinsmen—"has brought chaos down upon the world, and it is for the world that I take vengeance."

Back in the famine-wracked city of Luoyang, few now were left. Hearing of the death of their patriarch, Donghai's wife and son had fled, accompanied by most of what was left of the capital's guard units. "Gentlemen and commoners in the city," we are told, "struggled [to be allowed] to accompany them."[70] Traveling

---

68. ZZTJ 87.2755; JS 5.121.
69. ZZTJ 87.2760–61; JS 59.1625–26.
70. ZZTJ 87.2760.

east, however, they too soon encountered Shi Le. Battle took the son, while the wife was sold as part of the plunder, though in the end she made her way to the court-in-exile that had already begun to take shape at Jiankang, where she was well treated.[71] As for the emperor, though eager to take up an invitation to relocate to one of the remaining Jin outposts in the east, the plan fell through as his aides, clinging to their belongings 左右戀資財, delayed departure.[72] And then it was too late.

The end of this particular episode in the much longer tale of Luoyang's rises and falls came in the summer of the fifth year of Eternal Excellence, the year 311 of the Common Era. Sent south by Liu Cong from the Han capital of Pingyang in southern Shanxi (near mod. Linfen) was the campaign's main force of 27,000, led by the Xiongnu lord Huyan Yan. Unsuccessful in the past, on this occasion the army swept all resistance before it as it headed south.[73] Though it was planned they would be joined by allied armies after crossing the River, the others had not yet arrived, so after storing his cargo train at Zhang Fang's fortress, Huyan proceeded to the walls of Luoyang. The next day he launched attack on the central-southern gate in the city's outer walls.[74] Perhaps like the empire itself, it was still standing, though with no one left to protect it: despite the lack of much if any of a defense, it was a powerful physical structure, locked and bolted, which took the Xiongnu army two days to pry open. Having breached the outer walls, the army now proceeded to burn government offices and other outer gates. But though they had very little food there to feed them, the emperor and what remained of his party were protected by one, perhaps two sets of inner walls; and the areas of the outer city into which the Xiongnu had penetrated was itself a vast warren of walls within walls within walls.[75]

After just one day inside the city, Huyan withdrew, though in departure he burnt the boats sitting on the Luo River to forestall any attempt by the emperor to escape. Part of the motivation for his retreat may have been fear that he himself would be trapped inside the great urban maze. But the main reason given was that the supposed allies still had not arrived. The armies of the Xiongnu Han were not particularly well coordinated, major divisions being the individual possessions of several men with several ambitions. These included the Chinese Wang Mi, grandson of an imperial governor who had himself turned on the Jin; the Xiongnu Liu Yao (r. 318–329), a cousin of the House of Han who would years later take its throne, and change its name to Zhao; and Shi Le (r. 319–333), who at the same time would take for himself the eastern half of the realm, and then the whole of it. In the Luoyang campaign,

71. ZZTJ 87.2761–62.
72. ZZTJ 87.2762
73. ZZTJ 87.2763.
74. See the map provided in Xiong, *Capital Cities and Urban Form*, 67.
75. For the inner walls, see Xiong, *Capital Cities and Urban Form*, 66.

we see among these men some cooperation, as well as some conflict. Though the fall of Luoyang is occasionally ascribed to him by modern historians, Shi Le in fact never did join in the united attack on the city. Wang Mi did, arriving four days after Huyan's withdrawal to place his army at another gate on the southern outer wall, and the day after that Liu Yao encamped his men at a western gate. Here we get a sense of the enormity of the city, the attackers being little encampments at particular gates among the dozen that regulated traffic through the main, outer walls. Five days on, the forces of Huyan and Wang joined together. Entering the outer walls, they then forced their way into the inner city and entered the imperial palace, ascending to the Grand Culmen (Taiji 太極) throne hall, which in cosmological terms was held by those who believed these things to be at one and the same time the center, source, and peak of the entire universe.[76] Its loftiness did not prevent Wang and Huyan from releasing their troops to pillage, though as we have seen above there cannot have been much left to take. More practically, Liu Yao would soon after breach his gate in the west wall and head straight for the Armory.

Exiting as they entered, the emperor now fled out the Floral Grove Garden in the city's northeast corner, hoping to escape and make it to Chang'an. He was, however, soon tracked down and imprisoned in one of the city's gatehouses.[77] He would later be sent, with his great seals of office, up to the Xiongnu capital at Pingyang. The heir apparent was not so lucky, being killed immediately, along with numerous princes and lords. In all, we are told, some 30,000 died in the massacres that followed the taking of the city, perhaps a tenth of its original population.[78] The problem with this number comes from wondering why that many would have stayed in the city in the midst of repeated seizures and lootings over the past decade, more recently compounded by severe famine. Flight and vagrancy would, of course, have had their own problems: earlier in this same year, a brother of the Jin prime minister had solved a refugee crisis down in Hubei by drowning 8,000 of them in the Yangtze.[79] If the figure of 30,000 killed in Luoyang is correct, we might well assume that most of the remaining population died. For the eminent dead, death was given again, as the palace's ancestral shrine was burnt, and the bodies of former emperors disinterred from the imperial tombs in the hills north of the city.

The city had been destroyed before, and would of course be destroyed again. But these events do mark the final collapse of the first Chinese empire. The news

---

76. ZZTJ 87.2763. On the imperial palace, or "Southern Palace," see Xiong, *Capital Cities and Urban Form*, 66; on the Grand Culmen "Basilica," 63.

77. ZZTJ 87.2763. On the Floral Grove Garden, see Xiong, *Capital Cities and Urban Form*, 64.

78. Xiong, *Capital Cities and Urban Form*, 68, estimates a population that rose to the high 300,000s during the Jin period.

79. ZZTJ 87.2758.

shook the Asian world: "Saray (Luoyang)," wrote an eastern Iranian merchant in consternation to a friend in Samarkand, "is no more!"[80]

But though Luoyang, for a time at least, was "no more"—the empire's head lopped off of the body—the structures of empire, for organizing and taxing subjects, survived, in at least a vestigial form. Much of Northern Wei history is wrapped up in efforts to use these structures, as well as questions as to how much they should be used.

---

80. W. B. Henning, "The Date of the Sogdian Ancient Letters," *BSOAS* 12.3/4 (1948): 605; Arthur Waley, "Lo-yang and its Fall," in his *The Secret History of the Mongols, and Other Pieces* (New York: Barnes and Noble, 1964), 54–55.

9

The World Shegui Created

In the previous chapter we have seen the rich but ravaged world that Shegui would enter, in a series of snapshots of the past culminating in destruction of the city of Luoyang in 311. When Shegui arrived on the plains 85 years later, Luoyang was still in ruins. He did not even visit the site, although his descendant, the emperor Xiaowen, would a century later rebuild it and move his capital there. What Shegui did do, after conquest of the plains was complete in the first month of 398, was make a triumphal tour of his new holdings, lingering with particular interest in the great city of Ye.[1] He then gathered up a part of the riches he had won to carry back to the Datong Basin. This would have included grain and weapons seized in the cities taken from the Murong, who had themselves conquered them just a bit more than a decade before.[2] It also included tens of thousands of human beings, an early example of the many forced transportations by which Wei "filled out" an emerging "capital region" in the highlands.[3]

Ten thousand conscripts were sent to prepare a road leading from the region of modern Tangxian, Hebei, up into the mountains, which then connected with a string of valleys leading past the town of Lingqiu and on to the upper Sanggan.[4] Shortly thereafter, some 100,000 transportees were led north by Shegui and his army.[5] This must have been a grueling trek. The transportees were walking, in the dead of winter, along a just-cleared road some 300 miles long that rose thousands of feet up from the plains. In the *Wei shu* biography of Cui Hong, Shegui is depicted as something of a cheerleader, at one point climbing to the top of Mount Heng (the same peak Zhao's Merciless One had ascended) to urge his new subjects on. One can't help wondering what these people thought of

---

1. For an overview of Ye, see Niu Runzhen 牛润珍, *Gu du Yecheng yan jiu—zhong shi ji Dong Ya du cheng zhi du tan yuan* 古都邺城研究—中世纪东亚都城制度探源 (Beijing: Zhonghua shu ju, 2015).
2. WS 2.31.
3. WS 2.32. Lists of these transportations are seen in many sources: e.g., Su Bai 宿白, "Pingcheng shi li de ji ju he Yungang mo shi de xing cheng yu fa zhan" 平城实力的集聚和云岗模式的形成与发展, in *Zhongguo shi ku si yan jiu* (Beijing: Wen wu chu ban she, 1996), 115–18; Li, *Bei Wei Pingcheng shi dai*, 270–71. For a general discussion of these transportations, see Hori Toshikazu 堀敏一, *Kindensei no kenkyū: Chūgoku kodai kokka no tochi seisaku to tochi shoyūsei* 均田制の研究: 中国古代国家の土地政策と土地所有制 (Tokyo: Iwanami shoten, 1975), 99–107.
4. WS 2.31; and for further discussion of the road based on a tomb inscription, see Yin Xian 殷宪, "Gai Tianbao mu zhuan ming kao" 盖天保墓砖铭考, *Jinyang xue kan* (2008.3): 25–34.
5. ZZTJ 110.3462, 3463; WS 110.2849–50, 33.787, 2.31, 32. Various figures are given for these transportations: see WS, 46–47 note 9, which plausibly suggests the figure given in *Zi zhi tong jian*—100,000—is the more accurate.

him. Coming upon Cui Hong, the story continues, Shegui was so delighted to see him helping his aged mother cross the peaks on foot that he gave them rice and oxen for a cart, and insisted that others who could not proceed be allowed to ride in oxcarts as well.[6] Upon arrival several weeks later, most of these people were settled in the Datong Basin, the "royal domain" (*ji* 畿, or *jing yi* 京邑) that Shegui would formally establish shortly thereafter. Consisting essentially of the Datong Basin, the domain—the Land of Dai—extended from Yinguan in the south (which lay between the Sanggan and the north side of the Yanmen Pass) north to Shenhe; and from the hills of Shanwu (near mod. Youyu, Shanxi) east to the old Han Dai commandery (northeast of mod. Yuxian 蔚县, Hebei), which lay in one of the fingers of valley farmland that stretch east through the mountains.[7] In the middle of this domain, Shegui would half a year later begin work on a new "City of Pacification."

For a time all roads would lead up to Pingcheng.[8] While Daowu's Lingqiu Road led through the Taihangs from the southeast, more directly southern roads joined at the Yanmen Pass, their main point of access into the Datong Basin. From the east, a circuitous route rose precipitously up from the region now occupied by Beijing and its suburbs to the Upper Valley (Shanggu, mod. Yanqing), then proceeded up the Sanggan through the highlands to Pingcheng.[9] From Manchuria in the northeast was a route we have seen before, the one probably taken in 443 by Taiwu's envoy to the Gaxian Cave. From the steppe, one could enter the basin directly from the north, passing by the Shenhe Slope (near mod. Yanggao), or come from the northwest, crossing the Yinshan just north of the modern city of Hohhot through the "White Road" (Baidao 白道) Pass, which roughly followed the line of National Highway G209, then across the Tumed Plain to the upper Sanggan.[10] From the west, a key route came from the Gansu Corridor to cross the River in the region of modern Ningxia, then up along the edge of the Ordos past Tongwan and Yulin to cross the River again at the "Gentleman's Ford" (Junzi jin 君子津), where the Yellow River narrows south of the modern town of Lamawanzhen 喇嘛湾镇.[11]

---

6. WS 24.621.

7. WS 110.2850, 2.33. On the location of Shenhe as north of Yanggao, see Chapter 7 note 73.

8. To this assertion needs to be added that in another configuration of trade routes during this time, all roads certainly led to Jiankang, the hub of a vast array of waterworks and undoubtedly the richer of the two cities. See Liu Shufen 劉淑芬, *Liu chao de cheng shi yu she hui* 六朝的城市與社會 (Taibei: Taiwan xue sheng shu ju, 1992), Part 1. Reconstruction of the Pingcheng routes is taken from Maeda, *Heijō no rekishi chirigakuteki kenkyū*, Chapter 4, "Heijō o meguru kautsūro."

9. See map on Maeda, *Heijō*, 208.

10. Maeda, *Heijō no rekishi chirigakuteki kenkyū*, 145–50; and Matsushita Ken'ichi 松下憲一, "Baidao kao— Bei chao Sui Tang shi qi de cao yuan zhi dao" 白道考—北朝隋唐时期的草原之道, in *Wei Jin Nan bei chao shi de xin tan suo*, ed. Lou Jing (Beijing: Zhongguo she hui ke xue chu ban she, 2015), 489–99.

11. A recent volume of popular history on the Wei capital is called *"Starting Point for the Silk Roads": Si lu qi dian: Bei Wei Pingcheng* 丝路起点：北魏平城, ed. Datong gu cheng bao hu he xiu fu yan jiu hui (Taiyuan: Shanxi chu ban chuan mei ji tuan, 2016). The Datong Basin had long been an important trade center. Wang Yintian 王银田, "Si chou zhi lu yu Bei Wei Pingcheng" 丝绸之路与北魏平城, rpt. in *Bei Wei Pingcheng kao gu yan jiu*, ed. Wang

Some things would have gone out from Pingcheng—horses, furs, and the like—but almost certainly the largest export during this period was the army, which regularly marched forth to take possession of the stuff of richer worlds. A bridge over the Gentleman's Ford built by Taiwu was not to encourage commerce but for invasion of the Ordos.[12]

Pingcheng's imports, however, were voluminous and multivarious. From the north came sheep, cattle, and horses, herded past the Shenhe Slope, or down through Baidao Pass. A wave of cultural influence—objects to delight in and supposedly wise men and women to listen to—would come from the western lands seized with conquest of Northern Liang in 439, as monks and musicians and merchants with glass cups and silver plates decorated with Hellenistic themes came through the Gansu Corridor and then up past Yulin to Pingcheng. There they exercised significant influence for a generation or two, as seen in the spread of Buddhism, and the strongly Central Asian cast of the early Yungang caves.[13] Chinese influences from the south had, of course, begun even earlier with conquest of the Yellow River plains, when men of the book such as Cui Hong had been marched up to Pingcheng, along with much larger numbers of farmers, and the craftsmen who would do much of the building of monuments to Taghbach power. The influence would increase in later generations, as more and more manufactures and men, fashions, and ideas came north from the Chinese world.

Pingcheng was a rough cosmopolis, its streets filled with people of diverse sorts.[14] Moving along, on foot or on horse, would have been Serbi soldiers with their short jackets and trousers tucked into leather boots; Sogdian merchants, with beards and prominent noses; and Chinese gentlemen clad in gentlemen's robes.[15] It would have been a Babel, with people speaking Chinese and Eastern

---

Yintian et al. (Beijing: Ke xue chu ban she, 2017), 159, quotes a story of *Shi ji* (43.1818) from the Warring States period in which the King of Qi warned Zhao that if Qin was able to seize Dai, they could cut off trade from the region of the Kunlun Mountains in Central Asia.

12. WS 4A.72.

13. Okamura Hidenori 岡村秀典, *Unkō sekkutsu no kōkogaku: yūboku kokka no kyosekibutsu o saguru* 雲岡石窟の考古学: 遊牧国家の巨石仏をさぐる (Kyoto: Rinsen shoten, 2017), 51; Joy Lidu Yi, *Yungang: Art, History, Archaeology, Liturgy* (London and New York: Routledge, 2017), 38–48.

14. Yin Xian 殷宪 builds a description of the scene on the basis of a frieze found at Yungang: "Yungang shi ku suo fan ying de yi xie Bei Wei zheng zhi she hui qing kuang" 云岗石窟所反映的一些北魏政治社会情状, rpt. in his *Pingcheng shi gao*, 78–80. And see the section on the "Ethnic Complexity" of Pingcheng in Fan Zhang, "Cultural Encounters: Ethnic Complexity and Material Expression in Fifth-century Pingcheng, China" (PhD diss., New York University, 2018), 29–36.

15. For the dress of the Serbi, see Albert E. Dien, "Encounters with Nomads," in *Monks and Merchants: Silk Road Treasures from Northwest China; Gansu and Ningxia, 4th–7th Century*, ed. Annette L. Juliano and Judith A. Lerner (New York: Harry N. Abrams with the Asia Society, 2001), 62–63; and for clothing in this age more generally, Dien, *Six Dynasties Civilization*, Chapter 9, "Clothing." See also the excellent work by Zhu Dawei, *Wei Jin Nan bei chao she hui sheng huo shi*, Kindle ed., Chapter 2 and Chapter 12, Section 1, "Fu shi"; and Song Xin 宋馨 [Shing Müller], "Bei Wei Pingcheng qi de Xianbei fu" 北魏平城期的鲜卑服, in *4–6 shi ji de bei Zhongguo yu Ou Ya da lu*, ed. Zhang Qingjie et al. (Beijing: Ke xue chu ban she, 2006), 84–107. For Central Asians in Pingcheng, see Wang Yanqing 王雁卿, "Bei Wei Pingcheng Hu ren de kao gu xue guan cha" 北魏平城胡人的考古学观察, in *Zhongguo Wei Jin Nan Bei chao shi xue hui di shi jie nian hui ji guo ji xue shu yan tao hui lun wen ji*, ed. Zhongguo Wei Jin Nan bei chao shi xue hui, Shanxi da xue li shi wen hua xue yuan (Taiyuan: Beiyue wen yi chu ban she, 2012),

Iranian, the Khaghan's Serbi as well as other Inner Asian tongues. Moving freely among these men were women, who "filled the streets with their carriages, occupied the government offices with their fancy dresses, begged official posts for their sons and made complaints about injustice done to their husbands."[16] This was a world in continuous motion. Towers went up as places for announcement, and walls to surround populations. Fifty years later, pagodas stretched up to the sky, proclaiming a religion that great-grandfather had known only off-handedly. Moving among these were different groups, which were supposed to play different roles here, with distinct statuses defined by common as well as written law. And the authorities wished to keep it that way. But people from different classes and occupations mingled, sometimes married. Testament to their own ineffectiveness, one law after another was published banning such practices.[17]

Among the earliest to be forcibly transplanted into these environs had been true nomads, High Carts captured during the first decade of Shegui's reign and forcibly resettled in the band of grassland that lay between Pingcheng and the Gobi Desert to the north; having turned his own herdsmen into a soldiery, Shegui needed to impress steppe nomads to take over that role in his empire.[18] Most, at least, of these groups were left to govern themselves and raise livestock, while offering tribute each year to the khaghan.[19] Adding to these Inner Asian populations were Murong cavalrymen and their families, along with Koreans and other "assorted barbarians" 雜夷, all of whom had migrated onto the flatlands under the Yan regimes and were then brought north in the 398 forced march to serve their new Taghbach overlord.[20]

Various groups figured among the 100,000 thus relocated, but in terms of numbers—and in other ways as well—Chinese populations would play a particularly important role in the world Shegui was creating in the Datong Basin, and within the realm as a whole. The first Chinese participants in the Taghbach endeavor were adventurers who came willingly in the early fourth century, in the midst of the Jin collapse. One such figure was Wei Cao, seen above, a swashbuckling general who fleeing the disorders of the Eight Princes had come with his kith and kin seeking Taghbach protection, then after the death of Yituo

---

567-77; and Zhang Qingjie 张庆捷, *Min zu hui ju yu wen ming hu dong—Bei chao she hui de kao gu xue guan cha* 民族汇聚与文明互动—北朝社会的考古学观察 (Beijing: Shang wu yin shu guan, 2010), 141-227.

16. A famous comment made by Yan Zhitui 颜之推 in his book *Yan shi jia xun* (completed early Sui) regarding women at Ye, capital of the Northern Wei successor Qi: *Yan shi jia xun ji jie* 颜氏家训集解, comp. Wang Liqi (Shanghai: Shanghai gu ji chu ban she, 1980), 5.60; Teng Ssu-yü, tr. *Family Instructions for the Yen Clan* (Leiden: E. J. Brill, 1968), 19. Yan went on to say "Were these customs [not] handed down from Heng and Dai (i.e., the Pingcheng area)?"

17. E.g., WS 5.122.
18. See discussion of this in Chapter 7.
19. WS 103.2309.
20. See WS 2.32, 110.2849-50. In these passages, the Murong were referred to as Tuhe 徒何. Accompanying them were people from the Korean peninsula and "assorted barbarians," and craft workers.

wrote a series of ditties praising him and his brother Yilu for their support for the Sima against Liu Yuan. A contemporary was the rich merchant Mo Han, who living down by the Sanggan frequently went north to trade with the Taghbach, and then remained there when the Datong Basin was turned over to them by the Taiyuan governor.[21] Both of these men were valued by Yilu, the first King of Dai. Both fled after his death.

Several generations later, however, in the time of Daowu, the migrants had no choice. As seen in Chapter 3, involuntary transportations had also occurred under Qin and Han, including transportations to the frontier. But center and periphery had changed: while transportation under the Chinese empire was to solidify their northern edge against what men of Han at least considered a barbarian world, Shegui transported "new subjects" (*xin min* 新民) by the tens of thousands into his royal domain to help create the center of a new East Asian order. Within a few decades, it would grow to a million or more.[22]

While there were various kinds of new subjects—the High Carts also fell into that category—most were Chinese and most were set to till the soil in the Datong Basin, especially the more fertile land along the Sanggan. Counted, these people were given land 計口授田 and draft oxen.[23] In some sense an expansion of the Prince of Wey's *tuntian*, this would have led to a significant increase in grain cultivation within the royal domain. The men of the book to whom Shegui gave such attention—men such as Cui Hong—were separated out to do the counting of mouths and collecting of taxes.[24] Though not necessarily as swept away by the power of the Chinese classics propounded to him by Cui as some historians suggest, Shegui did make him director of a newly invented chancellery (*huang men shi lang*).

The power of this office, however, was very limited. This was the "outer court." Real power lay in the "inner court," and in the hands of princes and generals, who were overwhelmingly of Inner Asian descent. (The Inner Court will be discussed in more detail below.) Cui Hong's chancellery was, however, a platform on which Shegui wished to see development of institutions to control and tax the millions of households of farmers that had now come under Taghbach control.[25] Those

---

21. WS 23.600–2; WS 23.603–4.
22. Maeda, *Heijō no rekishi chirigakuteki kenkyū*, 28; Yin Xian, "Bei Wei Pingcheng shi lüe," 195; Ren Zhong 壬重, "Pingcheng de ju min gui mo yu Pingcheng shi dai de jing ji mo shi" 平城的居民規模与平城时代的经济模式, *Shi xue yue kan* (2002.3): 107–13.
23. WS 2.32, 24.621, 110.2850; ZZTJ 110.3465. Subjects of the now-absent Jin were not the only ones settled to farm: for an example of pastoralists who were also subjected to this, see the annals of Mingyuan in WS 3.53, which describes defeat of a group in the Ordos region, seizure of their horses and cattle, and then the forced transplantation of more than 20,000 families to farm in a high river valley northeast of the Shenhe Slope (near mod. Huaian).
24. As Peter Golden notes, the Mongols also regarded talented administrators as one of the spoils of war: *Central Asia*, 87.
25. Ge Jianxiong 葛劍雄 et al., *Zhongguo ren kou shi* 中国人口史, 6 vols. (Shanghai: Fudan da xue chu ban she, 2000–2002), 1: 475, points out that the population figures of *Wei shu* 106A&B, the "Di xing zhi," are not reliable, but estimates that the high point of Wei's population would have been about 35 million; the great majority, of course, were Chinese farmers. This figure is much lower than the 63 million of the (much larger) Former Han empire (1: 399), and approximately the (what Ge Jianxiong believes to be real) figure for Western Jin (1: 458).

transported into the domain directly under the khaghan's control became part of the "eight units (or cantons)" (*ba bu* 八部), whose leaders "encouraged them in their cultivation"—this must have included actually going out to inspect the villages—and collected taxes from them.[26] Though there is little direct evidence for the villages of Pingcheng, from the work of the modern scholar Hou Xudong in adjacent regions we can infer that down along the Sanggan there would have been dense networks of hamlets, perhaps some with low earthenware walls. The cottages, spaced out within the village, were small, 100–150 square feet, constructed of earthenware and wooden posts, with thatched roofs, or perhaps tile for the better-off.[27] Outhouses, corrals, and wells would have been adjacent.

Suitable for both farming and ranching, these lands were used for both. In the first several decades of Wei, stock-rearing and hunting continued to predominate, and to play an important role in feeding the army.[28] With continuing transportation of populations, however, the farming communities grew more numerous, and agriculture over time came to dominate the Dai economy.[29] Pastoralists themselves seem to have been turning more and more to agriculture, as seen in orders in the time of Taiwu for the well-off in settled groups to share oxen with their poorer kinsmen.[30] In one particularly dramatic incident, a Dai military man awaiting execution in the time of Taiwu is said to have told his younger brother that "the land north of the Sanggan is barren. [But] you can live south of the river and plough the good land [there]."[31] The rapid growth of agriculture in the basin of course had effects. In the fourth century the hills around the Datong Basin had had dense groves of elms and other trees, which seem to have had a religious dimension for the Taghbach. By the end of the fifth century, the peaks had been denuded as wood was cut there for construction. It seems likely that with growing population the less advantaged were forced to pick out a living on the sides of naked hillsides, which meant those hills no longer held

---

26. WS 110.2850; Yan, *Bei Wei qian qi zheng zhi zhi du*, 28–29. Though WS 110.2850 states these were settled in officially designated "hinterland" territories (*jiao dian* 郊甸) beyond the domain, those hilly territories could not have supported this influx of population. Quite sensibly, the early modern historian Hu Sanxing glosses a *Zi zhi tong jian* passage (114.3591) by simply saying "the eight units were distributed throughout the inner domain." For further discussion, see Li Ping, *Bei Wei Pingcheng shi dai*, 53–57; Yu, *Bei Wei zhi guan zhi du kao*, 23–27.

27. See Hou Xudong 侯旭东, "On Hamlets (cun) in the Northern Dynasties," *EMC* 13-14.1 (2007): 99–141, and esp. 132; this is a translation and adaptation of Hou's "Bei chao de cun luo" 北朝的村落, rpt. in his *Bei chao cun min de sheng huo shi jie—chao ting, zhou xian yu cun li* 北朝村民的生活世界-朝廷，州县与村里 (Beijing: Shang wu yin shu guan, 2005), 26–59. Care is needed here, since none of the examples raised by Hou in the piece is from the Datong Basin, and most are from the sixth century.

28. WS 25.644 tells us that hunting was used "to feed the army" 以充軍實.

29. Wang, *Zhuan xing qi de Bei Wei cai zheng yan jiu*, 46–48, et passim.

30. WS 4B.108–9; Yan, *Bei Wei qian qi zheng zhi zhi du*, 95.

31. WS 28.682 (in the text, it is the contemporary name of the Sanggan, Lei 灅, that is used); and for concentration of agriculture in this region, see Li Ping, *Bei Wei Pingcheng shi dai*, 55–57. The man to be executed in the story is called in *Wei shu* "He Ba." Yao Weiyuan (*Bei chao Hu xing kao*, 84) analyzes his clan name as Suhe, a group among the "White" (Bai) Serbi first defeated in the region by Liwei (see Chapter 5). The *Wei shu* text goes on to say that the statement by Ba-x-x of the Suhe clan was a hint that the brother should escape altogether, which he did. Enraged, Taiwu then killed all members of the family upon whom he could lay hands.

water as they had before, leading in turn to increasing difficulty for the farmers in the basin down below.³²

As for physical manufacture and construction, the goods produced by artisans for the Chinese empire had been an important basis for its power, and its capacity for centuries to influence and manipulate neighboring populations. The importance to Shegui of direct control over such producers cannot be overstated. It had been important to the Murong too—in 398, 36 units (*shu* 署) of "craftsmen and artisans of all sorts" that had previously been under Yan control were also marched north to the Datong Basin.³³ Though clearly under the control of monarchies, and transferable, very little is known of their internal organization. It can, however, be assumed that they were self-perpetuating, with children taking up parents' roles within the group, while knowledge and skills were passed down from generation to generation.³⁴ These groups were also the sine qua non of construction of Pingcheng, which would begin about half a year later. With direct control over groups of artisans, and a prevalence of top-down distribution of goods, there was little need for coinage, which was not minted by Wei monarchs until the move to Luoyang.³⁵

Specialized labor was thus under direct control, most at least in government workshops, while the "mouths that had been counted" farmed and paid taxes on their harvests to the administrators of the royal domain's eight cantons. In early Wei, these populations—though at times called up for logistics, or to build roads—were not part of the central armies. "Although they did not go on campaign, they served to farm and [produce] silk, in order to supply the army and the state."³⁶ And most of the state was army.³⁷

In the complex administration of early Wei, those who served in the regular army constituted a distinct population. This group, a "nation of a sort,"

---

32. As mentioned in Chapter 5 (note 67), the early fourth-century Taghbach khaghan Yituo is said to have spit upon the Shenhe Slope, causing elms to grow up there; while several generations later, elms again sprouted out on the slope where Madam Helan had given birth to Shegui: WS 1.7, 2.19. A century later, the situation was very different. Sagawa, "You mu yu nong geng zhi jian," 134, citing Li Daoyuan, *Shui jing zhu shu* 1: 3.235, mentions a trip made by Li in 494 accompanying Xiaowen into the Yinshan, where he saw "the mountains were without trees; just bare earth and that is all."

33. The 三十六署百工伎巧 were thus a part of the 100,000 marched north in 398: BS 1.17; *Ce fu yuan gui* 冊府元龜 486.5818. (And see note 5 in this chapter regarding apparent errors in WS 2.32). For one example, see mention of discovery of a Wei government tile factory outside of Pingcheng, at which are seen styles used in the city of Ye: Okamura, *Unkō sekkutsu no kōkogaku*, 14. Some of the crafts, on the other hand, were left down on the plains, such as foundries located near the resources needed to construct armor for the troops: WS 2.41. For the status of these workmen and their families, see Scott Pearce, "Status, Labor and Law: Special Service Households under the Northern Dynasties," *HJAS* 51.2 (1991): 89–138.

34. Comparison can, of course, be made to the "soldier" household that emerged in this period; and also with the *be* 部 of early Japan. The organization of these artisan units is a field of medieval East Asian history that needs more examination, to the extent that is possible on the basis of text or excavation. Some good work here has been done by Okamura, *Unkō sekkutsu no kōkogaku*, 51–55. For excellent work on the artisans of the first East Asian empire, see Anthony J. Barbieri-Low, *Artisans in Early Imperial China* (Seattle and London: University of Washington Press, 2007); and for early development of the Chinese "factory," Ledderose, *Ten Thousand Things*.

35. Yan, *Bei Wei qian qi zheng zhi zhi du*, 103.

36. WS 38.688.

37. See note 51 in Chapter 7.

enjoyed a shared set of special privileges, including a share in the booty taken on campaigns.[38] Their main obligation to the khaghan was reliable service in those campaigns. Special permission was needed from the khaghan to withdraw from that service.[39] Those who served in this way were the individuals and families—mostly of Inner Asian origin, and with long association with the Taghbach, such as the Helan—who were defined by their registration on special military rolls (see Chapter 11). While the "new subjects" who farmed lived for the most part at least in villages, much at least of the specialized military population apparently lived in cities—in Pingcheng itself, or garrisons down in the lowlands. The southern history *Nan Qi shu* ("Documents of Southern Qi," comp. early sixth century) mentions a Wei office called in transcription the *jiudouhe* (九豆和, MC *kyuw-tuw-hwa*), in charge of "all subjects within 3 *li* (about one mile) of Pingcheng's palace city whose household register was not attached to the armies or garrisons" 宮城三里內民戶籍不屬諸軍戍者, telling us, of course, that most within a mile of the city center were on the military registers.[40] There are hints in our texts that they may have been divided among six particular wards of the city.[41]

Supporting evidence for the registration of this specialized military population may come from the "Tale of Mulan," though the provenance of the text is not certain and it must be used with caution. We have only a Song-period Chinese-language version of the poem. Still, many scholars have argued the story was originally orally composed in an Inner Asian language—perhaps Taghbach—and later translated into Chinese and written down, perhaps in the sixth century.[42] In the earliest extant version a daughter takes the place of her father, who when

---

38. As seen with He Na in Chapter 7, these were "registered households" 編戶, on their own set of registers: WS 83A.1812. See Sagawa Eiji 佐川英治, "Bei Wei de bing zhi yu she hui: cong 'bing min fen li' dao 'jun min fen ji'" 北魏的兵制与社会——从"兵民分离"到"军民分籍", *Wei Jin Nan bei chao Sui Tang shi zi liao* (1996.1): 49–50. As we will see, this would change over time, with increasing recruitment of populations controlled by forms of local administration inherited from the Chinese empire. But still, more than a century later, it is reported that Gao Huan, the military leader of the successor state Eastern Wei, said to his Serbi military men, "the Han people, they are your slaves; the men plow for you, the wives weave for you" 漢人是汝奴,夫為汝耕,婦為汝織 (ZZTJ 157.4882).

39. For the need for the khaghan's permission, see Chapter 11 note 20. And for hints that some taxes were also collected on these groups, see Yan, *Bei Wei qian qi zheng zhi zhi du*, 109.

40. NQS 57.985; Yan, *Bei Wei qian qi zheng zhi zhi du*, 38–41.

41. Yan, *Bei Wei qian qi zheng zhi zhi du*, 37–43, suggests division of the inner following of the dynasty into six units, in contrast to the eight units of the "new subjects." It must be noted that we have very little information on this, and other quite different interpretations have been made (e.g., Koga Akimine 古賀昭岑, "Hokugi no buzoku kaisan ni tsuite" 北魏の部族解散について, *Tōhōgaku* 59 [1980]: 67, where he equates the six and the eight units, and sees them all as denoting settled pastoralists; this is one of several difficult issues we will not pursue in this book.) It is possible that this was based on actual settlement of these populations in "six wards" (liu fang 六坊), based on a mention in SS 24.675 in which we are told that with the final collapse of Northern Wei Luoyang in 534 that the emperor fled west to the emerging Western Wei regime with "less than ten thousand men" from the six wards, perhaps a reference to what remained of the inner guard units (see also ZZTJ 156.4857). It is, of course, difficult to be certain of the nature of the situation, with the paucity of sources and the fact that this is Luoyang, not Pingcheng. Cen Zhongmian 岑仲勉, *Fu bing zhi du yan jiu* 府兵制度研究 (Shanghai: Shanghai ren min chu ban she, 1957), 19, suggests that *liu fang* here is a euphemism for refugees from the Six Garrisons along the northern frontier, though it must be noted that in the *Sui shu* passage "Six Garrisons (liu zhen 六鎮)" is explicitly used just before *liu fang*.

42. All extant versions of this have been received in Chinese, and only in Chinese. Nonetheless, there is something of a consensus this is translation, from stories circulating among the Inner Asian populations of Wei or its

the "Khaghan is mobilizing all his troops" (Ch. 可汗大點兵) is too aged to take the place required of him on the "list of summoned men."[43] Hiding her identity, she mounts up to join a cavalry unit sent past the bend of the Yellow River to fight the nomads (if the poem does derive ultimately at least from Northern Wei, this would be the Rouran). Here we perhaps see fictional depiction of actual situation—the names of the "men of the nation" (*guo ren* 國人) were entered on military documents (*jun shu* 軍書). These documents would necessarily have been in Chinese, the language of administration, most at least of the names in transcribed form. It was in this manner that the *guo ren* were called up to provide military service for the khaghan.

Occasionally, women did so as well, as is portrayed in fictional form in "Mulan"—which could have been describing real events—but with more certainty in the historical record, as we see with the wife of the general "Big Eye" Yang, a woman of the Poduoluo clan skilled at horseback archery, who accompanied her partner on campaign. Making no effort to hide her identity, she strapped on battle gear and rode with the men, "[her horse's] bit in line [with those of the men] on the field of battle, and galloping alongside [them through] the forested gullies."[44] Most, of course, did not, "gallop alongside the men" to war, but participated in their own way, vicariously, as we shall see in Chapter 13 with another Poduoluo woman, portrayed in her tomb as overseeing her man's army on parade. For others, it might have been hearing recitation of the "Tale of Mulan."[45]

---

successors: see Shiamin Kwa and W. L. Idema, *Mulan: Five Versions of a Classic Chinese Legend with Related Texts* (Indianapolis: Hackett Pub. Co., 2010), xiii; and Wang Wenqian 王文倩 and Nie Yonghua 聂永华, "'Mulan shi' cheng shi nian dai, zuo zhe ji Mulan gu li bai nian yan jiu hui gu" 木兰诗成诗年代，作者及木兰故里百年研究回顾, *Shangqiu shi fan xue yuan xue bao* 23.1 (2007): 20, citing Liu Dajie 劉大杰, *Zhongguo wen xue fa zhan shi* 中國文學發展史 (Taibei: Taiwan Zhonghua shu ju, 1968), 306-8. Though perhaps true, these judgments are of course based on subjective reading; Xiaofei Tian urges caution in too readily assuming a northern origin to songs that were written down and preserved—perhaps actually composed—in the Yangtze region: "From the Eastern Jin through the Early Tang (317–649)," in *The Cambridge History of Chinese Literature: To 1375*, ed. Kang-i Sun Chang and Stephen Owen (Cambridge and New York: Cambridge University Press, 2010), 267.

43. Kwa and Idema, *Mulan*, 1; Sanping Chen suggests that the name Mulan transcribed the Taghbach name for "bull" or "stag," a nickname for military men: see his *Multicultural China in the Early Middle Ages* (Philadelphia: University of Pennsylvania Press, 2012), Chapter 2.

44. WS 73.1634. The name "Poduoluo" was later changed to Pan 潘, which is how it is given in the *Wei shu* passage: Yao, *Bei chao Hu xing kao*, 217–20. Shimunek, *Languages of Ancient Southern Mongolia and North China*, 135, reconstructs the Chinese transcription "Poduoluo" as "*Pʰatala." "Big Eye" Yang was a man of Qiang extraction, who entering the Wei army had risen through the ranks. There are, of course, other such tales from later periods of East Asian history: the most famous might be Khutulun, a great-great-granddaughter of Chinggis Khan, who according to Marco Polo could ride into the enemy ranks and snatch a captive "as deftly as a hawk pounces on a bird," and carry him to her father Caidu (Qaidu); Henry Yule, tr., *The Book of Ser Marco Polo the Venetian Concerning the Kingdoms and Marvels of the East*, 2 vols. (New York: Charles Scribner's Sons, 1903), 2: 465 (the main name given for her here is "Aijaruc"; she is, of course, the distant origin of Puccini's Turandot). And see also Michal Biran, *Qaidu and the Rise of the Independent Mongol State in Central Asia* (Surrey: Curzon Press, 1997), 2.

45. The relationship of woman to army is a long, complex and important story, which is perhaps in the 21st century undergoing decisive change. Until recent decades, however, though there may have been some Amazons in some places they are hard to pin down. See an attempt to do so in Adrienne Mayor's *The Amazons: Lives and Legends of Warrior Women across the Ancient World* (Princeton, NJ: Princeton University Press, 2014). Closer to the arena of our study here is the volume edited by Katheryn M. Linduff and Karen Sydney Rubinson, *Are All Warriors*

142   *Creating an Empire*

The *guo ren* who made up the inner core of the early Wei regime also came to be called the "people of Dai" 代人.⁴⁶ An ancient name of uncertain origin, "Dai" early on appeared in the written language of the Chinese world, representing there an "other" liable for seizure and exploitation. But though on one level a borrowing by the Taghbach from the Chinese literary tradition, the name also grew for that people into a powerful symbol of localism and local loyalty, presumably beginning when Yilu assumed the title King of Dai in 310. As seen above, Shegui attempted to set it aside in 386 in favor of Wei. Dai, however, had become a key mark of identity of the *guo ren* and the change was never fully imposed. Some had argued against it in 386, and 12 years later, after the armies had returned from conquest of the plains, some of the "officials"—that is, the generals—insisted that "We are of the mind that if we take long-standing [precedent], the name Dai should be used."⁴⁷ Shegui won the court debate by recruiting Cui Hong to argue that as opposed to little "Dai"—the barbarian statelet seized by Zhao 800 years before—"Wei" represented a great (and proper) state. A corollary of this was, of course, that a great state was lorded over by a great monarch. Despite formal victory on this matter, the throne still accepted use of "Dai," which continued to appear on a variety of eave tiles and funerary inscriptions, sometimes together with "Wei." Both terms were used through the life of the regime: "Great Wei" was perhaps the proper name of the monarch's realm as a whole; while "Great Dai" (*da Dai* 大代) was used more selectively to refer to the royal domain, or the men and women of that inner core, the "nation" or conquest polity of Dai.⁴⁸ It may

---

Male?: Gender Roles on the Ancient Eurasian Steppe (Lanham, MD: AltaMira Press, 2008). Among the articles in this work is one by Gideon Shelach, "He Who Eats the Horse, She Who Rides It?: Symbols of Gender Identity on the Eastern Edges of the Eurasian Steppe," in which the author examines the establishment in the early first millennium BCE of gender identity, and the warrior as "male," though this was of course not necessarily the same as biological nature. Parallel to the active role of woman as manpower in the army was woman playing a derivative role as leader of the army: see Walter L. Arnstein, "The Warrior Queen: Reflections on Victoria and Her World," *Albion* 30.1 (1998): 1–28, in which we are reminded that Victoria stressed that "I was always told to consider myself a soldier's child" and wore the colors of her father's unit while she reviewed them on horseback (4–5). While in the midst of the Crimean war she wrote that "I regret exceedingly not to be a man & to be able to fight in the war ... there is no finer death for a man than on the battlefield!" (10).

46. This could, of course, also be translated as "men of Dai," since the main glue binding these communities together into one was universal participation of its men in the Taghbach military. But as we shall see in more detail in Chapter 13, women were in various ways also ongoing and active participants in this militarized society.

47. See the Chinese translation of this statement in WS 2.32–33. For Cui Hong's counter-argument (in what language we do not really know), see WS 24.620–21.

48. For examples of use of Da Dai, see the book compiled by Yin Xian 殷宪, *Bei Wei Pingcheng shu ji* 北魏平城书迹 (Beijing: Wen wu chu ban she, 2017), passim. See also Matsushita Ken'ichi 松下憲一 "Hokugi no kokugō 'Dai Dai' to 'Dai Gi'" 北魏の国号'大代'と'大魏'; in his *Hokugi Kozoku taiseiron*, 111–59 (including the table of appearances of the term "Da Dai" on 146–57); and He Dezhang 何得章, "Bei Wei guo hao yu zheng tong wen ti" 北魏国号与正统问题, *LSYJ* (1992.3): 113–25. Others, in fact, put forth other suggestions for name change: a holy man (*fang shi*) whose name is given us as Qi Xian is said in the time of Taiwu to have put forth a proposal that the regional name "Dai" be changed to "Ten Thousand Years" 萬年: WS 35.822, 114.3054. Taiwu seems to have accepted the plan for a time (WS 113.2975), but having heard the counterargument of Cui Hao, the emperor in the end dismissed the idea. It should, however, be noted that part of Cui's argument was that it was appropriate that in referring to the regime both "Dai" and "Wei" be used 代魏兼用, as had been the case with the ancient Shang also being called "Yin" (WS 35.822).

have been the case that, informally at least, Wei's monarch was a *huang di*, while Dai's was a khaghan, though the two titles were, of course, held by the same man.

In recent years, Azar Gat in his book *Nations* has made clear that this has not been just a thing of modernity.[49] Dai—or better here, the "people of Dai"—are a good example of this, becoming a *Staatsvolk*, with shared loyalties and defining memories.[50] In *Wei shu*, the terms "people of Dai" (Dai ren 代人) and "people of the nation" (*guo ren* 國人) are effectively interchangeable.[51] Perhaps more troubling is the tendency of members of a "nation" to share a sense of common privilege and entitlement vis-à-vis the "other," the conquered. With this in mind, we might take another look at the rage directed at Cui Hao's history, in which an outsider had insulted the dynasty, and by insulting the dynasty an outsider had insulted the nation. Over the years, with expansion of the empire, and of the monarch's connections within that empire, such feelings of the men of Dai would increasingly vex the lords of Wei, and impede them in their planning.[52] But in the end, the nation outlived the dynasty. The term "Dai ren," and the concept, survived into early Tang, no doubt with an evolving form and scope.[53]

The conquest polity had grown over time. At the top was the ever-expanding imperial clan—the *tigin, which is to say all those descended from Liwei. These descent groups could be huge: one clan of Inner Asian descent in the Gansu

---

49. See again Azar Gat, *Nations*, 3, and the discussion among Gat, Chris Wickham, and others in "Debate on Azar Gat's Nations." Looking at the Chinese world, the modern scholars Gideon Shelach and Yuri Pines ("Secondary State Formation and the Development of Local Identity," 220) have come to recognize "undeniable common aspects of Qin in the period of the Warring States and the modern nation-state," suggesting that through a combination of social mobility (by rising through the ranks of the Qin army) and the social engineering of an activist state, "parochial identities" were eliminated, while the people of Qin developed a shared sense of "us" as opposed to the outside "them." William Honeychurch, "The Nomad as State Builder: Historical Theory and Material Evidence from Mongolia," *Journal of World Prehistory* 26.4 (2013): 283–321, has also pointed out the particular capacity for pre-modern state-building among mobile pastoralists. On the other end of Eurasia, recent studies suggest that two or three generations before the Norman conquest, "England" had taken shape as at least an "embryonic nation," in which every freeman took an oath of loyalty to the king: see Robert Tombs, *The English and Their History* (New York: Alfred A. Knopf, 2015), 36–37; and George Molyneaux, *The Formation of the English Kingdom in the Tenth Century* (Oxford: Oxford University Press, 2015), 11–13.

50. Explorations of different forms of loyalty within the East Asia would include Naomi Standen's *Unbounded Loyalty: Frontier Crossing in Liao China* (Honolulu: University of Hawai'i Press, 2007); Jennifer Jay's *A Change in Dynasties: Loyalism in Thirteenth-century China* (Bellingham: Western Washington University, 1991); and again with Shelach and Pines, "Secondary State Formation and the Development of Local Identity," 219–22. For such phenomena in another set of societies, see discussion of Ibn Khaldun's '*asabiyyah*, "bindedness," in Tim MacKintosh-Smith, *Arabs: A 3000-year History of Peoples, Tribes and Empires* (New Haven, CT: Yale University Press, 2019), xxi, and of Muhammed's creation of a "super-'*asabiyyah*, "a sense of solidarity and unity like none before" (148). Thomas Small, in a review of Robert Irwin's *Ibn Khaldun* (Princeton, NJ: Princeton University Press, 2018), in *Times Literary Supplement*, January 11, 2019, 11, carries on discussion of '*asabiyyah* in an interesting way, with fascinating parallels to the people of Dai, stating that "[t]his wasn't simply a sense of group identity.... Nor a sense of group homogeneity, since the societies he analysed, far from being homogeneous nations in the modern sense, were riven by ethnic tensions, class stratification and inter-tribal conflict, despite the presence of Islam as a unifying force. Rather, *asabiyyah* indicates a group's capacity for harnessing their collective identity in pursuit of political dominance over other groups."

51. See discussion of the *guo ren*, which he translates as "compatriots," in Klein, "Contributions of the Fourth Century Xianbei," 95–97.

52. See the excellent description of the situation given in Yan Gengwang, "Bei Wei shang shu zhi du," 89.

53. Matsushita, *Hokugi Kozoku taiseiron*, 139: e.g., *Xin Tang shu* 79.3545.

Corridor was said to have numbered some 10,000.[54] Men of this sort played prominent roles in the army's officer corps.[55] Alongside them were groups with longstanding social and political ties, such as the cadet clans, the groups that had early on joined the confederation (*nei ru*), and then groups forcibly incorporated, such as the Helan. But the army evolved generation by generation: by 407, Daowu had begun to recruit from among the "free families of the eight nations (cantons)" (*ba guo liang jia* 八國良家) of the Datong Basin and adjoining regions.[56] Over time, High Carts were brought in as well, as we shall see in Chapter 11. Internal distinctions no doubt persisted, with competing memories, overlapping loyalties, alternative ways of defining the self. But by entering service in the regular army, the body of the *guo ren* had changed. As Patrick Amory has said regarding his Goths, "[t]he edges of an ethnic group are always bleeding and healing as people leave it or join it."[57] Part of a unifying institution, these men now also shared a common, hybrid culture, "hybrid" used here with the particular meaning of "how newness enters the world," "derived from heterogeneous sources."[58] The best way to describe them is certainly to escape the duality of "Chinese" vs. "non-Chinese," and define them as they defined themselves, as the "people of Dai," a world, like all worlds, complete unto itself.

If not the "original equality" of the "Prefatory Annals," such militarized communities—such conquest polities—typically have a sense of shared meaning and entitlement. (Such a collective sense of shared privilege was certainly part of what the later reorganizer Xiaowen was trying to escape.) At the same time, hierarchy was deeply embedded in this society, with roots going back to emergence of hereditary lordship among the Serbi in the time of Tanshihuai. The Dai community took shape around the Taghbach khaghan, and for them the role of the khaghan was first and foremost as supreme commander of the armies. This was not an abstract title—for a century, Daowu's heirs mounted up to personally lead

---

54. This was the Juqu, of the "Lushui Hu." See Chapter 12; and JS 129.3189.

55. On the place of imperial kinsmen in the officer corps, see Liu Jun 刘军, "Lun Bei Wei qian qi zong shi zai jin jun zhong de di wei ji zuo yong" 论北魏前期宗室在禁军中的地位及作用, *Xuchang xue yuan xue bao* 32.1 (2013): 12-15. On the term "*tigin*," see Luo Xin, "Bei Wei zhi qin kao," 92. Taken from the Chinese transcription *zhi qin* 直勤, this term has also been reconstructed as *tegin, *tekin.

56. WS 113.2974. The recruiters, we are told, sought "talented and well-thought-of adult men" (*nian zhang you qi wang zhe* 年長有器望者)." It is not clear if the volunteers were in some way transferred into the six-unit system.

57. Patrick Amory, *People and Identity in Ostrogothic Italy, 489–554* (Cambridge and New York: Cambridge University Press, 1997), 16; and also the comments of Michael Nylan on multiple layers of "micro-identities": "Talk about 'Barbarians' in Antiquity," 590.

58. See Matthew Liebmann, "Parsing Hybridity: Archaeologies of Amalgamation in Seventeenth-century New Mexico," in *The Archaeology of Hybrid Material Culture*, ed. Jeb J. Card (Carbondale: Southern Illinois University Press, 2013), 31, and his quoting of the *Oxford English Dictionary* on p. 30. In the term as we use it in this study, the questions of colonialism and post-colonialism don't take on the significance described by Liebmann. See also discussion of when the term is not appropriately used in Bryan Miller, "The Southern Xiongnu in Northern China," along with his interesting comments at the end of the piece (186–87) of the undoing of the "precarious middle ground" between distinct cultures that had existed with the Southern Xiongnu, and development under Northern Wei and its successors of "new cultures," on a new "central ground."

the troops, and forge bonds with them, in a variety of ways.[59] For the men of Dai, the khaghan was *our* lord. Intense personal loyalty is described in tales scattered throughout *Wei shu*. One of these describes an event in the life of the second Wei monarch, Mingyuan (r. 409–423), before accession, when he was still heir apparent. On a winter hunting expedition, the young prince was crossing a river when the ice buckled and his horse went through. A member of his guard, Wang Luor, now jumped in and fished his lord out of the freezing water, in the process himself becoming chilled almost to the point of death.[60] The soon-to-be emperor reciprocated by removing his own clothing to warm and so save his loyal subject. "From this point on," we are told in this ancient propaganda tale, "the favor shown him grew by the day."

Such cultivation of ties with the military continued after Mingyuan had taken the throne. In 410, little more than a decade after Daowu had led the major campaign by which he took control of the plains to the south, Mingyuan personally led an army north against the Rouran. According to Mingyuan's annals, this was followed two months later by archery contests and military exercises. Such activities were perhaps a way for the recently enthroned 19-year-old to show his effectiveness as military leader and so solidify his mastery of the realm. Over the next few years, Mingyuan continued to reach out to his soldiery. In 411 he granted them a three-day drinking bout (*pu*), accompanied—as we so often see in Taghbach history—by the bestowal of textiles, a manufacture much prized by these people, which Mingyuan gave out in quantities determined on the basis of rank.[61] At the end of this same year the emperor held a great review of the troops, accompanied by training exercises, an act repeated a little over a year later, which all the young men 12 *sui* and up from the Dai region were expected to attend. Here we see a real example of the fictionalized version given in "Mulan" of the nature and duties of the Dai ren.[62]

Due to hostility—or ignorance, or indifference—the title "khaghan" (Chinese: *ke han*) is never used in *Wei shu* with reference to the Taghbach monarchs. As noted above, however, it does appear in the Gaxian Cave inscription (though not in the parallel text in *Wei shu*), and was undoubtedly the main honorific used by the men of Dai to refer to their ruler. The Taghbach lords, however, delighted in receiving, and later appropriating, titles from the Chinese

---

59. The last emperor to personally lead troops was the reformer Xiaowen. It is interesting to note that despite the deep cultural and institutional reforms he attempted to impose upon his realm, Xiaowen argued vigorously against the argument that he should not himself lead the army: see ZZTJ 138.4331. (Though it must also be noted that this was on the eve of his leading his troops south in 493 to relocate them to Luoyang.)

60. WS 34.799. Wang Luor was a man whose family came originally from the Wei River valley.

61. WS 3.51. And see the story of Mingyuan's great-grandfather, the Dai king Shiyijian, involving among other things concern over the paucity of silks: WS 1.16.

62. For the 411 rally, the editors of the Zhonghua shu ju edition of *Wei shu* give evidence that though originally present in the 12th month the event has dropped out of the *Wei shu* annals; see 66 note 4. For the review in the first month of 413, see WS 3.52.

world as well. Receiving the title "king" (*wang*) from the Jin court, Yilu had then turned name into reality by taking a swath of the dying empire and restoring to it the name "Dai." Appropriation of Chinese appellations and their incorporation into the titles of Inner Asian regimes is frequently seen; a well-known later example would be *Ong Qan* (*Khan* ∾ Khaghan), "King (Ch. *wang*) Khan," used in the twelfth century by the Kereyit lord To'oril.⁶³

The process by which the Taghbach dynasty appropriated the ultimate Chinese honorific, *huang di*—which in English we generally translate as "emperor," though it more literally means "august god-king," or in the Grekicized form "august thearch"⁶⁴—began on the eve of the southern conquests when the King of Wei, the 24-year-old Shegui, received from a Chinese scribe a memorial urging him to take the "venerable title." He did not go all the way with this in 396, but did adopt the pennons of a "Son of Heaven," a frequently used Chinese alternative to *huang di*, and tellingly changed the reign name to "Augustness's Commencement" (*huang shi*).⁶⁵ Two years later, the conquest of the plains complete, and work begun on a new capital at Pingcheng, Shegui was again urged to take the title. On this occasion, the letter came from the Prince of Wey and all the peers and officers of the realm. This one took, and in the last month of the year (398) Shegui entered more fully into the Chinese world of symbols (in a manner that could, perhaps, be compared to British appropriation of the title "raj"). In a newly finished Heaven's Order throne hall 天文殿, in the not-yet-finished city of Pingcheng, he was saluted by his officials and received the seals of office. A great pardon was given, while the dynasty was incorporated into Chinese cosmology with assignment of the Earth element and the color yellow.⁶⁶ The reign name was changed to "Heaven Prevails" (*tian xing*; 398–404). A growth and solidification of monarchical power had taken place here, to a significant extent drawing upon symbols and rituals of the Chinese tradition. And from this point forward, as a simple matter of convenience, we will generally refer to Taghbach rulers by the Chinese-style imperial titles bestowed on them after death. Thus Shegui becomes "Daowudi," "the Way of War Emperor," or simply Daowu. It is, however, important to remember that for many within the regime, the lord was seen as a "Khaghan," rather than an "August God-King"; and the reign title may have been imagined, and spoken, in a different language as "Tengri Prevails."

The mixing of elements in this hybrid culture is seen as well in the realm of religion. What was to be the shape of faith in the emerging Dai community? What was to be the "Book of Rules" for this newly emergent body of still uncertain shape? Here we will simply attend to the great state sacrifices, and the questions

---

63. Rachewiltz, *Secret History of the Mongols*, 1: 104 et passim. For more on borrowing of Chinese terms by the Mongols, see Ruth Dunnell, *Chinggis Khan: World Conqueror* (Boston: Longman, 2010), 17.
64. Kroll, *A Student's Dictionary of Classical and Medieval Chinese*, 84.
65. WS 2.27.
66. WS 108A.2734.

that emerged regarding to whom sacrifice should be given, and how and where that should be done. As the modern scholar Kang Le has well described, the core of Chinese state religion had taken shape around sacrifice to Heaven, Tian, at a shrine lying to the south of the capital city. The great tradition of the steppe, established in the age of the Xiongnu, also involved sacrifice to the high sky god—the Türks used the name Tengri—though in a sacred space to the west of the monarch's residence, be that palace or *ger*.[67] Daowu seems to have been undecided: at his enthronement with the Helan up at Niuchuan, his altar to Tengri had been to the west, and he followed this model again in the fourth month of 398 (the altar to the west of Shengle, since Pingcheng had not yet been designated); then in the first month of 399 and 400 he sacrificed to Shangdi, a term at times used interchangeably with the Chinese Tian, at a shrine south of Pingcheng; but then in 405, we see him once again sacrificing to Tengri in the shrine to the west.[68] This would continue for generations: diplomats from Jiankang visiting Pingcheng in the late fifth century remarked that the altar to Heaven lay to the west of the city.[69] At times at least, gods' names can be interchangeable—the Romans equated Jupiter with Zeus; and Tengri is the name by which some faithful modern Muslims in Turkey refer to God.[70] Among the Taghbach, this multivalent style of religion would persist until the forced culture change and rigid systematization of the emperor Xiaowen.

This is seen in the administration as well. In the Chinese historiographical tradition, one way of summarizing the unfolding of order in the world of humans lay in exhaustively tracing bureaucratic flow charts from ancient Zhou to the author's own age, a process that took full shape in the Tang with the *Tong dian* 通典, the "Comprehensive Institutions." Such summarization was not so easy for Wei Shou, two centuries before *Tong dian*, as he tried to compose a "Treatise on Officials and Clans" (Guan shi zhi) for *Wei shu*. Daowu, he said, had originally "wished to model after the pure and unadorned of antiquity. When he established an official title, he usually did not base it on the old names of the Zhou or the Han, [but instead would] sometimes take it from a person, sometimes take it from a thing, sometimes used an affair of the common people, all taking the meaning of the 'clouds and birds' (i.e., the officials) of distant antiquity."[71] Many of these were of course borrowings from Inner Asian tradition, which sounded very strange to

---

67. HS 94A.3752; Huang, "Tuoba Xianbei zao qi guo jia," 75.

68. Liu Puning, "Becoming the Ruler of the Central Realm: How the Northern Wei Dynasty Established Its Political Legitimacy," *JAH* 52.1 (2018): 104, makes the interesting point that the emperor conducted the southern—Chinese-style—sacrifice on his own, while the western sacrifice was conducted with kinsmen, and so was presumably the enactment of a shared mandate with his clansmen.

69. WS 2.32, 34, 108A.2734–36; NQS 57.985; Kang Le 康樂, *Cong Xi jiao dao Nan jiao: guo jia ji dian yu Bei Wei zheng zhi* 從西郊到南郊—國家祭典與北魏政治 (Taibei: Dao he chu ban she, 1995), 167–69.

70. Yves Bonnefoy and Wendy Doniger, eds., *Asian Mythologies* (Chicago: University of Chicago Press, 1993), 331.

71. WS 113.2972–73.

Chinese observers. But even when Chinese forms were taken up, this was an age of creative experimentation. Thus, Daowu took the number "36"—in the Chinese tradition representing "completeness"—as a basis for dividing his government into 36 offices (*bu*), which for some unexplained reason then ballooned into 360, and then a few years later retreated back to 36.[72] It would be a century before clear tables of office and rank were produced.

In early Wei, real power lay in the inner court, a holdover from the time of Shiyijian, if not before, whose inhabitants were overwhelmingly military men of Inner Asian descent.[73] As the modern scholar Yan Yaozhong has put it so well, to understand the nature of the early Wei state, we need "to attempt to return to its true face," which is to say, the Inner Court.[74] A scattering of these titles appear, in contemporary inscriptions, in the Jiankang histories, and occasionally in *Wei shu*. One was the *nei xing agan* 內行阿干, *nei xing* a Chinese translation of some Taghbach term for "internal affairs," *agan* a transcription of a term frequently seen in Inner Asian languages for "elder brother."[75] Though with antecedents within the Chinese empire, the *shi zhong* 侍中, "palace attendant," seems in early Wei to have been another important Inner Court post. Those who held the title were allowed into the palace as a member of the khaghan's Privy Council.[76] And linked with development of law in the regime, a body of independent judges had also taken shape, who dealt with disputes and charges that could not be solved by the leaders of still semi-autonomous vassal polities. Yan Yaozhong describes this as an important aspect of preserved forms of collegial office-holding.[77] As

72. WS 113.2972, 2974.
73. Discussing the *zhong san* post in particular (see just below), Zheng Qinren 鄭欽仁 finds that the Inner Court post was filled overwhelmingly with military men of Inner Asian derivation through the reign of Taiwu: *Bei Wei guan liao ji gou yan jiu* 北魏官僚機構研究 (Taibei: Dao he chu ban she, 1995), 191. And see also discussion in Yan, *Bei Wei qian qi zheng zhi zhi du*, 66–67; and in Kubozoe Yoshifumi 窪添慶文, *Boshi o mochiita Hokugi-shi kenkyū* 墓誌を用いた北魏史研究 (Tōkyō: Kyūkoshoin, 2017), Section III, Chapter 2, 447–89. Eight hundred years later, the Mongol *keshig*, "guard," similarly played a role in both military and civil affairs: David M. Farquhar, *The Government of China under Mongolian Rule* (Stuttgart: Steiner, 1990), 41–42.
74. Yan, *Bei Wei qian qi zheng zhi zhi du*, 50.
75. Yu, *Bei Wei zhi guan zhi du kao*, 34–46; Kawamoto, *Gi Shin Nanbokuchō jidai no minzoku mondai*, 192; Chen, *Multicultural China in the Early Middle Ages*, 61–65; Shimunek, *Languages of Ancient Southern Mongolia and North China*, 326. On the equivalent Mongol term, see Rachewiltz, *Secret History of the Mongols*, 1: 237, note 2, where he tells us that *aqa* meant "elder brother (*or* cousin)" and was "used also as a term of respect." Note that there are frequently variants for translations such as *nei xing*: see Zhang Jinlong 张金龙, *Wei Jin Nan bei chao jin wei wu guan zhi du yan jiu* 魏晋南北朝禁卫武官制度研究, 2 vols. (Beijing: Zhonghua shu ju, 2004), 2: 692. For attempted reconstruction of a number of titles in Serbi language, taken from the Jiankang history *Nan Qi shu*, see Shimunek, *Languages of Ancient Southern Mongolia and North China*, 148–62.
76. Kawamoto, *Gi Shin Nanbokuchō jidai no minzoku mondai*, 190, citing the late Wei case involving Yuan Cha, WS 16.406. And see also Yan, *Bei Wei qian qi zheng zhi zhi du*, 59.
77. See Yan, *Bei Wei qian qi zheng zhi zhi du*, 135–42; and Yu, *Bei Wei zhi guan zhi du kao*, 28–34. This system of judgeship was called in Chinese the *San du*, translation of a *guo yu* term for "the three metropolitan (judges)," one each for outer, central, and inner, with two prestigious figures chosen for each. Brief mention is made in WS 111.2874, where we are told that the "leader of the unit makes a full report, the grievance office investigates the accusation, and the *san du* decide it." This was apparently for *guo ren*; special pardons were regularly given them (Yan, *Bei Wei qian qi zheng zhi zhi du*, 132). See also Matsunaga Masao 松永雅生, "Hokugi no San to 北魏の三都," *Tōyōshi kenkyū* 29.2–3 & 29.4 (1970, 1971): 129–59 & 297–325, who suggests (323) that this was an institution inherited from the Xiongnu. For the possible *guo yu* name of these posts, see Shimunek, *Languages of Ancient Southern*

with most parts of the Inner Court, this was abolished in the course of Xiaowen's reorganization of the state.⁷⁸

Reflecting its origins, an important office of the Inner Court was known in Chinese as the "unit for managing horses" 典馬曹, in charge of the great imperial ranches, located among other places in the Ordos and in the Deer Park north of the palace.⁷⁹ On a junior level there was the "palace jack-of-all-trades," in Chinese *zhong san* 中散, recruited on a hereditary basis in early Wei from among sons of powerful Serbi officials and generals. Errand runners for the throne, these young men were occasionally sent on very important errands, as imperial inspectors of the provinces.⁸⁰ Regarding this post, and others, the modern scholar Zheng Qinren makes the key point that in contrast to the at least theoretically strict hierarchical organization of clearly demarcated posts of the Han bureaucracy, a position such as *zhong san* in the Inner Court was quite fluid, in terms both of function and of importance. The *zhong san* was a guard, an attendant and an errand boy for the khaghan, doing whatever the khaghan wished done.⁸¹ "The Inner Court," Yan Yaozhong tells us, "favored the military, the Outer Court favored civil affairs."⁸² Since in early Wei what the khaghans wished most to do was spend their time on war, Yan goes on to say that the Inner Court controlled the Outer Court.

These posts were dominated by imperial kinsmen and men of Dai, which in early Wei was also true of the outer court, whose administrative units were led by teams of three: an Inner Asian military man, aided in his efforts by an interpreter and a scribe.⁸³ Unsurprisingly, *Wei shu* contains little discussion of the "inner court"; the term *nei chao* 內朝 is mentioned only twice. In one of these, however, we see an interesting expression of its privileged nature: in early Wei, during

---

Mongolia and North China, 330, drawing on NQS 57.985. For discussion of the collegial nature of Taghbach government in early Wei, see Eisenberg, *Kingship in Early Medieval China*, Chapter 3; and for discussion of the collegial nature of Mongol rule in Persia, Michael Hope, *Power, Politics, and Tradition in the Mongol Empire and the Ilkhānate of Iran* (Oxford: Oxford University Press, 2016).

78. WS 21A.546. Yan, *Bei Wei qian qi zheng zhi zhi du*, 145, suggests that while this reflected general tendencies toward centralization of power, a part of the reason may have been the growth of an enormous backlog of cases under the San du system: 獄訟留滯 (WS 48.1089). Xiaowen's concern for the system is seen in the visits he made to prisons: WS 7A.148.

79. WS 26.654. For the role of Deer Park as government ranch, see Sagawa, "You mu yu nong geng zhi jian."

80. Zheng, *Bei Wei guan liao ji gou yan jiu*, 169–209, with useful tables showing inheritance of the post by members of the Baba ("Zhangsun") cadet clan and others, on 207–9. For inspection tours by *zhong san*, see Zheng, *Bei Wei guan liao ji gou yan jiu*, 180–81, citing WS 24.954, 41.937; and see also Yan, *Bei Wei qian qi zheng zhi zhi du*, 66–67. This term also has variant forms, including on Wencheng's "Southern Progress" inscription *nei xing nei xiao* 內行內小, "junior [official] for palace business," perhaps a more literal translation of the *guo yu* title (to be discussed more below): Matsushita, *Hokugi Kozoku teiseiron*, 76.

81. Zheng, *Bei Wei guan liao ji gou yan jiu*, 178.

82. Yan, *Bei Wei qian qi zheng zhi zhi du*, 73.

83. WS 113.2973. It is not recorded when this ended, but perhaps under Taiwu's reign. In early Wei, each province also had three Inspectors (*ci shi*); Yan, *Bei Wei qian qi zheng zhi zhi du*, 78–80, points out a difference, in that this consisted of a man of Dai, a Chinese from court, and a local man, who served as intermediary. This arrangement had disappeared by the 470s.

sacrifices to Tengri at the western altar, members of the inner court accompanied the monarch within the shrine's walls. Those of the outer court waited outside.[84]

Those down in the Yangtze region—engaged, of course, in their own processes of inventing tradition—looked askance at the highland culture that had emerged up in the Yinshan region: "Since the time of the Wolf [Lord]," said a culture critic whose work eventually made it into *Nan Qi shu*, "they have presumed to appropriate bits of the models of [our] civilization ('Hua') 稍僭華典, which they chaotically jumble together with barbarian manners and the mores of their nation."[85] As contacts of various sorts increased with Jiankang, Wei monarchs found such criticism increasingly difficult to bear. Seeking to establish a greater fidelity to at least the imagined structures of the old Chinese empire, the radical reformer Xiaowen would in the end unify the offices of his government within a schedule of Han-style official titles and ranks. In the process the Inner Court ceased to exist, at least in its full original sense.[86] The scribes, perhaps, breathed a sigh of relief. For early Taghbach monarchs, however, the jumble had been just fine: they came, they saw, they appropriated as they saw fit.[87]

The loyalties of the men of Dai did not, at any rate, apply so much to the monarchs' institutions as to the monarch himself, as seen in the story of Wang Luor above. It extended, as well, to the royal clan, to the *tigin*, as seen in the reaction of the "common people" to the forced suicide of a prince. In 508 this unfortunate had lost out in a deadly political struggle, but loudly insisted to the end that "I am loyal to the court. What crime have I committed that I should die?"[88] After his death, *Wei shu* tells us, men and women wept as they walked along the roads.

More fundamentally, however, these loyalties extended beyond the lord and his clan to a more general feeling for the manners and mores that had taken shape in the Land of Dai, for the "old ways." There were shared memories of particular events that had taken place in particular locations, such as the Shenhe Slope. This is where Daowu had been born, no doubt in a yurt.[89] But vivid recollection of this place did not belong only to the imperial house. All would have remembered that their people had been under mortal threat from the Murong, that the

---

84. Kawamoto, *Gi Shin Nanbokuchō jidai no minzoku mondai*, 189, citing WS 108A.2736.
85. NQS 57.990.
86. Wang, *Zhuang xing qi de Bei Wei cai zheng yan jiu*, 3–4.
87. See discussion of the complexity of such "multiethnic empires" in terms of later conquest dynasties in Francesca Fiaschetti and Julia Schneider, "Introduction," in their edited volume *Political Strategies of Identity Building in Non-Han Empires in China* (Wiesbaden: Harrassowitz Verlag, 2014), 1–5, where the authors say (1) that "[t]he multiculturalism of these empires is the result of the negotiation between the ethnic identity of the conquerors and the different ethnic awareness of the conquered peoples," and that "the ruling elites were very conscious of their traditions and used them for the construction of their political identities," though (2) "these dynasties undoubtedly integrated certain parts of Chinese culture, especially political and institutional, when shaping their own political identity."
88. WS 21B.582–83.
89. WS 2.19.

Murong had inexplicably retreated, and that with the aid of the gods—who froze the River—the men of Dai had tracked them down to Shenhe Slope and there destroyed them. "Familiar in [the] mouth as household words," the names of those men were certainly year after year in "flowing cups freshly rememb'red."⁹⁰ One of those recounting these tales was a *tigin*, a distant member of the imperial clan called in *Wei shu* Yuan Pi—a powerful official during the 480s—who is said to have sat bolt upright at the feasting table and "in a booming voice recounted in order past victories and defeats." Whether or not they wished to hear this yet again, the emperor Xiaowen and the Wenming empress dowager "listened respectfully."⁹¹ Though put forth as an offering to the monarch, these communal memories constrained the monarch as well. We will see this pivotal figure again, in later sections of this study.

Common loyalties and common action usually at least require a common language. Many groups entered the Dai community, speaking many languages: Turkic and Mongolic, Xiongnu and Chinese.⁹² When assembled for military service, however, the men of Dai would have had to acquire at least a working knowledge of the "national language" (*guo yu*), the language of the Khaghan and of the officers of his army.⁹³ This was needed to hear and act out orders, in the camp or in the field. But even greater fluency would have probably been needed for casual interaction in camp: to converse with the messmates, or argue with them, or sing drinking songs in the evening. This almost certainly would have been one of the major impediments to interaction between the central armies and auxiliary units called up from among the Xiongnu, or the High Carts. For some Chinese, knowledge of the *guo yu* could be a route to promotion, as seen in the story of Chao Yi, who "because he was good at the northerners' language [became] an Inner Court attendant 內侍左右."⁹⁴ And while transition to the central

---

90. The quote, of course, from the St. Crispin's day speech in *Henry V*. See also Pierre Nora, *Realms of Memory: Rethinking the French Past*, 3 vols. (New York: Columbia University Press, 1996–1998), 1: 1; and the work of Anthony Cohen, who in his *Symbolic Construction of Community* has powerfully described loyalties to *this* place, *this* set of experiences and symbols, noting (99) that "people emphasize local identity in times of intensive encounter with others, but paradoxically often choose to do so by choosing things, symbols and ideas that come from outsiders."

91. BS 15.554 (WS 14.358).

92. In his biography, one prince of the house was praised for his ability to serve as translator for "the languages of the many regions": WS 15.372. And several languages must have been used at court, since when Xiaowen in 495 banned use of Inner Asian languages at the new Luoyang court, he forbade use not just of the "national language" (*guo yu* 國語), but of "the various northern languages" (*zhu bei yu* 諸北語): WS 21A.536. There are several other references in *Wei shu* and histories of the successor regimes to "languages of the northerners" 北人語: WS 91.1944; BQS 41.539; BS 48.1760, 50.1838, 53.1926, 89.2923, these examples generally divided between Chinese who knew the language of the northerners and so won office (see note 94), and explaining the garbled nature of transcriptions from the northern languages into Chinese.

93. As a very rough comparison, it should be noted that for entry to the US Army: "Non-citizens must speak, read, and write English fluently": https://www.usa.gov/join-military, accessed 28 June 2018. One can't help wonder if similarly strict requirements are imposed upon citizens.

94. WS 91.1944. See also the well-known rejection by Yan Zhitui, much later, of the boast of an acquaintance at the Northern Qi court who had taught his son how to play the lute (*pi pa*) and speak the Serbi language that the boy was thereby on a path to success: *Yan shi jia xun ji jie* 2.21; Teng, tr., *Family Instructions for the Yen Clan*, 7.

army would have required working knowledge of the national language, men of different mother tongues would certainly have had different accents. Perhaps as in the United Kingdom, until recent times at least, this was an informal but very real way of determining origin and so status and possibility of rising through the ranks. At the same time, the emerging common language would not have been used only by fighting men (or the occasional Mulan). As we will see in Chapter 13, even within their generally accepted roles, women themselves were deeply involved in creation of the networks of interaction that took shape in Dai, and so would have been equal participants in use and development of the lingua franca.

As for the nature of this national language, the Khaghan's Serbi, as mentioned in Chapter 2 there has been debate for decades, though the dominant position is now that it was an early Mongolic form, or related to the Mongolic languages.[95] Others, however—among them Peter Boodberg—have argued for Turkic origins and it is fair to wonder if through centuries-long interactions among many different peoples, the national language that over centuries took shape in Dai was not a Serbi-based creole, drawing on Turkic ("böri"), perhaps Xiongnu, and as the modern scholar Zhu Dawei has pointed out, Chinese.[96] Though recovered contemporary texts such as Wencheng's "Nan Xun bei" (see below) show simultaneous use of characters to write Literary Chinese and to transcribe the national language, and interpreters of spoken language were in constant use in the early Wei,[97] it seems unlikely that there was a *guo yu* version of "Pingcheng." That and other borrowings from Chinese simply became part of Dai's evolving language, something like "Manhattan" in American English.

Efforts were also made to borrow from the Chinese writing system to develop a new writing system for the *guo yu*, Dai thus being an early example of a much broader phenomenon among neighbors of the Chinese world. As is well known, the Chinese character—the "Sinograph"—has a unique complexity, most of the tens of thousands of them being a mixture of phonetic and significant elements, in a manner that has, among other things, created a striking beauty in calligraphy and poetry. And although the Chinese spoken languages and its classical writing system did diverge early on, they come from the same roots, and can—as we've seen in recent times—fairly readily be reintegrated. For North Asian societies, the original spoken languages had no relationship at all to the

---

95. See discussion, Chapter 2 note 28.

96. Boodberg, an advocate for Turkic origins, in fact more or less makes this suggestion in his "Language of the T'o-pa Wei," 239; a similar insight on the distinctive nature of the *guo yu* is also made by Liu, *Xianbei shi lun*, 83–86. For the incorporation of Chinese into the *guo yu*, see Zhu, *Wei Jin Nan bei chao she hui sheng huo shi*, Kindle ed., Chapter 12, Section 3.

97. E.g., WS 113.2973; or the example given in WS 15.372, of a Taghbach kinsman who was noted not only for his skill at mounted archer but could also "interpret the languages of all the lands" 通解諸方之語. For more on the office of interpreter, see Chapter 2 note 24.

embedded phonetics of the borrowed writing system. Some instead turned to alphabetic systems derived ultimately from Aramaic. The source of writing for the early Türkic khaghanates, and then the Uyghurs, this was also used in one of the Mongols' writing systems.[98] Others, however, sought in one way or another to adapt the Chinese writing system in complex borrowed systems. In some, such as Japanese, with its *ōn* and *kun* readings, and use of *kana* alongside *kanji*, the Chinese language was incorporated along with its writing system to become "Sino-Xenic."[99] Though certainly not becoming Chinese, the Japanese language changed enormously through its borrowings.[100] Other peoples, such as the Tanguts, Khitans, and especially the Jurchen, excavated the Chinese script to create their own phonetic systems.[101] Although Sinographs were drawn upon in construction of the Khitan Large Script, unlike Japanese they were not incorporated whole into the evolving language but clearly modified, perhaps, according to Zev Handel, for cultural reasons, to differentiate them from Chinese script.[102]

It is possible that Taghbach use of modified Sinographs as a syllabary for their tongue is seen in Taiwu's announcement in 425 that "Now We firmly establish written characters . . . [that shall] eternally be our standard model."[103] More than a thousand "new characters" were said to have been created. But none of these have survived, so their nature remains unclear. We do, however, have a handful of examples of the use of conventional Chinese characters to transcribe names and terms—such as *zhi qin* (reconstructed as *"tigin,"* "member of the imperial clan," in the Taghbach *guo yu*)—particularly from outside sources such as the dynastic histories of the Yangtze regimes, or in surviving contemporary documents such as the "Nan xun bei" stele. And the "Bibliography Monograph" of *Sui shu* lists the names of several documents in the Sui libraries in the early seventh century, with brief notes. One was a "Classic of Filial Piety in the National Language" (*Guo yu Xiao jing*), concerning which it is explained to the reader that after relocation to Luoyang the *guo ren*—the commoners of Dai—did not understand Chinese, so Xiaowen had the gist of *Xiao jing* set in the "barbarian speech" (*yi yu* 夷語)—what had been the *guo yu*—so they could be taught. None of these texts

---

98. András Róna-Tas, "On the Development and Origin of the East Turkic 'Runic' Script," *Acta Orientalia Academiae Scientiarum Hungaricae* 41.1 (1987): 7–14; Findley, *The Turks*, 48. Other examples would be the use of Chinese characters as phonetics to convey the Mongols' *Secret History*; and a similar alternative used by some Uyghurs: Shōgaito Masahiro, "A Chinese Āgama Text Written in Uighur Script and the Use of Chinese," in *Trans-Turkic Studies: Festschrift in Honour of Marcel Erdal* (Istanbul: Mehmet Ölmez, 2010), 67–77.

99. This "Sino-Xenic" pronunciation of Chinese characters in Korean, Japanese, and Vietnamese is discussed in Zev Handel's *Sinography: The Borrowing and Adaptation of the Chinese Script* (Leiden and Boston: Brill, 2019), 13.

100. See Marc Hideo Miyake, *Old Japanese: A Phonetic Reconstruction* (London and New York: RoutledgeCurzon, 2003).

101. Beckwith, *Empires of the Silk Road*, 180–81.

102. Handel, *Sinography*, 273.

103. WS 4A.70.

survive, but we can assume that as seen repeatedly above, *guo yu* words had been transcribed using Chinese characters.[104]

This translation of a piece of the Chinese canon was a singular event, and we are not told how the men responded to the emperor's educational efforts. But different sorts of *guo yu* texts appear in a later section of the *Sui shu* catalog. These included half a dozen guides to northern tongues, some simply entitled "The National Language" (*Guo yu*), others—apparently lexicons—with titles such as "The Names of Things in the National Language" (*Guo yu wu ming*).[105] In the same section are two texts providing transcription of songs of the Pingcheng court, one named "Imperial Songs in the National Language" (*Guo yu yu ge* 國語御歌). As pointed out above, the modern scholar Tian Yuqing has suggested that this was an epic form of the Taghbach origin myth.[106] Unfortunately, nothing remains of it.

Another interesting set of *guo yu* documents in the *Sui shu* Bibliography consists of transcriptions of military commands. "When Later Wei first secured the Central Plain," the catalog's notes explain, "all of the orders and commands [employed to] marshal the army used barbarian speech (*yi yu*). Later, there was an intermixing with Chinese ways, and many could not understand. Therefore, the original commands have been recorded."[107] These changes, of course, took place for the most part down in Luoyang, where upper-class officers at best half-knew the *guo yu*, one part of the distancing that had grown up between the regime's elites and the men of Dai; those who remained in the north certainly had no need for books with names like "Orders and commands in the National Language."[108]

Despite efforts to draw the "language of the nation," the *guo yu*, into a written language, those efforts failed and nothing, unfortunately, has to this point been

---

104. SS 32, with the entry on p. 934 and the explanatory comments on p. 935; and see also Zheng, *Bei Wei guan liao ji gou yan jiu xu pian*, 229, where he points out that later Inner Asian rulers of Chinese territory also translated *Xiao jing* into the native language. The name of the Northern Wei translator was transcribed as Houfuhou Kexiling 侯伏侯可悉陵. Yao Weiyuan, *Bei chao Hu xing kao*, 81–87, examines the group name, which may have derived from the Jie people. It is a shame that we don't have more information on him. For the continued use of Chinese characters to transcribe the Dai *guo yu*, rather than development out of the Chinese system of a new phonetic system (as the Khitans and Japanese did, each in their own way), see He Dezhang 何德章, "'Xianbei wen zi' shuo bian zheng" 鮮卑文字"说辨正, rpt. in his *Wei Jin Nan Bei chao shi cong gao* (Beijing: Shang wu yin shu guan, 2010), 371–72. The received version of the Mongols' *Secret History* was, of course, created in the same way.

105. SS 32.945. The second of these was done by the same fellow who translated the *Guo yu Xiao jing*, Houfuhou Kexiling. Several texts, entitled "The Xianbei language," may date from the successor dynasties, when self-consciousness of ethnicity seems to have reappeared among the men of the garrisons who had come south and with it use of the term *Xianbei yu* 鮮卑語, which does not appear in *Wei shu*, but is seen repeatedly in *Bei Qi shu* (21.295, 34.341, 39.515) and *Zhou shu* (26.428).

106. See Chapter 2, note 11.

107. SS 32.947, 945.

108. Use of Serbi among the officers of the northern armies continued in the late Wei: an exile sent to one of the northern garrisons is said to have used "the old speech," that is, *guo yu*, to translate imperial edicts to the soldiers there: WS 30.732. This persisted after Luoyang's fall. In a story about Gao Huan, the power behind the Eastern Wei (534–550) throne, we are told when giving orders to his army he "regularly [used the] Serbi language" 常鮮卑語, with the exception of times when an important Chinese leader was in the ranks, when he used "Hua yan" 華言: BQS 21.295.

recovered of these documents. Oral traditions do, of course, have their own power. As the classicist Denis Feeney, in the midst of examining how the Romans based a literature of their own on that of the Greeks, has also pointed out, "it is quite possible for a highly sophisticated culture"—such as the Etruscans, who made "great works of sculpture, and had a complex set of religious practices and a sophisticated theatrical tradition"—to "produce nothing that we in the modern Western world would recognize as 'literature.'"[109] Unsatisfied, however, with their oral tradition, the Dai elites over time came increasingly to use written Chinese for practical purposes, and more than that, increasingly to place interest on the canon that had taken shape using that writing system. From early on, the Taghbach monarchs could read, and write, Chinese; Mingyuan, we are told, was the author of a 30-chapter book called "New Compilation" (*Xin ji* 新集).[110] But to the regret of some, perhaps, they did not go on to create a written form of their language, or their own literature. In conversation, most at least of the court elite were multilingual, speaking among other tongues a form of Chinese.[111] It is difficult to say, but when reading the conversations recorded in *Wei shu* it is useful to wonder in different periods what language was actually used, and how that changed over time.

* * *

In the first 12 years of Shegui's reign, the monarch had grown from a boy to a man who with great ambition relentlessly drove his army onward. Beginning by hobbling, eliminating, or absorbing his rivals on the frontier and the steppe, he then turned south to seize lands that were both much richer and very differently organized. During this period, the nature and identity of the regime he had inherited began enormous change, which took place in the midst of contest between different groups wishing different things.

If Shegui's mother's brother, Helan Na, had had any wishes apart from staying alive, it would have been preservation of the privileges enjoyed by the men of Dai within the realm as a whole, and of the collegial forms of decision-making which they expected in the court.

Cui Hao wished to use the Wei monarchs and their army to recover the order his own world had lost.

The Wei monarchs, of course, viewed the situation differently. Their main ambition was to consolidate and expand royal power, their attitude toward the

---

109. The quote taken from Emily Wilson's *Times Literary Supplement*, April 27, 2016, review of Denis Feeney's *Beyond Greek* (Cambridge, MA: Harvard University Press, 2016).
110. WS 3.64.
111. Shimunek, *Languages of Ancient Southern Mongolia and North China*, 81, calls the Chinese spoken at Pingcheng a "northeastern dialect of Early Middle Chinese." The multilingual nature of the Taghbach emperors from early times (it is hard to say how early) is another reality obscured by *Wei shu*; 1,000 years later, under the Manchu regime, it was made clear in the famous trilingual stelae.

world perhaps something like the Habsburgs of the Dual Monarchy, who saw themselves as neither Hungarians, nor even as Austrians, but as Habsburgs, and monarchs. For the Taghbach lords, one way to consolidate power was to play different groups against each other in the court, Serbi generals against Chinese scribes. Another would be eventually to shift the base of the empire away from the Land of Dai onto lands that if ravaged, were certainly richer and more reliable as a funding source.

10

Troubling Innovation

The great conquests of Shegui, the Way of War Emperor, ended when he was still a young man in his late twenties. From that time until his death at the age of 38 he looked increasingly within, at himself, with disastrous consequences for those without. For a year or two he engaged in the building of throne halls, and institutions, and rituals. But this gave way in the last years of Daowu's reign to struggle with real or imagined enemies, leading to rebellion real or perhaps at times also imagined. He had built the shell of a new city but, we are told, its streets were still largely deserted, those who did reside there increasingly lawless.[1] One wonders what the new inhabitants—both conquerors and transported conquered—turned to for comfort.

The emperor, our sources tell us, was turning to an ancient form of Viagra called "cold food powder."[2] Composed of five minerals—including fluorine, stalactite, and sulfur—as well as animal and plant products, this stimulant was of questionable reliability.[3] Over time, we are told, Daowu's dosages increased. Whether or not this was the cause, or the only cause, *Wei shu* tells us he was becoming more and more unstable, going days without eating and nights without sleeping, brooding over past successes and failures, fearing omens, and talking to himself as if in conversation with a demon. Whatever the precise nature of his mental state, the Wei emperor was increasingly isolated from his court and mistrustful of those around him.

Many died in Daowu's last years.[4] In 408 came the end of a leader of the Monalou people. The fellow had served Daowu well for years but decades before,

---

1. WS 2.44; ZZTJ 115.3614.
2. WS 2.44; ZZTJ 115.3614.
3. Ute Englehardt, "Cold Food Powder," in *The Encyclopedia of Taoism*, 2 vols. (London: Routledge, 2008), 1: 473; and Joseph Needham, *Science and Civilization in China*, Vol. 5. *Chemistry and Chemical Technology*: pt. 3. *Spagyrical Discovery and Invention: Historical Survey, from Cinnabar Elixirs to Synthetic Insulin* (Cambridge: Cambridge University Press, 1954–), 117–19, in which we are provided a passage from *Wei shu* (114.3049; Needham, 118) describing establishment of the post of an "Alchemist-Royal" who concocted medicines and elixirs, which were tested on individuals sentenced to death. "[S]ince it was not their original intention (to seek for immortality)," the translation tells us, "many died." This is confirmed by Akahori Akira, in his "Drug Taking and Immortality," in *Taoist Meditation and Longevity Techniques*, ed. Livia Kohn (Ann Arbor: Center for Chinese Studies, University of Michigan, 1989), 74, who describes cold-food powder as having been popularized by its association with the philosopher He Yan (d. 249), who used it "to gain relief from depression." Akahori goes on to say that there was no standard formula, and that "[i]t frequently caused severe adverse reactions and sometimes even led to death."
4. See the table of those killed or dismissed by Daowu in Li, *Bei Wei Pingcheng shi dai*, 74–77.

in the midst of the crucial events of 386, had sided with the rival claimant, Shegui's uncle. At that time, the Monalou man is reported to have given Shegui an arrow and said, "How can a three-year juvenile bull win over a heavy wagon?" Though the adolescent had resented being referred to as a juvenile bull, after winning the succession he needed the fellow's backing and so for the next twenty years employed him as a member of the guard. In 408, however, brooding over past successes and failures, he sent a messenger to the house of the Monalou man to present an arrow to him and ask, "The three-year juvenile bull—can it defeat the heavy wagon, or not?" The fellow was executed the next morning.[5] In addition to taking vengeance for an old grudge, Daowu also had the satisfaction of seizing all the man's property, which at this time still consisted mostly of herds.[6]

Of far more consequence was the command in 409 that the Prince of Wey must die, supposedly as punishment for a planned treason.[7] With our meager sources it is hard to know if the charge was true. But for reasons we've already seen, Daowu did have real cause to fear the succession would again be contested. Although he had five years before at least informally designated as heir his eldest son, the future Mingyuan emperor—naming him Prince of Qi and more tellingly setting him up as Minister of State (*xiang guo*)—the Prince of Wey was a close and powerful royal kinsman.[8] In 408 the prince had been summoned to the palace at night by the emperor to see the birth of the heir's putative heir, the future Taiwu. "When you heard the call in the middle of the night," asked the emperor, "weren't you surprised and frightened?" To which the prince is said to have replied, "Your subject with sincerity serves Your Highness. Your Highness being judicious, your subject has now calmed himself. There was surprise, but really there was no fear."[9] But the Prince of Wey did have reason to fear. In the next year he would be ordered to commit suicide. Needless to say, he was not buried among the Jinling tombs.

---

5. WS 28.683–84. The term here translated as "juvenile bull," *du* 犢, is the Chinese term that translated whatever the Monalou and Shegui actually said in their own *guo yu*; it would be fascinating to recover the original, taken as it is from the core of their traditional economy.

6. Zhang, *Bei Wei zheng zhi shi*, 2: 330.

7. WS 15.372; and see the discussion of this in Zhang, *Bei Wei zheng zhi shi*, 2: 323–27.

8. On the uncertain nature of Wey's relationship to Daowu, see Chapter 7 note 61. For the apparent existence already of clear heir apparency, see WS 2.41; and the comments of Li, *Bei Wei Pingcheng shi dai*, 71. It needs also pointed out that the Chinese name (or title) assigned Mingyuan was "Si" 嗣 (WS 3.49), which simply means "successor." WS 4A.69 also states that Taiwu was born to Mingyuan in the latter's "eastern palace," the Chinese designation of the heir apparent's residence; and see also discussion of Taiwu's designation as heir in Li, *Bei Wei Pingcheng shi dai*, 82. It is true, as Holmgren, "Harem in Northern Wei Politics," 73, correctly states, that Mingyuan "was never officially proclaimed heir-apparent in the Chinese manner." This does not, however, mean that he was not designated as heir; instead, here we see yet another sign of how this regime was still largely organized on the basis of Inner Asian tradition (or ad hoc invention), with key aspects not seen in the incomplete record provided in its Chinese history. Vertical succession had already clearly appeared in the Inner Asian world, among the Xiongnu: Di Cosmo, "Aristocratic Elites," 26. For a general discussion of contested succession in Northern Wei, see Eisenberg, *Kingship in Early Medieval China*, Chapter 2.

9. BS 15.562 (WS 15.371).

This served only to augment a tide of fear and panic that had been growing for years within the court. The bodies of officials killed by Daowu's own hand—supposedly for such offenses as walking off-stride, or losing their train of thought while speaking—were put up for display outside the Hall of Heaven's Peace.[10] After ordering the Prince of Wey's death, Daowu invited the other princes of the house to a feast to defuse tensions. Only one made an appearance. All the others, fearing they would be implicated by association with Wey, fled, some making plans to ride north to seek refuge with the Rouran. In the event, the prince who did attend was well treated, calming the imperial clan a bit.[11] But the issue of contested succession was not confined to the emperor's close relatives. From the time of Liwei, the Taghbach family had been an ever-expanding conical clan. Liwei's descendants, the *tigin*, were collective owners of this patrimony, and some seem to have held the view that all *tigin* were at least in theory eligible to succession as Liwei's heir.[12] Not surprisingly, the Northern Wei monarchs disagreed with this assertion, but still, for a century we see sporadic revolt of distant imperial kinsmen.[13] This issue would not be finally settled until the time of Xiaowen. But in 404, to provide a counterweight to threat from his own kinsmen, Daowu began to grant the title "prince" (*wang*) to men not of the imperial line.[14] Structures of status, of various sorts, had no doubt existed previously among the various groups brought together over the previous century to create the Dai polity. But by creating an externally imposed, top-down hierarchy alongside the persistence of grandees of the old polities, these peerages—though not of the special sort given the Erzhu, with actual bestowal of land—transformed the realm. Using a nomenclature borrowed from the Chinese empire, and linked with military rank, they brought heritable prestige and access at court and within the army, in a way not clearly described within the sources.[15]

The ways in which he used outsiders to shore up his power as monarch against kinsmen indicates a method in Daowu's madness. But this mind was undoubtedly troubled. Like all human beings, on the basis of feelings lodged deep inside our selfish genes, Daowu wanted to pass his enterprise on to his own progeny.

10. WS 2.44.
11. BS 15.575 (WS 15.382).
12. Luo Xin, "Zhi qin," 104–5; Albert Dien, "Elite Lineages and the T'o-pa Accommodation," 76–77, citing Marshall D. Sahlins, *Tribesmen* (Englewood Cliffs, NJ: Prentice-Hall, 1968), 24. On the broadly shared view of corporate ownership of the patrimony, see Biran, "Introduction," *Nomads as Agents of Cultural Change*.
13. Eisenberg, *Kingship in Early Medieval China*, 46.
14. WS 2.41–42, 113.2973. Chen, *Shi jia da zu yu Bei chao zheng zhi*, 3, points out the importance of this reform of peerage in development of the Taghbach state.
15. Though not receiving land, they did receive bound labor: WS 113.2974; Yan, *Bei Wei qian qi zheng zhi zhi du*, 180–82. See also Chen, *Shi jia da zu yu Bei chao zheng zhi*, 12–13; and discussion of the (partial) linkage between peerage and rank within military and administration in Daichi Seiko 大知圣子 (大知聖子), "Guan yu Bei Wei qian qi jue he pin xiang dui ying de ji chu kao cha—yi Nanxun bei wei zhong xin" 关于北魏前期爵和品相对应的基础考察——以南巡碑为中心, in *Zhongguo Wei Jin Nan Bei chao shi xue hui di shi jie nian hui ji guo ji xue shu yan tao hui lun wen ji*, ed. Zhongguo Wei Jin Nan Bei chao shi xue hui, Shanxi da xue li shi wen hua xue yuan (Taiyuan: Beiyue wen yi chu ban she, 2012), 92–107.

Not a cousin. And certainly not a wife, or a wife's father or brother. But apparently doubting his sons' ability, we see the emergence at the end of Daowu's reign of a particularly troubling practice called "exalting the son and so killing the mother," which consisted of formally designating the imperial heir and then forcing the mother to commit suicide. In this polygamous society, the designated empress and the birth-mother of the heir would be two different individuals. It should also be noted that none of the women killed in this way were Serbi.[16] By killing the heir's mother—and precluding a close bond between the empress and the heir—Daowu sought to prevent the rise to power of empresses and affines, which had occurred before in Taghbach history, with Madam Wei, and with Daowu's own mother.[17] Later, it must be said, killing of the heir's mother came to be used by prominent women at court to eliminate the birth-mother and so take control of the heir and ensure their own power.[18] Though referred to as an "ancient practice," this effort to dismantle family ties had no real precedents in earlier Taghbach history and seems to have been invented by Daowu; the reader can decide if it is plausible that he was inspired to do this by Cui Hong reading to him from *Han shu* a similar story from the reign of the Han emperor Wudi.[19]

The woman designated as Daowu's empress was the youngest daughter of Murong Bao, taken upon the fall of Zhongshan, along with several hundred of her kinsmen. They had then been marched north to Pingcheng, where the Murong daughter is said to have been "graced" (*xing* 幸) by the emperor, though no births are recorded for her. She died young, perhaps of natural causes. The year of her passing is unknown, but it was before 409, when just months before his own death Daowu killed all her kinsmen in Pingcheng on charges of an attempt to abscond.[20]

Bearing for Daowu his first son and putative heir, the future Mingyuan emperor (r. 409–423), was Madam Liu, a niece of the Xiongnu lord Liu Kuren (and so cousin of Daowu's bitter enemy, Liu Xian). Daowu made her a consort in 386, and in 392 she bore Mingyuan up on the Tumed Plain. She failed, however, to become empress, supposedly because of her inability to cast a golden statue (a

---

16. Yan, *Bei Wei qian qi zheng zhi zhi du*, 17. Though a woman of the Helan clan—close affines of the Taghbach—would meet her end this way, as we shall see just below, these were viewed as Xiongnu (see Yao, *Bei chao Hu xing kao*, 36).

17. Holmgren, "Women and Political Power," 62, makes the good point that this was linked with a shift from fraternal to filial succession. I do have a somewhat different view than that which she states on p. 63, that "the traditional T'o-pa [Tuoba] leadership structure was based on the concept of a male-dominated military dictatorship which allowed very little room for female or distaff participation in political affairs." In the opinion of this author, Daowu chose to kill the heir's mother precisely because women and distaff kinsmen had earlier participated in political affairs, and Daowu did not want them to continue to do so.

18. Tian, *Tuoba shi tan*, 15–68; and see also Scott Pearce, "Nurses, Nurslings, and New Shapes of Power in the Mid-Wei Court," *Asia Major*, 3rd ser., 22.1 (2009): 287–309.

19. WS 24.621; Zhang, *Bei Wei zheng zhi shi*, 2: 341. A theory was propounded in *EMC* in 2002 (8 [2002], 1–41) by Valentin Golovachev that the practice had roots in ancient Inner Asian practice ("Matricide among the Tuoba-Xianbei and Its Transformation during the Northern Wei"), to which this author wrote a rebuttal in *EMC* 9.

20. BS 13.492 (WS 13.325); WS 2.36, 44.

practice seen among other groups of Inner Asian origin that would not long outlive the reign).[21] And in 409—although she is said to have been much adored by Daowu—she was forced to commit suicide, apparently because the emperor felt his own days were numbered and did not wish to leave his son in the hands of a strong woman. At this point, the distraught 17-year-old designated heir fled his palace.[22] Daowu now turned to his next son, Shao, who had been born of another Helan woman, who happened to be sister of the emperor's mother. (While among the Helan, we are told, the early teen Daowu had been captivated by her beauty. Asked about this, his mother had said "No—she's too pretty for you. And besides, she has a husband."[23] Before long, the husband was dead and the aunt taken to wife.)

Despite his original infatuation, the father now moved to impose the "ancient practice" on Shao's mother as well. Before he could do so, however, the imprisoned woman sent her son a secret message asking, "How are you going to save me?" That night, while Daowu slept in the Hall of Heaven's Peace, Shao—described in *Wei shu* as a thuggish adolescent—forced his way in with a small party of his own followers as well as several palace eunuchs. The alarm having sounded, the Taghbach monarch leapt up out of bed, groping for sword or bow. Unable to lay his hands on a weapon, he died.[24]

The next day the gates of the palace did not open till noon, when Shao came out to say to those assembled, "I have uncles, and I have an elder brother—lords and ministers, whom do you wish to follow?"[25] Ashen-faced, none could make a reply until the old and loyal "'Song' of the Baba clan"[26] said "I will follow the prince." Though suspicion and uneasiness pervaded, Shao now attempted to buy loyalty by opening up the palace stores to give out reams of textiles, the coinage of the realm.[27]

One group that did rally to Shao's support was his mother's people, the Helan: "the remnants of the old tribe led their sons and brothers to rally their kinsmen, who gathered together everywhere."[28] But the Helan would lose once

---

21. BS 13.493 (WS 13.325). See the note on this by James Ware, "An Ordeal among the T'o-pa Wei," *T'oung Pao*, 2nd ser., 32.4 (1936): 205–9; and Cheng Ya-ju (Zheng Yaru) 鄭雅如, "Han zhi yu Hu feng: chong tan Bei Wei de 'huang hou,' 'huang tai hou' zhi du" 漢制與胡風：重探北魏的「皇后」、「皇太后」制度, *Zhong yang yan jiu yuan li shi yu yan yan jiu suo ji kan* 90.1 (2019): 6–7.
22. WS 34.799, 800; ZZTJ 115.3622.
23. WS 16.390.
24. WS 16.389–90.
25. ZZTJ 115.3623. This rendition of the quote is more plausible than that given in *Wei shu* (16.390), which says, "I have a father, and I have an elder brother." From the outlines of the story, it seems clear that the assembly knew that Daowu had died.
26. In *Wei shu* given under the anachronistic "Zhangsun Song."
27. See discussion of the use of textiles as currency in Wei Wenjiang 卫文江, "Bei Wei shi qi de huo bi liu tong" 北魏时期的货币流通, *Bei chao yan jiu* 4 (2004): 281–84; and Richard Von Glahn, *The Economic History of China: From Antiquity to the Nineteenth Century* (Cambridge: Cambridge University Press, 2016), 178. This would continue under Tang.
28. WS 16.390, 83A.1813. See also Tian, *Tuoba shi tan*, 73.

again. Hearing of his father's death, Mingyuan was hiding in the mountains that ring the basin, following the situation. His attempts to contact those within elicited eager response. As he approached the city, the guard seized Shao and handed him to Mingyuan, who now forced suicide upon both son and mother, and executed a dozen or so followers. Those who had affronted Daowu were taken to a plaza just outside the palace city, we are told, and while still alive flayed and eaten by the "host of officials."[29] Though primogeniture was still contested, Mingyuan clearly enjoyed broad support, and loyalty. Fleeing the palace after his mother's death, he had been protected by his guardsman Wang Luor—the one who had earlier fished him from the icy river. Keeping him safe in hiding, Wang had gone on to make contact with the court officials who eventually allowed Mingyuan to return to take power.[30]

So it was in this dramatic way that the 17-year-old took the throne. Though one of the southern histories gives his personal name as the transcription Mumo 木末 (MC *Muwk-mat), within the Chinese historiographical tradition he would go down as Emperor Mingyuan 明元帝 (r. 409–423).[31] Movingly, almost the first thing recorded in the new emperor's annals is posthumous elevation to the rank of empress of his mother, whom his father had forced to die. It would take more than a year for him to get the wife-killer buried among the Jinling tombs in the mountains east of the town of Shengle.[32] We are not told where the corpse was kept in the meantime.

The sixth-century *Wei shu* compiler Wei Shou closes Mingyuan's section of the annals by telling us that at the end of Daowu's reign "there was much enmity within" the court, but that though his son and heir had had "the calamity of encountering a monster"—perhaps referring as much to the father as the patricidal son—he had gone on to create "harmony within and concordance without."[33] Some of the ways in which he did this was by extending to major officials dismissed from office by Daowu invitations to resume service to the state, and more particularly, rehabilitating the line of the Prince of Wey by granting his heir a princely title.[34] During this reign came an assertion of the power of senior statesmen vis-à-vis that of the monarch, in a sort of regency by committee. Including key military men such as Song of the Baba clan, but also Cui Hong, this group sat outside the palace complex's main southern gate, the "Stop-Your-Cart-Here Portal" (*Zhichemen* 止車門), to decide government business.[35]

---

29. WS 16.390; Yin, "Bei Wei Pingcheng shi lüe," 194. These events were hopefully embellished by their chronicler.
30. WS 34.799.
31. For the transcribed name Mumo, see SoS 95.2322; NQS 57.983, 984.
32. WS 3.49, 50, 2.44. It may, of course, have taken time to build the tomb; but it will be noted that for Mingyuan himself it took only one month from death to burial: WS 3.64.
33. WS 3.64: 逢梟獍之禍. The terms *xiao* and *jing* each refer to a different mythological creature that will eat its own parent, more generally to one lacking all human feeling: see *HYDCD* 4: 1054b.
34. WS 3.49, 50.
35. ZZTJ 115.3624; WS 24.622, 25.643, 17.698, 113.2975. It is not clear how institutionalized this was; the *Wei shu* says that "the people of this age called them the eight lords" 世號八公 (WS 25.643). Some have suggested

Still, neither the realm nor the royal family was in a state of perfect harmony. Occupancy of the throne, in fact, continued to be contested. A few months after Mingyuan's accession, a cousin with a knife hidden in his robes was caught deep inside the palace with plans to assassinate him.[36] And toward the end of his reign come a series of cryptic mentions in *Wei shu* of deaths of the emperor's brothers. Apparently the court was eliminating the potential danger posed by siblings by eliminating siblings.[37] In these cases, however, the peerage was not abolished but inherited by the dead men's sons.

The fourteen years of Mingyuan's reign also saw a continuation of the general pause in Wei military activity that had begun in the last years of Daowu. There were occasional indecisive engagements with what remained of the Yan regime in Manchuria, though control had now fallen to the Feng, an ostensibly Chinese family heavily influenced by generations spent among Serbi (we will discuss the Feng in much more detail below). A more serious issue was the Rouran threat from the steppe, which led in the last year of Mingyuan's reign to construction of ramparts (*chang cheng*) along the Yinshan frontier, an early step in development of a string of garrisons north of the Yinshan.[38]

Wei showed the flag in 416 on the north bank of the Yellow River near Luoyang as the southern general Liu Yu—who would in 420 end the Eastern Jin and establish his own Song dynasty (420–479)[39]—sailed up it to seize from the crumbling Later Qin regime of the Qiang first Luoyang—or what remained of it, a century after its despoliation—and then briefly Chang'an and the Guanzhong region.[40] (It was during the course of this expedition that notes on forts along the Luo River were gathered, which eventually made their way into the late-Wei geography, *Shui jing zhu* 水經注.) Soon after the death of Liu Yu in 422, Mingyuan dispatched troops, then himself led the main army down to seize key strategic points on the south bank of the Yellow River, including the site of Luoyang, as

the term "eight lords" was borrowed from Wei and Jin (Liu Jun 刘军, "Bei Wei huang zu zheng zhi ti zhi zhi kao cha—yi zong shi ba gong wei zhong xin" 北魏皇族政治体制之考察——以宗室八公为中心, *Nandu xue tan* 34.6 [2014]: 21–27), though Hucker, *Official Titles*, 359 #4371, expresses skepticism. Be that as it may, Liu in the article makes a good case that this and related posts were important bases of power for the broader imperial clan vis-à-vis the emperor and his court. For a good guess of location of the Zhichemen as the main southern gate of the entire palace complex, see Duan and Zhao, *Tian xia da tong*, 55.

36. WS 3.50; 29.705.
37. Two deaths came in the year 416, and one each in 421 and 422. No detail is provided on how or why the young men died: WS 3.56, 61; WS 16.391, 395, 399. Not all of these necessarily derived from power struggles within the family; for one of the four deaths, the one in 421, Mingyuan is said to have expressed great grief, and to have paid for a well-stocked tomb. See discussion of "sib elimination" during the Mingyuan reign in Eisenberg, *Kingship in Early Medieval China*, 43.
38. WS 3.63. For broader discussion of the northern garrisons, see Scott Pearce, "The Land of Tai: The Origins, Evolution and Historical Significance of a Community of the Inner Asian Frontier," in *Opuscula Altaica: Essays Presented in Honor of Henry Schwarz*, ed. Edward H. Kaplan and Donald W. Whisenhunt (Bellingham: Western Washington University, 1994): 465–98.
39. This was, of course, quite distinct from the early modern Song dynasty of the Zhao family, 960–1279.
40. ZZTJ 117.3689ff.

well as the crucial military center of Hulao (northwest of Xingyang, Henan), a pass controlling traffic through a narrow passage between mountain and the River east of Luoyang.⁴¹ The emperor soon, however, returned north and this area would for years remain a contested no-man's-land.⁴² But sensing a threat from the Taghbach, leaders of the Qiang, the Gansu Corridor state of Northern Liang and the eastern Tibet state of the Tuyuhun began making efforts to establish alliance with the Jiankang regime.⁴³

Within territory more firmly under control, however, the new emperor did send out a party of inspectors to examine the deeds and misdeeds of regional administrators left over from Daowu's reign. Such efforts had been made sporadically since the conquest: in 398, immediately after the fall of Zhongshan, as he marched across the plains with his army Daowu had made a performance of asking about the well-being of his new subjects and ordering local officials there to care for the indigent elderly.⁴⁴ But efforts to gain secure control over the new provinces increased under Mingyuan. One of the agents reported to the throne that a tailor from the imperial armory, appointed as magistrate of Taiyuan, had illegally been engaged in trade.⁴⁵ He was punished, we are told, and the situation in the provinces improved, but in reality the twin problems of corruption and less than complete control over the conquered territories would persist. As we shall discuss in more detail in Chapter 15, though taxes were collected from these areas, they were brought in through the mediation of powerful locals.⁴⁶

More firmly under control of the monarchy was the royal domain. Daowu had begun work on Pingcheng in 398, after the conquest of the plains. But till the end of his reign, it was still a work in progress, a scene of cleared ground with a few new buildings scattered across. Though occasionally using it as a place of habitation—he died, of course, in the bedchamber of the Heavenly Peace Palace—we are told by the Jiankang history *Nan Qi shu* that Daowu was still a nomad, spending most of his time "following water and grass," and that it was only in the time of Mingyuan that the emperor truly settled to live in the palaces of Pingcheng.⁴⁷ Under Mingyuan much of the city's actual building was completed, including the city's outer walls, which were finally finished in 422.⁴⁸

41. ZZTJ 119, passim; Zhang, *Bei Wei zheng zhi shi*, 2: 500.
42. ZZTJ 119.3758–59.
43. ZZTJ 118.2724, 119.2753–54; SoS 95.2337.
44. WS 2.31.
45. WS 30.713.
46. Yan, *Bei Wei qian qi zheng zhi zhi du*, 79–83. And see the 415 edict berating corrupt officials and declaring that taxes from that year still unpaid would as punishment come from the official's own household budget, and were not to be levied on the peasantry: WS 3.55.
47. NQS 57.984.
48. WS 3.62. See also discussion in Guan Furong 管芙蓉, "Bei Wei Pingcheng gong dian jian zhu chu tan" 北魏平城宫殿建筑出探, rpt. in *Zou chu shi ku de Bei Wei wang chao*, ed. Jin Zhao and Alede'ertu (Beijing: Wen hua yi shu chu ban she, 2010), 740; and in Zhang, *Bei Wei zheng zhi shi*, 2: 381–85.

Administrators and army men now began to dwell in the city's wards, fed and served by populations forcibly resettled around the capital. These transportations were particularly large in scale with the conquests of Mingyuan's son and heir, Taiwu, leading to a population within the domain of a million or more.[49]

There were, of course, drawbacks to locating the capital in this high and rather dry region, in a time of general cooling of the weather of northeastern Asia, and the year 415 saw crop failure there.[50] When it was suggested the capital be moved down onto the plain, Mingyuan turned for advice to Cui Hao. The key to Cui Hao's argument against the move was that Taghbach power depended on mystery and terror: "Now, living in the northlands, if there is an incident in the lands east of the mountains [i.e., down on the plains], your light cavalry can go south and emerge, making a show of force amongst the mulberries and catalpas [of the Chinese village]. How does anyone know how many [of you there are]? The common folk see this, and beholding the [clouds of] dust are terrified into submission."[51] Writ large, Pingcheng was a castle on a hill.[52] These thoughts, said the emperor in reply, "are like Our own ideas." And so the capital was kept in the highlands, its most desperate inhabitants sent down as temporary refugees to the plains, where granaries were opened to feed them. Presumably, many of these starving people would have been trudging south on the same route along which they had been guided north some 17 years before. Immediate crisis was thus averted. But the basic problems continued to exist and grew worse over the years.

Cui Hao was not a unique example of Pingcheng's use of Chinese advisors and administrators. In early spring of 413, messengers were sent out to scour the realm for "talented recluses," selecting and sending to the capital for examination scions of eminent families, as well as individuals with various sorts of talents, such as decision-making and leadership skills, and more generally "civil or military skills."[53] Mingyuan received these men with both respect and affection, and seems himself to have become interested in the richness of the Chinese literary tradition. In the first year of his reign the emperor commanded Cui Hao to expound for him the meaning of the Chinese classics. And, as mentioned above, in the summation of his career at the end of his section of the annals he is said to have produced a work called "New Compilation," supposedly because of his dissatisfaction with the work of the Han scholar Liu Xiang.[54] Whoever actually drew the volume together, it is interesting to note that it was a pastiche

---

49. See Chapter 9 note 22.
50. WS 110.2850, 3.55. For associated climate change, see note 10 in Chapter 3.
51. WS 35.808, 110.2850, 3.55.
52. This perhaps dovetails with W. J. F. Jenner's description of Pingcheng as a "latifundium": *Memories of Loyang: Yang Hsüan-chih and the Lost Capital (493–534)* (Oxford: Clarendon Press, 1981), 25.
53. WS 3.52.
54. WS 35.825, 3.64.

of passages taken from the Chinese classics and the histories, "from which was drawn a wealth (of information) in both civil and military (matters)."[55] The book itself is lost, but here we see a key aspect of the Taghbach regime, and no doubt of regimes in general: the need to balance cultural capital with the capacity for physical coercion, the latter which we will examine in more detail in Chapter 11.

55. WS 3.64.

SECTION V.

Pingcheng as Center of a World

Perched in the northern highlands, the town of Pingcheng would for about a century be the center of *a* world, if not *the* world (since there is, of course, no particular center of *the* world).

It was an army town, and in Chapter 11 we discuss in detail the nature of that army. Though changing over time, it was originally composed of men of Inner Asian origin (alongside, perhaps, an occasional Mulan), who carrying on their ancestors' skills at shooting an arrow from the back of a horse, had taken up new technologies such as the stirrup, or armor for both man and horse. Their technologies were organizational as well as material: the groups from which the soldiery was drawn seem to have been rearranged to accord with institutionalization of army units based on 10s. As with other highly militarized societies—that of the Warring States' Qin, for instance, or Prussia—social mobility came with military service, which included a broad variety of activities, such as protecting the pennon of one's unit on the field of battle, or organizing the troops for the huge imperial hunts. In more immediate terms, those who fought well on the field of battle would receive a share of the loot.

As described in Chapter 12, the Wei emperor Taiwu (r. 426–451)—known among his men by the Inner Asian appellation, Böri Beg or "Wolf Lord"—led these troops forth to complete the conquests of the territories in and around the Yellow River plains. Over several decades the holdouts—mainly polities of Inner Asian origin—were one by one destroyed. At that point, the Wolf Lord led an army said—no doubt with hyperbole—to have numbered one million men south to confront his last major rival in East Asia, the rich, Yangtze-based empire of Jiankang. In the winter of 451 he arrived on the north bank of the river, where from a great tent perched up on a hill he could look across it at his enemies' capital. But the effort went no further; the Wei monarch then pulled up his tent stakes to return to Pingcheng. And there he would soon after meet his own end.

Hunting—of either animals, or other humans—was one of the great preoccupations of the society that took shape at Pingcheng. It was a way both to discipline the soldiery, and more practically, to feed those hungry men. In Chapter 13, drawing on murals from those people's tombs, we examine their great preoccupation with such undertakings, which is in the murals often paired with delight in the feast. Reflecting the power of women in this society, the feasts' hosts were often not generals, but generals' wives.

11

The Wei Army

With the decline of the Chinese empire in the early centuries CE had come a decline in its fighting forces. Formal abolition of universal conscription in the first century led to increasing use of professional soldiers or convicts sentenced to military service as punishment for crime.[1] With peripheralization from the larger society came a decline in the soldier's status. Another sort of peripheralization of military manpower came with increasing use of auxiliary units recruited from among non-Chinese groups. In this great age of poetry in the Chinese world, the point might be best made in a poem written in October 220 celebrating the southern campaign of the first emperor of the Wei of the third century, Cao Pi, who is said to have put "the six army regiments in order / Commanding the Xiongnu riders and their Khan / as well as the bow-carriers of Wuhuan and Xianbei." A bit later the piece goes on to say that "There is no need to renew conscription. / Farmers remain at ease in the fields; / Merchants effect no change to their shops."[2]

With collapse of the empire in the early fourth century, large standing armies no longer emerged from what remained of its subject populations, at least in the Yellow River region. Former junior partners of the empire—Qiang, Xiongnu, Serbi—now filled the breach, building armies—and so kingdoms—from the populations at the edges. In the end, the most successful of these regimes was Northern Wei. In this chapter we will look at how the Wei army was recruited and organized, particularly in the regime's early generations, when it was most effective. The key for Wei was ability of its leaders to reorganize at least some of the peoples and polities under their control to form a large and stable military force that also became the tight-knit community described in Chapter 9, serving as a new basis for identity, touchstone for loyalty, and source of rewards.

---

1. Lewis, "Han Abolition of Universal Military Service."
2. The poem is translated by Xiaofei Tian, *The Halberd at Red Cliff: Jian'an and the Three Kingdoms* (Cambridge, MA, and London: Harvard University Asia Center, 2018), 96–97, drawing on *Quan San guo wen* 全三國文, comp. Yan Kejun 嚴可均 (1762–1843). (Note that the term usually rendered "khaghan" in this volume is here given as "khan.") See also Lewis, "Han Abolition," 59–60, 47; He Ziquan 何玆全, "Wei Jin de zhong jun" 魏晉的中军, in his *Du shi ji* (Shanghai: Shanghai ren min chu ban she, 1982), 243; and Jin Fagen, *Yongjia luan hou*, 48. Based on the terracotta warriors of Qin's First Emperor it has, in fact, been suggested that fighting men from the grasslands were in the empire's armies from the very beginning: Rawson, "China and the Steppe," 386.

Unfortunately, as the archaeologist Xia Nai (1910–1985) has pointed out, "the military institutions of Northern Wei are without a clear written account, and cannot be studied in detail."³ This is not because of a lack of an army, of course, but instead lack of interest in (or access to) that army among contemporary chroniclers. Modern scholars, however, have made good effort to—as the skeptic Lü Simian 呂思勉 (1884–1957) put it so well—"spread the sand to pick out the gold" 披沙揀金,⁴ and reconstructed at least the rough outlines of the early Wei army.⁵

The original core of the Taghbach army came from among horse-riding populations of Inner Asian origin living in and around the Tumed Plain. For most of the fourth century this was a coalition of the cavalry of minor dynasts who followed—or, when they dared, declined to follow—the Taghbach overlord. During this period, however, the overlord was making efforts to extract from these populations (or others) a central force permanently under his own command. This eventually took shape as a huge imperial guard that functioned both to protect the monarch, and provide the core of most campaigns. And this army had changed rapidly, in a decade or two: while as seen in Chapter 6, Shiyijian's army seems to have been made up of light cavalry, with no sign yet of the stirrup, the Wei army that attacked Zhongshan in 397 is said to have numbered more than 300,000 in all, with 100,000 crack cavalry with armored mounts (and so presumably stirrups).⁶ Despite worthy efforts to pick gold out of sand, it is not quite clear how and when the newly recreated regime produced or obtained all that armor; presumably, a large part of it was extracted from piles of dead bodies after the battle of Shenhe Slope, just two years before.⁷ From this point on, these

---

3. This is from recent republication of comments by Xia Nai 夏鼐 that originated in a 1930s debate between him and the famous medievalist Chen Yinke: "Du shi zha ji: lun Bei Wei bing shi chu liu Yi ji Hu hua Han ren wai, si yi you Zhongyuan Han ren zai nei" 读史札记: 论北魏兵士除六夷及胡化之汉人外,似亦有中原汉人在内, *Qinghua da xue xue bao (Zhe xue she hui ke xue ban)* 17.6 (2002): 6. The same general point was made even earlier by the *Wei shu* author Wei Shou, when in the 550s in his "Treatise on Offices and Clans" he observed of the Wei system before Xiaowen's reforms, the "old regulations are lost; there is nothing we can depend on" (WS 113.2976); cited by Zhang, *Jin wei wu guan*, 2: 659, again, to make the point that we cannot have a full reconstruction of the early Wei state. Back in the 1930s, the scholar Gu Jiguang attempted to fill the gap by piecing together a "Supplemental *Wei shu* Monograph on the Army" 補魏書兵志 as part of Volume 4 of the *Er shi wu shi bu bian* 二十五史補編 (Beijing: Zhonghua shu ju, 1956) (despite the fact that none of the early standard histories has such).

4. In his *Du shi zha ji*, 809, quoting the Tang historian Liu Zhiji, *Shi tong tong shi*, 7.193.

5. In the following pages, many texts will be cited, but for this author probably the most helpful has been Zhang Jinlong's *Jin wei wu guan*.

6. WS 33.787 provides these figures in a question-and-answer session between a Wei envoy and a Jiankang official. It will be noted that the figure of the army in WS 2.27; ZZTJ 108.3430 is given as more than 400,000. Perhaps the difference lies in the *Zi zhi tong jian* statement that this was "more than 400,000 foot and horse," the larger figure thus including supporting units on foot.

7. "Armored horses" 鎧馬 were being used by Serbi and others fighting in the Jin civil war in the early fourth century: JS 39.1148, 63.1707; see David A. Graff, *Medieval Chinese Warfare, 300–900* (London and New York: Routledge, 2002), 41. Regarding the Murong in particular, in 403 53,000 "iron horsemen" 鐵騎 were serving a Murong group that had splintered off after the fall of Later Yan: Müller, "Horses of the Xianbei," 188–89 (JS 127.3172); and in SoS 1.20 we see mention of heavily armored Serbi cavalry in the Yangtze region serving as auxiliary units in the civil wars of the early 400s that led to the fall of Eastern Jin.

numbers for the Wei army seem to have become relatively fixed, with a central army as a whole with about 300,000 troops, of which elite guard units comprised one or two hundred thousand men.[8] Other troops were placed in garrisons, down on the plains, and later, north of the Yinshan.

The central army took shape within the northern sector of the Taghbach dual administration. On the other side was what remained of the old empire's system of local administration—districts and commanderies—that had been appropriated with Daowu's conquest of the plains.[9] Over decades in the fifth century, Wei monarchs came to draw on this as well for military service. At first conscripting them for support and logistics, by the late fifth century they were the source of infantry troops that came increasingly to outnumber what remained of cavalry. In this way, the army, like the regime, was transformed.

* * *

Into the fourth century the Taghbach lords were just one hub in a complex network of frequently changing alliances among many disparate groups that existed in the lands north and south of the Yinshan. Coalitions of fighting groups came and went. Effort to build a more stable military institution can be seen with Yilu's imposition of strict martial law in the early 300s, but his efforts, it will be remembered, failed. It is not until the late 330s that a distinct khaghan's army took shape under Shiyijian, with his establishment of what are called in Chinese in the *Wei shu* "close attendants of the left and right" 左右近侍.[10] Recruited from among the sons of the nobility and numbering about 100, these men combined civil and military functions. While distributing the lord's commands, they also served as his guards (it is perhaps only a coincidence that the Chinese term used here, "attendant," *shi*, is the *kanji* used for the Japanese "samurai"). Shiyijian's new institution is clearly a prologue to Pingcheng's Inner Court, and the first embodiment of the rough unity of army and state that so strongly characterizes the first century of the Wei regime.

Soon after, Shiyijian began the practice of regular summer assemblies for military training at Shenhe Slope, at which he seems to have had a platform erected from which he could watch the mounted archery contest.[11] It is said he could

---

8. Yan, *Bei Wei qian qi zheng zhi zhi du*, 155–56; He Ziquan 何兹全, "Fu bing zhi qian de Bei chao bing zhi" 府兵制前的北朝兵制, in his *Du shi ji*, 323.

9. See discussion of the Taghbach appropriation of Later Yan administration on the Yellow River plains in Wu, *Bei Wei zheng zhi di li yan jiu*, Chapter 2.

10. WS 113.2971; and Zhang, *Jin wei wu guan*, 2: 686. Similar titles would reappear under Daowu and later; it is quite possible that these were the same *guo yu* title, over time translated differently into Chinese by different scribes. This was, of course, a *comitatus*, seen in many societies. See Atwood's "Some Early Inner Asian Terms Related to the Imperial Family and the Comitatus"; and mention in SJ 110.2888 of the *zuo you* 左右 of the Xiongnu lord Modun.

11. WS 1.12. See Zhang Wenjie 張文杰, "Bei chao jiang wu tan lun" 北朝講武探論, *Guo fang da xue tong shi jiao yu xue bao* (2017.7): 38. Though having found use in this article, this author needs to disagree with the amount of time spent in it attempting to link these events with the *Zhou li*.

field an army of hundreds of thousands horsemen, with a million mounts.[12] As seen in Chapter 6, however, Shiyijian's own personal guard was relatively modest, and the great cavalry force was for the most part still a coalition of the personal followings of various Inner Asian lords. Such an army, we may assume, did not march on command, but could be fielded only through complex negotiation.

The situation would change enormously under Shiyijian's grandson, Daowu. The founder of Wei created a new military system—and a new conquest polity—through forced, top-down reorganization of at least some of the independent or semi-independent polities that had played a role in his grandfather's coalition. Among these was the Helan people, which as seen in Chapter 7 Daowu had taken from his mother's brother to place as registered populations on the military rolls. Interesting parallels can be seen here with Temujin's creation—800 years later and under quite different circumstances—of a new military loyal to the khan of khans from among the Tatars, Kereyids, and other peoples he had bested on the steppe.[13] The Taghbach program seems, however, to have been more gradual and incremental, unfolding over decades, and never really complete.[14] Multiple groups were enlisted into the growing central army, including early followers of the Taghbach, subdued neighbors, as well as transportees from the conquered lowlands.[15]

Much of the last category were Murong who, having been resettled by their own lords on the plains below, were now resettled in the Taghbach highlands. The populations from which the central army grew were predominantly of Inner Asian origin; there is no evidence of "men of Jin" in the early guard units, and in incidental mentions of troop transfers, whole units are referred to as "Serbi," or "Hu."[16] As for the Hu—referring here to Xiongnu and related groups (and not to Central Asians as in the Tang)—these were often auxiliary units, and not part of the central army. In the early years, some of these were loyal vassals, who brought to campaign the "groups they hereditarily led" 世領部落, though over time apparently more and more of these were incorporated into the central army, in a process not clearly described in *Wei shu*.[17] Irregular units from less trusted

---

12. WS 24.609.
13. Giovanni da Pian del Carpine noted that "the men are divided, Tartars and everyone else, among the generals": *The Story of the Mongols Whom We Call the Tartars*, tr. Erik Hildinger (Boston: Branden Publishing Company, 1996), 66. In his *The Desert Road to Turkestan* (Boston: Little, Brown, and Company, 1929), 21, Owen Lattimore described how in the process of being forced into Manchu banners, the Tumed Mongols "were hounded until they vanished."
14. The slow, complex process of reorganization of different polities into the Khaghan's Army is well described by Koga, "Hokugi no buzoku kaisan ni tsuite," 62–76; the persistence of older forms of social and political organization among these groups in Matsushita Ken'ichi 松下憲一, "Hokugi buzoku kaisan saikō — Gen Chō boshi o tegakari ni" 北魏部族解散再考—元萇墓誌を手がかりに, *Shigaku zasshi* 123.4 (2014): 35–59.
15. See Zou, "Bei Wei de bing zhi," 163–65.
16. For the ethnic makeup of the guard units, see Zhang, *Bei Wei zheng zhi shi*, 2: 691; for the troops mentioned for transfer, He, "Fu bing zhi qian," 330, citing WS 50.1113–14. For the Murong, see He, "Fu bing zhi qian," 323.
17. WS 40.901, 28.681. See also mention in WS 3.62 of how during a 422 progress of Mingyuan, as he crossed the Heng Mountains, "vassal lords of the four quarters each led their following to accompany" 四方蕃附大人各帥所部從 the Wei khaghan.

groups continued, however, to be called up, especially for major campaigns. At times they were used as expendable fodder for war. In one well-known story presented in the Jiankang history *Song shu*, during a major southern campaign conducted by Taiwu in 450 (to be discussed in more detail in Chapter 12), the Taghbach monarch sent a taunting note to the commander of a southern town he was besieging: "None of the men [I've sent against you now] are of my own nation (*fei wo guo ren* 非我國人). To the northeast of the walls are Dingling [Tiele] and Hu [Xiongnu]; to the south of the walls are Di and Qiang." It won't hurt me if you kill them, Taiwu went on to say, for that will rid me of bandits and rebels back north.[18]

The troops of the central army stood in stark contrast. Drawn from the "men of Dai" (Dai ren 代人), they were as seen above separately registered and had a role quite distinct from the auxiliary units, on the one hand, or on the other, the farming populations (the *min*), either in the Dai region or down on the plains.[19] The *Dai ren*'s main duty was generation after generation to supply manpower for the khaghan's army; if we accept that the received version of the Mulan tale contains elements from the Wei system, each family on the military registers was to provide one trooper for the khaghan's call-up. For most of the fifth century, this service in the military was a privileged path to promotion and prosperity. In the late Wei, however, it became a burdensome draft; special permission from the khaghan was needed to escape the hereditary obligation.[20] One possible example of these military registers—an officers' roll—has been recovered at Dunhuang, which some say came from Pingcheng, though it has been persuasively argued the piece comes from a successor regime.[21]

---

18. *SoS* 74.1912; ZZTJ 126.3963–64. Kikuchi Hideo 菊池英夫 discusses the clear separation between the inner guard units and auxiliaries in "Hokuchō gunsei ni okeru iwayuru kyōhei ni tsuite" 北朝軍制に於ける所謂鄉兵について, in *Shigematsu Sensei koki kinen Kyūshū Daigaku Tōyōshi ronsō* (Fukuoka: Kyūshū Daigaku Bungakubu [Shigakukai] Tōyō Shi Kyūken[sic]shitsu, 1957), 101.

19. It is not clear if Chinese settled to farm in the Datong Basin were also thought of as "Dai people"; according to Matsushita, *Hokugi Kozoku teiseiron*, 159, most at least were not, presumably because they did not give military service to the khaghan. As for military registration, this is not clearly described in our texts. There are anecdotal mentions in *Wei shu*, e.g., the mention of a figure who lived in Pingcheng, but "whose name was still with the garrison" 名猶在鎮 to which he had been assigned (WS 91.1970; see also the *bing hu* 兵戶 mentioned in WS 68.1520); and the mention of *jun guan* 軍貫 in a 524 edict ending the use of military registers, in the midst of the regime's collapse (WS 9.237).

20. The best example of release of *guo ren* from service is found in WS 7A.138. Other examples raised by Gao Min 高敏, *Wei Jin Nan bei chao bing zhi yan jiu* 魏晉南北朝兵制研究 (Zhengzhou: Da xiang chu ban she, 1998), 307, regard forgiveness given members who were not *guo ren*, but had in some way or another been forcibly incorporated into the garrison system: a 494 pardon for those 70 years of age, or infirm, who had been sent to the garrisons for crimes, WS 7B.174 (and see also 86.1884); as well as examples from late Wei of individuals impressed into service after conquest of their territory, who lived and worked in Pingcheng but whose "names were still on the garrison [register]" (as mentioned in the previous note): WS 91.1970, 68.1520. From the latter, and other evidence (see Scott Pearce, "The Yü-wen Regime in Sixth Century China" [PhD diss., Princeton University, 1987], 163–64), we can probably infer that *guo ren* assigned to the garrisons were also on those rolls, or a parallel set of them.

21. Yang Sen 楊森, "Dunhuang yan jiu yuan cang juan 'Bei Wei jin jun jun guan ji bo' kao shu" 敦煌研究院藏卷"北魏禁軍軍官籍薄"考述, *Dunhuang yan jiu* (1987.2): 20–24, has suggested the list came from Northern Wei. Zhang Jinlong, however, has made a good case that it probably belongs to Western Wei or Northern Zhou: *Jin wei wu guan*, 2: 671–74.

This central army was, as the modern scholar Yan Yaozhong has observed, the core of the early Wei state.[22] More than that, the worldview of the "men of Dai," and apparently the women as well, centered on war. The society that took shape in the Dai region was fundamentally militarized, defining the term "militarized" as reference to a society or sub-society in which culture and upbringing are actively geared to raising all young men for organized fighting, for war, borrowing here Hobbes's definition of "war" as consisting "not in actual fighting but in a known disposition thereto during all the time there is no assurance to the contrary."[23] Such groups certainly existed elsewhere in East Asia, as with the cohorts of fighting men who served patrons down in the Yangtze region.[24] But these were sub-societies; in Dai, the relationship of "the khaghan" to his soldiery defined the society.[25]

Though hunger drives men to war, they must eventually be fed, and one key question of any standing army is how to feed the men, or get them to feed themselves.[26] Early on, it had been relatively cheap to provision the khaghan's army.

22. Yan, *Bei Wei qian qi zheng zhi zhi du*, 151; and see the comments of Di Cosmo in "State Formation and Periodization," 18, 22.
23. Thomas Hobbes, *Leviathan; or, The Matter, Forme and Power of a Commonwealth, Ecclesiasticall and Civil*, ed. Michael Oakeshott (Oxford: Blackwell, 1957), 82. Edward Jones, in his "Militarisation of Roman Society, 400–700," in *Military Aspects of Scandinavian Society in a European Perspective, AD 1–1300: Papers from an International Research Seminar at the Danish National Museum, Copenhagen, 2–4 May 1996*, ed. Anne Nørgård Jorgensen and Birthe L. Clausen (Copenhagen: National Museum, 1997), 19, adds the following, which accords well with the Taghbach state: no clear distinction between soldier and civilian (with regard to the Taghbach society itself, as opposed to the larger realm), nor between military officer and government official; the head of state is also commander-in-chief; all adult free men have right to carry weapons; a certain group or class is expected by reason of birth to participate in the army; education of the young involves a military element; symbolism of warfare and weaponry are prominent in official and private life; and warfare is a predominant government expenditure and/or a major source of economic profit. All these are important, but it seems particularly regrettable that little is recorded of how the young men of Dai were raised to take on their military duty. For military expenditure in the Wei state see Chapter 7 note 51; and also Nicola Di Cosmo's discussion of military culture in his "Introduction" to *Military Culture in Imperial China*, ed. Nicola Di Cosmo (Cambridge, MA, and London: Harvard University Press, 2009), 3–4.
24. Chittick, *Patronage and Community in Medieval China*.
25. See the insightful comment of Zhu Weizheng 朱维铮, "Fu bing zhi du hua shi qi Xi Wei Bei Zhou she hui de te shu mao dun ji qi jie jue—jian lun fu bing de yuan yuan he xing zhi" 府兵制度化时期西魏北周社会的特殊矛盾及其解决—兼论府兵的渊源和性质, *LSYJ* (1963.6): 153, that coming from Inner Asian forms of organization, for the Taghbach the "soldiery and the people were one"; and Cen Zhongmian's reminder that this was a "unity of the soldiery and the herdsman" 兵牧合一: *Fu bing zhi du yan jiu*, 3. Cen goes on in the same text (10) to compare and contrast armies in the north and south, stressing that under Northern Wei and its successors leadership and control of the armies was unified and centralized, while in the south it was local and dispersed.
26. Good points have been made in the last couple decades by scholars—Nicola Di Cosmo, William Honeychurch, et al.—that agriculture existed on the eastern steppe, and that these regions were not necessarily dependent for grains on the farmlands to the south. The presence of some farming on the steppe, however, does not mean that hunger never became an issue, for particular groups at particular times and places, as with the formation by Daowu of a large military force that was effectively a standing army with an insufficient base of support. In discussing the formation of the royal domain, *Wei shu*'s "Shihuozhi," 110.2850, states that, "at this time the war chariots never paused, and though repeatedly there were [good] years, it was not enough to be seen for long" 是時戎車不息, 歲頻有年, 未足以久贍矣. Interesting comparisons can be made with Europe from the 1500s onward. Even if Europeans had enough food, they wished to eat it on something other than wooden plates, and taste it with added spice. And many were simply, really hungry: in E. M. Collingham's *The Hungry Empire: How Britain's Quest for Food Shaped the Modern World* (London: The Bodley Head, 2017), xv, we are told that "'Bring me food' became

Hunting, of course, played an ongoing role in feeding the troops, as we shall see in more detail below. Plunder and its distribution by the leader was also a source of provisions, as well as being a source of irregular pay (for services rendered).[27] Thus, after the fall of Shiyijian, in a report to Fu Jian the Qin lord was told that "the northern men are strong, and fearless ... their armies are without the hardship of baggage, or of gathering firewood to prepare a meal. Traveling light they travel fast. They rely on the enemy to get their supplies."[28] This travel-light approach continued for decades, not always with the best results: on the 450 campaign against Jiankang, we are told in the Jiankang history *Song shu*, Taiwu's army soon ran out of provisions. Feeding themselves by looting granaries, when they could no longer find granaries to loot, "man and horse were beset by starvation."[29] Even 50 years in, this could still become a "hungry empire"; these realities need to underlie our thinking when we examine the feast in Chapter 13.

In early Wei, efforts were soon made to supplement these ad hoc approaches to provisioning. Daowu in his early years had established agricultural colonies (*tun tian*) on the northern length of the Yellow River. By the time of Taiwu, these had been extended throughout the Yellow River loop, from the old Xiongnu stronghold of Tongwan to the region around modern Yinchuan.[30] At the end of the century, in the time of Xiaowen, with a more efficient local administration, 25,000 "field troops" (*tian zu* 田卒) could be called up from districts in the Yellow River plains to work government agricultural colonies (*tun tian*) along the southern frontier.[31] More fundamentally, by this time, provisions could be provided for both campaign troops and for garrisons on the basis of a newly instituted special tax for "army grain" 軍糧.[32]

From the meager evidence available, it seems that some sorts of taxes were also paid by the general Dai ren population, since the family of "a man who died for the king's business" was excused from any further obligations to the state

---

a persistent demand ... a metaphor for the relationship of Britain to its empire." Closer to home, Nicola Di Cosmo in "State Formation and Periodization in Inner Asian History," 23, states that the "first 'cry' of a new inner Asian state was one of great, insatiable hunger."

27. E.g., a campaign in 436, in which the enemy retreated. When the Wei general considered simply withdrawing, his commanders pointed out that "if we don't have loot, then [we'll] have nothing to provision the army, [or] reward the officers and soldiers": WS 17.413; ZZTJ 123.3863. And see also Wang, *Zhuan xing qi de Bei Wei cai zheng*, 35ff.

28. WS 24.609. For another such anecdote, from the Murong point of view, JS 124.3094 speaks of how the cavalrymen of the Wei army, during the 396–397 invasion of Later Yan, "[are] provided only 10 days of grain on the backs of their horses."

29. SoS 74.1912; ZZTJ 125.3959.

30. WS 38.867–68; Sakuma Kichiya 佐久間吉也, *Gi Shin Nanbokuchō suiri shi kenkyū* 魏晋南北朝水利史研究 (Tokyo: Kaimei Shoin, 1980), 364–66; He, "Fu bing zhi qian," 348.

31. WS 79.1756.

32. He, "Fu bing zhi qian," 347–48. This seems to have first been established on an ad-hoc basis for campaigns in the time of Xianwen (r. 465–471) (WS 60.1331, 7A.139; see Sagawa, "Bei Wei de bing zhi yu she hui," 49), but by 493 had become regularized to the point where Xiaowen was giving relief for this tax to specific districts (WS 7B.172).

死王事者，復其家。³³ The bereaved family also seems to have received "regular rewards" (*heng shang* 恆賞) of an unfortunately unspecified kind.³⁴ More generally, at times the Wei government assisted their troops with woolens for winter clothing.³⁵ But for the common soldiery, this seems to have been the limit: as far as we can tell, till the end of Wei many at least of the troops of the central armies supported themselves and their families in times of peace, and when called to war were expected to bring much of their own supplies.³⁶ Perhaps this is hinted at in the earliest version of the Mulan story, when after choosing to serve in her father's place, Mulan goes to:³⁷

> The eastern market: there she bought a horse;
> The western market: there she bought a saddle.
> The southern market: there she bought a bridle;
> The northern market: there she bought a whip.

More elite—or more isolated—elements of the military seem to have received more. Garrison troops and enlistees into the elite guard units may have been free of all taxation.³⁸ And officers seem to have been paid salaries, interestingly, long before that was done for civil officials. After Daowu's conquest of the southern plains, we are told, eight occupation armies were organized. Each had 5,000 men, and each also had 46 "salaried major commanders" 食祿主帥.³⁹ More than a

---

33. WS 7A.138; and see Sagawa Eiji's analysis of this 473 edict in "Bei Wei de bing zhi yu she hui," 50, and on p. 54, his discussion of the "rich rewards" given to families of men of the central armies who fell in battle. Regarding levies from the general military population of Dai, Yao Yanzhong suggests irregular, light taxation: *Bei Wei qian qi zheng zhi zhi du*, 109. Confirming this, after the move to Luoyang, in 494, an edict offered three-year remission of taxes for "households relocated from Dai" 代遷之戶 (WS 7B.176). As for those within the royal domain called up for corvée duties leading to death, who were not *guo ren*, they had only their funeral bill paid, by the district in which they were registered 詔畿內民從役死事者，郡縣為迎喪，給以葬費 (WS 7A.138).

34. See Sagawa Eiji, "Bei Wei de bing zhi yu she hui," 50, drawing on comments made in 524, in the last years of the regime, when hereditary military service was being dismantled, about how the preexisting *heng shang* would be continued for those who continued to serve (WS 9.237). In early times, most of these "rewards" would have been booty, but by 524 that had not been the case for generations: see Wang, *Zhuang xing qi de Bei Wei cai zheng yan jiu*, 108–9.

35. Zhang Min 张敏, "Shi liu guo Bei Wei jun dui dong zhuang bao zhang ji qi dui zhan zheng zhi ying xiang" 十六国北魏军队冬装保障及其对战争之影响, *Xuchang xue yuan xue bao* (2003.4): 51–53. At the Luoyang Museum are two late Wei statuettes (excavated from Beichen Village 北陈村, Luoyang, in 1989) showing men in heavy overcoats, perhaps examples of this winter apparel.

36. Yan, *Bei Wei qian qi zheng zhi zhi du*, 164. He, "Fu bing zhi qian," 349, quotes WS 44.996, stating that at least troops based in outposts of garrisons or provinces supplied their own food and clothing, so that they "frequently suffered from hunger and cold" 州鎮戍兵，資絹自隨，不入公庫，任其私用，常苦飢寒. This became at times insupportable, as we see with a 467 edict ordering that fabric (the main form of money in Wei) be given to the poor in the Six Garrisons: WS 6.128.

37. Kwa and Idema, *Mulan*, 1; Yan, *Bei Wei qian qi zheng zhi zhi du*, 164, supports this association of the Mulan tale with actual Wei practice.

38. See Tang Zhangru 唐长孺, *Wei Jin Nan bei chao Sui Tang shi san lun: Zhongguo feng jian she hui de xing cheng he qian qi de bian hua* 魏晋南北朝隋唐史三論：中國封建社會的形成和前期的變化 (Wuchang: Wuhan da xue chu ban she, 1993), 192, drawing on description of early recruits to the northern garrisons given in BS 16.617 (WS 18.429), that they were free of tax and could take office, which he suggests applies to the guard units as well.

39. WS 58.1287. In the same account, we are told of *tigin*, "sons of the [imperial] clan" (*zong zi* 宗子), posted to garrisons in provincial cities in the Chinese interior, who had 800 households to supply labor for their paddy fields.

century later, in the late Wei, the successors to these posts were still enjoying these benefits when the fellow describing the situation sent up to the throne a complaint that while these eight armies had been reduced in force by more than two-thirds, the number of officers in each remained the same. The expenses were "not small," he said, as he went on to ask that the number of officers be cut in half. As has been the case in many times and many places, the army seems to have become a reliable jobs program for those with access to such employment. In this case, at least, the emperor followed the advice, though this certainly must have been resented by the military establishment and the men who got the ax.

Such problems had deep roots. Assuming a central army of some 300,000 in the time of Taiwu, the modern economic historian Wang Wanying has estimated that the military took up about 75 percent of total tax revenues.[40] Thus, in the course of Taiwu's many campaigns, we are told that the court's treasury was almost emptied out. Such difficulties would persist. The march led south by Xiaowen in 493, putatively for a Yangtze campaign, led to a similar fiscal crisis and large cuts in the just-established system of salaries for civil officials.[41]

The nature of these expensive troops was compounded by their main means of transportation, the horses from whose backs they fought. After buying a mount and all its equipment, Mulan had ridden north across the Yellow River with her new comrades, to fight the "Hu of the Yan Mountains." This had long been the Taghbach mode of warfare: when fully mobilized the army of Shiyijian is said to have consisted entirely of mounted archers, with hundreds of thousands of cavalrymen, and a million horses.[42] As noted above, in the time of Shiyijian these seem to have been unarmored light cavalry, and probably still without stirrups. This was, however, precisely the time that the stirrup clearly appears, with worldwide consequences, though nothing at all is said on the matter in *Wei shu* or any other history from the period.[43]

According to findings in storehouses from the Han dynasty, with materials taken from the Xiongnu and Wusun (Central Asian allies of the Xiongnu), the earliest stirrup seems to have developed on the western steppe, though the technology's importance was not immediately recognized.[44] By the fourth century, however, it had become widely used in East Asia.[45] Skilled horsemen like the Taghbach had,

---

40. Wang, *Zhuan xing qi de Bei Wei cai zheng*, 66–67. These are, of course, very tentative figures.
41. For Taiwu, see WS 5.123. For Xiaowen, WS 7B.177, 31.743; and ZZTJ 141.4430. In the time of the latter, in fact, demands from the military budget forced the monarch to reduce the stipends given to peers (WS 7B.176); and made the Prince of Pengcheng feel a need to dip into his own fortune to help bail out the state, giving back a year's worth of "the stipend of his fief, his salary as an official, and the 'charity' given him as a kinsman" of the imperial clan 國秩, 職俸, 親恤: WS 21B.574; ZZTJ 141.4429.
42. WS 24.609; He, "Fu bing zhi qian," 319.
43. As has been noted, the stirrup seems to have had a more far-reaching import in Europe than in East Asia: see Dien, "The Stirrup"; Lynn White, *Medieval Technology and Social Change* (Oxford: Clarendon Press, 1964). For general discussion of the stirrup in East Asia, see also Dien, *Six Dynasties Civilization*, 334–36.
44. Yates, "The Horse in Early Chinese Military History," 62–63.
45. Dien, "The Stirrup," 37.

of course, for centuries been shooting arrows without stirrups, and for skilled riders, even cavalry shock combat can be done in this manner.[46] Nevertheless, secure support for the foot certainly facilitated both archery and shock combat, and the spread of the stirrup in the fourth century was accompanied by development of heavy cavalry in East Asian armies.[47] From this time, tomb art often shows a mix of both light and heavy cavalry in depictions of processions. As noted above, Taghbach use of armor for horse and horseman may have first taken place with the invasion of the Yellow River plains, and probably increased with subsequent transportation of Murong cavalry to Pingcheng and a new control of technicians skilled in iron manufacture. In a discussion of the army Shegui led against Zhongshan, we are told that it consisted of 100,000 crack cavalry, with armored horses. A mural made more than a century later, just a few years after the fall of Northern Wei, on the south wall of Cave 285 of the Dunhuang's Mogao Grotto, gives a highly detailed depiction of armored cavalry riding down light infantry, reliving reality in an illustration of the Buddhist tale of the Five Hundred Robbers.[48]

In terms of organization of the central army, the units to which these men and their families had been assigned were artificial creations, based on units of 10. Evidence of this among the Taghbach is already seen with Shiyijian, who it will be remembered had had a 100-man guard. Under Daowu we see proliferation of 100-man companies that rallied around "pennons" (Ch. *chuang*), and were led by "pennon commanders" (*chuangjiang* 幢將).[49] Ten pennons together formed a "regiment" (or "army": Ch. *jun* 軍), with (theoretically) 1,000 men. We know of this organization only through a few offhand remarks preserved in the histories, but it is confirmed by description of a parallel development among the Rouran—the steppe rival Mulan seems to have been sent off to fight—who are also said to have created 100-man companies and 1,000-man regiments. Told of this, Daowu is said to have boasted that they were "learning from the 'central states,'" viz., "from *us*."[50] The boast need not be accepted: decimal organization is

---

46. See Graff, *Medieval Chinese Warfare*, 42–43.
47. See note 7; and discussion of the Anak Tomb No. 3, dated 357, built for a man who fled the Murong into Koguryŏ, in the region that is now northern North Korea: So Tetsu (Su Zhe) 蘇哲, "Goko Jūrokkoku Hokuchō jidai no shukkōto roboyō" 五胡十六国・北朝 時代の出行圖と鹵簿俑, in *Higashi Ajia to Nihon no kōkogaku*, ed. Gotō Tadashi and Mogi Masahiro, 4 vols. (Tokyo: Dōseisha, 2002): 2: 115–120.
48. https://commons.wikimedia.org/wiki/File:Story_of_the_Five_Hundred_Robbers_(535%E2%80%93557 _CE),_Mogao_Cave_285,_Dunhuang,_China.jpg, accessed 26 August 2019; and the same image in Roderick Whitfield, Susan Whitfield, and Neville Agnew, *Cave Temples of Mogao: Art and History on the Silk Road* (Los Angeles: The Getty Conservation Institute and the J. Paul Getty Museum, 2000), 19. For discussion of Cave 285, with inscriptions dating it to 538, 539, in the Western Wei period (535–557), see Ma De 马德, *Dunhuang Mogao ku shi yan jiu* 敦煌莫高窟史研究 (Lanzhou: Gansu jiao yu chu ban she, 1996), 67–69.
49. Zhang, *Jin wei wu guan*, 2: 667–68. An early example would be a fellow referred to in *Wei shu* as Mo Ti 莫題, a man of Dai, who in the very earliest years of the regime under Daowu was a "banner commander, who commanded guard troops 禁兵": WS 28.683. For the apparently Serbi group from which he came, see Yao, *Bei chao Hu xing kao*, 122–24. In terms of the decimal units: needless to say, as with the units of every army, the theoretical number rarely matched the number on the ground.
50. Zhang, *Jin wei wu guan*, 2: 667–68; WS 103.2291.

widely seen in Inner Asian history, and had been used by the Xiongnu.[51] It seems quite possible that both the Taghbach and Rouran were separately drawing on this established model. Later Inner Asian groups would draw on it as well, among them the Türks and the Mongols.[52]

Though many have used the flag, it has been suggested that its use systematically to identify the army's basic units—the 100-man company—was a Taghbach innovation.[53] Unfortunately, so far at least none of these pennons has been uncovered, so we cannot directly see the object under discussion. But pennons, or banners, did play a key role in a more famous empire created 1,000 years later by another Inner Asian people, the Manchus. The units in the Wei army represented by the *chuang* were much smaller than those of the banner (for which we do have the [Manchu] *guo yu* term, *gūsa*, Ch. *qi*), and it is not clear if they had the same administrative importance.[54] Still, it is interesting to see continuation among Inner Asian peoples of the practice of using the flag to reorganize societies into armies.

It is also interesting to see the loyalty given the pennon as abstract symbol of a man's unit in the Northern Wei story of Han Mao (or getting closer to the name of the group to which he was attached, Poliuhan, MC *Pha-ljuwk-han), a man of Xiongnu descent who lived in the Yellow River's great loop, and submitted to the Taghbach in the early fifth century.[55] Highly skilled—as most of these men are said to be—at mounted archery, Mao of the Poliuhan was serving as pennon-bearer in a campaign led by Mingyuan against the Dingling ("High Carts"), when:[56]

> a gust came up and the flags of all the armies fell over flat. [But Poliu]han held onto his pennon on his horse, and from beginning to end it never toppled. Marveling at this, [Mingyuan] . . . summoned [Poliu]han to come to his stopping place, and tested his horseback archery. Deeply

---

51. David Sneath, "Introduction," in *Imperial Statecraft: Political Forms and Techniques of Governance in Inner Asia, Sixth-Twentieth Centuries*, ed. David Sneath (Bellingham: Center for East Asian Studies, Western Washington University and Mongolia and Inner Asia Studies Unit, University of Cambridge, 2006), 9–10; Di Cosmo, "Ethnogenesis," 47. Di Cosmo suggests that the ultimate origin may have been the Persian Achaemenids.

52. For the Mongols' units of 1,000s and 10,000s, see Rachewiltz, *Secret History of the Mongols*, 1: 133–34, nos. 202–3, and 2: 762–63.

53. Zhang, *Jin wei wu guan*, 2: 666. It will be noted, however, that the Rouran also defined their 100-man units by a flag, in a way similar to that of the Taghbach: "1,000 men were a regiment, . . . [and] 100 men a pennon; [for each] pennon one man was established as leader" 千人為軍, . . . 百人為幢, 幢置帥一人: WS 103.2290.

54. For the Manchu banners, see Mark C. Elliott, *The Manchu Way; The Eight Banners and Ethnic Identity in Late Imperial China* (Stanford, CA: Stanford University Press, 2001).

55. For the descent of the Han (Poliuhan) family, see Chen Lianqing 陈连庆, *Zhongguo gu dai shao shu min zu xing shi yan jiu: Jin Han Wei Jin Nan bei chao shao shu min zu xing shi yan jiu* 中国古代少数民族姓氏研究: 秦汉魏晋南北朝少数民族姓氏研究 (Changchun: Jilin wen shi chu ban she, 1993), 43–44. This is just one of a number of transcriptions of the same Xiongnu name. See Yao, *Bei chao Hu xing kao*, 136–38.

56. WS 51.1127. It needs noted here that Poliuhan Han "bore the pennon for the central army" 為中軍持幢, from which we can infer that "pennons" did not just mark 100-man companies, but larger military units as well.

impressed, [Mingyuan] made [Poliu]han Mao commander of the Huben palace guards 虎賁中郎將.

Being the core of the khaghans' armies, and numbering in the tens of thousands, the palace guards were for the Taghbach, perhaps, at least a rough equivalent of the Manchu banners. Following Shiyijian's practice, though on a much larger scale, Daowu recruited from the central army as a whole three elite guard units, called in Chinese the *sanlang* 三郎, the "three (units of) esquires." Of greatest prestige among these was the *nei san lang* 內三郎, who served in the inner precincts of the palace, to which were added two other divisions: the Yulin 羽林 (whose Chinese name is derived from a constellation, the "celestial water bearer") and the Huben 虎賁, the "Brave as Tigers" guard (of which Poliuhan was made commander).[57]

Later, under Taiwu, another, distinct set of guards units was established under the "palace steward" (*dian zhong shang shu* 殿中尚書).[58] These played a special role in the palace. While units such as the Yulin personally served and protected the monarch,[59] the palace stewards and the men under their command controlled the palace gates and were in charge of weapons and horses, as well as the palaces' granaries and storehouses. It seems that as a system of checks and balances on the position's power, there were always at least two palace stewards.[60] Such checks and balances may also have been the reason underlying the ongoing proliferation of guard units themselves. Though these posts were originally non-hereditary, there are hints that over the years inheritance of command of guards began to pass from father to son, or elder to younger brother.[61] Rather than eliminating entrenched power in the palace, an incoming, activist monarch such as Taiwu may have simply added new units, without removing the old ones. The expense of the army thus become even more problematic. But for Taiwu, the addition of a new set of guard commanders, put in place by he himself, might have brought assurance of direct, personal loyalty.[62]

---

57. Yan, *Bei Wei qian qi zheng zhi zhi du*, 154. See Zhang (*Jin wei wu guan*, 2: 680–81) on apparent earliest dates for establishment of the Huben. Though we don't have a systematic description of the organization of the guards, Zhang has labored to recover what he can from anecdotes and snippets taken from various sources, and general statements can be given about their interrelations, such as that the Yulin were more prestigious than the Huben.

58. Zhang, *Jin wei wu guan*, 2: 697–98; on the fact that this was a separate, distinct group, not under the Yulin or earlier units, see 2: 702.

59. See, for instance, the story of "Big Thousand" Lai: WS 30.725.

60. Zhang, *Jin wei wu guan*, 2: 696, 702; Yan, *Bei Wei qian qi zheng zhi zhi du*, 56. And see NQS 57.985, where the functions of the palace steward position are described. On the number of stewards, see Zhang, *Jinwei wuguan*, 2: 698.

61. Tang, *Wei Jin Nan bei chao Sui Tang shi san lun*, 193; Yan, *Bei Wei qian qi zheng zhi zhi du*, 154.

62. Such practices are found in other societies as well. See the comments by Armin Hohlweg on the appearance and disappearance of such units within the late Byzantine state (*Beiträge zur Verwaltungsgeschichte des Oströmischen Reiches unter den Komnenen*, 61), quoted in Marc C. Bartius, *The Late Byzantine Army: Arms and Society, 1204–1453* (Philadelphia: University of Pennsylvania Press, 1992), 272: a new ruler might doubt the loyalty of groups; there might be difficulties recruiting guards for certain units (particularly those based on ethnicity); an emperor might wish to create his own personal guard division.

As for officers' titles, what we have access to through *Wei shu* are given in Chinese, borrowed from structures of the Chinese empire. Since the guard units in fact emerged from within the Taghbach regime itself, these Chinese names would frequently have been pasted onto original titles in the *guo yu* (though since the Taghbach language, like its culture, was a creole, the "original" could certainly at times have been a borrowing from Chinese). In other sources, such as the Jiankang histories, we are given transcription of *guo yu* terms, though these transcriptions are not consistent—in several cases, two or three different Chinese renderings seem to point to the same Taghbach title.[63]

Another useful source, giving a few more hints of the words really spoken, is the "Nan xun bei," the "Stele of the Southern Progress." A badly damaged stone inscription recovered several decades ago near the town of Lingqiu, Shanxi, the "Nan xun bei" commemorated a 461 progress by Wencheng (r. 452–465) and his guard along Daowu's road from Pingcheng down onto the lowlands.[64] In the best-preserved text on the stele's verso, in a long string of titles and names, we see more clearly than in *Wei shu* the fascinating hybrid language used by these people, in which Chinese characters are partly used to convey the Chinese language, but partly as transcription of the Taghbach *guo yu*. One of the stele's transcribed titles is *tigin*, discussed in Chapter 9. Another is *huluozhen* 斛洛真, clearly a variant of the term 胡洛真 given in the southern history *Nan Qi shu* (57, p. 985), where the term—reconstructed by one scholar as **qoragčın*—is translated into Chinese as "people who carry weapons" 帶仗人.[65] *Zhen*, **čın*, found at the end of many such titles, is the transcription of a plural occupational suffix in the *guo yu* meaning "those who . . . ." In evolving form, the term carried on into later Mongolic languages. More generally, the list as a whole shows the strong militarism of the regime—most of the almost 300 men in the stele's name lists have some kind of military rank, which among other things would have brought salary.[66]

Apart from the guard, another important unit of the Wei military was the "Esquires of the Hunt" (Ch. *lielang* 獵郎), which had already separately taken

---

63. Zhang, *Jin wei wu guan*, 2: 692, points out that a series of titles in Chinese translation (in this case, not transcription)—*nei xing ling* 內行領, *nei xing zhang* 內行長, *nei xing zhang zhe* 內行長者, *nei xing a gan* 內行阿干—all apparently translate/transcribe the same original *guo yu* term.
64. See Zhang Qingjie 張慶捷 and Li Biao 李彪, "Shanxi Lingqiu Bei Wei Wenchengdi 'Nan xun bei'" 山西靈丘北魏文成帝《南巡碑》 *WW* (1997.12): 72; and Zhang, *Jin wei wu guan*, 2: 713–45.
65. NQS 57.985; Zhang Qingjie 張慶捷 and Guo Chunmei 郭春梅, "Bei Wei Wenchengdi 'Nan xun bei' suo jian Tuoba zhi guan chu tan" 北魏文成帝《南巡碑》所見拓跋職官初探, *Zhongguo shi yan jiu* (1999.2): 59–61. The reconstruction of *huluozhen* is by Shimunek, *Languages of Ancient Southern Mongolia and North China*, 151–52. Zhang Jinlong (*Jin wei wu guan*, 2: 717–20) has suggested that this term may refer to the Yulin or Huben; Boodberg ("Language of the T'o-pa Wei," 227), on the other hand, has suggested that this was a reference to the "officer who girdled (the ruler?) with weapons."
66. Zhang, *Jin wei wu guan*, 2: 716. The name lists on the stele are reproduced in many sources: see, e.g., Matsushita, *Hokugi Kozoku taiseiron*, 75–86. Di Nicola, "Aristocratic Elites," 27, points out that the highest-ranking Xiongnu aristocrats had dual titles: "one was a title linked to a specific political and government post and the other was a generic military title."

shape in the time of Daowu.⁶⁷ As Thomas Allsen has described, the hunt was central to states and armies across Eurasia, "a demonstration of the ability to rule, the means of projecting an image of vigor and authority."⁶⁸ The men enjoyed these activities, and these activities fed them large amounts of meat. Furthermore, while allowing personal development of martial skills, they also—being conducted by large numbers under strict discipline—trained them to fight in formation. An entire administrative apparatus was dedicated to organization of the imperial hunts.⁶⁹ According to the early modern historian Hu Sanxing, "First rising in the lands north of Dai, the Taghbach were by practice skilled at the hunt. For this reason, they (went on to) establish the Esquires of the Hunt, for which were taken the brave and talented sons and brothers of the prominent and esteemed houses."⁷⁰

Through the close ties that could be gained on the hunt with the Taghbach monarch, the office of Esquire of the Hunt took on a particularly important role, as a key steppingstone to higher rank within the military, and more generally in the regime.⁷¹ A fellow called in *Wei shu* Shusun Jun ("Shusun" being an anachronistic application of the late Wei designation for one of the royal clan's cadet branches, for most of Wei transcribed into Chinese as "Yizhan") had joined the inner guard at the age of 15 *sui*, and then because of his skill at bow and horse was transferred to be an esquire of the hunt.⁷² When the prince Shao locked the gates of the palace after killing his father, he pressed Shusun to support his claim

---

67. Zhang, *Jin wei wu guan*, 2: 682–83.

68. Thomas Allsen, *The Royal Hunt in Eurasian History* (Philadelphia: University of Pennsylvania Press, 2006), 129. I will point out that Allsen is drawing here on Mencius. More blunt about the linkage between hunting and war would be the statement made by Ernest Hemingway, in his article "On the Blue Water" (*Esquire*, April 1936): "Certainly there is no hunting like the hunting of man and those who have hunted armed men long enough and liked it, never really care for anything else thereafter." One way to get a taste of this state of mind would be examination of the scenes of hunting (and war) on the carved panels of Ashurbanipal (r. 669–ca. 631 BCE) that are kept in the British Museum, where showing "an image of vigor and authority," "The King Pursues a Herd of Wild Asses with a Pack of Hounds," or "Ashurbanipal, on Horseback, Kills a Lion with a Spear": Gareth Brereton, ed., *I Am Ashurbanipal, King of the World, King of Assyria* (New York: Thames and Hudson, 2018), 72–73 figure 78, 71 figure 77. Such themes are pervasive—"The royal lion hunt," the text tells us, "played a significant role in the artistic scheme of the carved reliefs of the North Palace." Somewhat reminiscent of the written account of how in 391 Shegui made the north loop of the Yellow River "run red with blood," on pp. 268–69, figure 279, of *I Am Ashurbanipal*, "The River Ulai Is Filled with Corpses, Horse Carcasses and Broken Chariots." The organization and large scale of the Manchu hunt, in many ways similar to that of the Taghbach, is described in Mark Elliott and Ning Chia, "The Qing Hunt at Mulan," in *New Qing Imperial History*, 66–83, esp. 77, where we are told that the hunt, as an "emblem of the warrior origins of the horse-riding, tiger-hunting Manchu nation," had become "a sacred Qing institution," for which, in both Chinese and Manchu, the Jiaqing emperor (r. 1796–1820) wrote a valedictory in 1807.

69. Zhang, *Jin wei wu guan*, 2: 401–6. Hunting would certainly fit in with "war and other types of conflict," which according to Walter Pohl were the ways in which in early medieval Europe "a community acquired the capacity to act as a collective": see his "Strategies of Identification: A Methodological Profile," in *Strategies of Identification: Ethnicity and Religion in Early Medieval Europe*, ed. Pohl et al. (Turnhout: Brepols, 2013), 45.

70. ZZTJ 115.3624.

71. See Zhang, *Jin wei wu guan*, 2: 682–83, for examples; and also Liu Meiyun 刘美云 and Wei Haiqing 魏海清, "Shou lie xi su dui Bei Wei qian qi zheng quan de ying xiang" 狩猎习俗对北魏前期政权的影响, in *Bei chao shi yan jiu*, ed. Yin Xian (Beijing: Shang wu yin shu guan, 2005), 423–27.

72. WS 29.705. And see Zhang's analysis of these events: *Jin wei wu guan*, 2: 682–83.

to succession. "Though outwardly he followed Shao, inwardly he was in reality sincerely loyal" ("loyalty" here, as always, a subjective standard). In the end, Shusun secretly joined with others to eliminate the claimant and instead place Mingyuan on the throne. He would subsequently rise to powerful posts within the Mingyuan court.

Apart from Poliuhan's loyalty to the flag, or Shusun's loyalty to his conception of proper succession, other anecdotes found in *Wei shu* tell of a much more personal kind of loyalty. As part of the Inner Court, guardsmen participated in state funerals and the great imperial rituals.[73] Their relationship to the monarch—leader of the army as well as the state—could take painfully personal forms. In 476, when Taiwu's great-grandson, Xianwen (r. 465–471, a retired emperor, 471–476), was killed in the course of palace power struggles, a deeply distressed member of his guard is quoted as saying that "[Our] wise lord has gone up, far away. How should I live this life?," whereupon he pulled his sword from off his belt and killed himself.[74] Though we are not told exactly how he used the blade, his self-destruction resembles the impromptu expression of feeling for lord as motivation for dramatic final act that was at least supposedly the basis of the samurai's *seppuku*.

Such feelings were reciprocated. Having impressed Mingyuan by single-handedly killing a tiger on a hunt, Lai Daqian 大千, "Big Thousand"—a Mahayana term describing the vast multiplicity of worlds—was raised to a high position in the palace administration. He later grew very close to Taiwu, whom he served as a constant attendant: "armed he would stand guard, not leaving (the emperor's) side night or day."[75] Trusting Big Thousand, Taiwu eventually sent him off as a field commander, where in the end he was killed in the Shanxi highlands by recalcitrant "mountain Hu." When his body was brought back to the capital, Taiwu came forth from the palace to see him and, we are told, "sighed with grief for a very long time."

This was, of course, seen on a lower level as well. As would be expected, the ties within these units, and the platoons that made them up, was close. As in any army, close bonding would have taken shape in the field or around the campfires on campaign.[76] Hints regarding this come, once again, from the Mulan story. In the Chinese world, "Mulan" has through arrangement and rearrangement evolved

---

73. WS 113.2972.

74. BS 85.2844 (WS 87.1891). After his death, the person who seems to have killed the wise lord—Empress Dowager Wenming—bestowed upon the guardsman's family 200 bolts of silk.

75. WS 30.725.

76. See Anthony D. Smith, "War and Ethnicity: The Role of Warfare in the Formation, Self Images and Cohesion of Ethnic Communities," *Ethnic and Racial Studies* 4.4 (1981): 375–97. An excellent description of these ties is given in Junger's *Tribe*, beginning with his definition of "tribe" as "the people you feel compelled to share your last bite of food with" (xvii); but it is perhaps summed up even more succinctly in the famous speech placed by Shakespeare in the mouth of Henry V at Agincourt: "We few, we happy few, we band of brothers; For he to-day that sheds his blood with me / Shall be my brother."

into a morality tale centered on *xiao*, "filial devotion." But the earliest version—which may derive from an Inner Asian song—is quite different (though we have received it in the Chinese language): there, upon returning home Mulan pays little actual attention to her parents; they are in fact little more than cardboard figures who speak no words. Instead, the most significant of her interactions are with her old messmates, who having accompanied their comrade home roar out when she re-emerges in a skirt that "We served in the same ranks for twelve long years, And absolutely had no clue that Mulan was a girl!"[77]

As seen with Big Thousand, the closeness of men who fought—or hunted—together could be a path to promotion. For some it was more than that, being a path to real social mobility. As we've already seen, Poliuhan Han was a Xiongnu, and so a member of a group generally less favored among the Taghbach. For his defense of the flag, he was promoted within the army, and so presumably more firmly established himself as a man of substance within the Dai community.

This assimilation and incorporation of new groups into a growing unity was an important function of the guard units. Though these units were at first filled with "young men of noble birth," taken from the imperial house and close allies (or defeated rivals),[78] by the last years of Daowu recruitment had been extended to the broader population of the Dai region, which included recent transportees from the lowlands (most apparently Murong, Koreans, or "miscellaneous barbarians"), who had been incorporated into the Eight Units.[79] And while most of the conquered and transported High Carts (Gaoche) were left intact as a group (if still in a sort of bondage), individuals from these groups were also allowed to enter the guard, though in lower-ranked, segregated units of the Yulin and Huben, led by officers with titles such as "Commander of the Gaoche Huben" 高車虎賁將軍. We later see appearance of specialized officers such as the "Huben recruiter" 募員虎賁.[80] One wonders what tactics these officers used to draw young men into service.

Over a few decades, the various guards established by Daowu and then Taiwu grew to be something on the order of 1,000 times what had served Shiyijian at Shengle, consisting of 100,000 men or more, out of a larger central military three

---

77. Loosely based on the translation given by Kwa and Idema, *Mulan*, 3; though otherwise fine, "marched" has been removed from their translation, since the poem itself makes clear they were on horseback. This incorporation of the concept of *xiao* in the course of the evolution of the Mulan story within the Chinese world is an interesting example of remaking in the course of cultural borrowing.

78. For the role of members of the imperial house and cadet branches in the guard units, as both leaders and soldiery, see Liu, "Lun Bei Wei qian qi zong shi zai jin jun zhong de di wei ji zuo yong."

79. WS 113.2974, 2.32; Zhang, *Jin wei wu guan*, 2: 688; Gao, *Wei Jin Nan bei chao bing zhi yan jiu*, 304. These groups are part of the 100,000 transported by Daowu.

80. WS 113.2983, 2985, 2988. See discussion of these recruitment issues in Zhang, *Jin wei wu guan*, 2: 681; and on p. 702, Zhang also cites an example of a palace steward recruiting High Carts (in this case referred to as Chile; BS 17.639 [WS 19A.450]). This expansion of recruitment, a very important issue, was, of course, true of the larger Wei armies as well, in which over the generations we see increasing numbers of Chinese recruited into the ranks. See Tang, *Wei Jin Nan bei chao Sui Tang shi san lun*, 190ff.

times that size. The core of the Wei army, they existed to serve their khaghan. When he was at home, they defended him, his family and his dwelling, be that grand felt yurt or timber-frame palace. But the early Wei emperors spent a great deal of time away from Pingcheng, and when the lord chose to go to war, a large part of the guard would go with him, as reliable core of the campaign's army. Thus, early in his reign Taiwu, thinking that a man of Dai, Lu Zhen, "was braver than any man, appointed him to the palace *san lang*." The record goes on immediately to say that Lu "repeatedly accompanied [the emperor] on campaigns, and wherever he went he would break [the enemy] and overrun their positions," repeatedly receiving special bestowals for his accomplishments.[81]

These core units of the Wei military are what Cui Hao had referred to as "those who live in the northern territories" (*ju bei fang* 居北方) in his 415 suggestion to Mingyuan that they be kept there, and the capital not be moved.[82] This ended in 493, when the reformer Xiaowen relocated a large part of the central army to Luoyang, his new capital in the Chinese interior. Long before this, however, beginning with Daowu's 398 campaign, parts had been detached and assigned to garrison towns and forts, in the south and on the northern frontier as well.[83] These "citadel men" (*cheng ren* 城人) had a different trajectory in Wei history.[84]

In terms of relocation of troops north of the Yinshan, units had from the earliest years of Wei been assigned to monitor and control the belt of grasslands that lay between the Yinshan and the Gobi.[85] These served to check Rouran incursion, and to control the resettled High Carts populations. Over time these solidified into permanent outpost towns on the northern edge of the Yinshan mountains, together with building (or rebuilding) of ramparts further north.[86] There were many of these defensive outposts on Wei's northern and northwestern frontier, running all the way into the region that is now Ningxia and beyond. But the best known, because of their critical role in checking incursions from the steppe empire, were the so-called Six Garrisons. These ran from Woye (near Ulad Qianqi, on the north loop of the Yellow River), to Huaishuo (just south of mod. Guyang, Inner Mongolia), to Wuchuan (near the village of the same name, across the mountains from Hohhot), then eventually to Huaihuang (mod. Zhangbei, Hebei).[87]

---

81. WS 30.730. Many other examples can be found of stewards leading their guard units out to war under the emperor's command: Zhang, *Jin wei wu guan*, 2: 703.

82. WS 35.808.

83. He, "Fu bing zhi qian," 327–30. The first major set of garrisons in Chinese territory were the "eight military headquarters" established by Daowu after the defeat of Later Yan: WS 58.1287.

84. On these see: Tang Zhangru 唐長孺, "Bei Wei nan jing zhu zhou de cheng min" 北魏南境諸州的城民, in his *Shan ju cun gao* (Beijing: Zhonghua shu ju, 1989), 96–109; and He Dezhang 何德章, "Bei Wei cheng ren yu nong geng" 北魏城人与农耕, in his *Wei Jin Nan bei chao shi cong gao* (Beijing: Shang wu yin shu guan, 2010), 346–54.

85. BS 16.617 (WS 18.429–30).

86. E.g., WS 54.1202.

87. For the garrison system in general, see Yan Gengwang 嚴耕望, *Zhongguo di fang xing zheng zhi du shi: Wei Jin Nan bei chao di fang xing zheng zhi du* 中國地方行政制度史: 魏晉南北朝地方行政制度, 2 vols. (Shanghai: Shanghai gu ji chu ban she, 2007), 2: Chapter 11; and Pearce, "Land of Dai."

Over time, the *guo ren* who served in the garrisons were supplemented by convict labor, and after move of the capital to Luoyang their position within the state was seen as much reduced, in relative terms at least.[88]

More generally, however, the move of the capital also led to a southward shift of the military's recruitment base. In the early Wei, the populations of the commandery system were conscripted for local police action, but for major campaigns were used mostly for logistics and support, and not as infantry troops.[89] A century or so later, however, during Xiaowen's reign, conscription of Chinese foot soldiers increased significantly, with overhaul of local government. The implementation of the Equal Fields system, of course, contributed significantly to this.[90] At the end of Wei, in the 520s, in one army involved in the fighting infantry outnumbered cavalry 15 to 1.[91] With a turn toward foot soldiers, the number of warhorses reared and maintained by Luoyang plunged.[92] And in an edict issued in 524, in the midst of the regime's collapse, the populations specially registered for military service were converted into "common subjects," *min* 民.[93]

In this way the Wei armies were profoundly remade. And the Wei state as well.

---

88. Tang, *Wei Jin Nan bei chao Sui Tang shi san lun*, 194, stresses that the decline was *relative*, insisting that their station was still much better than the indentured military labor of the Jiankang regimes.

89. WS 38.688. He Ziquan describes preponderance of cavalry in "Fu bing zhi qian," 318–20; and of occasional early use of Chinese infantry units on pp. 332–33.

90. WS 110.2857, describing development of corvée service; and He, "Fu bing zhi qian," 334–35; Tang, *Wei Jin Nan bei chao Sui Tang shi san lun*, 198. Sagawa, "Bei Wei de bing zhi yu she hui," 49, suggests it was first seriously implanted in 473 under Xiaowen's father, Xianwen.

91. WS 73.1638.

92. Müller, "Horses of the Xianbei," 185.

93. WS 9.237.

The Wolf Lord

Though it saw a buildup of the armies discussed in the last chapter, the reign of Mingyuan also saw a general lull in active campaigning. The second Wei monarch would die in 423, at the age of just 31.[1] If the death came from unnatural causes, they were probably unnatural causes of Mingyuan's own making; like his father, he was ingesting cold food powder. The modern scholar Zhang Jinlong, on the other hand, has suggested as a more proximate cause illness contracted during his exploratory campaign down in the Luoyang area, where in some places disease had taken a heavy toll on the Taghbach troops.[2] If so, he was another colonizer brought low by local disease.

Taiwu (r. 426–452) was the third Northern Wei *huang di*, the 17th Taghbach khaghan from the time of Liwei.[3] His father—already in decline—had the year before prepared succession well, naming his son Prince of Taiping, and then later a sort of vice-emperor, with authority over the government, effectively establishing a diarchy so as to expedite the transfer of power.[4] The plan met with a measure of success, and the transition from Mingyuan to Taiwu was the only in early Wei that did not lead to a struggle within the court. Taiwu's mother, of a minor branch of the Dugu, had died in 420, two years before Taiwu's designation, and there is no evidence that she did not die a natural death.[5] The heir had at any rate not been raised by his birth mother, but by a wet nurse who would come to be the first major female political actor at the Wei court, raised eventually to the palace rank of Empress Dowager (Ch. *tai hou* 太后), in Chinese history at least an act without precedent.[6]

---

1. WS 3.64.
2. WS 3.62; Zhang, *Bei Wei zheng zhi shi*, 2: 530–31; WS 3.63.
3. See Sagawa Eiji 佐川 英治, "Tō Gi Hoku Sei kakumei to 'Gisho' no hensen" 東魏北齊革命と『魏書』の編纂, *Tōyōshi kenkyū* 64.1 (2006): 37–64, on changing definitions of when the regime began, under Northern Wei and then the eastern successors under which Wei Shou finally compiled *Wei shu*.
4. WS 3.61, 62. This is the well-argued thesis of Li Ping, *Bei Wei Pingcheng shidai*, Chapter 2. See also discussion in Eisenberg, *Kingship in Early Medieval China*, Chapter 2. In this arrangement, the senior emperor retained authority over the army.
5. Pearce, "Nurses, Nurslings, and New Shapes of Power," 293; Yao, *Bei chao hu xing kao*, 219; BS 13.493 (WS 13.326).
6. In 425 she was made "nurse empress dowager": WS 4A.70; seven years later, she was given the more conventional title *huang tai hou*: WS 4A.80. For more detail, see Pearce, "Nurses, Nurslings, and New Shapes of Power." Though this was a Chinese title, see Cheng Ya-ju, "Han zhi yu Hu feng," 15–19, as to how this was an ad hoc invention, drawing together parts of the institutions of the old empire as well as practices used among the Taghbach people from the time of Madam Wei (see Chapter 5), if not before.

Being a "Great Martial Emperor"—or a Wolf Lord, a Böri Beg—Taiwu resumed large-scale military activity, eventually reunifying the northern territories of the Han empire, which had last briefly occurred half a century before under Fu Jian. His first major campaign was directed against that old enemy of the Taghbach, the Xiongnu. Liu Weichen's son, Helian Bobo, having retaken the Ordos and established his own Xia 夏 regime, seized Chang'an from the Eastern Jin army in 418 and declared himself emperor.[7] In 425, hearing of the death of Helian Bobo and an ensuing struggle for power in Xia, Taiwu led 20,000 light cavalry to sack and burn the fortified Xia capital of Tongwan 統萬 (some 65 miles southwest of mod. Yulin, Shaanxi, along the "Aimless" 無定 River).[8] Meanwhile, another Taghbach army took Chang'an, down in the Wei River valley.

In early 427, Helian Bobo's heir, Chang, who had reoccupied Tongwan, sent an army south to attempt to recover Chang'an, depleting his defenses in the north. Taiwu now led a much larger army—some 100,000 men—slowly down into the Ordos.[9] In early summer, they halted at a river north of Tongwan, where the emperor prayed to Tengri, informed his ancestors of his plans, and with his men swore an oath; we here perhaps see fuller description than usually provided by the chroniclers of how the early Wei lords prepared their army for battle. A week later they took the city, which seems to have served the still-mobile Helian lords primarily to store accumulated wealth (or in this case, reaccumulated, remembering the sacking just two years before).[10] Helian Chang's rich holdings were seized by Taiwu and according to the usual practice "distributed to the officers and men, each according to his rank."[11] Among the goods seized were 300,000 horses; most at least were left in the Ordos, which now became a huge imperial pasture for the Taghbach (as it would be two centuries later for the Tang).[12] Down in Guanzhong, however, the Helian continued to resist Serbi intrusion, and the Wei commander posted there eventually abandoned Chang'an.[13] Determined to extirpate the Xiongnu nemesis, and enraged at his general's failure, Taiwu had the fellow executed.

Before finishing Xia off, however, Taiwu chose to strike at what was quickly becoming a major rear threat for Pingcheng, the steppelands to the north where the Rouran had fully emerged as dominant power. Beginning again with sacrifice to Tengri, in 429 Taiwu led his armies north across the desert to rout the Rouran and drive their khaghan to the west, where much weakened he grew

---

7. See the history of this regime by Wu Honglin 吴洪琳, *Tiefu Xiongnu yu Xia guo shi yan jiu* 铁弗匈奴与夏国史研究 (Beijing: Zhongguo she hui ke xue chu ban she, 2011).
8. WS 95.2057; ZZTJ 120.3789–91. The walled complex took up something on the order of a quarter of a square mile. An appreciable share of the ruins survive; standing on the edge of desert, there has not been much reason over the last 1,500 years to build over.
9. WS 4A.72
10. For city as storehouse, see Chapter 5 note 36.
11. WS 4A.72–73; 95.2058–59.
12. WS 110.2857; see also Müller, "Horses of the Xianbei," 184. On the horse ranches of Tang two centuries later, see Skaff, *Sui-Tang China and Its Turko-Mongol Neighbors*, 259–62.
13. ZZTJ 121.3798–3801

ill and died.¹⁴ Rouran herds were now scattered untended across the grasslands and former vassals began to surrender. In the end, some half a million encampment groups (*luo*) submitted, while the Taghbach had taken more than a million warhorses.¹⁵ So many animals had suddenly entered the Dai markets, in fact, that prices dropped precipitously for livestock and for felt and hides.¹⁶ The captives, for their part, now stripped of their wealth, were settled in a great swathe in the grasslands north of the Yinshan, from the Chengde region to Wuyuan. Garrisons were established among these groups, to maintain control over them. They also served to defend the frontier, since it would not be long before the Rouran regrouped. This was the origin of the northern or Six Garrisons mentioned in the last chapter, which would play a very important role at the end of Northern Wei. What it marked was not so much power, but defensiveness, as dominance of the steppe began to slip out of the hands of the Taghbach khaghans. Perhaps in part to express his frustration at the matter, Taiwu—who could apparently pun in Chinese, probably several other languages as well—now tinkered with transcription of his steppe rivals' name. While Baldy's descendants had themselves taken up Sinographs to record their name as "Rouran" 柔然, Taiwu changed this to "Ruanruan" 蠕蠕, "the crawling bugs," as a deliberate attempt to belittle.¹⁷

Leaving the crawling bugs aside for a time, Taiwu now turned his attention back to the deteriorating situation in the south, where the Helian successor had made tactical alliance with Jiankang (now seat of Liu Yu's Song) in his effort to restore Xiongnu control over the northwest, suggesting to the Jiankang monarch that together they could destroy Pingcheng, and divide its territories between them, the Song regime taking all the lands east of Mount Heng, the Xiongnu all the lands to the west.¹⁸ The effort came to nothing and in the autumn of 430, Taiwu led another victorious campaign south across the Ordos and by 431 had solid control of more or less the entire region of modern Shaanxi province. Xia was no more, and the Taghbach now possessed Chang'an, which had for centuries been a major political and cultural center of the Chinese world, and though no longer of that importance had recently served, under Later Qin, as the site of the great project by which the Central Asian monk Kumārajīva (344–413) translated key Buddhist texts into Chinese.¹⁹ There followed the first of several large-scale transportations of

---

14. ZZTJ 121.3807ff. It will be noted that discussion of the Rouran campaign elicited a fierce debate of the kind seen 14 years later, as described in Chapter 1.

15. Uchida, *Kita Ajia shi kenkyū*, 2: 34, estimates the *luo* 落 as generally made up of 2–3 tents, and containing 10–20 individuals. If the number given for the number of High Carts taken in 429 is correct, this would have been at least 5 million individuals settled in the band of grassland north of the Yinshan.

16. WS 4A.75, 103.2293; ZZTJ 121.3811–12.

17. WS 103.2289, and see also the modern editors' comments on p. 2314 note 3. On Rouran use of scribes to record in Chinese, see SoS 95.2357.

18. WS 95.2059.

19. ZZTJ 121.3826. For Kumārajīva, see Valerie Hansen, *The Silk Road: A New History* (New York: Oxford University Press, 2012), Chapter 2; and his biography in the *Gao seng zhuan*, T. 2059, 50: 330a-333a. Translation of these texts into Chinese may, of course, have reinforced the dominance of this writing system in East Asia.

northwesterners to Pingcheng, where some would play important roles both in the Wei government and as proselytizers of the Buddhist faith.

In the next year, 432, Taiwu turned east to Manchuria to end another holdout, Yan. No longer under Murong rule, this version—conventionally called "Northern" Yan—survived in much diminished and very altered form, now under control of a man named Feng Hong (r. 430–436). The Feng family, though claiming origin in the Jin empire, had by this time served the Murong for generations and showed a heavy overlay of Serbi culture. Perhaps it is simply best to assume that—like many in this age—they were of mixed descent, in terms both of blood and of culture.[20] In a series of attacks stretching from 432 to 436, Wei armies hammered away at the northeastern state, seizing territory and transplanting populations back to the Pingcheng region. An early defector was a son of Feng Hong, Feng Lang, who surrendered in 433.[21] (This is a minor incident, though as we shall see below, it would later be of enormous consequence, when Feng Lang's daughter took power in the Wei court.) The final offensive commenced in 436. As the Wei armies approached Feng Hong's capital city of Helong (mod. Chaoyang), Yan's eastern neighbor Koguryŏ sent an army to rescue him.[22] Feng now followed them east, burning his city behind. Another Taghbach rival was gone.

Taiwu now turned his attentions west again, to Northern Liang (397–439), one of several regimes that had emerged over the previous century within the Gansu Corridor, that crucial passage between desert and mountain that linked the Tarim Basin with the Wei River valley. Though small in size, these states were strategically placed on the Silk Roads. Northern Liang was ruled by a people whose name has come to us in Chinese transcription as Juqu, a branch of a people called the "Hu of Lu River" (Lushui Hu), perhaps derived from Xiongnu who upon moving into the Gansu Corridor had mixed with various local populations; these were also called "Mixed Hu" (*za Hu*).[23] By the early decades of the fifth century, Northern Liang had extended its power up to Dunhuang, while making its capital at Guzang (mod. Wuwei, Gansu).

---

20. See JS 125.3127, where it is asserted that the family went back to Eastern Zhou's Spring and Autumn period (771–476 BCE). The former monarch, Feng Hong's elder brother, had however had a "cognomen," Qizhifa 乞直伐, that was clearly transcription from another language, presumably Inner Asian. See description of the tomb of another brother, Feng Sufu, with strong Inner Asian elements: Dien, *Six Dynasties Civilization*, 104–5. Questions of origin are raised by Holmgren, "Social Mobility in the Northern Dynasties," 19–32; Stanley Abe, *Ordinary Images* (Chicago: University of Chicago Press, 2002), 181–82; and Kubozoe, *Boshi o mochiita Hokugi-shi kenkyū*, 524–25.

21. WS 4A.81.

22. ZZTJ 123.3861–62. Feng Hong, it should be noted, was subsequently killed by the Koguryŏ king. For more on Wei relations with Koguryŏ, see Li Ping 李凭, *Bei chao yan jiu cun gao* 北朝研究存稿 (Beijing: Shang wu yin shu guan, 2006), 63–135, and for the flight of Feng Hong, 78–83. For a more general overview on Koguryŏ, see also *The History and Archaeology of the Koguryŏ Kingdom*, ed. Mark E. Byington (Cambridge, MA: Early Korea Project, Korea Institute, Harvard University, 2016); and Christopher I. Beckwith, *Koguryo: The Language of Japan's Continental Relatives* (Leiden: Brill, 2004).

23. Zhang, *Bei Wei zheng zhi shi*, 3: 137–46.

In 433, Taiwu bestowed titles upon the new lord of Liang, Juqu Mujian 沮渠 牧犍, and the sides exchanged wives.²⁴ But Taiwu already had designs here as well, privately commenting at the time of the bride exchange that "it won't be long before We conquer Liang."²⁵ From the year 435 he was unnerving the Juqu monarch by reaching past him to build ties with oasis states of the Tarim Basin.²⁶ Some Wei missions would go even further—years later, around 451, an envoy of the "Great Wei" scratched an inscription on a stone in the Gilgit-Baltistan region of Pakistan.²⁷ Taiwu clearly had a wish to get beyond Northern Liang, and in 439 that wish became action, when rumors surfaced of efforts at the Juqu court to poison the Wei princess residing there, and to turn the Wei flank through alliance with the Rouran.²⁸

Many of Taiwu's advisors opposed action against the Juqu, arguing the Gansu Corridor was a desiccated region without the grass or water needed to support a large cavalry force.²⁹ The emperor's position, however, was supported by Cui Hao, who put forth a quote from *Han shu* saying that the region was a rich grassland.³⁰ Perhaps of equal or greater import for Taiwu were the words of a *guo ren* guardsman, whose moniker in *Wei shu* transcription has been whittled down to "Yi Bo." A thoughtful individual, whatever his actual name, whose opinion was respected by the emperor, the guardsman remained behind with Taiwu after the others had left to say: "If Liangzhou (Gansu) is without water or grass, how could they make a country there?"³¹ And so in the summer of 439, Taiwu marshaled his troops in the western suburb—perhaps for an unrecorded sacrifice to Tengri—and then led them forth from Pingcheng. To the complaints of poisoning and collaboration with the Rouran that he put forward to convince his men of the righteousness of the cause, the emperor added another interesting

---

24. Although, as pointed out by Armin Selbitschka, "Tribute, Hostages and Marriage Alliances: A Close Reading of Diplomatic Strategies in the Northern Wei Period," *EMC* 25 (2019): 74–75, ties were also maintained with Jiankang.
25. ZZTJ 122.3848; WS 99.2206, 36.832.
26. Yu Taishan 余太山, *A History of the Relationships between the Western and Eastern Han, Wei, Jin, Northern and Southern Dynasties and the Western Regions* (Philadelphia: Department of East Asian Languages and Civilizations, University of Pennsylvania, 2004), 263–69; the book is a partial English translation of Yu's *Liang Han Wei Jin Nan bei chao yu Xi yu guan xi shi yan jiu* 兩漢魏晉南北朝与西域关系史研究 (Beijing: Zhongguo she hui ke xue chu ban she, 1995). See also the table of Central Asian envoys to Wei (alongside those of Song) in Itagaki Akira 板垣明, "Hokugi no Sei-iki tōbatsu o megutte" 北魏の西域討伐をめぐって, *Chuō daigaku Ajia shi kenkyū* 20 (1996): 104.
27. Nicholas Sims-Williams, "The Sogdian Merchants in China and India," in *Cina e Iran da Alessandro Magno alla dinastia Tang*, ed. Alfredo Cadonna and Lionello Lanciotti (Florence: Casa Editrice Leo S. Olschki, 1996), 57.
28. ZZTJ 123.3870–71.
29. ZZTJ 123.3871–72; WS 36.832; 28.690; 35.822–23.
30. HS 26B.1644–45. For a general overview of the physical conditions of the Gansu Corridor during this period, which though increasingly arid in the fourth and fifth centuries still had more vegetation than it does today, see Maeda Masana 前田正名, *Kasei no rekishi-chirigakuteki kenkyū* 河西の歴史地理學的研究 (Tokyo: Yoshikawa Kōbunkan, 1964), 1–13.
31. For Cui Hao's comment, see WS 35.823; for Yi Ba's, WS 44.989–90.

issue, a demand for free trade: Liang, he said, had disrupted international commerce with its transit taxes.[32]

The campaign was a complete success. The Liang lord locked himself up in Guzang, hoping to be saved by his Rouran allies.[33] They did not arrive and after some two months the city fell and Juqu Mujian surrendered. Brothers of Mujian fled west to Gaochang (southeast of mod. Turpan, Xinjiang), where for the next two decades they controlled this key stopping point on the Silk Roads. Forcibly transplanted the other way, thousands, including many monks, were marched north to Pingcheng.[34] And having seen the rich grasslands of Guzang, which supported the two-month siege, Taiwu on the one hand congratulated the wisdom of Cui Hao, and on the other ordered his main rival in the debate to commit suicide. As for the guardsman presented in *Wei shu* as Yi Bo, Taiwu "loved him and always treated him with a special warmth. Rich gifts were given him."[35]

Triumph over Northern Liang brought an end to the last of the Sixteen Kingdoms, and Wei now ruled over most at least of what had been Han's northern territories. In control of the Gansu Corridor, Taiwu sent forth forays into eastern parts of the Tarim Basin region, taking Shanshan in 445 and Karasahr (Ch. Yanqi; mod. Bayingol, Xinjiang) in 448.[36] Direct control, however, really only lasted a few years. The Juqu continued to hold out at Gaochang, just a few hundred miles to the northeast, and beyond them were the Rouran. The end of Taiwu's reign saw retreat back to Dunhuang; by the year 460 the Rouran had reasserted dominance over the Tarim Basin.[37] Still, contact continued at a lively pace. Northern Wei Buddhists played a prominent role at Khotan in the early 500s.[38] And needless to say, thriving trade continued for Wei with the oasis states, as well as diplomatic gifts. In a statement made some 50 years later, we are told that "Since the beginning of the Jingming reign-period (500 CE), carrying forward the cause of peace and prosperity, the four frontiers are tranquil and at peace, [those] near

---

32. WS 99.2207.
33. ZZTJ 123.3873–74;WS 99.2207.
34. WS 114.3032; Leon Hurvitz, tr., *Wei Shou: Treatise on Buddhism and Taoism; An English Translation of the Original Chinese Text of Wei-shu CXIV and the Japanese Annotation of Tsukamoto Zenryū* (Kyoto: Jimbunkagaku Kenkyusho, Kyoto University, 1956), 61; Liu Shufen 劉淑芬, *Zhong gu de Fo jiao yu she hui* 中古的佛教与社会 (Shanghai: Shanghai gu ji chu ban she, 2008), 30–32.
35. WS 44.990.
36. See Yu, *The Western Regions*, Chapter 7.
37. Rong, "The Rouran Qaghanate and the Western Regions," 77. A decade later, a request from Khotan for Wei help against Rouran raids was met with a diffident "we'll look into the possibilities," from which little real effort came: ZZTJ 132.4155. For a general discussion of the at times underestimated power of the Rouran, see also Sören Stark, "A 'Rouran Perspective' on the Northern Chinese Frontier during the Northern Wei Period," forthcoming in *Mounted Warriors in Europe and Central Asia*, ed. F. Daim, H. Meller, and W. Pohl.
38. Liu Xinru, "The Silk Road: Overland Trade and Cultural Interactions in Eurasia," in *Agricultural and Pastoral Societies in Ancient and Classical History*, ed. Michael Adas (Philadelphia: Temple University Press, 2001), 161–62; and for a Wei mission that in 520 made it all the way to Gandhāra (parts of mod. Afghanistan and Pakistan), see Jenner, *Memories of Loyang*, 265–66.

and [those] far come together [to our court]. Therefore the tributes [given us by the] barbarians follow one after the other on the roads, and the merchants enter by turns. The tribute and goods are twice as much as usual."³⁹

Much was coming into the Wei treasuries. But control was uneven in the newly seized territories. Rebellion repeatedly broke out, among High Carts, Han Chinese, and various other groups. The most recalcitrant region was the swathe of highlands that stretched from the Fen River in Shanxi west across the Yellow River and down to the Jing River in northern Shaanxi. Many groups inhabited these regions—Qiang and Di, Han Chinese, and Lushui Hu, of which as we have seen the Juqu were a branch.⁴⁰ In 445 rebellion broke out there, led by a man referred to in the Chinese sources as Gai Wu 蓋吳, from Apricot Town (Xingcheng, about 100 miles north of Chang'an, on the route now followed by Highway G65). A strategic point in the local geography, Apricot Town had in earlier times repeatedly been the origin of rebellion or the goal of military campaign.⁴¹

Gai Wu's rebellion broke out six years after the taking of Guzang, and may have been motivated by links with the Juqu, Gai himself being of the Lushui Hu. Other possibilities, quite probably overlapping, are resentment at newly asserted Wei control of trade or at the brutal suppression of other recent risings in the area.⁴² At any rate, the rebellion of Gai Wu was on a much larger scale than previous examples and met with early success. After Gai's defeat of a Wei army, several supportive insurrections broke out elsewhere in the northwest. Flush with victory, Gai Wu now took Chang'an, declared himself king, and opened up communications with Jiankang.⁴³

In February of the next year, 446, the emperor himself led an army down the Fen and then into the Wei valley, whereupon Gai Wu fled back into the highlands. Taiwu now visited the old Han capital, as well as the famous Kunming pond, constructed more than a half millennium before by the Han emperor Wudi; a century later, the regent of the Western Wei successor regime, Yuwen Tai, would make this visit too. Having restored control of the Wei Valley, he slowly led his procession back north, with 2,000 families of Chang'an's skilled artisans in tow. Though not captured by Taghbach troops, promises of amnesty eventually led kinsmen to eliminate the rebel Gai Wu.⁴⁴

* * *

---

39. WS 65.1438; tr. Yu, *Western Regions*, 306, with modifications. See also discussion of "tribute" and Wei diplomacy in Selbitschka, "Tribute, Hostages and Marriage Alliances."
40. Chen, *Multicultural China*, 90–92, quoting Tang Zhangru 唐长孺, "Wei Jin za hu kao" 魏晉雜胡考, in his *Wei Jin Nan bei chao shi lun cong*, 382–450.
41. JS 116.2964; ZZTJ 100.3161, 106.3363, 106.3369, 117.3677; WS 2.32. Zhang, *Bei Wei zheng zhi shi*, 4: 132–68, gives detailed information on Gai Wu and his rebellious predecessors.
42. Liu, *Zhong gu de Fo jiao yu she hui*, 10; Zhang, *Bei Wei zheng zhi shi*, 4: 147. For the immediately preceding events, see WS 4B.98–101; ZZTJ 124.3914–16.
43. WS 30.727–28; SoS 95.2339–40 gives copies of letters to the Song court.
44. WS 40.902–3; ZZTJ 124.3926–29.

Pingcheng's major conquests had now been completed, and from this time till the end of Northern Wei, East Asia's international politics would to a great extent at least be defined by the balance of power that lay between Wei in the north and Jiankang down on the Yangtze. As we have seen, the first significant contact with southern armies had begun in the time of Mingyuan. Various Taghbach enemies had subsequently sought Jiankang's support—Gai Wu, and before him the Feng and the Helian—though to no great effect in any of these cases.[45] His flanks now clear, Taiwu began to train his eye upon the rich lands south of the Yellow River.

The man inhabiting the Jiankang throne at this time was Liu Yilong, a son of the Song founder Liu Yu. Interestingly, his reign, from 424 to 453, almost exactly overlaps the 423 to 452 reign of Wei's Taiwu. Both were effective rulers, Liu through careful management and cultivation of his administrative apparatus. And both met their ends in struggle with a son.

In early 450, Taiwu led a force of 100,000 foot and horse down to Luoyang, then took them hunting in the no-man's land to the south, both to show the flag and as a way to feed the men.[46] The army continued the march south, taking a series of towns before bogging down in a siege of Runan (on the site of the mod. town of the same name in Henan). Although improvement can be seen in the Taghbach skill at siegecraft—portable towers were used to rain arrows down on the town, and huge hooks on siege engines pulled down sections of the town's walling— the town was not taken. Suffering heavy casualties, after about a month and a half Taiwu led his army back north, sending to Liu Yilong a letter—in Chinese— complaining about the Song emperor's earlier attempts to buy alliance with the rebel Gai Wu: "If you are a real man, why didn't you come yourself and take (those territories) rather than using your goods to seduce my border people?"[47]

Of the many things that can be found in this letter, perhaps the most interesting is the blunt statement of the enticing quality of Jiankang goods. Since the Bronze Age, the Chinese world had been a unique center for the manufacture of goods, and production and distribution had played an important role in Han manipulation and control of rivals and border populations. With the beginning in this period of a shift of the economic center of the Chinese world down to the Yangtze region, Taiwu would undoubtedly have been thinking not only of Jiankang's material seduction of the populations of contested borderlands, but also how beneficial it would be to control the growing centers of production along the Yangtze, rather than marching captured craftsmen up to Pingcheng.[48]

---

45. ZZTJ 124.3922.
46. ZZTJ 125.3937. For the location of the grounds on which the hunt was conducted, see Zhang, *Bei Wei zheng zhi shi*, 3: 210.
47. SoS 95.2346; ZZTJ 125.3938–40.
48. See discussion of the early development of mass manufacture in Lothar Ledderose's *Ten Thousand Things*. For the economic development of the south during this period, see Liu Shufen 劉淑芬, "Jiankang yu Liu chao li shi de fa zhan" 建康与六朝历史的发展, in her *Liu chao de cheng shi yu she hui* (Taibei: Taiwan xue sheng shu ju, 1992),

This rude letter was, of course, also an intentional provocation, showing Taiwu's pride in the midst of efforts to shame a rival. Reply came in the form of an advance by southern armies adding up to some 200,000. But here we see that one of the key differences between Wei and the Jiankang regimes lay in the ability to muster and maintain a large standing army. By this time, the lower Yangtze region was the richest in East Asia, perhaps the entire world. But the presence of wealth and the ability to extract it are two different things: Jiankang's methods of tax collection were (like those of Wei) not highly developed, and so the call-up of troops seriously strained the treasury. One way to fund the military campaign was to cut the salaries of Song officials by a third.[49]

Despite these difficulties, the Song army now advanced to the Yellow River, laying siege to the fortress at Hulao. Responding to demands at Pingcheng that an army be sent to protect "the grain and textiles along the River," Taiwu demurred, saying, "the horses have not yet plumped up, and it is still hot down there. It won't be to our benefit to set forth immediately." With great bombast he went on to say that "The men of our nation (*guo ren*) originally wore trousers made of sheepskin"—it is doubtful that many still did so—"what need have we for silks?"[50] In more practical terms, the emperor's attention was probably also distracted at this time by the difficult decision he had just made to execute his minister Cui Hao.

With the coming of autumn, however, his horses were sleek. Nor did he have difficulty raising a huge army from among the very willing men of the nation, despite the drain on the treasury. Having practiced them with a hunt in the Ordos and then gathered them again in Pingcheng's western suburb, Taiwu led his army south, adding to his core units auxiliaries including draftees from districts down in the plains.[51] No doubt with some exaggeration, we are told that he crossed the Yellow River "with an army of one million, the beating of the war-drums shaking heaven and earth." Defenders fled, abandoning their arms—and comrades—in heaps behind them.[52] Following multiple lines of advance the Wei armies moved south largely unopposed. En route, Taiwu arrived at Mount Zou (east of mod. Jining, Shandong). In 219 BCE—two years after his unification of the Chinese lands—the Qin First Emperor had ascended the mountain and placed a commemorative stele there. Taiwu now climbed the mountain himself, where he had his men push over his rival's monument. More courteously, representatives were sent to make sacrifice in Confucius' old hometown, which was just 15 or so miles away.[53]

3–34; and Shufen Liu, "Jiankang and the Commercial Empire of the Southern Dynasties: Change and Continuity in Medieval Chinese Economic History," in *Culture and Power in the Reconstitution of the Chinese Realm, 200–600*, ed. Scott Pearce, Audrey Spiro, and Patricia Ebrey (Cambridge, MA: Harvard University Press, 2001), 35–52.

49. SoS 5.98, 95.2349; ZZTJ 125.3938.
50. ZZTJ 125.3948.
51. WS 4B.104.
52. SoS 95.2350.
53. SoS 95.2350; WS 4B.104.

From Mount Zou they continued south, in mid-February 451 reaching the north bank of the Yangtze, just across the river from Jiankang. Taiwu's tent sat on top of a hill overlooking his army of some 600,000 men, in encampments stretching for miles.[54] Other Wei armies moving on parallel routes on the same day arrived at points west and east on the banks of the Yangtze, showing not only the Wei capacity for choreography but the weakness of the Song defense, at least north of the river. On the south side, martial law had been declared and defenses put in place for hundreds of miles along the south bank.[55] On the northern bank, Taghbach troops were bundling reeds into rafts for a great crossing. Terrified, Liu Yilong now presented tribute and begged for peace, and according to *Wei shu*, at least, marriage between the two royal houses.[56] No marriage took place, but three days later—by the Chinese calendar New Year's Day—the Wei emperor held a great feast for his officers, with bestowals to each according to his rank and peerage for more than 200 men. He went on to declare an end to hostilities. And on the day after that, he gathered the army together for return north. The river had not been crossed, the invasion not carried to completion. But the regions through which the Wei armies had marched were devastated, and as he withdrew, Taiwu gathered up more than 50,000 households of captives to take back to the Sanggan highlands.[57] Though it had survived, the Song regime was much weakened.

The question of why Taiwu did not push south rests probably on material limits. In terms of attack and defense, the Yangtze itself was a huge moat, more than half a mile wide at Jiankang. South bank defenses rested on sophisticated naval capacities; it is not clear how well the reed rafts would have done against them. Another issue was logistics. On the road back north, the "men and horses were hungry," and increasingly driven to attacks on grain stores in the cities they passed.[58] And while many of these walled towns had been abandoned, many were still held by defenders.[59] The Wei armies could turn from orderly procession to trapped prey. Furthermore, remembering why the emperor did not move south earlier, we perhaps hear the complaint of many men of Inner Asian origin

---

54. WS 4B.104–5, 105C.2406; ZZTJ 125.3960.
55. Described at length in Zhang, *Bei Wei zheng zhi shi*, 3: 268–95.
56. WS 4B.105, 95.2139, which go on to state that it was Taiwu who considered that marriage between the two dynasties would be "incorrect" 不禮. SoS 95.2352, 71.1849, state instead that it was Taiwu who asked for marriage (and also claims that earlier requests had been made as well, before the invasion: SoS 95.2334). ZZTJ 125.3961 takes the side of the latter. For further discussion of different perspectives on some of these events seen in different histories from this age, see Albert Dien, "The Disputation at Pengcheng: Accounts from the *Wei shu* and the *Song shu*," in *Early Medieval China: A Sourcebook*, ed. Wendy Swartz et al. (New York: Columbia University Press, 2014), 32–59.
57. WS 4B.105, 95.2140, 105C.2406.
58. WS 95.2140; SoS 74.1912.
59. In SoS 74.1913, we are told of one who challenged Taiwu by asking how he measured up to Fu Jian, to whom the enraged Taghbach khaghan responded by making a nail bed and saying when the city fell the defender would be lying on it.

regarding the heat of the southlands; spring was around the corner, and summer after that. Mingyuan, again, may have died of a disease picked up south of the Yellow River, while Taiwu, for his part, is said to have been unwilling to drink the region's water, and had his potables shipped down from the north on the backs of camels. These were, of course, real humans moving across unfamiliar parts of the world, with all the complaints and comments still heard today.[60] And finally, as noted above, the emperor had ordered the death of his minister Cui Hao just months before the campaign, certainly sending Pingcheng into a tumult. And so for all these reasons, and perhaps more, this practical commander-in-chief led his troops back north, with hundreds of thousands of new subjects in thrall. Perhaps this had been the point of the campaign from the beginning, together with a desire to intimidate Song and squelch efforts to retake northern Henan—which with the ongoing power struggles that unfolded in the Song after Liu Yilong's murder by his son in 453 did not occur again.

* * *

The Wolf Lord struggled with enemies on the field of battle. He also struggled with sets of symbols and beliefs, supporting some and rejecting others depending on whether, in his opinion, they strengthened the monarchy or weakened it. In looking at these matters, it must be remembered how new the nation was—in full form, at least, going back only a couple of generations to Daowu. Many little traditions may have existed among particular groups, but the nation as a whole—perhaps a bit like "Great Britain" in recent years—may have felt dangerously fragile, despite the unifying features of booty and the hunt, Tengri and the khaghan. Here it would be well to remember not only what we see, but what we don't see: though there were in Dai many cults of what *Wei shu* calls "petty gods" 小神, no powerful figures emerged from among their leaders of the sort we see with Temujin's rival, the Mongol holy man Kököčü.[61] And though there seem to have been shared songs and epics—perhaps including early *guo yu* versions of "Mulan"—there is no record at least of a bardic tradition that brought these from community to community to touch the heart of every compatriot.

---

60. SoS 95.2352. Discussion and complaint were often heard about the different cuisines of the Yellow River as opposed to the Yangtze regions: see Scott Pearce, Audrey Spiro, and Patricia Ebrey, "Introduction," in *Culture and Power in the Reconstitution of the Chinese Realm, 200–600*, ed. Scott Pearce, Audrey Spiro, and Patricia Ebrey (Cambridge, MA: Harvard University Press, 2001), 22.

61. WS 108A.2739. ZZTJ 124.3906 calls them "barbarian gods" 胡神, which in later times came to be applied to gods deriving from Central Asian religions. For the place of Kököčü Teb Tenggeri in the Mongol community, and his death by order of Temujin, see Rachewiltz, *Secret History of the Mongols*, 1: 168–74, and analytical discussion on 2: 869ff., including discussion of whether or not he should properly be called a "shaman"; "prophet" may be the more proper term. According to Rachewiltz (2: 870–72), "Teb Tenggeri" can be taken to mean "The Very Lord[-like]," here translating *tenggeri* (≈ *tengri*) not as "celestial" or "heaven," but by the derivative "lord." For discussion of the rivalry between Kököčü and Temujin, see the notes on 2: 878–79.

Buddhism had by this time for centuries been spreading into East Asian societies, having become well entrenched in the Yangtze region, in Manchuria in the east, and in the former nesting place of Kumārajīva in the northwest.[62] But in the mid-fifth century it was just beginning to take root in Dai, stimulated in large part by transportation from the recently conquered northwest of large numbers of proselytizing monks and nuns.[63] Living in the uncertainty of a newly created world, still rough in terms of content and definition, many of Pingcheng's inhabitants were fruit for the plucking of those who wished to spread the faith. Among those converted was the emperor's own son and heir, Huang.

But as for the emperor himself, he was uncomfortable with the growing influence of Buddhist proselytizers, and the potential power of their institutions, and of the religion itself.[64] His suspicions gained new focus in 446, down in the Wei valley, when in the course of a tour of Chang'an following suppression of Gai Wu's rebellion his men discovered an armory at a monastery there.[65] Saying, "These are not [things] that monks use—they must have been plotting with Gai Wu!," Taiwu's response was brutal: all the monks at the monastery were put to death, the temple razed, its objects of devotion destroyed. Shortly thereafter it was edicted that this would be extended throughout the realm.[66] In the event, this act was opposed by many at court, including of course Huang, who serving as viceroy of the capital delayed implementation long enough that the monks of Pingcheng were able to hide. The temples, on the other hand, seem largely to have been destroyed.

Buddhism represented to Taiwu a threatening alternative set of alliances, within the nation and across its borders. It also threatened as something new; though the younger generation—his son—found solace in the faith, for Taiwu it remained something foreign. And so, as his forebears had created Pingcheng, Taiwu now sought to create other ways to draw the credulousness of Pingcheng's folk to his own ends. As we have seen above, a first effort came in 443, with appearance of the Olakkô mission to Pingcheng. But in addition to efforts to plant roots beyond the pale, a larger effort was being made to map the regime's place

---

62. Tang Yongtong 湯用彤, *Han Wei Liang Jin Nan bei chao Fo jiao shi* 漢魏兩晉南北朝佛教史, 2 vols. (Beijing: Zhonghua shu ju, 1955), 2: 488; for Buddhism in the northwest, see Liu, *Zhong gu de Fo jiao yu she hui*, 25–35.

63. WS 114.3032 (Hurvitz, *Treatise on Buddhism and Taoism*, 56–62); Liu, *Zhong gu de Fo jiao yu she hui*, 30–32.

64. For discussion of the extraordinary powers—the "magic"—supposedly used by monks in these times, see John Kieschnick, *The Eminent Monk: Buddhist Ideals in Medieval Chinese Hagiography* (Honolulu: University of Hawai'i Press, 1997), 93; and Arthur Wright, "Fo-t'u-teng: A Biography," *HJAS* 11 (1948): 321–71. More mundanely, there are also reports of Buddhist monks leading occasional insurrections, both before Taiwu and after him, though none were major threats to the regime: e.g., WS 2.39, 7A.140, 150, 8.215. Taiwu's attempted suppression of Buddhism certainly was in part based on fears of such events, which would have motivated earlier attempts to forbid the private keeping by families of their own monks or shamans: see WS 4B.97; Liu, *Zhong gu de Fo jiao yu she hui*, 37.

65. ZZTJ 124.3923; WS 114.3033–34 (Hurvitz, *Treatise on Buddhism and Taoism*, 64–65); Kenneth Chen, *Buddhism in China: a Historical Survey* (Princeton, NJ: Princeton University Press, 1964), 149–50.

66. For an overall picture of Taiwu's suppression, see Liu, *Zhong gu de Fo jiao yu she hui*, 36–43.

and significance within worlds less distant, by turning to symbols and structures of the old Chinese empire. We have seen above the construction of a genealogy tracing the Taghbach lords back to the legendary Yellow Emperor.[67] The Chinese classics—themselves of course in their own way invented tradition—were also drawn upon, at first in a spotty fashion, but systematically from the time of the later Wei emperor Xiaowen. As a relatively early stage of this process, in 444 (immediately after banning Buddhism) Taiwu put forth an edict ordering that the sons of all his princes, dukes, and ministers attend the imperial academy to study them.[68] Cui Hao had been a key figure in these developments, seeking to subsume Taghbach lord and Taghbach army into the ideal blueprint of state and society he extracted in his own interpretation of the classics.[69]

Cui Hao had also played a key role in efforts to establish as state religion a school of the native Chinese religion of Daoism. In 424, Cui introduced the emperor to Kou Qianzhi, a Daoist prophet who while in hermitage at the sacred Mount Song (south of the Yellow River, in that still contested frontier zone between Wei and Song) had received revelation from Lord Lao, the deified Laozi.[70] Taiwu was drawn to Kou's brand of Daoism in part by its magic and immortality, in part because Kou presented himself as having been charged by the gods to go north to Pingcheng and aid Taiwu. Culmination came in 440 with Taiwu's adoption of a title Kou had suggested, Perfect Ruler of Great Peace (*Tai ping zhen jun*), which he also made his new reign name (440–451).[71]

Despite Taiwu's effort to foster a new religion—which he hoped would reach out from the capital to bind the disparate and often rebellious peoples of his recently created realm together in a new world order—there seems to have been little popular interest in Kou's concoctions. Over time, in fact, the emperor himself seems to have lost interest. When Kou died in 448, he was not replaced as leader of the Daoist church. The reign name was changed in 451, a few months after the emperor's return from the southern campaign.[72] Under Taiwu's successor, Buddhism would be assigned the role of key binding agent for the regime.

---

67. See discussion of this in Chapter 4.
68. WS 4B.97. For earlier examples, see WS 2.35, 4A.71.
69. Arthur Wright, *Buddhism in Chinese History* (Stanford, CA: Stanford University Press, 1959), 60, points out that Chinese advisors to the Taghbach lords were "striving always to persuade their alien masters to reconstitute a Confucian state in which the educated gentry would have the key role." From an earlier time, Mark Edward Lewis in his *Writing and Authority in Early China*, 4, describes how "the Chinese empire . . . was based on an imaginary realm created within texts."
70. For Kou Qianzhi, see WS 114.3049–54; Richard A. Mather, "K'ou Ch'ien-chih and the Taoist Theocracy at the Northern Wei Court, 425–451," in *Facets of Taoism: Essays in Chinese Religion* (New Haven, CT: Yale University Press, 1979), 103–22; David C. Yu, *History of Chinese Daoism* (Lanham, MD: University Press of America, 2000), 352–66.
71. WS 35.814, 114.3051–52; ZZTJ 119.3762, 123.3885; Mather, "K'ou Ch'ien-chih," 114–15. It will be noted that as heir he had been named King of the Great Peace (Taiping wang 泰平王); WS 112B.2954 ties these events together in an omen.
72. WS 4B.105.

Perhaps Taiwu tired of Kou's faith as he tired of Kou's mentor. The highly educated son of an eminent Chinese lineage, Cui Hao had served for decades as an important advisor to the throne. His execution in 450, at Taiwu's command, shook the Wei state. The cause stated in *Wei shu* was disgruntlement at the contents of Cui's "National Records" (*Guo ji*). As seen in Chapter 2, he had been charged to write this by the emperor, and when complete the history was carved onto tablets and put out for a grand display to the west of the outer walls of Pingcheng, on the avenue that led to the dynasty's Altar of Tengri. Complaints soon surfaced that passages were "inappropriate" (*bu dian*) and revealed "unseemly affairs of the nation" (*guo e*). These complaints then became formal charges.[73]

Various explanations have been put forth for Cui's execution in 450, with many emphasizing ethnic tension.[74] But the "National Records" were doubtlessly at least the proximate cause. Although we do not know what the inappropriate passages said, we can with some confidence assume that in describing the Taghbach, in assigning their role in his utopian empire, Cui wrote something that at least some of the *guo ren* did not like. One plausible explanation, put forth by the Jiankang history, *Nan Qi shu*, was a suggestion by Cui Hao that the Taghbach were descended not from the Yellow Emperor, but a renegade Han general who had gone over to the Xiongnu.[75] Whatever the cause, some correctly foretold the results: on hearing of the plan publicly to display the "National Records," one of the project's participants, the scribe Gao Yun, predicted that this would "be a calamity for the Cui for many generations. None of our lot will survive,"[76] the lot here referring to Chinese men of letters. Gao Yun himself did survive, the heir apparent Huang intervening to save his tutor's life. But Gao's prediction very much came true. More than 100 died in all. Placed in a caged carriage, Cui Hao was taken out to the execution grounds, in the same plaza south of the palace city's gate where the prince Shao had been sliced to death some forty years before.[77] As a prelude, several dozen *guo ren* guardsmen urinated on him; his piteous cry, we are told, was heard by passersby. Confirming the import of the "National Records" in the case, with the exception of Gao Yun all the assistant editors were put to death.[78]

Cui Hao's making of a tight-knit and powerful faction in the Wei government seems to have been another underlying reason for his killing: also executed were

---

73. WS 35.826.
74. Some such tensions clearly existed at the Wei court: see, e.g., WS 38.875. For the persistence of these not uncommon prejudices into the Tang, see Abramson, *Ethnic Identity in Tang China*.
75. In NQS 57.993: "The caitiffs were the descendants of Li Ling 李陵. The caitiffs shunned mention of this. There was someone who said that the [Taghbach] were descendants of [Li] Ling. He was promptly put to death."
76. WS 48.1070. For general overview of these events, see ZZTJ 125.3941–44; and Zhou Yiliang 周一良, "Cui Hao guo shi zhi yu" 崔浩国史之狱, in his *Wei Jin Nan bei chao shi zha ji* (Beijing: Zhonghua shu ju, 1985), 342–350, who gives several suggestions of possible affronts to the *guo ren*.
77. Yin, "Bei Wei Pingcheng shi lüe," 194.
78. WS 35.826; ZZTJ 125.3943–44.

his close kinsmen, and the families of Chinese affines, whom he had in large numbers raised to office. Cui also had marriage ties with southerners, which might explain his reluctance to move troops south, while he had regularly shown enthusiasm for campaigns in the north or west.[79] It will be remembered that it was only after executing Cui Hao that Taiwu led his huge army down to the banks of the Yangtze.[80]

More generally, as people often do, Cui seems over the decades to have grown increasingly arrogant and self-satisfied.[81] Or to put it another way, he had come to conceive himself not simply as servant of the dynasty, but more fundamentally as recipient of a charge—from Heaven perhaps, if not Tengri—to transform the realm in accordance with his vision. When Taiwu came to the throne at the age of just fifteen he had perhaps needed a reliable mentor—a "wise weakling" as Cui Hao was described—different from and yet able to stand against seasoned generals and scheming kinsmen.[82] But if Cui Hao can be said to have become a prideful man, it seems that over the years Taiwu grew in that direction as well. Perhaps he had come to see that he, the supposed lord, was playing pawn—or at best knight—in another man's game. And so even if truly angry to hear publicly announced who it was that great-grandfather had slept with, or whatever the inappropriate passages had said, Taiwu now in a calculating way used this as an excuse to sweep the board clean and begin again with other players upon it.

If that was the emperor's plan, it did not succeed; the new pieces on the board served Taiwu's interests much less well. Not long after the execution of Cui Hao and his kinsmen came the deaths first of Taiwu's heir apparent, Huang, and then Taiwu himself. Confusion would reign at court.

79. WS 35.813, 825–26. SoS 77.1991 directly states that Cui Hao was killed due to plotting with southern relations. The man's "emotional entanglements" with the south and with southerners are explored by Wang Yongping 王永平, "Cui Hao zhi nan chao qing jie ji qi yu nan shi zhi jiao wang kao xi 崔浩之南朝情结及其与南士之交往考析, in 1–6 shi ji Zhongguo bei fang bian jiang, min zu, she hui guo ji xue shu yan tao hui lun wen ji, ed. Jilin daxue gu ji yan jiu suo (Beijing: Ke xue chu ban she, 2008), 241–52.

80. Cui Hao had argued against the Jiankang campaign, which had apparently enjoyed strong support among the generals: ZZTJ 121.3817.

81. See the comment by Gao Yun, WS 48.1069. For other examples, see WS 35.815, 825; WS 48.1069, 1070.

82. Holmgren, "Northern Wei as Conquest Dynasty," 13–14, points out that more rather than fewer Chinese ministers were raised to high office under strongmen rulers such as Daowu and Taiwu, to serve as counterweights to generals and kinsmen.

13

Hunting and Gathering in the Land of Dai

Here, at the end of the Wolf Lord's reign, we turn again to the Land of Dai, the region in which Taiwu's army had been assembled and largely quartered over the previous fifty years, and which would—despite increasingly rapid change—remain as the Wei base of power for almost another half century. In this chapter, however, we look at Dai from another vantage point, focusing not on the army, or the nation, but more generally on how life was lived in and around the Datong Basin. Unfortunately, all we really have a view of is the rich, or at least those rich enough to hire a contractor to build a tomb for father, or mother. As is always the case, everywhere, most of this place's inhabitants have no history.

"Hunting" and "gathering" are the twin themes here. The terms took shape within the field of anthropology to describe a particular form of human adaptation, though they have now been largely abandoned in favor of other terminology. Here, they are borrowed for a different context, to be used in different ways, in a way that perhaps resembles appropriation of Jin titles in the early stages of the Wei state. In our discussions in this chapter, "hunting" will mean, as the OED states in one subsidiary definition, "to pursue with force, violence, or hostility," whether that be an animal, or booty, or territory and its populations.[1] Our "gathering" will diverge equally far, referring to the gathering of people "in one place or company" (OED), for the purpose of distributing and redistributing goods taken directly or indirectly from the hunt. Particular focus will be given in this connection to gathering for a feast, for which, as everywhere, "splendor was the aim,"[2] and the means by which one built community, and arranged that community along the lines of a clear hierarchy, with the feast's master, or mistress, at that hierarchy's top. For these subjects, we will for the most part draw on murals on the walls of the tombs of high-ranking *guo ren*, which have been excavated

---

1. Borrowing in part at least from the Chinese phrase, "chasing the deer" (*zhu lu* 逐鹿), which beginning with the power struggles that followed the Qin collapse, ca. 210 BCE, has been used in connection with predatory warfare undertaken in order to take control of taxable populations: SJ 92.2629. Among other places, it has appeared in a study of the later Northern Dynasties: Jiang Lang 姜狼, *Zhu lu tian xia: Bei Qi he Bei Zhou si shi nian zheng ba shi, 526-581* 逐鹿天下: 北齊和北周四十年爭霸史, 526–581 (Taibei: Da di chu ban she, 2012).

2. A phrase taken from the caption on an exhibit of 17th- and 18th-century Hanoverian dining silver, displayed in Gallery 250 of Boston's Museum of Fine Arts. Similar remarks are provided by Lothar Ledderose regarding the Han elite, which "defined and displayed social status through luxury tableware, just as the aristocracy in medieval Europe would" (*Ten Thousand Things*, 177–78).

outside the walls of a city that, for a century, was a major East Asian center of growth and change.

* * *

Pingcheng was always work in progress. Its palaces seem at first to have been scattered structures, visited only occasionally by a monarch—Daowu—constantly in the field. In subsequent years halls and walls proliferated, and were increasingly occupied by servants, and officials, and inhabitants of the women's quarters. Having filled up, the city in its precarious environment then became too full—the domain reaching something on the order of a million, or more[3]—with growing crime and ongoing fears of famine.[4] In 493, Pingcheng was abandoned by its ruler, with relocation of Great Wei's capital into the Chinese interior, and thirty years after that, with the state's collapse, by more or less everyone. Unlike its successor-town—Luoyang—Pingcheng had no book written to mourn its passing.[5] This does not, of course, mean that no one grieved its loss, but only that the people who at that time wrote books were not the ones who felt grief for the city's abandonment.

The Shamo Khaghan had been down to Luoyang in the late third century, and sixty years later, Shiyijian to Ye. But as we've seen with Shamo's fate—and the veto of Shiyijian's mother—citification was resisted by important elements of the Taghbach community. This resistance faded with Daowu's conquest of the plains in 398. Touring the great city of Ye, we are told, the conqueror triumphally "ascended the towers, and surveilled all the palaces and walls."[6] It was on this basis, we are told by the scribes who compiled his annals, that Daowu—apparently impressed by the grandness of the scene—decided to establish his own capital. And this he did as soon as he returned to the north. Some six months later, he relocated the seat of his rule from the Tumed Plain down to Pingcheng, ordering construction of royal halls and shrines to his forebears. The "Hall of Heaven's

---

3. See Chapter 9 note 22.
4. Treager, *Geography of China*, 213, points out persistent danger of famine in the loess lands.
5. Luoyang's rapid rise and rapid fall (493–534) were recorded by Yang Xuanzhi 楊衒之 (d. ca. 555) in his *Luoyang qie lan ji* 洛陽伽藍記 (published as *Luoyang qie lan ji jiao zhu* 校注 [Shanghai: Shanghai gu ji chu ban she, 1978]); translated by Jenner in his *Memories of Loyang*; and by Yi-t'ung Wang as *A Record of the Buddhist Monasteries in Lo-yang* (Princeton, NJ: Princeton University Press, 1984). As for Pingcheng, there was a poem, "Mourning Pingcheng" 悲平城, written shortly after the capital had been moved to Luoyang (see Lei Bingfeng 雷炳锋, "Wang Su 'Bei Pingcheng' shi chuang zuo shi jian kao bian" 王肃《悲平城》诗创作时间考辨, *Suzhou xue yuan xue bao* 30.8 [2015]: 64–66). The four-line poem, by Wang Su, whom we shall discuss in more detail in Chapter 16, was, however, more complaint about the region's weather than grief at the city's abandonment (WS 82.1799): "the Shadow Mountains (Yin shan) are always dark and snowy; desolate pine, wind without cease." It must also be made clear that Pingcheng was not entirely abandoned; it continued to play a role in East Asian history, as "western capital," for instance, of the Khitan state. In archaeological work done at Datong, Liao tiles are found atop those of the Wei (Joy Yi, *Yungang*, 23ff.).
6. WS 2.31, 23.604. Cao Chenming 曹臣明, "Bei Wei Pingcheng bu ju chu tan" 北魏平城布局初探, in *Bei Wei Pingcheng kao gu yan jiu: gong yuan wu shi ji Zhongguo du cheng de yan bian*, ed. Wang Yintian (Beijing: Ke xue chu ban she, 2017), 1.

Order" 天文殿 is said to have been completed three months later. For this and later projects, we are told, tens of thousands of men were put to work.[7] For the material that these men worked, millions of tree trunks were cut and taken to the city, part no doubt of the denuding of the surrounding hills, which would over time significantly affect the region's environment.[8] This was the hall in which, several months later, Daowu accepted symbolic seals and the borrowed Chinese title "August God-King," *huang di* 皇帝.[9] It would, of course, have been a grand event, a symbolic expression of intent to control and exploit the wealthy farmlands of the plains, as the Han lords had done before. The ceremony would also, however, have been a somewhat ad hoc affair, conducted by the leaders of a just-returned army, in the midst of an ongoing construction project. Logs, wood shavings, and tools were likely still scattered across the ground as dwelling units were built for the royal family, and walls of rammed earth laid around the new palace city. Labor for the latter may have been lessened by the fact that these walls—with a perimeter of about two-and-a-half miles—seem to have followed the lines of the still partially intact walls of the Han frontier outpost from which the Wei capital took its name.[10]

With the transportations, and settlement of the military in the city, the Pingcheng populations now began to grow. Already by the end of Daowu's reign, it has been estimated that more than half a million lived there, most clustered south of the palace city.[11] In 406, a set of city walls was added around these populations, and finally, we are told, Wei "met the requirements of a city [one could actually] live in."[12] A rough vertical rectangle, the walls of the city as a whole, also of rammed earth, were said to have extended some six miles, a little more than a mile east-west, and a bit less than two north-south, so about two square miles. It has been estimated that these walls were 35 to 40 feet high.[13] Most of the space within them consisted of residential units; repeated mentions are made in *Wei shu* of imperial visits to mansions of powerful members of the regime who lived within the city, just outside the palaces' southern gate.[14] A bit farther from the palace gates would have been the houses of military families,

---

7. See the statement made more than fifty years later by Gao Yun 高允 to the emperor Wencheng (r. 452–465), in opposition to a building project, that it would take 40,000 men six months to complete the project, bringing suffering upon the common people: WS 48.1073. In the same passage, Gao Yun expressed disapproval of the fact that Daowu had scheduled construction of Pingcheng without taking account of farmers' slack seasons.
8. WS 23.604.
9. WS 2.33–34.
10. WS 105C.2392; Cao, "Bei Wei Pingcheng bu ju chu tan," 3; Yin, "Bei Wei Pingcheng shi lüe," 193.
11. Yin, "Bei Wei Pingcheng shi lüe," 195.
12. WS 105C.2392.
13. See the figures given in Yin, "Bei Wei Pingcheng shi lüe," 196. A suggested reconstruction of the layout of the walls can be seen in Duan and Zhao, *Tian xia da tong*, 19; in this theory, the outer walls went around and contained the palace city. For wall height, see p. 28.
14. Duan and Zhao, *Tian xia da tong*, 17–18.

as discussed in Chapter 11, and probably some at least of the skilled and useful transportees.

While walls protected these growing populations from incursions from the steppe, they seem also to have served to control them: interior sets of walls were put up as well, creating an early example of the ward system well known later from the Tang capital of Chang'an. Pingcheng's "large wards," according to a southern visitor whose comments are recorded in *Nan Qi shu*, "contain four or five hundred families, the small ones sixty or seventy."[15] Though we do not know the names of these directly, later texts suggest names like "The Ward of Northern Pacification" (Bei ping fang 北平坊)—perhaps for military men—and the "Ward of the Employed Worthies" (Ren xian fang 任賢坊)—perhaps for transportees serving the state.[16] As gates in walls usually are, those of the wards were locked, on the outside, opening at dawn and closing at dusk with 1,000 beats of a great drum set atop a "white tower."[17] Each time the gates were closed, the Jiankang observer went on to write, "the wards are searched, to take precautions against perfidious schemes."[18] Among the "perfidious schemes" in the minds of inhabitants—particularly those forcibly relocated—must have been getting out of the place. One of Pingcheng's functions was then to serve as a huge detention camp, with a perilously unstable food base.

With the growth of yet more settlements south of the growing city, yet another set of walls—"barbicans" or *guo cheng* 郭城—were added in 422. With a perimeter estimated to be eight or nine miles, these were likely lower in height than the walls of the palace and inner city, though they still needed to be high enough to keep mounted Rouran raiders out, and the inhabitants in.[19] Wards were constructed within the barbican as well. Over time, rivers coming from north and west were redirected to flow through and around the growing city, for the practical purpose of irrigation but also simply for their beauty.[20] To the north of the palace city was the great Deer Park established in 399 by Daowu, which served not just as a hunting park but was also used for training and inspecting troops and holding court away from the city, and furthermore, as a huge imperial

---

15. NQS 57.985. Duan and Zhao, *Tian xia da tong*, 20–21, point out that this is the first textual mention of a system of walled wards, which went on to influence Wei's Luoyang, and from this the larger East Asian world. Dien, *Six Dynasties Civilization*, 31–32, cites Miyazaki Ichisada 宮崎市定 ("Rikuchō jidai Kahoku no toshi" 六朝時代華北の都市, *Tōyōshi kenkyū* 20.2 [1961]: 53–74) in discussion of use of walls in these cities as a control for restive, transplanted populations. Though the main NQS quote raises the issue with the *guo cheng* ("barbicans"), Yin Xian states this began with the city walls, the *wai cheng*: "Bei Wei Pingcheng shi lüe," 196.

16. Duan and Zhao, *Tian xia da tong*, 21.

17. Originally built in 416, the drum was added later: Duan and Zhao, *Tian xia da tong*, 67, citing *Shui jing zhu shu* 2: 13.1144–45.

18. NQS 57.985. Note suggestion for correction of this passage by the editorial authors of the Zhonghua shu ju edition.

19. WS 3.62; Yin, "Bei Wei Pingcheng shi lüe," 196. For estimates of the barbican's height see Duan and Zhao, *Tian xia da tong*, 27.

20. Song, *Bei Wei nü zhu lun*, 21; Sakuma, *Gi Shin Nanbokuchō suirishi kenkyū*, 363–64.

ranch for livestock brought down from the steppe, managed by captured High Cart people.[21]

Alongside pragmatic utility, structures are used to display power.[22] Taiwu thus had made for himself a portable hall of glass—a technology brought east by Central Asian Hephtalites—which no doubt glittered in the eyes and hearts of those received there.[23] Among the new town's early fixed landmarks would have been a five-story pagoda erected in 398, and the multistory structure that Taiwu lived atop, located among the residences in the rear of the palace city, close by the "Cloud Mother" 雲母—"Mica"—Hall, built back in the time of Daowu and apparently decorated with its namesake, which was believed to prolong life.[24] More immediately apparent to outsiders would have been the great "white terrace" 白臺—supposedly 200 feet tall—at the southern edge of the palace city, and the two detached towers that went up just outside its main southern gate. Of rammed earth, and standing some 100 feet tall, it would be from the top of one of these towers that the imperial will was decreed to those below, by the monarch himself or by his agents.[25] About the same size as the Tower of London, Pingcheng's towers apparently played much the same role, which in the English case is said to have been "to awe, subdue and terrify Londoners, and to deter foreign invaders."[26] The effect of Pingcheng's towers would have been especially powerful for men coming down from the northlands, who had never seen such monumental architecture; for men such as the Olakkô (Ch. Wuluohou) who came to Taiwu in the year 443. Erected by Daowu, in the year 406, the towers were still standing through the Tang period, when a poem was composed mentioning them. In the time of the Khitans—Inner Asian heirs to the Taghbach for whom Pingcheng was a "western capital"—it was said that "the pair of watchtowers are still there."[27]

The Two Towers are no longer with us—having been knocked over in the 1960s to fill in the city's old moat[28]—and at this point it must be noted that, with the obvious exception of the Buddhist cave temples at nearby Yungang, almost nothing of the Wei city has survived above ground. The dominant architecture of the Han empire—carried on in Pingcheng by the only ones there who knew how

21. Segawa, "You mu yu nong geng zhi jian," 104–5; Yin, "Bei Wei Pingcheng shi lüe," 198.
22. For discussion of the broader topic, see among many possibilities Louis Nelson's *Architecture and Empire in Jamaica* (New Haven, CT, and London: Yale University Press, 2016).
23. WS 102.2275; Bonnie Cheng, "Exchange across Media in Northern Wei China," in *Face to Face: The Transcendence of the Arts in China and Beyond* (Lisbon: Centro de Investigação e Estudos em Belas-Artes [CIEBA], 2014), 138.
24. WS 2.36; NQS 57.984. Fragments of this have been discovered: see Yin Xian 殷宪, "Datong Bei Wei gong cheng diao cha zha ji" 大同北魏宫城调查札记, *Bei chao yan jiu* 4 (2004): 153. And for discussion of belief that mica could prolong life, and prevent decomposition of the dead's flesh, see the article by Edward H. Schafer and E. H. Snafer, "Notes on Mica in Medieval China," *TP* 43.3/4 (1955): 265–86.
25. NQS 57.984; WS 2.42; Zhang Zhizhong 张志忠, "Bei Wei Pingcheng shuang que kao" 北魏平城双阙考, rpt. in *Bei Wei Pingcheng kao gu yan jiu*, 24–27.
26. https://www.hrp.org.uk/tower-of-london/explore/white-tower/#gs.WaiQ7xY; accessed 19 May 2018.
27. *Liao shi* 41.506.
28. Zhang, "Bei Wei Pingcheng shuang que kao," 26.

to do such things, transported craftsmen who were almost certainly Chinese—was timber frame resting on rammed-earth walls and foundations, with growing preponderance over the centuries of the former.[29] Wood decays, of course, much more quickly than stone, while what is left of rammed-earth foundation after erosion tends simply to become the base of new foundations built for new structures.[30] Important parts of Pingcheng rested on what had been laid in the Han, while Wei structures would in turn become the base of new construction done by Tang, or the Khitans, or the Ming state. This is most clearly apparent in the walls.[31] Though most of the information preserved about Pingcheng in texts is about the palaces, it is still difficult for modern scholars to fix exact location of what remains of the foundations of imperial halls and residences mentioned in scattered literary references, particularly since over the century of Wei use there were repeated major reorganizations and reconstructions. The most recent stage of seeking and losing Pingcheng has come in the past decade, with construction of walls for a faux-Ming inner city, to encourage tourists to come to the city now called Datong, which has until recently been the PRC's "Coal Capital."[32] Some archaeological finds were made in the process, but much was no doubt further covered by new layers of human fabrication.[33]

Still, a good case has been made that Pingcheng's palace city followed the pattern of Shi Le's fourth-century Ye, the palace complex as a whole, north of the larger city, made up of several distinct, parallel walled compounds—looking a bit like piano keys—each individually laid out on a north-south axis but placed side by side, from west to east.[34] In a classic East Asian fashion, within each of these separate compounds halls for reception and ritual were placed in front (at the compound's southern end), while personal residence was in back, in the north.

In the beginning at least, the Wei monarch's own walled compound was at the western end of the palace complex, though use seems to have been occasional. In the annals of both Daowu and Mingyuan are entries saying that they had "blessed

---

29. Fu Xinian, *Traditional Chinese Architecture: Twelve Essays* (Princeton, NJ, and Oxford: Princeton University Press, 2017), Chapter 4.

30. See the comments of Dien, *Six Dynasties Civilization*, 15, on why "[r]elatively little work has been done on urban archaeology in China."

31. For the loss of remains under new constructions, see the comments of Zhang, "Bei Wei Pingcheng shuang que kao." On the walls in particular, see Duan and Zhao, *Tian xia da tong*, 28–29.

32. See Ren Yuan's article "Back to the Future: The Fake Relics of the 'Old' Chinese City of Datong," in the *Guardian*, 15 October 2014. Insight into the changing nature of the town in the 21st century is given in Chris Buckley's *New York Times* article, "In China's Coal Capital, Xi Jinping's Dream Remains Elusive" (21 October 2017).

33. On difficulties involved in reconstructing city plans, see inter alia the general comments made by Dien at the beginning of his chapter on "Cities and Outposts," in his *Six Dynasties Civilization*, 15; and for Pingcheng the introductory comments in Zhang's "Bei Wei Pingcheng shuang que kao," 24; and Duan and Zhao, *Tian xia da tong*, 46. The latter is the most ambitious effort this author has seen to attempt, with much speculation, to describe Pingcheng, and follow it from Wei into later ages.

34. I have relied on the more detailed attempted reconstructions of Duan and Zhao, *Tian xia da tong*, 52–53. These are, however, tentative: somewhat different attempts are given in Yin, "Bei Wei Pingcheng shi lüe," 193; and Cao, "Bei Wei Pingcheng bu ju chu tan," 1, 5.

the western palace" 幸西宮, that is, "visited"; in other words, this was not their regular residence.³⁵ For Daowu in particular, "regular residence" was a campaign tent, though interspersed throughout the annals are also mentions of "visits" to other imperial residences, outside Pingcheng. Among other things, in early Wei the Taghbach khaghans and their entourage went north across the Yinshan every spring to "shake off the frost."³⁶ While the subjects were contained within the walls of the wards, the lords and ladies roamed free.³⁷ In its first decades, Pingcheng may, in fact, to a large part have been for them a storage center for goods taken in war—gold and silver, men and women, and in the Deer Park just north, herds taken from steppe nomads—in a way seen in the contemporary Xiongnu capital of Tongwan, and much later in the Mongols' Khara Khorum.³⁸

But though he spent most of his time on the road, it will be remembered that Daowu died in a palace bed chamber, groping for a weapon after being jolted awake by the forced entrance of a son bent on murder.³⁹ This was in a Hall of Heaven's Peace 天安殿, apparently the domestic quarters set up behind (north of) the Heaven's Order (Tianwen) throne hall.⁴⁰ It seems this (along with most other palace structures) was arranged something along the lines of the Heian *shinden-zukuri*—a main hall flanked by two connected wings—on the basis of mention made in *Wei shu*'s "omen monograph" that shortly before Daowu's death the "eastern wing" of the Hall of Heaven's Peace had been shaken by earthquake.⁴¹ (The unsettled monarch for some reason responded by having both wings torn down.) More generally, Pingcheng palace halls were of the classic East Asian column and beam—timber frame—style.⁴² Those built in the earlier reigns seem to have been of relatively modest size—perhaps seven or eight bays wide—though throne halls built at Pingcheng under Xiaowen—including a "Grand Culmen" (Taiji) Hall that we will see below—were much wider and taller.⁴³ The tops of the roofs were tiled, the eave-tiles inscribed with declarations such as "Great Dai—Ten Thousand Years! (i.e., Banzai!)"⁴⁴ At times at least, the halls' columns

---

35. WS 2.42, 3.52, 3.58. Ren Aijun 任爱君, "Bei Wei Xianbei ren woluduo yi zhi ling shi" 北魏鲜卑人斡鲁朵遗制零拾, *Bei chao yan jiu* 3 (1996) (cited in Sagawa, "You mu yu nong geng zhi jian," 106 note 2), suggests that Daowu's "palaces" at Pingcheng may in fact have been tents (see also Sagawa, 111). The issue of the "peripatetic rulership" of the Taghbach is discussed at length in Chapter 2 of Chin-yin Tseng's *Making of the Tuoba Northern Wei* (Oxford: BAR Publishing, 2013).

36. SoS 95.2322; He Dezhang 何德章, "'Yinshan que shuang' zhi su jie" "阴山却霜"之俗解, *Wei Jin Nan bei chao Sui Tang shi zi liao* 12 (1993): 102–16.

37. This can, of course, be connected with the forced sedentarization imposed upon the Helan and other groups, assignment to fixed location in the fixed space of the imperial domain; see this volume's Chapter 7.

38. For use of fortified cities as storage centers, see Chapter 5 note 36.

39. WS 2.44.

40. Duan and Zhao, *Tian xia da tong*, 54.

41. WS 112A.2910; Duan and Zhao, *Tian xia da tong*, 54, 56. The style did not, of course, originate on the archipelago but was borrowed from architectural developments on the continent.

42. See detailed discussion of timber frame architecture in Dien, *Six Dynasties Civilization*, Chapter 3.

43. Duan and Zhao, *Tian xia da tong*, 48–49.

44. Yin Xian 殷宪, "Bei Wei Pingcheng zhuan wa wen zi jian shu" 北魏平城砖瓦文字简述, rpt. in his *Pingcheng shi gao*, 147.

showed Bactrian—and so indirect Hellenistic—influence, while on the basis of miniature stone sarcophagi in tombs it has been suggested the doors had great knockers on them, presented as the faces of various fierce beasts, which may have come from Serbi mythology.[45] Fierce beasts also rode up to the palace doors on horseback: Taiwu's favorite, "Big Thousand," would on the occasion of audiences arrive in full armor to gallop his horse in circles before the throne hall. The court officials, we are told, all sighed.[46] This was apparently an ongoing activity since much later, down in Luoyang, a rule was instituted forbidding mounted entry to the court.[47] From the beginning, however, one needed to dismount the carriage at the "Stop-Your-Cart-Here Portal" (*Zhichemen* 止車門), the palace city's main southern gate.

As seen above, an interesting division of duties took shape in early Wei, in which the monarch kept to himself the most important role—supreme commander of the army—while delegating to his chosen heir the lesser duties of superintending the administration.[48] On this basis, the crown prince was allotted his own compound, the "eastern palace," separated from adjoining palace compounds by its own walls and corner towers.[49] This institution may have taken shape as early as the Daowu reign.[50] In the time of Taiwu, however, the palace city was completely rearranged, the monarch moving his own to the palace city's eastern side, where a new set of halls were built for him, while the so-called eastern palace of the heir— his son Huang—now actually lay on the west.[51] (The contradiction may not have been as acute for the actual participants in these events, since "eastern palace" is a Chinese term, derived from that classical tradition; it is not clear if there was a distinct *guo yu* term for the heir's compound, or if so, if that term had the same directional significance.) Formal designation of the heir as viceroy with his own distinct residential complex seems to have ended, at any rate, after the death of Taiwu's heir in 451.[52]

---

45. Duan and Zhao, *Tian xia da tong*, 35, 37; and more general discussion of such influences in the columns depicted at Yungang by Kateřina Svobodová, *Iranian and Hellenistic Architectural Elements in Chinese Art*, Sino-Platonic Papers No. 274 (Philadelphia: Department of East Asian Languages and Civilizations, University of Pennsylvania, 2018). The most famous example of the knockers would be found on the tomb of Song Shaozu (buried 477): see Liu Junxi 刘俊喜, ed., *Datong Yan bei shi yuan Bei Wei mu qun* 大同雁北师院北魏墓群 (Beijing: Wen wu chu ban she, 2008), Chapter 5; and Annette L. Juliano, *Unearthed: Recent Archaeological Discoveries from Northern China* (Williamstown, MA: Sterling and Francine Clark Art Institute, 2012), 35–53, esp. 43–46. For suggestion of origin, see Lin, "Bei Wei Shaling bi hua mu yan jiu," 17–20, who proposes possible links to the depictions of animals on the well-known belt buckles of the Xiongnu.

46. WS 30.725. He went on to serve in a high office in the guard units.

47. Duan and Zhao, *Tian xia da tong*, 58.

48. Li Ping, *Bei Wei Pingcheng shi dai*, Chapter 2. Kubozoe Yoshifumi 窪添慶文, "Guan yu Bei Wei de tai zi jian guo zhi du" 关于北魏的太子监国制度, *Wen shi zhe* (2002.1): 124–29, paints a little more complex picture of the situation, with the emperor having ultimate authority over the administration, and the heir some roles in military activity.

49. Cao, "Bei Wei Pingcheng bu ju chu tan," 14.

50. In Taiwu's annals, it is said that he was "born in the Eastern Palace" of his father, Mingyuan: WS 4A.69; Duan and Zhao, *Tian xia da tong*, 54.

51. Duan and Zhao, *Tian xia da tong*, 58, 60; Yin, "Bei Wei Pingcheng shi lüe," 193.

52. Cao, "Bei Wei Pingcheng bu ju chu tan," 14.

In between those of the west and those of the east seems to have been another, independently walled central compound.⁵³ On the western side of this central compound were the dynasty's great armories, where weaponry seized in war or manufactured by the khaghan's metal-workers was stored in more than forty buildings. Built in 399, this complex is, interestingly, one of the earliest constructions in Pingcheng.⁵⁴ Besides weapons, other palace storehouses held textiles—the main currency of the time—and clothing crafted from those textiles, as well as jewels and precious metals.⁵⁵

Taking up the central compound's middle section was the huge shared kitchen of the entire palace community, in which, the southern observer quoted in *Nan Qi shu* tells us, "there were dozens of sheds with tiled roofs, in which foodstuffs hung down, while set [nearby] were craft shops making [dining utensils] of metal and wood."⁵⁶ Meat remained an important part of the imperial diet, but so apparently were grains. In the vicinity of the kitchens, we are told in the same text, were more than 80 great grain pits, which, as described in Chapter 11, would have been under the control of the palace stewards (in Chinese, the *dian zhong shang shu*).⁵⁷ Traces of the pits have been discovered by archaeologists, and one modern scholar has estimated that each of these held something on the order of 158,000 metric liters, so if these figures are correct, and all were full, more than 12 million in toto.⁵⁸ According to the southern visitor, half was millet, half rice.

From the time they've been around, kitchens have been central to human life: in Chinese, since the time of the first empire, the imperial kitchen was called the "Great Office" (Taiguan 太官), rendered by the modern scholar Charles Hucker in the less literal but clearer translation of "[Office of the] Provisioner."⁵⁹ The *guo yu* term for a part at least of the kitchens is presented in *Nan Qi shu* as *Azhen chu* 阿真廚, a mix of *guo yu* transcription—"*azhen*"—and proper Chinese—*chu* for "kitchen."⁶⁰ Under Taiwu, the man controlling these kitchens

---

53. This placement is based on the theories of Duan and Zhao, *Tian xia da tong*. For other attempted reconstructions, see, e.g., Cao, "Bei Wei Pingcheng bu ju chu tan"; or Zhang Zhuo 张焯, "Pingcheng ying jian shi mo" 平城营建始末, *Shi zhi xue kan* (1995.1): 51–55.

54. WS 2.35; NQS 57.984; Duan and Zhao, *Tian xia da tong*, 24. Regarding transportation of the craftsmen who produced these goods, see Wang, *Zhuan xing qi de Bei Wei cai zheng yan jiu*, 60–61; and Pearce, "Status, Labor and Law." For the establishment of metalworking factories down on the plains, see WS 2.41; ZZTJ 110.2857.

55. See Yan, *Bei Wei qian qi zheng zhi zhi du*, 107.

56. NQS 57.984. For interpretation of *shang fang* 尚方 as government factory, Duan and Zhao, *Tian xia da tong*, 51, make reference to an anecdote of Wencheng in 462 establishing a *shang fang* to produce twelve golden serving trays (WS 110.2851). For suggestion that this was the shared kitchen of the entire palace city, see Duan and Zhao, *Tian xia da tong*, 51.

57. Yan, *Bei Wei qian qi zheng zhi zhi du*, 112.

58. Zhang Qingjie 张庆捷, "Datong Caochangcheng Bei Wei Taiguan liang chu yi zhi chu tan" 大同操场城北魏太官粮储遗址初探, *WW* (2010.4): 53–58; Duan and Zhao, *Tian xia da tong*, 51. These were apparently built atop ruins from Han and from the Warring States period Zhao: Zhang Xibin 张喜斌 et al., "Datong Bei Wei Taiguan liang jiao yi zhi chu tu de Zhan guo Qin Han wa dang" 大同北魏太官粮窖遗址出土的战国秦汉瓦当, *Wen wu shi jie* (2009.6): 10–14; and Yin Xian, "Bei Wei Pingcheng shi lüe," 192.

59. Hucker, *Official Titles*, 479, no. 6185.

60. NQS 57.984. Shimunek, *Languages of Ancient Southern Mongolia and North China*, 158, offers several possible reconstructions of the Taghbach word transcribed by "azhen," and translates the term as "food." So if the term

was a captured southerner, Mao Xiuzhi. For a time, this fellow served by leading a unit of southern ("Wu") soldiers, but he was as good or better as a cook. According to the southern history, *Song shu*, he first gained Taiwu's attention by sharing a mutton stew with a "caitiff palace steward" 虜尚書 who passed it on to the emperor with praise that it was "great tasting."[61] Whatever the reason, *Wei shu* gives a somewhat different account, stating that Mao was good at making the "food and drink of the southerners." It may, of course, have been a bit of both, something like a French chef making haggis, if and when circumstances demanded. At any rate, the emperor gave Mao a ducal title and made him head chef. He was, we are told, "always in the Great Office, overseeing presentation of the emperor's meals."[62]

The kitchen was also of interest to empresses. One of these, the main wife of Taiwu, a captured daughter of Helian Bobo, had been assigned residential quarters at the back of the central compound, apparently between the armories and the kitchens. This individual, at least, was more interested in the latter, since according to the visitor from Jiankang she was constantly there "seeking food" 求食.[63] This is obviously reference not to her own snacking, but more generally to management of meals and banquets, an important aspect of the responsibility and power of women in this society (and many others as well).[64] It is to be noted that her apartment in the central compound was later taken over by the powerful empress dowager, Wenming.[65]

Unfortunately, just as barbarian qua barbarian was of little interest to the men who compiled the records that came out in *Wei shu*, so too were the activities of women. Little if any detail is supplied as to who organized Mingyuan's feast of 412, when the emperor "visited" the Heaven's Order reception hall, in the courtyard of which a temporary plank hall 板殿 had been erected. It was here that the emperor feted his officials and officers, distributing to them meat taken in a great hunt of the month before; it had presumably been smoked or in some way dried in the intervening time.[66] As mentioned above, modern studies of human

---

"azhen chu" was actually used in Pingcheng, it would be a bit like a weaving together of English and French such as "the food cuisine." The *NQS* quote states that this was to the west, but Duan and Zhao, *Tian xia da tong*, 51, state that there is a clear link between the Taiguan and *Azhenchu*; perhaps the latter was a western section of the larger whole.

61. SoS 48.1429.
62. WS 43.960–61.
63. NQS 57.984; Duan and Zhao, *Tian xia da tong*, 59.
64. One famous expression of this came with Judy Chicago's "Dinner Party," which she described as "a reinterpretation of the Last Supper from the point of view of women, who, throughout history, had prepared the meals and set the table. In my 'Last Supper,' however, the women would be the honored guests." This is a permanent exhibit at the Brooklyn Museum; the quote comes from her *A Dinner Party: A Symbol of Our Heritage* (Garden City, NY: Anchor Press/Doubleday, 1979), 11.
65. Duan and Zhao, *Tian xia da tong*, 61–62.
66. WS 3.52. He did much the same in 420: see WS 3.60. For an overview of the Wei imperial feast, see Zhang Hequan 張鶴泉 and Wang Meng 王萌, "Bei Wei huang di ci yan kao lüe" 北魏皇帝賜宴考略, *Shi xue ji kan* (2011.1): 26–33. For the 412 feast, which was followed by an East Asian Saturnalia, Zhang and Wang (28) quite sensibly suggest this was held not for the broader population, but for Serbi, or probably more specifically, men of Dai.

remains in Pingcheng tombs have made clear that among that city's complex populations some groups—presumably soldiers of Inner Asian derivation—still ate a great deal of meat, while others—farmers—lived mainly on grain.[67] Piles of animal bones found by archaeologists in and around the supposed locations of Wei palaces indicate that attendees of feasts such as that held in 412 ate a great deal of meat—pig, oxen, sheep, occasionally even tiger taken from the tiger pit in the Deer Garden—then threw the bones on the ground, where they apparently remained.[68]

It is not clear if women were involved in the organization of the 412 event, but 70 years later—in the time of Wenming and Xiaowen—there is no doubt the empress dowager wielded great power, in the kitchen and outside of it as well. On one occasion Wenming—feeling unwell—waited to be brought a bowl of congee, while the emperor dutifully stood in attendance at her side.[69] Failing to notice that a dragonfly had settled in the gruel, the server—said to be a simple-minded soul—presented the meal to the dowager, who fished the creature out with her spoon while Xiaowen—enraged—moved to have the offender punished "in a manner most severe." At times, though, power over others lies in our choice not to use it: Wenming laughed, and the wretch was released.[70]

A much grander event later took place at an imperial dacha north of the city, beside Divine Spring Pond (Lingquan chi) at the foot of Fangshan hill, where as we shall see below tombs were also built for the emperor and the dowager.[71] There, we are told in the dowager's biography, she and Xiaowen held a banquet for the realm's officials, foreign envoys, and the local leaders of outlying regions, each of whom were commanded to perform one of their homeland's dances.[72] After Xiaowen had led all in wishing Wenming long life, the delighted empress dowager began to sing. First Xiaowen and then all the others joined in to follow her song, until 90 or more were singing harmony 和 to the tune of the diva at

---

67. See the article by Hou Liangliang 侯亮亮 et al., based on carbon tests of bodies found in Northern Wei tombs, showing persistence in the diet of significant amounts of meat: "Nong ye qu you mu min zu yin shi wen hua de zhi hou xing—ji yu Datong Dongxin guangchang Bei Wei mu qun ren gu de wen ding tong wei su yan jiu" 农业区游牧民族饮食文化的滞后性——基于大同东信广场北魏墓群人骨的稳定同位素研究, *Ren lei xue xue bao* 36.3 (2017): 359–69. It would, of course, be fair to point out to Dr. Hou and the other authors of this fascinating study that this "debatable land" was not necessarily an "agricultural region" (*nong ye qu*).

68. Yin, "Datong Bei Wei gong cheng diao cha zha ji," 156, suggests the tigers in the Deer Park garden were for eating as well as spectacle.

69. BS 13.496. Holmgren, "Harem in Northern Wei politics," 88, points out that as Xiaowen grew older, Wenming's power over him only increased.

70. Song, *Bei Wei nü zhu lun*, 201, sums the situation up well, saying that when she saw the necessity she would move quickly to punish, but that her punishments were not gratuitous (the identification of "offense" for which another should be "punished" being, of course, a subjective judgment). One example of her capacity for graciousness would be the official Liu Fang. Because Liu was implicated in a holy man's misdeeds, Wenming ordered that he be brought into the palace and beaten 100 strokes. Learning that he had been slandered, however, she regretted her action and promoted him to high office (WS 55.1219–20).

71. *Shui jing zhu shu* 2: 13.1138.

72. BS 13.496–97 (WS 13.329–30). For another example where Xiaowen danced before the empress dowager at a feast, see WS 54.1203.

the main table. Here we see a concrete example of a broad tendency by which women were incorporating men into elaborate, evolving structures of rituals and fashions, norms and expectations.

At times, of course, women were also singing solo songs of grief, as we see in analysis by Kate Lingley of a niche in the Guyang Cave at Longmen. This was dedicated in 495—just after the move to Luoyang—by a woman named Lady Yuchi, wife of a powerful Wei general, whose son had died. Though niches dedicated by women in the Guyang Cave are, according to Lingley, more modest than those done by men, and the inscriptions of all of them are generally quite formulaic, in this one, in a "distinctive language . . . in which she seems to take a mother's care to ensure that her son will be protected," Lady Yuchi called upon the future Buddha Maitreya, "in the hope that Niujue"—presumably a transcription of the boy's Serbi name—"will be released from the domain of transmigration to soar through the realms of non-delusion. If he is reborn again, may he be reborn in heaven above."[73] Flanking a statue of Maitreya are images that seem, on one side, to depict Lady Yuchi, and on the other side, the husband and the dead son, all dressed in Serbi garb, which in Lingley's view show "a family unit centered around Lady Yuchi herself," but omitting the husband's other wife, and the other wife's son. Here, perhaps, we see "a society in which mother-son relationships were not necessarily seen as subordinate to father-son relationships."[74]

The Divine Spring song was a happier event, in which, able to induce all the court figures present to cooperate in her endeavors, it seems that in some sense at least Wenming ruled the realm. The growth of women's power in the Wei court seems to have come alongside their command of the kitchen, and of the gathering for feast. At the end of this event, Wenming turned beyond her inner circle to pay respects to those esteemed by her subjects 外禮民望, "subjects," min, here undoubtedly referring to the men of Dai, the military establishment.[75] The first on the list was the fellow named Yuan Pi, the distant imperial kinsman and powerful official who, as we have seen in Chapter 9, would at times at feast "in a booming voice recount in order past victories and defeats." As with "Yi Bo," the name given in *Wei shu* is misleading. Though his names have been rebottled by later chroniclers as "Yuan Pi," assigning him the new, Chinese-style imperial surname "Yuan" established later by Xiaowen, Pi would in fact become a fierce opponent of Xiaowen's efforts to Sinicize the realm. The personal "Pi" is

---

73. Kate A. Lingley, "Lady Yuchi in the First Person: Patronage, Kinship and Voice in the Guyang Cave," *EMC* 18 (2012): 40, 38, 31.
74. Lingley, "Lady Yuchi in the First Person," 43, 45.
75. BS 13.496–97 (WS 13.330). Interestingly, the derivative *Wei shu* passage uses *min* rather than the *ren*, "people," used in *Bei shi*. In this case, I will take the *Wei shu* version as correct even though it is from a reconstructed chapter, assuming that assembled in the Tang period *Bei shi* was avoiding *min* as part of the personal name of the Tang emperor Taizong.

also certainly a later fabrication, once again, probably the first character in transcription of a multi-syllable name from the *guo yu*: "Pi-x-x."

The Fangshan feast, however, came before such matters had broken out into the open. Relations there were still civil, though seemingly already with a hint of tension. At the end of the gathering, Wenming gave Pi gifts of gold and silk, horses and carriages, and made a point to include him in her words when she praised her own favorites, to "show that she was without bias." Apparently, some were already on the lookout for bias against a favorite of the men of Dai.

* * *

At least one form of woman's ability to organize and influence the Dai community, then, seems to have lain in control of the kitchen, and of the in-gathering that takes place at a feast, while that of men is depicted as coming more directly from the physical domination that takes place in the course of the hunt. And domination is clearly the point of the armed procession of a lord and his soldiery that is a central theme in the daily-life depiction seen on the murals of Pingcheng tombs. Monumental architecture in motion, the procession is intended to "awe, subdue and terrify" the locals, and not so much to deter invasion by others as to proclaim the imminence of one's own, or at least the possibility of such.

The Xiongnu may have had their own version of such rituals, though it would seem that for the procession to have much meaning it needs large numbers of bystanders to watch as the train marches by, which might not happen much on the steppe. Within the more densely populated Chinese empire, however, these practices had already taken clear shape, as seen in repeated depiction in Later Han tomb murals of a powerful man riding carriage, with troops around him.[76] Along with much else from Han, such physical depictions had spread to the regimes that took shape on the edges of its collapse, though with increasing detail and focus on organized military purpose.[77] A dramatic example is seen in the 357 northeastern tomb of a man whose name is given as Dong Shou, who had fled east from the Murong to take up a powerful position with the Koguryŏ state that had grown up in southern Manchuria and down across the Yalu.[78] Now in the territory of the North Korean state, the tomb—Anak No. 3—contains an

---

76. A famous example is an Eastern Han tomb from Horinger, built for a Han commandant of the Wuhuan. See *Helin'geer Han mu bi hua tu mo xie tu ji lu* 和林格爾漢墓壁畫孝子傳圖摹寫圖輯錄, ed. Chen Yongzhi 陳永志 et al. (Beijing: Wen wu chu ban she, 2015), 76–81; or Anneliese Gutkind Bulling, "The Eastern Han Tomb at Ho-lin-ko-êrh (Holingol)," *Archives of Asian Art* 31 (1977–1978): 90, 93.

77. For suggestion of this spread to adjacent regions, see Su (So), "Goko Jūrokkoku Hokuchō jidai no shukkōto to roboyō," 2: 120; and Seo Yunkyung 徐润庆, "Cong Shaling bi hua mu kan Bei Wei Pingcheng shi qi de sang zang mei shu" 从沙岭壁画墓看北魏平城时期的丧葬美术 in *Gu dai mu zang mei shu yan jiu*, ed. Wu Hung and Zheng Yan, 3 vols. (Beijing: Wen wu chu ban she, 2011), 1: 171–72.

78. For an overview of Anak No. 3, see Su, "Goko Jūrokkoku Hokuchō jidai no shukkōto to roboyō," 115–20. Su raises debates as to whether the tomb was actually for Dong Shou, or for a local king. These debates may derive in part from competing modern myths of nationhood, and borders.

elaborate mural showing the protagonist in his carriage, surrounded by 40 cavalry (including on each side four heavily armed and armored flankers) with many more infantry, and in the front, footmen beating drums and displaying pennons. While Han depictions seem at times to be random assemblage of images—spread over multiple surfaces, with a footman here, a horseman there—the styles taking shape on the periphery have a new coherence and intensity. The march represents, as one modern scholar has said, not a parade but a "call to arms."[79] This may show real change from relatively loose control of auxiliary units by Han border commanders, in contrast to the "nations" that emerged there after the empire's collapse; or may, of course, simply be change in artistic convention.

Exerting their rule over the atomized communities of the plains, each of which could muster forces only in the dozens or hundreds, the early Wei lords and generals liked to display, in tomb art and reality, their ability to field forces that were large, well-organized, and aggressive. In *Wei shu*'s "Monograph on Ritual" we are provided with a description of an imperial march designed for Daowu in 405.[80] It "was to be square, with a guard of honor." In the march, "infantry and cavalry were arrayed in ranks. Inside out, there were layers (of marchers), the flags arrayed, the standards straight up, marching through the gate and out across the whole empire, with chariots and flags of all colors, each in its own place. The princes, some in front and some behind, (marched) surrounded by the armored cavalry; the dukes surrounded by the pennons; the marquises surrounded by the pike-men (*bushuo* 步矟)[81]; and the viscounts surrounded by the sword-and-shield-men."

The prominent presence of infantry at this early time needs to be viewed skeptically; this may well simply have been an ideal, put forth by a Chinese scribe drawing on Han precedents.[82] Tellingly, we are told in the *Sui shu* ritual treatise that in carriage and attire—as in much else—in early Wei "much of barbarian arrangement was mixed in" 多參胡制 with "proper" ritual practice.[83] Whether or not these were neatly and symmetrically arranged tableaux in motion, grounded in ancient Chinese ritual, Taghbach monarchs and their generals certainly rode at the center of intimidatingly prominent processions that would leave bystanders

---

79. Lin, "Bei Wei Shaling bi hua mu yan jiu," 13, 26.
80. WS 108D.2813; Zhang, *Jin wei wu guan*, 2: 666–67.
81. *Shuo* 矟 is a variant form of 槊, with the meaning of "long spear." See *Bei chao wu shi ci dian* 北朝五史辭典, ed. Jian Xiuwei 簡修煒 et al., 2 vols. (Jinan: Shangdong jiao yu chu ban she, 2000), 2: 1346. For a general overview of weaponry in this period, see Dien, *Six Dynasties Civilization*, Chapter 10, "Armor and Weapons."
82. See the astute comment made by Jenny Liu in her discussion of "Status and the 'Procession' Scene on the Sloping Path in Tang Princess Tombs (643–706)," *Mei shu shi yan jiu ji kan* 41 (2016): 241, raising the need with these murals to distinguish real processions from idealized forms for the funerary march; the same issue has been raised in personal communication to this author by the scholar Fan Zhang. Something of the same can be said of what is portrayed in *Wei shu*, as opposed to the actual arrangement of the procession.
83. SS 12.254; and see similar comments in WS 108.2811, both having been quoted by Lin, "Bei Wei Shaling bi hua mu yan jiu," 16–17, to support his suggestion that Daowu's procession was made up more of "barbarian arrangement" than the "old forms."

awestruck, "terrified into submission," as Cui Hao had told Mingyuan in response to suggestion that the capital be moved.[84]

The most elemental form of "pursuit with force and violence" is of course animal hunting itself. As discussed above, this has always been a habit of military elites across all of Eurasia, serving as both training for war and as an arena for personal bonding. Early Han emperors pursued it with relish, as no doubt did the Xiongnu lords.[85] For the men of the Taghbach military, in early times, it trained them for war, while also giving them food to eat. Even in later, more prosperous times, the meat thus gathered, and dried or seasoned, was the centerpiece of Taghbach feasts.[86]

The scale of these hunts could be huge: in the year after Mingyuan's 412 feast he traveled west with his hunting party to the upper corner of the Yellow River, then up into the hills to take 100,000 beasts. In 431, Taiwu is said to have led a hunt in which millions of deer were driven to their deaths by tens of thousands of his cavalrymen.[87] Prey might, however, be arranged more conveniently. In the Deer Park north of the palace city was a big cat enclosure, which Mingyuan visited in 412 "to shoot tiger," which they then perhaps ate.[88]

Mingyuan's time in power was the high point for the imperial hunt; over just 15 years (409–423), he is recorded as hunting on 22 occasions, the most recorded for any reign.[89] After that the imperial hunt tailed off, until ceasing altogether in the time of Xiaowen, who actively chose to end it on moral grounds.[90] Interestingly, the feast as a major theme for Pingcheng tomb art disappeared at about the same time.[91] The two seem to have been tightly knit in the minds of those paying for such undertakings. But this does not, of course, mean that the hunt—or the feast—necessarily ended among the common folk; only that elites were advertising themselves in other ways. Population pressure in the Datong Basin may have made it more difficult, and the gradual stripping of the woodlands up on the hills. But for many, if they did not hunt they did not eat.[92]

---

84. For similar practices under the Manchus, see Michael G. Chang, *A Court on Horseback: Imperial Touring & the Construction of Qing Rule, 1680–1785* (Cambridge, MA: Harvard University Asia Center, 2007).

85. For Han, see the "Western Capital Rhapsody," in Knechtges, tr., *Wen xuan*, 1: 134–41, where "staging the grandest of spectacles," the emperor "rouses a martial fervor in the imperial preserve."

86. See discussion in Zhu et al., *Wei Jin Nan bei chao she hui sheng huo*, Kindle ed., Chapter 12, Section 2. And again, see the article by Hou et al. based on carbon tests of bodies found in Northern Wei tombs, showing persistence in the diet of significant amounts of meat: "Nong ye qu you mu min zu yin shi wen hua de zhi hou xing."

87. WS 3.53; 4A.79; 24.635. For other examples, of the great circle-round hunts (in Chinese, *xian* 獮), see WS 3.52, 56, 61. For an overview of the hunt in early Wei, see Li Hu 黎虎, "Bei Wei qian qi de shou lie jing ji" 北魏前期的狩猎经济, *LSYJ* (1992.1): 106–18.

88. WS 3.51; *Shui jing zhu shu* 2: 13.1141; Yin Xian, "Datong Bei Wei gong cheng diao cha zha ji," 156.

89. Li Hu, "Bei Wei qian qi de shou lie jing ji," 108.

90. Li Hu, "Bei Wei qian qi de shou lie jing ji," 108.

91. Seo, "Cong Shaling bi hua mu," 183–84. This came with more and more influence from the Yangtze world. Kitchen and hunt were replaced by filial scenes, and images of the immortals.

92. See discussion in Liu Meiyun 刘美云 and Wei Haiqing 魏海清, "Shou lie xi su dui Bei Wei qian qi zheng quan de ying xiang" 狩猎习俗对北魏前期政权的影响, in *Bei chao shi yan jiu: Zhongguo Wei Jin Nan Bei chao shi guo ji xue shu yan tao hui lun wen ji*, ed. Yin Xian (Beijing: Shang wu yin shu guan, 2005), 425–26, where they repeat the story of a Wei prince, who living in difficult times in the wake of the wars that caused Luoyang's fall served as

For high-ranking members of the Dai elite, for several generations the hunt—on a more personal basis than the great imperial efforts—appeared prominently in murals on walls of brick laid against the rough walls of a vertical pit dug out by the construction team's journeyman laborers. Sometimes they were painted on the coffin as well as the walls, while those of the lesser elites had to make do with coffin alone. We see the latter in the Zhijiabao tomb, excavated in 1997, a simpler tomb without brick lining. Though it had been robbed and the remaining contents scattered, all three of the prominent early Wei themes—the hunt, the procession, the feast—were found painted on the planks that remained from the pine-wood coffin.[93] The painting on the left-side planking portrays, on the left, a grand progression, with a variety of servants and entertainers surrounding a fine ox-drawn carriage, with a cloth covering on top and a robe-covered figure within. At the other end of the plank, down by where the dead person's feet were once located, is a remarkable scene of hunting, in which a bearded man wearing Serbi dress pulls a compound bow to shoot an arrow at a wild boar racing by, while a white rabbit running the other way takes a fearful glimpse at the unfolding scene. Further to the right are mounted archers, shooting at other beasts and birds.[94]

---

a governor under the successor regime Eastern Wei, and though having 100 hawks and hounds, and more than 10 supply carts, is still quoted as saying that if he was "idle for three days there will be no food; I can't not hunt every day" (BQS 28.384). A demonstration of the continuation of hunting among even some elite groups, who had not joined the move to Luoyang, can be seen in the dramatic murals of hunting found in a tomb discovered near the town of Xinzhou, in the valley of the Hutuo River, just south of the Yanmen Pass: Shanxi sheng kao gu yan jiu suo et al., "Shanxi Xinzhou Jiuyuangang Bei chao bi hua mu," 51–74. The tomb was located in the center of power of the Erzhu clan, and though the previously cited piece makes a preliminary dating of Eastern Wei/Northern Qi, one scholar suggests it was actually a tomb for a member of the Erzhu clan, at the end of the Northern Wei: Xu Jinshun 徐锦顺, "Erzhu Rong huo Erzhu Zhao?—cong 'Shou lie tu' kan Xinzhou Jiuyuangang Bei chao bi hua mu mu zhu" 尔朱荣或尔朱兆？—从《狩猎图》看忻州九原岗北朝壁画墓墓主, *Zhongyuan wen wu* (2015.6): 82–86. It will also be noted that this is the tomb from which this book's cover photo comes.

93. Liu Junxi 刘俊喜 and Gao Feng 高峰, "Datong Zhijiabao Bei Wei mu guan ban hua" 大同智家堡北魏墓棺板画, *WW* (2004.12): 35–47.

94. For another example, a mural, see the preliminary report, "Shanxi Datong Yunbolilu Bei Wei bi hua mu fa jue jian bao" 山西大同云波里路北魏壁画墓发掘简报, by the Datong shi kao gu yan jiu suo 大同市考古研究所, *WW* (2011.12): 13–25. For overall discussion of the hunt in Pingcheng tombs, see Lin, "Bei Wei Shaling bi hua mu yan jiu," 27–28.

From Liu Junxi & Gao Feng. "Datong Zhijiabao Bei Wei mu guan ban hua." *Wen wu* (2004.12): 41, fig. 9.

From Liu Junxi & Gao Feng. "Datong Zhijiabao Bei Wei mu guan ban hua." Wen wu (2004.12): 44, detail of fig. 14.

Since the meat taken by the hunters was to be eaten, the right side of the Zhijiabao coffin shows preparation of the food, as well as its serving, in an outdoor setting. On the right side are cooks, servants, and a great cauldron. The scene is then divided, as it no doubt was in life, by standing fabric partitions, and on the other side of the partition are lines of guests, standing, the men in trousers, the women in skirts, all wearing the classic black cap of the Serbi (somewhat resembling a modern hairnet, with a short train down the back of the neck), which would for centuries be a way to speak identity.[95] These would be the good folk of Dai, arrived for feast, standing to pay honor to their host (the deceased).[96]

These themes of early Pingcheng burials are stated with particular force in the richly detailed and well-preserved murals found on the walls of a tomb discovered in 2005 in the district of Shaling, just across the Yuhe River in the eastern outskirts of Datong. One of a group of twelve, it is called Shaling M7.[97] On the basis of a partial inscription found on lacquer scrap in the tomb, the occupant seems to have been the mother of a high-ranking Wei general, who was also a Palace Attendant (*shi zhong*) to Taiwu. The brief passage dates her death to 435— Taiwu's 12th year on the throne, in the midst of the campaigns against Northern Yan—making this the earliest-dated Wei tomb found so far in the Pingcheng area.[98] This and the generally good state of its murals' preservation are what make this relatively modest tomb distinctive.

Also in the fragmentary inscription is the name Poduoluo (*P^{h}atala), though it is not entirely clear whether this was the woman's people, or the name of the group she had married into.[99] No matter, we shall from this point on simply call her the Poduoluo Lady, meaning either "the lady of the Poduoluo clan," or "the lady who married into the Poduoluo clan."[100] As for the Poduoluo people, they had entered the Taghbach orbit only a few years before, when they had been forcibly incorporated into the Wei war machine. Originally minor players in the

---

95. An identity that would, as identities do, continually evolve. For those who defined themselves as "Serbi," the cap was a key way of declaring who one was, since "the evanescent mystique of the ethnic community has to be made evident in everyday life": Pohl, "Introduction," in *Strategies of Identification*, 25 (and see also p. 46). For a more general description of "Xianbei-style attire," see Lingley, "Lady Yuchi in the First Person," 42; Dien, *Six Dynasties Civilization*, 317–19. See the persistence and spread among various groups of a broader set of such symbols in Scott Pearce, "The Way of the Warrior in Early Medieval China, Examined through 'the Northern *Yuefu*,'" *EMC* 13–14 (2008): 87–113.

96. Liu and Gao, "Datong Zhijiabao Bei Wei mu guan ban hua," 45, suggest these are servants, lined up to attend upon the feast. This is possible, but one would think such a picture would depict the guests as well as the staff, as we see in the Shaling M7 piece. And so, it seems more likely these are people who have just arrived (in the damaged section to the left, horses are shown) and are waiting to begin.

97. For an overview on stages of tomb construction in this area in this period, see Cao Chenming 曹臣明, "Pingcheng fu jin Xianbei ji Bei Wei mu zang fen bu gui lü kao" 平城附近鲜卑及北魏墓葬分布规律考, *WW* (2016.5): 61–69; and Zhang, "Cultural Encounters," 41–50.

98. Yin Xian 殷宪 discusses this date, before accepting it, in his "Shanxi Datong Shaling Bei Wei bi hua mu qi hua ti ji yan jiu" 山西大同沙岭北魏壁画墓题画记研究, in *4–6 shi ji de bei Zhongguo yu Ou Ya da lu*, ed. Zhang Qingjie et al. (Beijing: Ke xue chu ban she, 2006), 348.

99. For the name and its reconstruction in the *guo yu*, see Shimunek, *Languages of Ancient Southern Mongolia and North China*, 135. He gives the name as either *P^{h}atala or *P^{h}atara. Some suggest she was the general's wife: see Shing Müller, "A Preliminary Study of the Lacquerware of the Northern Dynasties, with a Special Focus on the Pingcheng Period (398–493)," *EMC* 25 (2019): 54, citing Zhang Qingjie 張慶捷, "Bei Wei Poduoluo shi bi hua mu suo jian wen zi kao shu" 北魏破多羅氏壁畫墓所見文字考述, *LSYJ* (2007.1): 174–79. Yin Xian gives a rebuttal to this position in his "Shanxi Datong Shaling Bei Wei bi hua mu qi hua ti ji yan jiu," 349–51; and see also Zhang, "Cultural Encounters," 70. As with so many features of this age (and others), certainty is difficult to obtain.

100. Borrowing here the usage of Tseng, *The Making of the Tuoba Northern Wei*, 74.

region of modern Guyuan, Ningxia, the Poduoluo had allied with one regional power after another before finally attaching to the Xiongnu leader Helian Bobo. The ethnicity of the Poduoluo is not clear; they are often referred to as Serbi, but at one point are referred to as a "distinct people (affiliated with) the Serbi" (Xianbei bie zhong 鮮卑別種), which leaves the field wide open and certainly allows old ties with the Xiongnu.[101] Defeated by a Wei army in 402, many Poduoluo were on this occasion captured and transported to Pingcheng. More fled to Pingcheng following the murder of the Poduoluo leader by Helian Bobo in 406, and a third wave came with final destruction of the Helian Xia regime by Taiwu in 428, when the rest of the Poduoluo were brought to the Wei capital.[102] If it was the general (and not his mother) who was of Poduoluo stock, one might guess linkage with the earlier groups of transportees, or defectors; with the tomb dated to 435, it seems that seven years would be a short time to climb so high in rank.

Beginning with a 30-foot downward-sloping passage leading east, the tomb then levels off and on the other side of a brick barrier enters a four- or five-foot-long brick-lined entrance corridor.[103] On either side of the entrance to the tomb itself are paintings of guardians; some half-man, half-beast. In the burial chamber, which is about 15 feet long and 10 across, are other kinds of fantastic beasts, which some have suggested come out of Serbi mythology.[104] The burial chamber's walls, also of brick, were arranged on a slightly outward arc, as Pingcheng tombs generally were.[105] The murals on the walls of the main chamber are painted on plaster over the brick.

As was the norm in Dai society, Shaling M7 is a creative assembly of elements drawn from a variety of sources and traditions.[106] Some seem to derive from Inner Asia, with expression of pastoral life in the bones of an ox, or placement so that the tomb faces west, on an east-west axis, which it has been suggested is linked with the ancient Serbi belief that the dead go to a western Red Mountain (Chi shan).[107] Others—such as the sloping ramp leading into subterranean chambers,

---

101. WS 103.2313.

102. See discussion of this by Yin Xian, "Shanxi Datong Shaling Bei Wei bi hua mu," 351–54; Yao, *Bei chao Hu xing kao*, 200–4. Yao (202) points out that the line continued to be eminent under Northern Qi and Tang, under the name assigned to them by Xiaowen: WS 113.3012. In a related article, Yin Xian 殷憲 suggests a possible correspondence between the Poduoluo mentioned on the lacquer fragment in the tomb (and various received sources as well), and a man with the transcribed name of Heduoluo, who held a similar (though not identical) set of posts for the Wei regime, at more or less the same time: "Heduoluo ji Poduoluo kao" 贺多罗即破多罗考, *Xue xi yu tan suo* (2009.5): 227–33.

103. Or "entryway": see discussion of terminology for analyzing tombs in Dien, *Six Dynasties Civilization*, 76–80.

104. Lin, "Bei Wei Shaling bi hua mu yan jiu," 17–25; discussed in terms of apotropaic figures in Dien, *Six Dynasties Civilization*, 208–12.

105. Wang Yanqing 王雁卿, "Datong Bei Wei mu zang chu tu yong qun de shi dai te zheng" 大同北魏墓葬出土俑群的时代特征, in *Bei Wei Pingcheng yan jiu wen ji*, ed. Dong Ruishan (Taiyuan: Shanxi ren min chu ban she, 2008), 301; Dien, *Six Dynasties Civilization*, 77.

106. See Seo, "Cong Shaling bi hua mu," 185; and Cheng, "Exchange across Media," 122, who describes how in the hybridity of Guyuan and adjacent regions, Confucians dressed in Serbi apparel, and artistic expression mixed together Buddhist, Confucian, Sasanian, and Serbi elements.

107. Zhang, "Cultural Encounters," 93, suggests the bones were an offering rather than remains of an animal sacrifice. For the tombs' directional arrangement, see Seo, "Cong Shaling bi hua mu," 177. Mentions of Red Mountain come from early Chinese efforts to describe the Serbi and their Wuhuan cousins, in SGZ 30.832. Lin, "Bei

or, of course, the Chinese inscription found on lacquer scrap—derived from the Chinese world, whether directly or indirectly. It is dangerous, however, to place too fixed a label on such things. As the Romanist Dick Whittaker has pointed out—in the midst of discussion of the complexity of identity on the frontiers of Roman Africa—just because one drinks Coke doesn't mean one is an American.[108] Much of the intricate reality of the many communities of East Asia during this period have been lost within the traditional Chinese historiographical tradition, and at times perhaps ignored in modern archaeological analysis, which is, of course, true of many times and many places.[109] Design and construction of Shaling M7, or any Pingcheng tomb, would have been an intricate relationship between sponsor and contractor. Though we have little information on this subject, it is fair to assume that on the side of the contractor—often at least a master and apprentices brought up from the Chinese world—there was a restricted set of forms and designs he and his men knew and were able to make. As for the sponsor, Shaling M7's general, it is proper to wonder how much the fellow actually knew about the sets of objects and symbols given in the package he was purchasing to safeguard mother, and provide her ease in the afterlife.[110] What he chose does not necessarily describe his "culture"; Charles I eagerly sought paintings by Titian and Raphael without being Italian. For the Poduoluo man, it might have sufficed to insist that an offering of ox meat be added in to the creative hodgepodge for which he was paying.

Furthermore, many of the elements linked to Han tradition that entered Dai in early Wei seem to have come by circuitous routes, not necessarily directly up from the plains—where with the collapse of Western Jin we largely cease to see tomb-building, along with most large-scale, organized activity—but from peripheral societies to the west and east that had themselves digested these styles

Wei Shaling bi hua mu yan jiu," 8–9, points out that arrangement of the 12 Shaling tombs was mixed, some with east-west orientation, some with the Chinese preference for north-south; he adds that within a century, at the new capital at Luoyang, the Chinese north-south arrangement predominated; on this topic, see the figure given on p. 6 of "Shanxi Datong Shaling Bei Wei bi hua mu fa jue jian bao"; and also Zhang, "Cultural Encounters," 67–68, who suggests these were two different cemeteries, with the north-south tombs made later in time.

108. Dick Whittaker, "Ethnic Discourses on the Frontiers of Roman Africa," in *Ethnic Constructs in Antiquity: The Role of Power and Tradition*, ed. Ton Derks and Nico Roymans (Amsterdam: Amsterdam University Press, 2009), 202.

109. The guiding principle of Zhang's "Cultural Encounters" is that the Land of Dai cannot be pigeonholed; and that although its arts drew on both, those artistic expressions were "an idiosyncratic production that cannot be defined by or interpreted through either the Chinese or the Inner Asian traditions" (13).

110. A fascinating piece of evidence giving at least a hint of these transactions has been found in another Pingcheng tomb, a billing report giving hours worked that was left inside the 477 burial of Song Shaozu: Zhang Qingjie 张庆捷 and Liu Junxi 刘俊喜, "Bei Wei Song Shaozu mu chu tu zhuan ming ti ji kao shi" 北魏宋绍祖墓出土砖铭题记考释, in *Datong Yan bei shi yuan Bei Wei mu qun*, ed. Liu Junxi (Beijing: Wen wu chu ban she, 2008), 200–4 (and 106 figure 86 in the same volume); and Fan Zhang raises details on this and other reports of transactions in "Cultural Encounters," 51–52. See also comments on production and producers in Lin, "Bei Wei Shaling bi hua mu yan jiu," 26ff. More work needs done on this topic, along the lines of Anthony Barbieri-Low's *Artisans in Early Imperial China*. Various questions present themselves, only some of which could be resolved. One wonders, for instance, if sketches were presented before the actual production of the murals. An exception proving the rule may be in a 495 niche at Longmen's Guyang cave, in an inscription Kate Lingley has suggested showed that Lady Yuchi "took

and techniques and developed them in their own way.¹¹¹ In the Gansu Corridor, a key eastern stretch of the Silk Roads, mixed populations had combined Chinese styles with Central Asian influences. It was from here that Bactrian columns came, and the stiff and solid style of the early Yungang Buddha-emperors.¹¹² A separate regional line of development lay in southern Manchuria and lands to the east, with the emerging Yan states and Koguryŏ.¹¹³ (Still further east, an even more peripheral regime—Yamato—was beginning to take shape, in its own ways drawing on and adapting elements of the Chinese world.) Since all roads—for a time at least—led to Pingcheng, these elements became incorporated into rapid changes in tomb design taking shape there, at least among elites who could afford such things. As was the case with the well-off general who buried mother at Shaling, some within the Pingcheng community now hired contracting teams to construct the brick-lined tombs that were becoming a new mark of elite status throughout northeastern Asia.¹¹⁴ Others, perhaps more conservative Serbi, continued to set their dead in traditional Inner Asian pit burials.¹¹⁵

Among the borrowings from the northeast—the Murong states, and Koguryŏ—was a newly vivid depiction of the tomb's inhabitants, which we certainly see at Dai with the master and mistress of the Shaling tomb. Although the man may have been buried elsewhere,¹¹⁶ wife and husband are—as is regularly seen in Pingcheng tombs, though of course in highly stylized form—depicted together on the tomb chamber's back (eastern) wall, the woman on the left and the man on the right. They are the master—and mistress—of all they survey. This seems to have been a style in life as well as death. In the biography of a Dai man of the Qiumuling clan, who served in the government along with Cui Hao, we are told of how "husband

---

a more active role in its design than the average Guyang patron" in avoiding typical formulaic language in expressing grief at the death of her son and a desire that he pass to a better world ("Lady Yuchi in the First Person," 41).

111. Seo, "Cong Shaling bi hua mu," 169-70; and see the table given by Ni Run'an 倪潤安, *Guang zhai zhong yuan: Tuoba zhi Bei Wei de mu zang wen hua yu she hui yan jin* 光宅中原：拓跋至北魏的墓葬文化与社会演进 (Shanghai: Shanghai gu ji chu ban she, 2017), 169-70.

112. See Zhang Mingyuan 张明远, "Yungang Tanyao wu ku zhong de wai lai yin su" 云岗昙曜五窟中的外来因素, in *4-6 shi ji de bei Zhongguo yu Ou Ya da lu*, ed. Zhang Qingjie et al. (Beijing: Ke xue chu ban she, 2006), 247-62; and for tombs, Ni Run'an 倪潤安, "Bei Wei Pingcheng mu zang zhong de Hexi yin su" 北魏平城墓葬中的河西因素, in *Wei Jin Nan bei chao shi de xin tan suo*, ed. Lou Jing (Beijing: Zhongguo she hui ke xue chu ban she, 2015), 603-23.

113. See Lin, "Bei Wei Shaling bi hua mu yan jiu," 26; and with a particular focus on borrowings from northeast, Seo, "Cong Shaling bi hua mu." For overall discussion of the cultural overlap of Koguryŏ and the Murong Serbi Yan regimes, see Tian Likun 田立坤, "San Yan wen hua yu Gaogouli kao gu yi cun zhi bi jiao 三燕文化与高句丽考古遗存之比较, in *Qing guo ji: Jilin da xue kao gu xi jian xi shi zhou nian ji nian wen ji*, ed. Jilin da xue kao gu xi (Beijing: Zhi shi chu ban she, 1998), 328-41.

114. Seo, "Cong Shaling bi hua mu," 168; Lin, "Bei Wei Shaling bi hua mu yan jiu," 7-8.

115. For description of the old burial practices of the people of Dai, see SoS 95.2322, which among other things relates that the deceased's clothing, as well as horse gear, was burnt as part of the funeral. We will see this practice below with the death of the emperor Wencheng. See also Ni, *Guang zhai Zhongyuan*, Chapter 2. In personal communication, the archaeologist Fan Zhang points out that choice of tomb style was not simply a matter of wealth, since some Pingcheng pit tombs (including M107 and M109 of the Nanjiao cemetery) contained "luxury burial goods, including the imported gilt silver vessels."

116. Tseng, *Making of the Tuoba Northern Wei*, 74.

and wife sat side by side, eating together 並坐共食," though in this case the story then turns to the haughty manner in which the two allowed the man's uncles to eat only the scraps, leading to criticism and mockery of the couple.[117]

Back in Shaling M7, on the back wall, we see the pair seated on a dais within a belvedere of classic Chinese style, with owl-tail roof ornament. Wearing flowing robes, they are apparently reveling here in their own brand of Chinoiserie.[118] Their core identities are, however, asserted by the black Serbi caps painted onto their heads. As important as asserted group identity—perhaps more—is hierarchy, which as the modern scholar Lin Sheng-Chih has pointed out pervades the depictions of life shown in the murals of this—and similar—tombs.[119] Servants stand on either side, also wearing the cap and the associated northern clothing of tight jackets and trousers. Quite pointedly, however, they are half the size.[120]

Beyond their servants, what the lord and the lady look out upon are apparently the two great preoccupations of the early Pingcheng elite, the doings by which they earned, maintained, and displayed status: on the wall on the couple's right (the northern wall) is formulaic display of the powerful male, leading an army on the move, hunting for the takings of war; and on their left is depiction of a great outdoor feast, presided over by an individual in another belvedere. The identity of this person is hard to make out because of the mural's decay. This author will, however, argue that the individual overseeing the gathering is the Poduoluo Lady.[121] This position is at least indirectly supported by two sets of evidence. First is reliable documentary evidence given above of the power exercised by women at Pingcheng feasts, already from the time of Taiwu. And second is the positioning of the tomb's compositions in and of themselves, which the modern scholar Fan Zhang characterizes as arranged in a "symmetrical way," in which the "rest of the paintings are organized" around the pair depicted on the wall in the back.[122] This author strongly agrees with that position; it would be quite unsymmetrical if the male depicted in the back-wall portrait alongside the Poduoluo Lady was shown on the side walls as both presiding over the feast and leading the procession.

---

117. WS 27.665, in which the man's surname is given in Sinicized form as Mu 穆, an eminent family within Dai. For this lineage, see Yao, *Bei chao Hu xing kao*, 25–28.

118. Tseng, *The Making of the Tuoba Northern Wei*, 85, suggests that placement of the subjects in fixed structures may be convention rather than accurate description of the reality of these events. It should be noted that a second image of the couple was also produced for the tomb, on the lacquer covering of the coffin: see "Shanxi Datong Shaling Bei Wei bi hua mu fa jue jian bao," 13, figure 19.

119. Lin, "Bei Wei Shaling bi hua mu yan jiu," 1, 42.

120. This creative pictorial depiction of hierarchy was, of course, not confined to Dai tombs, being well known in the south as well, in the paintings of such as Gu Kaizhi; see Müller, "Lacquerware," 56, citing Furuta Shinichi 古田真一, on the exchange of paintings between Pingcheng and the Yangtze region: "Rikuchō kaiga ni kansuru ichi kōsatsu—Shiba Kinryū bo shutsudo no shiga byōbu o megutte" 六朝絵画に関する一考察—司馬金龍墓出土の漆画屏風をめぐって, *Bigaku* 42.4 (1992): 57–67.

121. I do this cautiously, keeping in mind caution given by Fan Zhang in personal communication that it is problematic "to link a depicted figure with a specific personage," since the images are fundamentally "part of the formulaic composition available at the workshops."

122. Zhang, "Cultural Encounters," 70.

Replica of the Shaling M7 mural exhibited at the Sackler Museum, Peking University. Photo, Fan Zhang, 2017.

Instead, we will argue that these wall paintings, surrounding the body of the Poduoluo Lady on a stone couch in the middle—the only clear physical presence in the tomb—present a unified, unspoken narrative of the activities that defined her life, and the lives of those around her, in a manner somewhat like the diplomas, certificates of achievement, and sports trophies that fill the walls of middle-class American households.[123]

Status and power in the Land of Dai derived first and foremost from successful military command. Early Wei emperors' roles centered on active leadership on the field of battle, while virtually all major officials, no matter what their function, held a generalship in the military establishment, whether they actually led troops or not.[124] In the Shaling mural, on the north wall, the lady's kinsman is leading an organized unit of troops, in the middle of which he rides in a canopied carriage. The pennons (*chuang* 幢) on the back are presumably those of his own unit. As in the Anak No. 3 tomb, in Koguryŏ, what is shown here is not a parade, but a disciplined march to war.[125] Though elements of the scene are displayed in the manner seen in the old Chinese empire, there is here a clear increase in scale and organization, and in unity of action. Central to the early Wei army, of course,

---

123. Tseng, *Making of the Northern Wei*, 82, puts this well in her suggestion that we see in this and other Pingcheng sites the tomb as "functional space in which a myriad of performances intersected to define the deceased by his or her role in society," which she contrasts with the "module" style of Han funerary art (75–76).

124. This began with the princes: see Zhang Hequan 张鹤泉, "Bei Wei qian qi feng shou zhu wang jue wei jia bai jiang jun hao zhi du shi tan" 北魏前期封授诸王爵位加拜将军号制度试探, *Shi xue yue kan* (2012.11): 14–21. Miyazaki Ichisada 宮崎市定, *Kyūhin kanjinhō no kenkyū: kakyo zenshi* 九品官人法の研究: 科擧前史 (Kyōto: Tōyōshi Kenkyūkai, 1956), 408, discusses the reduction of most at least of generalships to prestige titles (*san guan* 散官). This will be seen in concrete form in Chapter 14's discussion of Emperor Wencheng's "Nan xun bei." Based on conclusions reached in Chapter 11, it seems fair to infer that part of the reason for assignment of military rank was probably the salary that accompanied such titles.

125. Lin, "Bei Wei Shaling bi hua mu yan jiu," 26; Wang, "Datong Bei Wei mu zang chu tu yong qun de shi dai te shu," 302; Tseng, *The Making of the Tuoba Northern Wei*, 87–88.

was cavalry, and though the Shaling mural depicts spearmen and other sorts of infantry, horsemen are the more prominent. Different sorts are shown: light cavalry, with their characteristic cockscomb headdresses; and heavy cavalry, just a century or so old in East Asia, with armor and barding for their horses.[126] Ahead of the carriage, in array, are drummers and pipers, whose incorporation into depiction of advancing military formations also seems to derive from developments in southern Manchuria.[127] The banging of drums and whistles of pipes has served, of course, to promote both discipline and ferocity in many societies.[128]

Although the story of Mulan adds an interesting wrinkle to the issue, we can assume that it was not the case that the lady of the Shaling tomb exchanged skirt for uniform to serve in her kinsman's army (and then, as with Mulan, reverted to become manager of a household).[129] As an integral and central part of the clan, however, she drew prestige from his activities. So did the clan as a whole, which with these depictions on her tomb wall was stating its position in the Dai society, briefly for mourners who walked down the ramp to pay farewell, and then presumably for denizens of the world beyond. In his work on the inscribed ritual biographies that became increasingly common in late Wei tombs, and especially down in Luoyang, the modern scholar Timothy Davis has pointed out the parallel way in which those epitaphs served the tomb's lord or lady, but also the family as a whole.[130]

The Shaling lady was, of course, more directly involved in the other great enterprise depicted in murals of early Wei tombs: gathering people together for a feast. In Dai, as in all societies, food was more than feed, to borrow the key insight of the anthropologist Mary Douglas.[131] It was an important way of binding individuals together within families and communities. Down in the belly, it seems, *Gesellschaft* can be digested to become *Gemeinschaft*; or to put it more bluntly, "the way to a man's heart is through his stomach." Perhaps the way to his loyalty as well.[132]

---

126. See a clear portrayal of the distinctions based on miniature statuary in Liu Junxi and Li Li, "The Recent Discovery of a Group of Northern Wei Tombs in Datong," *Orientations* 33.5 (2002): 44.

127. Lin, "Bei Wei Shaling bi hua mu yan jiu," 14.

128. In the Ming dynasty, see Kenneth Swope, "The Beating of Drums and Clashing of Symbols: Music in Ming Dynasty Military Operations," *Chinese Historical Review* 16:2 (2009): 147–77; and further afield, Kate Van Orden, *Music, Discipline and Arms in Early Modern France* (Chicago: University of Chicago Press, 2005).

129. Examples of female cavalry are given in Chapter 11.

130. Timothy Davis, *Entombed Epigraphy and Commemorative Culture in Early Medieval China* (Leiden: Brill, 2015), 354.

131. Mary Douglas, cited by Kaori O'Connor in her *The Never-ending Feast: The Anthropology and Archaeology of Feasting* (London and New York: Bloomsbury Academic, 2015), 15. Or as Epicurus said: "We should look for someone to eat and drink with before looking for something to eat and drink" (3). And once we've done so, says Ian Sansom in his *Times Literary Supplement* 18 December 2018 article titled "Jubilant Devastation," we should remember that according to a magazine called *Good Housekeeping*, Christmas dinner is "instrumental, a way of asserting one's dominance over the food, oneself and one's guests."

132. Or at least his "cynical acquiescence": Michael Dietler, "Clearing the Table: Some Concluding Reflections on Commensal Politics and Imperial States," in *The Archaeology of Food and Feasting in Early States and Empires*, ed. Tamara L. Bray (New York: Kluwer Academic/Plenum, 2003), 272. In connection with this, Dietler points out how the feast has played a powerful, ongoing role within the arena created by fixed monuments and institutions, and never could be entirely replaced by them.

The feast has long played a crucial role in defining—or redefining—the place of groups and individuals within a larger whole, snugly intertwining hierarchy and commonality in a seamless, and delicious, whole.[133]

The "hunt" and the feast have been closely paired in many societies. The famous "Standard of Ur" (ca. 2600 BCE) in the British Museum, for instance, shows war on one side and banquet on the other.[134] Within the Chinese worldview, they could be seen as complementary *yang* and *yin* in the construction of hierarchy. For precisely this reason, though women in most societies have been the ones who generally prepared and presented food, men have often taken control of the grand occasions, and so taken the lead in forging alliance, asserting hierarchy, and resolving conflict.[135] In depictions of such events in Han tombs, women were shown as second-floor onlookers, while in those of third-century Chinese successor states females had their own, separate dining space.[136] But in the fifth century, in the Land of Dai, women had come to control the feast: as Taiwu's empress oversaw the palace kitchens, and the empress dowager Wenming led the singing from the main table at a feast held with her foster-grandson, the emperor, so this author argues it was the Shaling matriarch who conducted the feast depicted on the tomb's wall. During this time, in this place, some women at least were deeply and openly involved in the networks of interaction that took shape at such events; within the domain formally allowed them, they drew power from the connections made there. (As with Wenming, so the Poduoluo Lady, mother of a powerful son, in this way took on a power of her own.) On the north wall, a male Other had occupied the center of a campaigning army, whose glory the Poduoluo Lady took as reflection. On the south wall she herself takes center stage, in a belvedere inhabited by her alone, reigning over a feast presumably attended by key figures in her kinsman's army, who sit kneeling in ranks below, and, as at Wenming's Divine Spring feast, look up to and seek to harmonize with her.[137]

---

133. In another piece, Michael Dietler argues that the "potential of food and hospitality to be manipulated as a toll in defining social relations lies at the crux of the notion of commensal politics": "Feasts and Commensal Politics in the Political Economy," in *Food and the Status Quest: An Interdisciplinary Perspective*, ed. Polly Wiessner and Wulf Schiefenhövel (Providence: Berghahn Books, 1996), 91.

134. O'Connor, *Never-ending Feast*, 46. See also Martin Jones, *Feast: Why Humans Share Food* (Oxford: Oxford University Press, 2007), 191–92.

135. Tamara L. Bray, "Commensal Politics of Early States and Empires," in *The Archaeology of Food and Feasting in Early States and Empires*, 6; on p. 1 of the same work, Bray defines "feasting" as a "communal food consumption event that differs in some way from everyday practice." For the multiple purposes of the feast, see O'Connor, *Never-ending Feast*, 9.

136. Tseng, *The Making of the Tuoba Northern Wei*, 76; and for depiction in poetry of the feast as the man's, see Tian, *Halberd at Red Cliff*, 89. See general discussion of male appropriation of food and its presentation by Carolyn Clark ("Land and Food, Women and Power in Nineteenth Century Kikuyu," *Africa* 50 [1980]: 357–70, cited by Michael Dietler, "Clearing the Table," 279). In her article (367), Clark asks whether women are "controllers of resources or themselves resources controlled by men?" In the Poduoluo Lady's tomb, at least, it seems to be the former, which Dietler goes on in his discussion of Clark's question to note occurs in at least some cases.

137. Though in the palace, we are told by a critical observer from Jiankang, they would sit on chairs with their legs splayed out: Jenner, *Memories of Loyang*, 25, citing NQS 57.986.

Though this is a stylized depiction of the woman's funeral meal in particular, a broader reality is certainly portrayed here.¹³⁸

Replica of the Shaling M7 mural exhibited at the Sackler Museum, Peking University. Photo, Fan Zhang, 2017.

As has been the case within most human societies, these women governed the internal operations of their household (*zhu jia shi* 主家事).¹³⁹ Some at least also stepped outside to serve as family ambassador. The empress dowager Wenming is said at times to have retired to the back rooms with the matriarch of a powerful family to have a woman-to-woman discussion of matters small, and great.¹⁴⁰ For the Poduoluo Lady to play that role—to chat, or toast, or, more purposefully, negotiate larger issues behind the curtains of the belvedere—she would, of course, have had to be conversant in the shared creole of the Dai domain. As for establishment of hierarchy at feasts, that would show itself clearly in seating rules.¹⁴¹ But even before seating, it can be seen in obligation to attend.¹⁴² It is hard to say what might have happened to one absent from the feast of the

---

138. Seo, "Cong Shaling bi hua mu," 177.

139. This is said of a woman who had married Wenming's brother, Feng Xi: BS 13.499 (WS 13.332). It certainly extended beyond this family, applying to most at least of the elite households of Pingcheng, and later Luoyang as well. Drawing upon funerary inscriptions, Wang Yongping 王永平 describes the power of women within elite households in Chapter 17 of *Qian Luo Yuan Wei huang zu yu shi zu she hui wen hua shi lun* 迁洛元魏皇族与士族社会文化史论 (Beijing: Zhongguo she hui ke xue chu ban she, 2017).

140. WS 30.803. This anecdote is raised by Song, *Bei Wei nü zhu lun*, 196, in discussion of the power of feasting. And see Alice Gregory's mention of "the archetype of woman as family ambassador" in her article "Finished: Life at the Last Swiss Bastion of Etiquette Training," *New Yorker*, 8 October 2018.

141. Zhang and Wang, "Bei Wei huang di ci yan kao lüe," 29. In WS 2.33 see creation of an officer for manners at feasts, at least for Daowu's feasts. For broader study of feast and hierarchy, see O'Connor, *Never-ending Feast*, 50; and Bray, who in her "Commensal Politics of Early States and Empires," 9, speaks powerfully on "pots as functioning objects and the relationship between pottery and food in articulating, defining, and negotiating identity and power," helping us gain further insight into why Daowu took the craftsmen and forcibly brought them up into the highlands.

142. Mauss, *The Gift*, 41: "*The obligation to accept* is no less constraining. One has no right to refuse a gift, or to refuse to attend the potlatch" (the italics are Mauss's). This is, of course, an essential part of Mauss's vision of "the gift."

Poduoluo Lady—perhaps she would induce her son to pass the offender over for promotion—but we know what happened two centuries before to the one lord who refused to accept Liwei's invitation, or the trepidation of the princes to accept Daowu's summons to a feast after the death of the Prince of Wey.

While the protagonist in the Shaling feast scene sits within a piece of fixed architecture, the scene as a whole is al fresco, ringed again by cartoonish little depictions of mountains and trees, that once again remind one of—and are certainly linked to—broader developments in painting technique in the Yangtze region, as seen for instance in work attributed to the painter Gu Kaizhi. Nonetheless, the modern scholar Chin-yin Tseng has made a good case in seeing a distinctive nature of such themes in Dai culture, and so Dai tomb art.[143] The feasters in the Shaling mural seem to revel in the outdoor barbeque. One can almost hear compliments from the floor about the delicious mutton stew, or—increasingly insistent—requests that the servers bring more kumis; though for the most part no longer practicing herdsmen, these people delighted in lamb flesh and fermented mare's milk. The food was often served on large pieces of lacquerware, as seems to be represented in the round plates placed before the guests in Shaling M7's feast mural.[144]

A variety of activities were carried on at Pingcheng feasts, including archery contests and riddle games.[145] As would be expected, toasts and salutes of the sort seen at Wenming's Divine Spring feast were central. It also seems likely that—though portrayed on the wall of no tomb—a more informal pastime was quarreling, or brawling. But at the moment captured in the Shaling mural, the diners are being entertained by dancers and singers, perhaps performing a just-arrived piece from a land far away. A report on music played at Daowu's court says that in addition to songs celebrating the dynasty's myths of origin, tunes were also played that came from southern Manchuria and the Wei River valley, from the Xiongnu down in the Ordos, and the Yangtze region south beyond that.[146] The Shaling lady would, alas, die a few years too early to hear perhaps even more popular waves of music, Central Asian tunes played by musicians forcibly transported to Pingcheng after conquest of Northern Liang.

We will, unfortunately, never actually hear the music that vivified these people. Still, in tombs just a few years after Shaling M7, with Taiwu's opening up of direct access to the Silk Roads by taking Chang'an, we find an increasing inflow of goods. Among these was a quite new style of apparel decoration from Sasanid Persia, in the form of roundels and pearls along robes' borders.[147] One of the indicators of

---

143. Tseng, *Making of the Tuoba Northern Wei*, 76–78.
144. See discussion of manufacture of these goods in Müller, "Lacquerware."
145. For discussion of entertainments, see Zhang and Wang, "Bei Wei huang di ci yan kao lüe," 30; and more broadly still, focusing on the Tang, Wang Yongping 王永平, *You xi, jing ji yu yu le: zhong gu she hui sheng huo tou shi* 游戏、竞技与娱乐: 中古社会生活透视 (Beijing: Zhonghua shu ju, 2010).
146. WS 109.2828.
147. Cheng, "Exchange across Media," 117–18, as part of a broader discussion of west-east exchange throughout the article.

elite status in Dai, the pearl appears in the relatively modest Shaling tomb only as ceiling decoration, in a Manichaean form adopted into Central Asian Buddhist art.[148] Other status markers were the utensils of silver or glass—many imported from Central Asia or Iran—from which the rich *Dai ren* took food and drink.[149] These items were so desirable, in fact, and private production of them seen as such a threat to the khaghan's control of distribution, that in 444 Taiwu issued an edict making the presence of craftsmen in the private households of nobles and magnates a crime punishable by death.[150] Though such things aren't seen in the tomb of the Poduoluo Lady—it was a bit too early to get the full flood of western exotica—at least she is shown in the mural with sets of plates to put out for her guests. Some of the pottery jars and jugs recovered from her tomb might have been used at her feasts.[151] As for what was put on those plates, though grain had become more accessible, meat was still a central part of the diet, and much of the meat was lamb and mutton—sometimes even sashimi, in the form of slices of raw sheep meat. Dairy products abounded, with use of yogurts, and butters, and kumis.[152] In describing general differences between Chinese food traditions and those deriving from Inner Asia, the modern scholar Lü Yifei points out the focus on grain as opposed to meat, and the Chinese blending of flavors as opposed to northerners' preference for keeping the items on the plate separate, so as to enjoy the distinct taste—and meaty smell—of each on its own.[153]

But strangers could, of course, always adapt, as we see in an anecdote about the southern expatriate Wang Su (463–501). Arriving in the northlands in 493, he was greeted with honor by emperor Xiaowen. In the beginning, Wang was unable to stomach lamb or goat's milk and preferred to eat the more familiar fish and drink tea. Several years later, however, at another imperial feast, it was noted that he was

---

148. Tseng, *Making of the Tuoba Northern Wei*, 88–89; Seo, "Cong Shaling bi hua mu," 174.

149. These imports are much discussed: inter alia, see Wang Yanqing 王雁卿, "Bei chao shi dai de yin shi qi ju" 北朝时代的饮食器具, *Bei chao yan jiu* 4 (2004): 158–68; examples of these vessels in Liu Junxi, ed., *Datong nan jiao Bei Wei mu qun*, 224–43; Boris I. Marshak, "Central Asian Metalwork in China," in *China: Dawn of a Golden Age, 200–750 AD*, ed. James C. Y. Watt et al. (New York: The Metropolitan Museum of Art; New Haven, CT: Yale University Press, 2004), 46–55; and Dien's discussion of "exotics" in *Six Dynasties Civilization*, 275–86. For a more general discussion of the influx of goods with direct opening of Pingcheng to the Silk Roads, see Wang, "Si chou zhi lu yu Bei Wei Pingcheng," 143–61. Fan Zhang, "Silver Handled Cup: Syncretism, Materiality, and Banquets in Northern Wei Art," *Artibus Asiae* 82.1 (2022): 6, notes that while popular among Serbi, such objects were apparently resisted by Chinese living in the Pingcheng area.

150. WS 4B.97. Private maintenance of Buddhist monks and other sorts of sorcerers were banned in the same pronouncement.

151. See pictures of the ceramics found in the tomb in "Shanxi Datong Shaling Bei Wei bi hua mu fa jue jian bao," 8, 10, 11.

152. See discussion of the foodstuffs eaten at feasts in Lü Yifei 吕一飞, *Hu zu xi su yu Sui Tang feng yun: Wei Jin Bei chao bei fang shao shu min zu she hui feng su ji qi dui Sui Tang di ying xiang* 胡族习俗与隋唐风韵：魏晋北朝北方少数民族社会风俗及其对隋唐的影响 (Beijing: Shu mu wen xian chu ban she, 1994), Chapter 2; and Zhang and Wang, "Bei Wei huang di ci yan kao lüe," 29–30. In viewing these materials, we need to remember the findings on meat eating among some—but only some—of the people of Dai of Hou Liangliang et al., "Nong ye qu you mu min zu yin shi wen hua de zhi hou xing."

153. Lü, *Hu zu xi su yu Sui Tang feng yun*, 51.

now consuming both lamb and yogurt. When the emperor asked how this had come to be, Wang replied that "mutton is the fine product of the land, and fish the best of the watery tribe. They are both delicacies in their different ways."[154] Even if unable to cook the two kinds, as Mao Xiuzhi had done, he would at least savor both.

Turning from the left side of the Poduoluo south-wall mural—where the lady and her guests feast—to the right, the other side of the temporary fabric partition, we see matters of equal or even greater interest. There, in temporary kitchen tents, the salt of the earth toiled for those who sat and dined. The belvedere is immediately left (east) of the screen, while just on the other side—on the servants' side—is parked what seems to be the grand carriage of the belvedere's occupant, with a red canopy and a horse grazing nearby.[155] This closeness to the kitchen is in fact another argument that the person in the belvedere is the Poduoluo Lady: though her back is to the staff, the Poduoluo Lady was ruler of the kitchen, and like the Helian empress, very aware of the doings there; it is hard to imagine the man leading the military procession on the opposite wall doing the same. If we accept this premise, having gotten down from her carriage on the servants' side, the Poduoluo Lady would presumably have given a final set of general instructions to her major-domo before passing through the gap in the screens to meet and greet the good folk. Ensconced there in a dominant position in her belvedere, she presumably would not have wanted to cross back over unless there had been a major gaffe of some sort. In which case, like Wenming, she would need to decide whether to be merciful, or not.

The servants' work was multivarious. At the top of the scene are three portable granaries, and to their right a number of parked carts, which had been used to convey foodstuffs, vessels, and utensils to the event; the lady of the household would have controlled all these household resources.[156] Below these are a line of four little tents, in two of which maids are working. In the most dramatic element of the scene, below the tents are two men who, surrounded by various scattered pots and jugs, have slaughtered a sheep and are now holding it up to let the blood drain into a cauldron just beneath.[157]

The modern scholar Lin Sheng-Chih has made the interesting suggestion that the distinctive juxtaposition in Pingcheng tomb murals of feasting and hunting was rooted in uncertainty that came from lack in Dai of a stable economic base.[158]

---

154. *Luoyang qie lan ji jiao zhu* 3.147–48; with modification, the translation comes from Jenner, *Memories of Loyang*, 215–16. See also the discussion in Pearce, Ebrey, and Spiro, "Introduction," in *Culture and Power in the Reconstitution of the Chinese Realm, 200–600*, 21–22.

155. Lin, "Bei Wei Shaling bi hua mu yan jiu," 25.

156. See discussion of women's control of grain stores among the Kikuyu in Kenya, by Clark, "Land and Food, Women and Power," 365–66.

157. See detailed discussion given in Lin, "Bei Wei Shaling bi hua mu yan jiu," 25. Bunker, *Ancient Bronzes*, 91–92, discusses a Serbi bronze cauldron excavated from the Hohhot region, dated to the fourth century.

158. Lin, "Bei Wei Shaling bi hua mu yan jiu," 26; and discussion of this general concept in Collingham's *The Hungry Empire: How Britain's Quest for Food Shaped the Modern World*.

Originally, at least, this had been a hungry empire, with uncertainty about food and its production. For those without the deep grain pits of the palace, livestock—or prey taken in the hunt—was the most reliable source of calories available. The sheep being slaughtered by the Poduoluo Lady's butchers—the mutton enjoyed by the diners—could have been obtained in various ways. It could be bought in a Pingcheng bazaar, having been driven down from the steppe by herdsmen, or sold off from the imperial house's Deer Park, which was also a huge ranch.[159] More likely, however, the Poduoluo Lady's household had herds of its own. In the time of the Wei collapse, in the early sixth century, a Chinese official by the name of Yang Chun reminded his offspring how their ancestor had long before come to serve Daowu, who in return "gave him land and a dwelling, and bestowed slaves, both male and female, horses and oxen and sheep—so that we became a wealthy household."[160] Under such circumstances, a mixed economy was to be expected: while some of the slaves would have been scratching grain out of the soil of the Datong Basin, another part—perhaps resettled nomads—would have been herding the sheep and oxen and horses up in the hills, while the Yangs lived in their dwelling, and at times went out for al fresco feasts, where they consumed part of the herd as mutton stew.[161]

The lives of most at least of the slaves and bound retainers would, of course, have been quite different. A fascinating set of grave goods has turned up in another Pingcheng tomb, M2 among those found in the year 2000 in the course of work at Yanbei Teachers College, again on the eastern outskirts of Datong. Among the terracotta figurines of horses, oxen, and camels found in this brick-lined tomb there also turned up three little terracotta models of nomad tents. One, a bit over seven inches tall, represents a classic round yurt—or *ger*—much like those still used in Mongolia today, while close by were slightly larger clay models of two square tents, showing ceiling flaps to let the smoke out.[162] It is not at all surprising that while Han dinner parties are depicted as occurring within the manor, those of the Dai people are shown as grand outdoor BBQs. Though members of the Dai elite had manor houses to which they returned after these events, and from which the great cauldrons were brought by ox-cart, they

---

159. Sagawa, "You mu yu nong geng zhi jian." On markets, see Li Hu 黎虎, ed., *Han Tang yin shi wen hua shi* 汉唐饮食文化史 (Beijing: Beijing shi fan da xue chu ban she, 1998), 185–86.

160. WS 58.1289. For a survey of stock rearing down on the Yellow River plains during this period, see Keith Knapp, "The Use and Understanding of Domestic Animals in Early Medieval Northern China," *EMC* 25 (2019): 85–99.

161. Huang, "Tuoba Xianbei zao qi guo jia de xing cheng," 84–90, discusses the use of slaves as among other things herdsmen. This would have been the "herdsman husbandry" described by Khazanov, *Nomads and the Outside World*, 22.

162. See Liu, ed., *Datong Yan bei shi yuan Bei Wei mu qun*, 66–67 and color plates 41 and 42; and mention in an English-language article by Liu and Li, "The Recent Discovery of a Group of Northern Wei Tombs in Datong," 46–47. A yurt model was also found in the tomb of Sima Jinlong: see Wang Yanqing 王雁卿, "Bei Wei Sima Jinlong mu chu tu de you tao zhan zhang mo xing" 北魏司马金龙墓出土的釉陶毡帐模型, *Zhongguo guo jia bo wu guan guan kan* (2012.4): 56–62.

had men who herded their sheep—and as needed, brought sheep to feasts to be slaughtered.[163] Those men—the modern scholar Koga Akimine suggests they still lived in autonomous units, organized on the basis of kinship—would have been spending much of their lives in yurts, as they moved the herds in spring up to rich highland meadows, or in winter down into the valleys (crossing lines of the ancient ramparts that no one now wished to enforce). Another elite family, the Pilou, "counted their household servants by the thousands; their oxen and horses were measured by the valley."[164]

Such herdsmen would have led hard, marginalized lives. Some became leaders of the uprisings that in the end brought down Luoyang.[165] In the period under discussion, however, they were just caring for their masters' livestock, out in their own kind of open air. They would not have used the great cauldrons we see in the murals, but a more compact, Inner Asian cooking vessel—frequently found in Northern Dynasty tombs, though not at Shaling M7—called in Chinese the *fu* 鍑.[166] Made of bronze or iron, these were relatively small but had wide mouths, a deep belly, and handles like ears through which a shaft could be inserted to hold over the flames. Some were designed for particular convenience on horseback: with one side flat, such pieces were easier to hang against the side of a horse, for al fresco cooking while herding, or hunting, or warring.

163. For an overview of pastoralism under Wei, see Zhang Yanli 张艳丽, "Qian lun Bei Wei xu mu ye de fa zhan ji ying xiang" 浅论北魏畜牧业的发展及影响, *Jincheng zhi ye ji shu xue yuan xue bao* 8.4 (2015): 51–53.
164. Koga, "Hokugi no buzoku kaisan ni tsuite," 6. For the Pilou: BQS 15.196, where the name transcription Pilou 疋娄 is given in abbreviated Chinese form as "Lou"; see Yao, *Bei chao Hu xing kao*, 98–99.
165. WS 9.237, 74.1645.
166. Wang, "Bei chao shi dai de yin shi qi ju," 161.

SECTION VI.

End Games

In Section II, we traced our story back to its origins. In Section VI we follow it to its end, looking at the games—played by various persons—by which it arrived there. The polity first set in place by Liwei was yet again transformed in the late fifth and early sixth centuries, in ways that certainly contributed to collapse in the 520s. But neither can we with any certainty say it would have survived by remaining unchanged in the rapidly changing East Asian world of the early sixth century.

As we see in Chapter 14, with the completion of the major conquests under Taiwu, and then the death of Taiwu himself, the central place of the army and its leadership declined in the Wei court. In the vacuum, women came to play ever more prominent roles. These powerful figures were not, it needs noted, those who had actually borne the reigning monarch—forced suicide was still imposed on those unfortunates—but senior women within the dynastic family, whether raised to that position because they had been wet-nurse for the emperor as a baby, or because they had been primary wife of a former emperor. The most important figure thus to emerge was the Wenming Empress Dowager, who having taken control of the rearing of her step-son's son, eventually killed the father and in the name of the nine-year-old on the throne took over as regent.

In Chapter 15 we look at how Wenming and her step-grandson, the emperor Xiaowen (r. 471–499), co-ruled as "two Buddhas," in a realm ever more shaped by the Buddhist religion. From a probably mixed-blood frontier family, Wenming knew the Chinese classical tradition, and as she raised the boy, she inculcated him with a strong sense of the duty of "filial piety," *xiao*, in this case directed not to his actual parents, who were both dead, but to the one who had raised him, Wenming. Showing a strong affinity toward Chinese tradition, not previously seen among Taghbach monarchs, Xiaowen obeyed her without reservation. With the empress dowager frequently the final voice on matters, they together began reform of the administration. Of particular importance was the Equal Fields system, by which, using the power of the Wei army, they reimposed on the farmer new configurations of the old practices of control and taxation that had first emerged under the Qin and Han. Equal Fields would continue to play an important role in East Asian states for centuries to come.

Though an innovator, Wenming was in some ways more conservative than her step-grandson. In particular, she wished to keep the capital at Pingcheng, up in the highlands. As described in Chapter 16, however, after Wenming's death in 490, Xiaowen mourned her according to Chinese ritual stipulations. When mourning was done, he finally did put her wishes aside and in 493 moved his capital down to the ancient Chinese city of Luoyang. From Luoyang he reached out in a variety of ways to the poets and statesmen of the rival empire of Jiankang. He simultaneously attempted to remake his dynasty's original following, the Dai ren, ordering that Chinese needed to be the language spoken in his new court at Luoyang, and that those who attended wear the robes of the Chinese gentleman, rather than the Serbi cap. Some of Inner Asian extraction who accompanied Xiaowen south liked these changes; others did not.

In the last chapter, 17, we see the dynasty's fall. The essential issue here was separation of the court from the military, the most significant part of which remained up in the frontier highlands. After decades of power struggle within the court, Empress Dowager Ling emerged to control it as regent for her son (forced suicide of the heir's mother having finally ended). Things went well at first. Drawing on the vast tax wealth brought in through Equal Fields, the empress dowager helped build a Buddhist paradise in Luoyang. In 523, however, the northern garrisons collapsed, many of the men rising in mutiny. Abandoning their frontier posts, the troops began to pour down into the Chinese interior. Five years later, one of the leaders of those mutineers and refugees came to Luoyang. Calling Empress Dowager Ling up to his camp on the Yellow River, he listened impatiently to her words, then had her thrown into the waters to drown.

A Transitional Age

Taiwu's original heir, his eldest son, whom we know by the Chinese appellation Huang 晃, was born in 428 to a Madam He, the name an abbreviated version of that of the old affinal Helan clan.[1] She died in the year of his birth, perhaps in childbirth. There is no reason to suspect other than natural causes; Huang was not explicitly designated heir until 432. In 444, when Huang was 16, Taiwu followed his father's precedent by affirming him as heir and then turning over to him government administration, with the support of four major officials, including Cui Hao.[2] This did not work out as successfully as it had for Mingyuan, Huang frequently arguing with Cui over policy and appointments.

Taiwu also did not get along with his son. He does, however, seem to have dearly loved his son's first son. The grandson is known to us by the Chinese name Jun 濬 or in Jiankang histories by a transcribed version of the *guo yu* title, *'Ulwoj tigin 烏雷直懃 (Wu lei zhi qin), which seems to mean something like "heir among the imperial clansmen."[3] After death, he received the Chinese imperial title Completed Culture Emperor (Wenchengdi 文成帝; r. 452–465). He was born on 4 August 440, the initial year of his grandfather's True Lord of Great Peace (Taiping zhenjun 太平真君) reign period (440–451). His father would at this time have been about 12 years of age. His mother was a Rouran princess.[4] The grandson is described in *Wei shu* as being a precocious boy, who at the age of five *sui* was in a group following Taiwu in a progress through the northern territories, when they encountered an Inner Asian commander who was about to beat a chained slave as punishment for some offense. Taken aback, the youngster rebuked the officer, saying, "The slave has now met with me; it is proper that you turn him loose."[5] Hearing of this, the grandfather is quoted as saying, "This

---

1. BS 13.494 (WS 13.327); and Zhang, *Bei Wei zheng zhi shi*, 4: 368, who points out that she was the last Helan woman to marry into the royal house.
2. WS 4B.96–97.
3. This is the name given in SoS 95.2353; NQS 57.984; and see ZZTJ 126.3981. Peter Boodberg suggests the translation "Prince and Descendant (or posterity), presumably meaning 'heir'" ("Language of the T'o-pa Wei," 230), basing "prince" on *tigin* (p. 137 of the same book). But as discussed above, Luo Xin ("Bei Wei zhi qin kao," 133) has plausibly suggested that *tigin* has the broader meaning of descendant of Liwei.
4. Of the Yujiulü 郁久閭 (Lü 閭), the royal clan of the Rouran, see Chen, *Zhongguo gu dai shao shu min zu xing shi yan jiu*, 196–98.
5. WS 5.111.

boy, though young, is taking for himself [the role of] Son of Heaven," implying assumption that the first-born son of his own son and heir, Huang, would take the throne after the father. If this story is true, stable succession was firmly fixed in Taiwu's mind. In fact, however, it would not be a smooth succession.

Left for extended times in charge of the capital while Taiwu was on campaign, Huang had become estranged from his father, and perhaps begun to plot his overthrow. In 451 the powerful eunuch Zong Ai set charges against the heir's favorites, whom Taiwu then had executed in Pingcheng's marketplace. The son died soon thereafter. Although the *Wei shu* annals provide no significant detail on this matter, the same book's Astrology chapter and the Jiankang-derived *Song shu*—in somewhat different terms—portray fierce argument between Taiwu and Huang, perhaps in part involving Taiwu's treatment of Buddhism. Eventually these conflicts opened the way for Zong Ai to persuade the father to put his heir apparent to death.[6] 'U-lwoj tigin, the grandson, would at this time have just turned 11. Subsequently, we are told, Taiwu came increasingly to grieve the death of his son. In early 452, fearing the emperor's wrath would fall upon him as well, Zong Ai killed his master.[7]

Zong Ai was a man of unknown origin, castrated for an unknown crime. Under Taiwu, he had received appointment as Palace Attendant-in-ordinary 中常侍 and a ducal title down on the banks of the Yangtze. After Taiwu's death, he took for himself a number of impressive offices and a princely title, and interestingly at least formal overall control of the Imperial Guard.[8] This situated him well in the power struggle that followed, in which he is said to have forged an edict by Taiwu's empress, the daughter of Helian Bobo, summoning those who supported succession for Taiwu's third son, Han, to the palace. There they were killed, Han himself dying in an alleyway between the walls of palace compounds. Zong Ai then raised up his own favorite, Taiwu's sixth son, the Prince of Southern Peace, Yu.

Relations between puppet and eunuch, however, soon soured. Late in that same year, 452, Southern Peace went to an ancestral shrine up at Baideng Hill, to sacrifice a horse, an ox, and a sheep to Shiyijian, Daowu, and Daowu's father. There he was killed by a eunuch sent by Zong Ai.[9] When the story leaked out to Liu Ni, the commander of the Yulin unit of the Imperial Guard, he urged Zong to

---

6. WS 4B.105–6, 109, 105C.2406; SoS 95.2353; WS 48.1072. Presumably involved is the death just before Huang of two princes of the house, tersely reported in *Wei shu*: WS 4B.105, 14.350. In ZZTJ 126.3981, Sima Guang cites comments in SoS 95.2353 (and see also NQS 57.984) stating that Huang had planned to rebel against his father, who then killed him; Sima dismisses these, suggesting they were groundless rumors. Li Ping (*Bei Wei Pingcheng shi dai*, 120–29), in turn, rejects Sima's interpretation and has constructed a complex argument suggesting not the plot of a eunuch, but the will of the monarch. Regarding the power struggles between the two palace households of emperor and heir apparent, see ZZTJ 126.3970–72; and WS 94.2012.

7. ZZTJ 126.3973–74; WS 4B.106; 94.2012.

8. ZZTJ 126.3980; WS 94.2012–13.

9. See ZZTJ 126.3980, including the Hu Sanxing commentary there.

put the imperial grandson on the throne, in order to preserve stability.[10] Rebuffed by Zong Ai—who is said to have called him a "great fool"—Liu quietly went to a key associate in the guard units, Yuan He, one of the two palace stewards 殿中尚書, with whom he "together controlled the troops of the imperial guard." The two then went to Lu Li, the Minister of the South (Nan bu shang shu),[11] suggesting to him that "Zong Ai set up the [Prince of] Southern Peace, and then killed him. If now we again don't set up the imperial grandson, it will not be good fortune for the dynasty's altars."[12] They then went to talk with the other palace steward, Zhangsun Kehou.

Here it would be good to pause to look at the Dai military men who played key roles in Wencheng's accession as commanders of the palace guard, to get some sense of their distinctive personalities.

Zhangsun ("Baba") Kehou, the second palace steward, was the closest relation of the imperial line, being a member of one of its cadet branches.[13] Perhaps the least involved of the four, he would be executed shortly after Wencheng's accession, for reasons not described.

The fellow referred to in our texts with the Sinicized name of Liu Ni 劉尼 was another member of the prominent Xiongnu Dugu clan, which would be one of the eight groups of early submissions to Wei that later, under Xiaowen, would be formally designated as the Eight Lineages of Meritorious Officials 勳臣八姓.[14] In earlier times, however, members of the Liu line seem to have gone primarily under their Inner Asian name; on the "Nanxun bei" (to be discussed below), Liu Ni appears as Dugu Hou-ni-xu 獨孤侯尼須.[15] Here again, we see the personal name given in *Wei shu* as one character taken from a more complex transcription. Of the clan of Liu Kuren and Liu Xian—whom we saw in the early years of Shegui—this fellow was also a "man of Dai," that is to say, on the military rolls

---

10. For comments on Liu Ni's title, see Zhang, *Jin wei wu guan*, 2: 678.

11. This would be the same office, though assigned a different translated name here, as that described in Chapter 7 as given by Shegui to Zhangsun Song (which in BS 22.805 [WS 25.643] is called Nan bu da ren); for the name change, see Yan, *Bei Wei qian qi zheng zhi zhi du*, 46 (and for evolution of these administrative units in general, see the table on p. 49). The office oversaw administration of the farmlands of the royal domain.

12. ZZTJ 126.3981. The (more) original variant given in Liu Ni's biography (WS 30.721) is interesting in adding that if the imperial grandson is not enthroned, "so as to accord with the hopes of the people" 以順民望, then the dynasty's altars will be endangered. This is, of course, a claim that the *guo ren* expected this to be done. If true, this is not necessarily a borrowing from the Chinese world; many societies have developed primogeniture. And the argument being asserted here is that it was the first son of the first son who should take the throne. There is at least one clear point that we can take from these stories: these guardsmen wished to forestall further struggle within the court by establishing what they seem to have viewed as regular succession.

13. Zhangsun Kehou is without a biography of his own. On his title, see WS 4A.106. It is interesting to note in the annals that it is Zhangsun and Lu who are cited (WS 4B.106) as having put Wencheng on the throne, with no reference to Liu or Yuan; apparently they were at the time at least the most prominent of the group. It should also be noted that in some passages, Zhangsun is listed as palace steward 殿中尚書 and Yuan He simply as "steward" (or "minister" 尚書; WS 40.907); in others vice versa (WS 30.721).

14. These changes were imposed by Xiaowen in the year 496: ZZTJ 140.4393.

15. On the Dugu and their alternative use of the surname "Liu," see Hu, *Bei chao Hu xing kao*, 43; Chen, *Xing shi yan jiu*, 52. For Dugu Hounixu's appearance on the "Nanxun bei," see Matsushita, *Hokugi Kozoku taiseiron*, 78.

of the royal domain. Despite Liu Xian's hostility, members of the "Battle-axe" clan had gone on for generations to serve the Taghbach regime. Liu Ni's great-grandfather had established himself under Daowu, while Liu Ni himself was appointed as a commander of the Yulin guard by Taiwu, who had been impressed by the fellow's physical strength and skill at archery.[16] Following the besting of Zong Ai and enthronement of Wencheng, he was raised to Duke and then Prince. From there, however, it was a downhill slide. Sent by Wencheng down to Zhongshan as governor of that district, he proved refreshingly incorrupt. This may, however, have been because he was drunk most of the time and not giving attention to much of anything else. Although Wencheng's heir, Xianwen (r. 465–471, d. 476), wished to honor Liu for his earlier accomplishments, in the year 470, during a great marshaling of the troops in preparation for a campaign against the Rouran, Liu was drunk once again, his unit in disarray. Feeling for the hero of 452, Xianwen simply dismissed him from office. Liu died four years later.

Doing much better in his career than the Baba or the Dugu was Yuan He 源賀, who would remain a major figure of the regime for decades after the Zong Ai affair. He had first appeared at the Taghbach court with the claim—not necessarily true—that he was a son of the last monarch of the Southern Liang (397–414) regime of the Tufa clan (apparently a branch of the Taghbach, as discussed in Chapter 5, that had long before migrated to the Gansu Corridor).[17] Taiwu, upon encountering him, had said that "You and We are of the same origin 源同. Because of events, our family names were distinguished. Now, you may be Mister Yuan 源氏."[18]

Recruited as a local guide in the campaign in which Taiwu seized control of the Gansu Corridor, Yuan had gone on to participate in campaigns against the Rouran and the Song regime to the south, again and again showing himself a redoubtable warrior, until finally he was made palace steward.[19] After the Zong Ai affair, he remained a major Wei figure until the early years of Xiaowen's Taihe reign period (476–499), when he grew ill and was honored by being treated by the imperial physician. He died in 478, receiving great accolades and numerous impressive titles.

---

16. WS 30.721.
17. WS 41.919. The way in which the statement is framed implies, of course, that it was not true.
18. For Yuan He's biography, see WS 41.919–23; and regarding the kinship group of which he claimed to be a part, see Yao, *Bei Wei Hu xing kao*, 238–41; and Chen, *Zhongguo gu dai shao shu min zu xing shi yan jiu*, 79–80. Boodberg, "Language of the T'o-Pa Wei," 229–30, points out apparent reference to Yuan He in SoS 95.2356, where he is referred to as a *tigin* (*zhi qin*, a member of the royal clan, though this fellow is not described as a descendant of Liwei). Boodberg also suggests that the name "He," bestowed upon Yuan by Taiwu, replacing his earlier name, Po-Qiang, "Smasher of the Qiang," is part for the whole of a Serbi name meaning something like "Name and Omen." Note also the interesting resemblance of the bestowed surname, "Yuan" 源, "origin," to the name later adopted by Xiaowen for the imperial clan, "Yuan" 元, "paramount," or "primal."
19. WS 41.919–20.

As for Lu Li 陸麗—the one figure among these who was not a guards officer—his clan name was properly Buliugu 步六孤, which has been tentatively reconstructed as *Buluwkku.[20] Li of the Buluwkku was a "man of Dai," grandson of a leader who had led his people to follow Daowu in the late fourth century, and son of "Lu Si" 陸俟, who had established himself as a major military man under Mingyuan and Taiwu. One of Lu Si's younger sons, Lu Li was enlisted into the palace guard on account of his "loyalty and respectful nature," and no doubt on the basis of legacy preference. Taiwu, we are told, was especially fond of the young man, and because he did his tasks with great care, with no mistakes, he was appointed Minister of the South. This prominent family would later also be included by Xiaowen among the Eight Lineages of Meritorious Officials.

These then are at least the key elements of the cast of characters who responded to the vacuum of power created by the deaths in quick succession of Cui Hao, Huang, Taiwu, and then of the Prince of Southern Peace. It was a confused and confusing situation. As the news of Yu's death spread, the officialdom in the capital fell into a state of panic; no imperial princes are seen coming to the fore.[21] There seems to have been both a lack of certainty as to who would next take the throne, and at the same time a certainty that the decision would be made in a bloody way. The Palace Steward Yuan He now "marshaled the guard, and calmly took control within [the palace] and [of the larger city] outside."[22] After Yuan went with Liu Ni to tell Lu Li that Zong Ai had killed Southern Peace, as recounted above, arguing that succession must pass to Huang's son, Lu Li replied that "the only thing we can do is secretly receive the imperial grandson."[23] Hereupon, the two palace stewards, Yuan He and Zhangsun Kehou, deployed the guard to secure the palace, while the Yulin commander Liu Ni and Minister of the South Lu Li rode out to the capital's Deer Park, where Wencheng had fled, to receive the boy.[24] Suddenly Lu reappeared before the palace, with the 12-year-old

20. See his biography, WS 40.907-9; and discussion of the Buliugu clan in Yao, *Bei chao Hu xing kao*, 28-31; Chen, *Zhongguo gu dai shao shu min zu xing shi yan jiu*, 99. The name as it appeared on the Nanxun bei—步六孤 伊[麗]—is given in Matsushita, *Hokugi Kozoku taiseiron*, 75; we will discuss this in more detail just below. For reconstruction of Buliugu as *Buluwkku, see Shimunek, *Languages of Ancient Southern Mongolia and North China*, 144. Though Shimunek states that there are no known cognates, Peter Boodberg has hypothesized that the name Buliugu is one of a number of different transcriptions of the Xiongnu name "Bulgar," which later appeared in Russia and Eastern Europe; see his "Two Notes on the History of the Chinese Frontier," 257-59. For a history of this clan, see Jennifer Holmgren, "The Lu Clan of Tai Commandery and Their Contribution to the T'o-pa State of Northern Wei in the Fifth Century," *TP* 69.4-5 (1983): 272-312; in the piece (290), Holmgren suggests that Lu Li was less a military man than a part of the emerging civil bureaucracy.
21. WS 40.907.
22. WS 41.920; ZZTJ 126.3981.
23. WS 30.721. Note that in Lu's biography (WS 40.907) it is said that it was he who insisted that primogeniture must be honored and Wencheng brought to court, and that this was the reason why he became a peerless figure at the court.
24. For a description of the Deer Park, see Li Ping 李凭, "Bei Wei Wenchengdi chu nian de san hou zhi zheng" 北魏文成帝初年的三后之争, in his *Bei chao yan jiu cun gao* (Beijing: Shang wu yin shu guan, 2006), 151-53, in which he tentatively suggests that the place that Wencheng hid might have been the same place his son, Xianwen, later set up his retired emperor's headquarters.

on the horse with him. In command of the gates as a palace steward, Yuan He opened them to receive the two. Liu Ni, in the meantime, went to the Baideng temple where Southern Peace had recently been dispatched, and is said to have given a rousing speech, thundering out that "Zong Ai has killed the Prince of Southern Peace. Treason! The imperial grandson has already ascended to the throne."[25] This rousing speech was, of course, originally in *guo yu*, and apparently directed to a group of guardsmen who had abandoned the palace, and were in the foothills to the east: "It has been declared—the troops of the guard may all return to the palace!" In response, the troops all shouted out the *guo yu* equivalent of "Ten Thousand Years!" Having seized Zong Ai in the palace, Yuan He and Zhangsun Kehou then arrayed the troops to receive Wencheng outside the palace gates and take him to be enthroned in the Eternal Peace Hall in the heir apparent's palace complex.[26] Zong Ai and his allies, on the other hand, were put to death, their families extirpated within three degrees of relationship.[27]

Liu Ni, Yuan He, and Lu Li no doubt truly did feel that they were loyal defenders of the royal house. But through their actions they had not just followed but invented tradition, making the dynasty what it would become. And for themselves, they had gained high position; for his part in the accession, Lu Li received the extraordinary title "without peer at the court" 無出其右.[28] Others contested Wencheng's enthronement, because they supported lateral succession, or wished power for themselves, or perhaps both. A series of purges followed Wencheng's accession.[29] The first to die were Zhangsun Kehou and a distant member of the ruling house, the Prince of Eternal Joy, who were raised to high office and then immediately put to death.[30] A week later, the possibility of lateral succession was ended, with the deaths of Wencheng's two surviving uncles.[31] But the struggle would continue for months, with further unexplained deaths of princes and high officials.

It was, of course, not the newly enthroned 12-year-old boy who was making these decisions, a position supported by the fact that on the day after the killing of the imperial uncles, it was Wencheng's own mother, the Rouran lady, who died.[32] Two and a half weeks after her death, she and the father—Huang—were given

---

25. WS 30.721; ZZTJ 126.3981.
26. WS 30.721; ZZTJ 126.3981. This was the same hall in which Taiwu had been killed: WS 4B.106.
27. WS 94.2013.
28. WS 40.907.
29. For the following purges, see WS 5.111–12; ZZTJ 126.3982ff.
30. For the Prince of Eternal Joy, see BS 15.544 (WS 14.346).
31. For the Prince of Linhuai, see BS 16.605 (WS 18.418–19). For the Prince of Guangyang, see BS 16.615 (WS 18.428).
32. In a rather speculative manner, Song Qirui in her *Bei Wei nü zhu lun*, 104–12, suggests that this was engineered by Taiwu's formal empress, Madam Helian; Holmgren, "The Lu Clan of Tai Commandery," 191–92, offers a similar possibility. Li Ping, "Bei Wei Wenchengdi chu nian de san hou zhi zheng," 156, suggests that while Madam Helian had the authority to do this, it was Wencheng's wet nurse Madam Chang who induced her to do so, and then despatched her as well in the next year.

posthumous titles, while Wencheng's wet nurse—like Taiwu's—was given the rank of "nurse dowager" 保太后. She was later promoted to bear what was—in the Chinese tradition at least—the more conventional title of "empress dowager" 皇太后. It has been suggested that it was, in fact, she who had fled with the boy to the Deer Park. Be that as it may, she had now become a key power within the Inner Court, in charge of the growing palace community.[33]

* * *

This was the bloody beginning of a new phase of Northern Wei history. The great age of military conquest was over; from this point on military activity would consist mainly of dogged border conflict, with the Rouran to the north and Jiankang to the south. Despite the role of the guard in securing the throne for Wencheng, military men would no longer dominate the regime as they had heretofore. During this period we see a rapid rise of Buddhism as both an intense focus of individuals' devotion and as the main justification for the monarchy. We also see a growing role of women in the court; Daowu's efforts to escape the household had failed, or to put it another way, a vast household had grown up around the monarchic line. The state would no longer be based around the commander-in-chief's war tent, but around the palaces of Pingcheng. The intimidation of the progress was still seen there, but now in part at least led by Pingcheng's powerful women: according to an observer from the south, when the "empress dowager"—most likely referring to Wenming—went forth from the palaces she was accompanied by a troupe of armored cavalrywomen.[34] The dramatic reorganization of the state and its institutions that took place under Xiaowen had roots in the reign of his grandfather, Wencheng.[35]

Still, like it or not—and they may not have always liked it—there was an enduring and ongoing closeness of the early Taghbach emperors with men of the Inner Court, of the military fratry. We have seen this above, in the story of the guardsman Yi Bo and Taiwu. We see it as well under Taiwu's successor, Wencheng, who in 461 led a progress from Pingcheng down into the central plain. As we have touched on in Chapter 11, on the way back, near the town of Lingqiu in the mountains southeast of Pingcheng, they stopped for an archery contest. The "Nan Xun bei," or as the title appears at the top of the stele, the "Huang di nan xun zhi song" 皇帝南巡之頌, "Paean for the Emperor's Southern Progress," was then inscribed on stone and placed at the site. Though badly damaged, broken

---

33. WS 5.111–12. And see Pearce, "Nurses, Nurslings and New Shapes of Power," 301–2; Li, "Bei Wei Wenchengdi chu nian de san hou zhi zheng," 149–53; Song, *Bei Wei nü zhu lun*, 107–8.
34. NQS 57.985. This book, "Documents of Southern Qi," is based on materials compiled under Southern Qi (479–502), and so is likely referring back to the most eminent of the dowager empresses of this period, Wenming (d. 490). And see discussion in Cheng Ya-ju, "Han zhi yu Hu feng," 20–23, of the broad range of authority of dowager empresses from the time of Taiwudi, if not before, both within the inner palace and in policy decisions in the court.
35. See the comments of Gao Yun, looking back from the Xiaowen reign: WS 48.1081.

into multiple pieces, the stele, discovered in the 1980s, is a helpful supplement to the received texts, providing among other things a sense of how names and titles seem actually to have been voiced in the multilingual world of the Pingcheng court, as well as fascinating details on the composition of the imperial entourage in general, and this one in particular.[36]

On the stele's verso, we are given more than 280 names, which seems to have been the typical size of an early Wei entourage (there may, of course, have been many people in the train of too little importance to be put up on the stele).[37] In the long list of names and titles given there we see much more clearly than is revealed in *Wei shu* the fascinating use of the Chinese writing system, in which characters are partly used to represent the Chinese language, and partly as transcription of the Taghbach *guo yu*, as seen above in the title for "weapon bearer," *huluozhen* or *quragčın*. Of equal interest are the names of those accompanying the 21-year-old emperor. The very first to appear on the first column of text was Lu Li, the man of Dai who nine years before had carried Wencheng into the palace on the back of his horse, an act that had made him a centerpiece of the new administration. Here his name was written in transcription of how it was actually spoken, as "Buliugu Yi[]" 步六孤 伊[], the unreadable character in the box [] probably being the *li* 麗 that later became his abbreviated personal name in the post-Xiaowen version "Lu Li" 陸麗. Supposing this to be the case, the Middle Chinese transcription of the characters of the personal name, perhaps a little closer to the original name in the Taghbach *guo yu*, is *'Jij-[lej].

Upon 'Jijlej of the Bʊluwkkʊ clan had been bestowed the irregular honorific "without peer at the court" (which interestingly does not appear on the stele).[38] But he held more conventional titles as well, with the ranking of prince, a generalship, and assignment as a Palace Attendant. The man whose name follows that of 'Jijlej on the stele was of the surname *'Jit-pyut-bu (Yifubu 一弗步).[39] Though the personal name has been lost in damage to the stone surface, modern scholars have concluded that this was the figure called Yi Hun in *Wei shu*, who four years later, in the power struggles following the death of Wencheng, would kill the peerless one and briefly seize power.[40]

---

36. This progress is described in WS 5.119; ZZTJ 129.4053. The *Shui jing zhu shu* (1: 11.1048–49) mentions the tableland where archery was practiced and the inscription—there called "Imperial Archery Stele" 御射碑—raised for Wencheng.

37. On the front of the stele there is mention of "several hundred people"; Zhang Qingjie 张庆捷, "Bei Wei Wenchengdi 'Nan xun bei' bei wen kao zheng" 北魏文成帝《南巡碑》碑文考证, *Kao gu* (1998.4): 83, cites other Wei progresses with a similar number, inferring that this might have been the norm.

38. WS 40.907.

39. "Yifubu" was also sometimes abbreviated into Chinese in the less radical abbreviation "Yifu" 乙弗: Yao, *Bei chao Hu xing kao*, 175–80.

40. For identification of both of these figures with their different names on the stele, see Zhang, *Jin wei wu guan*, 2: 714.

Under Wencheng, the guard continued to play a key role and a large part of the emperor's entourage on this progress were guardsmen; about a third of the names on the stele were commanders of various units. We also see the enduring militarism of the regime in the fact that those who hold substantial "civil" rank also have military rank, with the salary of an officer.[41] At the end of the first row of names, we are told "the fifty-one people to the right are inner attendant officials."[42] Almost half of the names listed were members of the royal clan or closely related Serbi groups. The others were of Xiongnu, Turkic, Korean, and Tibetan extraction.[43] Though the regime was by 461 already changing in significant ways, the core of the regime remained Dai ren. What we don't find are many at all accompanying the emperor on this progress from among the Chinese populations.[44] Despite real change from the time of Wencheng on, the dominance of *guo ren* would continue throughout the regime.[45]

Two major sets of events are described on the stele, which run roughly parallel to brief comments in the *Wei shu* annals. The first of these was a tour of the lowlands, including the cities of Zhongshan and Ye. One purpose of the progress was to build support for the regime among the agrarian populations there, with Wencheng receiving local elders, and perhaps participating with them in a spring festival.[46] Another purpose may have been to intimidate the Jiankang regime to the south, a decade after Taiwu's advance to the Yangtze: in the midst of the 461 journey, we are told, the Song monarch sent up a tribute mission.

In the course of the return to Pingcheng, the procession stopped on a mesa by the town of Lingqiu, where both the stele and the account in "Wei documents" describe an archery contest. "South of Lingqiu," *Wei shu* says, "there is a mountain more than 4,000 feet high. [The emperor] proclaimed that all the officials (accompanying him) should shoot up to the mountain peak. There were none who could shoot over it. The emperor [then] bent his bow and loosed an arrow that went more than 300 feet above the mountain, and (landed) 1,000 feet past the mountain's south side. Subsequently, they cut a stone to engrave an inscription."[47]

---

41. Zhang, *Jin wei wu guan*, 2: 716.
42. See Matsushita, *Hokugi Kozoku taiseiron*, 77.
43. Zhang, *Jin wei wu guan*, 2: 735–40. On p. 745 of the same text, Zhang mentions that on the stele we see almost all the Inner Asian groups attached to the Taghbach.
44. Zhang, *Jin wei wu guan*, 2: 735–37, 691. Regarding *Han ren*, Zhang (739) reprimands the archaeologist Zhang Qingjie for in his reports on the "Nanxun bei" too uncritically taking those with Chinese-style monosyllabic names as being ethnic Chinese; and see also Klein, "Contributions of the Fourth Century Xianbei States," 107ff..
45. Holmgren, "Northern Wei as a Conquest Dynasty," 13–15, points out that even under the Sinicizing emperor Xiaowen, Chinese occupied only about a third of government offices.
46. WS 5.119; Zhang, "Bei Wei Wenchengdi 'Nan xun bei' bei wen kao zheng," 83.
47. WS 5.119. It is, of course, quite likely that the stele was made later, in Pingcheng, the stele then transported back to Lingqiu and raised up there. The figures given here are "more than 30 *zhang*," a Wei *zhang* being about 3 meters; and "220 *bu* 步," a *bu* being about half a *zhang*. Though they may be for other dynasties, measures for Northern Wei are not necessarily consistent and variants are regularly seen in reference works.

The stone itself, in fragmentary form, tells the story a bit differently, beginning with a recollection of a 453 trip, when "we had pulled (the bows) and shot at the cap of the mountain."[48] Apparently referring to the 461 procession, the stele then goes on to say that "the several hundred men all (shot their arrows) several dozen feet over the mountain."[49] This clashes, of course, with the *Wei shu* text, which tells how the emperor had bested them all. The modern scholar Zhang Qingjie sensibly says that he believes the stele—composed near to the event—and that what we see in *Wei shu* is just later flattery given to the monarch or his lineage.[50] Here, at any rate, we do see continuation of a core element of the militarized Taghbach society: competition over skill with the bow.[51]

* * *

But the Taghbach court was changing. Although the core of the emperor's entourage was Serbi, or related northern populations, the emperor was not necessarily happy with the generals and guardsmen accompanying him, in part no doubt because of the drain their salaries imposed upon the treasury. An anecdote from the biography of the Chinese minister Gao Yun describes Wencheng's scolding of his *guo ren* retainers: "You all are on Our left and on Our right, [but] We never hear from you a straightforward comment. You just wait for when We are in a good mood to seek for office, to beg for a posting. You all hold your bows and your swords, on the right and left attending Us—you get 'merit' for just standing there and all become dukes or princes. This fellow, [Gao Yun,] takes up a brush to save my realm and my dynasty (*guo jia*)"—perhaps from bankruptcy—"and he's nothing more than an attendant. Don't you all feel ashamed?"[52] Hereupon the peerless one, "Jij-lej of the Buluwkku" (or "Lu Li"), confirmed the monarch's concerns, saying: "Though Gao Yun receives your fondness, his household is poor, he wears garments of coarse cloth." Infuriated, the emperor now himself went to confirm the humble nature of Gao's dwelling. The problem lay in the fact that in the early Wei civil office did not bring salary. Reward had heretofore lain in the great distributions of booty taken in war, the salaries given military officers, and the growth among the Taghbach elite of land-holdings. As these dried up, officeholders would turn increasingly to activities the monarch at least might call corrupt. Apparently a genuinely good man, Gao—the lone survivor of the *Guo ji* scandal—had not pursued such options.[53] Being a rather good man himself, Wencheng now bestowed upon his beloved

---

48. See brief mention in WS 5.113.
49. See the recto inscription in Zhang and Li, "Shanxi Lingqiu Bei Wei Wenchengdi 'Nanxun bei,'" 72.
50. Zhang, "Bei Wei Wenchengdi 'Nan xun bei' bei wen kao zheng," 83.
51. For a broader view of the archery contest, or hunting, as "A Measure of Man," see the chapter by that name in Allsen, *The Royal Hunt in Eurasian History*.
52. WS 48.1075–76.
53. Ad hoc assistance was given, when the emperor so willed: for another example, see the story of aid to a salary-less Li Biao in WS 62.1397. And note that in early Wei, local officials did at least receive land and supplies: Yan, *Bei Wei qian qi zheng zhi zhi du*, 113–16.

attendant—his father's tutor and mentor—generous gifts of cloth and grain. Gao's son was given a generalship—and so a salary—and appointment as governor of a commandery, apparently a reliable source for the Gao family of goods and services, though we are not told of the methods used to obtain them.

Having been written by Gao's peers, men of the educated service class, this anecdote must, of course, be taken with a grain of salt. And even if the incident happened as described, it is certainly true that most humans tire of kith and kin. It does not necessarily mean that Wencheng did not also enjoy riding or pulling the bow with 'Jij-lej and the boys, or that Gao Yun was all the young emperor needed in order to survive and thrive. Nevertheless, from this brief anecdote we do get a glimpse of a broad and uneven field of development within the Taghbach state as it groped forward, from one generation to the next. With the end of the age of major expansion, although they remained a major drain on the treasury the military and the inner court inevitably began to decline in importance, their members increasingly focusing on their own business.

What was now emerging was an "inner court" of a different sort, the palaces and their inhabitants who lived in continuous propinquity to the one who sat on the throne. As we have seen, eunuchs had already begun to play an important role. But of greater importance for Northern Wei would be the role played by palace women. Basing his kingship primarily on his role as commander-in-chief of the armies, Taiwu had spent a great deal of his time in camp, physically removed from the capital. From the time of Wencheng emperors spent more time in the palace, where power was more diffused and action based on attention to ever more elaborate procedure, which included the feasts we have seen with Wenming, and the Poduoluo Lady. Paralleling development and systematization of the state bureaucracy was growth within the palace of a parallel women's administrative hierarchy.[54] Some women at least thrived in this environment. Men, for their part, seem to have been becoming increasingly peripheral figures. As we shall see below, this is certainly the case in the court. It was also the case with the men in the field. With less and less booty being taken, the emperor was less and less able to play the role of the great dispenser of captured goods.

Daowu's wish to exclude heirs' mothers from the court had already begun to unravel when his grandson, Taiwu, raised his wet nurse—in effect, his foster mother—to Empress Dowager. Even more import lay in repetition of this act by his successor, Wencheng.[55] Having nursed Wencheng, and perhaps been the

---

54. Song, *Bei Wei nü zhu lun*, 203; Stephanie Balkwill, "When Renunciation Is Good Politics," *Nan Nü* 18.2 (2016): 235–37. Unfortunately, we have little clear sense of the functions of these posts.

55. WS 4A.70, 80; and Pearce, "Nurses, Nurslings and New Shapes of Power." For a more general view of the wet nurse in the Chinese world, see Jender Lee, "Wet Nurses in Early Imperial China," *Nan Nü* 2.1 (2000): 1–39; and beyond East Asia, Ruby Lal, *Domesticity and Power in the Early Mughal World* (Cambridge: Cambridge University Press, 2005), 188–94, on the power of foster-community in the Mughal court, where "the ties formed by the bountiful milk were crucial," pushing "the boundaries of what would normally be recognized as blood-relations and relationships of marriage and birth" (194).

one who protected him during the power struggle that followed his grandfather's death, Madam Chang went on to exert real power in his court, revealed (and reinforced) by her ability to order the suicide of Wencheng's most beloved concubine, a southern woman taken in war who had birthed the future emperor Xianwen.[56] A transportee from Northern Yan, Madam Chang also married Wencheng to a daughter of that dynasty's ruling Feng family, who as the Empress Dowager Wenming would emerge as the dominant figure of the late fifth century.[57]

From being booty taken from fallen states, who feared rather than wished for the birth of a boy, some women in the later Wei court learned to raise another woman's son, gaining enormous authority if and when he was set upon the throne. Some have suggested this political role of women was of Inner Asian origins, though an obvious counterexample would be the wife of the founder of the Chinese Han dynasty, who played a vigorous and powerful role in that state's politics. Perhaps the distinction lay not so much in contrast of the Inner Asian and the Chinese worlds, as in cultural developments in the increasingly urbanized areas of the Yangtze region, where over time much more efficient and enduring social and physical constraints came to be placed upon women than those provided by Daowu's "ancient practice."[58]

Women were also deeply involved in the spread of Buddhism in the Land of Dai. As we've seen, Taiwu had become very hostile to the religion. His proscription of Buddhism, however, had not been particularly successful, and with Wencheng's accession the policy was reversed and Buddhism embraced, by the throne and by the people.[59] Thus began the recasting of Northern Wei as a Buddhist state. Though this would reach its point of highest development decades later in Luoyang, key early steps in the process began during Wencheng's reign, with the cave temples at Yungang.[60]

Located on a river about ten miles west of Pingcheng, Yungang provided the more or less vertical rock face needed to carry on the tradition of the cave temple that had come to East Asia from India via Bamiyan, and nearer to hand Dunhuang and Maijishan (in mod. Gansu province).[61] With production beginning under Wencheng (it is not clear precisely when these were finished), the

---

56. Li, *Bei Wei Pingcheng shi dai*, 149–53; Song, *Bei Wei nü zhu lun*, 107–8; Pearce, "Nurses, Nurslings and New Shapes of Power," 301, 303–4.
57. Pearce, "Nurses, Nurslings and New Shapes of Power," 296–97; and for the close ties between Madam Chang and the Fengs, Li Ping, *Bei Wei Pingcheng shi dai*, 177ff. More generally for the Fengs, see Jennifer Holmgren, "Social Mobility in the Northern Dynasties: A Case Study of the Feng of Northern Yen."
58. See the comments of Jennifer Holmgren, "Women and Political Power in the Traditional T'o-pa Elite," 33–34. Different but comparable sets of constraints were, of course, placed on women in other urbanizing societies in Eurasia.
59. WS 5.112, 114.3035–36; Hurvitz, *Treatise on Buddhism and Taoism*, 69–71.
60. WS 114.3037; Hurvitz, *Treatise on Buddhism and Taoism*, 72; Tsukamoto Zenryū, "The Śramana Superintendent T'an-yao and His Time," *Monumenta Serica* 16.1–2 (1957): 374–75.
61. Hansen, *The Silk Road*, Chapter 6; Michael Sullivan, *The Cave Temples of Maichishan* (Berkeley: University of California Press, 1969).

project involved excavation of five adjoining grottoes with statues representing Wei emperors as Buddhas. Showing strong Central Asian influence, these were quite likely created by stonemasons and artists transported to Dai after Taiwu's conquest of Northern Liang.[62] Enormous work was dedicated to these figures, which stood between 40 and 50 feet high, but they were not originally meant for large-scale public display. Though parts of the caves have since collapsed, people were originally meant to behold these figures within tightly confined excavated space. Still, many were drawn there, for ritual circumambulation within the caves or to hear tales read them by monks, and Yungang became a major East Asian Buddhist center.[63] Even after removal of the capital to Luoyang in 493, work—on a smaller scale—continued there, until the area was largely abandoned 30 years later.[64]

Yungang was a colossal physical manifestation of the astonishingly rapid growth of Buddhism within the Taghbach realm, and of attempts to use it to justify the monarchy. One seems to have been sponsorship of a new sutra called the "Humane King Perfection of Wisdom Sutra" (*Ren wang bo re bo luo mi jing* 仁王般若波羅蜜經), which described the monarch as protector of the faith.[65] On the surface, this was clearly a rejection of Taiwu's proscription. But looking for underlying policy, it could also be seen as continuation of the grandfather's efforts to use religion as a way—in this case a more effective way—of reconciling recently conquered populations to the state, a new phase in the ongoing project of defining and redefining the polity. It was Taiwu who had first begun actively to experiment with the use of religion to prop up the state, even if his own particular effort at it failed.

Under these circumstances, the state now patronized Buddhism, while at the same time attempting to control it through the imposition of administrative structures.[66] There would for centuries be ongoing issues of state control in different East Asian regimes. But despite such efforts, the religion grew rapidly. In 477, Pingcheng had 100 temples and 2,000 monks and nuns; in the realm as a whole, there were some 6,500 temples and more than 75,000 clergy. Fifty years later, at the end of the dynasty, there were 2 million monks and nuns and the number of temples had almost quintupled.[67] Work at Yungang carried on as well,

---

62. Yi, *Yungang*, 38–39. Okamura Hidenori suggests, however, that tile work at the Yungang grottos seems to have been done by tile-makers transported to Pingcheng from the city of Ye, down on the plains: see his *Unkō sekkutsu no kōkogaku*, 14.

63. See an interesting discussion of these practices in Yi, *Yungang*, Chapter 5.

64. Su Bai 宿白, "Yungang shi ku fen qi shi lun" 雲岡石窟分期試論, rpt. in his *Zhong guo shi ku si yan jiu* (Beijing: Wen wu chu ban she, 1996), 84–88 (originally in *Kao gu xue bao* 1978.1).

65. Charles Orzech, "The Scripture on Perfect Wisdom for Humane Kings Who Wish to Protect Their States," in *The Religions of China in Practice*, ed. Donald Lopez (Princeton, NJ: Princeton University Press, 1996), 372–73. It needs noted that the apparently Northern Wei text discussed by Orzech is just one of several different versions with similar titles.

66. Tsukamoto, "T'an-yao," 383; and see also Dorothy C. Wong, *Chinese Steles: Pre-Buddhist and Buddhist Use of a Symbolic Form* (Honolulu: University of Hawai'i Press, 2004), esp. Chapter 3.

67. WS 114.3039, 3048; Hurvitz, *Treatise on Buddhism and Taoism*, 79, 103.

then later continued at the Longmen caves outside of Luoyang. Yungang itself served not just the elite, but as a much broader center for proselytization, where preachers chanted to large numbers of those drawn to the faith: "The cadence of their voices rises and falls.... When they talk of death, it makes everyone's heart tremble with fear. When they talk of hell, it makes everyone weep.... When they talk about joy, everyone is happy."[68] In a more spontaneous way, such things also occurred in towns and villages throughout the Wei domain, with proliferation of societies of the faithful, which produced the stelae decorated with scenes from the life of Buddha that are familiar from museums throughout the modern world. From the time of the initial building at Yungang on, with great rapidity, Buddhism would become an inextricable element of Wei culture, and of Wei politics.[69]

* * *

Madam Chang died in 460. Her foster son, the Wencheng emperor, died five years later, after a reign of thirteen years, which though ushered in by a fierce struggle for power, was one in which, as Wei Shou, the author of *Wei shu* put it, he "gave his age rest."[70] Though just 25 at the time of his death, there is no suggestion given in the texts that his was not a natural death, though its causes are unknown.

Born in 454, Wencheng's successor, the emperor Xianwen (r. 465–471), was designated heir in 456 at the same time that Madam Chang—employing Daowu's ancient practice for her own purposes—ordered the mother's death. He was not even 11 when he took the throne in 465. A power struggle immediately broke out, the most visible participant being the man who had stood second on the Southern Progress list: Yi Hun 乙渾, the fellow of the Yifubu clan. Of obscure background—but probably of Serbi derivation[71]—Yi Hun had risen to be a close companion and advisor to Wencheng, being a Palace Attendant with princely title and high rank in the military.[72] With the death of Wencheng and accession of Xianwen, again in the midst of a power vacuum, Yi Hun turned quickly to seize power, conducting a purge of opponents. Among the victims of the second name on the Southern Progress stele was the fellow whose name had come first, Lu Li, 'Jij-lej of the Buluwkku. It is not clear how old Lu Li was at this time. He had been a favorite of Taiwu, and under him had risen to be Minister of the South. But no mention is made of his participation in the campaigns of that age, so perhaps we could assume that he was fairly young—perhaps in his mid-20s at the

---

68. Yi, *Yungang*, 117. This passage comes from a chapter on monks who "lead by singing" (*chang dao* 唱導) in Huijiao's *Gao seng zhuan* (T2059:50:418a), which was compiled shortly after the fall of Luoyang.
69. Tsukamoto, "T'an-yao," 370.
70. WS 5.123.
71. Eisenberg, *Kingship in Early Medieval China*, 64; Zhang, *Bei Wei zheng zhi shi*, 5: 174–81.
72. WS 5.120; ZZTJ 130.4073. Li Ping, *Bei Wei Pingcheng shi dai*, 189–91, suggests he was also closely tied to Madam Chang.

time of Taiwu's death in 452. We might guess that 13 years later, in 465, he was around 40. At any rate, at the time of Wencheng's death, Lu Li had some sort of ailment, which he was treating at the hot springs of Dai, south of Pingcheng near the Sanggan River.

Yi Hun, we are told, feared and hated Lu Li, because the latter had repeatedly criticized Yi for violation of court protocol. Apparently feeling confident in his control of the guard and its officers, Yi now dispatched one of the overseers of the guard, Mu Duohou, to summon Lu Li back to the capital.

Duohou 多侯 was a scion of the Qiumuling 丘穆陵 (MC *Khjuw-mjuwk-ling), or Mu clan, which since the time of Daowu had provided the realm with many generals and statesmen, including Duohou's elder brother, Mu Shou.[73] Duohou himself was unwilling to follow Yi Hun, and in his biography we are told he made the following speech to Lu Li: "Hun [of the Yifubu clan] has the ambition to be subject to no lord. [And you,] great prince, are the one the multitude look up to (*wang* 望). If you go, it will certainly be dangerous. [You] should tarry in making your return [to Pingcheng], and plan [what to do about] this."[74] Lu Li's biography gives a rather different account, telling us that while at the hot springs, Lu heard of the secret doings at court and wished to go there. His attendant (referring to Mu Duohou?) stopped him saying, "The emperor has died, and the virtue and fame of the prince (Lu) have long been substantial. If the traitorous official resents the praise of the people, I fear an unimaginable catastrophe [for you]. I would that you delay a bit your return [to the court]. After the court has calmed, then hurry back. That will still not be too late." Lu Li replied, "How could there be a fellow who, when he has heard his lord has died, just worries about calamities and does not go [to court] like a rushing wave?"[75]

However these discussions actually proceeded, whatever precisely the advice given was, Lu Li did not take it. Instead he went immediately from the hot springs to the court, where he was killed by Yi Hun. The guardsman, Mu Duohou, was killed as well. Later, when Yi Hun was gone, Xianwen posthumously entitled Lu Li the Simple Prince, and buried him among the Jinling tombs. Lu's son Dingguo, having been raised in the imperial palace, was under his old playmate Xianwen specially given princely title, and rapidly raised to the status of Palace Attendant and Palace Steward. Becoming, unfortunately, overly dependent on imperial favor and not strictly following the laws and regulations, he was in 471 stripped

---

73. For Mu Duohou, see WS 27.674. Mu Shou (d. 447) was the cocky fellow seen in Chapter 13, who had sat dining with his wife, leaving only the scraps for his own uncles. Serving in the time of Taiwu, during Cui Hao's heyday, he was also one of the few who dared treat Cui with contempt: see WS 27.665. For a sense of the widespread involvement of the Mu clan in the Wei regime, see Yao, *Bei chao Hu xing kao*, 29–32; and *Wei shu* 27, which is devoted entirely to this descent group, containing biographies of dozens of its members. It will also be noted that thirty years later, it was a Mu who led rebellion up at Pingcheng against Xiaowen's relocation of the capital to Luoyang.
74. WS 27.674.
75. WS 40.908. These two dialogues are fused in ZZTJ 130.4073.

of rank and sent out as a common soldier. After the death of Xianwen in 476, however, his offices and princely title were restored.

A day after the killing of Lu Li and Mu Duohou, Yi Hun was given the honorary status of one of the Three Dukes, Defender-in-chief (*tai wei*), a prestige title borrowed from the Chinese empire, as well as overall control of the Outer Court administration as Overseer of State Affairs (*lu shang shu shi*).[76] "Many others," we are told, "were executed."[77] One was a distant cousin of the imperial house, Yu 郁 (not to be confused with the Prince of Southern Peace), who had begun as an officer of the Yulin guard, and then served as a Palace Steward during the reign of Wencheng, receiving a ducal title. When Yi Hun seized power and cut off communication with the palace city,[78]

> The officials were all panic stricken; no plans were forthcoming. Yu [then] led several hundred guardsmen of the palace administration into the palace through the Shunde Gate.[79] His wish was to execute Yi Hun. Terrified, Yi Hun came out to meet him, asking Yu, "Why, sir, have you entered [the palace]?" Yu replied, "Not having seen the Son of Heaven, the servants [of the state] are all worried and frightened. We seek to see the lord." Desperately frightened, [Yi] Hun said to Yu, "Now the Great Progress (i.e., the late emperor) is in his coffin, and the [new] Son of Heaven in the mourning hut. It is for this reason that he has not received officialdom. What is making you gentlemen so suspicious?"

Yi Hun escaped immediate danger by presenting the new emperor, Xianwen, to the court, and shifting blame onto a eunuch. Later, however, Yu resumed his plans to eliminate Yi Hun, working with his brother Muchen. The *tigin* duke was, however, slow and undecided. And then time ran out: the plans leaked and Yu was executed. His brother was luckier: Muchen escaped and was able to hide out until Yi Hun's death, when he returned to the court to serve with some prominence.[80]

The power of Yi Hun in the vacuum of the court lasted for about nine months, during which time he made efforts to win support with tax relief and a pardon for convicts in the capital zone.[81] His time would, however, run out too. An

---

76. WS 6.125.
77. ZZTJ 131.4104; WS 33.793; Eisenberg, *Kingship in Early Medieval China*, 67–68.
78. This is from Yu's biography in WS 14.347. Though *Wei shu* 14 is one of the reconstructed chapters, the account of this man's life in BS 15.544 is much less detailed; perhaps this is part of the *Wei shu* chapter that survived.
79. In the reconstruction of Duan and Zhao, *Tian xia da tong*, 60, this led through government offices up to the actual palaces.
80. The eunuch to whom Yi Hun had shifted the blame was soon put to death; incidentally, he was the uncle of a Madam Lin who later became an empress of Xiaowen, and gave birth to the heir who died for resisting his father's move to Luoyang: BS 13.498 (WS 13.332); WS 44.993. For Muchen's biography, see BS 15.544–45 (WS 14.348). Muchen began his career in the Yulin guard, then rose to Palace Attendant and Vice Director of State Affairs (*shangshu zuo puye*). After these events, he was involved in arranging transfer of the throne in 471 from Xianwen to Xiaowen; and later under Xiaowen was stripped of his titles, apparently on the basis of corruption charges.
81. WS 6.125–26. See Eisenberg, *Kingship in Medieval China*, 69ff., for a theory that Yi Hun's power was based on support from key figures in the imperial clan.

interesting anecdote from the end of this period, showing diffusion of power throughout the expanding government and the limits of Yi Hun's control, despite his best efforts, is found in the biography of an official named Jia Xiu. Yi Hun had by this time tried at least to take up dictatorial powers, having raised himself up to "Chancellor, with station above that of all the princes. All matters," we are told, "both big and small, were decided by Hun."[82] This was, however, not entirely true. Around this time, Yi Hun's wife, of commoner status, entered the scene, seeking to get for herself the title of princess (*gong zhu*). Repeated mentions were made of this wish to Jia Xiu, perhaps by the wife herself. (And if so, these points might well have been raised at feasts.) Jia's response was stony silence.[83] Later, when Jia Xiu had gone to the couple's mansion on government business, it was said to him that "There are no government affairs that you do not attend to. [But when] I ask for [the title of] princess, you don't respond—what's the point?" The furious Jia Xiu then shouted back, "the appellation of princess is a title for the daughters of the king. It is the highest honor and not something appropriate for commoners. If you improperly assume this title, you certainly must take the crime upon yourself. Xiu would rather die in the present court, and not invoke laughter in later days."[84] Shocked at this, Yi Hun's followers all blanched, while Jia Xiu remained of perfectly calm composure. "Silently, Hun and his wife swallowed their rage." Jia seems to have survived only because of Yi Hun's fall soon thereafter.

In spring of 466, a conspiracy took shape involving several of the boy-emperor's uncles—the princes whom Yi Hun had ranked himself above; Wencheng's empress, the future empress dowager Wenming; and a Palace Attendant whom we have repeatedly seen before, the *tigin* Yuan Pi. These three groups now formed an alliance to have Yi Hun charged with treason and executed.[85]

---

82. WS 6.126; ZZTJ 130.2074.

83. See the biography of Jia Xiu, WS 33.792–93, and the editors' comments in note 13, pp. 797–98, pointing out although *juan* 33 is not one of the chapters known to have been reconstructed in the Song, that it does have discrepancies with a slightly fuller version given in BS 27.981, presumably on the basis of materials available in Tang when *Bei shi* was compiled. Though originally from the Gansu Corridor region, Jia's father had entered Wei service as one among the few selected out of the Murong army after the defeat at Shenhe Slope, before the rest were slaughtered. Although ZZTJ 131.4104 text says explicitly that it was Yi Hun who raised the issue to Jia Xiu, *Wei shu* (33.793) does not specify the requester: 渾妻庶姓而求公主之號，屢言於秀，秀默然. In the slightly fuller version given in *Bei shi* (27.981), we are told that after Jia Xiu's stony silence he went on official business to the mansion of Yi Hun and his wife, where the couple sat together, and that one of them (it is not really clearly stated which one), "with a face contorted with anger" then demanded to know why the wife's wishes had not been accorded with. It does seem possible that Sima Guang has viewed this from an early modern, Song perspective, and simply assumed that the man had raised the point; and so, perhaps, we see here another example of the active role of women in Pingcheng's politics and government. More clearly, we also see that Yi Hun (or his wife) would need to go through a particular official to have their way.

84. Note that this is the version given in WS 33.793; the BS 27.981 version is slightly different.

85. ZZTJ 131.4104; BS 13.495 (WS 13.328); BS 15.553 (WS 14.357); WS 33.793. And as for the princes, see notice of the arrival in court of several imperial princes in WS 6.126; pointing this out is Zhang, *Bei Wei zheng zhi shi*, 5: 184. Modern scholars have different views as to who was the real leader of the plan to get rid of Yi Hun: Song, *Bei Wei nü zhu lun*, 140, holds it was the empress. Zhang, *Bei Wei zheng zhi shi*, 5: 186–87; and Eisenberg, *Kingship in Early Medieval China*, 71, lean more toward the princes, despite the fact that they are little mentioned in the primary accounts. Most likely, it was a bit of both.

The empress was a granddaughter of the last lord of Northern Yan, Feng Hong, and as described in Chapter 12, of a family of mixed descent. After defecting to Wei, her father was sent to govern Chang'an, where Wenming was born.[86] He was later executed—for unknown reasons—and Wenming brought into the palace's women's quarters, where an aunt was already present to take the niece under wing.

As frequently happened, Wenming was raised to empress as a symbol of conquest. As was also the norm, she did not bear him a son, perhaps because Wencheng preferred not to visit a symbol at night. Her life came to bear more meaning with his leaving it. Others in the palace were impressed by her effort to hurl herself upon the fire set to ritually dispose of her late husband's clothing and knickknacks.[87] Elevated to Empress Dowager, she then joined the plan to be rid of Yi Hun.

For a year after the dictator's death, Wenming played the role of regent for her stepson, Xianwen. But with the birth in October of 467 of the 13-year-old's first son, she withdrew into the rear apartments of the palace, taking the child with her.[88] The birth mother died two years later; we are not told of what cause, but her brief biography tells us all were struck with grief at her passing.[89]

Strange doings were not the property of Pingcheng alone. In 464, the Song throne down in Jiankang was taken over by an apparently troubled teenager named Liu Ziye, who among other things bestowed upon his rotund uncle Liu Yu the title "Prince of the Pigs."[90] The reign lasted just over a year. After the young man's assassination, he was succeeded by the Prince of the Pigs—known posthumously by the more elegant title "Brilliant Emperor" (Mingdi, 465–472). The throne was, however, contested by another nephew and though the rising was ultimately squelched, Mingdi's harsh treatment of his nephew's supporters led in 467 to defection of several Song frontier governors, the most important holding the crucial town of Pengcheng (on the site of mod. Xuzhou, Jiangsu). Both Pingcheng and Jiankang now sent armies to the scene. When they met east of Pengcheng in winter of 467, the northerners had the best of the battle; the heads of tens of thousands of southern soldiers were taken.[91] The Song lord Mingdi now sued for peace, but in a series of mop-up operations led by a scion of the old Yan ruling house, Murong Baiyao, Pingcheng over the next year took control of all the

---

86. BS 13.496 (WS 13.328, 329 note 10); Holmgren, "Social Mobility in the Northern Dynasties," 28–29; Zhang, *Bei Wei zheng zhi shi*, 5: 194ff.

87. BS 13.495 (WS 13.328).

88. See Ruby Lal's discussion of "adoption," or perhaps "taking charge," of other women's children by senior females at the Mughal court: *Domesticity and Power in the Early Mughal World*, 120–23.

89. BS 13.498 (WS 13.331). Some modern scholars have even suggested that Wenming was actually Xiaowen's biological mother. This is effectively debunked by Li, *Bei Wei Pingcheng shi dai*, 195–208; Zhang, *Bei Wei zheng zhi shi*, 6: 62.

90. SoS 72.1871.

91. WS 6.127, 50.1110; SoS 8.159–60; ZZTJ 132.4129–30.

lands north of the Huai River. Perhaps because of lack of confidence that these territories could be held—or perhaps to solidify control—a large part of the local population was now reduced to servitude and transported north to Pingcheng. There they were eventually reassigned to serve the Buddhist monasteries.[92]

The Song dynasty would last just a little more than a decade.

For four years after Wenming's retirement from regency, Xianwen sat on the throne and exercised power in his own right. In 471, however, presumably under pressure from his uncles and his stepmother, the 17-year-old emperor convened the main figures of the court to propose that he would step aside for his uncle, the Prince of Jingzhao, Zitui. Appearing stunned at the suggestion that the issue of succession be reopened, the assemblage stood mute until another of Xianwen's uncles, the Prince of Rencheng, with the Chinese name Yun, perhaps remembering some fairly recent power struggles, spoke up to insist that this would destabilize the dynasty.[93] Perhaps never serious in the first place, the emperor now agreed and had his seals taken off to the four-year-old heir, the soon-to-be emperor Xiaowen (r. 471–499).[94] Xianwen then retired to a lodge in the Deer Park north of the city. There he is said to have engaged in Buddhist meditation, while at the same time continuing to play a leading role in the government, regularly hearing reports on affairs of state.[95] Building on the basis of male power, he also conducted great reviews of the troops, perhaps as a way of making a statement to his stepmother down in the city.[96]

For her part, Wenming was raising the future Xiaowen in the back apartments of the Pingcheng palaces. The son visited the father up in the Deer Park just once a month.[97] Like any good politicker, Wenming also used this time to build connections throughout court and government.[98] And it was rumored that one of these connections—for whom she'd gotten a plum post—was also her lover.[99] Although the Heir Apparent Huang, who died at the age of 23, had by that time sired 14 sons by 11 or 12 different women (and of course an unknown number

---

92. ZZTJ 132.4148–49; Chen, *Buddhism in China*, 154–55; Huang Wen-Yi, "Negotiating Boundaries: Cross-Border Migrants in Early Medieval China" (PhD diss., McGill University, 2017), 28–42.

93. WS 19B.461; ZZTJ 133.4164–65. See the overview of the abdication in Zhang, *Bei Wei zheng zhi shi*, 5: 308–20; and Eisenberg, *Kingship in Early Medieval China*, 72–76, who argues that the abdication was a scripted event, in which Wenming played only a minor role.

94. WS 41.921.

95. WS 6.132; ZZTJ 133.4166; WS 114.3038; Hurvitz, *Treatise on Buddhism and Taoism*, 75. Eisenberg, *Kingship in Early Medieval China*, 81–84, suggests that though Xianwen had not himself effected the abdication, this being undertaken by powerful members of the imperial family, once he was in the Deer Park he successfully built power, becoming able to evade and from a distance control the court. Song, *Bei Wei nü zhu lun*, 149–50, describes a sharing of power that she compares to those earlier seen between Mingyuan and his heir, Taiwu; or Taiwu and his son Huang.

96. WS 7A.142; Song, *Bei Wei nü zhu lun*, 152.

97. WS 7A.138.

98. Song, *Bei Wei nü zhu lun*, 156–58.

99. This was Li Yi, a son of Li Shun, Cui Hao's rival in the debate over the Northern Liang campaign whom Taiwu had put to death: WS 36.841.

of daughters),[100] the suggestion that the empress dowager was traveling a similar road caused scandal: the retired emperor now executed her lover, causing his stepmother to feel, as *Wei shu* puts it, a "lack of satisfaction" (*bu de yi*).[101] If she had previously lacked the will or the way to hold and exercise power, it seems that she had at this point gotten both. Having her stepson killed with poison, she now emerged again from the inner palace, with the nine-year-old monarch in tow.[102]

---

100. BS 17.629 (WS 19A.441). Of course, toward the end of the dynasty there were emperors who had the opposite problem.

101. BS 13.495 (WS 13.328); ZZTJ 134.4187.

102. Though not so clear in the annals (WS 6.132, 7A.142), we are told Xianwen was poisoned in other parts of *Wei shu*: 105C.2413; BS 13.495 (WS 13.328). In the last pair of texts, Wenming's biographies, *Bei shi* bluntly states the empress dowager "harmed the emperor (Xianwen)" 害帝, while *Wei shu* says Xianwen "suddenly expired 暴崩. At the time [people] said the empress dowager had done it." Accompanying the death of Xianwen was the death of his uncle, Zitui, who had been sent off to govern a province and "unexpectedly died" en route: WS 7A.144; BS 17.632 (WS 19A.443); Song, *Bei Wei nü zhu lun*, 154.

The Two Buddhas

Born in 442, Wenming had still been a young woman of 23 when her husband, Wencheng, died in 465. Eleven years later, at the age of 34, she reappeared in very different circumstances, now a key actor at Pingcheng who wielded power with a new confidence. This power derived from three sources: the first, based on her title Empress Dowager, was her designated position as matriarch of the imperial house, with control over among other things the women's palace administration; the second was the body of informal allies with which she filled the court, beginning with her brother Feng Xi, who married an imperial princess and rose to be a Palace Attendant, with a princely title; and the third, perhaps of greatest significance, was the emotional control she wielded over the monarch, whom she had raised from birth and would continue to guide until her own death in 490.[1]

It is an obvious fact of life that for all humans of all human groups, our most important and fundamental relationships are generally our earliest ones. And for most this is the relationship with the mother, or the person who played the nurturing role in childhood. In the Chinese tradition the parent-child relationship was systematized around the concept of *xiao*, "filiality," which in the Ru classics tended to focus on relationship between the son and the father, perhaps because that relationship is by nature more tenuous. But with the addition of Buddhism to the cultural mix of medieval East Asia, the relationship of child to mother—which had of course been there all along—was given a new centrality in the realm of public discourse.[2] At any rate, Xiaowen's relationship with Wenming—his step-grandmother, whom we could also call his foster mother—was self-consciously defined by *xiao*. For one who vested authority in the Chinese classics—which was certainly the case with Xiaowen, if not all his kinsmen—this gave great authority to Wenming as well.

---

1. See a parallel analysis of her sources of power in Holmgren, "The Harem in Northern Wei Politics," 89–90; and the comment of Balkwill, "When Renunciation Is Good Politics," 247, on how the empress dowager "benefitted politically by being the only woman in the emperor's life."

2. For *xiao* in general during this period, see Knapp, *Selfless Offspring*. For the mother-child relationship in particular, within the Buddhist context, see Alan Cole, *Mothers and Sons in Chinese Buddhism* (Stanford, CA: Stanford University Press, 1998). A powerful embodiment of such feeling was the much-loved "Tale of Turnip," in which a young Buddhist monk goes to Hell to save his mother: see Victor Mair, *Tun-huang Popular Narratives* (Cambridge and New York: Cambridge University Press, 1983), Chapter 2.

For her part, the empress maintained firm control over her ward, the ultimate basis of her power within the court. At one point in the boy's early life she is said to have begun thinking he was clever—too clever—and at some point in the future might "not be to the advantage of the Feng family" 不利於馮氏.[3] A "wise if stern" individual,[4] she thereupon decided to depose him, beginning the process by locking the boy up in an unheated room in the middle of winter, clad in the barest of apparel. For three days he was given no food. Wenming was about to replace him with a brother (apparently presuming he would die soon) when she was convinced to abandon this course of action by the strong objections of the eminent *tigin* Yuan Pi—the dinner guest seen in Chapter 13—and Mu Tai, who much later would lead rebellion against Xiaowen's relocation of the capital.[5]

Not unexpectedly, Xiaowen felt deep and complex emotions for his self-assigned caretaker. But in a manner most filial, in his public stance he held nothing against his mother-figure, deferring to her on matters of state and attending to her while she ate her congee.[6] In fact, they came to be called the "two sages" (*er sheng*), a relationship that seems to have been mirrored at Yungang by frequent depiction of two Buddhas sitting one beside the other, a theme taken from the *Lotus Sutra*.[7] When the empress dowager died in 490, the emperor—now without doubt a man, who had long before taken up the responsibility of actually running the state[8]—of his own accord put off all food and water for five days, and then to the concern of his officials insisted on entering into a prolonged and elaborate period of mourning according to dictates of the Ru tradition.[9] It

---

3. WS 7B.186.
4. BS 13.496 (WS 13.329).
5. Eisenberg, *Kingship in Early Medieval China*, 88. Building on the work of Li Ping and other scholars, Eisenberg quite persuasively also demonstrates that in general Yuan Pi had been an ally of Wenming, though the leader of his own faction based in the military: pp. 85–87. Jennifer Holmgren, "The Harem in Northern Wei Politics," 88, also points out a passage in *Zi zhi tong jian* (134.4194) describing how in 477 an heir, angry at the dowager empress, tried to poison her, though was in the end dissuaded. This passage, however, has been misread (in part because it is a rare example of sloppy arrangement in the Zhonghua shu ju ed.). The passage does not refer to Xiaowen, but to the Song heir down in Jiankang; see also the same passage in the *Wei shu* chapter on the "Island Barbarians," WS 97.2151.
6. BS 13.496 (WS 13.329); WS 7B.186.
7. Yin, "Yungang shi ku suo fan ying de yi xie Bei Wei zheng zhi she hui qing kuang," 75–77; and Eugene Wang, *Shaping the Lotus Sutra: Buddhist Visual Culture in Medieval China* (Seattle and London: University of Washington Press, 2005), 7, 10, who cautions against viewing "the twin Buddhas as iconic portraits of the reigning Twin Sages (though such an analogy may have been intended and exploited by the imperial spin doctors)." Also see the very interesting article examining the use of Buddhism by Wenming in Yungang by Guan Furong 管芙蓉, "Fo mu ta dong yu Feng Taihou—Yungang shi ku wen hua nei han jie du" 佛母塔洞与冯太后—云冈石窟文化内涵解读, in *2005 nian Yungang guo ji xue shu yan jiu hui lun wen ji, yan jiu juan* (Beijing: Wen wu chu ban she, 2006), 733–36 (rpt. in her *Bei chao san lun*, 352–59).
8. Though Wenming exerted real power at court, for all his deference Xiaowen was by 485 clearly taking a more significant role himself. See Zhang Jinlong 张金龙, "'Feng shi gai ge' shuo shang que" "冯氏改革"说商榷, in his *Bei Wei zheng zhi yu zhi du lun gao* (Lanzhou: Gansu jiao yu chu ban she, 2002), 28–51 (originally in *LSYJ* 1986.2).
9. BS 13.497 (WS 13.330); ZZTJ 136.4290.

was for good reason that he was posthumously entitled the "filial and cultured emperor," Xiaowendi.

* * *

The Xiaowen reign is best known for a broad and radical set of changes in policy and institution that are usually referred to as "reforms," with a clear assumption that they made the regime better. These came in two major clumps: the first, of a practical sort, in the mid-480s—while the court still lay under the "two sages"; the second, after Wenming's death in 490, of a more visionary bent, an attempt to create on earth a utopia drawn from Chinese tradition.

It is an oft-heard argument—some may contest it—that a strong state rests on a strong army; and that a strong army rests on reliable economic support. Early efforts in this direction were seen with the Prince of Wey's Wuyuan agricultural colonies. While the *guo ren* soldiery for the most part supported themselves and their families up in Dai, they needed to be supported when on campaign. A few years later, of course, much vaster farmlands were brought under Wei control, where the old empire's systems of organization and taxation of farm households survived in at least a vestigial form, having been tapped into by the regimes of Fu Jian and the Murongs and taken over by the Taghbach as soon as they seized the lowlands.[10] They came to Wei, however, in a rudimentary and undependable form and in the early decades seizure and distribution of booty seemed to have been more important, serving not only to reinforce the troopers' loyalties but also to fill the Wei treasury.[11] But after the great conquests of Taiwu, there was not much more booty to take. And though bringing in much wealth, the great conquests—and in particular, the march to the bank of the Yangtze—had in fact expended more, so that at the end of Taiwu's reign the treasury was almost empty.[12] Ad hoc efforts to improve agricultural production and to bring more of that production into state coffers and granaries had already begun under Taiwu, who in 444 decreed that farmers post their names over their fields, to make clear who was—or was not—producing grain from it. This may not have had much effect. Eleven years later, Wencheng sent a team of 30 men to the provinces to inspect "the many untilled fields" that still remained.[13] A more reliable system was needed to support the army and the state, which finally took full shape a generation later. Economic necessity was at least one of the things pulling the court deeper and deeper into what was—potentially at least—the most productive and prosperous sector of its realm.

---

10. See WS 2.28, 2.31; and Wang, *Zhuan xing qi de Bei Wei cai zheng yan jiu*, 46–47.
11. Wang, *Zhuan xing qi de Bei Wei cai zheng yan jiu*, 5–8; Han, *Bei chao jing ji shi tan*, 36–38. And see comments on the economics of "army and state" in WS 110.2851–52.
12. WS 5.123.
13. WS 4B.109, 5.114.

The centerpiece of the reforms of the 480s was establishment of a new system of allocation of farmland by the state called Equal Fields (*jun tian*). If not truly resting on the assumption that all land belonged to the monarch, as some have suggested, Equal Fields did use Pingcheng's power to at least partially limit large-scale accumulation of farmland, while re-establishing the taxpaying, registered small farmer base of Qin and early Han.[14] In territories recovering from protracted warfare and disorder, production was increased and social stability enhanced by placing refugees on land that had over the previous two centuries been abandoned.

The origins of this system are complex: apparently with roots in experiments toward the end of the first Chinese empire, closer in time Equal Fields was an expansion to the realm as a whole of the policy of census and land allocation (*ji kou shou tian*) implemented to settle hundreds of thousands relocated to the Dai region.[15] Much has been said on the matter by modern scholars, but to state it simply, Equal Fields seems to have been a fusion of forms of social control and extraction of production developed under the Chinese empire, imposed in a more systematic and efficient manner through the coercive capacity of outsiders, of the Taghbach.

Formal proposal of the Equal Fields system was presented to Wenming and Xiaowen in 485, when a Chinese official put forth a memorial asking for measures to deal with two intertwined problems down on the lowlands, the first being populations uprooted by crop failure, and the second, the large-scale evasion of taxation by the wealthy.[16] The latter was a problem that went back to the beginning of Northern Wei, and really long before. Although the local administration of the Chinese empire, with its commanderies (*jun*) and districts (*xian*), had survived the Western Jin collapse, eventually to be inherited by Northern Wei, it no longer functioned as the statecraft experts had long before conceived. Rather than a system of control for central government, it had instead become an institutional support for the power of the local elites seen in Chapter 8.

In 404, Daowu had edicted that of the districts (*xian*) in the recently conquered territories, any with fewer than 100 households should be abolished.[17] Some of these may have been significantly depopulated in the course of the wars of the fourth century.[18] Many, however, would have actually still contained populations

---

14. See Von Glahn, *The Economic History of China*, 175, where building on Hori Toshikazu (see note 15) he rejects the notion that Equal Fields was an assertion that the monarch owned all land within the empire.
15. Hori, *Kindensei no kenkyū*, 99–114; WS 2.47, 3.53. For the Northern Wei Equal Fields, see also Yang Jiping 杨际平, *Bei chao Sui Tang jun tian zhi xin tan* 北朝隋唐均田制新探 (Changsha: Yuelu shu she, 2003) 38–60.
16. WS 53.1176; ZZTJ 136.4268.
17. WS 2.41. In fact, one commandery (*jun*, near the mod. Shaoyuanzhen, Henan) contained four districts but in all just 52 households, with 158 registered subjects on the rolls (WS 106A.2484–85).
18. Lewis, *China between Empires*, 51, suggests that as many as a million people may have fled the Yellow River region in the midst of the wars that brought Western Jin down. As noted above, however, Andrew Chittick in his *Jiankang Empire* has expressed doubt at the size of these migrations.

much larger than those recorded on what remained of census forms, with dozens, sometimes hundreds of families evading Wei levies by being incorporated into the "household" of a "clan master" (*zong zhu* 宗主), a designated local man who before Equal Fields served as the basic unit of Wei local administration in these territories.[19] These fellows had, of course, mixed interests. In the view of Wencheng, at least, local officials were corrupt: they "seize the food of the commoners in order to build up their own households, without fulfilling the royal taxes."[20] With implementation of the Equal Fields system in 485, central agents were sent out to guide local officials in implementation of the new policy. Previously, with only indirect control over the Yellow River plains through the *zong zhu*, Pingcheng had tried to create a reliable tax base by forcing populations to move up into the royal domain of the Datong Basin. Now, central power was—in theory at least—to be directly inserted into every village in the realm.[21]

The essential elements of the Northern Wei plan mandated that to each male 15 *sui* and over was assigned about 6.5 acres of "open land" (*lu tian* 露田) for grain production (with, where possible, another 6.5 acres as fallow ground). This land had been assigned to him; it would be taken back and redistributed when the fellow reached the age of 70. Women were allotted half the amount given men and—for those who could afford these things—allocations of land were also given for slaves and for plowing oxen. The allocated lands need not have been contiguous; this policy was implemented within the patchwork pattern of land holding seen on the Yellow River plains since Han, and obviously worked better within such a system. In some regions, however, the family was also permanently allotted smaller portions to plant mulberry trees for silk production.[22]

The tax system was reorganized around these innovations, taking as its basic measure the joint-filing husband and wife, who yearly owed to the state 7 bolts of fabric—silk or hemp depending on the region—and 13 bushels of grain.[23] To this were added smaller levies for unmarried inhabitants of the households, slaves,

---

19. WS 53.1180: This description of the status quo was presented in a memorial from the architect Li Chong, from the Gansu Corridor region, who argued here for establishment of the Three Headmen system, and would go on to serve as chief designer for the new capital at Luoyang. Yan, *Bei Wei qian qi zheng zhi zhi du*, 95–99, suggests this was a new system established by the Taghbach within the Chinese world, and compares the *zong zhu* to the local headmen (*ling min qiu zhang* 領民酋長) set up over the High Carts, and other groups.

20. WS 5.117. This does clash with the well-known position of Tanigawa Michio; see discussion in Chapter 2 note 2.

21. Hori, *Kindensei no kenkyū*, 97.

22. WS 110.2853–55, 7A.156, 53.1176; ZZTJ 136.4268–69. The figure used to measure land is *mu* 畝; in WS 110.2853 we are told that the main allocation to a man was 40 *mu*. Hou, "Bei chao de cun luo," 48, provides the figure of 677.4 square meters per *mu*. If this is correct—and Northern Wei figures are sparse and not always reliable—forty *mu* would figure to about 6.5 acres, or about 2.5 hectares.

23. Hori, *Kindensei no kenkyū*, 121–22. Only a few Northern Wei measuring devices have been found, and none for capacity: Qiu Guangming 丘光明, *Zhongguo li dai du liang heng kao* 中國歷代度量衡考 (Beijing: Ke xue chu ban she, 1992), 258. Going on the basis of Han measures, for which a *dan* 石 was about 20 liters, we can say roughly that the 22.9 *dan* which Hori, including additional taxes to pay official salary, calculates were required of the taxed couple would equal about 460 dry liters, or 13 US bushels. As for the bolts of fabric (pi 匹), these were 4 *zhang* long (WS 110.2852), which in this time would be about 40 feet (see Qiu, 69), so about 280 feet of fabric in all.

and oxen. Corvée service was also due, which could include participation in local militias, the beginning of a fundamental change in the nature of the Wei military touched upon in Chapter 11. Taxation was, however, now somewhat equalized, along with the fields, as part of a larger plan to atomize the farming population into small households, and so, of course, make them easier to control. By the end of Wei, these taxes were being levied on some 5 million households.[24] The system was more complex than this, of course, and it evolved over time. It never worked perfectly, and was always adapted for local conditions; officeholders, for instance, were allowed more extensive holdings than the average family. It was nevertheless a groundbreaking innovation—dependent on the new state strength Pingcheng drew from its solid and reliable armies—that for more than two centuries, long after the fall of Northern Wei itself, would tap the productive power of the Chinese farmlands to provide a stable fiscal basis for a series of increasingly powerful dynasties, culminating, of course, in Tang.[25]

Interlocking with the full implementation of government control and taxation of the land was the nature and organization of the local administration.[26] Previously, local officials had had to negotiate with the "clan master" to collect taxes. A year after publication of the Equal Fields edict, however, the prominent official Li Chong sent up a memorial proposing another, indispensable aspect of this broad reform package, establishment of the system of "three headmen" (*san zhang*), who had a vertical relationship stretching from the neighborhood up to the village and above that to a "unit" (*dang*) of 125 families.[27] The headmen had the onerous duties of counting heads, collecting taxes, organizing corvée and militia service, and overseeing the community in general. The situation was made easier by a related, earlier reform. As seen above, a major problem confronting the Wei state was lack of salary for civil officials, leading to corruption or, as with Gao Yun, straitened circumstances for those who chose to follow the regulations. Efforts were made to rectify this with establishment in 484 of salary for government officials.[28] This was, in fact, no doubt part of the motivation for instituting Equal Fields in the next year, 485. Establishment of a salary system was a dramatic

---

24. See Ge, *Zhongguo ren kou shi*, 1: 474, drawing on WS 106.2455, where we are told that the Wei population in the early 520s was something like twice that of Jin in Wudi's Taikang period (280–289), which had been about 2,450,000 households.

25. Denis Twitchett, "Introduction," in *Cambridge History of China*, Vol. 3, *Sui and T'ang China, 589–906*, Part 1, ed. Denis Twitchett (Cambridge: Cambridge University Press, 1979), 24–25; Victor Cunrui Xiong, *Emperor Yang of the Sui Dynasty: His Life, Times, and Legacy* (Albany: State University of New York Press, 1999), 180–82.

26. See Hori, *Kindensei no kenkyū*, 124–28, on the linking of Equal Fields and three headman policies.

27. WS 53.1180, 7B.161, 110.2855; ZZTJ 136.4271–72; and Hou Xudong 侯旭东, "Bei chao 'san zhang zhi'" 北朝三长制, in his *Bei chao cun min de sheng huo shi jie* (Beijing: Shang wu yin shu guan, 2005), 112–25.

28. WS 7A.153–54. WS 110.2852; Koga Noboru 古賀登, "Hoku-Gi no hōroku sei shikō ni tsuite" 北魏の俸禄制施行について, *Tōyōshi kenkyū* 24.2 (1965): 152–76; Wang Daliang 王大良, *Fan fu bai: lai zi gu dai Zhongguo de qi shi: yi Bei Wei guan li shou ru yu jian cha ji zhi wei li* 反腐败：来自古代中国的启示：以北魏官吏收入与监察机制为例 (Beijing: Min zu chu ban she, 2001), Chapter 2. A year after this, salaries were also established for peerages held by members of the imperial family: WS 7A.155.

change for civil officials, bringing them on a par with military officers, which in particular favored Chinese officeholders, especially those of lower tiers, who generally lacked the power and connections of army men.

Equal Fields was a radical proposal, opposed by many at court who felt the threat of growing central control. In the end, however, it was decreed that it would be. Though we are told that Xiaowen "received [the memorial proposing the innovation] with a deep sense of its significance," and that this was the basis for implementation,[29] it is clear that the other Buddha was deeply involved in these discussions as well. Things had changed somewhat since the time Xiaowen was a child, 10 or 15 years before, when "all matters big or small were turned over to the Empress Dowager. . . . [When it was needed that] things be decided in haste, there were many in which the emperor was not involved," which, we are told, had "shocked those within the court and beyond it."[30] By the time of implementation of the Equal Fields, however, Xiaowen was 17 or 18 years old, and much more involved in court activities. Still, in 486, when the three headman proposal was sent up to the throne, it was Wenming who read it, declared it a good idea, and summoned the regime's leadership for discussion.[31] While Yuan Pi approved the plan, saying, "it will be to the benefit of both the public and the private," others were staunchly opposed, expressing concern that "it will in fact be difficult to implement," or "I fear it will cause chaos." Unswayed by these arguments, Wenming replied that "If we establish the three headmen, then the levies (ke 課) will have regular criteria, the land-taxes (fu 賦) permanent apportionment, the concealed households can come forth, and those who have been presumptuous can cease. How is this not possible?" The plan was now implemented.

Implementation of the three headmen system—and the institutional package as a whole—gave Wei an enormous increase in control over the farming populations down on the plains and a much more efficient system for extracting wealth therefrom.[32] Some at least of the old rural leadership adapted to the changing times by entering state service and drawing those newly established salaries. At any rate, seeing that taxes came to just a tenth of the previous rates (for those who paid taxes), in the end "all between the seas were at peace."[33]

Xiaowen was not, however, at peace when the elder of the two sages died in 490. A pause now came in all major matters of state, while the emperor mourned her death in dramatic fashion over several years.[34] Her body was placed in a

---

29. WS 53.1176.
30. BS 13.496 (WS 13.329).
31. WS 53.1180; ZZTJ 136.4271–72.
32. For its continuing success even at the end of Wei, as the regime collapsed, see the article by Zhou Yiliang 周一良, "Cong Bei Wei ji ge jun de hu kou bian hua kan san zhang zhi de zuo yong" 從北魏几个郡的户口变化看三长制度的作用, rpt. in his *Wei Jin Nan Bei chao shi lun ji xu bian* (Beijing: Beijing da xue, 1991), 52–66.
33. WS 110.2856. This statement is certainly an exaggeration.
34. ZZTJ 137.4296–98, 4323.

mounded tomb sitting on Fangshan hill some 20 miles northeast of Pingcheng. Begun in 481, this Eternally Resolute (Yonggu) Mausoleum was one of the largest of the Wei tombs, with two chambers under a mound standing some 75 feet tall.[35] It is interesting to note that we see in this a break with the past. The empress dowager was buried not in the traditional complex of Jinling tombs in the hills northwest of the Datong Basin but in her own designated site, apart from and independent of the graves of the royal house.[36] There was precedent for this, established by other recent dowager empresses. But there was no precedent for the further decision made while Wenming was still living that her ward, the emperor, would also not be laid to rest among the Jinling but on Fangshan hill as well, in a mound next to hers that—quite interestingly—is appreciably smaller. In the end, the young emperor had been to the advantage of the Feng family.

---

35. WS 7A.147, 114.3039; Dien, *Six Dynasties Civilization*, 182–84; A. G. Wenley, *The Grand Empress Dowager Wên Ming: And the Northern Wei Necropolis at Fang Shan* (Washington, DC: Freer Gallery of Art, 1947), 10–12.
36. Li, *Bei Wei Pingcheng shidai*, 260–62; Pearce, "Nurses, Nurslings and New Shapes of Power," 308.

To Luoyang

Looking south from Fangshan hill during Wenming's funeral, the emperor should have been able to glimpse his capital city, a thousand feet below and some 15 miles away, and in between the Deer Park where his father had for a time lived as Retired Emperor. But the dense zone of cultivation down along the Sanggan, almost 50 miles away, would have been out of sight, much less the plains of the Yellow River far below. With construction of the Fangshan tombs, the Two Buddhas had recentered the world of the imperial dead to Pingcheng from the hills south of Shengle. Xiaowen was now about to embark on a much grander project to recenter the throne itself, and place it at a location almost 500 miles away. His actions would represent radical divergence from the way of his forebears who had created the empire.

Out of physical sight, the farmers along the Sanggan seem to have been generally out of mind of those in the Pingcheng palaces. This essential economic base for the Wei capital had been created by forced transportations, beginning with Daowu's enthusiastic guidance of tens of thousands of people to the precarious environment of the highlands. These transplantations had then continued for more than half a century. For many of those transported, things were not going well. The rich in the city thrived. Even their slaves, complained a Confucian moralist, wore silks. But the farmers down in the Sanggan valley, he went on, are hungry and half-naked.[1] Vagrancy and crime had led in 479 to the institution of a new capital police force; this did not, however, prevent plots of rebellion in and around the court, some by men of the cloth.[2]

As it was becoming harder and harder to control, so this marginal agrarian region was becoming harder and harder simply to support. The city could no longer depend on local agriculture to feed it, in part because of its rapid growth over two or three generations, in part because of the understandable wish of the half-naked transportees to abscond whenever possible, and in part because of a significant cooling of the area's climate.[3] Having under Taiwu peaked at around a

---

1. WS 60.1332–33. One effort to cope with the situation involved opening up the mountain game reserves to let commoners hunt there: Song, *Bei Wei nü zhu lun*, 159.
2. WS 111.2877; WS 7A.150; WS 44.994.
3. *NQS* 57.990. See Chapter 10 note 50; as well as Hsu Shengi, "From Pingcheng to Luoyang: Substantiation of the Climatic Cause for Capital Relocation of the Beiwei Dynasty," *Progress in Natural Science* 14.8 (2004): 725–29.

million, the region's population then began a slow decline. The city was, however, still painfully crowded: a 491 edict described it as a place where "the wards and apartments are like the teeth of a comb, and men and spirits throng together."[4] All those men and spirits needed fed, and already in the late 460s, Xianwen had adjusted the tax code to mandate that the three highest categories in the newly won Shandong territories would deliver grain up to the capital.[5] These efforts were obviously continuing twenty years later when, in 482, 50,000 men were called up to improve the old Lingqiu Road, built originally by Daowu, and a generation before used by grandfather Wencheng on his Southern Progress. No longer a staging ground for archery, the road was now a delivery route for grain, laboriously brought up from the plains down below.[6] (In more recent times, more or less the same road has been traveled by convoys of coal trucks, carrying their cargo east.) This did not, however, solve the problem and in 487 the capital was beset with a disastrous drought, combined with another cattle plague. An edict was given permitting subjects to depart for richer fields and, we are told, perhaps with exaggeration, that 50 or 60 percent of what remained of the population fled south.[7]

Slow decline in the populations of the Pingcheng region thus accelerated and after this—that is, for the six or seven years that would pass before relocation of the capital—there were no major famines.[8] But the 487 famine and the difficulty of controlling and supporting Pingcheng had added impetus to ideas that seem already to have been developing in the young emperor's mind. The Chinese lands had been from the beginning an object of attention for the Taghbach in material terms—the reader may remember bits of lacquerware found in Serbi graves up by Hulun Nur, or more recently, Taiwu's comments to the Song emperor on desired commodities. Interest had certainly grown in Pingcheng regarding the Yangtze as an alternative and superior hub of commerce down in the East Asian heartlands.[9] By the time of Xiaowen, for some at least of the Taghbach elite it had also become a center of culture and—whatever one makes of this word—"civilization." Schooled in the Chinese classics, one of the great traditions, Xiaowen now took a

---

4. WS 113.3055. In terms of difficulty of support, Wang, *Zhuan xing qi Bei Wei de cai zheng yan jiu*, 146–47, puts forth desire for a more stable tax base as one at least of the reasons for Xiaowen's move; Jenner, *Memories of Loyang*, 37, emphasizes the twin motivations of transportation and "civilization." Discussing the Bronze Age Shang monarchy, Victor Mair points out that it was cheaper for the king to go to the grain, than to bring the grain to him and his court: "The North(west)ern Peoples and the Recurrent Origins of the 'Chinese' State," 67.

5. WS 110.2852, 7A.151.

6. WS 110.2858; Yan, *Bei Wei qian qi zheng zhi zhi du*, 114.

7. WS 110.2856.

8. WS 110.2857.

9. These trends are depicted in the famous "Tribute Scroll" (*Zhi gong tu* 職貢圖), painted in the 520s or 530s by Xiao Yi 蕭繹 (508–555), who under unfortunate circumstances became emperor of the doomed Liang dynasty from 552 to 554. The version we have is an early modern copy, but shows that Persians and Hephtalites came to Jiankang just as eagerly as they came to Luoyang, or perhaps more. For a recent set of studies on the scroll, see Suzuki Yasutami 鈴木靖民 and Kaneko Shūichi 金子修一, *Ryō shokukōzu to tōbu yūrashia sekai* 梁職貢図と東部ユーラシア世界 (Tokyo: Bensei shuppan, 2014).

path many had followed before—and would in the future—in the Chinese lands, and in neighboring regions such as Korea or Japan: ascribing authority to that canon.[10] But while this "great tradition" had for him taken up a centrality in both physical and metaphorical senses, it is also clear that in Xiaowen's view the "central states" would be centered on and ruled by him and his progeny. Though he enjoyed reading Zhuangzi, he did not seek that thinker's relativism.[11] Much of what attracted Xiaowen to the Chinese tradition was the absolute power he at least imagined that the Han monarch had possessed.

For the monarch, the benefits of ruling from the edge—pointed out long before by Cui Hao—had thus become less significant and less attractive, and as the mourning period for Wenming came to an end he began actively to look for a new capital, in the interior of the Chinese world. Though there were several possibilities, including the city of Ye—which had mesmerized Daowu almost a century before—in the end Xiaowen chose as his new capital the old Zhou city of Luoyang, where 1,500 years before the Duke of Zhou had in the midst of hectoring the conquered officers of Shang put forth the idea that the rightful ruler was called forth by the Chinese version of the high sky god, Tian. For some, Luoyang was close by the very center of the physical world.[12] In more practical terms, it was at the center of a network of waterways for efficient transportation that, if not the equal of Jiankang, was certainly an improvement on the Lingqiu Road.[13] The city was also close to the southern marches, to which Xiaowen's attention had come increasingly to turn.

Interest in making the ancient Zhou monarchy a model for once again perfecting an increasingly imperfect world had become popular among Chinese thinkers during the crumbling of Han and its successors. Occasionally seen in early Northern Wei, such interests became more systematic under Xiaowen, who in a regime without clear cultural roots seems to have taken a personal interest in using these ancient models to justify new institutions and new systems of political and social organization.[14] Efforts to "resurrect antiquity"—invent tradition—reached their high point under the successor regime Western Wei (535–557), when an entirely new table of bureaucratic organization would be drawn up on the basis of the archaic nomenclature of *The Rites of Zhou* (*Zhou li*), a Warring States text that presented itself as describing the ideal world of Zhou.[15]

---

10. Goody, *The Power of the Written Tradition*, 56, 59, discusses how the "power of a single form"—the books of a literate culture—plays a central role in efforts to establish a single, fixed hierarchical order.

11. For his reading of Zhuangzi (and Laozi), see WS 7B.187.

12. Jenner, *Memories of Loyang*, 45.

13. WS 79.1754; ZZTJ 140.4384.

14. For an early example, an effort by the doomed crown prince Huang to promote cooperative agriculture based on the prescriptions of the "Documents of Zhou," "Zhou shu" 周書 (viz., "Zhou li" 周禮, for which see just below), see WS 4B.108–9. At the same time, the crown prince attempted to ban drinking, itinerant peddlers, and "wild entertainments" 雜戲. For Xiaowen, a generation or two later, see his use of *Zhou li* to justify establishment of salary for civil officials (WS 7A.153) and changes in his dynasty's system of weights and measures (WS 7B.178).

15. Scott Pearce, "Form and Matter: Archaizing Reform in Sixth-century China," in *Culture and Power*,

For Xiaowen that ideal world was centered on Luoyang. It had not been for Wenming. Before death, she had explained that the reason she wanted her tomb on Fangshan hill, just north of Pingcheng, was that she wanted him regularly to come to honor her tomb. "My spirit," she had gone on to say, "will be here for a hundred years."[16] Xiaowen, however, would not, perhaps wishing among other things to escape from that spirit.[17] In 493, at the end of mourning for the matriarch done in accordance with the Chinese book of rules, he initiated discussion with members of the court of his wish to march his army south.[18] As we see in the account below, it is likely the invitees intuited that his real aim was to relocate the capital to Luoyang. These encounters took place in the midst of a new array of borrowings to Pingcheng that Daowu, even Taiwu, would have barely understood, beginning with a retreat to the left verandah of the new Hall of Light (Mingtang) Xiaowen had built in homage to the traditions of Han, about a mile and a half south of the city's outer walls.[19] There the Chief Minister of the Court of Imperial Sacrifices (Tai chang qing) was ordered to do a divination using the "Book of Changes" (*Yi jing*), a central text of the Ru canon.[20] The hexagram the prognosticator came up with was "Ge" 革—"recasting," "molting," perhaps "revolution"—whereupon Xiaowen is said to have restated a passage from the commentary: "Tang [the founding ruler of Shang] and Wu [of Zhou] recast the mandate by being obedient to Heaven and in accord with men" 湯武革命, 順乎天而應乎人.[21]

Such sayings can be interpreted in various ways. While Xiaowen was apparently reading Ge as referring to a "molting," or shedding of old skin—"removal of that which is antiquated"—it seems that the listeners at the Mingtang conference

---

149–78; Benjamin A. Elman and Martin Kern, ed., *Statecraft and Classical Learning: The "Rituals of Zhou" in East Asian History* (Leiden: Brill, 2010).

16. BS 13.495–96 (WS 13.328–29); Wenley, *The Grand Empress Dowager Wên Ming*, 5.

17. Li Ping, *Bei Wei Pingcheng shi dai*, 268–74, discusses the frictions that had existed between the dowager and the emperor; Song, *Bei Wei nü zhu lun*, 172, argues that his mourning for his foster mother was sincere. Probably both are true. There were, of course, an array of reasons why Xiaowen would have wished to leave, including a much broader network of irksome relationships within the Pingcheng community.

18. For the process of Xiaowen's mourning for Wenming, see WS 108C.

19. See Duan and Zhao, *Tian xia da tong*, 19. Victor Xiong, in his "Ritual Architecture under the Northern Wei," in *Between the Han and Tang: Visual and Material Culture in a Transformative Period*, 69, suggests the Pingcheng Mingtang was based on a "synthesist model" drawn from competing schools of thought in the Chinese world; Tseng, *Making of the Tuoba Northern Wei*, 27, resists attempting to place this structure within Chinese tradition and argues instead that "we should interpret this architectural compound based on its actual functions rather than on its name."

20. WS 19B.464–65. Description of these events is taken largely from WS 19B, which contains the biography of Cheng, the Prince of Rencheng 任城王澄, of whom we shall see more just below. The version of these exchanges on the Luoyang move given in ZZTJ 138.4329–31 draws on brief comments in NQS 57.990 on negative aspects of weather in the Datong Basin, before going on to borrow wholesale from Rencheng's biography. Rencheng, near mod. Jinan, Shandong, came under Wei control during the lifetime of Cheng's father, Yun, who in 464 was enfeoffed as the first Prince of Rencheng; as with most peerages, until 483 it was an "empty fief," from which the peer himself did not personally extract taxation (see Chapter 15 note 28).

21. For comments on this by Richard Wilhelm, and a different translation, see his *The I Ching: or Book of Changes*, tr. Cary F. Baynes, 3rd ed. (Princeton, NJ: Princeton University Press, 1967), 189–192, 635–640.

heard something more like "revolution."[22] "None among the officials," we are told in the biography of Xiaowen's kinsman Cheng, the Prince of Rencheng, "dared speak," until the prince himself did, pointing out that "What the *Yi[jing]* says of Ge is that it is change. For Tang and Wu that was propitious, since they were about to respond to Heaven and obey the people by changing [the heavenly] mandate of [who will be] ruler and [who] subject. But Your Majesty, the Emperor, already possesses all-under-Heaven. . . . This is not a hexagram for a lord. This can't be entirely propitious." Enraged, his face turning red, the 26-year-old monarch now barked out that "The dynasty's altars are Our altars! Rencheng, you're wanting to block the army [from proceeding south]!," to which the prince replied that "the altars—I know they are Your Majesty's altars. But your servant is a servant to those altars. When joining in discussions, I will dare put forth all the foolish thoughts in my head." A long pause intervened before the emperor, who seems to have deeply resented his kinsman's response, smiled and said, "Each shall speak his mind—and what harm then in that?"

The conversation continued one-on-one after Xiaowen had returned to the palace, summoning Rencheng to tell him that "the fuss at the Hall of Light was because I was afraid that the group would argue, and block my grand design." Then having dismissed the servants, he talked to the prince alone; the report of the matter that eventually reached *Wei shu* presumably came from Rencheng, and was quite possibly now actually spoken between the two men in Chinese. "The undertaking [discussed] today—" Xiaowen went on to say, "know for sure that it's not changing. But—the dynasty rose in the northern lands, and then [we] moved to dwell in Pingcheng. Though we have all [within] the four seas, the ways [of the different regions] are not one. This space [here at Pingcheng]—it's a land for making war. One can't govern [here on the basis of] the perfect patterns (*wen* 文)."

On the basis of his biography in *Wei shu*, the Prince of Rencheng seems at first to have had real misgivings about the emperor's proposed relocation. But he too was a part of real change within the Land of Dai, particularly within the court's elite. The prince's father, with the Chinese name Yun, had grown up in difficult circumstances, being just five *sui* old when his own father, Taiwu's crown prince, Huang, was killed by grandfather. Hearing of the unceasing crying that followed, Taiwu had hugged the little one and himself teared up, saying, "what is it that you know, that you have the thoughts of a grownup?"[23] When grown up, the little one became under his brother Wencheng a key figure of the inner court and major military figure, and was enfeoffed as the first Prince of

---

22. See Wilhelm, *The I Ching*, 635 (and note that he translates the name of the hexagram itself as "Revolution [Molting]"), and his translation on p. 636 of *ge ming* 革命 as "political revolution." Not all agree with this reading. For translation of *ge* as "recasting," see Kroll, *A Student's Dictionary of Classical and Medieval Chinese*, 132.

23. WS 19B.461.

Rencheng. Under his nephew, the emperor Xianwen, he received appointment as commander-in-chief of the entire army (Du du zhong wai zhu jun shi). His son, our Prince of Rencheng, was a different sort. Though also playing an important military role for Xiaowen, Rencheng the Younger had when young loved to study the Ru classics, and when grown served in leading civil posts in an outer court, based increasingly on the forms of the Chinese empire, that under Xiaowen completely displaced the old inner court.[24] An observer from Jiankang is said to have commented that "Wei's previous Rencheng made his name with war, while Wei's current Rencheng shows beauty with his cultural refinement (wen)," on the basis of the latter's fine demeanor, and the elegance of the tone of his (Chinese) speech.

Rencheng the Younger was then perhaps already inclined to be won over by Xiaowen's concealed plans. So in the private chat in the palace that followed the Mingtang flare-up, the emperor went on to say, "I know it will be very hard to shift the winds, change the customs. [But] Mount Xiao and the Han Valley are the dwellings of emperors (di); the [Yellow] and Luo Rivers are the hamlets of kings (wang).[25] Pursuing this great undertaking; to have all of the central plains:[26] Rencheng—what are your feelings on this?"[27] The desired response was forthcoming. "The central district [through which run] the Yi and Luo Rivers," said the prince, "is the place to take hold of regulating all the world. Your Majesty controls the Chinese world [Hua Xia], has pacified its nine regions (jiu fu). When the commoners hear this, there should be great celebration." Conceding reality in the midst of his idealism, the emperor then went on to point out that, "The northerners love things as they are. When they suddenly hear we are about to move, we can't be without panic and disorder." To which the prince responded that "since this is an extraordinary matter, it ought to be managed by an extraordinary man. All we need is to have it decided by your wise mind—what then can this sort do?" "Rencheng," said the monarch, "you then are my Zifang."[28]

About a month later, Xiaowen's firstborn son Xun was named heir apparent. Announcement of a southern campaign was then sent throughout the realm, and to Jiankang as well, causing panic in Southern Qi (479–502), which was already in the midst of power struggles, certainly part of the reason for the planned offensive.[29] Xiaowen now went to visit Wenming's tomb on

---

24. WS 19B.464. Though not mentioned in Wei shu, evidence from an inscription suggests that Xiaowen dismantled the old inner court in 492: Wang, Zhuan xing qi de Bei Wei cai zheng, 4. He had not been completely idle while mourning Wenming.

25. Mount Xia and the Han Valley are just to the west of Luoyang, close by the Sanmen Ravine; the Luo River runs through Luoyang, while the Yellow River is a bit north.

26. This phrase—guang zhai zhong yuan 光宅中原 has become the title of a recent work by Ni Run'an, Guang zhai zhong yuan: Tuoba zhi Bei Wei de mu zang wen hua yu she hui yan jin.

27. WS 19B.464–65; ZZTJ 138.4330.

28. The name Zifang was a cognomen of Zhang Liang, who had supported the founder of the Han dynasty in his decision 600 years before to move his capital to Chang'an. See his biographies in SJ 55; HS 40.

29. ZZTJ 138.4331.

Fangshan hill, and having bade her farewell headed south, leading hundreds of thousands of men on foot and horse. The lesser tomb he had built for himself alongside would not be filled; he would be buried down at Luoyang.[30] Left in charge of the soon-to-be-abandoned northern capital was the *tigin* Yuan Pi.[31]

The troops were told that this would be another great march on Jiankang, like the one led by Taiwu 42 years before. But though Xiaowen did have real southern ambitions, the immediate aim was quite different.[32] Reaching Luoyang, an apparently scripted performance was staged, in which the emperor insisted that they continue further south while the Prince of Rencheng, together with the statesman Li Chong, insisted that the troops were not willing. The emperor now declared that "if the imperial carriage is not to continue south, then we should move the capital to this place."[33] To which Li Chong replied, "Your Highness has now remade the institutions of the Duke of Zhou, and made your capital at Chengzhou [Luoyang]."

But doubts persisted, even in Xiaowen's own retinue. "What do you have to say about your thoughts?," he asked Yu Lie, scion of an old and eminent Dai clan.[34] "If I take measure of my heart, and speak" said Yu, "I'm just right down the middle. Half of me likes the move, half longs for the old." "I feel very strongly," said the emperor, "that it would be better not to talk of that." More concretely, nothing had yet been rebuilt in the city ruined almost two centuries before and there was really nowhere for the hundreds of thousands of sudden arrivals to live. So though he praised the relocation, Li Chong went on to suggest it would be a good idea for the emperor to return north to wait for completion of the palace. Declining this, Xiaowen instead announced that he would go on a tour of the provinces, then stay for a time in the still-standing palaces at Ye, returning to Luoyang in the spring.[35] Li Chong was left at Luoyang to oversee construction, much of which was no doubt done by the transplanted army of Dai men, who perhaps felt some disgruntlement, doing backbreaking work in a world of heat and illness to which they were not at all habituated. In successive waves over the next year or two, more guardsmen were brought south, and then the imperial women and the bureaucracy.[36] These people now ceased to be "people of Dai," and were re-registered at Luoyang. They were now to live there, and be buried

---

30. WS 7B.170, 171; ZZTJ 140.4387.
31. BS 15.554 (WS 14.358–59). Pi was left with a half-brother of Xiaowen, the Prince of Guangling: WS 21A.546. Though Xiaowen is said to have much loved his brothers, and had Guangling accompany him down to the Yanmen Pass, the prince was dissatisfied with the situation, and at one point asked to withdraw from the court.
32. WS 53.1183, 7B.172–73; ZZTJ 138.4329–31.
33. WS 53.1183–84; ZZTJ 138.4339–41. And see Pearce, "Form and Matter," 164.
34. See WS 31.738; ZZTJ 138.4340. The original name of the Yu was transcribed as "Wanniuyu": Yao, *Bei chao Hu xing kao*, 58–60.
35. WS 53.1184.
36. ZZTJ 140.4389–90.

there as well, rather than in their original homeland.[37] This applied to monarchs as well—Xiaowen and his successors would not be buried in tombs near those of their ancestors in the Shengle area, but in mounded tombs in the hills north of Luoyang. Some of those who had by edict been moved south, finding the climate unbearable, were eventually permitted to maintain a sort of alternate attendance at court, coming down in the autumn and returning north in the spring.[38]

There was also discontent among the military men left in the north. Having used the Prince of Rencheng to help act out a scripted portrayal of forced halt at Luoyang, followed by public proclamation of relocation, the emperor then ordered that Rencheng go back north, where it was "necessary to visit the troops," who, we are told, were to a man unhappy with their monarch's choice.[39] The prince was able to calm them some, but in the second month of 494 the emperor himself went to hear the words of the officials he had left at Pingcheng.[40] The process began upon his arrival, when the leader of the caretaker government, Yuan Pi, asked leave to sing for the emperor. We are, unfortunately, not told what the song was—perhaps one of the "Songs of Dai," certainly in *guo yu*—but when it was done the emperor stated that "Having swayed Us to bring Our carriage back [north], the Duke[41] himself then sang to put forth what is on his mind. Now since the construction [down at Luoyang is proceeding] in stages, I have temporarily returned to the old capital." Shortly thereafter the emperor was assailed not by one but many, in a conference convened in the Hall of the Grand Culmen (Tai ji dian), which Xiaowen had finished just a few years before.[42] Some of the arguments were of a practical sort, such as statement of the reality that the world was still at war, and that "to raise a campaign, we will need war horses. If we have no horses, then we can't succeed in these things."[43] To which the emperor replied that, "Horses are always coming down from the northern regions, and we'll set stables up here. My dear sir—why worry about having no horses! Now, Dai is

---

37. There seem, however, to have been a few exceptions, including a man named Feng Hetu 封和突, a man of Dai relocated to Luoyang who when he died in 501 was granted special permission for burial in Pingcheng: see Datongshi bowuguan 大同市博物馆, "Datongshi Xiaozhancun Huage ta tai Bei Wei mu qing li jian bao" 大同市小站村花圪塔台北魏墓清理简报, *WW* (1983.8): 1–4; and discussion in Zhang, "Cultural Encounters," Chapter 5.

38. BS 54.1965; ZZTJ 141.4410.

39. WS 19B.465. In the biography of Xiaowen's half-brother, the Prince of Guangling, we are told that "many among the men and barbarians of the northern frontier could not understand" the justification for removal of the capital: WS 21A.546.

40. According to ZZTJ 139.4351 it took Xiaowen 29 days to go the approximately 450 miles from Luoyang to Pingcheng, which means his train was traveling at about 15 miles a day.

41. It should be noted that the emperor's reference to Yuan Pi as "duke" was a statement of reduction of his peerage; for further discussion, see below.

42. WS 7B.171.

43. WS 14.359. Though this chapter was, as mentioned above, reconstructed during the early modern Song period on the basis of *Bei shi* and other sources, this anecdote, and the one regarding Yu Guo just below, are not found in *Bei shi*'s much briefer account of these events (BS 15.554–55). Since some lines in the Yu Guo story are also garbled, it is fair to wonder if the Song scholars who reconstructed *Wei shu*'s Chapter 14 did not rely, in part at least, on a damaged version of the original. It should also be noted that the *Zi zhi tong jian* version of these events (139.4351–52) is quite different. A close study of this might be needed.

north of the Hengshan, and outside of the Nine Regions (of the Chinese world). It is on the basis of this that we move to the central plains."⁴⁴ The steward (*shang shu*) Yu Guo raised a more emotional issue, saying:

> Your Vassal really does not know what happened in ancient times, [but] if one hears the words of the common folk, [they say] the previous monarchs established their capital here [in Pingcheng]. There's no reason that one should want to move. I hold that we can't do it. The Central Plain . . . ⁴⁵ has had many usurpations. Since establishing the capital at Pingcheng, Heaven and Earth have both been steadfast, the sun and the moon regularly bright. It is true that your servant is shallow and narrow-minded, by nature dull in my understanding. In the end, [if we do this, I myself] will [no doubt] not cling to the lands of Dai and the Heng [Mountains], but instead take up the beauty of the [land between the] Yi and Luo Rivers. It is, however, the regular nature of things to feel at peace with [their own] land and sad about moving. If one morning I relocated south, I'm afraid that I would not be happy.

There is little one could say to rebut this heartfelt statement, and no evidence in the text that the emperor tried. For all the others, however, he attempted both to answer and give comfort, one by one, until the arguments had exhausted themselves.⁴⁶ And then he, no doubt exhausted himself, withdrew to the Pingcheng palace, and then to the new one in Luoyang. Some at least of those he left behind remained unconvinced, and more than that felt abandoned and betrayed.

* * *

The removal of the capital to the interior of the Chinese world undoubtedly had clear practical purposes: to draw closer to—compete more effectively with—the cultural and economic hub taking shape at Jiankang. It was only down in Luoyang that Wei monarchs began to mint their own coins, and attempt at least to incorporate their state into the growing, monetized trade networks taking shape in the Yangtze region.⁴⁷ It also allowed easier access to lands desired for incorporation into the Wei empire. Since the time in which Taiwu had docked his reed rafts and returned to Pingcheng, there had been increasing amounts

---

44. On efforts to establish new horse pastures nearer Luoyang, and the later decline of these pastures, see Shing Müller, "Horses of the Xianbei," 184; ZZTJ 139.4369. See also suggestions on importation of horses into the plains region in Knapp, "Use and Understanding of Domestic Animals."
45. The Zhonghua shu ju editors point out that this passage is garbled: see *Wei shu*, 368 note 13.
46. BS 15.555 (WS 14.360).
47. WS 110.2863. After the move, Xiaowen ordered the minting of *wu zhu* coins, which had first been made under the Former Han. These seem to have had limited circulation. See Wei, "Bei Wei shi qi de huo bi liu tong," 281–84. Some foreign coinage—Iranian or old Han—circulated privately. Underlying this was the situation described by Yan, *Bei Wei qian qi zheng zhi zhi du*, 118, who points out the early Wei treasurer of the Inner Court functioned only as a royal butler, storing and maintaining the treasury. More sophisticated fiscal authorities emerged only under Xiaowen.

of intercourse and interaction across the loose frontiers between Wei and the Jiankang regimes. Efforts to curb trade could lead to rebellion, while diplomats going both directions eagerly explored their hosts' marketplaces.[48]

But ideas and beliefs were also moving across the frontier, and overwhelmingly in one direction. Some within the Wei regime, including of course Xiaowen, saw a perfect order in the institutions and rituals and literary forms that came north. One particular figure involved in Xiaowen's reign has been put forth as symbol and embodiment of the process in its most complete form. This was a man named Wang Su, of a branch of the Wangs of Langye commandery (near mod. Linyi, Shandong) that had long before fled south with the Western Jin collapse and risen to great eminence under the Eastern Jin.[49] Almost two centuries later Wang Su and his father were still serving at Jiankang, now under the Southern Qi lord Xiao Ze (Wudi; r. 482–493). The situation ended badly for the Wangs, however, the father put to death by the Qi emperor, while the son, Wang Su, in 494 fled north to the city of Ye, within Wei territory. It would be the beginning of a prolonged period of instability in the Yangtze region.

Coincidentally, the Wei emperor was also in Ye when Wang Su appeared, waiting for his palace to be built down in Luoyang, 200 miles to the south. A sophisticated man, Xiaowen had in the course of his 27 years met many eminent figures of many different backgrounds. But whether because of the nature of the man, who was just a few years older, or the nature of the moment, the texts convey a special quality to the monarch's encounter with the expatriate, who had since youth "hunted"—not for deer or rabbits, but—"through the classics and histories," with a particular interest in the ritual texts and the *Book of Changes*. Even as a boy, we are told, Wang Su had had "something of a great ambition." At Ye, Xiaowen put aside formality to receive the gentleman scholar with deference, weeping, we are told, at the southerner's story of the killing of his father and his flight north.[50] "In smooth and elegant tones," Wang then went on to put forth his ideas on the origins of order and chaos, no doubt in abstract form drawing on the Ru canon, but in more immediate terms as well, "speaking of signs of the perils of a collapse of the House of Xiao," the ruling house of Southern Qi. This was, said Wang, "an opportunity that could be taken up" by Wei, as he "urged Gaozu (Xiaowen) to raise a major" offensive.[51] "Deeply," we are told, did these ideas "concur with the emperor's own opinions," which he "received with a sigh."

---

48. See further discussion in Pearce, Spiro, and Ebrey, "Introduction," in *Culture and Power*, 23. For the rebellion of a border district in reaction to attempts to shut trade down, see *Liang shu* 16.272; ZZTJ 147.4598-99.

49. See Wang Su's *Wei shu* biography (63.1407-12); there is also a scattering of mentions in Jiankang histories. Wang Su was a descendant of Wang Dao, a powerful statesman of Eastern Jin. For a general study of the Wang of Langye, see Mao Hanguang 毛漢光, "Zhong gu da shi zu zhi ge an yan jiu—Langye Wang shi" 中古大士族之個案研究—琅琊王氏, in his *Zhongguo zhong gu she hui shi lun* (Taibei: Lian jing chu ban shi ye gong si, 1988), 365–404.

50. NQS 57.998.

51. WS 63.1407.

In another reference to the Chinese past, they are said then to have compared their relationship to that between Liu Bei, founder in 221 CE of the Shu regime in Sichuan, and his famous advisor Zhuge Liang. A minor, but interesting, feature of the relationship is put forth in the southern history, *Nan Qi shu*, which states that part of what drew the Wei emperor to Wang was the perfume the southerner had daubed onto the walls of his new abode.[52]

Wang Su is remembered for two sorts of activity in the north: as a major commander on the southern front, and for leading the way in remaking Wei government along the lines of the old empire. In terms of the former, Wang was installed by Xiaowen as a regional commander-in-chief down in the region of Runan, in the far south of what is now Henan province. There he was permitted to raise troops on his own, from among the locals, and to a certain level himself bestow rank, with particular privilege for Qi defectors. The no-man's-land between Wei and Qi was a complex honeycomb of interests. Loyalty was local, and locals repeatedly jumped sides, seeking the best for their families and their neighbors. Others showed a fierce regional pride. In a situation where the days of the rapid, effective offensive were over, ties with a prestigious southerner were to Wei benefit. "On the frontier, those far and near came to give allegiance," to Wang Su, we are told. "Those who had submitted were like a marketplace."[53] He was eventually given the great honor of his own pipe and drum unit, and under Xiaowen's successor, Xuanwu (r. 499–515), a Wei princess.[54] Among an array of military and civil posts given Wang was Senior Rectifier (Da zhong zheng)—in charge of recommending locals for government office—and later a title containing more hope than substance: Inspector of Yangzhou, which is to say Jiankang.[55]

Great attention is thus given in *Wei shu* to Wang Su's military role. The southern histories make reference to this as well, but also claim the existence of another dimension of Wang's activity. Fifty years later, in 548, a Jiankang ambassador was attending a feast in the capital of Eastern Wei when the historian Wei Shou—whom we met in Chapter 2—snidely remarked that "today's heat must have come up with you," to which the southerner replied, "Previously, when Wang Su came here, he first established ceremony and ritual for Wei. Now I come on a diplomatic mission to make you remember hot and cold."[56] This is taken further in the

---

52. NQS 57.998.
53. WS 63.1411.
54. WS 63.1409, 1410. But note that for setbacks in the field, he was also chided by Xiaowen, and temporarily demoted (WS 63.1410), and later that the Prince of Rencheng, resenting the man's power, also laid claim that Wang retained ties with Qi, though these were rejected by Xuanwu and Rencheng punished instead (WS 63.1410, 19B.470).
55. WS 63.1408. There was a Northern Wei "province" of Yangzhou, with its seat south of mod. Shangqiu, Henan: WS 106B.2581–83. It will be noted, however, that unlike real Wei administrative units, no population figures are given; this was a statement of intent. See also Mou et al., *Zhongguo xing zheng qu hua tong shi: Shi liu guo Bei chao juan*, 1: 733–34.
56. *Chen shu* 26.326.

chapter on the "Wei Caitiffs" in *Nan Qi shu*, where it is stated that "for the caitiffs, Wang Su arranged their officials' bureaucratic ranks, completely like the central states," the term "central states" here having been transplanted to Jiankang. "In all there were nine ranks, each rank with two steps."[57]

Interestingly, however, there is no mention in *Wei shu* of any such activity at all on the part of Wang Su, despite long descriptions of other Chinese officials' involvement in reorganization of the court and the government.[58] While the relationship between Xiaowen and Wang Su was, to some extent, one of real effect, it seems (like the scripted halting of the army at Luoyang the year before) to also have been a form of theater, propaganda intended in this case to reassure the border populations, and to try to induce them to submit. The central theme of this performance was deferral of the monarch to the wise and learned gentleman, a frequently seen leitmotif within the Chinese literary tradition, ascent to the latter role being, of course, the ambition of those who wrote these tales. No doubt something of this sort did at times actually take shape. But caution is advisable, for Xiaowen and Wang Su, and perhaps for Liu Bei and Zhuge Liang as well. It seems that an East Asian form of Clifford Geertz's "theatre state" was being presented here, by which Xiaowen attempted "to construct a state by constructing a king," or a *huang di*, in a play performed before a Chinese audience in the loose borderlands between Jiankang and Luoyang.[59] But plays aren't always well received. Despite some defections (going both ways), this performance did not result in widespread submission to the Confucian sage-king at Luoyang. The fierce defender of a siege laid by Xiaowen on the border town of Xinye (on the site of mod. Xinye, Henan; about 170 miles south of Luoyang) responded to calls for surrender by saying, "There's still a lot of soldiers and food within these walls; I don't have time to follow your petty caitiff words 小虜語." When captured, he made up a ditty: "[I'd] rather be a southern ghost / [I] won't be a northern slave" 寧為南鬼 / 不為北臣. His wish was fulfilled.[60]

---

57. NQS 57.998. These southern statements are emphasized in Wang Wanying's generally useful economic history, *Zhuan xing qi de Bei Wei cai zheng*, 4–5, with little attention to the lack of any such mention in the *Wei shu* account.

58. Though the *Nan Qi shu* account (57.998) asserts Wang Su played a role in establishing the 9-rank system for Wei, there is no mention of Wang Su at all in the "Monograph on Offices and Clans" (WS 113), or regarding bureaucratic reorganization anywhere in *Wei shu*, while in WS 68.1521 we are told that Xiaowen "keenly wanted a southern campaign, and exclusively consulted Wang Su on [such] military matters."

59. Clifford Geertz, *Negara: The Theatre State in Nineteenth-century Bali* (Princeton, NJ: Princeton University Press, 1980), 124. The author of this volume has recently discovered that a colleague, Andrew Chittick, has in his book *The Jiankang Empire* also drawn upon Geertz's insights to discuss the object of his study in the "Sino-Southeast Asian Zone." There certainly are more direct links between the Jiankang empire and the Southeast Asian state of Negara. But after mulling over abandonment of the term in this study, this author has come to the conclusion that, in some sense, all states are theatre states, basing effective rule—in part at least—on their capacity to induce most people most of the time to accept that rule. Here Geertz's insights into a particular regime have been drawn into a broader discourse.

60. NQS 57.997. Perhaps these were early seeds of the broad national feeling that according to Nicolas Tackett emerged more fully among Chinese in early modern Song: see his *The Origins of the Chinese Nation: Song China and the Forging of an East Asian World Order* (Cambridge and New York: Cambridge University Press, 2017).

With the move to Luoyang, and the public wooing of Wang Su, came a series of other changes, which in their symbolism did contain substance. Thus in 491, still in Pingcheng, the emperor reorganized his ancestral temple to conform to what commentators said was the model of the ancient Zhou dynasty, while in the next year he designated three of his palace halls with terminology taken from *Zhou li*.[61] Also in 492 the dynasty's element was changed to water, a claim within the Chinese world that succession had passed to Wei from Jin, with its metal element (and so that the current Jiankang regime was illegitimate).[62] This might have interested some in the southern borderlands. It is safe to say that such issues were of little or no interest to most at least of the military men still living up in Dai.

Regarding Dai, wishing to make real the "great harmony" (*tai he* 太和) of the realm that had since 477 been his reign name, Xiaowen's main intent was to eliminate its distinctive culture and identity and render nugatory the practices and habits of "the homeland the northerners held dear to their hearts" 北人戀本; the "webs of significance they themselves had spun."[63] What he wished was to move from being leader of a national kingdom to overlord of the diverse constituent parts of an empire.

A key example of this is abolition of sacrifice to Tengri in the capital's western outskirts. The rite was still being performed at Pingcheng in 492—the year before removal to Luoyang—when envoys from Jiankang described Xiaowen and his ministers in military dress and on horseback circling the western altar.[64] After the move, in 494, the ceremony was replaced by the classic Chinese model of sacrifice to Heaven on an altar south of the new capital city.[65]

In the same year, Xiaowen forbade at the Luoyang court the traditional "barbarian garb," the cape, hood, and trousers often seen on Wei tomb statuary, and in the next year use of "the northern languages" (*zhu bei yu*), at least for all those 30 and under. As for codgers above 30, whose "habits are already long entrenched," it was conceded they, unfortunately, just might not be able to change.[66] Though we have no detailed discussion of time frame or how this happened, it is clear

---

61. WS 7B.171, 108A.2749; Kawamoto Yoshiaki 川本芳昭, "Goko Jūrokkoku Hokuchō ki ni okeru Shūrai no juyō o megutte" 五胡十六国・北朝期における周礼の受容をめぐって, *Saga daigaku kyōyōbu kenkyū kiyō* 23 (1991), 10. For change of weights and measures to accord with Zhou models, see WS 7B.178.

62. WS 107A.2661, 108A.2747; ZZTJ 137.4318. For a view of these issues from within the Chinese historiographical tradition, see Liu, "Becoming the Ruler of the Central Realm," 89–93.

63. The first quote: WS 19B.465; the second is a paraphrase of the words of Clifford Geertz in his *Interpretation of Cultures: Selected Essays* (New York: Basic Books, 1973), 5. Having put forth this quote of Geertz in his book *Belonging*, 4, Anthony Cohen goes on to say on p. 9 of his object of study, the fishermen of Whalsay, among the Shetland Islands: "Whalsaymen never think of themselves as merely 'fishermen': they are *Whalsay* fishermen."

64. NQS 57.985, 991; Kang, *Cong xi jiao dao nan jiao*, 167–69.

65. WS 108A.2751; WS 7B.174. For the beginnings of use of the southern altar, see WS 7B.164. This is the central theme of Kang Le's book, cited in the previous note.

66. For clothing: ZZTJ 139.4370; Dien, *Six Dynasties Civilization*, 317–19. For language: WS 21A.536; ZZTJ 140.4386–87.

that by this time Chinese had become the main language spoken by the dominant figures at court—Xiaowen, his brothers, et al. Most, at least, of the speeches put forth in *Wei shu* during this period were spoken in the language in which they were written down, even if tidied up for Literary Chinese. But Chinese was still not the language of most *guo ren*. Thus, as seen above, "correct learning" was encouraged for those relocated to Luoyang who did not know Chinese, through translation into the *guo yu* of the *Classic of Filial Piety*.[67] But Xiaowen's efforts to "civilize" his troops don't seem to have been particularly successful (which is perhaps why no samples of these texts survive). "Northerners (*bei ren*)," Xiaowen at one point complained, "are always saying 'Why do northerners need to know books?' When We hear this, We are deeply disappointed."[68]

Up to this point, the imperial clan had been an ever-expanding lineage group, including all those descended in the male line from Liwei. Some of the *tigin* served the regime well, such as the princes of Rencheng, father and son, or the more distantly related Yuan Pi, the influential military man who had been a key figure in the enthronement of Xianwen and then argued Wenming out of deposing Xiaowen. But they were clearly also a source of bother to the emperors, with expectations of inclusion in collegial decision-making, threats of rebellion by the few who did not accept primogeniture, and in more prosaic terms, more privileged *tigin* households to support. "You get 'merit' for just standing there," it will be remembered Wencheng had said, 30 years before, "and all become dukes or princes." The issue would grow worse in the time of Xiaowen, who began to turn these titles from mere markers of status, into real sources of income.[69] In 492, the year before the move to Luoyang, Xiaowen began to deal with the problem by issuing an edict saying: "Distant kinsmen—not descendants of Taizu (Daowu)—and members of different lineages (*xing*) who are princes: all will be reduced to dukes; dukes will be marquises, marquises will be earls," etc.[70] For Yuan Pi, descended not from Daowu but from Daowu's grand-uncle, Yihuai, this meant demotion to be a *gong* ("duke"). Though specially excused from the stipend reduction so that he "still enjoyed (the income of) his fief," Yuan Pi, who had been left up north, still was not happy.[71]

In addition to pruning his own overgrown family bush, Xiaowen was more ambitiously attempting by fiat to construct a new elite, centered of course on himself and the now more narrowly defined royal line. In 495 he issued another

---

67. SS 32.935. This interest in the book continued under Xiaowen's son and heir, Xuanwu: WS 8.203.
68. WS 21A.550; ZZTJ 139.4359.
69. See WS 7A.155; ZZTJ 136.4266; and the discussion of substantial grants with peerage in Zhang Hequan 张鹤泉, "Bei Wei hou qi zhu wang jue wei feng shou zhi du shi tan" 北魏后期诸王爵位封授制度试探, *Zhongguo shi yan jiu* (2012.4), 73–96.
70. WS 7B.169.
71. BS 15.555 (WS 14.360). Another opponent of the move was Mu Tai, who had long before also opposed Wenming's plan to remove Xiaowen: WS 27.663.

edict explicitly identifying certain lineages—*Dai ren* as well as Chinese—on the basis of previous service to the throne (officeholding, and in the case of the *Dai ren*, peerage), which were then given privileged access to high office. In this way, Xiaowen merged particular groups from the two kinds of elites to create a new court elite, defined by and directly dependent upon state service, while limited by the Chinese grades of mourning (and so not endlessly expanding, as the imperial clan had been doing). Though this edict attempted to reorganize non-Chinese kinship on the basis of Chinese structures—perhaps to make them easier to register on census forms—it also guaranteed chosen Serbi groups a continuing role in the state and placed a sort of quota on Chinese access to key government posts.[72] (At the same time, however, it significantly reduced possibilities for promotion within the general *guo ren* population; the days of "original equality" were now entirely done.) In 496 the process was completed by replacing the old names of non-Chinese kinship groups with (mostly) single-syllable Chinese names. Thus "Taghbach" (Tuoba) became Yuan, "the Paramount," and so down the line for at least the vast majority of Serbi and other such groups.[73] These are the Sinicized names—Zhangsun, Lu, etc.—anachronistically attached by *Wei shu* to actors in the first century of Wei. Some liked these dramatic changes: a son of Lu Li, the "peerless one," who married a girl of the eminent Chinese Cui family of Boling, is said previously to have resented the multisyllabic nature of his family name.[74] Some, such as "Yuan" Pi, did not like it at all.

It might also be presumed that it was during this time that the monarchic title "khaghan" ceased to be formally used as well, though, never having been acknowledged in *Wei shu*, we cannot expect the book to tell when it was formally abandoned. And anyway, it wouldn't have been abandoned by all: the common *guo ren*, who did not know Chinese, would have continued to use the term to refer to his far-off lord.

In these ways, Xiaowen redrew the main lines of the socio-political map, attempting to replace a divide between conquest polity and the subject populations with distinctions based on class, class as defined by the monarchy. This was a bold experiment by an innovative Young Turk. With the benefit of hindsight, we know that it would within a generation lead to disaster for the dynasty.

---

72. WS 113.3014–15; ZZTJ 140.4393–94; Albert Dien, "Elite Lineages and the T'o-pa Accommodation"; and Eisenberg, *Kingship in Early Medieval China*, 90. Regarding reorganization of kinship groups along lines established long before under Qin and Han, the comments of a northern visitor to Jiankang needs noted: "I am a Serbi and do not have a surname" 我是鮮卑，無姓 (SoS 59.1600). For Inner Asian populations, forms of organization other than the family name had regularly been seen: Xiongnu are said to have only had personal names (HS 94A.3743; SJ 110.2879); while early on, Wuhuan and Xianbei took their "surname" from their leader (HHS 90.2975; SGZ 30.832). For Xiaowen and his evolving government, assignment of surnames of the Chinese style would certainly make such people easier to register on government forms, and would also undercut the persistence of old ties that had bound together groups such as the Helan after their forced incorporation into the Wei state.

73. ZZTJ 140.4393; WS 7B.179; WS 113.3006. It must here be restated that since "Serbi do not have surnames," it seems likely that "Taghbach" had not previously been used as a surname in the Chinese manner.

74. WS 40.911.

Accompanying—and clearly related to—these attempts to redesign the nature of the officeholding elite were various measures to reform the administration itself, to weed incompetents out of a bloated bureaucracy: this may have included a *tigin* or two, who, as Wencheng had said, "when We are in a good mood" had sought office, begged for a sinecure, thus draining the treasury. Firings need done, Xiaowen at one point lectured his ministers—and you haven't been doing them. Regular evaluation of officials was now instituted, and those who could not speak Chinese removed from court.[75] The system of civil exams was enormously expanded, paving the way for Sui and Tang.[76] Salaries were also cut for unassigned officials—those with bureaucratic rank but no real posting.[77]

At the same time, though apparently sans Wang Su, this systematizing visionary directly confronted the confusing patchwork that was itself the administration (or better, administrations). From the time of Daowu until the early years of Xiaowen's reign, *Wei shu*'s "Monograph on Office and Clan" tells us, the "inner and outer bureaucracies regularly had [offices] removed and added, such things perhaps done on an *ad hoc* basis. There was no regular catalog."[78] Or, the catalog existed in the mind of the Taghbach khaghan. Seeking, as always, an ideal order of the sort described in the texts he had taken as scripture, in 493 Xiaowen established the first complete and regular catalog we have of official titles for Wei. Creation of a single, unified government system meant, of course, an end to the inner court that had for more than a century been the conquerors' control system over the expanding government; as noted above, this seems to have been done in 492.[79] Much that Xiaowen considered dead wood would have been left up at Pingcheng when he moved his capital the next year. Though it must have seemed quite clear on paper, when applied to the actual, complex workings of the Wei government—with, among other things, different administrative structures for different sections of the population—the 493 plan was unworkable. A second list was published in 499, the year of the emperor's death.[80] It was implemented by his heir, Xuanwu, as an "eternal institution" (*yong zhi*).

Some *Dai ren* within the regime—the lucky ones with newly locked-in privilege—welcomed these changes, or at least adapted to them. Others— even some both young and privileged—rebelled. Perhaps most prominent was Xiaowen's own adolescent son, the heir apparent Xun. Born in 483, Xun had ten

---

75. ZZTJ 139.4353; 140.4387.

76. Dai Weihong 戴卫红, *Bei Wei kao ke zhi du yan jiu* 北魏考课制度研究 (Beijing: Zhongguo she hui ke xue chu ban she, 2010), 39–58; and for an overview of the issue during this age, Albert Dien, "Civil Service Examinations: Evidence from the Northwest," in *Culture and Power*, 99–121.

77. ZZTJ 139.4358–59; 140.4386. Bloating of salary for redundant and unnecessary posts is a problem seen in many societies, including those of the Manchus and Tokugawa Japan (see, e.g., the depiction of this in Tetsuko Craig, tr., *Musui's Story: The Autobiography of a Tokugawa Samurai* [Tucson: University of Arizona Press, 1988]).

78. WS 113.2976.

79. See this chapter's note 24.

80. WS 113.2977–3003; WS 7B.172.

years later been raised to the status of heir apparent.⁸¹ He seems to have been a troubled young man, perhaps in part because when the 10-year-old was declared heir his reformist father had fallen back to the regime's "ancient practice" of despatching the mother. The father, for his part, was unhappy about the boy's dislike for books. After the move to Luoyang, we are told, the plump young man is said to have hated the hot southern weather, and wished to return north; he wore his hair in the traditional Taghbach braid, and when not around father, wore the banned apparel of a Dai cavalryman.⁸² Eventually in 496 he attempted to flee up to Pingcheng.⁸³ Captured before he even got out of the gates, the 13-year-old was beaten more than 100 times with a club by his father and an uncle, then deposed and imprisoned. In the end he was ordered to commit suicide.

Xun seems to have been attempting to go to Pingcheng to join a rebellion there that was already brewing. In 495, while Yuan Pi was still in Pingcheng, two of his sons who opposed the move to Luoyang had tried to keep him in the north to raise troops to cut off the Yanmen Pass and establish a secessionist regime with Xun as their khaghan.⁸⁴ Nothing came of this scheme and Xun was moved south later that same year with the rest of the palace inhabitants.⁸⁵ In the next year, however, after Xun's failed effort to return north, resentment became real action. The leader was Mu Tai, the governor of Hengzhou province (i.e., Pingcheng), a man of the Qiumuling clan and kinsman of the fellow seen in Chapter 14 visiting Lu Li at the hot springs.⁸⁶ Xiaowen had previously felt gratitude to Mu Tai, who long before had joined Yuan Pi in opposing Wenming's plan to dethrone him. By 496, however, that gratitude had completely disappeared. "Feeling in their hearts that Our move to Luoyang was not to be countenanced," complained Xiaowen, "they pulled together the princes and discussed calling on [my] son, Xun," to come join them.⁸⁷ Unable to accomplish this, they turned to other princes of the house. Some waited and watched.⁸⁸ The rebels' choice for the northern throne, however, the Prince of Yangping, then serving as governor of Shuozhou province (seat at Shengle), pretended to join the movement while sending a secret message down to Luoyang.⁸⁹ Xiaowen now summoned from sickbed his trusted aide, Rencheng, saying to him that "Mu Tai schemes to break our laws; he entices [to

---

81. WS 7A.152; BS 19.713-14 (WS 22.587-89).
82. NQS 57.996.
83. BS 19.713-14 (WS 22.588); ZZTJ 140.4400-1, 141.4410.
84. BS 15.556 (WS 14.361).
85. WS 7B.178.
86. WS 7A.180; and see his biography, WS 27.663. Note that also involved in the plot was a kinsman of Lu Li, Lu Rui 陸叡, the governor of Dingzhou (seat at Zhongshan, down on the plains). See his biography in WS 40.911-13; and overview of these events in ZZTJ 140.4402-4.
87. WS 40.913.
88. One of these was the Prince of Leling (adopted son of an imperial clansman named "Son of a Hu," Huer 胡兒), who "knew (about Mu Tai's plans) but did not report": WS 19C.516. For this he was reduced to commoner status, though this was reversed at the end of Xiaowen's reign.
89. ZZTJ 140.4402. See Yangping's biographies in BS 17.630 (WS 19A.442).

his cause members of] the royal house. Perhaps for Us it must be thus. The relocation of the capital has just been done, [while] the men of the north ache for the old. North and south struggle. Our Luoyang is not [firmly] in place."[90] To which Rencheng replied that "Tai and the others are fools. It is just because of their love for their homeland 戀本 that they do this; they don't have a long-range plan."

Rencheng was now sent north with an army. Separatist feeling seems to have been strong in Pingcheng. Apart from removal of the capital, deep resentment had grown among *guo ren* that the emperor was using more and more Chinese Ru scholars in his bureaucracy.[91] Among "the old families of the Dai countryside, those who joined in the plot were many."[92] The feelings of these people seem to have been summed up by the old codger, the *tigin* Yuan Pi. Unhappy with reduction of his peerage, he was also perturbed by many other changes Xiaowen had made. "He had always," we are told, "loved the old customs, and did not understand the new ways. Changing the government posts and regulating the clothes, forbidding the old speech—he could not accept any of these."[93] But the leader of the movement, Mu Tai, hesitated. And even if he had moved more decisively when Rencheng's force arrived, there was not much of an army at Pingcheng to raise. The core guard units had already been moved south, while most of the rest lived to the north in the garrisons, which don't seem to have been deeply involved in these events.[94] Realizing his cause was lost, and seeking one last victory, Mu Tai now led a force of just a few hundred to attack a negotiator sent by the Prince of Rencheng who had holed up in a gatehouse of Pingcheng's barbicans. Failing even that, he fled west alone on his horse. He and all the others were soon taken.

Xiaowen himself arrived on the scene a few months later, early in 497, en route collecting Yuan Pi, who had been living down in Taiyuan. Though Pi was not directly involved in the rising, his sons had kept him informed as it unfolded, and though he was "outwardly concerned it would not succeed, and with words argued [against it], his heart tended to affirm it."[95] This carried on into the interrogations of Mu Tai and the others, which Yuan Pi attended and during which the emperor constantly needed to tell him to sit down and observe, which is to say, shut up. In the end, it was ordered that all the major actors—Mu Tai, and Yuan Pi's two sons—would die for plotting treason.[96] Though implicated as well, Yuan Pi had earlier been granted a document forgiving him from any death penalty, and was spared, though he was reduced to commoner status. There was

---

90. WS 19B.468; ZZTJ 140.4402–3.
91. ZZTJ 140.4402. Though again, the government was still made up largely of men of northern extraction; see Chapter 14 note 45.
92. A comment made in the biography of one of the few who resisted involvement in the rebellion: WS 31.738; ZZTJ 141.4410.
93. BS 15.555 (WS 14.360); ZZTJ 141.4408–9.
94. WS 27.663.
95. BS 15.556 (WS 14.361).
96. BS 15.556 (WS 14.361); WS 27.663; ZZTJ 141.4408–9.

sorrow at the fate of the old man, who by this time had lived through 80 years. He accompanied the monarch's train back to Luoyang, where he was kept for a time. While Yuan Pi lived in the capital that had caused him such discomfort, Xiaowen sent attendants to do what they could to comfort the fellow. He later returned to Taiyuan, where he died a few years later.

Neither the failure of the aborted uprising, nor the death of Yuan Pi, put a total end to "love of the homeland" or to the old ways. True of the northern highlands, this was seen even down in Luoyang, as we see in a conversation Xiaowen had with Rencheng in 499 upon his return from his last campaign, in which the emperor complained that in his own capital he had seen women wearing the cap and short jacket of the old Serbi garb.[97] And despite Xiaowen's radical visions, the real power of the regime still actually rested on armies drawn from increasingly dissatisfied populations.

As for lands to the south, Luoyang now served Xiaowen as base for a complex relationship with Jiankang, which would for a few more years be under Southern Qi control. Diplomatic exchange between the two courts, revived in the late 480s, turned to war almost immediately after establishment of the new capital,[98] as living up to his original 493 claims Xiaowen personally led southern campaigns in 494 and 497.[99] Neither had great practical effect. The first began in the 12th month of 494 (January 495 in the Western calendar), spurred by rumors that the new Qi monarch was viewed as illegitimate, and more concretely, by an offer of surrender from the Qi governor holding the key city of Xiangyang (mod. Xiangfan, Hubei), on the Han River about 200 miles south of Luoyang.[100] Despite objections by the Prince of Rencheng and others that the troops and their families were not yet properly settled in Luoyang, the emperor still led his unhappy troops forth for half a year into the no-man's-land between Jiankang and Luoyang.[101] While on tour, Xiaowen lodged each night in a black felt "traveling palace" capable of holding 20 men.[102] Having noted this, the southern observer gathering information on the invading caitiffs went on to say that when on the road the carriage of the Wei monarch was surrounded by heavy cavalry guards, with "lances (decorated with) much pure white plumage."[103] Accompanying foot

---

97. WS 19B.469.
98. WS 55.1214; ZZTJ 136.4290.
99. It would be decades before diplomacy with Jiankang revived: see the tables in Cai Zongxian 蔡宗憲's *Zhong gu qian qi de jiao pin yu nan bei hu dong* 中古前期的交聘與南北互動 (Taibei: Dao xiang chu ban she, 2008), 400–1.
100. Xiangyang as military center is the subject of Chittick's *Patronage and Community in Medieval China: The Xiangyang Garrison, 400–600 CE*. For the rumors that Xiaowen heard that the new lord of Jiankang was a usurper, see NQS 57.993.
101. WS 19B.466.
102. NQS 57.994.
103. Peter Boodberg, "Selections from *Hu T'ien Yan Yüeh Fang Chu*," 137, links a term used in this passage—*he la zhen* 曷剌真—to the Mongol *atlačin, "horseman"; while Bao Yuzhu, "Kalaqin yuan liu," links this "Halaqin" ("Karqin") guard to later Inner Asian groups. Yan, *Bei Wei qian qi zheng zhi zhi du*, 174, suggests that for all the great changes made by Xiaowen, the military was changed the least.

soldiers, for their part, all had black shields and spears, and hanging from the latter were dark "toad streamers." In living black-and-white, and no doubt on a vaster scale, we see here the triumphal procession depicted on the walls of the Poduoluo Lady's tomb. Still, not much triumph came from Xiaowen's procession. Though not having made it as far south as his great-great-grandfather Taiwu, still more than 100 miles northwest of Jiankang, Xiaowen rather closely followed the elder's script. Climbing a hill to look down upon the city he had wanted to take, Xiaowen wrote a poem and then departed.

The next campaign lasted a full year, from the fall of 497 till the fall of 498. The army on this occasion was made up in part at least of infantry from the Yellow River Plain, some 200,000 of whom were called up for the offensive from the "provinces and commanderies" (*zhou jun*) through the new system of local administration.[104] But once again not much was accomplished: though a number of battles were won and the emperor briefly in the spring of 498 "graced Xiangyang with his presence," after a "display of arms" (*yaowu*) along the Han River, Xiaowen—who had fallen seriously ill—led his forces back north. It would be another 50 years before a successor state—the Western Wei—was able permanently to seize this critical steppingstone to the Yangtze region.

* * *

Underlying the occasional exploratory incursion was a lively cultural and economic rivalry between Luoyang and Jiankang. Xiaowen's claims to occupy at Luoyang the center of the world, to have received from Jin the mandate to rule that world, were of course contested by Jiankang, where new maps were created reapplying the names of famous sites under the Han empire to places in the Yangtze world, and the claim was made that possession of the Grand Jade Seal of the Qin Dynasty proved that legitimacy lay in the south.[105] And Xiaowen seems in some ways convinced of southern superiority. According to the southern authors of *Nan Qi shu*, Xiaowen "deeply valued the men of Qi," at one point gushing to his own officials that "there are so many good officials down in the land south of the Yangtze." To the emperor's great embarrassment, one of his men—an ethnic Chinese—snapped back that "In the land south of the Yangtze there are so many good officials—and they change their ruler annually. In the land north of the Yangtze there aren't any good officials—and we've had the same ruling family for one hundred years."[106]

---

104. WS 7B.184 speaks of this troop levy in 498, while Sima Guang has moved it back to 497, ZZTJ 141.4411.
105. Pearce, Spiro, and Ebrey, "Introduction," in *Culture and Power*, 14.
106. NQS 57.992.

Downfall of a Theatre State

One way to describe a state—any state—is on the basis of the two legs that support it. One of these is physical force, or the threat of physical force; in its most fully institutionalized form, the army. The other leg is the set of symbols and rituals that have been assembled, and more importantly actively displayed and performed, to be accepted by those who accept them. When enough are willing to do so, the state machinery can come to operate almost automatically, the lord simply folding his arms into his robes.[1] In its broader sense, the "theatre state" described by Clifford Geertz down in Bali extends far beyond Indonesia. One drawback, of course, appears when "organized spectacle" encounters armed men, who care neither for the spectacle nor the principles of its organization.

As a visionary, Cui Hao had wanted to reconstruct the state in which he found himself around symbols and rituals taken from his own tradition; as a realist, he had wanted to have a strong army up in the hills, which would maintain that state by "terrifying the people into submission." Another visionary, Xiaowen, apparently missed that point. The forced transplantation of most of his army down to Luoyang led to its slow decay, at the same time that spectacles grew grander, and imperial tax receipts grew larger. When a major civil war broke out 30 years later, the theatrics of symbol and ritual did not suffice. As the modern scholar Kang Le has said, in the title of his Yale thesis, it was "an empire for a city."[2]

* * *

Unlike visions, visionaries last only so long. This we have seen in Cui Hao's violent and sudden end. The life of Xiaowen was brought to an end by the illness he began to suffer from on the 497–498 campaign. Hearing news of a retaliatory offensive launched by Southern Qi in 499, he roused himself to lead troops south once again. Having rebuffed the southern army, he died on the road back to Luoyang, at the age of just 31. The 499 campaign was Xiaowen's last endeavor. It was also the last time that a Wei emperor led an army into the field, which

---

1. According to Confucius, the sage-king Shun ruled "simply by reverently and properly facing to the south" (*Analects* 15:4). This idea continued to develop in the Warring States period, taking its fullest shape in such Qin thinkers as Han Fei and Li Si.
2. Kang Le, "Empire for a City: Cultural Reforms of the Hsiao-wen Emperor (A.D. 471–499)" (PhD diss., Yale University, 1983).

Xiaowen did in the midst of a new form of entangling court debate in which a text master insisted that "since before the Wei and Jin dynasties, in a time of peace there has not been an emperor who in his carriage personally directed his armies."[3] To which Xiaowen had pointed out that Cao Cao won the day by "gathering up virtue and righteousness from within."

Xiaowen was succeeded by his son, Yuan Ke, the seventh Wei *huang di* (r. 499–515). The posthumous title assigned him after his death, Xuanwudi—meaning something like "god-king exuding might"—does not describe the reality of his reign particularly well. Yuan Ke was born in 483 to Xiaowen and a woman of the Gao clan from the region of modern Korea. He was named heir in 497, after the death of his rebellious sibling Xun, and assumed the throne two years later at the age of 16. This was not, of course, young for a Taghbach monarch—the oldest at accession had been the 17-year-old Mingyuan. But Xuanwu was not an effective leader. Power struggles raged throughout his reign and beyond, while the court grew increasingly divorced from its real power base—the armies of *guo ren* who had by organized force created the state.[4]

The state had by this time become almost entirely a family affair, the court struggles of Xuanwu's reign to a great extent animated by wives and in-laws, fighting over and around the emperor. One measure of Wenming's power over Xiaowen had been that during her life he never formally appointed a wife, but when he had finished his mourning for her, Xiaowen honored her yet again by raising one of her nieces to the status of empress.[5] Subsequently, a half-sister of the new empress, Feng Run, entered the harem and displaced her kinswoman, who was sent off to a nunnery.[6] In 497, Feng Run herself became Xiaowen's empress.[7] Though he is said originally to have loved her, the bond was in the end not a happy one. But the emperor was unwilling to depose another Feng empress.[8] He did, however, withhold all affections and, perhaps more important, ensured that despite her express wishes she had no contact with his new heir apparent, who no longer had a mother since Madam Gao had been killed, according to rumor by an agent of Feng Run. Decades after her death, on order of her son Xuanwu, Madam Gao would be immortalized by her presence on one of the most beautiful works of art to come from this age, a relief from the Binyang cave excavated down

---

3. WS 47.1047–48; ZZTJ 138.4331.

4. Skaff, *Sui-Tang China and Its Turko-Mongol Neighbors*, 14, points out that in East Asia during this period political identity was based on personal allegiance. Thus, the loyalty of the Northern Wei soldiers came from the monarch's personal leadership. When that leadership ended, so did the effective base of their loyalty.

5. BS 13.499 (WS 13.332). This was at the suggestion of Yuan Pi. See discussion in Holmgren, "Harem in Northern Wei Politics," 89.

6. For more detail on these events, see Balkwill, "When Renunciation is Good Politics," 247–49.

7. WS 7B.182. See her biography in BS 13.499–501 (WS 13.333–35).

8. ZZTJ 142.4435–36; Holmgren, "The Harem in Northern Wei Politics," 92–96, suggests exaggeration of the situation based on gender bias, particularly questioning the hints that she had been involved in the death of Madam Gao (see just below).

along the Yi River, at Longmen, which shows her with her attendants making faithful devotion to the Buddha.⁹

Madam Gao died in 497, Xiaowen two years later. His vacillation about what do with Feng Run ended on his deathbed, from which an order was issued that she die. Whether it actually came from Xiaowen is questionable: a brother is reported later to have said, "Even if we hadn't had that final command, my brothers and I would have had to make a plan to get rid of her ourselves. How could we let that immoral wife"—it is fair to wonder if this is the term actually used—"rule the realm, and kill us all?"¹⁰ Though the Feng line continued to play a part in politics into the Tang period, the family would never again reach the level of power it had held under Wenming.¹¹

As was touched on in Chapter 9, in Northern Wei collegial government of close kinsmen underlay the power of the monarchy. Never having worked perfectly, this increasingly unraveled down in Luoyang, which is perhaps part of the reason for increasing ascendency of palace women. In the beginning of Xuanwu's reign, uncles formed the core of a regency council. Here we see both the model and its failure. Never achieving even the pretense of a unified front, the regency council came to an end in 501 through the scheme of one of the royal uncles, the Prince of Beihai, who collaborated with Yu Lie, a commander of the palace guard, to persuade the young emperor to abolish the council and institute direct rule with the aid of Beihai. Xiaowen's closest sibling, Yuan Xie, the Prince of Pengcheng, was then pushed out of the government.¹² A niece of Yu Lie was taken as concubine and later promoted to be Xuanwu's first empress.¹³ In 504, the Prince of Beihai fell in turn, while Pengcheng's situation worsened with house arrest. The winner in these struggles was Gao Zhao, brother of Xuanwu's murdered mother, who upon his nephew's accession had married a sister of Xiaowen, while Xuanwu was given as concubine a niece of Gao Zhao (and of his late mother).

Marital politics now dominated the court, with a complexity that is perhaps wearisome for the modern reader, and was perhaps just as wearisome for contemporary participants. This was now less a struggle between the imperial house and its in-laws than among the various in-law families themselves. While Feng Run in 497 may have engineered the death of Xuanwu's mother née Gao, a decade

---

9. ZZTJ 141.4411. Liu Jinglong 刘景龙, *Bin yang dong: Longmen shi ku di 104, 140, 159 ku* 宾阳洞: 龙门石窟第 104、140、159 窟 (Beijing: Wen wu chu ban she, 2010), 8–10; and see also Amy McNair, "The Relief Sculptures in the Binyang Central Grotto at Longmen and the 'Problem' of Pictorial Stones," in *Between Han and Tang: Visual and Material Culture in a Transformative Period*, ed. Wu Hung (Beijing: Wen wu chu ban she, 2003), 157–86. The relief has been removed from the cave, and is now—controversially—at the Nelson-Atkins Museum in Kansas City; the matching relief featuring Xiaowen is at the Metropolitan Museum of Art, in New York.

10. WS 13.335 (BS 13.501). Holmgren suggests, on the basis of inference, that the emperor may not have actually given the command, and that this represented instead a power struggle between the Feng empress and the princes of the blood: "The Harem in Northern Wei Politics," 95.

11. Holmgren, "Social Mobility in the Northern Dynasties."

12. WS 21A.537–38; WS 8.193. For Yu Lie, see WS 31; Zhang, *Jin wei wu guan*, 2: 680

13. BS 13.502 (WS 13.336).

later it seems to have been the Gao family that caused the 507 deaths of Xuanwu's first empress—Yu Lie's niece—and her son, who was at that time Xuanwu's only possible heir.[14] Gao Zhao's niece was then elevated to empress. Opposing the elevation, Xuanwu's uncle, the Prince of Pengcheng, was charged with rebellion and forced to drink a cup of poisoned wine.[15] But Gao Zhao would not have final victory. While his niece the empress bore a daughter, in 510 a consort, a woman of the northwestern Chinese Hu family, gave birth to a son, Xuanwu's only available heir. Remembering the ancient practice, her consœurs in the harem urged Madam Hu to abort when she first showed pregnancy. "I will not," she replied, "shrink from my duty."[16] In the end, she was not put to death with her son's designation as heir, perhaps simply because there was no figure at court sufficiently strong to force Daowu's rule upon her. Still, Madam Hu was denied access to the baby boy, as were members of the Gao family. Control of the heir was the path to power, and Xuanwu would not give him over to anyone.[17]

Power struggles had also broken out in the Yangtze region, leading in 502 to replacement of Qi by the Liang dynasty (502–557) of a distant cousin, Xiao Yan (this dynasty conventionally called "Southern Liang"). But the Luoyang court made little serious effort to take advantage of the tumult in Jiankang, perhaps because it now lacked a strong-willed commander-in-chief. There were some border wars, but these too became entangled in court politics. In 514, Xuanwu tardily took up an option to have Wei forces push south from the Wei River valley into the rich rice bowl of Sichuan, which Jiankang had temporarily lost control of. He did not, however, follow the way of his forebears and head the army himself, but instead selected Gao Zhao as commander, perhaps trying to get him out of Luoyang. In 515, while the army was en route, Xuanwu died and after a brief factional struggle—made easier by Gao Zhao's absence—Madam Hu's five-year-old son was placed on the throne (this was Yuan Xu, the emperor Xiaoming, who would reign from 515 to 528, but never in any sense actually rule). Recalled to court, Gao was killed by the Prince of Rencheng, and a son of Yu Lie, Yu Zhong. With control of the guard, Yu Zhong for a time emerged as the dominant figure of the court.

For her part, Madam Hu was protected immediately after Xuanwu's death by the eunuch Liu Teng, and so survived to take the title of Empress Dowager and personal power as regent for her son.[18] The Gao empress became a nun.[19]

* * *

---

14. ZZTJ 146.4575, 147.4581.
15. WS 8.206, 21B.582–83.
16. BS 13.503 (WS 13.337); Jennifer Holmgren, "Empress Dowager Líng of the Northern Wei and the T'o-pa Sinicization Question," *PFEH* 18 (1978): 161.
17. BS 13.503 (WS 13.337).
18. ZZTJ 148.4611–18.
19. See discussion of this in Balkwill, "When Renunciation Is Good Politics," 240–46.

Madam Hu, conventionally entitled Empress Dowager Ling, came from an ethnically Chinese family originally from the town of Anding on the Jing River, near modern Jingchuan in Gansu. With Taiwu's conquest of the region, various members of the family had come to serve the Wei.[20] Descended from these was an aunt of Madam Hu, the first-known formally ordained nun in Northern Wei, invited into court as spiritual advisor by Empress Dowager Wenming. Later, while preaching in the palace, she caught the attention of Xuanwu, who was then induced to bring the niece, Miss Hu, into the harem.[21]

With removal of the Gao clan, and instatement as empress dowager, Madam Hu now took power in Luoyang, managing the imperial household and so managing the realm. Fascinatingly, she began with efforts to frame her power in the realm of ceremony, of performance, making her own use of the *Rituals of Zhou* by claiming that precedent could be found there that would allow her to conduct the national rituals on behalf of her five-year-old. When this was rejected by the Ministry of Rites, she pressured the Palace Attendant Cui Guang (a distant relative of Cui Hao[22]) to dig through the classics to find some justification for her to take on the role of the dynasty's high priest. To her delight the fellow did so.[23] Seemingly now reassured, Madam Hu began herself issuing imperial edicts (*zhao*), rather than putting them in the name of the child on the throne. Seeking to secure a place among the generals, she also made public displays of her martial talents in archery.[24] Through such performance she built support, or at least acquiescence. But there was, as we shall see, a rickety quality to this ruler's power.

For a time, though, at least for those of wealth and status in Luoyang, this was a glorious age, a time of peace in which were reaped the rich fruits of the reforms made under Wenming and Xiaowen. Developing from within the Chinese architectural tradition, Xiaowen's rebuilt Luoyang consisted of walls within walls within walls. The outer walls were more than 6 miles east-west and more than 4.5 north-south; the population contained within reached half a million, or more.[25] The 30 or so square miles of the outer city contained walled wards, as at Pingcheng.[26] Along the city's main north-south avenue were lodgings for foreign

---

20. WS 52.1149; WS 83B.1833.
21. BS 13.503 (WS 13.337). For more detail, see Stephanie Balkwill, "A Virtuoso Nun in the North: Situating the Earliest-Known Dated Biography of a Buddhist Nun in East Asia," *Hualin International Journal of Buddhist Studies* 3.2 (2020): 129–61.
22. For the Cui clan, again see Holmgren, "The Making of an Élite."
23. BS 13.503 (WS 13.338); ZZTJ 148.4621; discussed in Holmgren, "Empress Dowager Ling," 162. For later examples of a better-known female ruler seeking support from authoritative scripture, see R. W. L. Guisso, *Wu Tse-t'ien and the Politics of Legitimation in T'ang China* (Bellingham: Western Washington University, 1978), Chapter 4.
24. BS 13.503–4 (WS 13.338–39).
25. See Xiong, *Capital Cities and Urban Form*, 87–101. Making the claim that the Wei Luoyang was the largest city in the world in the early sixth century (95), Xiong suggests the registered population was over 500,000, while upward of 200,000 lived there without proper forms. A counterclaim is made for Jiankang by Liu Shufen in her "Jiankang and the Commercial Empire of the Southern Dynasties," 35. For further discussion of the population size, and a much more detailed discussion of Luoyang, see Jenner, *Memories of Loyang*, Chapter 6.
26. Xiong, *Capital Cities and Urban Form*, 100–1, suggests, however, that ward bosses at Luoyang had much less power than their predecessors in Pingcheng.

visitors, while nearby wards had names like "White Elephant"—taken from a creature of that sort that lodged there, which had been sent as gift by a Gandhāran king.[27] Close by was the "Marketplace of the Four Directions," where Inner Asians and Koreans, Central Asians or Yangtze folk could, according to a contemporary ditty, buy "Carp of the Luo (River), / Bream of the Yi, / Costlier than / Beef and lamb!"[28] This and other markets were on schedule opened and closed by the beating of great drums, which could supposedly be heard 15 miles away. The largest of the markets in the outer city was the aptly named Great Market, which lay to the west of the inner city and was some 250 acres in size. This was ringed by wards with names like "Circulation of Trade," inhabited by tradesmen who made all the things that humans need: jewelry, and wine, and coffins.[29] While some of these merchants were rich, with great mansions, most, no doubt, were not.[30] Nevertheless, we see here a combination of commerce and cosmopolitanism that, if not the equal of Tang's Chang'an, was certainly a predecessor.

Within the outer city was an inner city with government offices. With permission from the emperor, powerful figures of the regime also resided there. One had been Xuanwu's uncle, Gao Zhao, who lived in a mansion just outside the main southern gate of the palace city.[31] This inner city had been planned by an agent of Xiaowen sent down to examine the plans of Jiankang, which had itself been based on the plans of Western Jin's Luoyang.[32] Centered on a new Grand Culmen (Taiji) throne hall, the Luoyang palace complex was of a more unified nature than the three or four parallel and separately walled structures of Pingcheng. Based on the southern model, Xiaowen's version of the Taiji Hall also surpassed it, being 13 bays (14 columns) across, one more than Jiankang. "The increase in dimensions," says the modern scholar Nancy Steinhardt, "was probably intended to assert the supremacy of Northern Wei and its new capital."[33]

Perhaps inspired by her aunt, the nun, Madam Hu was a lavish patron of Buddhism. She and others funded many Buddhist centers in the late Wei capital, these being the organizational basis, in fact, for Yang Xuanzhi's nostalgic

---

27. Xiong, *Capital Cities and Urban Form*, 99; citing *Luoyang qie lan ji jiao zhu* 3.161.
28. *Luoyang qie lan ji jiao zhu* 3.161; tr. Wang, *A Record of Buddhist Monasteries in Lo-yang*, 151.
29. Xiong, *Capital Cities and Urban Form*, 99; *Luoyang qie lan ji jiao zhu* 4.202.
30. For the rich, see for instance the story of Liu Bao, whose "chariots, horses, dresses, and ornaments were comparable to those of princes": *Luoyang qie lan ji jiao zhu* 4.202–3; Wang, *A Record of Buddhist Monasteries in Lo-yang*, 182–83.
31. *Luoyang qie lan ji jiao zhu* 1.52; Wang, *A Record of Buddhist Monasteries in Lo-yang*, 51; Xiong, *Capital Cities and Urban Form*, 96. The gate was the Changhemen. For an English-language report, see Qian Guoxiang et al., "Changmen Gate-site of the Northern Wei Palace-city in Han-Wei Luoyang City, Henan," *Chinese Archaeology* 4 (2004): 49–56.
32. Steinhardt, *Chinese Architecture in an Age of Turmoil*, 184. For the architects' journey south, see WS 91.1971.
33. Steinhardt, *Chinese Architecture in an Age of Turmoil*, 185; see also Xiong, *Capital Cities and Urban Form*, 92, who translates Taiji as "Grand Culmen," and on p. 93 also points out that overall, the Northern Wei palace complex was smaller than earlier precedents in the Chinese architectural tradition.

remembrance of the short-lived Wei capital, *Record of Buddhist Monasteries in Luoyang (Luoyang qie lan ji)*.[34] The most magnificent example of the city's Buddhist holy sites was the pagoda of the Yongning ("Eternal Peace") Temple (not far from what had been Gao Zhao's mansion), construction of which began in the empress dowager's second year of regency, 516.[35] Located in the southwest section of the walled inner city, the nine-storied structure stretched upward hundreds of feet.[36] It was said that it could be seen some 30 miles away.[37] At the top of the pagoda's mast was a golden jar containing precious stones, and below this on the mast 11 golden dishes to collect the dew. Golden bells—the size of "bushel pots"—were placed on the iron chains that supported the mast from the corners of the top story, and decorated the eaves of each of the other floors. The doors were of vermillion lacquer, with golden nails and knockers.[38] After completion, the empress dowager took her son up to the top of the tower, where they "gazed down upon the national capital [as if] in their own courtyard," which in a sense it was: since the pagoda overlooked the palace, commoners were forbidden.[39] For Madam Hu, looking down from on top, surveillance of the world below undoubtedly represented possession as well.[40]

The author of the *Record of Buddhist Monasteries*, Yang Xuanzhi, himself was once given the privilege of going up to the top of the pagoda, where "in truth, it seemed as if the clouds and rain were below us!"[41] This delightful recollection, put forth in a book written some 20 years after the city's collapse and abandonment, portrays the glory of the age in context of sorrow at its passing. Built in 516, the pagoda burnt to the ground just eighteen years later, in 534.

But looking down from the pagoda, at temples and markets and mansions, the future would have been hard to discern. In addition to the Yongning pagoda, Madam Hu also carried on work at Longmen, which would of course continue on an even grander scale under the Tang.[42] Nor was this the limit. By the end of Wei there were almost 1,400 Buddhist temples in Luoyang, and upward of 40,000 monks and nuns; it would seem that the capital's entire *sangha* turned out in 518,

---

34. Serving under the Wei successor, Eastern Wei, Yang wrote the book between 547 and 550 (shortly before Wei Shou's compilation of *Wei shu*): Jenner, *Memories of Loyang*, Chapter 1.

35. Jenner, *Memories of Loyang*, 132; *Luoyang qie lan ji jiao zhu*, 1.1–12.

36. Following the texts, the tower would have been more than 800 feet tall, almost two-thirds the height of the Empire State Building. Dien, *Six Dynasties Civilization*, 72, lists this figure, then suggests a more conservative estimate of about 250 feet is "still an impressive height." See also Jenner, *Memories of Loyang*, 148 note 10. As with the Taiji dian, there had been a temple of the same name in Pingcheng.

37. *Luoyang qie lan ji jiao zhu* 1.1; Wang, *A Record of Buddhist Monasteries in Lo-yang*, 15–16. Steinhardt, *Chinese Architecture in an Age of Turmoil*, 200, says it was "the most spectacular landmark in Luoyang."

38. Fu, *Traditional Chinese architecture*, 83; Jenner, *Memories of Loyang*, 148.

39. *Luoyang qie lan ji jiao zhu* 1.5; Wang, *A Record of Buddhist Monasteries in Lo-yang*, 20.

40. D. Fairchild Ruggles, *Women, Patronage and Self-representation in Islamic Societies* (Albany: State University of New York Press, 2000), 7: "vision is a form of power, and seeing implies possession."

41. *Luoyang qie lan ji jiao zhu*, 1.5; Wang, *Record of Buddhist Monasteries*, 20.

42. Amy McNair, *Donors of Longmen: Faith, Politics, and Patronage in Medieval Chinese Buddhist Sculpture* (Honolulu: University of Hawai'i Press, 2007), 60–67.

when Empress Dowager Ling visited the Yongning temple, accompanied by "several tens of thousands" of monks and nuns.[43] And when the Buddha's Birthday was celebrated each spring, the emperor scattered flowers before them as images of the Buddha were brought forth from the hundreds of temples in a great carnival-like parade: "Banners were as numerous as trees in a forest, and incense smoke as thick as fog. Indian music and the din of chanted Buddhist scriptures moved heaven and earth alike.... Throngs formed around renowned monks and virtuous masters, each of whom carried a staff."[44] One of them may have been the "Persian barbarian" Bodhidharma, the semi-legendary monk said to have brought at least the seeds of East Asian Buddhism's School of Meditation (Chan, or in Japanese Zen) from western lands, but who, according to Yang Xuanzhi, was so entranced "seeing the golden disks on the pole on top of Yongning's stupa reflecting in the sun, the rays of light illuminating the surface of the clouds, the jewel-bells on the stupa blowing in the wind, the echoes reverberating beyond the heavens, [that] he sang its praises [exclaiming]: 'Truly this is the work of spirits.... Even the distant Buddha-realms lack this.' "[45]

Some objections were raised to the lavish nature of the court's patronage of Buddhism, and the large amounts of corvée labor assigned the projects.[46] But these heavy workloads did not lead to widespread resistance or rebellion among the Chinese farmers on whom most of the burden no doubt fell.[47] More active expressions of resentment had, however, begun to appear among those left over from the conquest polity, the *guo ren*. Although the men of the garrisons resented the privileges enjoyed by their cousins down south, the guardsmen of Luoyang had their own complaints. In 519, enraged by a Chinese official's proposal that they be categorically excluded from promotion into the bureaucracy's higher ranks, the capital guard rioted, killing the official's father and brother.[48] Fearing further rioting, the court did little in response, simply arresting a few ringleaders, while offering the guardsmen new advantages in competition for office.[49]

---

43. BS 13.504 (WS 13.338); Tang, *Han Wei Liang Jin Nan bei chao Fo jiao shi*, 2: 70; Jenner, *Memories of Loyang*, 118.

44. Wang, *Record of Buddhist monasteries*, 126, with slight emendations. See the detailed discussion of these events in Po Yee Wong, "Acculturation as Seen through Buddha's Birthday Parades in Northern Wei Luoyang: A Micro Perspective on the Making of Buddhism as a World Religion" (PhD diss., University of the West, 2012).

45. *Luoyang qie lan ji jiao zhu* 1.5; Wang, *Record of Buddhist Monasteries*, 20–21; this translation taken from Jeffrey L. Broughton, *The Bodhidharma Anthology: The Earliest Records of Zen* (Berkeley: University of California Press, 1999), 54–55.

46. WS 66.1471–72; ZZTJ 148.4628–29; McNair, *Donors of Longmen*, 64.

47. Jenner, *Memories of Loyang*, 72–73.

48. WS 64.1432, 9.228–29.

49. WS 66.1479. In WS 81.1793 we are told of efforts by the dictator Yuan Cha (whom we shall see just below) to give jobs to frustrated (and apparently un- or underemployed) Dai commoners who had come down to Luoyang 代來寒人 by sending them back north with announcements seeking to mollify rebels there. The effort was thwarted by unemployed sons of officials who wanted the jobs themselves, and had the connections to demand them. Here we see hints of a situation resembling that of the Manchu "orphan warriors" described in the book of that name by Pamela Crossley: *Orphan Warriors: Three Manchu Generations and the End of the Qing World* (Princeton, NJ: Princeton University Press, 1990).

More troubling if less noticed was a gradual decay among such men of the old Taghbach martial culture. One who did notice, the Prince of Rencheng, voiced concern for weakening of the central armies that protected Luoyang.[50] Such concerns were also voiced by a young man from the Huaishuo garrison (near mod. Guyang, Inner Mongolia) who was on an official errand in the capital when the riot broke out. This was Gao Huan, who would later be the power behind the throne of the successor state Eastern Wei (534–550). In Luoyang he saw not only the riot but also the staggering wealth of the Wei princes, and the grand shows they made of that wealth in competition with each other, with hundreds of singing girls, and painters for each egg they consumed.[51] Upon returning north, Gao began spending in a different way, to build up a personal following of the military populations of the garrisons. With Luoyang in such a state, he said, "How will one be able to hang on to wealth?"[52]

In the midst of such circumstances, the empress dowager doubtless wished to have dependable support at court. Occasionally she would simply open up the overflowing royal treasuries to let her officials take what they would, in a modified form of the old practice of booty distribution.[53] Perhaps seeking more personal support, the young widow also built with a son of Xiaowen, Yuan Yi, the Prince of Qinghe, a partnership that was both political and personal.[54] The relationship seems to have been an effective one, for the two individuals as well as for the state: the Prince of Qinghe was not only a handsome fellow but is also said to have given careful attention to matters of state, unlike various of his kinsmen who spent their time worrying about singing girls and decorated eggs.[55] And in a way not usually seen in the histories, the empress dowager is for her part praised in her biographies for being both bright and talented.[56] Together the couple now emerged as competent rulers, sitting atop a vast machinery of tax collection that even after leadership failed would for a time at least continue operations.

In ancient times and modern, no matter the organizational flow chart, politics is actually based on personal bonds. Thus, in addition to the empress dowager's paramour, the Prince of Qinghe, other key figures of the coalition were drawn

---

50. WS 19B.475. A contemporary, Yuan Yuan (due to the rule of avoidance the name has been changed in both texts to Shen 深), spoke of how "the men are without fighting spirit" 人無鬪情: BS 16.620 (WS 18.433). See further discussion of this issue in Liu Jun 刘军, "Lun Tuoba zu shang wu xi su zhi shuai tui—yi Bei Wei hou qi zong shi dan ren jin wei wu zhi wei li" 论拓跋族尚武习俗之衰退——以北魏后期宗室担任禁卫武职为例, Bei fang wen wu (2015.1): 54–59; He, "Fu bing zhi qian," 322. For description of the changes among the transplanted guoren, see WS 78.1724; Wang Zhongluo 王仲犖, Wei Jin Nan bei chao shi 魏晋南北朝史, 2 vols. (Shanghai: Shanghai ren min chu ban she, 1979–1980), 2: 565.
51. See the examples given in Jenner, Memories of Loyang, 68–69.
52. BQS 1.2.
53. BS 43.1598; WS 13.338 (note that this passage is not in the BS version of her biography); ZZTJ 149.4645–46; Luoyang qie lan ji jiao zhu 4.206; Wang, Record of Buddhist Monasteries, 195–96.
54. BS 13.504 (WS 13.339); for an estimate of her age at this time, see Zhang, Bei Wei zheng zhi shi, 9: 151.
55. BS 19.716–17; and see his epitaph, quoted in Zhang, Bei Wei zheng zhi shi, 9: 151.
56. BS 13.503 (WS 13.338). See, however, discussion by Holmgren, "Empress Dowager Ling," of her characterization as a "bad last" ruler.

from more conventional ties of marriage. The most important of these was the empress dowager's brother-in-law, Yuan Cha.[57] Yuan Cha had ties on both sides, being the husband of Madam Hu's younger sister, while at the same time a distant relation of the boy-emperor Xiaoming. Yuan Cha's father, the Prince of Jiangyang, had under Xiaowen been a major commander of the northern garrisons, entrusted with the difficult tasks of checking Rouran incursion and maintaining control over the nomads resettled there. At times headquartered in the north, he was at other times called south to the new capital to serve as a commander of the Luoyang guard. This line of imperial cousins would be a useful plum for the empress dowager, and so she ousted Yu Zhong from the key position of General of the Palace Guard (*ling jun jiang jun*), installing instead Yuan the Father. In 519, completing a meteoric rise in rank, the son took this same position. He now "completely controlled the imperial guard," the core of the dynasty's army.[58]

Madam Hu, we are told, came to "deeply trust and depend on" Yuan Cha.[59] This was a mistake. A power struggle now erupted between the empress dowager's lover and her brother-in-law, as the Prince of Qinghe sought to check his rival's ample ambitions. Yuan Cha responded by building an alliance with another trusted aide of the empress dowager, the powerful eunuch Liu Teng, who took to Xiaoming charges that his mother's lover planned to poison him and take the throne.[60] With the boy's permission, Yuan Cha now locked his sister-in-law up in her suite, and had the Prince of Qinghe executed. A son of Xianwen, the Prince of Gaoyang, was put forward as chancellor (*cheng xiang*). But Yuan Cha was the real power behind the throne, whose occupant called him "uncle."

Though hundreds of *guo ren*, we are told, slashed their faces to mourn Qinghe, and several countercoups were attempted, Yuan Cha was able to keep his power with support of the guard, and in the inner palace that of his ally Liu Teng.[61] Acquiescence was also won from imperial princes, including a brother of Qinghe, and the seemingly always available Prince of Gaoyang, who though given the title of Chancellor functioned as little more than a yes-man.[62] Though it had certainly existed under Madam Hu, corruption became even more widespread, with the dictator's kinsfolk taking the lead. The father is depicted as a grasping old man,

---

57. See his biography in WS 16.403–8. Two variant readings of the personal name are given in the sources: see Jenner, *Memories of Loyang*, 164 note 82; Wang, *Records of Buddhist monasteries*, 43 note 158. Pace Jenner, I will follow Wang's model and use the form given in *Wei shu*.

58. WS 16.404; *Luoyang qie lan ji jiao zhu* 1.39; Wang, *Record of Buddhist monasteries*, 43–44, 165. For the importance of the post of *ling jun jiang jun* 領軍將軍 in later Wei, see Zhang Jinlong 张金龙, "Ling jun jiang jun yu Bei Wei zheng zhi" 领军将军与北魏政治, in his *Bei Wei zheng zhi yu zhi du lun gao*, 350–53.

59. WS 16.404.

60. ZZTJ 149.4656–58.

61. For the slashing of faces, see BS 19.717 (WS 22.592); and Holmgren, "Empress Dowager Ling," 157. For the uprisings, see WS 94.2028, 2029.

62. BS 19.718 (WS 22.593); WS 21A.557.

the yes-man Chancellor, Gaoyang, as an East Asian Crassus, who received special permission to have feathered curtains in his carriage, surrounded by 100 men of the imperial guard, with painted swords.[63] Yuan Cha's chief ally within the palace, Liu Teng, engaged in profitable trade on the frontiers while "skinning the Northern Garrisons."[64]

Some of this may be exaggeration put forth by hostile parties. We lack solid evidence to seriously compare the situation under Yuan Cha with the situation 20 years before, or 50. Nevertheless, it does seem that things were beginning to fall apart. Though this certainly involved the personal inadequacies and misdeeds of various leaders, the fundamental issue lay in the growing physical and social distance that lay between the elite at the capital and the regime's main military centers on the frontier; this would of course be seen again 250 years later, with the Tang emperor Xuanzong and Rokhshan the Sogdian (Ch. An Lushan).[65] Despite the links he had through his father with the garrisons, Yuan Cha gave no more attention than had Madam Hu to the growing problems of men such as Gao Huan. These problems certainly began with memory of suppression of the 497 uprising, and so alienation of the northern soldiery from the monarch, who was no longer their khaghan but "something other than themselves."[66] Though Xiaowen had wished to remake them through learning from a particular set of books, "these northerners," he complained, are always saying "what is the point of knowing books?"[67] More practically, those northerners were of a declining status up in their military outposts, which had become dumping grounds for convicts.[68] Increasingly subject to the malfeasance of officers coming up from Luoyang, they were also very aware that their own possibilities for promotion through the ranks were increasingly limited. According to one commentator, a Wei prince, "in a whole life of pushing, [one] won't rise above regiment commander (*jun zhu*)."[69] Underlying this relative decline in career opportunities was,

---

63. *Luoyang qie lan ji jiao zhu* 3.176; Wang, *Record of Buddhist Monasteries*, 156.
64. Jenner, *Memories of Loyang*, 69; WS 94.2028. The generally poor quality of the men sent to command the garrisons was commented on by a number of court figures in the early sixth century: BS 16.617 (WS 18.430); WS 19B.476.
65. I have relied upon Edwin G. Pulleyblank, *The Background of the Rebellion of An Lu-shan* (Westport, CT: Greenwood Press, 1955), Chapter 2, for these suggestions as to the names behind the Chinese transcription "An Lushan." See also the convincing argument made by Edward H. Schafer, *Golden Peaches of Samarkand: A Study of T'ang Exotics* (Berkeley: University of California Press, 1963), 4, regarding the need to refer to the man by his original name, "Rokhshan." He seems in fact to have been a mix of Türk and Sogdian: Graff, *Medieval Chinese Warfare*, 212. During his well-known mid-eighth century rebellion, Rokhshan would establish his own Yan dynasty.
66. Tanigawa Michio 谷川道雄, *Zui Tō teikoku keisei shiron* 隋唐帝国形成史論 (Tokyo: Chikuma Shobō, 1971), 214.
67. WS 21A.550; ZZTJ 139.4359.
68. The convicts occasionally being princes of the imperial house: BS 16.605 (WS 18.419).
69. BS 16.617. As discussed in Chapter 11, these units theoretically numbered 1,000 men. Tang, *Wei Jin Nan Bei chao Sui Tang shi san lun*, 194, points out that these are complaints about promotion; the situation of the bound, hereditary soldiery of the Yangtze regions was in reality far worse.

of course, an absolute: the difficulty of life in an artificially constructed community in a hard environment.[70]

Fostering power struggle on the steppe, Yuan Cha had in the early 520s harbored in Luoyang a contender for the Rouran khaghanate, whose name is given in the Chinese transcription as Anagui (r. 520–552), eventually assisting his return north to take up rule.[71] The plan backfired, however, as drought and a severe depletion of livestock led to starvation and turmoil in the Rouran lands. In 523, Anagui returned to Wei territory to seize 100,000 head of stock in the frontier region and drive them back to the steppe north of the Gobi, in the process evading a Wei army of 150,000. Echoing the comments made by Gao Huan four years before, the Prince of Guangyang now commented that having seen the poor showing of the imperial army, the men of the border region had conceived a contempt for the weakness of the Luoyang regime that based its power on the "central states."[72] This would be the beginning of the end for Wei, as the afflictions of drought and continuing raids from the steppe led to mutiny, rebellion, and perhaps more fundamentally a mass exodus down into the lowlands of the garrisons' populations, who cared little for the spectacles of Luoyang, or the symbols and assumptions around which they had come to be organized.

These men would in successor regimes re-establish the centrality of what had survived of the Northern Wei military establishment. But a sense of the deterioration of ties between Luoyang and the Northern Garrisons might be given in the story of Yu Jing, a brother of Yu Zhong, who had resisted Yuan Cha and as typical in late Wei was punished by being sent north to command the Huaihuang garrison (mod. Zhangbei, Hebei). In 523, under Rouran attack the inhabitants of the garrison—which was also suffering drought—asked their commander to open the granaries to feed them. Yu Jing refused, whereupon they killed him and took the food for themselves.[73] Shortly thereafter a soldier of Xiongnu origin, whose name is given us in Chinese transcription as Poliuhan Baling, led a mutiny at Woye Garrison (on the northern bend of the Yellow River, west of Baotou) that began the dominos' falling. Echoing the garrison mutinies came rebellions in the old lands of Gai Wu, in the northwest; while risings among the hill folk of Shanxi and Henan encouraged Jiankang to send armies north.

The lands to the north thus became battlegrounds or wastelands, their resources largely lost to Luoyang.[74] At least one loyalist center, however, did hold

70. For more detail on these issues, see Tang Zhangru 唐長孺 and Huang Huixian 黄惠賢, "Shi lun Wei mo Bei zhen zhen min bao dong de xing zhi" 試論魏末北鎮鎮民暴動的性質, in Tang's *Shan ju cun gao* (Beijing: Zhonghua shu ju, 1989), 25–59; and Pearce, "The Yü-wen Regime in Sixth Century China," 141–79.
71. ZZTJ 149.4660–69. Giving a sense of Luoyang's capacity for manufacture, the Rouran lord was upon his departure given by the Wei emperor 18 "hundred man tents": WS 103.2300; Andrews, *Felt Tents and Pavilions*, 1: 84, 92.
72. BS 16.617 (WS 18.430).
73. ZZTJ 149.4674–75; WS 31.747.
74. "Pingcheng (Heng-Dai) and north, now is (just) ruins," we are told in WS 106A.2455.

out, the autonomous domain of the Erzhu in northern Shanxi, established it will be remembered in the course of Daowu's southern campaign, where they had come to raise "ox and sheep, camels and horses . . . by the valley full."[75] During the rebellions that broke out in the 520s, their leader Erzhu Rong represented himself as a defender of the old order, and many of the refugees from the garrisons flocked to him, among them Huaishuo's Gao Huan, who would go on to become the power behind the throne of the Eastern Wei successor regime.

In the midst of these convulsions, in 525 an old ally of Yuan Cha who held for Wei the key southern border town of Pengcheng (mod. Xuzhou, Jiangsu), fearing power change in Luoyang, surrendered to Xiao Yan. This led to rapid decay in Yuan Cha's position at court. Madam Hu's house arrest had by this time loosened and now the Prince of Gaoyang, no longer a mere yes-man, found a way secretly to talk with her about his fears of Yuan Cha.[76] Confronting Yuan, the empress dowager now took advantage of his deep embarrassment with the Pengcheng affair to force him to step down from his post as General of the Palace Guard, while keeping his other titles. After he had physically departed from the palace, however, he was stripped of the post of Palace Attendant as well, and so denied reentry.[77] Concerned with her personal ties with Yuan Cha—and feelings for her sister—the empress dowager resisted for a time taking this matter any further. In the end, however, pressed by complaints—including one from a son of the Prince of Rencheng, just then able to return to court after having earlier been forced out by Yuan Cha—the empress dowager gave in and charged her brother-in-law with inciting rebellion among the Man people.[78] He was now ordered to commit suicide in his home. Liu Teng, who had died in 523, was disinterred, his bones scattered.[79]

Madam Hu was again the court's main power. But although taxes were still being collected in unaffected districts to the south and west, the court's power as a whole was slipping away.[80] The empress dowager was no more able than Yuan Cha to stem the empire's disintegration. While the garrison troops were reorganizing around new leaders such as Erzhu or Gao Huan, Luoyang's armies' troubles grew. Troops were now defecting, some turning to banditry.[81] And while the armies lost men to desertion or as casualties of war, the regions available for recruitment shrank almost daily. Where they could be gotten hold of, more and

---

75. WS 74.1644; Jenner, *Memories of Loyang*, 86ff.
76. WS 16.406.
77. WS 16.406; BS 13.504 (WS 13.339); ZZTJ 150.4695–97.
78. WS 19B.482; ZZTJ 150.4697.
79. WS 94.2028.
80. For continuation of tax collection in regions to the south and west, see Zhou, "Cong Bei Wei ji ge jun de hu kou bian hua kan san zhang zhi de zuo yong," 140–46; but see also WS 56.1255, where a man sent north to hold a province up on the plains (Yinzhou 殷州; seat in the vicinity of mod. Longyao, Hebei) insisted he needed troops, and food for them, but "in the end nothing was given him."
81. See the edict issued in the 12th month of 525: WS 9.242.

more of those liable for military service fled into the sangha. By the dynasty's end, there were some 2 million monks and nuns.[82] Perhaps even more troubling, there were few if any effective commanders for what troops were left.[83] And those who were, perhaps, effective were mistrusted, their efforts undercut by court rivals, leading in some cases to their deaths.[84] Not surprisingly, the consequence was a largely unbroken string of defeats for the imperial armies.[85]

Back at court, dictatorship had been replaced by clique. Madam Hu had a new lover, a handsome Chinese fellow from the Zhengzhou region by the name of Zheng Yan, whom she allowed to conduct government affairs on her behalf. Zheng did this working together with Xu He, an ambitious up-and-comer who gained power by tying himself to the empress's lover.

During this period, most major edicts and commands came from Xu's brush.[86] A few, apparently, did not. In 526 and 527, we see issuance of three edicts stating that the emperor would personally lead troops against the rebels.[87] None of these plans, presumably concocted in the young man's mind, came to fruition, certainly quashed by Madam Hu. For his part, Xiaoming spurned the Hu girl mother gave him as empress, instead giving all his attention to a young woman from the Pan family.[88]

The struggle intensified in 528. In early March of this year, seeking to clip her son's wings, Madam Hu had several of his allies at court killed.[89] Open struggle now broke out between mother and son—the one who ruled and the one who reigned—to which Xiaoming responded by seeking a new ally from beyond the walls of the city, the self-proclaimed loyalist Erzhu Rong, who had in the tumult of the last several years expanded his power in Shanxi, with his base now at the key town of Taiyuan.[90]

The plan did not work out as Xiaoming had hoped and he was poisoned by the empress dowager. A bizarre chain of events then commenced, in which Madam Hu first put on the throne the infant daughter birthed a month before by the concubine, Madam Pan, then immediately realizing that would not work replaced the baby with a great-grandson of Xiaowen who had lived through three years.[91] Erzhu responded by voicing outrage and leading his troops down to Luoyang to "save the court." On the north shore of the Yellow River, with an army of

---

82. WS 114.3048; Hurvitz, *Treatise on Buddhism and Taoism*, 103.
83. WS 72.1619; ZZTJ 151.4271.
84. BS 16.618–21; WS 18.431–34; ZZTJ 151.4713, 4716.
85. Zhang, *Bei Wei zheng zhi shi*, 9: 331–32.
86. WS 93.2007–9.
87. WS 9.243, 246; ZZTJ 151.4712, 4721, 4723.
88. BS 13.506 (WS 13.340).
89. BS 13.505 (WS 13.339–40); Holmgren, "Empress Dowager Ling," 168–69.
90. BQS 1.3; ZZTJ 152.4737–39. Note that Jenner, *Memories of Luoyang*, 89, suggests that the claim that Xiaoming invited Erzhu into Luoyang needs taken with a grain of salt.
91. ZZTJ 152.4739.

10,000 men, he received a rival candidate for the Wei throne, Yuan Ziyou, a son of Xiaowen's brother, the Prince of Pengcheng. The next day, 15 May 528, they crossed the River, camping at Heyin ("South of the River"), where Yuan Ziyou was proclaimed the new Wei emperor.[92] Zheng Yan and Xu He now fled, as did some commanders of what remained of the palace guard. Those who did not surrendered to Erzhu, and the city gates were opened. The empress dowager now gave the women of Xiaoming's harem the tonsure, attempting to save them by turning them into nuns.

But though she cut her own hair as well, Madam Hu was not to retire to a quiet life in a convent. Two days after crossing the river Erzhu Rong sent horsemen to seize the empress dowager and her three-year-old claimant and bring them up to Heyin. There Madam Hu pleaded her case at length before Erzhu Rong. Her case rejected, the two were then drowned in the Yellow River.[93] At this point one of the recently defected guard officers pointed out that Erzhu's army was not even 10,000 in number, and went on to suggest that they would not be able to physically control the court and its very numerous officers and officials.[94] And so, telling these officers and officials that he wished them to accompany him in making sacrifice to Tengri, Erzhu summoned them out of Luoyang to Heyin, where he berated them for their greed and corruption and for allowing the murder of Xiaoming.[95] He then set upon them his horsemen, who cried out "The House of Yuan is Dead. The House of Erzhu has Uprisen." Thousands died, in their fine robes, their hands held together in supplication. Among them was most of the ruling family, including the ever adaptable prime minister, the Prince of Gaoyang, who could adapt to the situation no more.[96]

Here we close our narrative of the history of the Northern Wei dynasty. Erzhu in the end curbed his ambition, deciding it would be more prudent to be the power behind the throne. Though understandably terrified, Yuan Ziyou continued as Erzhu's puppet for two years, before he personally killed the man, and then was killed by Erzhu clansmen in turn. The Erzhu were soon replaced by men from the garrisons—including Gao Huan—who would have Yuan puppets sit on the thrones of successor regimes—Western Wei and Eastern Wei—into the mid-550s. But these were other men's states, whose centers of power lay neither in Shengle, nor Pingcheng, nor Luoyang. The state created by Shiyijian almost 200 years before, which had changed repeatedly on its way to becoming the House of Yuan, was finally extinct.

---

92. WS 74.1646–47; ZZTJ 152.4739, 4741.
93. BS 13.505 (WS 13.340); ZZTJ 152.4741.
94. WS 44.1004; ZZTJ 152.4742.
95. WS 74.1648; ZZTJ 152.4742.
96. Jenner, *Memories of Loyang*, 90, lists a range of numbers given in different sources between 1,300 and 3,000. See also discussion in Chinese translation of the work of Kubozoe Yoshifumi 窪添庆文, *Wei Jin Nan bei chao guan liao zhi yan jiu* 魏晋南北朝官僚制研究, Kindle ed. (Shanghai: Fudan da xue chu ban she, 2017), Chapter 15.

Summing Up; Looking Ahead

In this final offering we will need to summarize the main points made in, and underlying, this study and on that basis look forward to future study that will pursue such issues into later periods. Though in some sense standing on its own, this work has been intended also to serve as a first step in tracing—as Chen Yinke did long ago—links between the Serbi state of the Taghbach and the Tang, an indirect heir, which emerged several generations after the Wei fall.

While its legitimacy within the Chinese world was questioned almost from the beginning, in more recent years the dynasty of the Taghbach (ca. 258–534[1]) has come to be seen as an important part of the history of East Asia, and of the important subset of East Asia that has been the Chinese world. This book has attempted to expand at least a bit our understanding of the regime that took shape in the Yinshan highlands in the mid-third century, using a mix of narrative and thematic study.

The Taghbach dynasty was a complex entity, which in the almost three centuries it persisted repeatedly saw dramatic reorganization, accompanied by dramatic physical relocation. About midway through these processes the dynasty retitled itself as "Wei," or the "Great Wei." To arrange it neatly in the classification scheme of traditional Chinese historiography—to distinguish it from other dynasties with the same name—it was later assigned the title "Northern Wei." But the reader needs to realize that the Taghbach lords never themselves used this name; sometimes, in fact, they had used different names altogether.

This was, of course, just one of many ways in which this dynasty was tucked and trimmed, renamed and reimagined to fit into another people's tradition, and to be given a place within writings that came from that tradition. And as is the case with all traditions, that of the ancient Chinese world had its own set of assumptions and preoccupations. Some of the later dynasts actively encouraged such preoccupations, or were at least pleased by them. Earlier Taghbach lords seem not fully aware what was being written about them; or, on discovering what had been written, became very unhappy about it. But they had no real choice—at

---

1. "Northern" Wei a subset of this: 386–534.

this time, in East Asia, Literary Chinese was the only available option for keeping records, or recording and describing events.

Thus, this book began with two chapters looking at the dynasty's relationship to history—and to the ways in which history is constructed, and fabricated. In Chapter 2, we see the difficulties met by writers attempting to place their lords in the Chinese tradition. This was a long process, and deadly for at least one, Cui Hao. As these writings took final shape in *Wei shu*, in the sixth century, the process involved (among other things) wholesale, anachronistic renaming of historical figures with appellations in the Chinese style, appellations the actual individual might never have heard or understood. One example would have been the Wolf Lord, Böri Beg, who posthumously received the Chinese title of Taiwudi (r. 426–451). Bowing in this case to tradition, we have taken the latter as main form of reference. Manufacture of history does not, of course, belong to just one group. In Chapter 1, we see how Taiwu himself made such efforts, for his own aims.

There are many complexities to these issues, perhaps the first being what name should be placed upon the tradition from which sprouted what we have of recorded Wei history. Such issues are first addressed in the book's Prologue. In recent years, several scholars have examined the meaning of the terms "China" and "Chinese," and how they should be used (or not). These are, of course, labels of outside invention, reimposed back upon the worlds of continental East Asia. Different individuals will have different views. But for this author, the decision has been to set aside "China" as containing the implication of a congruence of cultural and political boundaries that did not really exist in the period under discussion. As for later periods, there may be need for continuing discussion as to whether or not Ming is really part of a larger whole with the empires of the Mongols or Manchus.

As will be obvious from its use above, however, the term "Chinese" has been retained, at times used in reference to a "Chinese world" that certainly did exist (though other worlds existed alongside). As used in this volume, "Chinese" takes on a quite particular meaning, which may not be applicable to other periods (or as Andrew Chittick has made clear, other parts of continental East Asia). For our purpose, the term refers to: use of Chinese language, both spoken and written; existence of a culture built around the classical tradition in Literary Chinese, with a significant role within communities played by "text masters," Ru; claims at least of origin within the former territories of Han and its successors, which to some extent created an early form of identity; and more particularly, definition of lineage based on the old empire's administrative map.

Being an important part of the Taghbach empire, definition of "Chinese" and Chinese tradition provide necessary background. But the main goal of this book has been to see the Taghbach in and of themselves, as much as that can be done with the limitation of our sources. For that reason, we began by tracing origins—the origins of the people itself, but also of the region they made their own, the Datong Basin or "Land of Dai." Attention was then directed to the Taghbach origin myth found in Chinese in *Wei shu*—perhaps based partly on their own oral tales—which tells of a great migration, possibly from the Khingan Mountains and apparently in the early centuries CE. We then turn to more reliable accounts of the first appearance of the Taghbach in the Yinshan region in the mid-third century. These were the "old lands of the Xiongnu," left empty by collapse of the Xiongnu empire a century or so before. At the time of their arrival another empire was teetering, that which for centuries had ruled the rich lowlands to the south. The first clear leader of the Taghbach was an interloper, Liwei. Though his origins—*pace* the author of the *Wei shu* myths—are not quite clear, we can say he began the process of establishing a new dynasty among the mostly Inner Asian peoples that had gathered in and around the Yinshan region. It could be argued that Liwei's effort began in earnest in the year 258, when Chinese historians date Liwei's first sacrifice to Tengri, "Heaven." Other local lords were invited to this event; one who refused was killed. It was probably through these events that Liwei assumed the title of "khaghan," which began to appear at this time among various Serbi groups, linked with a new notion of dynastic rule.

Liwei came to his end some 20 years later, in the midst of resistance to his efforts to build the dynasty. The line survived, however, and 50 years later a grandson established rule over the Datong Basin; another half century after that, Liwei's great-great-grandson, Shiyijian (r. 338–376), created something more like a stable state, in particular with formation of a standing guard. After Shiyijian's death, and a decade-long interregnum, his grandson Shegui (r. 386–409) took the family enterprise to a new level, incorporating subject Inner Asian peoples into a much larger army than grandfather had had and leading that army in 396 down onto the Yellow River plains. Having more clearly established an empire—as in a complex state organized in hierarchical terms—Shegui also fundamentally rearranged his state, renaming the dynasty with the Chinese "Wei," and moving his capital to Pingcheng in the Datong Basin. At the same time, he took for himself the Chinese title *huang di*, "emperor"—though he was certainly still a "khaghan" to the horsemen of his army. Conquests continued under Shegui's heirs—most notably his grandson, the emperor Taiwu, the Wolf Lord (r. 426–451)—until the entire Yellow River region had been brought under their control.

The Taghbach dynasty had existed for more than a century before conquest of lowlands. But when it did so, it became a dramatically new form of East Asian state. Under Han, goods, ideas, and texts had long been moving outward into neighboring regions, such as Manchuria, the Korean peninsula, or the archipelago that became Japan. This was one way that Han established influence and hegemony. With Han collapse in 220, followed a century later by collapse of its last successor Western Jin (266–316), new states and new dynasties began to take shape along the periphery, of which that of the Taghbach was but one, though physically one of the closest to the core lands of the now-vanished empire. Much of the rest of East Asian history would be taken up by efforts of such northern states to seize control of the heavily populated and richly productive lowlands to the south. These are sometimes called "conquest dynasties," though that is something of a misnomer, describing them only in terms of their conquest of territories dominated by Chinese populations (and also ignoring the fact that native Chinese dynasties also took power through organized violence). Taking shape over centuries, under different circumstances, each of these conquest dynasties had a character of its own. There were, however, certain shared features that from the time of Wei appeared and reappeared. These included the use of multiple languages—Inner Asian, Chinese, and others—as well as use of several different monarchic titles, all placed upon the same person. Though there was borrowing from the Chinese world, it was selective, the borrowings incorporated into something new and distinct. And one of the forms this took was in administrative complexity, with different institutions organizing, regulating, and taxing farmers and pastoralists.

Northern Wei can be described as the first major example of these complex East Asian empires. But it can and should also be seen in and of itself, as a particular group that at a particular time formed a "nation" of a sort, whose people were quite aware of themselves in distinction to others. Not simply Chinese, nor was it simply "Inner Asian." The bulk of these "people of Dai" were settled in and around "Dai," the Datong Basin, where grew deep loyalties for particular places, and for "old ways" that—as is so often the case—were not really all that old. Pingcheng—the "city of pacification"—was transformed from being a frontier citadel in Han into the political and social center of a very different sort of empire. As the dwelling place of many of the military men of Dai, it had a distinctive culture all its own, their tombs showing a strong preoccupation with the hunt, on the one hand, and on the other, the feast.

Centered for a century on the huge military base of Pingcheng, the Northern Wei state was organized around the army the men of Dai could consistently field for their khaghan. Those men, of course, also gained from the situation: service in the military was an important path for promotion for soldiers who had served well, leading some at least to peerage, or to a place in the "inner court," the khaghan's Privy Council, which though ignored in *Wei shu* was the actual core of the early Wei state. The army that took shape under Shegui was very large (and very expensive), consisting in all of some 300,000 men, with elite guard units of 100,000. Highly organized in decimal units, each was marked by its own distinctive pennon. The power of the Wei army also derived from adoption of recent innovations in material technology, with use by its mounted archers of the stirrup, and for some units at least, barding for both man and horse. The "gatherings of clouds" that had been the armies of the Western Jin civil war were no match, nor were the militias that remained down on the plains after Jin's collapse. Long after Northern Wei, in fact, armies of mounted archers would continue to be a dominant force in Eurasia.

A cavalry army was thus the heart of the Wei regime. Inversely, decline in its cavalry army accompanied the dynasty's decline. This was a gradual and complex process, no doubt with internal change and decay within the army itself. But overriding all such issues would be the growing wish of later Wei monarchs to get themselves out from underneath the power and influence of their generals. This wish took on full significance under the "filial and cultured" monarch, Xiaowen (r. 471–499). A *huang di*, but apparently no longer a khaghan, Xiaowen and his co-ruler, the empress dowager Wenming, had in the 480s with their Equal Fields program rebuilt a strong tax base in the farmlands of the Yellow River plains. A devotee of the Chinese classical tradition, Xiaowen preferred its neatly unitary principles of organization to the ad hoc approach his ancestors had taken, the diversity they had allowed. Most dramatically, desiring to be away from the Pingcheng establishment, and wishing instead to dwell in the "central states," he in 493 moved his capital from the highlands down onto the plains, to the ancient city of Luoyang. Bringing south a large part of his army, this began a process of change in the military, of deterioration. In the Luoyang area, it was more difficult to maintain the herds of horses needed by a large force of cavalry. It was also harder to keep the men, who began melting into the larger population. A large part of the old army based in the south thus disappeared, to be replaced with infantry drawn through the new forms of local administration that had been imposed on the populations of the Yellow River plains. As for the army left in the northern highlands—taking shape there was a growing sense of distance and abandonment from the now faraway court at Luoyang; and a mourning for the passing of the "old ways." A generation later, the northern garrisons would collapse, their inhabitants disgorge in a second, and much more chaotic migration down onto the lowlands. Not long after, we see the fall of Luoyang and the tragic death of Madam Hu and the child she had raised up to be, if not a khaghan, then a *huang di*.

* * *

Focus on the army was one of the things that bound this dynasty together over the almost three centuries of its existence. It was only in the last years of the dynasty that men were formally taken off the special military rolls. Another of the things giving continuity would have been the dynastic line's genes, though those of Liwei had, of course, been a mixture from the beginning—of the line of Jiefen and that of the "daughter of Heaven"—and they would mix and mix again. Also implanted in the heirs of Liwei, though in a less physical form, would have been the idea of dynastic succession as family possession, as in some sense property of the *tigin*: it was the lot of the clan to be "rulers of the earth," or more prosaically, to maintain and manage the complex structures of a complex empire.

This approximation of unity is lost, however, in the world of names. Long ago the thinker Zhuang Zhou pointed out the slippery nature of those inventions of the human mind, with changing application to the real world as they pass from generation to generation. Because humans have emotional needs for them, names often persist, hovering over changing substance long after original import has been lost. In the case here under discussion, however, while something of the substance did endure the names applied changed, again and again, crossing the boundaries of languages and cultures from "Dai" to "Wei," from "Taghbach" to "Tuoba," from "Tuoba" to "Yuan."

These processes took shape over centuries, but the name-shifter par excellence was, of course, Xiaowen, who moved his court deep into the interior of the Chinese territories where he attempted to remake the realm. The up-and-coming generation of his super-elite was instructed to speak Chinese before the monarch, to shed the distinctive cap by which the identity of the men of Dai had for generations been "made evident in everyday life,"[2] and instead dress in a new and what he considered "proper" way, in the way the expatriate Wang Su did. Such sudden cultural remaking is occasionally seen in human history, often moving from the top down; in East Asia one might think of the sudden shift to Western apparel under Meiji (or more recently in the Zhonghua ren min gong he guo). Culture choice is, of course, always embedded in a material base.

Top-down culture change can be ferociously opposed, though frequently with no success, as we have seen in Northern Wei with the *tigin* "Yuan Pi." More to the point, Xiaowen's changes were never complete. This was true even in Northern Wei, and under its immediate successors, in the mid-sixth century, Serbi continued to be used as soldiers and efforts were made to restore Inner Asian names. While Yuan scions are seen in the Tang empire—among them the poet and statesman Yuan Zhen (779–831)—the clan's original name continued to be seen in the eighth-century Orkhon inscriptions in the Turkic pronunciation of "Tabgatch," as reference to a Northern Wei successor: Tang. And Tang emperors again wore the Serbi cap.

Spiritual heirs of Wang Su, the peoples of the economic and cultural hubs of the Yangtze region played an important role in the Tang world, and following the patterns established by Xiaowen became deeply woven into that evolving tapestry. But Tang's bone and sinew—as long as it had bone and sinew—had been shaped by the Northern Wei military men originally stationed in the Yinshan

---

2. Again, to borrow the words of Walter Pohl in the "Introduction" to his *Strategies of Identification*, 25.

military colonies who emerged out of Luoyang's collapse. This is the main line that leads from Wei into Tang.

In its own way, Tang carried on the new forms of dual government invented by the Serbi; at times, Tang monarchs took on two titles: that of Khaghan alongside that of August God-King, much as had the Taghbach monarchs. It is no accident that the great Tang catastrophe—the rebellion of the Tang general Rokhshan the Sogdian—emerged from more or less the same frontier region that had birthed the Dai regime.

Much good work has been done on the complex nature of the Tang empire, and also on the derivation of its core institutions from Northern Wei's sixth-century successors. But more work is needed, with particular attention to the war machine that had taken shape in the Yinshan region: its re-emergence to dominance in the course of the Northern Wei collapse, its development over the next several centuries, and the evolving nature and origin of the manpower of these armies. For this author, the next phase of this project will begin with close examination of the sixth-century successor states, the Taiyuan-based regime of Eastern Wei/Northern Qi, created by Gao Huan, the disconsolate visitor to Luoyang, and its rival in the Wei River valley, Western Wei/Northern Zhou, both formed by officers from the Northern Wei military fleeing south after the northern garrisons' collapse in the 520s.

Bibliography

PRIMARY SOURCES

Bei Qi shu 北齊書. Li Baiyao 李百藥; completed 636. Zhonghua shu ju ed. Beijing, 1972.
Bei shi 北史. Li Yanshou 李延壽; completed 659. Zhonghua shu ju ed. Beijing, 1974.
Ce fu yuan gui 冊府元龜; presented to the throne 1013. Zhonghua shu ju ed. Beijing, 1960.
Chen shu 陳書. Yao Silian 姚思廉; completed 636. Zhonghua shu ju ed. Beijing, 1972.
Dongguan Han ji 東觀漢記. Comp. by multiple editors during Later Han period (25–220 CE). Edition used *Dongguan Han ji jiao zhu* 東觀漢記校注. Zhengzhou: Zhongzhou gu ji chu ban she, 1987.
Gao seng zhuan 高僧傳. Comp. Hui Jiao 慧皎; ca. 530. *Taishō shinshū Daizōkyō*. Ed. Takakusu Junjirō and Watanabe Kaigyoku. Tokyo: Taishō Shinshū Daizōkyō Kankōkai, 1990. Vol. 50; T. 2059.
Han shu 漢書. Ban Gu 班固; completed 111 CE. Zhonghua shu ju ed. Beijing, 1962.
Hou Han shu 後漢書. Fan Ye 范曄 et al.; completed ca. 440. Zhonghua shu ju ed. Beijing, 1962.
Jin shu 晉書. Fang Xuanling 房玄齡 et al.; completed 648. Zhonghua shu ju ed. Beijing, 1974.
Jiu Tang shu 舊唐書. Liu Xu 劉昫 et al.; presented to the throne 945. Zhonghua shu ju ed. Beijing, 1975.
Luoyang qie lan ji 洛陽伽藍記. Yang Xuanzhi 楊衒之 (d. ca. 555). Edition used *Luoyang qie lan ji jiao zhu* 洛陽伽藍記校注. Comp. Fan Xiangyong 范祥雍. Shanghai: Shanghai gu ji chu ban she, 1978.
Nan Qi shu 南齊書. Xiao Zixian 蕭子顯; completed ca. 520. Zhonghua shu ju ed. Beijing, 1972.
San guo zhi 三國志. Chen Shou 陳壽 and Pei Songzhi 裴宋之; completed 429. Zhonghua shu ju ed. Beijing, 1959.
Shi ji 史記. Sima Qian 司馬遷; completed ca. 94 BCE. Zhonghua shu ju ed. Beijing, 1982.

Shi shuo xin yu 世說新語. Liu Yiqing 劉義慶; completed ca. 430. Edition used *Shi shuo xin yu jiao jian* 世說新語校箋. Comp. Xu Zhen'e 徐震堮. Taibei: Wen shi zhe chu ban she, 1985.

Shi tong 史通. Liu Zhiji 劉知幾 (661–721). Edition used *Shi tong tong shi* 史通通釋. Comm. by Pu Qilong 浦起龍 (1679–ca. 1762). Taipei: Jiusi chu ban you xian gong si, 1978.

Shui jing zhu 水經注. Li Daoyuan 酈道元 (d. 527). Edition used *Shui jing zhu shu* 水經注疏. Comm. by Yang Shoujing 楊守敬 (1839–1915) et al. 3 vols. Nanjing: Jiangsu gu ji chu ban she, 1989.

Song shu 宋書. Shen Yue 沈約; completed ca. 500. Zhonghua shu ju ed. Beijing, 1974.

Wei shu 魏書. Wei Shou 魏收; completed 554. Zhonghua shu ju ed. Beijing, 1974.

Yan shi jia xun 顏氏家訓. Yan Zhitui 顏之推; completed ca. 591. Edition used *Yan shi jia xun ji jie* 顏氏家训集解. Comp. Wang Liqi 王利器. Shanghai: Shanghai gu ji chu ban she, 1980.

Zhan guo ce 戰國策. Ascribed to Liu Xiang 劉向 (ca. 77–ca. 6 BCE). Edition used Shanghai: Shanghai gu ji chu ban she, 1978.

Zi zhi tong jian 資治通鑒. Sima Guang 司馬光; presented to the throne 1084. Zhonghua shu ju ed. Beijing, 1959.

SECONDARY STUDIES

Abe, Stanley. *Ordinary Images*. Chicago: University of Chicago Press, 2002.

Abramson, Marc. *Ethnic Identity in Tang China*. Philadelphia: University of Pennsylvania Press, 2008.

Akahori Akira. "Drug Taking and Immortality." In *Taoist Meditation and Longevity Techniques*. Ed. Livia Kohn, 73–98. Ann Arbor: Center for Chinese Studies, University of Michigan, 1989.

Alizadeh, Abbas. "Archaeology and the Question of Mobile Pastoralism in Late Prehistory." In *The Archaeology of Mobility: Old World and New World*. Ed. Hans Barnard and Willeke Wendrich, 78–114. Los Angeles: Cotsen Institute of Archaeology, University of California, 2008.

Allard, Francis. "Introduction: Power, Monumentality, and Mobility." In *Social Complexity in Prehistoric Eurasia: Monuments, Metals, and Mobility*. Ed. Bryan K. Hanks and Katheryn M. Linduff, 323–29. Cambridge and New York: Cambridge University Press, 2009.

Allsen, Thomas T. *The Royal Hunt in Eurasian History*. Philadelphia: University of Pennsylvania Press, 2006.

Amory, Patrick. *People and Identity in Ostrogothic Italy, 489–554*. Cambridge and New York: Cambridge University Press, 1997.

Andrews, Peter A. *Felt Tents and Pavilions: The Nomadic Tradition and Its Interaction with Princely Tentage*. 2 vols. London: Melisende, 1999.

Anthony, David. "Migration in Archaeology: The Baby and the Bathwater." *American Anthropologist*, n.s., 92 (1990): 895–914.

Árnason, Jóhann Páll. *The Peripheral Centre: Essays on Japanese History and Civilization*. Melbourne: Trans Pacific Press, 2002.

Arnstein, Walter L. "The Warrior Queen: Reflections on Victoria and Her World." *Albion* 30.1 (1998): 1–28.

Atwood, Christopher. "Historiography and Transformation of Ethnic Identity in the Mongol Empire: the Öng'üt Case." *Asian Ethnicity* 15.4 (2014): 514–34.

Atwood, Christopher. "Some Early Inner Asian Terms Related to the Imperial Family and the Comitatus." *Central Asiatic Journal* 56 (2012–2013): 49–86.

Balazs, Étienne. "History as a Guide to Bureaucratic Practice." In his *Chinese Civilization and Bureaucracy*. Ed. Arthur F. Wright, tr. H. M. Wright, 129–49. New Haven, CT: Yale University Press, 1964.

Balkwill, Stephanie. "A Virtuoso Nun in the North: Situating the Earliest-known Dated Biography of a Buddhist Nun in East Asia." *Hualin International Journal of Buddhist Studies* 3.2 (2020): 129–61.

Balkwill, Stephanie. "When Renunciation Is Good Politics: The Women of the Imperial Nunnery of the Northern Wei (386–534)." *Nan Nü* 18.2 (2016): 224–56.

Bao Yuzhu 宝玉柱. "Kalaqin yuan liu: Bei Wei shi qi de Helazhen 喀喇沁源流：北魏时期的曷剌真." *Man yu yan jiu* (2013.1): 96–104.

Barbieri-Low, Anthony J. *Artisans in Early Imperial China*. Seattle and London: University of Washington Press, 2007.

Barfield, Thomas. *The Perilous Frontier: Nomadic Empires and China*. Cambridge, MA: Blackwell, 1989.

Barnes, Gina Lee. *Archaeology of East Asia: The Rise of Civilization in China, Korea and Japan*. Oxford and Philadelphia: Oxbow Books, 2015.

Bartius, Marc C. *The Late Byzantine Army: Arms and Society, 1204–1453*. Philadelphia: University of Pennsylvania Press, 1992.

Baxter, William H., and Laurent Sagart. *Old Chinese: A New Reconstruction*. Oxford: Oxford University Press, 2014.

Beazley, John. *Herodotus at the Zoo*. Oxford: Gaisford Prize, 1907.

Beckwith, Christopher I. *Empires of the Silk Road: A History of Central Asia from the Bronze Age to the Present*. Princeton, NJ: Princeton University Press, 2009.

Beckwith, Christopher I. *Koguryo: The Language of Japan's Continental Relatives*. Leiden: Brill, 2004.

Beckwith, Christopher I. "On the Chinese Names for Tibet, Tabghatch and the Turks." *Archivum Eurasiae Medii Aevi* 14 (2005): 7–22.

Bei chao wu shi ci dian 北朝五史辭典. Ed. Jian Xiuwei 簡修煒 et al. 2 vols. Jinan: Shangdong jiao yu chu ban she, 2000.

Biran, Michal. "Introduction: Nomadic Culture." In *Nomads as Agents of Social Change: The Mongols and Their Eurasian Predecessors*. Ed. Reuven Amitai and Michal Biran, 1–9. Honolulu: University of Hawai'i Press, 2015.

Biran, Michal. *Qaidu and the Rise of the Independent Mongol State in Central Asia*. Surrey: Curzon Press, 1997.

Birtalan, Agnew. "The Tibetan Weather-magic Ritual of a Mongolian Shaman." *Shaman* 9.2 (2001): 119–42.

Bodde, Derk. "The State and Empire of Ch'in." In *Cambridge History of China*, Vol. 1, *The Ch'in and Han Empires, 221 B.C.–A.D. 220*. Ed. Denis Twitchett and Michael Loewe, 20–102. New York: Cambridge University Press, 1986.

Bonnefoy, Yves, comp., Wendy Doniger, tr. and ed. *Asian Mythologies*. Chicago: University of Chicago Press, 1993.
Boodberg, Peter. "The Language of the T'o-Pa Wei." *Harvard Journal of Asiatic Studies* 1 (1936). Rpt. in *Selected Works of Peter A. Boodberg*. Ed. Alvin P. Cohen., 221–39. Berkeley: University of California Press.
Boodberg, Peter. "Marginalia to the Histories of the Northern Dynasties." *Harvard Journal of Asiatic Studies* 3 (1938), 4 (1939). Rpt. in *Selected Works of Peter A. Boodberg*. Ed. Alvin P. Cohen, 265–349. Berkeley: University of California Press, 1979.
Boodberg, Peter. *Selections from Hu T'ien Han Yüeh Fang Chu*. Berkeley, CA, 1932. Rpt. in *Selected Works of Peter A. Boodberg*. Ed. Alvin P. Cohen, 41–172. Berkeley: University of California Press, 1979.
Boodberg, Peter. "Two Notes on the History of the Chinese Frontier." *Harvard Journal of Asiatic Studies* 1 (1936). Rpt. in *Selected Works of Peter A. Boodberg*. Ed. Alvin P. Cohen, 240–64. Berkeley: University of California Press, 1979.
Boyang 柏杨 (Guo Dingsheng 郭定生). *Zi zhi tong jian: Shenhe sha fu* 资治通鉴：参合杀俘. Shenyang: Wan juan chu ban gong si, 2015.
Boyle, John Andrew. "Turkish and Mongol Shamanism in the Middle Ages." *Folklore* 83.3 (1972): 177–93.
Bray, Tamara L. "Commensal Politics of Early States and Empires." In *The Archaeology of Food and Feasting in Early States and Empires*. Ed. Tamara L. Bray, 1–13. New York: Kluwer Academic/Plenum, 2003.
Brereton, Gareth, ed. *I Am Ashurbanipal, King of the World, King of Assyria*. New York: Thames and Hudson, 2018.
Broadbridge, Anne F. *Women and the Making of the Mongol Empire*. Cambridge: Cambridge University Press, 2018.
Brose, Michael. *Subjects and Masters: Uyghurs in the Mongol Empire*. Bellingham: Center for East Asian Studies, Western Washington University, 2007.
Broughton, Jeffrey L. *The Bodhidharma Anthology: The Earliest Records of Zen*. Berkeley: University of California Press, 1999.
Brown, R. Allen. *English Castles*. London: B. T. Batsford, 1962.
Buckley, Chris. "In China's Coal Capital, Xi Jinping's Dream Remains Elusive." *New York Times*, 21 October 2017. https://www.nytimes.com/2017/10/21/world/asia/china-xi-jinping-datong.html. Accessed 1 March 2021.
Bulling, Anneliese Gutkind. "The Eastern Han Tomb at Ho-lin-ko-êrh (Holingol)." *Archives of Asian Art* 31 (1977): 79–103.
Bunker, Emma. *Ancient Bronzes of the Eastern Eurasian Steppes from the Arthur M. Sackler Collections*. New York: Arthur M. Sackler Foundation, 1997.
Byington, Mark E., ed. *The History and Archaeology of the Koguryŏ Kingdom*. Cambridge, MA: Early Korea Project, Korea Institute, Harvard University, 2016.
Cai Zongxian 蔡宗憲. "Bei Wei Taiwudi de ji si ji qi yi xiang de zhuan bian 北魏太武帝的祭祀及其意象的轉變－以兩宋之間的佛狸祠為中心." *Zao qi Zhongguo shi yan jiu* 6.1 (2014): 1–28.
Cai Zongxian 蔡宗憲. *Zhong gu qian qi de jiao pin yu nan bei hu dong* 中古前期的交聘與南北互動. Taibei: Dao xiang chu ban she, 2008.

Campany, Robert Ford. *Making Transcendents: Ascetics and Social Memory in Early Medieval China*. Honolulu: University of Hawai'i Press, 2009.

Cao Chenming 曹臣明. "Bei Wei Pingcheng bu ju chu tan" 北魏平城布局初探. In *Bei Wei Pingcheng kao gu yan jiu: gong yuan wu shi ji Zhongguo du cheng de yan bian*. Ed. Wang Yintian, 1–23. Beijing: Ke xue chu ban she, 2017.

Cao Chenming 曹臣明. "Pingcheng fu jin Xianbei ji Bei Wei mu zang fen bu gui lü kao" 平城附近鮮卑及北魏墓葬分布規律考. *Wen wu* (2016.5): 61–69.

Carneiro, Robert L. "The Chiefdom: Precursor to the State." In *The Transition to Statehood in the New World*. Ed. Grant D. Jones and Robert R. Kautz, 37–79. Cambridge and New York: Cambridge University Press, 1981.

Cen Zhongmian 岑仲勉. *Fu bing zhi du yan jiu* 府兵制度研究. Shanghai: Shanghai ren min chu ban she, 1957.

Chang, Michael G. *A Court on Horseback: Imperial Touring & the Construction of Qing Rule, 1680–1785*. Cambridge, MA: Harvard University Asia Center, 2007.

Chen Bo and Gideon Shelach. "Fortified Settlements and the Settlement System in the Northern Zone of the Han Empire." *Antiquity* 88 (2014): 222–40.

Chen Cheng-siang (Chen Zhengxiang) 陳正祥. *Cao yuan di guo: Tuoba Wei wang chao zhi xing shuai* 草原帝國: 拓跋魏王朝之興衰. Hong Kong: Zhonghua shu ju (Xianggang) you xian gong si, 1991.

Chen, Kenneth. *Buddhism in China: A Historical Survey*. Princeton, NJ: Princeton University Press, 1964.

Chen Lianqing 陈连庆. *Zhongguo gu dai shao shu min zu xing shi yan jiu: Jin Han Wei Jin Nan bei chao shao shu min zu xing shi yan jiu* 中国古代少数民族姓氏研究: 秦汉魏晋南北朝少数民族姓氏研究. Changchun: Jilin wen shi chu ban she, 1993.

Chen Linguo 陈琳国. *Zhong gu bei fang min zu shi tan* 中古北方民族史探. Beijing: Shang wu yin shu guan, 2010.

Chen, Sanping. *Multicultural China in the Early Middle Ages*. Philadelphia: University of Pennsylvania Press, 2012.

Chen Shuang 陈爽. "Lue lun Bei chao de xiang cun wu zhuang" 略论北朝的乡村武装. In *1-6 shi ji Zhongguo bei fang bian jiang, min zu, she hui guo ji xue shu yan tao hui lun wen ji*. Ed. Jilin daxue gu ji yan jiu suo, 299–311. Beijing: Ke xue chu ban she, 2008.

Chen Shuang 陈爽. *Shi jia da zu yu Bei chao zheng zhi* 世家大族与北朝政治. Beijing: Zhongguo she hui ke xue chu ban she, 1998.

Chen Yinke 陳寅恪. "Tao hua yuan ji pang zheng" 桃花源記旁證. In his *Chen Yinke xian sheng quan ji*, 2: 1169–78. 2 vols. Taibei: Jiu si chu ban you xian gong si.

Chen Yongzhi 陳永志 et al., eds. *Helin'geer Han mu bi hua tu mo xie tu ji lu* 和林格爾漢墓壁畫孝子傳圖摹寫圖輯錄. Beijing: Wen wu chu ban she, 2015.

Chen Yongzhi, Song Guodong, and Ma Yan. "The Results of the Excavations of the Yihe-Nur Cemetery in Zhengxiangbai Banner (2012-2014)." *The Silk Road* 14 (2016): 42–57 + Color Plates IV-VI.

Chen Yuping 陈玉屏. *Wei Jin Nan bei chao bing hu zhi du yan jiu* 魏晋南北朝兵户制度研究. Chengdu: Ba Shu shu she, 1988.

Cheng, Bonnie. "Exchange across Media in Northern Wei China." In *Face to Face: The Transcendence of the Arts in China and Beyond*. Ed. Rui Oliveira Lopes, 114–45. Lisbon: Centro de Investigação e Estudos em Belas-Artes (CIEBA), 2014.

Cheng Fangyi. "Remaking Chineseness: The Transition of Inner Asian Groups in the Central Plain during the Sixteen Kingdoms Period and Northern Dynasties." PhD diss., University of Pennsylvania, 2018.

Cheng, Ya-ju (Zheng Yaru) 鄭雅如. "Han zhi yu Hu feng: chong tan Bei Wei de 'huang hou,' 'huang tai hou' zhi du" 漢制與胡風：重探北魏的「皇后」、「皇太后」制度. *Zhong yang yan jiu yuan li shi yu yan yan jiu suo ji kan* 90.1 (2019): 1–76.

Chicago, Judy. *A Dinner Party: A Symbol of Our Heritage*. Garden City, NY: Anchor Press/Doubleday, 1979.

Chittick, Andrew. *The Jiankang Empire in Chinese and World History*. Oxford: Oxford University Press, 2020.

Chittick, Andrew. *Patronage and Community in Medieval China: The Xiangyang Garrison, 400–600 CE*. Albany: State University of New York Press, 2009.

Clark, Carolyn. "Land and Food, Women and Power in Nineteenth Century Kikuyu." *Africa* 50 (1980): 357–70.

Clark, Hugh. "What's the Matter with China? A Critique of Teleological History." *Journal of Asian Studies* 77.2 (2018): 295–314.

Cohen, Anthony P. *Belonging: Identity and Social Organisation in British Rural Cultures*. St. John's: Institute of Social and Economic Research, Memorial University of Newfoundland, 1982.

Cohen, Anthony P. *Symbolic Construction of Community*. London and New York: Tavistock Publications, 1985.

Cole, Alan. *Mothers and Sons in Chinese Buddhism*. Stanford, CA: Stanford University Press, 1998.

Collingham, E. M. *The Hungry Empire: How Britain's Quest for Food Shaped the Modern World*. London: The Bodley Head, 2017.

Craig, Tetsuko, tr. *Musui's Story: The Autobiography of a Tokugawa Samurai*. Tucson: University of Arizona Press, 1988.

Crossley, Pamela. *Orphan Warriors: Three Manchu Generations and the End of the Qing World*. Princeton, NJ: Princeton University Press, 1990.

Crump, J. I., tr. *Chan-kuo ts'e*. Oxford: Clarendon, 1970.

Cunliffe, Barry. *By Steppe, Desert, and Ocean: The Birth of Eurasia*. Oxford: Oxford University Press, 2015.

Dai Weihong 戴卫红. *Bei Wei kao ke zhi du yan jiu* 北魏考课制度研究. Beijing: Zhongguo she hui ke xue chu ban she, 2010.

Daichi Seiko 大知圣子 (大知聖子). "Guan yu Bei Wei qian qi jue he pin xiang dui ying de ji chu kao cha—yi Nanxun bei wei zhong xin" 关于北魏前期爵和品相对应的基础考察——以南巡碑为中心. In *Zhongguo Wei Jin Nan Bei chao shi xue hui di shi jie nian hui ji guo ji xue shu yan tao hui lun wen ji*. Ed. Zhongguo Wei Jin Nan Bei chao shi xue hui, Shanxi da xue li shi wen hua xue yuan, 92–107. Taiyuan: Beiyue wen yi chu ban she, 2012.

Darby, Brian J., Gregory A. Davis, and Zheng Yadong. "Structural Evolution of the Southwestern Daqing Shan, Yinshan Belt, Inner Mongolia, China." In *Paleozoic and Mesozoic Tectonic Evolution of Central Asia: From Continental Assembly to Intracontinental Deformation*. Ed. Marc S. Hendrix and Greg Davis, 199–214. Boulder, CO: Geological Society of America, 2001.

Datong gu cheng bao hu he xiu fu yan jiu hui 大同古城保护和修复研究会, ed. *Si lu qi dian: Bei Wei Pingcheng* 丝路起点：北魏平城. Taiyuan: Shanxi chu ban chuan mei ji tuan, 2016.
Datongshi bowuguan 大同市博物馆. "Datongshi Xiaozhancun Huage ta tai Bei Wei mu qing li jian bao" 大同市小站村花圪塔台北魏墓清理简报. *Wen wu* (1983.8): 1–4.
Datongshi kao gu yan jiu suo 大同市考古研究所. "Shanxi Datong Yunbolilu Bei Wei bi hua mu fa jue jian bao" 山西大同云波里路北魏壁画墓发掘简报. *Wen wu* (2011.12): 13–25.
Davis, Timothy. *Entombed Epigraphy and Commemorative Culture in Early Medieval China.* Leiden: Brill, 2015.
De Crespigny, Rafe. *Fire over Luoyang: A History of the Later Han Dynasty, 23–220 AD.* Leiden and Boston: Brill, 2017.
De Crespigny, Rafe. *Imperial Warlord: a Biography of Cao Cao, 155–220.* Leiden: Brill, 2010.
De Crespigny, Rafe. *Northern Frontier: The Policies and Strategy of the Later Han Empire.* Canberra: Faculty of Asian Studies, Australian National University, 1984.
De Crespigny, Rafe, tr. *Emperor Huan and Emperor Ling: Being the Chronicle of Later Han for the Years 157 to 189 AD as Recorded in Chapters 54 to 59 of the "Zizhi tongjian" of Sima Guang.* Canberra: Faculty of Asian Studies, Australia National University, 1989. Revised Internet Edition 2018: https://openresearch-repository.anu.edu.au/handle/1885/42048.
Di Cosmo, Nicola. *Ancient China and Its Enemies.* Cambridge and New York: Cambridge University Press, 2002.
Di Cosmo, Nicola. "Ancient Inner Asian Nomads: Their Economic Basis and Its Significance in Chinese History." *Journal of Asian Studies* 53.4 (1994): 1092–1126.
Di Cosmo, Nicola. "Aristocratic Elites in the Xiongnu Empire as Seen from Historical and Archaeological Evidence." In *Nomad Aristocrats in a World of Empires.* Ed. Jürgen Paul, 23–53. Wiesbaden: Ludwig Reichert, 2013.
Di Cosmo, Nicola. "China-Steppe Relations in Historical Perspective." In *Complexity of Interaction along the Eurasian Steppe Zone in the First Millennium CE.* Ed. Jan Bemmann and Michael Schmauder, 49–72. Bonn: Vor- und Frühgeschichtliche Archäologie, Rheinische Friedrich-Wilhelms-Universität, 2015.
Di Cosmo, Nicola. "Ethnogenesis, Co-evolution and Political Morphology of the Earliest Steppe Empire: The Xiongnu Question Revisited." In *Xiongnu Archaeology: Multidisciplinary Perspectives of the First Steppe Empire in Inner Asia.* Ed. Ursula Brosseder and Bryan K. Miller, 35–48. Bonn: Vor- und Frühgeschichtliche Archäologie, Rheinische Friedrich-Wilhelms-Universität Bonn, 2011.
Di Cosmo, Nicola. "Ethnography of the Nomads and 'Barbarian' History in Han China." In *Intentional History: Spinning Time in Ancient Greece.* Ed. Lin Foxhall, Hans-Joachim Gehrke, and Nino Luraghi, 297–324. Stuttgart: Franz Steiner, 2010.
Di Cosmo, Nicola. "Introduction." In *Military Culture in Imperial China.* Ed. Nicola Di Cosmo, 1–22. Cambridge, MA, and London: Harvard University Press, 2009.
Di Cosmo, Nicola. "The Northern Frontier in Pre-imperial China." In *Cambridge History of Ancient China.* Ed. Michael Loewe and Edward L. Shaughnessy, 885–966. Cambridge and New York: Cambridge University Press, 1999.
Di Cosmo, Nicola. "The Origins of the Great Wall." *The Silk Road* 4.1 (2006): 14–19.

Di Cosmo, Nicola. "State Formation and Periodization in Inner Asian History." *Journal of World History* 10.1 (1999): 1–40.
Dien, Albert E. "Civil Service Examinations: Evidence from the Northwest." In *Culture and Power in the Reconstitution of the Chinese Realm, 200–600*. Ed. Scott Pearce, Audrey Spiro, and Patricia Ebrey, 99–121. Cambridge, MA, and London: Harvard University Asia Center, 2001.
Dien, Albert E. "The Disputation at Pengcheng: Accounts from the *Wei shu* and the *Song shu*." In *Early Medieval China: A Sourcebook*. Ed. Wendy Swartz, Robert Ford Company, Yang Lu, and Jessey J. C. Choo, 32–59. New York: Columbia University Press, 2014.
Dien, Albert E. "Elite Lineages and the T'o-pa Accommodation: A Study of the Edict of 495." *Journal of the Economic and Social History of the Orient* 19.1 (1976): 61–88.
Dien, Albert E. "Encounters with Nomads." In *Monks and Merchants: Silk Road Treasures from Northwest China; Gansu and Ningxia, 4th–7th Century*. Ed. Annette L. Juliano and Judith A. Lerner, 54–115. New York: Harry N. Abrams with the Asia Society, 2001.
Dien, Albert E. "A New Look at the Xianbei and Their Impact on Chinese Culture." In *Ancient Mortuary Traditions of China: Papers on Chinese Ceramic Funerary Sculptures*. Ed. George Kuwayama, 40–59. Los Angeles: Los Angeles County Museum of Art, 1991.
Dien, Albert E. *Six Dynasties Civilization*. New Haven, CT: Yale University Press, 2007.
Dien, Albert E. "The Stirrup and Its Effect on Chinese Military History." *Ars Orientalia* 16 (1986): 33–56.
Dien, Albert E. "Wei Tan and the Historiography of the *Wei-shu*." In *Studies in Early Medieval Chinese Literature and Cultural History*. Ed. Paul W. Kroll and David R. Knechtges, 399–466. Provo, UT: T'ang Studies Society.
Dietler, Michael. "Clearing the Table: Some Concluding Reflections on Commensal Politics and Imperial States." In *The Archaeology of Food and Feasting in Early States and Empires*. Ed. Tamara L. Bray, 271–82. New York: Kluwer Academic/Plenum, 2003.
Dietler, Michael. "Feasts and Commensal Politics in the Political Economy." In *Food and the Status Quest: An Interdisciplinary Perspective*. Ed. Polly Wiessner and Wulf Schiefenhövel, 87–125. Providence, RI: Berghahn Books, 1996.
Domrös, Mandred, and Peng Gongbin. *The Climate of China*. Berlin: Springer-Verlag, 1988.
Drompp, Michael R. "The Lone Wolf in Inner Asia." *Journal of the American Oriental Society* 131.4 (2011): 515–26.
Du Shiduo 杜士铎, ed. *Bei Wei shi* 北魏史. Taiyuan: Shanxi gao xiao lian he chu ban she, 1992.
Duan Zhijun 段智钧 and Zhao Nuodong 赵娜冬. *Tian xia da tong: Bei Wei Pingcheng Liao Jin Xijing cheng shi jian zhu shi gang* 天下大同: 北魏平城辽金西京城市建筑史纲. Beijing: Zhongguo jian zhu gong ye chu ban she, 2011.
Dunnell, Ruth. *Chinggis Khan: World Conqueror*. Boston: Longman, 2010.
Dunnell, Ruth. *The Great State of High and White: Buddhism and State Formation in Eleventh-Century Xia*. Honolulu: University of Hawai'i Press, 1996.
Dunnell, Ruth. Review of Thomas Barfield, *The Perilous Frontier*. *Journal of Asian Studies* 50.1 (1991): 126–27.
Durrant, Stephen, Wai-Yee Li, Michael Nylan, and Hans Van Ess. *The Letter to Ren An & Sima Qian's Legacy*. Seattle: University of Washington Press, 2016.

Duthie, Nina. "The Nature of the *Hu*: Wuhuan and Xianbei Ethnography in the *San guo zhi* and *Hou Han shu*." *Early Medieval China* 25 (2019): 23–41.
Ebrey, Patricia. *The Aristocratic Families of Early Imperial China: A Case Study of the Po-ling Ts'ui Family*. Cambridge and New York: Cambridge University Press, 1978.
Eisenberg, Andrew. *Kingship in Early Medieval China*. Leiden and Boston: Brill, 2008.
Elliott, Mark (C.). "*Hushuo*: The Northern Other and the Naming of the Han Chinese." In *Critical Han Studies: The History, Representation, and Identity of China's Majority*. Ed. Thomas S. Mullaney et al., 173–90. Berkeley: University of California Press, 2012.
Elliott, Mark (C.). "Manchu (Re)Definitions of the Nation in the Early Qing." *Indiana East Asian Working Papers on Language and Politics in Modern China* 7 (1996): 46–78.
Elliott, Mark C. *The Manchu Way: The Eight Banners and Ethnic Identity in Late Imperial China*. Stanford, CA: Stanford University Press, 2001.
Elliott, Mark C. "Whose Empire Shall It Be? Manchu Figuration of Historical Process in the Early Seventeenth Century." In *Time, Temporality and Imperial Transition*. Ed. Lynn A. Struve, 31–72. Honolulu: Association for Asian Studies and University of Hawai'i Press, 2005.
Elliott, Mark C., and Ning Chia. "The Qing Hunt at Mulan." In *New Qing Imperial History: The Making of Inner Asian Empire at Qing Chengde*. Ed. James Millward, Ruth W. Dunnell, Mark C. Elliott, and Philippe Forêt, 66–83. London and New York: Routledge, 2004.
Elman, Benjamin A., and Martin Kern, eds. *Statecraft and Classical Learning: The "Rituals of Zhou" in East Asian History*. Leiden: Brill, 2010.
Englehardt, Ute. "Hanshi san (Cold Food Powder)." In *The Encyclopedia of Taoism*. Ed. Fabrizio Pregadio, 1: 473. 2 vols. London: Routledge, 2008.
Fan Zhaofei 范兆飞. "Yongjia luan hou de Bingzhou ju shi—yi Liu Kun ci Bing wei zhong xin" 永嘉乱后的并州局势—以刘琨刺并为中心. *Xue shu yue kan* (2008.3): 122–30.
Fan Zhaofei 范兆飞. *Zhong gu Taiyuan shi zu qun ti yan jiu* 中古太原士族群体研究. Beijing: Zhonghua shu ju, 2014.
Farquhar, David M. *The Government of China under Mongolian Rule: A Reference Guide*. Stuttgart: Steiner, 1990.
Fedosenko, Alexander K., and David A. Blank. "Ovis ammon." *Mammalian Species* 773 (July 15, 2005): 1–15.
Feeney, Denis. *Beyond Greek: The Beginnings of Latin Literature*. Cambridge, MA: Harvard University Press, 2016.
Fentress, James, and Chris Wickham. *Social Memory*. Cambridge, MA: Blackwell, 1992.
Fiaschetti, Francesca, and Julia Schneider. "Introduction." In their edited volume *Political Strategies of Identity Building in Non-Han Empires in China*, 1–5. Wiesbaden: Harrassowitz, 2014.
Findley, Carter V. *The Turks in World History*. Oxford: Oxford University Press, 2005.
Fingarette, Herbert. *Confucius: The Secular as Sacred*. New York: Harper & Row, 1972.
Fogel, Joshua. *Medieval Chinese Society and the Local "Community."* Berkeley: University of California Press, 1985.
Ford, (Randolph) R. A. "The Gaxian Cave 嘎仙洞 Inscription: The Perpetuation of Steppe Tradition under the Northern Wei Dynasty." *Archivum Eurasiae Medii Aevi* 20 (2013): 23–66.
Fox, Robin Lane. *Augustine: Conversion to Confessions*. New York: Basic Books, 2015.

Frachetti, Michael. "Differentiated Landscape and Non-uniform Complexity among Bronze Age Societies of the Eurasian Steppe." In *Social Complexity in Prehistoric Eurasia: Monuments, Metals, and Mobility*. Ed. Bryan K. Hanks and Katheryn M. Linduff, 19–46. Cambridge and New York: Cambridge University Press, 2009.

Fridley, David, tr. "Xianbei Remains in Manchuria and Inner Mongolia: Record of Xianbei remains, Part One." *Chinese Studies in Archaeology* 1.2 (1980): 18–27.

Fried, Morton. *The Notion of Tribe*. Menlo Park, CA: Cummings, 1975.

Fu, Xinian. *Traditional Chinese Architecture: Twelve Essays*. Princeton, NJ, and Oxford: Princeton University Press, 2017.

Furuta Shinichi 古田真一. "Rikuchō kaiga ni kansuru ichi kōsatsu—Shiba Kinryū bo shutsudo no shiga byōbu o megutte" 六朝絵画に関する一考察—司馬金龍墓出土の漆画屏風をめぐって. *Bigaku* 42.4 (1992): 57–67.

Gai Shanlin 盖山林 and Lu Sixian 陆思贤. "Yinshan nan lu de Zhao chang cheng" 阴山南麓的赵长城. In *Zhongguo chang cheng yi ji diao cha bao gao ji* 中国长城遗迹调查报告集. Ed. Wen wu bian ji wei yuan hui, 21–24. Beijing: Wen wu chu ban she, 1981.

Gang Ge'er 钢格尔 et al., comp. *Nei Menggu zi zhi qu jing ji di li* 内蒙古自治区经济地理. Beijing: Xin hua chu ban she, 1992.

Gao Min 高敏. *Wei Jin Nan bei chao bing zhi yan jiu* 魏晋南北朝兵制研究. Zhengzhou: Da xiang chu ban she, 1998.

Gardiner, K. H. J., and R. R. C. (Rafe) de Crespigny. "T'an-shih-huai and the Hsien-pei Tribes of the Second Century A.D." *Papers on Far Eastern History* 15 (1977): 1–44.

Gat, Azar. *Nations: The Long History and Deep Roots of Political Ethnicity and Nationalism*. Cambridge: Cambridge University Press, 2013.

Ge Jianxiong 葛剑雄 et al. *Zhongguo ren kou shi* 中国人口史. 6 vols. Shanghai: Fudan da xue chu ban she, 2000–2002.

Geertz, Clifford. *Interpretation of Cultures: Selected Essays*. New York: Basic Books, 1973.

Geertz, Clifford. *Negara: The Theatre State in Nineteenth-century Bali*. Princeton, NJ: Princeton University Press, 1980.

Giele, Enno. "Evidence for the Xiongnu in Chinese Wooden Documents from the Han Period." In *Xiongnu Archaeology: Multidisciplinary Perspectives of the First Steppe Empire in Inner Asia*. Ed. Ursula Brosseder and Bryan K. Miller, 49–75. Bonn: Vor- und Frühgeschichtliche Archäologie, Rheinische Friedrich-Wilhelms-Universität Bonn, 2011.

Giovanni da Pian del Carpine. *The Story of the Mongols Whom We Call the Tartars*. Tr. Erik Hildinger. Boston: Branden Publishing Company, 1996.

Golden, Peter B. *Central Asia in World History*. New York: Oxford University Press, 2011.

Golden, Peter B. "Imperial Ideology and the Sources of Unity among the Pre-Činggisid Nomads of Western Eurasia." *Archivum Eurasiae Medii Aevi* 2 (1982): 37–76.

Golden, Peter B. *An Introduction to the History of the Turkic Peoples: Ethnogenesis and State-formation in Medieval and Early Modern Eurasia and the Middle East*. Wiesbaden: Harrassowitz, 1992.

Golden, Peter B. "Wolves, Dogs and Qïpchaq Religion." *Acta Orientalia Hungarica* 50.1–3 (1997): 87–97.

Golovachev, Valentin. "Matricide among the Tuoba-Xianbei and Its Transformation during the Northern Wei." *Early Medieval China* 8 (2002): 1–41.

Goodman, Howard L. "Sites of Recognition: Burial, Mourning, and Commemoration in the Xun Family of Yingchuan, AD 140–305." *Early Medieval China* 15 (2009): 49–90.

Goody, Jack. *The Power of the Written Tradition*. Washington, DC: Smithsonian Institution Press, 2000.

Graff, David A. *Medieval Chinese Warfare, 300–900*. London and New York: Routledge, 2002.

Grafflin, Dennis. "Great Family in Medieval South China." *Harvard Journal of Asiatic Studies* 41 (1981): 65–74.

Gregory, Alice. "Finished: Life at the Last Swiss Bastion of Etiquette Training." *New Yorker*, 8 October 2018. https://www.newyorker.com/magazine/2018/10/08/lessons-from-the-last-swiss-finishing-school. Accessed 1 March 2021.

Gruen, Erich. *Rethinking the Other in Antiquity*. Princeton, NJ: Princeton University Press, 2011.

Gu Jiguang 谷霽光. "Bu Wei shu bing zhi" 補魏書兵志. In *Er shi wu shi bu bian* 二十五史補編, 4: 4665–68. Ed. Er shi wu shi kan xing wei yuan hui 二十五史刊行委員會. 6 vols. Beijing: Zhonghua shu ju, 1956.

Guan Furong 管芙蓉. "Bei Wei Pingcheng gong dian jian zhu chu tan" 北魏平城宮殿建築出探. In her *Bei chao san lun*. Taiyuan: Shanxi jing ji chu ban she, 2007. Rpt. in *Zou chu shi ku de Bei Wei wang chao*, edited by Jin Zhao and Aledeʾertu, 739–50. Beijing: Wen hua yi shu chu ban she, 2010.

Guan Furong 管芙蓉. "Fo mu ta dong yu Feng Taihou—Yungang shi ku wen hua nei han jie du" 佛母塔洞与冯太后—云冈石窟文化内涵解读. In *2005 nian Yungang guo ji xue shu yan jiu hui lun wen ji, yan jiu juan*. Ed. Yungang shi ku yan jiu yuan, 733–36. Beijing: Wen wu chu ban she, 2006. Rpt. In her *Bei chao san lun*. Taiyuan: Shanxi jing ji chu ban she, 2007: 352–59.

Guisso, R. W. L. *Wu Tse-tʾien and the Politics of Legitimation in Tʾang China*. Bellingham: Western Washington University, 1978.

Halsall, Guy. *Barbarian Migration and the Roman West, 376–568*. Cambridge: Cambridge University Press, 2007.

Hämäläinen, Pekka. *The Comanche Empire*. New Haven, CT: Yale University Press, 2008.

Han Guopan 韓國磐. *Bei chao jing ji shi tan* 北朝經濟試探. Shanghai: Shanghai ren min chu ban she, 1958.

Han Maoli 韩茂莉. "Li shi shi qi Zhongguo jiang yu shen suo de di li ji chu" 历史时期中国疆域伸缩的地理基础. *Zhongguo wen hua yan jiu* (2016.2): 71–79.

Han Xiang 韩香. "Shi lun zao qi Xianbei zu de yuan shi sa man chong bai" 试论早期鲜卑族的原始萨满崇拜. *Heilongjiang min zu cong kan* (1995.1). Rpt. in *Zou chu shi ku de Bei Wei wang chao*. Ed. Jin Zhao and Aledeʾertu, 600–607. Beijing: Wen hua yi shu chu ban she, 2010.

Han yu da ci dian 汉语大词典. 12 vols. Shanghai: Han yu da ci dian chu ban she, 1993.

Handel, Zev. *Sinography: The Borrowing and Adaptation of the Chinese Script*. Leiden and Boston: Brill, 2019.

Hansen, Valerie. *The Silk Road: A New History*. New York: Oxford University Press, 2012.

He Dezhang 何德章. "Bei Wei cheng ren yu nong geng" 北魏城人与农耕. In his *Wei Jin Nan bei chao shi cong gao*, 346–54. Beijing: Shang wu yin shu guan, 2010.

He Dezhang 何得章. "Bei Wei guo hao yu zheng tong wen ti" 北魏国号与正统问题. *Li shi yan jiu* (1992.3): 113–25.

He Dezhang 何德章. "'Xianbei wen zi' shuo bian zheng" "鲜卑文字"说辨正. *Bei chao yan jiu* (1992.2). Rpt. in his *Wei Jin Nan Bei chao shi cong gao*, 369–75. Beijing: Shang wu yin shu guan, 2010.

He Dezhang 何德章. "'Yinshan que shuang' zhi su jie" "阴山却霜"之俗解. *Wei Jin Nan bei chao Sui Tang shi zi liao* 12 (1993): 102–16.

He Ziquan 何兹全. "Fu bing zhi qian de Bei chao bing zhi" 府兵制前的北朝兵制. In his *Du shi ji*, 317–53. Shanghai: Shanghai ren min chu ban she, 1982.

He Ziquan 何兹全. "Wei Jin de zhong jun" 魏晋的中军. *Li shi yu yan yan jiu so ji kan* 17. Rpt. in his *Du shi ji*. 242–68. Shanghai: Shanghai ren min chu ban she, 1982.

Heather, P. J. (Peter J.). *Empires and Barbarians: The Fall of Rome and the Birth of Europe*. London: Macmillan, 2009.

Heather, P. J. (Peter J.). *Goths and Romans, 332–489*. Oxford: Clarendon Press, 1991

Hein, Anke, ed. *The "Crescent-shaped Cultural-communication Belt": Tong Enzheng's Model in Retrospect*. Oxford: Archaeopress, 2014.

Helms, Mary. *Craft and the Kingly Ideal: Art, Trade and Power*. Austin: University of Texas Press, 1993.

Hemingway, Ernest. "On the Blue Water." *Esquire*, April 1936.

Henning, W. B. "The Date of the Sogdian Ancient Letters." *BSOAS* 12.3/4 (1948): 601–15.

Hobbes, Thomas. *Leviathan; or, The Matter, Forme and Power of a Commonwealth, Ecclesiasticall and Civil*. Ed. Michael Oakeshott. Oxford: Blackwell, 1957.

Holcombe, Charles. *The Genesis of East Asia: 221 B.C.–A.D. 907*. Honolulu: University of Hawai'i Press, 2001.

Holcombe, Charles. *In the Shadow of the Han: Literati Thought and Society at the Beginning of the Southern Dynasties*. Honolulu: University of Hawai'i Press, 1994.

Holcombe, Charles. "The Xianbei in Chinese History." *Early Medieval China* 19 (2013): 1–38.

Holmgren, Jennifer. *Annals of Tai: Early T'o-pa History According to the First Chapter of the Wei shu*. Canberra: Australian National University Press, 1982.

Holmgren, Jennifer. "Empress Dowager Ling of the Northern Wei and the T'o-pa Sinicization Question." *Papers on Far Eastern History* 18 (1978): 123–70.

Holmgren, Jennifer. "The Harem in Northern Wei Politics." *Journal of the Economic and Social History of the Orient* 26.1 (1983): 71–96.

Holmgren, Jennifer. "Lineage Falsification in the Northern Dynasties: Wei Shou's Ancestry." *Papers on Far Eastern History* 21 (1980): 1–16.

Holmgren, Jennifer. "The Lu Clan of Tai Commandery and Their Contribution to the T'o-pa State of Northern Wei in the Fifth Century." *T'oung Pao* 69.4–5 (1983): 272–312.

Holmgren, Jennifer. "The Making of an Élite: Local Politics and Social Relations in Northeastern China during the Fifth Century A.D." *Papers on Far Eastern History* 30 (1984): 1–79.

Holmgren, Jennifer. "The Northern Wei as a Conquest Dynasty." *Papers on Far Eastern History* 40 (1989): 1–50.

Holmgren, Jennifer. "Social Mobility in the Northern Dynasties: A Case Study of the Feng of Northern Yen." *Monumenta Serica* 35 (1981–1983): 19–32.

Holmgren, Jennifer. "Women and Political Power in the Traditional T'o-Pa Elite: A Preliminary Study of the Biographies of Empresses in the *Wei-Shu*." *Monumenta Serica* 35 (1981–1983): 33–74.

Honeychurch, William. "Alternative Complexities: The Archaeology of Pastoral Nomadic States." *Journal of Archaeological Research* 22.4 (2014): 277–326.

Honeychurch, William. "From Steppe Roads to Silk Roads: Inner Asian Nomads and Early Interregional Exchange." In *Nomads as Agents of Social Change: The Mongols and Their Eurasian Predecessors*. Ed. Reuven Amitai and Michal Biran, 50–87. Honolulu: University of Hawai'i Press, 2015.

Honeychurch, William. *Inner Asia and the Spatial Politics of Empire: Archaeology, Mobility, and Culture Contact*. New York: Springer, 2015.

Honeychurch, William. "The Nomad as State Builder: Historical Theory and Material Evidence from Mongolia." *Journal of World Prehistory* 26.4 (2013): 283–321.

Hong Tao 洪涛. *San Qin shi* 三秦史. Shanghai: Fudan da xue chu ban she, 1992.

Hope, Michael. *Power, Politics, and Tradition in the Mongol Empire and the Ilkhānate of Iran*. Oxford: Oxford University Press, 2016.

Hori Toshikazu 堀敏一. *Kindensei no kenkyū: Chūgoku kodai kokka no tochi seisaku to tochi shoyūsei* 均田制の研究: 中国古代国家の土地政策と土地所有制. Tokyo: Iwanami shoten, 1975.

Hou Liangliang 侯亮亮 et al. "Nong ye qu you mu min zu yin shi wen hua de zhi hou xing—ji yu Datong Dongxin guangchang Bei Wei mu qun ren gu de wen ding tong wei su yan jiu" 农业区游牧民族饮食文化的滞后性—基于大同东信广场北魏墓群人骨的稳定同位素研究. *Ren lei xue xue bao* 36.3 (2017): 359–69.

Hou Xudong 侯旭东. "Bei chao de cun luo" 北朝的村落. In his *Bei chao cun min de sheng huo shi jie—chao ting, zhou xian yu cun li* 北朝村民的生活世界-朝廷，州县与村里, 26–59. Beijing: Shang wu yin shu guan, 2005. (An earlier version appeared in *Qing zhu He Ziquan xian sheng jiu shi sui lun wen ji*, 161–82. Beijing: Beijing shi fan da xue chu ban she, 2001.)

Hou Xudong 侯旭东. "Bei chao 'san zhang zhi'" 北朝"三长制". In his *Bei chao cun min de sheng huo shi jie—chao ting, zhou xian yu cun li* 北朝村民的生活世界-朝廷，州县与村里, 108–33. Beijing: Shang wu yin shu guan, 2005.

Hou Xudong 侯旭东. "On Hamlets (cun) in the Northern Dynasties." *Early Medieval China* 13–14.1 (2007): 99–141.

Hsu, Shengi. "From Pingcheng to Luoyang: Substantiation of the Climatic Cause for Capital Relocation of the Beiwei Dynasty." *Progress in Natural Science* 14.8 (2004): 725–29.

Huang Lie 黄烈. "Tuoba Xianbei zao qi guo jia de xing cheng" 拓拔鲜卑早期国家的形成. In *Wei Jin Sui Tang shi lun ji*, Vol. 2. Ed. Zhongguo she hui ke xue yuan li shi yan jiu suo, Wei Jin Nan Bei chao Sui Tang shi yan jiu shi, 60–94. Beijing: Zhongguo she hui ke xue chu ban she, 1983.

Huang, Wen-Yi. "Negotiating Boundaries: Cross-Border Migrants in Early Medieval China." PhD diss., McGill University, 2017.

Hucker, Charles O. *A Dictionary of Official Titles in Imperial China*. Stanford, CA: Stanford University Press, 1985.

Hurvitz, Leon, tr. *Wei Shou: Treatise on Buddhism and Taoism; An English Translation of the Original Chinese Text of Wei-shu CXIV and the Japanese Annotation of Tsukamoto Zenryū*. Kyoto: Jimbunkagaku Kenkyusho, Kyoto University, 1956.

Hutchinson, John, Chris Wickham, Bo Stråth, and Azar Gat. "Debate on Azar Gat's *Nations: The Long History and Deep Roots of Political Ethnicity and Nationalism*." *Nations and Nationalism* 21.3 (2015): 383–402.

Indrisano, Gregory G. "Subsistence, Environment Fluctuation and Social Change: A Case Study in South Central Inner Mongolia." PhD diss., University of Pittsburgh, 2006.

Irwin, Robert. *Ibn Khaldun: An Intellectual Biography*. Princeton, NJ: Princeton University Press, 2018.

Itagaki Akira 板垣明. "Hokugi no Sei-iki tōbatsu o megutte" 北魏の西域討伐をめぐって. *Chuō daigaku Ajia shi kenkyū* 20 (1996): 103–19.

Jackson, Peter. "Beg." In *Encyclopædia Iranica*. Originally published in Vol. 3, 1989. Accessed in online edition, 17 December 2018. https://www.iranicaonline.org/

Jacobson-Tepfer, Esther. *The Hunter, the Stag, and the Mother of Animals: Image, Monument, and Landscape in Ancient North Asia*. Oxford and New York: Oxford University Press, 2015.

Janhunen, Jan. *Manchuria: An Ethnic History*. Helsinki: Finno-Ugrian Society, 1996.

Jay, Jennifer. *A Change in Dynasties: Loyalism in Thirteenth-century China*. Bellingham: Western Washington University, 1991.

Jenner, W. J. F. (William John Francis). *Memories of Loyang: Yang Hsüan-chih and the Lost Capital (493–534)*. Oxford: Clarendon Press, 1981.

Jiang Lang 姜狼. *Zhu lu tian xia: Bei Qi he Bei Zhou si shi nian zheng ba shi, 526–581* 逐鹿天下：北齊和北周四十年爭霸史, 526–581. Taibei: Da di chu ban she, 2012.

Jin Fagen 金發根. *Yongjia luan hou bei fang de hao zu* 永嘉亂後北方的豪族. Taibei: Zhongguo xue shu zhu zuo jiang zhu wei yuan hui, 1964.

Johnson, David. *The Medieval Chinese Oligarchy*. Boulder, CO: Westview Press, 1977.

Jones, Edward. "Militarisation of Roman Society, 400–700." In *Military Aspects of Scandinavian Society in a European Perspective, AD 1–1300: Papers from an International Research Seminar at the Danish National Museum, Copenhagen, 2–4 May 1996*. Ed. Anne Nørgård Jorgensen and Birthe L. Clausen, 19–24. Copenhagen: National Museum, 1997.

Jones, Martin. *Feast: Why Humans Share Food*. Oxford: Oxford University Press, 2007.

Ju Shengji 具聖姬. See Ku Saek-hŭi.

Juliano, Annette L. *Unearthed: Recent Archaeological Discoveries from Northern China*. Williamstown, MA: Sterling and Francine Clark Art Institute, 2012.

Junger, Sebastian. *Tribe: On Homecoming and Belonging*. New York and London: Twelve, 2016.

Kang Le 康樂. *Cong Xi jiao dao Nan jiao: guo jia ji dian yu Bei Wei zheng zhi* 從西郊到南郊—國家祭典與北魏政治. Taibei: Dao he chu ban she, 1995.

Kang Le. "Empire for a City: Cultural Reforms of the Hsiao-wen Emperor (A.D. 471–499)." PhD diss., Yale University, 1983.

Kawakatsu Yoshio 川勝義雄. *Chūgoku kizokusei shakai no kenkyū* 中國貴族制社會の研究. Kyoto: Kyōto Daigaku Jinbun Kagaku Kenkyūjo, 1987.

Kawamoto Yoshiaki 川本芳昭. *Gi Shin Nanbokuchō jidai no minzoku mondai* 魏晋南北朝時代の民族問題. Tokyo: Kyūko Shoin, 1998.

Kawamoto Yoshiaki 川本芳昭. "Goko Jūrokkoku Hokuchō ki ni okeru Shūrai no juyō o megutte" 五胡十六国・北朝期における周礼の受容をめぐって. *Saga daigaku kyōyōbu kenkyū kiyō* 23 (1991): 1–14.

Kern, Martin. Review of David Schaberg, *A Patterned Past*. *Harvard Journal of Asiatic Studies* 63.1 (2003): 273–89.

Kessler, Adam Theodore. *Empires beyond the Great Wall: The Heritage of Genghis Khan*. Los Angeles: Natural History Museum of Los Angeles County, 1994.

Khazanov, Anatoly. *Nomads and the Outside World*. Cambridge and New York: Cambridge University Press, 1984.

Kidder, Edward J. *Himiko and Japan's Elusive Chiefdom of Yamatai: Archaeology, History, and Mythology*. Honolulu: University of Hawai'i Press, 2007.

Kieschnick, John. *The Eminent Monk: Buddhist Ideals in Medieval Chinese Hagiography*. Honolulu: University of Hawai'i Press, 1997.

Kikuchi Hideo 菊池英夫. "Hokuchō gunsei ni okeru iwayuru kyōhei ni tsuite" 北朝軍制に於ける所謂郷兵について. In *Shigematsu Sensei koki kinen Kyūshū Daigaku Tōyōshi ronsō*. Ed. Hino Kaisaburō, 95–139. Fukuoka: Kyūshū Daigaku Bungakubu (Shigakuka) Tōyō Shi Kyūken[sic]shitsu, 1957.

Klein, Kenneth. "The Contributions of the Fourth Century Xianbei States to the Reunification of the Chinese Empire." PhD diss., UCLA, 1980.

Knapp, Keith. *Selfless Offspring: Filial Children and Social Order in Early Medieval China*. Honolulu: University of Hawai'i Press, 2005.

Knapp, Keith. "The Use and Understanding of Domestic Animals in Early Medieval Northern China." *Early Medieval China* 25 (2019): 85–99.

Knechtges, David R., tr. *Wen xuan: Or, Selections of Refined Literature*. 3 vols. Princeton, NJ: Princeton University Press, 1982–1996.

Koga Akimine 古賀昭岑. "Hokugi no buzoku kaisan ni tsuite" 北魏の部族解散について. *Tōhōgaku* 59 (1980): 62–76.

Koga Noboru 古賀登. "Hoku-Gi no hōroku sei shikō ni tsuite" 北魏の俸禄制施行について. *Tōyōshi kenkyū* 24.2 (1965): 152–76.

Kornicki, Peter. *Languages, Scripts and Chinese Texts in East Asia*. Oxford: Oxford University Press, 2018.

Kost, Catrin. "Heightened Receptivity: Steppe Objects and Steppe Influences in Royal Tombs of the Western Han Dynasty." *Journal of the American Oriental Society* 137.2 (2017): 349–81.

Kramers, Robert P. "The Development of the Confucian Schools." In *Cambridge History of China*, Vol. 1, *The Ch'in and Han Empires, 221 B.C.–A.D. 220*. Ed. Denis Twitchett and Michael Loewe, 747–65. Cambridge: Cambridge University Press, 1986.

Kroll, Paul. *A Student's Dictionary of Classical and Medieval Chinese*. Leiden and Boston: Brill, 2015.

Ku Saek-hŭi 具聖姬. *Liang Han Wei Jin Nan Bei chao de wu bi* 两汉魏晋南北朝的坞壁. Beijing: Min zu chu ban she, 2004.

Kubozoe Yoshifumi 窪添慶文. *Boshi o mochiita Hokugi shi kenkyū* 墓誌を用いた北魏史研究. Tokyo: Kyūko Shoin, 2017.

Kubozoe Yoshifumi 窪添庆文. "Guan yu Bei Wei de tai zi jian guo zhi du" 关于北魏的太子监国制度. *Wen shi zhe* (2002.1): 124–29.

Kubozoe Yoshifumi 窪添庆文. *Wei Jin Nan bei chao guan liao zhi yan jiu* 魏晋南北朝官僚制研究. Kindle ed. Shanghai: Fudan da xue chu ban she, 2017. (Original in Japanese: *Gi Shin Nanbokuchō kanryōsei kenkyū* 魏晋南北朝官僚制研究. Tokyo: Kyūko Shoin, 2003.)

Kwa, Shiamin, and W. L. Idema. *Mulan: Five Versions of a Classic Chinese Legend with Related Texts*. Indianapolis: Hackett Pub. Co., 2010.

Lal, Ruby. *Domesticity and Power in the Early Mughal World*. Cambridge: Cambridge University Press, 2005.

Lattimore, Owen. *The Desert Road to Turkestan*. Boston: Little, Brown, and Company, 1929.

Lattimore, Owen. *The Inner Asian Frontier of China*. Boston: Beacon Press, 1951.

Ledderose, Lothar. *Ten Thousand Things: Module and Mass Production in Chinese Art*. Princeton, NJ: Princeton University Press, 2000.

Lee, Jen-der. "Wet Nurses in Early Imperial China." *Nan Nü* 2.1 (2000): 1–39.

Lei Bingfeng 雷炳锋. "Wang Su 'Bei Pingcheng' shi chuang zuo shi jian kao bian" 王肃《悲平城》诗创作时间考辨. *Suzhou xue yuan xue bao* 30.8 (2015): 64–66.

Lewis, Mark Edward. *China between Empires: The Northern and Southern Dynasties*. Cambridge, MA: Belknap Press of Harvard University Press, 2009.

Lewis, Mark Edward. *The Construction of Space in Early China*. Albany: State University of New York Press, 2006.

Lewis, Mark Edward. *The Early Chinese Empires: Qin and Han*. Cambridge, MA: Belknap Press of Harvard University Press, 2007.

Lewis, Mark Edward. "Han Abolition of Universal Military Service." In *Warfare in Chinese History*. Ed. Hans J. van de Ven, 33–74. Leiden and Boston: Brill, 2000.

Lewis, Mark Edward. "The Mythology of Early China." In *Early Chinese Religion*, Part 1, *Shang through Han*. Ed. John Lagerwey and Marc Kalinowski, 1: 543–94. Leiden and Boston: Brill, 2008.

Lewis, Mark Edward. *Writing and Authority in Early China*. Albany: State University of New York Press, 1999.

Li Hu 黎虎. "Bei Wei qian qi de shou lie jing ji" 北魏前期的狩猎经济. *Li shi yan jiu* (1992.1): 106–18.

Li Hu 黎虎, ed. *Han Tang yin shi wen hua shi* 汉唐饮食文化史. Beijing: Beijing shi fan da xue chu ban she, 1998.

Li Jizhong 李继忠 and Niu Jin 牛劲. *Bei Wei she hui sheng huo zhi liu bian* 北魏社会生活之流变. Changchun: Jilin da xue chu ban she, 2009.

Li Junqing 李俊清. "Bei Wei Jinling di li wei zhi de chu bu kao cha" 北魏金陵地理位置的初步考察. *Wen wu ji kan* (1990.1): 67–74, 38.

Li Ping 李凭. *Bei chao yan jiu cun gao* 北朝研究存稿. Beijing: Shang wu yin shu guan, 2006.

Li Ping 李凭. *Bei Wei Pingcheng shi dai* 北魏平城时代. Beijing: She hui ke xue wen xian chu ban she, 2000.

Li Ping 李凭. "Bei Wei Wenchengdi chu nian de san hou zhi zheng" 北魏文成帝初年的三后之争. In his *Bei chao yan jiu cun gao*, 137–61. Beijing: Shang wu yin shu guan, 2006.

Li Yanong 李亞農. *Zhou zu de shi zu zhi yu Tuoba zu de qian feng jian zhi* 周族的氏族制與拓跋族的前封建制. Shanghai: Hua dong ren min chu ban she, 1954.

Liebmann, Matthew. "Parsing Hybridity: Archaeologies of Amalgamation in Seventeenth-century New Mexico." In *The Archaeology of Hybrid Material Culture*. Ed. Jeb J. Card, 25–49. Carbondale: Southern Illinois University Press, 2013.

Ligeti, Lajos (Louis). "Le Tabghatch, un dialecte de la langue Sien-pi." In *Mongolian Studies*. Ed. Lajos Ligeti, 265–308. Budapest: Akadémiai Kiadó, 1970.

Lim, An-king. "On the Etymology of T'o-pa." *Central Asiatic Journal* 44.1 (2000): 30–44.

Lin Gan 林幹. *Xiongnu tong shi* 匈奴通史. Beijing: Ren min chu ban she, 1986.

Lin Gan 林幹, ed. *Xiongnu shi liao hui bian* 匈奴史料彙編. 2 vols. Beijing: Zhonghua shu ju, 1988.

Lin Sheng-Chih (Lin Shengzhi) 林聖智. "Bei Wei Shaling bi hua mu yan jiu" 北魏沙嶺壁畫墓研究. *Zhong yang yan jiu yuan li shi yu yan yan jiu suo ji kan* 83.1 (2012): 1–95.

Linduff, Katheryn M., and Karen Sydney Rubinson. *Are All Warriors Male?: Gender Roles on the Ancient Eurasian Steppe*. Lanham, MD: AltaMira Press, 2008.

Lingley, Kate A. "Lady Yuchi in the First Person: Patronage, Kinship and Voice in the Guyang Cave." *Early Medieval China* 18 (2012): 25–47.

Liu Dajie 劉大杰. *Zhongguo wen xue fa zhan shi* 中國文學發展史. Taibei: Taiwan Zhonghua shu ju, 1968.

Liu, Jenny Chao-Hui. "Status and the 'Procession' Scene on the Sloping Path in Tang Princess Tombs (643–706)." *Mei shu shi yan jiu ji kan* 41 (2016): 239–374.

Liu Jinglong 刘景龙. *Bin yang dong: Longmen shi ku di 104, 140, 159 ku* 宾阳洞: 龙门石窟第104、140、159窟. Beijing: Wen wu chu ban she, 2010.

Liu Jun 刘军. "Bei Wei huang zu zheng zhi ti zhi zhi kao cha—yi zong shi ba gong wei zhong xin" 北魏皇族政治体制之考察——以宗室八公为中心. *Nandu xue tan* 34.6 (2014): 21–27.

Liu Jun 刘军. "Lun Bei Wei qian qi zong shi zai jin jun zhong de di wei ji zuo yong" 论北魏前期宗室在禁军中的地位及作用. *Xuchang xue yuan xue bao* 32.1 (2013): 12–15.

Liu Jun 刘军. "Lun Tuoba zu shang wu xi su zhi shuai tui—yi Bei Wei hou qi zong shi dan ren jin wei wu zhi wei li" 论拓跋族尚武习俗之衰退——以北魏后期宗室担任禁卫武职为例. *Bei fang wen wu* (2015.1): 54–59.

Liu Junxi 刘俊喜, ed. *Datong Yan bei shi yuan Bei Wei mu qun* 大同雁北师院北魏墓群. Beijing: Wen wu chu ban she, 2008.

Liu Junxi 刘俊喜 and Gao Feng 高峰. "Datong Zhijiabao Bei Wei mu guan ban hua" 大同智家堡北魏墓棺板画. *Wen wu* (2004.12): 35–47.

Liu Junxi and Li Li. "The Recent Discovery of a Group of Northern Wei Tombs in Datong." *Orientations* 33.5 (2002): 42–47.

Liu Meiyun 刘美云 and Wei Haiqing 魏海清. "Shou lie xi su dui Bei Wei qian qi zheng quan de ying xiang" 狩猎习俗对北魏前期政权的影响. In *Bei chao shi yan jiu: Zhongguo Wei Jin Nan Bei chao shi guo ji xue shu yan tao hui lun wen ji*. Ed. Yin Xian, 423–27. Beijing: Shang wu yin shu guan, 2005.

Liu Puning. "Becoming the Ruler of the Central Realm: How the Northern Wei Dynasty Established Its Political Legitimacy." *Journal of Asian History* 52.1 (2018): 83–117.

Liu, Shufen. "Jiankang and the Commercial Empire of the Southern Dynasties: Change and Continuity in Medieval Chinese Economic History." In *Culture and Power in* the Reconstitution of the Chinese Realm, 200–600. Ed. Scott Pearce, Audrey Spiro, and Patricia Ebrey, 35–52. Cambridge, MA, and London: Harvard University Asia Center, 2001.

Liu Shufen 劉淑芬. "Jiankang yu Liu chao li shi de fa zhan" 建康与六朝历史的发展. *Da lu za zhi* 66.4 (1983). Rpt. in her *Liu chao de cheng shi yu she hui* 六朝的城市與社會, 3–34. Taibei: Taiwan xue sheng shu ju, 1992.

Liu Shufen 劉淑芬. *Liu chao de cheng shi yu she hui* 六朝的城市與社會. Taibei: Taiwan xue sheng shu ju, 1992.

Liu Shufen 劉淑芬. *Zhong gu de Fo jiao yu she hui* 中古的佛教与社会. Shanghai: Shanghai gu ji chu ban she, 2008.

Liu Xinru. "The Silk Road: Overland Trade and Cultural Interactions in Eurasia." Washington, DC: American Historical Association, 1998. Rpt. in *Agricultural and Pastoral Societies in Ancient and Classical History*. Ed. Michael Adas, 151–79. Philadelphia: Temple University Press, 2001.

Liu, Yan. "Emblems of Power and Glory: The Han Period Chinese Lacquer Wares Discovered in the Borderlands." In *Production, Distribution and Appreciation: New Aspects of East Asian Lacquer Ware*. Ed. Patricia Frick and Annette Kieser, 30–63. Boston: Brill, 2018.

Lü Simian 呂思勉. *Du shi zha ji* 讀史札記. Taibei: Muduo chu ban she, 1983.

Lü Yifei 吕一飞. *Hu zu xi su yu Sui Tang feng yun: Wei Jin Bei chao bei fang shao shu min zu she hui feng su ji qi dui Sui Tang de ying xiang* 胡族习俗与隋唐风韵：魏晋北朝北方少数民族社会风俗及其对隋唐的影响. Beijing: Shu mu wen xian chu ban she, 1994.

Lung, Rachel. *Interpreters in Early Imperial China*. Amsterdam and Philadelphia: John Benjamins Publishing Company, 2011.

Luo Tonghua 羅彤華. *Han dai de liu min wen ti* 漢代的流民問題. Taibei: Taiwan xue sheng shu ju, 1989.

Luo Xin 罗新. "Bei Wei Taiwudi de Xianbei ben ming" 北魏太武帝的鲜卑本名. *Min zu yan jiu* (2006.4). Rpt. in his *Zhong gu bei zu ming hao yan jiu*, 166–74. Beijing: Beijing da xue chu ban she, 2009.

Luo Xin 罗新. "Bei Wei zhi qin kao" 北魏直勤考. *Li shi yan jiu* (2004.5). Rpt. in his *Zhong gu bei zu ming hao yan jiu*, 80–107. Beijing: Beijing da xue chu ban she, 2009.

Luo Xin. "Chinese and Inner Asian Perspectives on the History of the Northern Dynasties (386–589) in Chinese Historiography." In *Empires and Exchanges in Eurasian Late Antiquity: Rome, China, Iran, and the Steppe, ca. 250–750*. Ed. Nicola Di Cosmo and Michael Maas, 166–75. Cambridge: Cambridge University Press, 2018.

Luo Xin 罗新. "Kehan hao zhi xing zhi" 可汗号之性质. *Zhongguo she hui ke xue* 2005.2. Rpt. in his *Zhong gu bei zu ming hao yan jiu*, 1–26. Beijing: Beijing da xue chu ban she, 2009.

Luo Xin 罗新. "Min zu qi yuan de xiang xiang yu zai xiang xiang—yi Gaxian dong de liang ci fa xian wei zhong xin 民族起源的想像与再想像—以嘎仙洞的两次发现为中心." *Wen shi* (2013.2): 5–25.

Ma Changshou 馬長壽. *Wuhuan yu Xianbei* 烏桓與鮮卑. Shanghai: Shanghai ren min chu ban she, 1962.

Ma De 马德. *Dunhuang Mogao ku shi yan jiu* 敦煌莫高窟史研究. Lanzhou: Gansu jiao yu chu ban she, 1996.

MacDonald, George Fraser. *The Steel Bonnets: The Story of the Anglo-Scottish Border Reivers.* New York: Knopf, 1972.

MacKintosh-Smith, Tim. *Arabs: A 3000-year History of Peoples, Tribes and Empires.* New Haven, CT: Yale University Press, 2019.

Maeda Masana 前田正名. *Heijō no rekishi-chirigakuteki kenkyū* 平城の歴史地理学的研究. Tokyo: Kazama Shobō, 1979.

Maeda Masana 前田正名. *Kasei no rekishi-chirigakuteki kenkyū* 河西の歴史地理學的研究. Tokyo: Yoshikawa Kōbunkan, 1964.

Mair, Victor. "The North(west)ern Peoples and the Recurrent Origins of the 'Chinese' State." In *Teleology of the Modern Nation-State: Japan and China.* Ed. Joshua Fogel, 46–84. Philadelphia: University of Pennsylvania Press, 2005.

Mair, Victor. *Tun-huang Popular Narratives.* Cambridge and New York: Cambridge University Press, 1983.

Major, John S., and Constance A. Cook. *Ancient China: A History.* Abingdon and New York: Routledge, 2017.

Mallory, J. P. *In Search of the Indo-Europeans: Language, Archaeology and Myth.* London: Thames and Hudson, 1989.

Mao Han-kuang (Mao Hanguang). "The Evolution in the Nature of the Medieval Genteel Families." In *State and Society in Early Medieval China.* Ed. Albert E. Dien, 73–109. Stanford, CA: Stanford University Press, 1990.

Mao Hanguang 毛漢光. *Liang Jin Nan bei chao shi zu zheng zhi zhi yan jiu* 兩晉南北朝士族政治之研究. Taibei: Taiwan shang wu yin shu guan, 1966.

Mao Hanguang 毛漢光. "Zhong gu da shi zu zhi ge an yan jiu—Langye Wang shi" 中古大士族之個案研究—瑯琊王氏. In his *Zhongguo zhong gu she hui shi lun*, 365–404. Taibei: Lian jing chu ban shi ye gong si, 1988.

Marcus, Joyce. "The Peaks and Valleys of Archaic States: An Extension of the Dynamic Model." In *Archaic States.* Ed. Gary M. Feinman and Joyce Marcus, 59–94. Santa Fe, NM: School of American Research Press, 1998.

Marshak, Boris I. "Central Asian Metalwork in China." In *China: Dawn of a Golden Age, 200–750 AD.* Ed. James C. Y. Watt et al., 46–55. New York: Metropolitan Museum of Art; New Haven, CT: Yale University Press, 2004.

Mather, Richard B. "K'ou Ch'ien-chih and the Taoist Theocracy at the Northern Wei Court, 425–451." In *Facets of Taoism: Essays in Chinese Religion.* Ed. Holmes Welch and Anna Seidel, 103–22. New Haven, CT: Yale University Press, 1979.

Mather, Richard B., tr. *A New Account of Tales of the World.* Minneapolis: University of Minnesota Press, 1976.

Matsunaga Masao 松永雅生. "Hokugi no San to" 北魏の三都. *Tōyōshi kenkyū* 29.2–3 & 29.4 (1970, 1971): 129–59 & 297–325.

Matsushita Ken'ichi 松下憲一. "Baidao kao—Bei chao Sui Tang shi qi de cao yuan zhi dao" 白道考—北朝隋唐时期的草原之道. In *Wei Jin Nan bei chao shi de xin tan suo.* Ed. Lou Jing, 489–99. Beijing: Zhongguo she hui ke xue chu ban she, 2015.

Matsushita Ken'ichi 松下憲一. "Hokugi buzoku kaisan saikō—Gen Chō boshi o tegakari ni" 北魏部族解散再考—元萇墓誌を手がかりに. *Shigaku zasshi* 123.4 (2014): 35–59.

Matsushita Ken'ichi 松下憲一. *Hokugi Kozoku taiseiron* 北魏胡族体制論. Sapporo: Hokkaidō Daigaku Daigakuin Bungaku Kenkyūka, 2007.

Matsushita Ken'ichi 松下憲一. "Hokugi no kokugō 'Dai Dai' to 'Dai Gi'" 北魏の国号'大代'と'大魏'. In his *Hokugi Kozoku taiseiron*, 111–59. Sapporo: Hokkaidō Daigaku Daigakuin Bungaku Kenkyūka, 2007.

Mauss, Marcel. *The Gift: The Form and Reason for Exchange in Archaic Societies*. Tr. W. D. Halls. New York and London: W. W. Norton, 1990.

Mayor, Adrienne. *The Amazons: Lives and Legends of Warrior Women across the Ancient World*. Princeton, NJ: Princeton University Press, 2014.

McNair, Amy. *Donors of Longmen: Faith, Politics, and Patronage in Medieval Chinese Buddhist Sculpture*. Honolulu: University of Hawai'i Press, 2007.

McNair, Amy. "The Relief Sculptures in the Binyang Central Grotto at Longmen and the 'Problem' of Pictorial Stones." In *Between Han and Tang: Visual and Material Culture in a Transformative Period*. Ed. Wu Hung, 157–86. Beijing: Wen wu chu ban she, 2003.

Mi Wenping 米文平. "Gaxian dong Bei Wei shi ke zhu wen kao shi" 嘎仙洞北魏石刻祝文考釋. In *Wei Jin Nan bei chao shi yan jiu* 魏晋南北朝史研究, edited by Zhongguo Wei Jin Nan Bei chao shi xue hui, 352–63. Chengdu: Sichuan sheng she hui ke xue yuan chu ban she, 1986.

Mi Wenping 米文平. "Wuluohou yan jiu" 烏洛侯研究. In his *Xianbei shi yan jiu* 鮮卑史研究, 188–209. Zhengzhou: Zhongzhou gu ji chu ban she, 1994.

Mi Wenping 米文平. "Xianbei shi shi de fa xian yu chu bu yan jiu" 鮮卑石室的發現與初步研究. *Wen wu* (1981.2): 1–7.

Mi Wenping 米文平. *Xianbei shi shi xun fang ji* 鮮卑石室尋訪記. Jinan: Shandong hua bao chu ban she, 1997.

Miao Linlin 苗霖霖. "Xianbei shan di li wei zhi kao lue" 鮮卑山地理位置考略. *Bei Hua da xue xue bao (She hui ke xue ban)* (2015.2): 60–63.

Miller, Bryan Kristopher. "The Southern Xiongnu in Northern China: Navigating and Negotiating the Middle Ground." In *Complexity of Interaction along the Eurasian Steppe Zone in the First Millennium CE*. Ed. Jan Bemmann and Michael Schmauder, 127–98. Bonn: Vor- und Frühgeschichtliche Archäologie, Rheinische Friedrich-Wilhelms-Universität, 2015.

Millward, James, Ruth W. Dunnell, Mark C. Elliott, and Philippe Forêt, eds. *New Qing Imperial History: The Making of Inner Asian Empire at Qing Chengde*. London and New York: Routledge, 2004.

Misaki Yoshiaki 三崎良章. "Bei Wei zheng quan xia de Wuhuan" 北魏政權下的烏桓. In *Wei Jin Nan bei chao shi de xin tan suo*. Ed. Lou Jing, 173–84. Beijing: Zhongguo she hui ke xue chu ban she, 2015.

Miščevič, Dušanka Dušana. "Oligarchy or Social Mobility. A Study of the Great Clans of Early Medieval China." *BMFEA* 65 (1993): 5–256.

Miyakawa Hisayuki 宮川尚志. *Rikuchō shi kenkyū: seiji, shakai hen* 六朝史研究: 政治・社会篇. Tokyo: Nihon Gakujutsu Shinkōkai, 1956.

Miyake, Marc Hideo. *Old Japanese: A Phonetic Reconstruction*. London and New York: RoutledgeCurzon, 2003.

Miyazaki Ichisada 宮崎市定. *Kyūhin kanjinhō no kenkyū: kakyo zenshi* 九品官人法の研究: 科舉前史. Kyoto: Tōyōshi Kenkyūkai, 1956.

Miyazaki Ichisada 宮崎市定. "Rikuchō jidai Kahoku no toshi" 六朝時代華北の都市. *Tōyōshi kenkyū* 20.2 (1961): 53–74.

Molyneaux, George. *The Formation of the English Kingdom in the Tenth Century*. Oxford: Oxford University Press, 2015.

Mou Fasong 牟发松. "Bei Wei jie san bu luo zheng ce yu ling min qiu zhang zhi zhi yuan yuan xin tan" 北魏解散部落政策与领民酋长制之渊源新探. *Huadong shi fan da xue xue bao: zhe xue she hui ke xue ban* 49.5 (2017): 1–12.

Mou Fasong 牟发松, Wu Youjiang 毋有江, and Wei Junjie 魏俊杰. *Zhongguo xing zheng qu hua tong shi, Shi liu guo Bei chao juan* 中國行政區劃通史, 十六国北朝卷. 2 vols. (Vols. 6 and 7 of the set). Shanghai: Fudan da xue chu ban she, 2017.

Mullaney, Thomas S., et al., eds. *Critical Han Studies: The History, Representation and Identity of China's Majority*. Berkeley, CA: University of California Press, 2012.

Müller, Shing. "Horses of the Xianbei, 300–600 AD: A Brief Survey." In *Pferde in Asien: Geschichte, Handel und Kultur = Horses in Asia: History, Trade and Culture*. Ed. Bert G. Fragner et al., 181–94. Vienna: Verlag der Österreichischen Akademie der Wissenschaften, 2009.

Müller, Shing. "A Preliminary Study of the Lacquerware of the Northern Dynasties, with a Special Focus on the Pingcheng Period (398–493)." *Early Medieval China* 25 (2019): 42–63.

Müller, Shing. See also Song, Xin.

Needham, Joseph. *Science and Civilization in China*, Vol. 5. *Chemistry and Chemical Technology*: pt. 3. *Spagyrical Discovery and Invention: Historical Survey, from Cinnabar Elixirs to Synthetic Insulin*. Cambridge: Cambridge University Press, 1974.

Nelson, Louis. *Architecture and Empire in Jamaica*. New Haven, CT, and London: Yale University Press, 2016.

Ni Run'an 倪润安. "Bei Wei Pingcheng mu zang zhong de Hexi yin su" 北魏平城墓葬中的河西因素. In *Wei Jin Nan bei chao shi de xin tan suo*. Ed. Lou Jing, 603–23. Beijing: Zhongguo she hui ke xue chu ban she, 2015.

Ni Run'an 倪润安. *Guang zhai zhong yuan: Tuoba zhi Bei Wei de mu zang wen hua yu she hui yan jin* 光宅中原: 拓跋至北魏的墓葬文化与社会演进. Shanghai: Shanghai gu ji chu ban she, 2017.

Nie Hongyin 聂鸿音. "Xianbei yu yan jie du shu lun" 鲜卑语言解读述论. *Min zu yan jiu* (2001.1): 63–70.

Niu Runzhen 牛润珍. "Bei Wei shi guan zhi du yu guo shi zuan xiu" 北魏史官制度与国史纂修. *Shi xue shi yan jiu* (2009.2): 16–29.

Niu Runzhen 牛润珍. *Gu du Yecheng yan jiu—zhong shi ji Dong Ya du cheng zhi du tan yuan* 古都邺城研究—中世纪东亚都城制度探源. Beijing: Zhonghua shu ju 2015.

Nora, Pierre. *Realms of Memory: Rethinking the French Past*. 3 vols. New York: Columbia University Press, 1996–1998.

Norman, Jerry. *Chinese*. Cambridge and New York: Cambridge University Press, 1988.

Nylan, Michael. *The Five "Confucian" Classics*. New Haven, CT: Yale University Press, 2001.

Nylan, Michael. "Review: Talk about 'Barbarians' in Antiquity." *Philosophy East and West* 62.4 (2012): 580–601.

O'Connor, Kaori. *The Never-ending Feast: The Anthropology and Archaeology of Feasting*. London and New York: Bloomsbury Academic, 2015.

Okamura Hidenori 岡村秀典. *Unkō sekkutsu no kōkogaku: yūboku kokka no kyosekibutsu o saguru* 雲岡石窟の考古学: 遊牧国家の巨石仏をさぐる. Kyoto: Rinsen shoten, 2017.

Olberding, Garett P. S. *Dubious Facts: The Evidence of Early Chinese Historiography*. Albany: State University of New York Press, 2012.

Orzech, Charles. "The Scripture on Perfect Wisdom for Humane Kings Who Wish to Protect their States." In *The Religions of China in Practice*. Ed. Donald Lopez, 372–80. Princeton, NJ: Princeton University Press, 1996.

Parker, Bradley. "What's the Big Picture? Comparative Perspectives on the Archaeology of Empire." In *The Archaeology of Imperial Landscapes: A Comparative Study of Empires in the Ancient Near East and Mediterranean World*. Ed. Bleda S. Düring and Tesse Dieder Stek, 324–50. New York and Cambridge: Cambridge University Press, 2018.

Pearce, Scott. "Form and Matter: Archaizing Reform in Sixth-century China." In *Culture and Power in the Reconstitution of the Chinese Realm, 200–600*. Ed. Scott Pearce, Audrey Spiro, and Patricia Ebrey, 149–78. Cambridge, MA, and London: Harvard University Asia Center, 2001.

Pearce, Scott. "The Land of Tai: The Origins, Evolution and Historical Significance of a Community of the Inner Asian Frontier." In *Opuscula Altaica: Essays Presented in Honor of Henry Schwarz*. Ed. Edward H. Kaplan and Donald W. Whisenhunt, 465–98. Bellingham: Western Washington University, 1994.

Pearce, Scott. "Nurses, Nurslings, and New Shapes of Power in the Mid-Wei Court." *Asia Major*, 3rd ser., 22.1 (2009): 287–309.

Pearce, Scott. "A Response to Valentin Golovachev's 'Matricide during the Northern Wei.'" *Early Medieval China* 9 (2003): 139–44.

Pearce, Scott. Review of Andrew Chittick, *The Jiankang Empire*. *Early Medieval China* 26 (2020): 114–19.

Pearce, Scott. "Status, Labor and Law: Special Service Households under the Northern Dynasties." *Harvard Journal of Asiatic Studies* 51.2 (1991): 89–138.

Pearce, Scott. "The Way of the Warrior in Early Medieval China, Examined through 'the Northern *Yuefu*.'" *Early Medieval China* 13–14 (2008): 87–113.

Pearce, Scott. "Who and What Was Hou Jing?" *Early Medieval China* 6 (2000): 49–73.

Pearce, Scott. "The Yü-wen Regime in Sixth Century China." PhD diss., Princeton University, 1987.

Pearce, Scott, Audrey Spiro, and Patricia Ebrey. "Introduction." In *Culture and Power in the Reconstitution of the Chinese Realm, 200–600*. Ed. Scott Pearce, Audrey Spiro, and Patricia Ebrey, 1–32. Cambridge, MA: Harvard University Press, 2001.

Pelliot, Paul. "Les mots à h initiale, aujourd'hui amuie, dans le mongol des XIIIe et XIVe siècles." *Journal Asiatique* 206 (1925): 193–263.

Perdue, Peter. "Military Mobilization in Seventeenth and Eighteenth Century China, Russia, and Mongolia." *Modern Asian Studies* 30.4 (1996): 757–93.

Pines, Yuri. "Beasts or Humans: Pre-imperial Origins of the 'Sino-Barbarian' Dichotomy." In *Mongols, Turks and Others: Eurasian Nomads and the Sedentary World*. Ed. Reuven Amitai and Michal Biran, 59–102. Leiden and Boston: Brill, 2005.

Pines, Yuri, Gideon Shelach, Lothar von Falkenhausen, and Robin D. S. Yates. *Birth of an Empire: The State of Qin Revisited*. Berkeley: University of California Press, 2014.

Pohl, Walter. *The Avars: A Steppe Empire in Central Europe, 567–822*. Ithaca, NY, and London: Cornell University Press, 2018.
Pohl, Walter. "Introduction—Strategies of Identification: A Methodological Profile." In *Strategies of Identification: Ethnicity and Religion in Early Medieval Europe*. Ed. Walter Pohl and Gerda Heydemann, 1–64. Turnhout: Brepols, 2013.
Průšek, Jaroslav. *Chinese Statelets and the Northern Barbarians in the Period 1400–300 B.C.* New York: Humanities Press, 1971.
Pulleyblank, Edwin G. *The Background of the Rebellion of An Lu-shan*. Westport, CT: Greenwood Press, 1955.
Pulleyblank, E. G. (Edwin G.). "The Chinese and Their Neighbors in Prehistoric and Early Historic Times." In *The Origins of Chinese Civilization*. Ed. David N. Keightley, 411–66. Berkeley: University of California Press, 1983.
Pulleyblank, Edwin G. "Ji Hu: Indigenous Inhabitants of Shaanbei and Western Shanxi." In *Opuscula Altaica: Essays Presented in Honor of Henry Schwarz*. Ed. Edward H. Kaplan and Donald W. Whisenhunt, 499–531. Bellingham: Center for East Asian Studies, Western Washington University, 1994.
Qian Guoxiang et al. "Changhemen Gate-site of the Northern Wei Palace-city in Han-Wei Luoyang City, Henan." *Chinese Archaeology* 4 (2004): 49–56.
Qiu Guangming 丘光明. *Zhongguo li dai du liang heng kao* 中国歷代度量衡考. Beijing: Ke xue chu ban she, 1992.
Rachewiltz, Igor de. *The Secret History of the Mongols: A Mongolian Epic Chronicle of the Thirteenth Century*. 2 vols. Leiden and Boston: Brill, 2004.
Rawson, Jessica. "China and the Steppe: Reception and Resistance." *Antiquity* 91 (2017): 375–88.
Ren Aijun 任爱君. "Bei Wei Xianbei ren woluduo yi zhi ling shi" 北魏鲜卑人斡鲁朵遺制零拾. *Bei chao yan jiu* 3 (1996): 3–8.
Ren, Yuan. "Back to the Future: The Fake Relics of the 'Old' Chinese City of Datong." *The Guardian*, 15 October 2014. https://www.theguardian.com/cities/2014/oct/15/datong-china-old-city-back-to-the-future-fake-relics. Accessed 1 March 2021.
Ren Zhong 壬重. "Pingcheng de ju min gui mo yu Pingcheng shi dai de jing ji mo shi" 平城的居民规模与平城时代的经济模式. *Shi xue yue kan* (2002.3): 107–13.
Robb, Graham. *The Debatable Land: The Lost World between Scotland and England*. New York and London: W. W. Norton, 2018.
Robinson, Tim. *Connemara: Listening to the Wind*. Dublin and New York: Penguin Ireland, 2006.
Rogers, Michael. *Chronicle of Fu Chien: A Case of Exemplar History*. Berkeley: University of California Press, 1968.
Róna-Tas, András. "On the Development and Origin of the East Turkic 'Runic' Script." *Acta Orientalia Academiae Scientiarum Hungaricae* 41.1 (1987): 7–14.
Rong Xinjiang. "The Rouran Qaghanate and the Western Regions during the Second Half of the Fifth Century Based on a Chinese Document Newly Found in Turfan." In *Great Journeys across the Pamir Mountains: A Festschrift in Honor of Zhang Guangda on His Eighty-fifth Birthday*. Ed. Huaiyu Chen and Xinjiang Rong, 59–82. Leiden and Boston: Brill, 2018.

Ross, E. Denison, and Vilhelm Thomsen. "The Orkhon Inscriptions: Being a Translation of Professor Vilhelm Thomsen's Final Danish Rendering." *Bulletin of the School of Oriental Studies, University of London* 5.4 (1930): 861–76.

Ruggles, D. Fairchild. *Women, Patronage and Self-representation in Islamic Societies*. Albany: State University of New York Press, 2000.

Sagawa Eiji 佐川 英治. "Bei Wei de bing zhi yu she hui: cong 'bing min fen li' dao 'jun min fen ji'" 北魏的兵制与社会——从"兵民分离"到"军民分籍". *Wei Jin Nan bei chao Sui Tang shi zi liao* (1996.1): 48–58.

Sagawa Eiji 佐川 英治. "Tō Gi Hoku Sei kakumei to 'Gisho' no hensen" 東魏北齊革命と『魏書』の編纂. *Tōyōshi kenkyū* 64.1 (2006): 37–64.

Sagawa Eiji 佐川 英治. "You mu yu nong geng zhi jian—Bei Wei Pingcheng lu yuan de ji neng ji qi bian qian" 游牧与农耕之间—北魏平城鹿苑的机能及其变迁. *Zhongguo zhong gu shi yan jiu: Zhongguo zhong gu shi qing nian xue zhe lian yi hui hui kan* 中國中古史研究: 中国中古史青年学者联谊会会刊 1 (2011): 102–36. Original version: "Yūboku to nōkō no aida—Hokugi Heijō no Rakuen no kinō to sono hensen" 遊牧と農耕の間—北魏平城の鹿苑の機能とその変遷. *Okayama Daigaku bungaku bu kiyo* 47 (2007): 49–76.

Sahlins, Marshall D. *Tribesmen*. Englewood Cliffs, NJ: Prentice-Hall, 1968.

Sakuma Kichiya 佐久間吉也. *Gi Shin Nanbokuchō suiri shi kenkyū* 魏晉南北朝水利史研究. Tokyo: Kaimei Shoin, 1980.

Salzman, Philip Carl. *When Nomads Settle: Processes of Sedentarization as Adaptation and Response*. New York: Praeger, 1980.

Schaberg, David. *A Patterned Past: Form and Thought in Early Chinese Historiography*. Cambridge, MA: Harvard University Press, 2001.

Schafer, Edward H. *Golden Peaches of Samarkand: A Study of T'ang Exotics*. Berkeley: University of California Press, 1963.

Schafer, Edward H. "Notes on Mica in Medieval China." *T'oung Pao* 43.3/4 (1955): 265–86.

Scheidel, Walter. *Escape from Rome: The Failure of Empire and the Road to Prosperity*. Princeton, NJ, and Oxford: Princeton University Press, 2019.

Schmidt-Glintzer, Helwig. "The Scholar-Official and His Community: The Character of the Aristocracy in Medieval China." *Early Medieval China* 1 (1994): 60–83.

Schreiber, Gerhard. "The History of the Former Yen Dynasty." *Monumenta Serica* 14 & 15 (1949–1956): 374–480, 1–141

Scott, James. *Against the Grain: A Deep History of the Earliest States*. New Haven, CT: Yale University Press, 2017.

Selbitschka, Armin. "Tribute, Hostages and Marriage Alliances: A Close Reading of Diplomatic Strategies in the Northern Wei Period." *Early Medieval China* 25 (2019): 64–84.

Sen, Tansen, and Victor Mair. *Traditional China in Asian and World History*. Ann Arbor, MI: Association for Asian Studies, 2012.

Seo Yunkyung 徐润庆. "Cong Shaling bi hua mu kan Bei Wei Pingcheng shi qi de sang zang mei shu" 从沙岭壁画墓看北魏平城时期的丧葬美术. In *Gu dai mu zang mei shu yan jiu*. Ed. Wu Hung and Zheng Yan, 1: 163–90. 3 vols. Beijing: Wen wu chu ban she, 2011.

Shanxisheng kao gu yan jiu suo 山西省考古研究所 and Xinzhoushi wen wu guan li chu 忻州市文物管理处. "Shanxi Xinzhoushi Jiuyuangang Bei chao bi hua mu" 山西忻州市九原岗北朝壁画墓. *Kao gu* (2015.7): 51–74.

Shao Zhengkun 邵正坤. "Shi lun Xianbei zao qi de zong jiao xin yang ji qi zhuan bian" 试论鲜卑早期的宗教信仰及其转变. *Dong bei shi di* (2007.2). Rpt. in *Zou chu shi ku de Bei Wei wang chao*. Ed. Jin Zhao and Aledeʾertu, 632–44. Beijing: Wen hua yi shu chu ban she, 2010.

Shelach, Gideon. "He Who Eats the Horse, She Who Rides It?: Symbols of Gender Identity on the Eastern Edges of the Eurasian Steppe." In *Are All Warriors Male?: Gender Roles on the Ancient Eurasian Steppe*. Ed. Katheryn M. Linduff and Karen Sydney Rubinson, 93–110. Lanham, MD: AltaMira Press, 2008.

Shelach, Gideon. *Prehistoric Societies on the Northern Frontiers of China*. London and Oakville, CT: Equinox, 2009.

Shelach, Gideon, and Yuri Pines. "Secondary State Formation and the Development of Local Identity: Change and Continuity in the State of Qin (770–221 B.C.)." In *Archaeology of Asia*. Ed. Miriam T. Stark, 202–30. Malden, MA: Blackwell, 2006.

Shen Changyun 沈长云. *Zhao guo shi gao* 赵国史稿. Beijing: Zhonghua shu ju, 2000.

Shimunek, Andrew. *Languages of Ancient Southern Mongolia and North China: A Historical-Comparative Study of the Serbi or Xianbei Branch of the Serbi-Mongolic Language Family*. Wiesbaden: Harrassowitz, 2017.

Shiratori Kurakichi 白鳥庫吉. *Dong Hu min zu kao* 東胡民族考. Shanghai: Shang wu yin shu guan, 1934.

Shōgaito Masahiro. "A Chinese Āgama Text Written in Uighur Script and the Use of Chinese." In *Trans-Turkic Studies: Festschrift in Honour of Marcel Erdal*. Ed. Matthias Kappler, Mark Kirchner, and Peter Zieme, 67–77. Istanbul: Mehmet Ölmez, 2010.

Sims-Williams, Nicholas. "The Sogdian Merchants in China and India." In *Cina e Iran da Alessandro Magno alla dinastia Tang*. Ed. Alfredo Cadonna and Lionello Lanciotti, 45–67. Florence: Casa Editrice Leo S. Olschki, 1996.

Sinor, Denis. "The Inner Asian Warriors." *Journal of the American Oriental Society* 101.2 (1981): 133–44.

Sinor, Denis. "The Making of a Great Khan." In *Altaica Berolinensia: The Concept of Sovereignty in the Altaic World*. Ed. Barbara Kellner-Heinkele, 241–58. Wiesbaden: Harrassowitz, 1993.

Skaff, Jonathan. Review of Nicolas Tackett's *Destruction of the Medieval Chinese Aristocracy*. *Journal of Chinese Studies* 61 (2015): 365–69.

Skaff, Jonathan. *Sui-Tang China and Its Turko-Mongol Neighbors*. Oxford: Oxford University Press, 2012.

Small, Thomas. "Sinewy Strength: A Muslim Polymath in His Cultural Context." *Times Literary Supplement*, 11 January 2019. https://www.the-tls.co.uk/articles/sinewy-strength/. Accessed 20 March 2021.

Smith, Anthony D. "War and Ethnicity: The Role of Warfare in the Formation, Self-Images and Cohesion of Ethnic Communities." *Ethnic and Racial Studies* 4.4 (1981): 375–97.

Sneath, David. *The Headless State: Aristocratic Orders, Kinship Society, and Misrepresentations of Nomadic Inner Asia*. New York: Columbia University Press, 2007.

Sneath, David. "Introduction: Imperial Statecraft: Arts of Power on the Steppe." In *Imperial Statecraft: Political Forms and Techniques of Governance in Inner Asia, Sixth–Twentieth Centuries*. Ed. David Sneath, 1–22. Bellingham: Center for East Asian Studies, Western Washington University and Mongolia and Inner Asia Studies Unit, University of Cambridge, 2006.

Snodgrass, Anthony. "Archaeology in China: A View from the Outside." In *China's Early Empires: A Re-appraisal*. Ed. Michael Nylan and Michael Loewe, 232–50. Cambridge: Cambridge University Press, 2010.

So Tetsu (Su Zhe) 蘇哲. "Goko Jūrokkoku Hokuchō jidai no shukkōto to roboyō" 五胡十六国・北朝時代の出行圖と鹵簿俑. In *Higashi Ajia to Nihon no kōkogaku*. Ed. Gotō Tadashi and Mogi Masahiro, 2: 113–63. 4 vols. Tokyo: Dōseisha, 2002.

Song Qirui 宋其蕤. *Bei Wei nü zhu lun* 北魏女主论. Beijing: Zhongguo she hui ke xue chu ban she, 2006.

Song Xin 宋馨 (Shing Müller). "Bei Wei Pingcheng qi de Xianbei fu" 北魏平城期的鲜卑服. In *4-6 shi ji de bei Zhongguo yu Ou Ya da lu*. Ed. Zhang Qingjie et al., 84–107. Beijing: Ke xue chu ban she, 2006.

Sonoda Shunsuke 園田 俊介. "Hokugi Tō Seigi jidai ni okeru Senpi Takubatsushi (Genshi) no sosen densetsu to sono keisei" 北魏・東西魏時代における鮮卑拓跋氏(元氏)の祖先伝説とその形成. *Shiteki* 27 (2005): 63–80.

Standen, Naomi. *Unbounded Loyalty: Frontier Crossing in Liao China*. Honolulu: University of Hawai'i Press, 2007.

Stark, Sören. "A 'Rouran Perspective' on the Northern Chinese Frontier during the Northern Wei Period." Forthcoming in *Mounted Warriors in Europe and Central Asia*. Ed. F. Daim, H. Meller, and W. Pohl.

Starrs, Roy. "The *Kojiki* as Japan's National Narrative." In *Asian Futures, Asian Traditions*. Ed. Edwina Palmer, 23–36. Folkestone, Kent: Global Oriental, 2005.

Steinhardt, Nancy. *Chinese Architecture in an Age of Turmoil, 200–600*. Honolulu: University of Hawai'i Press, 2014.

Strange, Mark. "An Eleventh-Century View of Chinese Ethnic Policy: Sima Guang on the Fall of Western Jin." *Journal of Historical Sociology* 20.3 (2007): 235–58.

Su Bai 宿白. "Dong bei, Nei Menggu di qu de Xianbei yi ji—Xianbei yi ji ji lu zhi yi" 东北、内蒙古地区的鲜卑遗迹—鲜卑遗迹辑录之一. *Wen wu* (1977.5). Rpt. in *Zou chu shi ku Bei Wei wang chao*. Ed. Jin Zhao and Alede'ertu, 391–402. Beijing: Wen hua yi shu chu ban she, 2010.

Su Bai 宿白. "Pingcheng shi li de ji ju he Yungang mo shi de xing cheng yu fa zhan" 平城实力的集聚和云岗模式的形成与发展. In his *Zhongguo shi ku si yan jiu*, 114–44. Beijing: Wen wu chu ban she, 1996.

Su Bai 宿白. "Shengle, Pingcheng yi dai de Tuoba Xianbei—Bei Wei yi ji—Xianbei yi ji ji lu zhi er" 盛乐、平城一带的拓跋鲜卑—北魏遗迹—鲜卑遗迹辑录之二. *Wen wu* (1977.11): 38–46.

Su Bai 宿白. "Yungang shi ku fen qi shi lun" 雲岡石窟分期試論. *Kao gu xue bao* (1978.1). Rpt. in his *Zhong guo shi ku si yan jiu*, 76–88. Beijing: Wen wu ban she, 1996.

Sullivan, Michael. *The Cave Temples of Maichishan*. Berkeley: University of California Press, 1969.

Sun Wei 孙危. *Xianbei kao gu xue wen hua yan jiu* 鲜卑考古学文化研究. Beijing: Kexue chubanshe, 2007.

Sun Xianfeng 孙险峰. "Yinshan shan mai yu 'Qian Qin fa Dai'" 阴山山脉与"前秦伐代". *Shi xue yue kan* (2014.12): 127–29.

Suzuki Yasutami 鈴木靖民 and Kaneko Shūichi 金子修一. *Ryō shokukōzu to tōbu yūrashia sekai* 梁職貢図と東部ユーラシア世界. Tokyo: Bensei shuppan, 2014.

Svobodová, Kateřina. *Iranian and Hellenistic Architectural Elements in Chinese Art*. Sino-Platonic Papers No. 274. Philadelphia: Department of East Asian Languages and Civilizations, University of Pennsylvania, 2018.

Swope, Kenneth. "The Beating of Drums and Clashing of Symbols: Music in Ming Dynasty Military Operations." *Chinese Historical Review* 16:2 (2009): 147–77.

Tackett, Nicolas. *Destruction of the Medieval Chinese Aristocracy*. Cambridge, MA: Harvard University Asia Center, 2014.

Tackett, Nicolas. *The Origins of the Chinese Nation: Song China and the Forging of an East Asian World Order*. Cambridge and New York: Cambridge University Press, 2017.

Tala 塔拉, ed. *Cao yuan kao gu xue wen hua yan jiu* 草原考古学文化研究. Hohhot: Nei Menggu jiao yu chu ban she, 2007.

Tamura, Jitsuzō 田村實造. *Chūgoku shijō no minzoku idōki: Goko, Hokugi jidai no seiji to shakai* 中国史上の民族移動期: 五胡・北魏時代の政治と社會. Tokyo: Sōbunsha, 1985.

Tan Qixiang 谭其骧 et al., eds. *Zhongguo li shi di tu ji* 中国历史地图集. 8 vols. Shanghai: Di tu chu ban she, 1982.

Tang Yongtong 湯用彤. *Han Wei Liang Jin Nan bei chao Fo jiao shi* 漢魏兩晉南北朝佛教史. 2 vols. Beijing: Zhonghua shu ju, 1955.

Tang Zhangru 唐長孺. "Bei Wei nan jing zhu zhou de cheng min" 北魏南境諸州的城民. In his *Shan ju cun gao*, 96–109. Beijing: Zhonghua shu ju, 1989.

Tang Zhangru 唐长孺. "Tuoba guo jia de jian li ji qi feng jian hua" 拓跋國家的建立及其封建化. In his *Wei Jin Nan bei chao shi lun cong*, 193–249. Beijing: Sheng huo, du shu, xin zhi san lian shu dian, 1955.

Tang Zhangru 唐长孺. *Wei Jin Nan bei chao Sui Tang shi san lun: Zhongguo feng jian she hui de xing cheng he qian qi de bian hua* 魏晋南北朝隋唐史三論: 中國封建社會的形成和前期的變化. Wuchang: Wuhan da xue chu ban she, 1993.

Tang Zhangru 唐长孺. "Wei Jin za hu kao" 魏晉雜胡考. In his *Wei Jin Nan bei chao shi lun cong*, 382–450. Beijing: San lian shu dian, 1955.

Tang Zhangru 唐長孺 and Huang Huixian 黃惠賢. "Shi lun Wei mo Bei zhen zhen min bao dong de xing zhi" 試論魏末北鎮鎮民暴動的性質. *Li shi yan jiu* (1964.1). Rpt. in Tang's *Shan ju cun gao*, 26–59. Beijing: Zhonghua shu ju, 1989.

Tanigawa Michio 谷川道雄. *Chūgoku chūsei shakai to kyōdōtai* 中国中世社会と共同体. Tokyo: Kokusho Kankōkai, 1976.

Tanigawa Michio 谷川道雄. *Zui Tō teikoku keisei shiron* 隋唐帝国形成史論. Tokyo: Chikuma Shobō, 1971.

Tapper, Richard. *The Conflict of Tribe and State in Iran and Afghanistan*. London: Croom Helm; New York: St. Martin's Press, 1983.

Teng Ssu-yü, tr. *Family Instructions for the Yen Clan: Yen-shih chia-hsün. An Annotated Translation*. Leiden: E. J. Brill, 1968.

Thonemann, Peter. "Sex and Elephants: Unpicking Some Hellenic Historiography." *Times Literary Supplement*, 31 May 2019. https://www.the-tls.co.uk/articles/sex-and-elephants/. Accessed 20 March 2021.

Tian Likun 田立坤. "San Yan wen hua yu Gaogouli kao gu yi cun zhi bi jiao" 三燕文化与高句丽考古遗存之比较. In *Qing guo ji: Jilin da xue kao gu xi jian xi shi zhou nian ji nian wen ji*. Ed. Jilin da xue kao gu xi, 328–41. Beijing: Zhi shi chu ban she, 1998.

Tian, Xiaofei. "From the Eastern Jin through the Early Tang (317–649)." In *The Cambridge History of Chinese Literature: To 1375*. Ed. Kang-i Sun Chang and Stephen Owen, 199–285. Cambridge and New York: Cambridge University Press, 2010.

Tian, Xiaofei. *The Halberd at Red Cliff: Jian'an and the Three Kingdoms*. Cambridge, MA, and London: Harvard University Asia Center, 2018.

Tian, Xiaofei. "Remaking History: The Shu and Wu Perspectives in the Three Kingdoms Period." *Journal of the American Oriental Society* 136.4 (2016): 705–32.

Tian Yuqing 田余庆. "'Dai ge,' 'Dai ji,' he Bei Wei guo shi" 《代歌》、《代记》和北魏国史. In his *Tuoba shi tan* 拓跋史探, 217–43. Beijing: Sheng huo, du shu, xin zhi san lian shu dian, 2003.

Tian Yuqing 田余庆. *Tuoba shi tan* 拓跋史探. Beijing: Sheng huo, du shu, xin zhi san lian shu dian, 2003.

Tombs, Robert. *The English and Their History*. New York: Alfred A. Knopf, 2015.

Treager, T. R. *A Geography of China*. London: University of London Press, 1965.

Tseng, Chin-yin. *Making of the Tuoba Northern Wei: Constructing Material Cultural Expressions in the Northern Wei Pingcheng Period (398–494 CE)*. Oxford: BAR Publishing, 2013.

Tsukamoto Zenryū. "The Śramana Superintendent T'an-yao and His Time." *Monumenta Serica* 16.1–2 (1957): 363–96.

Tuan, Yi-fu. *A Historical Geography of China*. Piscataway, NJ: AldineTransaction, 2008.

Twitchett, Denis. "Introduction." In *Cambridge History of China*, Vol. 3, *Sui and T'ang China, 589–906*, Part 1. Ed. Denis Twitchett, 1–47. Cambridge: Cambridge University Press, 1979.

Uchida Ginpū 内田吟風. *Kita Ajia shi kenkyū* 北アジア史研究, Vol. 2, *Senpi Jūzen Tokketsu hen* 鮮卑柔然突厥篇. Kyoto: Dōhōsha, 1975.

Van Orden, Kate. *Music, Discipline and Arms in Early Modern France*. Chicago: University of Chicago Press, 2005.

Von Glahn, Richard. *The Economic History of China: From Antiquity to the Nineteenth Century*. Cambridge: Cambridge University Press, 2016.

Vovin, Alexander. "Once Again on the Tabgač Language." *Mongolian Studies* 29 (2007): 191–206.

Vovin, Alexander. "A Sketch of the Earliest Mongolic Language: The Brāhmī Bugut and Khüis Tolgoi Inscriptions." *International Journal of Eurasian Linguistics* 1 (2019): 162–97.

Waldron, Arthur. *The Great Wall of China: From History to Myth*. Cambridge and New York: Cambridge University Press, 1990.

Waley, Arthur. "Lo-yang and Its Fall." In his *The Secret History of the Mongols, and Other Pieces*, 47–55. New York: Barnes and Noble, 1964.

Waley-Cohen, Joanna. *The Culture of War in China: Empire and the Military under the Qing Dynasty*. London and New York: I. B. Tauris, 2006.

Wang Daliang 王大良. *Fan fu bai: lai zi gu dai Zhongguo de qi shi: yi Bei Wei guan li shou ru yu jian cha ji zhi wei li* 反腐败：来自古代中国的启示：以北魏官吏收入与监察机制为例. Beijing: Min zu chu ban she, 2001.

Wang, Eugene. *Shaping the Lotus Sutra: Buddhist Visual Culture in Medieval China*. Seattle and London: University of Washington Press, 2005.

Wang Kai 王凯. *Bei Wei Shengle shi dai* 北魏盛乐时代. Hohhot: Nei Menggu ren min chu ban she, 2003.

Wang Lihua 王利華. *Zhongguo nong ye tong shi: Wei Jin Nan bei chao juan* 中國農業通史：魏晉南北朝卷. Beijing: Zhongguo nong ye chu ban she, 2009.

Wang Wanying 王万盈. *Zhuang xing qi de Bei Wei cai zheng yan jiu* 转型期的北魏财政研究. Beijing: Guang ming ri bao chu ban she, 2006.

Wang Wenqian 王文倩 and Nie Yonghua 聂永华. "'Mulan shi' cheng shi nian dai, zuo zhe ji Mulan gu li bai nian yan jiu hui gu" 木兰诗成诗年代，作者及木兰故里百年研究回顾. *Shangqiu shi fan xue yuan xue bao* 23.1 (2007): 17–21.

Wang Yanqing 王雁卿. "Bei chao shi dai de yin shi qi ju" 北朝时代的饮食器具. *Bei chao yan jiu* 4 (2004): 158–68.

Wang Yanqing 王雁卿. "Bei Wei Pingcheng Hu ren de kao gu xue guan cha" 北魏平城胡人的考古学观察. In *Zhongguo Wei Jin Nan Bei chao shi xue hui di shi jie nian hui ji guo ji xue shu yan tao hui lun wen ji*. Ed. Zhongguo Wei Jin Nan bei chao shi xue hui, Shanxi da xue li shi wen hua xue yuan, 567–77. Taiyuan: Beiyue wen yi chu ban she, 2012.

Wang Yanqing 王雁卿. "Bei Wei Sima Jinlong mu chu tu de you tao zhan zhang mo xing" 北魏司马金龙墓出土的釉陶毡帐模型. *Zhongguo guo jia bo wu guan guan kan* (2012.4): 56–62.

Wang Yanqing 王雁卿. "Datong Bei Wei mu zang chu tu yong qun de shi dai te zheng" 大同北魏墓葬出土俑群的时代特征. In *Bei Wei Pingcheng yan jiu wen ji*. Ed. Dong Ruishan, 298–312. Taiyuan: Shanxi ren min chu ban she, 2008.

Wang, Yi-t'ung, tr. *A Record of the Buddhist Monasteries in Lo-yang*. By Yang Xuanzhi. Princeton, NJ: Princeton University Press, 1984.

Wang Yintian 王银田. *Bei Wei Pingcheng kao gu yan jiu—gong yuan wu shi ji Zhongguo du cheng de yan bian* 北魏平城考古研究—公元五世纪中国都城的演变. Beijing: Ke xue chu ban she, 2017.

Wang Yintian 王银田. "Si chou zhi lu yu Bei Wei Pingcheng" 丝绸之路与北魏平城. *Jinan da xue xue bao (zhe xue she ke ban)* 2014.1. Rpt. in *Bei Wei Pingcheng kao gu yan jiu*. Ed. Wang Yintian et al., 143–61. Beijing: Ke xue chu ban she, 2017.

Wang Yongping 王永平. "Cui Hao zhi nan chao qing jie ji qi yu nan shi zhi jiao wang kao xi" 崔浩之南朝情结及其与南士之交往考析. In *1-6 shi ji Zhongguo bei fang bian jiang, min zu, she hui guo ji xue shu yan tao hui lun wen ji*. Ed. Jilin daxue gu ji yan jiu suo, 241–52. Beijing: Ke xue chu ban she, 2008.

Wang Yongping 王永平. *Qian Luo Yuan Wei huang zu yu shi zu she hui wen hua shi lun* 迁洛元魏皇族与士族社会文化史论. Beijing: Zhongguo she hui ke xue chu ban she, 2017.

Wang Yongping 王永平. *You xi, jing ji yu yu le: zhong gu she hui sheng huo tou shi* 游戏, 竞技与娱乐: 中古社会生活透视. Beijing: Zhonghua shu ju, 2010.

Wang Zhongluo 王仲荦. *Wei Jin Nan bei chao shi* 魏晋南北朝史. 2 vols. Shanghai: Shanghai ren min chu ban she, 1979–1980.

Wapner, Jessica. "Do Walls Change How We Think?" *New Yorker*, 28 March 2019. https://www.newyorker.com/culture/annals-of-inquiry/do-walls-change-how-we-think. Accessed 17 March 2021.

Ware, James. "An Ordeal among the T'o-pa Wei." *T'oung Pao*, 2nd ser., 32.4 (1936): 205–9.

Watson, Burton, tr. *Records of the Grand Historian of China*. New York: Columbia University Press, 1961.

Watson, Burton, tr. *Records of the Grand Historian, Han Dynasty II*. Rev. ed. Hong Kong and New York: Columbia University Press, 1993.

Watt, James, et al., eds. *China: Dawn of a Golden Age, 200–750 AD*. New Haven, CT: Yale University Press, 2004.

Wei Jian 魏坚, ed. *Nei Menggu di qu Xianbei mu zang de fa xian yu yan jiu* 内蒙古地区鲜卑墓葬的发现与研究. Beijing: Ke xue chu ban she, 2004.

Wei Wenjiang 卫文江. "Bei Wei shi qi de huo bi liu tong" 北魏时期的货币流通. *Bei chao yan jiu* 4 (2004): 281–84.

Wells, Peter. *Beyond Celts, Germans and Scythians: Archaeology and Identity in Iron Age Europe*. London: Duckworth, 2001.

Wen Haiqing 温海清. "Bei Wei, Bei Zhou, Tang shi qi zhui zu Li Ling xian xiang shu lun" 北魏，北周，唐时期追祖李陵现象述论. *Min zu yan jiu* (2007.3): 73–80.

Wenley, A. G. (Archibald Gibson). *The Grand Empress Dowager Wên Ming: And the Northern Wei Necropolis at Fang Shan*. Washington, DC: Freer Gallery of Art, 1947.

White, Lynn. *Medieval Technology and Social Change*. Oxford: Clarendon Press, 1964.

Whitfield, Roderick, Susan Whitfield, and Neville Agnew. *Cave Temples of Mogao: Art and History on the Silk Road*. Los Angeles: The Getty Conservation Institute and the J. Paul Getty Museum, 2000.

Whittaker, Dick. "Ethnic Discourses on the Frontiers of Roman Africa." In *Ethnic Constructs in Antiquity: The Role of Power and Tradition*. Ed. Ton Derks and Nico Roymans, 189–205. Amsterdam: Amsterdam University Press, 2009.

Wilbur, C. M. *Slavery in China during the Former Han Period, 206 B.C.–A.D. 25*. Chicago: Field Museum, 1943.

Wilhelm, Richard. *The I Ching: or Book of Changes*. Tr. Cary F. Baynes. 3rd ed. Princeton, NJ: Princeton University Press, 1967.

Wilson, Emily. "Web of Rome: How the Romans Adopted Greek Culture." *Times Literary Supplement*, 19 April 2016. https://www.the-tls.co.uk/articles/web-of-rome/. Accessed 20 March 2021.

Wolfram, Herwig. *History of the Goths*. Berkeley: University of California Press, 1988.

Wong, Dorothy C. *Chinese Steles: Pre-Buddhist and Buddhist Use of a Symbolic Form*. Honolulu: University of Hawai'i Press, 2004.

Wong, Po Yee. "Acculturation as Seen through Buddha's Birthday Parades in Northern Wei Luoyang: A Micro Perspective on the Making of Buddhism as a World Religion." PhD diss., University of the West, 2012.

Wright, Arthur F. *Buddhism in Chinese History*. Stanford, CA: Stanford University Press, 1959.
Wright, Arthur F. "Fo-t'u-teng: A Biography." *Harvard Journal of Asiatic Studies* 11 (1948): 321–71.
Wright, Joshua, William Honeychurch, and Chunag Amartuvshin. "The Xiongnu Settlements of Egiin Gol, Mongolia." *Antiquity* 89 (2009): 372–87.
Wu Honglin 吴洪琳. *Tiefu Xiongnu yu Xia guo shi yan jiu* 铁弗匈奴与夏国史研究. Beijing: Zhongguo she hui ke xue chu ban she, 2011.
Wu Youjiang 毋有江. *Bei Wei zheng zhi di li yan jiu* 北魏政治地理研究. Beijing: Ke xue chu ban she, 2018.
Xia Nai 夏鼐. "Du shi zha ji: lun Bei Wei bing shi chu liu Yi ji Hu hua Han ren wai, si yi you Zhongyuan Han ren zai nei" 读史札记:论北魏兵士除六夷及胡化之汉人外,似亦有中原汉人在内 edited by Wang, Shimin 王世民, *Qinghua da xue xue bao (Zhe xue she the hui ke xue ban)* 17.6 (2002): 6–8.
Xia Yan 夏炎. *Zhong gu shi jia da zu Qinghe Cui shi yan jiu* 中古世家大族清河崔氏研究. Tianjin: Tianjin gu ji chu ban she, 2004.
Xiao Ke 晓克 et al. *Tumote shi* 土默特史. Hohhot: Nei Menggu jiao yu chu ban she, 2008.
Xiong, Victor Cunrui. *Capital Cities and Urban Form in Pre-modern China: Luoyang, 1038 BCE to 938 CE*. London and New York: Routledge, 2017.
Xiong, Victor Cunrui. *Emperor Yang of the Sui Dynasty: His Life, Times, and Legacy*. Albany: State University of New York Press, 1999.
Xiong, Victor Cunrui. "Ritual Architecture under the Northern Wei." In *Between Han and Tang: Visual and Material Culture in a Transformative Period*. Ed. Wu Hung, 31–95. Beijing: Wen wu chu ban she, 2003.
Xu Jinshun 徐锦顺. "Erzhu Rong huo Erzhu Zhao?—cong 'Shou lie tu' kan Xinzhou Jiuyuangang Bei chao bi hua mu mu zhu" 尔朱荣或尔朱兆？—从《狩猎图》看忻州九原岗北朝壁画墓墓主. *Zhongyuan wen wu* (2015.6): 82–86.
Yan Gengwang 嚴耕望. "Bei Wei shang shu zhi du" 北魏尚书制度. *Li shi yu yan yan jiu suo ji kan* 18 (1948). Rpt. in his *Yan Gengwang shi xue lun wen xuan ji*, 116–22. Taibei: Lian jing chu ban shi ye gong si, 1991.
Yan Gengwang 嚴耕望. *Tang dai jiao tong tu kao* 唐代交通圖考. 6 vols. Taibei: Zhongyang yan jiu yuan li shi yu yan yan jiu suo, 1985–.
Yan Gengwang 嚴耕望. *Zhongguo di fang xing zheng zhi du shi: Wei Jin Nan bei chao di fang xing zheng zhi du* 中國地方行政制度史: 魏晋南北朝地方行政制度. 2 vols. Shanghai: Shanghai gu ji chu ban she, 2007.
Yan Yaozhong 严耀中. *Bei Wei qian qi zheng zhi zhi du* 北魏前期政治制度. Changchun: Jilin jiao yu chu ban she, 1990.
Yang Jiping 杨际平. *Bei chao Sui Tang jun tian zhi xin tan* 北朝隋唐均田制新探. Changsha: Yuelu shu she, 2003.
Yang Jun 样军. "Tuoba Xianbei zao qi li shi bian wu" 拓拔鲜卑早期历史辩误. *Shi xue ji kan* (2006.4): 124–31.
Yang Sen 杨森. "Dunhuang yan jiu yuan cang juan 'Bei Wei jin jun jun guan ji bo' kao shu" 敦煌研究院藏卷"北魏禁军军官籍薄"考述. *Dunhuang yan jiu* (1987.2): 20–24.

Yang Shao-yun. "Becoming Zhongguo, Becoming Han: Tracing and Reconceptualizing Ethnicity in Ancient North China, 770 B.C.–A.D. 581." MA thesis, National University of Singapore, 2007.

Yang Yongjun 杨永俊. "Lun Tuoba Xianbei de dong wu chong bai yi cun" 论拓跋鲜卑的动物崇拜遗存. *Qiu suo* (2007.1). Rpt. In *Zou chu shi ku de Bei Wei wang chao*. Ed. Jin Zhao and Alede'ertu, 621–31. Beijing: Wen hua yi shu chu ban she, 2010.

Yano Chikara 矢野主稅. "Mochi no igi ni tsuite" 望の意義について. *Nagasaki daigaku kyōiku gakubu shakai kagaku ronsō* 21 (1972): 1–16.

Yao Congwu 姚從吾. *Liao Jin Yuan shi lun wen (shang)* 遼金元史論文(上). In Vol. 5 of *Yao Congwu xian sheng quan ji* 姚從吾先生全集. Taibei: Zheng zhong shu ju, 1981.

Yao Dali 姚大力. "Lun Tuoba Xianbei bu de zao qi li shi: Du 'Wei shu Xu ji'" 论拓跋鲜卑部的早期历史—读《魏书序纪》. *Fudan xue bao (She hui ke xue ban)* (2005.2): 19–27.

Yao Weiyuan 姚薇元. *Bei chao Hu xing kao* 北朝胡姓考. Beijing: Zhonghua shu ju, 1962.

Yates, Robin D. S. "The Horse in Early Chinese Military History." In *Jun shi zu zhi yu zhan zheng* 軍事組織與戰爭. Ed. Huang Kewu 黃克武, 1–78. Taibei: Zhong yang yan jiu yuan li shi yu yan yan jiu suo, 2002.

Yates, Robin D. S. "Introduction: Empire of the Scribes." In *Birth of an Empire: The State of Qin Revisited*. Ed. Yuri Pines et al., 141–53. Berkeley: University of California Press, 2014.

Yi, Joy Lidu. *Yungang: Art, History, Archaeology, Liturgy*. London and New York: Routledge, 2017.

Yin Xian 殷宪. "Bei Wei Pingcheng shi lüe" 北魏平城事略. In his *Pingcheng shi gao* 平城史稿, 185–212. Beijing: *Ke xue chu ban* she, 2012.

Yin Xian 殷宪, comp. *Bei Wei Pingcheng shu ji* 北魏平城书迹. Beijing: Wen wu chu ban she, 2017.

Yin Xian 殷宪. "Bei Wei Pingcheng zhuan wa wen zi jian shu" 北魏平城砖瓦文字简述. *Shanxi Datong da xue xue bao* (2009.1). Rpt. in his *Pingcheng shi gao*, 145–54. Beijing: Ke xue chu ban she, 2012.

Yin Xian 殷宪. "Datong Bei Wei gong cheng diao cha zha ji" 大同北魏宫城调查札记. *Bei chao yan jiu*, n.s. 4 (2004): 147–57.

Yin Xian 殷宪. "Gai Tianbao mu zhuan ming kao" 盖天保墓砖铭考. *Jinyang xue kan* (2008.3): 25–34.

Yin Xian 殷宪. "Heduoluo ji Poduoluo kao" 贺多罗即破多罗考. *Xue xi yu tan suo* (2009.5): 227–33.

Yin Xian 殷宪. *Pingcheng shi gao* 平城史稿. Beijing: *Ke xue chu ban* she, 2012.

Yin Xian 殷宪. "Shanxi Datong Shaling Bei Wei bi hua mu qi hua ti ji yan jiu" 山西大同沙岭北魏壁画墓漆画题记研究. In *4-6 shi ji de bei Zhongguo yu Ou Ya da lu*. Ed. Zhang Qingjie et al., 346–60. Beijing: Ke xue chu ban she, 2006.

Yin Xian 殷宪. "Yungang shi ku suo fan ying de yi xie Bei Wei zheng zhi she hui qing kuang" 云岗石窟所反映的一些北魏政治社会情状. *Bei chao shi yan jiu* (2004). Rpt. in his *Pingcheng shi gao*, 75–80. Beijing: Ke xue chu ban she, 2012.

Yoshida Jun'ichi 吉田順一. "Hangai to Kageyama" ハンガイと陰山. *Shikan* 102 (1980): 48–61.

Yu Changchun 于长春 et al. "Tuoba Xianbei he Xiongnu zhi jian qin yuan guan xi de yi chuan xue fen xi" 拓拔鲜卑和匈奴之间亲缘关系的遗传学分析. *Yi chuan/Hereditas* (2007.10): 1223–29.

Yu, David C., tr. *History of Chinese Daoism*. By Qing Xitai. Lanham, MD: University Press of America, 2000.

Yu Lunian 俞鹿年. *Bei Wei zhi guan zhi du kao* 北魏職官制度考. Beijing: She hui ke xue wen xian chu ban she, 2008.

Yu Taishan. *A History of the Relationships between the Western and Eastern Han, Wei, Jin, Northern and Southern Dynasties and the Western Regions*. Philadelphia: Department of East Asian Languages and Civilizations, University of Pennsylvania, 2004.

Yu Taishan 余太山. *Liang Han Wei Jin Nan bei chao yu Xi yu guan xi shi yan jiu* 兩汉魏晉南北朝与西域关系史研究. Beijing: Zhongguo she hui ke xue chu ban she, 1995.

Yü, Ying-shih. "Han Foreign Relations." In *Cambridge History of China*, Vol. 1, *The Ch'in and Han Empire 221 B.C.–A.D. 220*. Ed. Denis Twitchett and Michael Loewe, 377–462. Cambridge: Cambridge University Press, 1986.

Yule, Henry, tr. *The Book of Ser Marco Polo the Venetian Concerning the Kingdoms and Marvels of the East*. 2 vols. New York: Charles Scribner's Sons, 1903.

Zhang, Fan. "Cultural Encounters: Ethnic Complexity and Material Expression in Fifth-century Pingcheng, China." PhD diss., New York University, 2018.

Zhang, Fan. "Silver Handled Cup: Syncretism, Materiality, and Banquets in Northern Wei Art." *Artibus Asiae* 82.1 (2022): 5–34.

Zhang Hequan 张鹤泉. "Bei Wei hou qi zhu wang jue wei feng shou zhi du shi tan" 北魏后期诸王爵位封授制度试探. *Zhongguo shi yan jiu* (2012.4): 73–96.

Zhang Hequan 张鹤泉. "Bei Wei qian qi feng shou zhu wang jue wei jia bai jiang jun hao zhi du shi tan" 北魏前期封授诸王爵位加拜将军号制度试探. *Shi xue yue kan* (2012.11): 14–21.

Zhang Hequan 张鹤泉 and Wang Meng 王萌. "Bei Wei huang di ci yan kao lüe" 北魏皇帝赐宴考略. *Shi xue ji kan* (2011.1): 26–33.

Zhang Jihao 張繼昊. *Cong Tuoba dao Bei Wei—Bei Wei wang chao chuang jian li shi de kao cha* 從拓跋到北魏—北魏王朝創建歷史的考察. Taibei: Dao xiang chu ban she, 2003.

Zhang Jingming 张景明. "Nei Menggu Liangchengxian Xiaobazitan jin yin qi jiao cang" 内蒙古凉城县小坝子滩金银器窖藏. *Wen wu* (2002.8): 50–52, 69.

Zhang Jingming 张景明. *Zhongguo bei fang cao yuan gu dai jin yin qi* 中国北方草原古代金银器. Beijing: Wen wu chu ban she, 2005.

Zhang Jinlong 张金龙. *Bei Wei zheng zhi shi* 北魏政治史. 9 vols. Lanzhou: Gansu jiao yu chu ban she, 2008.

Zhang Jinlong 张金龙. "'Feng shi gai ge' shuo shang que" 冯氏改革"说商榷. *Li shi yan jiu* (1986.2). Rpt. in his *Bei Wei zheng zhi yu zhi du lun gao*, 28–51. Lanzhou: Gansu jiao yu chu ban she, 2002.

Zhang Jinlong 张金龙, "Ling jun jiang jun yu Bei Wei zheng zhi" 领军将军与北魏政治. *Zhongguo shi yan jiu* (1995.1). Rpt. in his *Bei Wei zheng zhi yu zhi du lun gao*, 343–60. Lanzhou: Gansu jiao yu chu ban she, 2002.

Zhang Jinlong 张金龙. *Wei Jin Nan bei chao jin wei wu guan zhi du yan jiu* 魏晋南北朝禁卫武官制度研究. 2 vols. Beijing: Zhonghua shu ju, 2004.

Zhang Li 张莉. *Wei shu yan jiu* 魏书研究. Beijing: Hua wen chu ban she, 2009.

Zhang Min 张敏. *Sheng tai shi xue shi ye xia de Shi liu guo Bei Wei xing shuai* 生态史学视野下的十六国北魏兴衰. Wuhan: Hubei ren min chu ban she, 2004.

Zhang Min 张敏. "Shi liu guo Bei Wei jun dui dong zhuang bao zhang ji qi dui zhan zheng zhi ying xiang" 十六国北魏军队冬装保障及其对战争之影响. *Xuchang xue yuan xue bao* (2003.4): 51–53.

Zhang Mingming 张明明 and Fan Zhaofei 范兆飞. "Shi liu guo Bei Wei shi qi de wu bi jing ji" 十六国北魏时期的坞壁经济. *Zhongguo she hui jing ji shi yan jiu* (2011.2): 14–21.

Zhang Mingyuan 张明远. "Yungang Tanyao wu ku zhong de wai lai yin su" 云岗昙曜五窟中的外来因素. In *4-6 shi ji de bei Zhongguo yu Ou Ya da lu*. Ed. Zhang Qingjie et al., 247–62. Beijing: Ke xue chu ban she, 2006.

Zhang Qingjie 张庆捷. "Bei Wei Poduoluo shi bi hua mu suo jian wen zi kao shu" 北魏破多羅氏壁畫墓所見文字考述. *Li shi yan jiu* (2007.1): 174–79.

Zhang Qingjie 张庆捷. "Bei Wei Wenchengdi 'Nan xun bei' bei wen kao zheng" 北魏文成帝《南巡碑》碑文考证. *Kao gu* (1998.4): 79–86.

Zhang Qingjie 张庆捷. "Datong Caochangcheng Bei Wei Taiguan liang chu yi zhi chu tan" 大同操场城北魏太官粮储遗址初探. *Wen wu* (2010.4): 53–58.

Zhang Qingjie 张庆捷. *Min zu hui ju yu wen ming hu dong—Bei chao she hui de kao gu xue guan cha* 民族汇聚与文明互动—北朝社会的考古学观察. Beijing: Shang wu yin shu guan, 2010.

Zhang Qingjie 张庆捷 and Guo Chunmei 郭春梅. "Bei Wei Wenchengdi 'Nan xun bei' suo jian Tuoba zhi guan chu tan" 北魏文成帝《南巡碑》所见拓跋职官初探. *Zhongguo shi yan jiu* (1999.2): 57–69.

Zhang Qingjie 张庆捷 and Li Biao 李彪. "Shanxi Lingqiu Bei Wei Wenchengdi 'Nan xun bei'" 山西灵丘北魏文成帝《南巡碑》. *Wen wu* (1997.12): 70–80.

Zhang Qingjie 张庆捷 and Liu Junxi 刘俊喜. "Bei Wei Song Shaozu mu chu tu zhuan ming ti ji kao shi" 北魏宋绍祖墓出土砖铭题记考释. In *Datong Yan bei shi yuan Bei Wei mu qun*. Ed. Liu Junxi, 200–4. Beijing: Wen wu chu ban she, 2008.

Zhang Wenjie 張文杰. "Bei chao jiang wu tan lun" 北朝講武探論. *Guo fang da xue tong shi jiao yu xue bao* (2017.7): 33–52.

Zhang Xibin 张喜斌, Wang Pujun 王普军, and Xu Guodong 徐国栋. "Datong Bei Wei Taiguan liang jiao yi zhi chu tu de Zhan guo Qin Han wa dang" 大同北魏太官粮窖遗址出土的战国秦汉瓦当. *Wen wu shi jie* (2009.6): 10–14.

Zhang Yanli 张艳丽. "Qian lun Bei Wei xu mu ye de fa zhan ji ying xiang" 浅论北魏畜牧业的发展及影响. *Jincheng zhi ye ji shu xue yuan xue bao* 8.4 (2015): 51–53.

Zhang Zhizhong 张志忠. "Bei Wei Pingcheng shuang que kao" 北魏平城双阙考. In *Bei Wei Pingcheng kao gu yan jiu*. Ed. Wang Yintian et al., 24–27. Beijing: Ke xue chu ban she, 2017.

Zhang Zhuo 张焯. "Pingcheng ying jian shi mo" 平城营建始末. *Shi zhi xue kan* (1995.1): 51–55.

Zhao Songqiao. *Physical Geography of China*. Beijing: Science Press; New York: John Wiley and Sons, 1986.

Zhao Xiaolong 赵晓龙. "Bei Wei Jinling xin tan" 北魏金陵新探. *Xue shu wen ti yan jiu* (2015.2): 13–17.

Zheng Jingyun 鄭景雲, Man Zhimin 满志敏, Fang Xiuqi 方修琦, and Ge Quansheng 葛全胜. "Wei Jin Nan bei chao shi qi de Zhongguo dong bu wen du bian hua" 魏晉南北朝時期的中國東部溫度變化. *Di si ji yan jiu* (2005.2): 129–40.

Zheng Qinren 鄭欽仁. *Bei Wei guan liao ji gou yan jiu* 北魏官僚機構研究. Taibei: Dao he chu ban she, 1995.

Zheng Qinren 鄭欽仁. *Bei Wei guan liao ji gou yan jiu xu pian* 北魏官僚機構研究續篇. Taibei: Dao he chu ban she, 1995.

Zheng Yaru 鄭雅如. See Cheng Ya-ju.

Zhou Weizhou 周伟洲. *Chile yu Rouran* 敕勒与柔然. Shanghai: Shanghai ren min chu ban she, 1983.

Zhou Yiliang 周一良. "Cong Bei Wei ji ge jun de hu kou bian hua kan san zhang zhi de zuo yong" 从北魏几个郡的户口变化看三长制度的作用. *She hui ke xue zhan xian* (1980.4). Rpt. in his *Wei Jin Nan Bei chao shi lun ji xu bian*, 52–66. Beijing: Beijing da xue chu ban she, 1991.

Zhou Yiliang 周一良. "Cui Hao guo shi zhi yu" 崔浩国史之狱. In his *Wei Jin Nan bei chao shi zha ji*, 342–50. Beijing: Zhonghua shu ju, 1985.

Zhou Yiliang 周一良. "Wei Shou zhi shi xue" 魏收之史学. In his *Wei Jin Nan bei chao shi lun ji*, 236–72. Beijing: Zhonghua shu ju, 1963.

Zhu Dawei 朱大渭 et al. *Wei Jin Nan bei chao she hui sheng huo shi* 魏晋南北朝社会生活史. Kindle ed. Beijing: Zhongguo she hui ke xue chu ban she, 1998.

Zhu Weizheng 朱维铮. "Fu bing zhi du hua shi qi Xi Wei Bei Zhou she hui de te shu mao dun ji qi jie jue—jian lun fu bing de yuan yuan he xing zhi" 府兵制度化时期西魏北周社会的特殊矛盾及其解决—兼论府兵的渊源和性质. *Li shi yan jiu* (1963.6): 151–72.

Zou Da 鄒達. "Bei Wei de bing zhi—Wu Hu Bei chao bing zhi zhi er" 北魏的兵制—五胡北朝兵制之二. *Da lu za zhi shi xue cong shu di yi ji* 4 (1970): 162–73.

Zou Yi, Zhou Huijie, Chen Jianxian, and Kuang Yaoqiu. "The Decline of Pingcheng: Climate Change Impact, Vulnerability and Adaptation in the Northern Wei Dynasty, China." *Journal of Historical Geography* 58 (2017): 12–22.

Index

For the benefit of digital users, indexed terms that span two pages (e.g., 52-53) may, on occasion, appear on only one of those pages.

For those who reigned, reign years are given; for those who didn't, date of death, or lacking that, n.d. for "no dates." And no dates for modern scholars.

Note that where possible there has been an effort to consolidate entries under major categories: agriculture, armies, culture and change, dynasty and succession, economy, government, identities, natural surroundings, society.

agriculture
    early conditions, 87, 102–4, 106–7, 137–39, 175, 230–31, 257
    Equal Fields 均田, 258–61
    tian zu 田卒 ("field troops"), 175
    tun tian 屯田, 106–7, 175
    the village, 137–38
    See also pastoralism; transportation, of populations
Allsen, Thomas, 181–82
Altan Khan, 26–27
Amory, Patrick, 143–44
An Lushan. *See* Rokhshan the Sogdian
Anagui 阿那瓌 (r.520–552), 294
ancestral worship, 64–65, 236–37, 275
the "ancient practice" (of forcing death of heir's mother), 159–61, 187, 235, 240–41, 246, 248–49, 252, 278–79, 285–86
Apricot Town (Xingcheng 杏城), 193
Aramaic, 152–53
aristocracy. *See* dynasty and succession; eminent lineages

armies, 120–21, 126–27, 169–86
    archery, 31–32, 141, 145, 171–72, 177–78, 179–80, 182–83, 217f, 228, 237–38, 243–44, 287
    arms and armor, 66, 170–71, 176, 177–78, 214–15
    auxiliary units, 111–12, 151–52, 172–73, 195
    cavalry, xxiii, 31–32, 39, 40, 48, 66, 86, 106, 109, 140–41, 165, 170–71, 177–78, 191–92, 214–15, 224–25, 281–82, 302
    composition, 64, 139, 143–44, 172–73, 184
    decimal organization, 30–31, 37–38, 178–79
    decline, 245, 283, 291, 293–94, 295–96
    draft and recruitment, 41, 76, 87–88, 102–4, 124, 169, 173, 184, 185–86, 195
    expense, 177, 195, 245
    fear of, 165, 195, 215–16
    guard units, 86, 170–71, 179–80,

armies (cont.)
    184–85, 236–37, 239–40, 241, 243, 290
    infantry, 171, 186, 215–16, 281–82
    martial culture, 37–38, 174, 181, 188, 291
    military registration, 102–4, 139–41, 172, 173
    officers, 86, 173, 176–77, 181, 184
    salaries of officers, 176–77, 181, 244–45
    private armies (*bu qu* 部曲), 124–25
    provisioning, 105, 106–7, 128–29, 174–75, 191–92, 196–97, 216
    riverine warfare, 196–97
    siegecraft, 112–13, 194
    size, 66, 71–72, 86, 118, 119–20, 170–72, 195
    status of soldier, 169, 173, 185–86, 293–94
    training, 86, 145, 171–72, 181–82, 195
    as unifying institution of *Taghbach, 76n.79, 143–44, 172, 174
    women in, 141, 241 (*see also* Tale of Mulan)
    See also armories; campaigns; clothing, military; Esquire of the Hunt; garrisons; horses; *huluozhen*; *khaghan*: as commander of armies; pennon commander; *shi ling bu luo*
armor. *See* armies: arms and armor
armories, 130–31, 210
artisans, 105, 135, 139, 193, 194, 202, 203–4, 206–7, 220–21, 228–29, 246–47
    See also timber-frame architecture; tombs
'*asabiyyah* ("bindedness"), 143n.50
Augustine, 113

Baba 拔拔 clan, 65n.29, 95, 238
    See also Zhangsun
Bai 白 people, 67, 74
Baidao白道(White Road) Pass, 134–35
Baideng Hill 白登山 (White Top Hill), 38, 236–37, 239–40
Bamiyan, 246–47

banner, 179
    See also flags
Battle of the Fei River 淝水, 96
Bei shi 北史, xxiv, 15n.14, 16–17, 97n.22, 251n.83, 254n.102, 270n.43
Beihai, Prince of, Yuan Xiang 北海王元詳 (d. 504), 285
bestowals, 68n.49, 145, 192, 244–45, 291
    of booty, 105, 111, 174–75, 188, 196, 197, 257
Big Thousand. *See* Lai Daqian
Binyang 賓陽 (Central) Cave, 284–85
Bodhidharma, 289–90
"Book of Changes" (*Yi jing* 易經), 51–52, 266, 272–73
booty. *See* bestowals
Böri Beg ("Wolf Lord"), 4–5
    See also Taiwu, Emperor
Buddhism, 135–36, 189–90, 192–93, 198, 199, 241, 246–48, 256–57, 287, 288–90, 295–97
    suppression, 198
    See also "Humane King. . ."; Yungang

calendars, xxiv–xxv, 127–28
campaigns
    steppe, 8–10, 71, 87–88, 101–2, 106, 140–41, 145, 188–89
    Yangtze, 194–97, 268–69, 281–82, 286
    Yellow River region, 86–87, 111–13, 188–93
Caneiro, Robert, 75–76
Cao Cao 曹操 (155–220), 48–49, 115–17, 126–27, 283–84
Cao Pi 曹丕 (r. 220–226), 169
Cathay, xxi, 3–4
census. *See* government: census
Central Asia, xix, 135–36, 191, 206, 228–29, 246–47
centralization of state power. *See* government: centralization
central states (*zhong guo* 中國), xx, 30, 51, 55n.41, 178–79, 264–65, 273–74, 294
Chang, Madam 常氏 (d. 460), 240n.32, 245–46, 248–49

Chang'an 長安, 119-20, 163-64, 188, 189-90, 193, 198
Changsha, Prince of, Sima Yi 長沙王, 司馬乂 (d. 304), 119-20
chanyu 單于, of the Xiongnu, 37-38, 39, 47-48, 72, 101
    Southern Chanyu, 41-43, 45-46, 72, 120
Chao Yi 晁懿 (n.d.), 151-52
Cheng, Bonnie, xxiv
Chengdu, Prince of, Sima Ying 成都王, 司馬穎 (d. 306), 119-22
China, discussion, xx-xxii, 126n.56
    Chinese world, xix-xxii, 125-26
    and Qin 秦, xxi
    See also central states
Chinese classics 經, 35, 115, 165-66, 198-99, 255, 264-65, 267-68, 272-73
    See also "Book of Changes"; "Classic of Filial Piety..."; Ru; Zhou li
Chittick, Andrew, xx
cities, 85-86, 114, 130-31, 203-4
    as storehouses, 66, 207-8
    wards, 164-65, 205-6, 207-8, 287-88
    See also Jiankang; Luoyang; Pingcheng; Tongwan; villages; walls; Ye; Zhongshan
"Classic of Filial Piety in the National Language" (Guo yu Xiao jing 國語孝經), 153-54, 275-76
    See also filial piety
clothing
    banning *Serbi clothing, 275-76, 281
    military, 128-29, 175-76
    *Serbi, 41-42n.94, 135-36, 195, 217-19, 223, 278-79, 281, 303
cold food powder 寒食散, 157, 187
Confucius 孔夫子, 195
conquest dynasties, xviii, 114, 150n.87, 300-1
conquest polity. See nation
Cui Guang 崔光 (d. 523), 287
Cui Hao 崔浩 (d. 450), 9, 15-16, 116-17, 155, 165-66, 185, 191-92, 195, 196-97, 198-201, 235, 283

Cui Hong 崔宏 (d. 418), 12-13, 116-17, 133-34, 135, 137, 162
Cui Liang 崔亮 (d. 521), 116
Cui Lin 崔林 (d. 244), 116-17
the Cui of Qinghe 清河崔, 12-13, 115-17, 200
Cui Yan 崔琰 (d. 216), 115-16
culture and change, 69, 82, 135
    borrowing, 74-75, 81, 146, 150, 215, 220-22, 228-29, 264-65, 266, 272
    generational, 78, 198-99, 278-79
    Hellenistic influences, 135, 208-9
    hybridization, 143-44, 146-48, 150, 215-16, 220-22
    See also Central Asia; identities; invention of tradition; Jiankang; interaction with Wei; the "old ways"

Da Dai 大代, 142-43, 209
    See also Dai
Dai 代
    early history, 30-31
    Land of Dai, 3, 142-43, 150-51
    See also Dai people
Dai people 代人, 142-44, 173, 213-14, 218-19, 228-29, 269-70
    taxation, 175-76
    See also guo ren; nation
Danhan Mountain 彈汗山, 46
Daoism, 199
    Lord Lao 老君, 199
Daowu, Emperor 道武帝 (r. 386-409), 12-14, 93-113, 133-34, 155, 157-61, 162, 215, 276
    See also Shegui
Da Wei 大魏, 142-43
    See also Wei
the Deer Park 鹿苑, 101-2, 149, 205-6, 216, 230-31, 239-40, 253-54, 263
Defoe, Daniel, 64
deforestation. See natural surroundings: trees
Deng Yuan 鄧淵 (d. 403), 13-15
Di 氏 people, 89, 172-73
Di Cosmo, Nicola, xviiin.4, 36

Dien, Albert, xxiv, 117n.17
diplomacy, 39, 107–8, 120–21, 163–64, 189–90, 191–93, 194–95, 243, 273–74
   tribute, 39, 41–43
   vassalage, 39
   See also marital politics; propaganda; seals
Disorders of the Eight Princes 八王之亂, 72, 118–22, 127
divine beast, 28–29, 55, 67, 72–73, 208–9
   See also wolves
Divine Spring Pond (Lingquan chi 靈泉池), 212–13
Dong Hu 東胡 ("Eastern Hu"), 34–35, 37, 44–45
Dong Shou 佟壽 (d. 357), 214–15
Dong Zhuo 董卓 (d. 192), 118, 121–22, 126–27
Donghai, Prince of, Sima Yue 東海王, 司馬越 (d. 311), 119–20, 122, 127–29
Dongying, Duke of, Sima Teng 東嬴公司馬騰 (d. 307), 72–73, 120–21, 128
Douglas, Mary, 225–26
dual administration. See government: dual administration
Dual Monarchy (of the Habsburgs), 155–56
Dugu 獨孤, 93, 97, 187, 237–38
Duke of Zhou 周公, 265, 269
Dunhuang 敦煌, 173, 190, 192–93, 246–47
dynasty and succession, 28–29, 47–48, 49, 60–61, 62–64, 66–67, 69–70, 76, 78–81, 83–84, 93, 97–101, 158, 159–63, 187, 209, 235–36, 239–40, 253, 268–69, 275, 285–86, 296–97
   cadet branches, 64–65, 95, 182–83
   enthronement, 78–79, 98
   *tigin (zhi qin 直勤), 143–44, 150, 153–54, 159, 235–36, 238n.18, 276
   See also guo

Eastern Wei (534–550), 291, 297
economy
   centers, 134, 194–95, 264–65, 271–72
   currency, 105, 139, 161, 271–72
   prices, 188–89
   taxation (see government)
   See also agriculture; cities; Luoyang: Great Market; pastoralism; trade
elms. See natural surroundings: trees
eminent lineages, 114–18
Empress Dowager Ling. See Madam Hu
Equal Fields. See agriculture: Equal Fields
Erzhu 尒朱 family, 111–12, 294–95
Erzhu Rong 尒朱榮 (d. 530), 294–95, 296–97
Esquire of the Hunt (lielang 獵郎), 181–83
ethnic tensions. See identities: ethnic tensions
Etruscans, 154–55

Fangshan 方山 hill, 212–13, 261–62, 263, 266
Fanzhi 繁畤, 82–84
the feast, 202–3, 211–13, 222–23, 225–31, 226f–27
   al fresco, 228, 232
   games, 228
   women's roles, 211, 212–13, 226–28, 230
   See also food; fu; government: Office of the Provisioner; kitchens; Mao Xiuzhi; music
Feeney, Denis, 154–55
Feng 馮 family, 163, 190, 256, 261–62, 285
Feng Hong 馮弘 (r. 430–436), 190, 252
Feng Lang 馮朗 (n.d.), 190
Feng Run 馮潤 (d. 499), 284–86
Feng Ta 封沓 (n.d.), 9–10
Feng Xi 馮熙 (d. 495), 255
filial piety (xiao 孝), 125–26, 183–84, 216n.91, 255, 256–57
   See also "Classic of Filial Piety..."; Ru
flags, 146, 178–80, 215, 301–2
food, 197n.60, 210–12, 216, 225–26, 228–30
   See also fu
Former Qin 前秦 (351–394), 13–14, 93, 95–96
fortresses (wu bi 塢壁), 122–28

See also walls

fu 鍑, 232

Fu 弗 (son of Shamo Han; r. 293–294), 70–71, 74, 78–80

Fu Jian 苻堅, of Former Qin (r. 357–385), 89–90, 95–96, 102–4, 106n.59, 188

Gai Wu 蓋吳 (d. 446), 193, 194, 198, 294

Gao, Madam 高氏 (Xuanwu's mother, d. 497), 284–85

Gao Huan 高歡 (d. 547), 291, 293–96, 297

Gao Yun 高允 (d. 487), 200, 204n.7, 244–45

Gao Zhao 高肇 (d. 515), 285–86, 288

Gaochang 高昌, 192–93

Gaoche 高車 ("High Carts"), 87–88, 89, 101–2, 136, 179, 184, 188–89, 193, 205–6

Gaoyang, Prince of, Yuan Yong 高陽王元雍 (d. 528), 292–93, 295, 297

garrisons, 139–40, 170–71, 175, 176–77, 176n.36, 185–86
    Six Garrisons, 154n.108, 163, 185–86, 188–89, 291, 292–95 (*see also* Huaihuang; Huaishuo; Woye)

Gat, Azar, 143

gathering, 202–3
    See also the feast

Gaxian Cave 嘎仙洞, 6–8, 10, 114–15

"Ge" 革 (hexagram), 266–67
    See also "Book of Changes"

Geertz, Clifford, 274, 283

genealogy, 50–55, 198–99

Gentleman's Ford (Junzi jin 君子津), 134–35

Gilgit-Baltistan, 191

The Golden Mounds. *See* Jinling tombs

government
    access to office, 276–77, 290
    bureaucracy, 147–48, 273–74, 278
    census registration, 31–32, 35, 40–41, 102–4, 137, 258 (*see also* armies: military registration)
    centralization, 35n.59, 77–78, 146, 155–56, 264–65, 275–78
    collegial rule, 77–78, 144–45, 148–49, 155, 162–63n.35, 276, 285
    corruption, 164, 180, 244–45, 258–59, 260–61, 292–93
    decline in first empire, 43, 124–25
    dual administration, 49, 76–78, 84, 171
    eight units (*ba bu* 八部), 137–38, 143–44
    examination system, 278
    law, 76, 84–85, 148–49
    local administration, 258–59, 260–61, 273, 282 (*see also* three headmen)
    Office of the Provisioner (Tai guan 太官), 210–11
    originating in Qin and Han, 35, 132, 257
    recruitment, 12–13, 18, 165–66
    salaries, 176–77, 195, 244–45, 260–61, 278 (*see also* armies: officers: salaries of officers)
    *Taghbach adaptation, 132, 147–50, 215–16, 258
    taxation, xxi, 31–32, 76, 137–38, 164, 191–92, 195, 258, 259–61, 263–64, 295n.80
    treasury, 102n.40, 177, 195, 244–45, 257, 271n.47, 278
    Wei population, 137n.25, 259–60
    See also agriculture; Equal Fields; *jiudouhe*; *nei xing agan*; Palace Attendant; Palace Steward; *zhong san*

Grand Culmen Hall. *See* Hall of the Grand Culmen

the Great Proscription of 169 黨錮, 115, 125

Great Wall. *See* long ramparts

Gu 孤 (n.d.), 82–84, 89–90

Gu Kaizhi 顧愷之 (d. 406), 228

Guangwu, Emperor 光武帝, of Later Han (r. 25–57), 124

Guangyang, Prince of, Yuan Yuan (in Tang changed to Shen) 廣陽王元淵 (深) (d. 526), 294

guo 國, meanings, 81n.98

guo ren 國人 ("men of the nation"), 64–65, 140–41, 143, 185–86, 195, 202–3, 243, 244–45, 276–77, 280, 292–93
  See also Dai people; identities; nation
guo yu. See language: *guo yu*
Guzang 姑臧, 190, 192

Habsburgs, 155–56
Hall of Heaven's Order 天文殿, 146, 203–4, 208–9
Hall of Heaven's Peace 天安殿, 159, 161, 208–9
Hall of Light (Ming tang 明堂), 266–67
Hall of the Grand Culmen (Tai ji dian 太極殿), 130–31, 208–9, 270–71, 288
Han 漢 empire, xxi, 38–43
  Later Han, 41, 48, 124–25
Han 翰 (Taiwu's son), 236–37
Han ren 漢人, xx–xxi, 114–15n.6, 243n.44
Handel, Zev, 152–53
Han shu 漢書, 191–92
Heaven (sky god of various peoples), 67, 74–75, 98, 146–47, 201, 265
  sacrifice to, 67, 98, 146–47, 149–50, 188–89, 191–92, 275, 297
Heaven's Order Hall. *See* Hall of Heaven's Order
Heaven's Peace Hall. *See* Hall of Heaven's Peace
heir apparency. *See* the "ancient practice"; dynasty and succession
Hejian, Prince of, Sima Yong 河間王, 司馬顒 (d. 306), 119–20, 121, 122
Helan 賀蘭 people, 80–81, 94, 102–4, 161–62, 172
Helan, Madam 賀[蘭]氏 (Daowu's mother, d. 396), 94
Helan, Madam 賀[蘭]氏 (Daowu's aunt and wife, n.d.), 160–62
Helian Bobo 赫連勃勃 (r. 407–425), 104–5, 188
Helian Chang 赫連昌 (r. 425–428, d. 434), 188
Helian, Madam 赫連氏 (d. 453), 211, 236
Helong 和龍, 190

Heluo 紇羅 (n.d.), 97
Hena 紇那 (r. 325– 329, 335– 337), 80–81
He Na 賀訥 (n.d.), 97–98, 102–4, 155
Hengshan 恆山 mountain, 30–31, 189–90
He Ran'gan 賀染幹 (n.d.), 97–98, 102
Heru 賀傉 (r. 321–325), 79–80
Heyin 河陰, 296–97
High Carts. *See* Gaoche
historiography, 5–8, 12–19, 50–55, 79–80n.90, 83–84, 85n.17, 97n.22, 103n.44, 110n.75, 177, 191–92, 200, 220–21, 243–45, 270n.43, 274, 275n.62, 293–94
  Jiankang histories, 53n.35, 59, 61, 89n.35, 93, 128, 148–49, 181, 200, 235–36, 273–74, 274n.58
  See also Bei shi; invention of tradition; *Jin shu*; *Wei shu*
Hobbes, Thomas, 174
Holmgren, Jennifer, 50–51, 83–84
Honeychurch, William, 75–76
horses, 8, 28–29, 31–32, 38–39, 55, 66, 72–73, 84–85, 87–89, 95, 101–2, 105–6, 107, 135, 149, 176, 177, 188–89, 195, 270–71
  sacrifice, 67, 236–37
  See also pastoralism
Hou Xudong 侯旭东, 137–38
Hu 胡 ("mounted nomad"), 31, 114–15n.6, 172–73
Hu, Madam 胡氏 (Empress Dowager Ling 靈皇后; d. 528), 285–97
Hu Sanxing 胡三省 (d. 1302), 101, 181–82
Huaidi 懷帝, of Western Jin (r. 307–311, d. 313), 127–32
Huaihuang 懷荒 garrison, 294
Huaishuo 懷朔 garrison, 291, 294–95
Huang 晃 (Taiwu's son and heir, d. 451), 198–99, 200, 201, 235, 236, 253–54
huang di 皇帝 ("emperor," "august god-king"), 121–22, 142–43, 146, 169, 203–4
Huben 虎賁 guards. *See* armies: guard units
Huidi 惠帝, of Western Jin (r. 290–301, 301–307), 119–22, 127–28

Hulao 虎牢, 163–64, 195
Hulun Nur 呼倫湖, 53–55
huluozhen 斛洛真/胡洛真, 181
"Humane King Perfection of Wisdom Sutra" (*Ren wang bo re bo luo mi jing* 仁王般若波羅蜜經), 247
hunting, 138–39, 181–83, 197, 202–3, 216–19, 217f
hungry empires, 105–7, 174–75, 230–31
  See also armies: provisioning
Huyan Yan 呼延晏 (n.d.), 130–31

identities, 5–6, 14n.10, 27–29, 47, 115, 125–26, 142–44, 150–52, 169, 174, 218–19, 220–21, 224, 225, 303
  ethnic tensions, 15–16, 77–78, 128n.64, 143, 154n.105, 200
  ethnogenesis, 63–64
  group identity, 111–12, 183n.76, 225–26
  See also clothing: *Serbi; Dai people; guo ren;* Han ren
Inner Asia, definition, xix
Inner Court 內朝, 84, 137–38, 148–50, 171, 183
interpreter. *See* translation
invention of tradition, 6–7, 150, 240

Japan, 171, 183
  See also Yamato
Japanese language, 152–53
Jia Xiu 賈秀 (d. 469), 250–51
Jiangyang, Prince of, Yuan Ji 江陽王元繼 (d. 528), 291–93
Jiankang 建康, 150, 193, 196–97, 288
  interaction with Wei, 200–1, 241, 271–72, 281–82, 286, 288
  See also southern campaigns
Jiefen 詰汾, 23, 55
Jin dynasty
  Eastern Jin 東晉 (317–420), 72, 118–19
  Western Jin 西晉 (266–316), 48–49, 118–22, 127–32
Jingzhao, Prince of, Zitui 京兆王子推 (d. 477), 253, 254n.102
Jinling 金陵 tombs (the "Golden Mounds"), 89–90, 158, 162, 249–50, 261–62, 263
Jin shu 晉書, 59
jiudouhe 九豆和, 139–40
Juqu 沮渠 people, 190, 192–93
Juqu Mujian 沮渠牧犍 (r. 433–439), 191–92
Jurchen, xviii, 152–53

Kang Le 康樂, 146–47, 283
Karasahr (Yanqi 焉耆), 192–93
Kawamoto Yoshiaki 川本芳昭, xxiv
Kebineng 軻比能 (d. 235), 49
khaghan, 7, 47–48, 53n.31, 67–69, 140–41, 142–43, 145–46
  as commander of armies, 144–45, 169, 183, 184–85, 191–92, 193, 241–42, 253, 283–84, 296
  end of term's use,, 277
  ties with, 144–45, 174, 183, 184–85, 293–94
khaghtun, 7
Khitans, 3–4, 18, 152–53, 206–7
Khotan, 192–93
kitchens, of the palace, 210–11, 213–14
  See also food; *fu*; government: Office of the Provisioner; Mao Xiuzhi
Koga Akimine 古賀昭岑, 231–32
Koguryŏ 高句麗 (37 BCE–668 CE), 190
Kojiki 古事記, 64
Köke qota (Hohhot, Huhehaote 呼和浩特), 26–27
Kököčü, 197
Koreans, 136, 284, 285–86
Kou Qianzhi 寇謙之 (d. 448), 199
Kuduo 窟咄 (d. 386), 100–1
Kumārajīva (d. 413), 189–90, 198
Kunming Pond 昆明池, 193

Lai Daqian 來大千 (d. 447), 183, 208–9
language, 135–36, 151–52, 241–42
  banning Inner Asian, 151n.92, 275–76, 278
  Chinese, 155n.111, 267, 275–76
  creole, 152, 181, 210–11

language (*cont.*)
  guo yu 國語 ("national language" of the Taghbach), xxiin.10, 18, 151–55, 158n.5, 227–28
  written language, 18, 73–74, 140–41, 152–55, 171n.10, 181, 210–11, 241–42
  See also oral tradition; translation
Later Qin 後秦 (384–417), 96, 163–64, 189–90
Lattimore, Owen, 27–28
Liang, Northern 北涼 (397–439), 5, 135, 163–64, 190–93
Liangcheng 涼城, 33, 34–35
Liao 遼, origin of name, 3–4
Li Chong 李沖 (d. 498), 260–61, 269–70
Lin Sheng-Chih 林聖智, 230–31
Lingley, Kate, 213
Lingqiu 靈丘, 181, 241–42, 243
Lingqiu 靈丘 Road, 133–34, 263–64, 265
Lingquan chi. *See* Divine Spring Pond
Liu Bang 劉邦, of Han (r. 202–195 BCE), 38
Liu Bei 劉備, of Shu (r. 221–223), 272–73, 274
Liu Cong 劉聰, of (Xiongnu) Han (r. 310–318), 120, 127–28
Liu Hu 劉虎 (d. 341), 88–89
Liu Jie 劉潔 (d. ca. 443), 9–10
Liu Kun 劉琨 (d. 318), 74, 78, 116–17
Liu Kuren 劉庫仁 (d. 385), 93, 95
Liu, Madam 劉氏 (d. 409), 160–61, 162
Liu Ni 劉尼 (d. 474), 236–38, 239–40
Liu Teng 劉騰 (d. 523), 286, 292–93, 295
Liu Weichen 劉衛辰 (d. 391), 88–89, 93, 100–1, 102, 104–5
Liu Wenbo 劉文伯 (n.d.), 41
Liu Wuhuan 劉務桓 (d. 356), 88–89
Liu Xian 劉顯 (d. 394), 95–96, 97, 99–101
Liu Xiang 劉向 (d. 6 BCE), 165–66
Liuxiu 六修 (Yilu's son; d. 316), 76–77
Liu Yao 劉曜, of Han/Zhao (r. 318–329), 130–31
Liu Yilong 劉義隆, of Song (r. 424–453), 194, 196–97
Liu Yu 劉裕, of Song (r. 420–422), 163–64
Liu Yu 劉彧, of Song (r. 466–472), 252–53
Liu Yuan 劉淵, of (Xiongnu) Han (r. 304–310), 72, 120–21, 128
Liu Ziye 劉子業, of Song (r. 464–466), 252–53
Liwei 力微 (r. ca. 240–277), 59–69, 143–44, 159, 276
Li Yanong 李亞農, 102–4
Longmen 龍門 caves, 284–85, 289–90
long ramparts (*chang cheng* 長城), 23–25, 27–28, 33–35, 36, 37–38, 163, 185–86
  See also walls
loyalty, 87–88, 95, 142–45, 150–51, 161–62, 179, 180, 182–83, 225–26, 273
Luguan 祿官 (r. 294–307), 70–71
Lu Li 陸麗 (d. 465), 236–37, 239–40, 242, 244–45, 248–50
Lü Simian 呂思勉, xxiv, 51–52, 170
luo 落 ("encampment group"), 189n.15
Luo Xin 罗新, xxi–xxii, xxiv
Luoyang 洛陽, 41, 68, 115, 118, 119–20, 121–22, 124, 127–32, 163–64, 203, 265–71, 285, 287–97
  Great Market, 287–88
  opposition to move, 269–71, 278–80
  See also cities; Hall of the Grand Culmen; wards
Lushui Hu 盧水胡, 190, 193
Lu Zhen 陸真 (d. 472), 184–85

Maeda Masana 前田正名, xxiv
Maijishan 麥積山, 246–47
Mao 毛, the "completing emperor," 51–52
Mao Xiuzhi 毛脩之 (d. 446), 210–11
marital politics, 39, 61, 72, 87, 117, 191, 196, 285–86
  See also diplomacy
Matsushita Ken'ichi 松下憲一, xxiv
Mayi 馬邑 ("Horse Town"), 38, 73–74n.67, 100
memory, shared, 151n.90
  And see the "old ways"
Meng Tian 蒙恬 (d. 210 BCE), 36

Mica Hall 雲母堂, 206
migration. *See* movement, of humans
military. *See* armies
military registration. *See* armies: military registration
Mingyuan, Emperor 明元帝 (r. 409–423), 144–45, 154–55, 158, 160–66, 179–80, 187, 216
Mo Han 莫含 (n.d.), 136–37
Modun 冒頓 (r. 209–174 BCE), 37–39
Moluhui 沒鹿回 people, 62–63, 66
Monalou 莫那婁 people, 157–58
Mongols, 71–72, 145–46, 152–53, 172
"Monograph on Offices and Clans" 官氏志, of *Wei shu*, 64–66, 147–48
Mote, Frederick, xx
movement, of humans
    migration, 43, 52–55, 114
    academic debate on migration, 52
    refugees, 64n.25, 71, 78, 123, 125, 131, 258, 294–95
    settlement of nomads, 102–4, 136, 172, 277n.72
    transportation, forced, 36, 40–41, 43, 74, 133–34, 137, 189–90, 196–97, 252–53, 258, 263
    See also new subjects
Mu 穆 family. *See* Qiumuling family
Mu Chong 穆崇 (d. 406), 100
Mu Duohou 穆多侯 (d. 465), 249–50
Mulan. *See* "Tale of Mulan"
Mumo 木末, 162
    See also Mingyuan, Emperor
Murong 慕容, 49
    Murong within Wei, 136, 172–73, 252–53
    See also Yan
Murong Baiyao 慕容白曜 (d. 470), 252–53
Murong Bao 慕容寶, of Later Yan (r. 396–398), 107–13
    daughter, 160
Murong Chui 慕容垂, of Later Yan (r. 384–396), 96–97, 99, 100–1, 107–11
music, 14–15, 228–29

Mu Tai 穆泰 (d. 497), 256, 279–81
myth, nature of, 50, 52

"The Names of Things in the National Language" (*Guo yu wu ming* 國語物名), 154
"Nan Xun bei" 南巡碑, 152, 153–54, 181, 237–38, 241–44
nation, 63–64, 143
    and privilege, 144–45
    of the *Taghbach, 62–63, 139–41, 197
    See also armies: as unifying institution; Gat, Azar; Dai people; identities; *guo*; *guo ren*
National Records (*Guo ji* 國記), 15, 200
natural afflictions
    disasters, 127–28, 165, 208–9, 294
    disease, 187, 196–97
natural surroundings (regions and rivers)
    climate, 25–28, 263–64, 269–70
    Datong Basin 大同盆地, 27, 74, 133–34 (*see also* Pingcheng; royal domain)
    Fen River 汾水, 193
    Gansu Corridor, xix, 60–61, 134, 135, 143–44, 190–93, 221–22, 238
    Great Black River 大黑河, 25–26
    Guanzhong 關中, 119–20, 126–27, 163–64, 188, 193
    Jing River 涇川, 193, 287
    Lake Daihai 岱海, 33, 34–35, 40–41
    loess, 24–25
    Luo River 洛水, 123, 130–31, 163–64
    Manchuria, xix, 3, 48, 49, 86–87, 112–13, 134, 190, 198, 214–15, 221–23, 224–25
    the Ordos, 25, 36, 37–38, 40, 42–43, 104–5, 108–9, 149, 188, 189–90
    Ox Creek 牛川, 98, 102
    Sanggan River 桑乾河, 24, 27
    trees, 73–74n.67, 138–39, 203–4, 216
    Tumed Plain, 25–27, 36, 40–41, 43n.105, 46, 55, 66, 70–71, 80–81, 87, 160–61, 170–71 (*see also* Shengle)
    Yangtze River, 196–97
    Yellow River 黃河, 24, 25

natural surroundings (regions and rivers) (*cont.*)
    Yellow River plains, xx, 5, 12–13, 25, 48–49, 86–87, 96, 111–13, 124–25, 128–29
        See also Hulun Nur; Shenhe Slope; *Shui jing zhu*
nei ru xing 內入姓, 65–66, 74–75, 143–44
nei san lang 內三郎. See armies: guard units
nei xing agan 內行阿干, 148–49
"New Compilation" (*Xin ji* 新集), 154–55, 165–66
new subjects (*xin min* 新民), 137
nurse dowager, 187n.6, 240–41, 245–46

*Olakkô. See Wuluohou
the "old ways," 69, 76, 143–44, 150–51, 268, 269–71, 275, 279–80, 301, 302
    See also Dai people; identities; Luoyang: opposition to move; Shenhe Slope
omens, 100, 108, 109, 110
Ong Qan, 145–46
oral tradition, 37n.66, 50–51, 154–55
"Orders and commands in the National Language" 國語號令, 154
Original Equality (Shijun 始均), 51, 76, 144–45, 276–77
    See also government: centralization; society: hierarchy; the "old ways"

Palace Attendant (*shi zhong* 侍中), 84, 148–49, 171, 219, 242–43, 248–49, 251, 255, 295
Palace Steward (*dian zhong shang shu* 殿中尚書), 180, 210–11, 236–37, 239–40, 249–50, 270–71
Pan, Madam 潘氏 (n.d.), 296–97
pastoralism, 8, 28–29, 101–2, 138–39, 205–6, 230–32, 294–95
    the yurt (*ger*), 231–32
"Peach Blossom Spring" 桃花源記, 124
peerage, 111–12, 159, 162–63, 244–45, 276–77
Pengcheng 彭城, 252–53, 295

Pengcheng, Prince of, Yuan Xie 彭城王元勰 (d. 508), 285–86
pennon commander (*chuangjiang* 幢將), 178–79
pennons (*chuang* 幢). See flags
Perfect Ruler of Great Peace (*Tai ping zhen jun* 太平真君; reign title, 440– 451), 199
Pilou 疋婁 family, 231–32
Pingcheng 平城, 3–4, 133–36, 139–40, 146, 157, 164–65, 185, 198–99, 202–10
    city design, 207, 208–9
    palaces, 207–10
    precarious nature, 165, 263–64
    Stop-Your-Cart-Here Portal (Zhichemen 止車門), 162, 208–9
    the Two Towers 雙闕, 206–7
    See also cities: wards; Hall of Heaven's Order; Hall of Heaven's Peace; Hall of Light; walls
Poduoluo 破多羅 Lady, Shaling M7 (d. 435), 219–30
Poduoluo 破多羅 Lady, wife of "Big Eye" Yang (n.d.), 141
Poduoluo 破多羅 people, 219–20
Poliuhan Baling 破六韓拔陵 (d. 525), 294
Poliuhan Mao 破六韓茂 (Han Mao 韓茂), 179–80
Prefatory Annals 序紀, of *Wei shu*, 14–15, 50–55
Prince of the Pigs. See Liu Yu 劉彧
the progress (of the lord), 214–16, 224f–25, 243, 281–82
propaganda, 10–11, 199, 247
provisioning. See armies: provisioning
pu 酺 ("drinking festival"), 145
Pugen 普根 (r. 316), 76–77, 78–79

Qiang 羌 people, 13–14, 15–16n.15, 63n.17, 96, 126–27, 141n.44, 163–64, 169, 172–73
Qifu 乞伏, 67–68
Qin 秦, 35, 36
Qin First Emperor 秦始皇, 195

Qinghe, Prince of, Yuan Yi 清河王元懌 (d. 520), 291–93
Qiumuling 丘穆陵 (Mu 穆) family, 249

raiding, on northern frontier, 30, 33–34, 39
Record of Buddhist Monasteries in Luoyang (*Luoyang qie lan ji* 洛陽伽藍記), 203, 288–89
Red Mountain 赤山, 220–21
religion, 97, 197
   See also ancestral worship; Buddhism; Daoism; Heaven: sacrifice to; horses: sacrifice; omens; rituals of state
Rencheng, Prince of (the elder), Yun 任城王雲 (d. 481), 253, 267–68
Rencheng, Prince of (the younger), Cheng 任城王澄 (d. 520), 266–68, 269, 270–71, 279–80, 286, 291
Rites (Rituals) of Zhou. See *Zhou li*
rituals of state, 146–47
rivers and lakes. See natural surroundings
Rokhshan the Sogdian (An Lushan 安祿山) (d. 757), 293–94
Rouran 柔然, 8–10, 87–88, 101–2, 159, 163, 178–79, 188–89, 192–93, 294
the Rouran lady (Wencheng's mother, 郁久閭氏; d. 452), 235–36, 240–41
royal domain, of Wei, 133–34
   population, 137, 164–65, 203
   See also Pingcheng
Ru 儒 ("Confucians"), xix, 12, 59–60, 115–16, 117, 125–26, 256–57, 263, 283–84
   See also Chinese classics; filial piety
Ruanruan 蠕蠕, 188–89
   See also Rouran
Runan 汝南, 194, 273

salaries. See armies: officers: salaries of officers; government: salaries
Samarkand, 131–32
samurai, 171, 183
san zhang. See three headmen
Saray, 131–32
   See also Luoyang

Scott, James, 34–35
seals, 72–73, 74–75
   See also diplomacy; titles
Secret History of the Mongols, xvii–xviii
*Serbi (Chinese: Xianbei), 37, 44–46, 47–48
servants. See societies: slaves and servants
settlement of nomads. See movement: of humans
Shamo Han 沙漠汗, 68–69
Shangdi 上帝, 146–47
Shanggu 上谷. See Upper Valley
Shangguan Si 上官巳 (n.d.), 119–20
Shanshan 鄯善, 192–93
Shao 紹 (Daowu's son), 160–62, 182–83, 200
Shegui 涉珪 (d. 409), 93
   See also Daowu, Emperor
Shelach, Gideon, 28–29
Shengle 盛樂, 27n.14, 66, 70–71, 76–77, 80, 85–86, 99, 106, 263
   See also Tumed Plain
Shenhe Slope 參合陂, 70–71, 73–74n.67, 85–86, 109–10, 111, 133–34, 135, 150–51, 171–72, 251n.83
Shi Hu 石虎, of Zhao (r. 334–349), 80–81, 86–87
Shijun 寔君 (d. 376), 89–90
Shi Le 石勒, of Zhao (r. 319–333), 78–79, 128–31
shi ling bu luo 世領部落 ("hereditary control of military populations"), 102–4, 172–73
shi zhong 侍中. See Palace Attendant
Shiyijian 什翼犍 (r. 338–376), 81, 82–90, 171–72
Shui jing zhu 水經注, 163–64
Shusun Jun 叔孫俊 (d. 416), 182–83
si fang xing 四方姓, 65–66, 143–44
Silk Roads, 190–93
Sima Qian 司馬遷 (d. ca. 86 BCE), 13–14, 29
Sima Teng. See Dongying, Duke of
Sima Ying. See Chengdu, Prince of
Sima Yue. See Donghai, Prince of

Sinograph, 152–54
Sinosphere, xx
Sixteen Kingdoms 十六國, 72, 120–131 passim, 169, 192–93
society
 hierarchy, 35n.59, 144–45, 149, 202–3, 223, 225–28, 230, 265n.10
 intermarriage, 46, 135–36
 patronage, 12n.2
 slaves and servants, 87–88, 124–25, 128, 230–32, 235–36, 263
 social mobility, 121, 182–83, 184, 185–86
 See also eminent lineages; Original Equality
Sogdians, 135–36
Song dynasty, of the Liu 劉宋 (420– 479), 163–64, 194–97, 252–53
Song嵩 of the Baba clan. See Zhangsun Song
Songshan mountain 嵩山, 199
Songs of Dai (Dai ge 代歌), 14–15, 50–51, 154, 228, 270–71
Southern Peace, Prince of, Yu 南安王余 (d. 452), 236–37
Standard of Ur, 226–27
state, definition of, 23–24, 37–38, 75–76
Steinhardt, Nancy, 284
stirrups. See armies: arms and armor
stock-rearing. See pastoralism
succession. See dynasty and succession

Tabgatch, 10–11
 See also *Taghbach
*Taghbach, xxii–xxiii, et passim
Taihang Mountains 太行山, 25
Taiwu, Emperor 太武帝 (r. 423–452), 3–11, 153–54, 158, 183, 187–201, 216, 235–36, 238
 See also Böri Beg
Taiyuan 太原 (≈ Jinyang 晉陽), 27n.14, 38, 68, 72, 74, 78, 107–8, 111–12, 120–21, 280–81, 296
"Tale of Mulan" 木蘭辭, 140–41, 145, 173, 175–76, 177, 183–84, 197

Tamura Jitsuzō 田村實造, xxiv
Tang Zhangru 唐長孺, xxiv
Tanshihuai 檀石槐 (ca. 137– ca. 181), 46, 48
Tao Yuanming 陶淵明 (d. 427), 124
Tapper, Richard, 75–76
Tarim Basin, xix, 37, 190–91, 192–93
taxation. See government
Tengri. See Heaven
theatre state, 274, 283
three headmen (san zhang 三長), 260–61
Tian 天. See Heaven
Tian Yuqing 田余庆, 154
Tiele 鐵勒, 87–88, 172–73
 See also Gaoche
tigers, 28–29, 88–89, 183, 211–12, 216
*tigin. See dynasty and succession: *tigin
timber-frame architecture, 206–7, 208–9
titles, 5, 31–32, 44–45, 46, 47–48, 67, 69–70n.53, 72, 74–75, 84, 98, 101, 121–22, 145–46, 181
 See also huang di; khaghan; peerage; seals
tombs, 202–3, 217, 220–22
 Anak No. 3, 214–15
 Hulun Nur, 53–55
 Shaling M7, 219–30
 Yanbei M2, 231–32
 Zhijiabao, 217–19
Tong dian 通典, 147–48
Tong Enzheng 童恩正, 27–28
Tongwan 統萬, 134, 188
Touman 頭曼 (r. ca. 220–209 BCE), 36
trade, 31–32, 33–34, 38–39, 41–42, 54–55, 68, 134–35, 136–37, 191–93, 230–31, 271–72, 287–88
 glass ware, 135, 206, 228–29
 lacquer, 41–42n.94, 54–55, 219, 220–21, 228
 pearls, 228–29
 silver ware, 135, 222n.115, 228–29
translation, 17–18, 79–80n.90, 149–50, 152–54, 189–90
transportation, forced. See movement, of humans

"Treatise on Officials and Clans." See "Monograph on Offices and Clans"
tribe, discussion of term, 45n.115, 75–76, 86n.19, 89–90n.36
Tseng, Chin-yin, xxiv, 228
Tufa 禿髮, 60–61, 238
Tuiyin 推寅, 52–53, 55
Tuoba 拓跋, xxii
  See also *Taghbach
Türks, 10–11, 152–53
Tuyuhun 吐谷渾, 69–70n.53, 163–64

Upper Valley (Shanggu 上谷), 111, 134
Uyghurs, 152–53

walls, 122–27, 130–31, 137–38, 203–8, 287–88
  See also fortresses; long ramparts
Wang Jun (of Taiyuan) 太原王浚 (d. 314), 120–21
Wang Luor 王洛兒 (d. 413), 144–45, 161–62
Wang, Madam 王氏 (d. 355), 83–84, 85–86
Wang Mang 王莽, of Xin (r. 9–23), 41, 124
Wang Mi 王彌 (d. 311), 130–31
Wang Su 王肅 (d. 501), 203n.5, 229–30, 272–74
Wei Cao 衛操 (d. 310), 71, 72, 78, 136–37
Wei Guan 衛瓘 (d. 291), 68, 69
Wei, Madam 惟氏 (n.d.), 78–80
Wei, Northern 北魏 (386–534), passim
  origin of name, 3–4
Wei 魏, of the Cao family (220–266), 48–49
Wei Shou 魏收 (d. 572), 16, 273–74
Wei shu 魏書, xxiv, 16–17, 19, 191–92
Wencheng, Emperor 文成帝 (r. 452–465), 239–48, 252
Wenming empress dowager 文明太后 (d. 490), 150–51, 212–14, 245–46, 251–52, 253–54, 255–62, 266
  basis of her power, 253–54, 255
  See also Feng family
Western Qin 西秦 (385–400, 409–431), 68
Western Wei 西魏 (535–557), 193, 265, 282, 297
Wey (Wei), Prince of, Yi 衛王儀 (d. 409), 106–7, 108, 158
White Road Pass. See Baidao
White Top Hill. See Baideng shan
Whittaker, Dick, 220–21
Wolf Lord. See Böri Beg
wolves, 4–5, 100–1
  See also divine beast
women, political roles, 7, 47, 60, 61, 79–80, 135–36, 140–41, 151–52, 159–60, 187, 211–14, 241, 245–46, 255, 285
  See also the "ancient practice"; the feast: women's roles; Helan, Madam; Hu, Madam; khaghtun; Poduoluo Lady; Wang, Madam; Wei, Madam; Wenming empress dowager
Woye 沃野 garrison, 294
wu bi 塢壁. See fortresses
Wudi 武帝, of Han (r. 141–87 BCE), 40, 193
Wudi 武帝, of Western Jin (r. 266–290), 118–19
Wuhuan 烏桓, 37, 41–43, 69, 128
Wuling 武靈 of Zhao (r. 325–299 BCE), 31–33
Wuluohou 烏洛侯 (*Olakkô), 3, 8, 9, 10
Wuwan 烏丸. See Wuhuan
Wuxu 毋恤 ("The Merciless") of Zhao (d. 425 BCE), 30–31

Xia 夏 (407–431), 188–90
Xia Nai 夏鼐, 170
Xianbei 鮮卑. See *Serbi
Xiangyang 襄陽, 127–28, 281–82
Xianwen, Emperor 獻文帝 (r. 465–471; d. 476), 183, 248–49, 252, 253–54
xiao. See filial piety
Xiaoming, Emperor 孝明帝 (r. 515–528), 286, 292, 296–97

Xiaowen, Emperor 孝文帝 (r. 471–499), 5–6, 146–47, 150–51, 153–54, 212–13, 216, 241, 252, 253–54, 255–62, 263–82, 283–84
  reforms, 257–62, 275–77
  response to reforms, 278–79
  surname bestowal, 276–77
  See also Luoyang
Xiao Yan 蕭衍, of Liang (r. 502–549), 286, 295
Xiao Ze 蕭賾, of Southern Qi (r. 482–493), 272
Xiaozhuang, Emperor, Yuan Ziyou 孝莊帝 元子攸 (r. 528–531), 296–97
Xiongnu 匈奴, 33, 36–46, 49, 88–89, 172–73, 177–78
  name, 128
Xu He 徐紇 (n.d.), 296–97
Xuanwu, Emperor 宣武帝 (r. 499– 515), 273, 284, 285–86
Xuanzong 玄宗, of Tang (r. 712–756), 293–94
Xun 恂 (Xiaowen's son and heir; d. 497), 268–69, 278–80
Xunzi 荀子, 8

Yamato, 221–22
Yan, 86–87, 96–97, 107–13, 163, 190
  Western Yan (384– 394), 101, 107–8
Yang, "Big Eye" 楊大眼 (d. 518), 141
Yang Chun 楊椿 (d. 531), 230–31
Yan Gengwang 严耕望, 109–10
Yang Xuanzhi 楊衒之 (fl. early sixth century), 288–90
Yanmen Pass 雁門關, 27–28, 30, 35, 134, 279–80
Yan Yaozhong 严耀中, xxiv, 148–49, 174
Ye 鄴, 81, 96–97, 119–21, 133, 203–4, 207, 265, 269–70, 272–73
Yellow Emperor 黃帝, 50–51, 198–99, 200
Yellow Turbans 黃巾, 48, 115–16, 126–27
Yi Ba 伊馛 (d. 459), 191–92, 213–14, 241–42
Yihuai 翳槐 (r. 329–335, 337–338), 80–81, 82–83, 276

Yi Hun 乙渾 (d. 466), 242, 248–51
Yilu 猗盧 (r. 295–326), 70–72, 74–77, 120–21, 136–37
Yingchuan 潁川, 124–25
Yinshan 陰山 mountains, 23–24, 134, 163, 171
  early history, 27–29
  grasslands north of, 136, 188–89
  Xiongnu loss of, 40
Yituo 猗㐌 (r. 295–305), 70–74, 120–21, 136–37
Yonggu Mausoleum 永固陵, 261–62
Yongjia 永嘉 (Western Jin reign title, 307–311)
  See also Huaidi
Yongning Temple 永寧寺, 288–90
Yu, Madam 于氏 (d. 507), 285–86
Yu 郁 (imperial kinsman), 250
Yu (Taiwu's son). See Southern Peace, Prince of
Yuan Cha 元叉[or 乂] (d. 525), 291–95
Yuan He 源賀 (d. 478), 236–37, 238, 239–40
Yuan Ke. See Xuanwu, Emperor
Yuan Pi 元丕 (d. 503), 150–51, 213–14, 251, 256, 261, 268–69, 270–71, 276–77, 279–81
Yuan Shao 袁紹 (d. 202), 115–16
Yuan Ziyou. See Xiaozhuang, Emperor
Yuchi, Lady (Madam) 尉遲氏 (n.d.), 213
Yuezhi 月氏, 37
Yu Guo 于果 (n.d.), 270–71
Yu Jing 于景 (d. 526), 294
Yu Lie 于烈 (d. 501), 269–70, 285–86
Yulin 羽林 guards. See armies: guard units
Yulü 鬱律 (r. 316–321), 74, 78–80
Yungang 雲岡, 135, 221–22, 246–47, 256–57
Yunzhong 雲中. See Tumed Plain
Yuwen Tai 宇文泰, 193
Yu Zhong 于忠 (d. 518), 286, 291–92

Zhang, Fan, xxiv, 223
Zhang Fang 張方 (d. 306), 119–22
Zhang Jinlong 张金龙, 187

Zhang Liang 張良 (d. 186 BCE), 268
Zhang Qingjie 张庆捷, 244
Zhangsun 長孫, 65n.29, 95, 149n.80
Zhangsun Fei 長孫肥 (d. 408), 95
Zhangsun Kehou 長孫渴侯 (d. 452), 236–37, 240
Zhangsun Song 長孫嵩 (d. 437), 98, 99, 161, 162
Zhao 趙, Warring States period, 30–35
Zheng Qinren 鄭欽仁, 149
Zheng Xuan 鄭玄 (d. 200), 115–16
Zheng Yan 鄭儼 (d. 528), 296–97
zhong san 中散 ("palace jack-of-all-trades"), 149
Zhongshan 中山, 96–97, 99, 112–13
Zhou 周 dynasty (ca. 1046–256 BCE), 265–57, 275
Zhou li 周禮, 115–16, 265, 275, 287
Zhuang Zhou 莊周 (Zhuangzi 莊子), xvii, 264–65
Zhu Dawei 朱大渭, 152
Zhuge Liang 諸葛亮 (d. 234), 272–73, 274
Zifang. *See* Zhang Liang
Zong Ai 宗愛 (d. 452), 236–37, 239–40
Zou, Mount 鄒山, 195